The Prentice-Hall Series in Marketing
Philip Kotler, Series Editor

Abell/Hammond	Strategic Market Planning
Corey	Industrial Marketing: Cases and Concepts, 3rd ed.
Green/Tull	Research for Marketing Decisions, 4th ed.
Keegan	Multinational Marketing Management, 3rd ed.
Kleppner/Russell/Verrill	Otto Kleppner's Advertising Procedure, 8th ed.
Kotler	Marketing for Nonprofit Organizations, 2nd ed.
Kotler	Marketing Management, 4th ed.
Kotler	Principles of Marketing, 2nd ed.
Myers/Massy/Greyser	Marketing Research and Knowledge Development
Ray	Advertising and Communications Management
Stern/El-Ansary	Marketing Channels, 2nd ed.
Stern/Eovaldi	Legal Aspects of Marketing Strategy: Antitrust and Consumer Protection Issues
Urban/Hauser	Design and Marketing of New Products

Marketing Essentials

Philip Kotler
NORTHWESTERN UNIVERSITY

Prentice-Hall, Inc.
Englewood Cliffs, New Jersey

Library of Congress Cataloging in Publication Data

Kotler, Philip.
  Marketing Essentials

  Includes bibliographical references and indexes.
  1. Marketing. I. Title.
HF5415.K63114   1984   658.8   83-19235
ISBN 0-13-557232-0

Printed in the United States of America

10 9 8 7 6 5 4 3 2 1

Prentice-Hall International, Inc., *London*
Prentice-Hall of Australia, Pty. Ltd., *Sydney*
Editora Prentice-Hall do Brasil Ltda., *Rio de Janeiro*
Prentice-Hall Canada Inc., *Toronto*
Prentice-Hall of India Private Limited, *New Delhi*
Prentice-Hall of Japan, Inc., *Tokyo*
Prentice-Hall of Southeast Asia Pte. Ltd., *Singapore*
Whitehall Books Limited, *Wellington, New Zealand*

Credits

Art Director: Florence Dara Silverman
Development Editor: Deirdre Silberstein
Production Editor: Eleanor Perz
Photo Researcher: Christine A. Pullo
Manufacturing Buyer: Ray Keating
Interior Designer: Jules Perlmutter
Cover Designer: Florence Dara Silverman/Jules Perlmutter
Cover Photo: The Image Bank/Michael DeCamp
Line Art: Danmark and Michaels, Inc.

Photo credits: Title page, pp. ii-iii—Citibank, Ehrhart-Babic Associates, Inc., Anita Duncan, and Marc Anderson; Chap. 1, p. xx—Teri Leigh Stratford; Chap. 2, p. 28—AT&T Photo Center; Chap. 3, p. 52—U.S. Census Bureau; Chap. 4, p. 74—New York Convention & Visitors Bureau; Chap. 5, p. 104—Tim Davis/Photo Researchers, Inc.; Chap. 6, p. 136—Monroe Systems for Business; Chap. 7, p. 158—Hershey Park; Chap. 8, p. 184—IBM; Chap. 9, p. 212—AT&T Photo Center; Chap. 10, p. 236—Teri Leigh Stratford; Chap. 11, p. 256—Ford *Dealer World* Magazine; Chap. 12, p. 272—American Airlines; Chap. 13, p. 296—The Galleria/Photo by David Nance; Chap. 14, p. 330—Teri Leigh Stratford; Chap. 15, p. 350—© Christine A. Pullo, 1983; Chap. 16, p. 378—Marc Anderson; Chap. 17, p. 398—AT&T Photo Center; Chap. 18, p. 424—United Nations/Photo by B. Wolff; Chap. 19, p. 442—American Museum of Natural History; Chap. 20, p. 458—Minneapolis Convention & Tourism Commission.

ISBN 0-13-557232-0

About the Author

Philip Kotler is the Harold T. Martin Professor of Marketing at the J. L. Kellogg Graduate School of Management at Northwestern University. He received a master's degree at the University of Chicago and a Ph.D. degree at M.I.T., both in economics. He did postdoctoral work in mathematics at Harvard and in behavioral science at the University of Chicago.

Dr. Kotler is the author of *Marketing Management: Analysis, Planning, and Control*, now in its fourth edition. This text has been translated into nine languages and is the most widely used marketing textbook in graduate schools of business. His *Marketing for Nonprofit Organizations*, now in its second edition, is the most widely used textbook in that specialized area. Dr. Kotler's other books are *Marketing Decision Making: A Model Building Approach; Marketing Management and Strategy: A Reader; Creating Social Change;* and *Simulation in the Social and Administrative Sciences*. In addition, he has written over seventy articles for leading journals, including the *Harvard Business Review, Journal of Marketing, Journal of Marketing Research, Management Science,* and *Journal of Business Strategy*. He is the only three-time winner of the coveted Alpha Kappa Psi award for the best annual article published in the *Journal of Marketing*.

Dr. Kotler has served as chairman of the College on Marketing of The Institute of Management Sciences (TIMS) and as director of the American Marketing Association. He is currently on the board of trustees of the Marketing Science Institute and is a director of the Management Analysis Center (MAC) and Deltak, Inc. He received the 1978 Paul D. Converse Award given by the American Marketing Association to honor "outstanding contributions to science in marketing."

Contents

10 Pricing Products: Pricing Objectives and Policies

11 Pricing Products: Pricing Strategies

Vignettes and Cases

Preface

In the complex world we live in, all of us need to know about marketing. Whether we are selling our car, looking for a job, raising money for a charity, or promoting a cause, we engage in marketing. We need to know what the market is like, who is in it, how it functions, what it wants.

We also need to know marketing as consumers and citizens. People are always trying to sell us something, and we need to recognize the methods they use. Studying marketing helps us behave more intelligently as consumers, whether we are buying toothpaste, frozen pizza, a personal computer, or a new car.

Marketing is an essential subject for professional marketers, such as sales representatives, retailers, advertising executives, marketing researchers, new-product managers, brand managers, and so on. They need to know how to define and segment a market; assess the needs, wants, and preferences of consumers in the target market; design and test need-satisfying products for that market; price products to convey their values to customers; select capable middlemen so that the products will be widely available and well represented; and advertise and promote the products so that customers know about and want them. Clearly, marketers need a broad range of skills.

Students who want to learn marketing can find many books on the subject. Even the large textbooks only skim the surface, since there is so much to learn about each marketing tool. Most students new to a subject want a broad picture of its essentials. They don't want to drown in a sea of details. *Marketing Essentials* has been written with this objective in mind.

Marketing Essentials, however, is not written just as an outline of marketing. The subject is far too fascinating to be displayed only in skeletal form. *Marketing Essentials* tells the stories that make up the drama of modern marketing: the failure of CBS cable television; the never-ending war between Coca-Cola and Pepsi-Cola; Miller Beer's successful rise from seventh to second place in the beer market; the Avon lady's impact on home shopping; Columbia Records' promotion strategy for the band Men at Work; the price war in the home computer market; and so on. Each chapter begins with a vignette describing some important marketing event or battle. Throughout each chapter, real-life examples make the world of marketing come alive to the reader.

In writing *Marketing Essentials,* I followed several principles. The book should be interesting to read, cover the main topics that the marketer and citizen need to know, flow logically from chapter to chapter, describe scientific findings rather than hearsay, and adopt a management orientation. My goal was to prepare the reader to make better decisions in the marketing arena.

Pedagogical Aids

This book contains many aids to help students learn about marketing. The main ones are:

- **Objectives.** Each chapter begins with objectives that prepare students for the chapter material.
- **Opening vignette.** Each chapter presents a marketing story that leads students into the chapter material.
- **Figures, tables, and photographs.** Throughout the text, key points and principles are illustrated.
- **Boxed exhibits.** Additional examples and interesting material are featured throughout the text.
- **Summary.** Each chapter concludes with a review of the main points and principles.
- **Review questions.** Each chapter has a set of questions covering the material presented.
- **Key terms.** Each chapter has a list of definitions to review the key terms in the chapter.
- **Case studies.** The text includes twenty cases for class and/or written discussion. The cases challenge students to apply marketing principles to real companies in real situations. Notes at the end of each chapter direct students to the appropriate cases.
- **Appendixes.** Two appendixes, "Marketing Arithmetic" and "Careers in Marketing," provide additional, practical material for students.
- **Glossary.** At the end of the book, there is a complete glossary of the key terms found in the book.
- **Indexes.** A name index and a subject index help in finding information and examples in the text.

Supplements

A successful course in marketing requires more than a well-written textbook. It requires a dedicated teacher and a set of useful teaching/learning aids. The following aids support *Marketing Essentials:*

- **Instructor's Manual.** The Instructor's Manual is available to all professors who adopt the book. It contains: an overview, list of features and key terms, lecture outline, and answers to discussion questions for each chapter; analyses of all twenty cases; and transparency masters for the major figures and tables.
- **Test Item File.** The Test Item File contains approximately 1,800 multiple-choice and true-false questions. The questions are available either on a computer tape or through the Prentice-Hall Computerized Testing Service.
- **Study Guide and Workbook.** The Study Guide and Workbook for students contains a review of each chapter, exercises to test students' knowledge, and cases with questions that ask students to apply the concepts presented in the chapter.
- **80 full-color transparencies.**

- **Prentice-Hall Marketing Slides (PH-200).** Prentice-Hall offers a self-contained set of 200 slides for the teaching of marketing essentials.
- **Introduction to Marketing filmstrips and audio cassette.** This full-color, ten-module audiovisual program introduces the major principles of marketing, and uses definitions, diagrams, charts, and photographs to connect the principles with real-life situations. Available through Prentice-Hall Media.
- **Great Marketing Wars Videotapes.** Prentice-Hall also offers a set of three videotapes describing how a functional analogy can be drawn between military strategy and marketing practices in competitive industries, such as the soft-drink wars and the blue-jeans wars.

Acknowledgments

No book is the work of a single author. Every author draws on the predecessors in his or her field who have pioneered its territory and developed its concepts, theories, and techniques. Every author relies also on his or her immediate colleagues who have lent their support by discussing various marketing ideas. In this connection, my thanks go to my colleagues at the J. L. Kellogg Graduate School of Management: Bobby J. Calder, Richard M. Clewett, Lakshman Krishnamurthi, Stephen A. LaTour, Sidney J. Levy, Prabha Sinha, Louis W. Stern, Brian Sternthal, Alice M. Tybout, and Andris A. Zoltners. Thanks also go to my Dean and longtime friend, Donald P. Jacobs, for his generous support of my research and writing efforts.

This book has also benefited from the comments of reviewers at other colleges: Jack Forrest, Belmont College; Sandra Heusinkveld, Normandale Community College; Eric Kulp, Middlesex County College; Thomas Paczkowski, Cayuga Community College; and Robert L. Powell, Gloucester County College.

I owe a great debt to two talented people at Prentice-Hall who aided the birth of this book. Elizabeth Classon, marketing editor, analyzed the market and convinced me that this book would make a contribution to undergraduate education in marketing. Deirdre Silberstein, development editor, helped me understand the needs and interests of undergraduate students and write the text in a way that would be lively without sacrificing substance. Many others at Prentice-Hall contributed to the book. My production editor, Eleanor Perz, copyedited manuscript and supervised galleys and proofs. Christine A. Pullo researched and gathered the text photos. The art director, Florence Dara Silverman, directed the design and layout of the text and cover. Sara Lewis aided in research and the preparation of new material. My thanks also go to Paul Misselwitz, marketing manager, and Ray Keating, manufacturing buyer.

Others at Prentice-Hall have been so helpful over the years that I want to celebrate my seventeen years of working with the company by dedicating this book to Prentice-Hall.

P. K.

Chapter 1

Social Foundations of Marketing: Meeting Human Needs

Objectives

After reading this chapter, you should be able to:

1. Define marketing and discuss its role in our economy.
2. Compare the five marketing management philosophies.
3. Discuss what buyers, sellers, and citizens want from a marketing system.
4. Explain how marketing is used by organizations.

Marketing touches all of us every day of our lives. We wake up to a Sears radio alarm clock, which begins to play a Barbra Streisand song followed by a United Airlines commercial advertising a Hawaiian vacation. We go into the bathroom where we brush our teeth with Colgate, shave with Gillette, gargle with Listerine, spray our hair with Revlon, and use other toiletries and appliances produced by manufacturers around the world. We put on our Calvin Klein jeans and Bass shoes. We enter the kitchen and drink Minute Maid orange juice, and pour Kellogg's Rice Krispies and Borden's milk into a bowl. Later we drink a cup of Maxwell House coffee with two teaspoons of Domino sugar while munching on a slice of Sara Lee coffee cake. We consume oranges grown in California, coffee imported from Brazil, a newspaper made of Canadian wood pulp, and radio news coming from as far away as Australia. We get our mail and find a Metropolitan Museum of Art shoppers' catalog, a letter from a Prudential insurance sales representative offering various services, and coupons saving us money on our favorite brands. We step out of our homes and drive to the Northbrook Court Shopping Center with its Neiman-Marcus, Lord & Taylor, Sears, and hundreds of other stores brimming with goods from floor to ceiling. Later we exercise at a Nautilus Fitness Center, have our hair cut at Vidal Sassoon, and plan a Caribbean trip at a Thomas Cook travel agency.

The marketing system has made all of this possible, with little effort on our part. It has delivered to us a standard of living that would have been inconceivable to our ancestors.

What Is Marketing?

What does the term **marketing** mean? Most people mistakenly think marketing is the same as selling and promotion.

No wonder! Americans are bombarded with television commercials, newspaper ads, direct mail, and sales calls. Someone is always trying to sell something. It seems that we cannot escape death, taxes, or selling.

Therefore many students are surprised to learn that the most important part of marketing is not selling! Selling is only the tip of the marketing iceberg. Selling is only one of several marketing functions, and often not the most important one. If the marketer does a good job on the marketing functions of identifying consumer needs, developing appropriate products, and pricing, distributing, and promoting them effectively, these goods will sell very easily.

Everyone knows about "hot" products to which consumers flock in droves. When Eastman Kodak designed its Instamatic camera, when Atari designed its first video games, and when Mazda introduced its RX-7 sports car, these manufacturers were swamped with orders because they had designed the "right" product. Not me-too products, but distinct ones offering new benefits.

Peter Drucker, one of the leading management theorists, put it this way:

> The aim of marketing is to make selling superfluous. The aim is to know and understand the customer so well that the product or service fits him and sells itself.[1]

This is not to say that selling and promotion are unimportant, but rather that they are part of a larger "marketing mix" or set of marketing tools that must be orchestrated for maximum impact on the marketplace.

Here is our definition of marketing:

> **Marketing** is human activity directed at satisfying needs and wants through exchange processes.

To explain this definition, we will look at the following terms: *needs, wants, demands, products, exchange, transactions,* and *markets.*[2]

Needs The most basic concept underlying marketing is that of human needs. We define a human need as follows:

> A **human need** is a state of felt deprivation in a person.

Human needs are plentiful and complex. They include basic physiological needs for food, clothing, warmth, and safety; social needs for belonging, influence, and affection; and individual needs for knowledge and self-expression. These needs are not created by Madison Avenue but are a basic part of human makeup.

When a need is not satisfied, the person feels deprived and unhappy. The more important the need to the person, the stronger these feelings are. An unsatisfied person will do one of two things—look for an object that will satisfy the need or try to extinguish the need. People in industrial societies try to find or develop objects that will satisfy their needs. People in poor societies, however, try to reduce their needs to what is available.

Wants   A second basic concept in marketing is that of human wants.

> **Human wants** are the form that human needs take as shaped by a person's culture and individuality.

A hungry person in Bali wants mangoes, suckling pig, and beans. A hungry person in the United States wants a hamburger, French fries, and a Coke. Wants are described in terms of culturally defined objects that will satisfy needs.

As a society evolves, the wants of its members expand. The people are exposed to more objects that arouse their curiosity, interest, and desire. Producers in turn take specific actions to build desire for their products. They try to form a connection between what they produce and people's needs. They promote their product as a satisfier of one or more particular needs. The marketer does not create the need; it exists.

Sellers often confuse wants and needs. A manufacturer of drill bits may think that the customer needs a drill bit, but what the customer really needs is a hole. If another product comes along that can make a better hole for less money, the customer will have a new want (the other product) but the same need (a hole). Manufacturers who focus only on existing wants and fail to recognize the underlying needs may find other products serving these needs better than their own products do.

Demands   People have almost unlimited wants but limited resources. They will choose those products that will produce the most satisfaction for their money.

> Their wants become **demands** when backed by purchasing power.

It is easy to list the demands in a given society at a given point in time. In the late 1970s, 200 million Americans purchased 67 billion eggs, 250 million chickens, 5 million hair dryers, 133 billion domestic air travel passenger miles, and over 20 million lectures by college English professors. These and other consumer goods and services led in turn to a demand for more than 150 million tons of steel, 4 billion tons of cotton, and many other industrial goods. These are a few of the demands that get expressed in a $1.5 trillion economy.

A society could plan next year's production by using this year's mix of demand. The USSR and other centrally planned economies plan production on

A woman may want a fur coat to satisfy a need for warmth. If the woman can afford the fur coat, the want becomes a demand.

©Alexander's Fur Vault

this basis. Demands, however, are not that reliable. People get tired of some things they are currently consuming, and they seek variety for its own sake. They also make new choices in response to changing prices and incomes. Lancaster has pointed out that products are really bundles of attributes, and people choose the products that give them the best bundle of benefits for their money.[3] Thus a Volkswagen represents basic transportation, low purchase price, fuel economy, and European ride; and a Cadillac represents high comfort, luxury, and status. A person chooses the product whose combined attributes deliver the most satisfaction for the price, given the person's wants and resources.

Products Human needs, wants, and demands suggest that there are products to satisfy them. We define product as follows:

> A **product** is anything that can be offered to a market for attention, acquisition, use, or consumption that might satisfy a want or need.

Suppose a woman feels a need to look attractive. We will call all the products that are capable of satisfying this need the *product choice set*. This set includes cosmetics, new clothes, a Caribbean suntan, a beautician's services, plastic surgery, and so forth. These products are not all equally desirable. The more

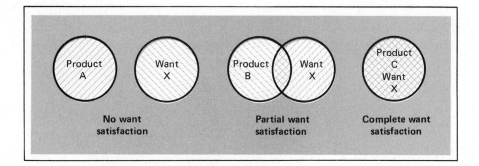

FIGURE 1-1

Three Degrees of Want Satisfaction

accessible and less expensive products, such as cosmetics, clothing, and a new haircut, are more likely to be purchased first.

We can represent a specific product and a specific human want as circles and represent the product's want-satisfying ability by the degree that it covers the want circle. Figure 1-1 shows that product A does not satisfy want X, that product B partially satisfies want X, and that product C completely satisfies want X. Product C would be called an *ideal product.*

The closer a product matches the consumer's desire, the more successful the producer will be. Suppose an ice-cream producer asks a consumer how much "creaminess" and "sweetness" he or she likes in ice cream. And suppose the consumer's answer is represented by "ideal" in figure 1-2. Now the consumer is asked to taste three competitive brands of ice cream and describe their levels of creaminess and sweetness. These are also represented by points in figure 1-2. We would predict that the consumer would prefer brand B because it comes closer than the other brands to "packaging" the ideal levels of the two attributes the consumer wants. If the ice-cream producer offered an ice cream closer to the consumer's ideal than brand B, the producer's new brand should outsell B, if the price, availability, and other conditions are similar.

FIGURE 1-2

Ice-Cream Brands Compared in Terms of Creaminess and Sweetness

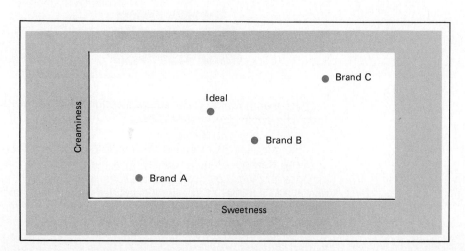

KIDS ARE ANIMALS TOO!

And we at The Bronx Zoo believe that children, like animals, thrive in environments not confined by walls or bars, environments as open as their minds. Not that a classroom is analogous to a cage, but there are some learning experiences as big as all outdoors. Our animals roam freely in their natural habitats. And our Children's Zoo encourages youngsters to do the same...to run and roar and touch and feel and slip and slide and learn. When a child "tries on" the ears of a fennec fox and hears for the first time the heightened sound perceived by that breed, the sensory impression is something no textbook can describe.

No teacher can explain how a turtle feels in its shell. Or how a gopher burrows through the ground. And could you describe just how a skunk smells? One sniff is worth a thousand words! And one climb in our giant spiderweb and no child will ever take those lacy creations for granted again.

In a time of such economic stress, when cutbacks in school funding are the norm rather than the rule, The Bronx Zoo is proud that one of the most vivid and enriching encounters is affordable to every child—the opportunity to learn from the animals. Special programs in the public school system may be a thing of the past, but The Bronx Zoo is growing every day.

And every child can grow with us.

THE NEW BRONX ZOO

Products do not have to be physical objects. A visit to the zoo can satisfy a need for adventure, an educational experience, or entertainment.
New York Zoological Society

The moral is that producers should find the consumers they want to sell to and their wants and should then prepare a product that comes as close as possible to satisfying these wants.

The concept of product is not limited to physical objects. Anything capable of giving service—that is, satisfying a need—can be called a product. This includes *persons, places, organizations, activities,* and *ideas,* in addition to goods and services. A consumer decides which entertainers to watch on television, places to go on a vacation, organizations to contribute to, and ideas to support. From the consumer's point of view, these are alternative products. If the term *product* seems unnatural at times, we can substitute the term *satisfier, resource,* or *offer.* All of these terms describe something of value to someone.

Exchange Marketing occurs when people decide to satisfy needs and wants through exchange.

> **Exchange** is the act of obtaining a desired object from someone by offering something in return.

Exchange is one of four ways in which individuals can obtain a desired object. For example, a man who is hungry can try to obtain food in the following ways. He can find his own food by hunting, fishing, or fruit gathering (*self-production*). He can steal food from someone else (*coercion*). He can beg for the food (*begging*). Finally, he can offer some resource such as money, another product, or some service for the food (*exchange*).

Of these four ways of satisfying needs, exchange has a great deal in its favor. People do not have to prey on others or depend on alms from others. Nor do they have to produce every necessity, regardless of skill. They can concentrate on producing things that they are good at producing and trade them for needed items produced by others. The members of a society end up producing a greater total number of products.

Exchange is the core concept of the discipline of marketing. For a voluntary exchange to take place, five conditions must be satisfied:

1. There are at least two parties.
2. Each party has something that may be of value to the other party.
3. Each party is capable of communication and delivery.
4. Each party is free to accept or reject the other party's offer.
5. Each party believes it is appropriate or desirable to deal with the other party.

These five conditions set up a potential for exchange. Whether exchange actually takes place depends upon the parties' coming to an agreement on the terms. If they agree, we conclude that the act of exchange leaves all of them better off (or at least not worse off) because each was free to reject or accept the offer.

Transactions As exchange is the core concept of the discipline of marketing, a transaction is its unit of measurement.

> A **transaction** consists of a trade of values between two parties.

We must be able to say, A gives X to B and gets Y in return. Jones gives $400 to Smith and obtains a television set. This is a classic *monetary transaction,* although transactions do not require money as one of the traded values. A *barter transaction* would consist of Jones giving a refrigerator to Smith in return for a television set. A barter transaction can also consist of the trading of services instead of goods, as when lawyer Jones writes a will for physician Smith in return for a medical examination (see exhibit 1-1).

A transaction involves several factors: (1) at least two things of value, (2) conditions that are agreed to, (3) a time of agreement, and (4) a place of agreement. Usually a legal system supports and enforces the terms of the transaction.

Exhibit **1-1**

Going Back to Barter

In the United States today, thousands of people are returning to the primitive practice of barter, thanks to high prices. Many people find that they can trade services or goods for other services or goods they need. Lawyers, doctors, and accountants swap services, and some adroit barterers obtain haircuts, dry cleaning, dental care, and other services without paying any cash. Many would-be barterers are joining the growing number of swapping clubs.

Some large companies are also resorting to barter. A few years ago Xerox offered to trade two hundred desktop copiers, worth about $800,000, for needed goods such as forklift trucks and airline tickets for employees traveling on company business. Not surprisingly, some specialist bartering companies have arisen to help individuals and companies achieve their bartering goals. One is Barter Systems Inc. of Oklahoma City, which operates sixty-two trading centers around the United States. A letter that it sent to a select number of its twenty-five thousand clients contained the following statement: "Wanted: $300,000 worth of dried milk or cornflakes, in return for an airplane of equal value." These bartering organizations are using computers to locate parties that may want to make a trade, and they give moneylike credits for future deals. They usually pay their employees in cash but prefer to pay them in the form of hard goods and services if the employees are willing.

Source: Written by the author based on "Swapathon," *Time*, November 9, 1981, pp. 74–75, and other sources.

A transaction differs from a transfer. In a transfer, A gives X to B but receives nothing explicit in return. Transfers include gifts, subsidies, and charitable acts and are also forms of exchange. The transferrer gives a gift in the expectation of some benefit, such as a good feeling, relief from a sense of guilt, or the wish to put the other party under an obligation. Professional fund-raisers are acutely aware of the "reciprocal" motives underlying donor behavior and try to provide the benefits sought by the donors. If they neglect the donors or show no gratitude, they will soon lose the donors' support. As a result, marketers have recently broadened the concept of marketing to include the study of transfer behavior as well as transaction behavior.

In the broadest sense, the marketer in a transfer is seeking to bring about a response to some offer; the response is not "buying" or "trading" in the narrow sense. A political candidate wants a response called "votes," a church wants a response called "joining," a social action group wants a response called "adopting the idea." Marketing consists of actions undertaken to elicit a desired response in any form from a target audience toward some object, service, or idea.

Markets The concept of transactions leads to the concept of a market.

A **market** is the set of actual and potential buyers of a product.

To understand the nature of a market, imagine a primitive economy consisting of four persons: a fisher, a hunter, a potter, and a farmer. Figure 1-3 shows three different ways in which these traders could meet their needs. In the first case, *self-sufficiency,* each person is able to gather the needed goods. Thus, the fisher spends more time fishing but also takes time to hunt, make pottery, and farm to obtain the other goods. The fisher is therefore less efficient at fishing, and the same is true of the other traders. In the second case, *decentralized exchange,* each person sees the other three as potential "buyers" and therefore making up a market. The fisher may make separate trips to the hunter, the potter, and the farmer to trade fish for their goods. In the third case, *centralized exchange,* a new person called a merchant appears, who locates in a central area called a marketplace. The traders bring their special goods to the merchant and trade for the things they need. Thus the fisher transacts with one "market" rather than with three other persons to obtain other goods. The emergence of a merchant substantially reduces the total number of transactions required to accomplish a given volume of exchange. In other words, merchants and central marketplaces increase the **transactional efficiency** of the economy.[4] (Transactional efficiency is discussed further in chapter 12.)

As the number of persons and transactions increases in a society, the number of merchants and marketplaces also increases. In advanced societies, markets need not be physical places where buyers and sellers interact. With modern communications and transportation, a merchant can advertise a product on late evening television, take orders from hundreds of customers over the phone, and

FIGURE 1-3

Evolution toward Centralized Exchange

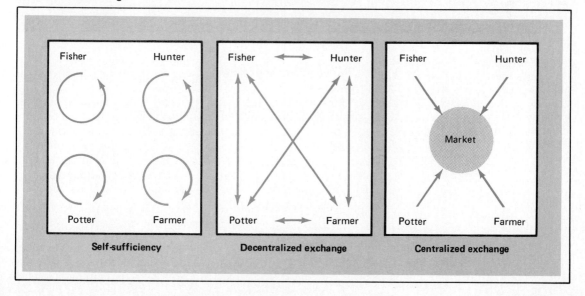

| Self-sufficiency | Decentralized exchange | Centralized exchange |

Markets, such as this farmers' market in Washington, D.C., bring buyers and sellers together to make transactions.
USDA Photo by Wm. E. Carnahan

mail the goods to the buyers on the following day without having had any physical contact with the buyers.

A market can grow up around a product, a service, or anything else of value. For example, a labor market consists of people who are willing to offer their work in return for wages or products. Various institutions such as employment agencies and job-counseling firms will grow up around a labor market to help its functioning. The money market is another important market that emerges to meet the needs of people so that they can borrow, lend, save, and safeguard money. And the donor market emerges to meet the financial needs of nonprofit organizations so that they can carry out their efforts.

Marketing The concept of markets finally brings us full circle to the concept of marketing. Marketing means human activity that takes place in relation to markets. Marketing means working with markets to create exchanges for the purpose of satisfying human needs and wants. Thus we return to our definition of marketing as human activity directed at satisfying needs and wants through exchange processes.

Exchange processes involve work. Sellers have to search for buyers, identify their needs, design appropriate products, promote them, store and transport them, negotiate prices, and so on. Such activities as product development, research, communication, distribution, pricing, and service are core marketing activities.

Although we normally think of marketing as being carried on by "sellers," buyers also carry on marketing activities. Homemakers do their "marketing," that is, they search for the goods they need at prices they are willing to pay. A company's purchasing agent who needs a commodity in short supply has to track down sellers and offer attractive terms. A *sellers' market* is one in which the sellers have more power and the buyers have to be the more active "marketers." A *buyers' market* is one in which the buyers have more power and the sellers have to be the more active "marketers."

In the early 1950s the supply of goods began to grow faster than the demand, and marketing became identified with sellers trying to find buyers. This book will take this point of view and examine the marketing problems of sellers in a buyers' market.

Marketing Management

Those who engage in the exchange process learn how to do it better over a period of time. In particular, sellers learn how to become more professional in their marketing management. We define marketing management as follows:

> **Marketing management** is the analysis, planning, implementation, and control of programs designed to create, build, and maintain beneficial exchanges with target buyers for the purpose of achieving organizational objectives, such as profit, sales growth, market share, and so on.

The popular image of the marketing manager is that of someone who finds enough customers for the company's current output. This, however, is too limited a view of the range of marketing tasks carried out by marketing managers. Marketing managers are concerned not only with creating and expanding demand but also with modifying and occasionally reducing it. *Marketing management seeks to influence the level, timing, and character of demand in a way that will help the organization achieve its objectives.* Simply put, marketing management is *demand management.*

The organization forms an idea of a desired demand level for its products. At any point in time, the actual demand level may be below, equal to, or above the desired demand level. That is, there may be no demand or there may be weak demand, adequate demand, excessive demand, and so on. Marketing management has to cope with these different states of demand. (See exhibit 1-2.)

Exhibit **1-2**

States of Demand and the Corresponding Marketing Tasks

1. *Negative demand*: A market is in a state of negative demand if a major part of the market dislikes the product and may even pay a price to avoid it. People have a negative demand for vaccinations, dental work, vasectomies, and gall bladder operations. Employers feel a negative demand for ex-convicts and alcoholic employees. The marketing task is to analyze why the market dislikes the product and whether a marketing program can change the market's beliefs and attitudes through product redesign, lower prices, and more positive promotion.

2. *No demand*: Target consumers may be uninterested in or indifferent to the product. Thus farmers may not be interested in a new farming method, and college students may not be interested in taking foreign language courses. The marketing task is to find ways to connect the benefits of the product with the person's natural needs and interests.

3. *Latent demand*: Many consumers may share a strong desire for something that cannot be satisfied by any existing product or service. There is a strong latent demand for nonharmful cigarettes, safer neighborhoods, and more fuel-efficient cars. The marketing task is to measure the size of the potential market and develop effective goods and services that will satisfy the demand.

4. *Falling demand*: Every organization, sooner or later, faces falling demand for one or more of its products. Churches have seen their membership decline, and private colleges have seen their applications decline. The marketer must analyze the causes of market decline and determine whether demand can be restimulated by finding new target markets, changing the product's features, or developing more effective communications. The marketing task is to reverse the declining demand through creative remarketing of the product.

5. *Irregular demand*: Many organizations face demand that varies on a seasonal, daily, or even hourly basis, causing problems of idle capacity or overworked capacity. In mass transit, much of the equipment is idle during the off-peak hours and insufficient during the peak travel hours.

By **marketing managers**, we mean personnel within the company who are involved in marketing analysis, planning, implementation, and/or control activities. The group includes sales managers and salespeople, advertising executives, sales promotion specialists, marketing researchers, product managers, and pricing specialists. We will say more about these marketing job positions in chapter 2 and in appendix B.

Museums are undervisited during weekdays and overcrowded during weekends. Hospital operating rooms are overbooked early in the week and underbooked toward the end of the week. The marketing task is to find ways to alter the time pattern of demand through flexible pricing, promotion, and other incentives.

6. *Full demand:* Organizations face full demand when they are pleased with their amount of business. The marketing task is to maintain the current level of demand in the face of changing consumer preferences and increasing competition. The organization must preserve its quality and continually measure consumer satisfaction to make sure it is doing a good job.

7. *Overall demand:* Some organizations face a demand level that is higher than they can or want to handle. Thus the Golden Gate Bridge carries a higher amount of traffic than is safe, and Yellowstone National Park is overcrowded in the summertime. The marketing task, called *demarketing,* requires finding ways to reduce the demand temporarily or permanently. General demarketing seeks to discourage overall demand and consists of such steps as raising prices and reducing promotion and service. Selective demarketing consists of trying to reduce the demand coming from those parts of the market that are less profitable or less in need of the service. Demarketing does not aim to destroy demand but only to reduce its level.

8. *Unwholesome demand:* Unwholesome products will attract organized efforts to discourage their consumption. Unselling campaigns have been conducted against cigarettes, alcohol, hard drugs, handguns, X-rated movies, and large families. The marketing task is to get people who like something to give it up, using such tools as fear communications, price hikes, and reduced availability.

Note: For a fuller discussion, see Philip Kotler, "The Major Tasks of Marketing Management," *Journal of Marketing,* October 1973, pp. 42–49; and Philip Kotler and Sidney J. Levy, "Demarketing, Yes, Demarketing," *Harvard Business Review,* November-December 1971, pp. 74–80.

Marketing Management Philosophies

We have described marketing management as the carrying out of tasks to achieve the desired demand levels in various markets. Now the questions arise: What philosophy should guide these marketing efforts? What weight should be given to the interests of the organization, customers, and society? Very often these conflict. Clearly, marketing activities should be carried out under some philosophy.

There are five basic concepts under which business and other organizations conduct their marketing activity: the production, product, selling, marketing, and societal marketing concepts. These concepts reflect different periods in American economic history and major social, economic, and political changes in the past 50 years. The general trend has been from a production/product to a selling, to a consumer, and increasingly to a consumer/societal orientation.

The Production Concept

The production concept is one of the oldest philosophies guiding sellers.

> The **production concept** holds that consumers will favor those products that are available and highly affordable, and therefore management should concentrate on improving production and distribution efficiency.

The production concept is an appropriate philosophy in two types of situations. The first is where the demand for a product exceeds the supply. Here management should concentrate on finding ways to increase production. The second situation is where the product's cost is high and has to be brought down and improved productivity is needed. Henry Ford's whole philosophy was to perfect the production of the Model T so that its cost could be brought down and more people could afford it. He joked about offering people any color car as long as it was black. Today Texas Instruments (TI) practices this philosophy of pursuing production volume and lower costs in order to bring down prices. It succeeded in winning a major share of the American hand-calculator market with this philosophy. However, when TI applied the same strategy in the digital watch market, it failed. Customers did not find TI's watches attractive, although they were priced low.[5]

Some service organizations also follow the production concept. Many medical and dental practices are organized on assembly-line principles, as are some government agencies such as unemployment offices and license bureaus. Although this results in handling many cases per hour, this type of management is open to the charge of impersonality and consumer insensitivity.

The Product Concept

The product concept is another major concept guiding sellers.

> The **product concept** holds that consumers will favor those products that offer the most quality, performance, and features, and therefore the organization should devote its energy to making continuous product improvements.

Many manufacturers believe that if they can build a better mousetrap, the world will beat a path to their door.[6] But they are often rudely shocked. The buyers are looking for a solution to a mouse problem and not necessarily a better mousetrap. The solution might take the form of a chemical spray, an exterminating service, or something that works better than a mousetrap. Furthermore, a better mousetrap will not sell unless the manufacturer takes positive steps to design, package, and price this new product attractively, place it into convenient distribution channels, bring it to the attention of people who need it, and convince them that it has superior qualities.

The product concept leads to "marketing myopia"—sellers liking their products so much, they lose sight of customers' needs.[7] Railroad management thought that users wanted trains rather than transportation and overlooked the growing challenge of airlines, buses, trucks, and automobiles. Slide-rule manufacturers thought that engineers wanted slide rules rather than calculating capacity and overlooked the challenge of pocket calculators. Colleges assume that high-school graduates want a liberal arts education and overlook the shift of preference to vocationally-oriented education.

The Selling Concept

Many producers follow the selling concept.

The **selling concept** holds that consumers will not buy enough of the organization's products unless the organization undertakes a substantial selling and promotion effort.

Sell anything

The selling concept is followed most aggressively with "unsought goods," those goods that buyers normally do not think of buying, such as insurance, encyclopedias, and funeral plots. These industries have perfected various sales techniques to track down prospects and hard-sell them on the benefits of their product.

Hard selling also occurs with sought goods, such as automobiles.

From the moment the customer walks into the showroom, the auto salesman "psychs him out." If the customer likes the floor model, he may be told that there is another customer about to buy it and that he should decide on the spot. If the customer balks at the price, the salesman offers to talk to the manager to get a special concession. The customer waits ten minutes and the salesman returns with "the boss doesn't like it but I got him to agree." The aim is to "work up the customer" to buy on the spot.[8]

The selling concept is also practiced in the nonprofit area. A political party will vigorously sell its candidate to the voters as being a fantastic person for the job.[9] The candidate stumps through voting precincts from early morning to late evening, shaking hands, kissing babies, meeting donors, making breezy speeches. Countless dollars are spent on radio and television advertising, posters, and mailings. Any flaws in the candidate are shielded from the public because the aim is to get the sale, not worry about post-purchase satisfaction.

The Marketing Concept

The marketing concept is a more recent business philosophy.[10]

The **marketing concept** holds that the key to achieving organizational goals consists in determining the needs and wants of target markets and delivering the desired satisfactions more effectively and efficiently than competitors.

The marketing concept has been expressed in colorful ways, such as "Find wants and fill them"; "Make what you can sell instead of trying to sell what you

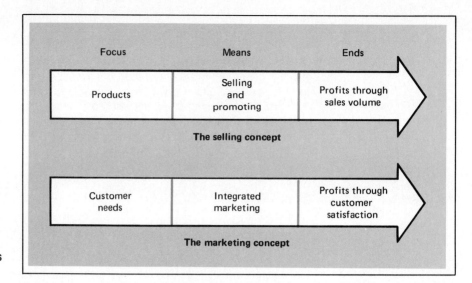

FIGURE 1-4

The Selling and
Marketing Concepts
Contrasted

can make"; "Love the customer and not the product"; "Have it your way" (Burger King); and "You're the boss" (United Airlines). J. C. Penney's motto summarizes this attitude: "To do all in our power to pack the customer's dollar full of value, quality, and satisfaction."

The selling concept and the marketing concept are frequently confused. Levitt contrasts the two:

> Selling focuses on the needs of the seller; marketing on the needs of the buyer. Selling is preoccupied with the seller's need to convert his product into cash; marketing with the idea of satisfying the needs of the customer by means of the product and the whole cluster of things associated with creating, delivering and finally consuming it.[11]

Figure 1-4 compares the two concepts. The selling concept starts with the company's existing products and calls for heavy selling and promotion to achieve profitable sales. The marketing concept starts with the company's target customers and their needs and wants. The company integrates and coordinates all the activities that will affect customer satisfaction, and achieves its profits through creating and maintaining customer satisfaction. In essence, *the marketing concept is a customer-needs-and-wants orientation backed by integrated marketing effort aimed at generating customer satisfaction as the key to satisfying organizational goals.*

The marketing concept expresses the company's commitment to *consumer sovereignty.* The companies produce what consumers want, and in this way they maximize consumer satisfaction and earn their profits.

Many companies have adopted the marketing concept. We know that Procter & Gamble, IBM, Avon, and McDonald's follow this concept faithfully (see exhibit 1-3). We also know that the marketing concept is practiced more in

Exhibit **1-3**

McDonald's Corporation Applies the Marketing Concept

McDonald's Corporation, the fast-food hamburger retailer, is a master marketer. In its short twenty-eight years, McDonald's has served over 40 billion hamburgers to people here and abroad! With over 5,500 outlets (1,100 abroad), it commands an 18% share of the fast-food market, far ahead of its next rivals, Burger King (5.7%), Kentucky Fried Chicken (5.5%), and Wendy's (4.1%). Credit for this leading position belongs to a thoroughgoing marketing orientation. McDonald's knows how to serve people and adapt to changing consumer needs.

Before McDonald's, Americans could get hamburgers in restaurants or diners. In many places, the consumer encountered poor hamburgers, slow service, unattractive decor, unfriendly help, unsanitary conditions, and a noisy atmosphere. In 1955, Ray Kroc, a 52-year-old salesman of milk shake mixers, became excited about a string of seven restaurants owned by Richard and Maurice McDonald. Kroc liked their concept of a fast-food restaurant and negotiated to buy the chain and its name for $2.7 million.

Kroc decided to expand the chain by selling franchises to others. Franchisees buy a twenty-year license for $150,000. They take a ten-day training course at McDonald's "Hamburger University" in Elk Grove Village, Illinois. They emerge with a degree in "Hamburgerology," with a minor in "French Fries."

Kroc's marketing strategy is captured in the initials "QSC," which stand for quality, service, and cleanliness. Customers enter a spotlessly clean restaurant, walk up to a friendly hostess, order and receive a good-tasting hamburger within no more than five minutes, and eat it there or take it out. There are no jukeboxes or telephones to create a teenage hangout. Nor are there any cigarette machines or newspaper racks. McDonald's became a family affair, particularly appealing to the children.

As time changed, so did McDonald's. McDonald's expanded its sit-down sections, improved the decor, launched a breakfast menu, added new food items, and opened new outlets in high-traffic areas.

McDonald's has mastered the art of franchise service marketing. It chooses locations carefully, selects highly qualified franchise operators, gives complete management training at Hamburger University, supports its franchisers with a high-quality national advertising and sales promotion program, monitors product and service quality through continuous customer surveys, and puts great energy into improving the technology of hamburger production to simplify operations, bring down costs, and speed up service.

consumer goods companies than in industrial goods companies, and more in large companies than in small companies.[12] Also, many companies profess the concept but do not practice it. They have the forms of marketing—such as a marketing vice-president, product managers, marketing plans, marketing research—but not the substance.[13] Several years of hard work are necessary to turn a sales-oriented company into a market-oriented company.

The Societal Marketing Concept

The societal marketing concept is the newest concept.

> The **societal marketing concept** holds that the organization's task is to determine the needs, wants, and interests of target markets and to deliver the desired satisfactions more effectively and efficiently than competitors in a way that preserves or enhances the consumer's and the society's well-being.

The societal marketing concept arises from questioning whether the pure marketing concept is adequate in an age of environmental deterioration, resource shortages, explosive population growth, worldwide inflation, and neglected social services.[14] Is the firm that senses, serves, and satisfies consumers' wants always acting in the best long-run interests of consumers and society? The pure marketing concept sidesteps possible conflicts between consumer wants and long-run consumer welfare.

Consider the Coca-Cola Company. People see it as being a highly responsible corporation producing fine soft drinks that satisfy consumer tastes. Yet consumer and environmental groups have leveled the following complaints:

1. Coke delivers little nutritional benefit to its consumers.
2. Coke's sugar and phosphoric acid harm people's teeth.
3. The brominated vegetable oil in colas has been removed from the Federal Drug Administration's list of products "generally recognized as safe."
4. In some instances, it has been found that the caffeine in colas produces tremors, insomnia, gastrointestinal disorders, and possible cellular damage.
5. The saccharine in Coca-Cola's diet soft drink, Tab, was banned by the FDA.
6. The soft-drink industry has increased the use of one-way disposable bottles. The one-way bottle presents a great waste of resources in that approximately seventeen bottles are necessary where one two-way bottle would have made seventeen trips before it could no longer be used. Many one-way bottles are not biodegradable and often are a littering element.

These and similar situations led to the formulation of the societal marketing concept.[15] The societal marketing concept calls upon marketers to balance three considerations in setting their marketing policies (see figure 1-5). Originally, companies based their marketing decisions largely on the profit the company would make. Then they began to recognize the long-run importance of satisfying consumer wants, and this introduced the marketing concept. Now they are beginning to think of society's interests when making decisions. The societal marketing concept calls for balancing all three considerations—company profits, consumer wants, and society's interests. A number of companies have made

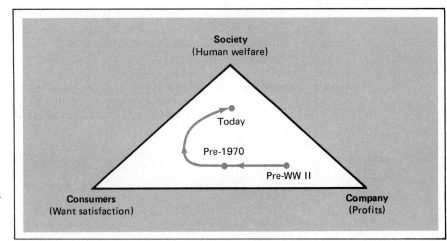

substantial sales and profit gains by adopting and practicing the societal marketing concept.

The Goals of a Marketing System

We know that marketing affects everyone—the buyer, the seller, the citizen. And their goals may conflict. Consider the following case.

THE BUYER. John Smith, a college student, wants to buy stereo equipment. At a large stereo retail outlet, he sees several stereo components. Several questions come to his mind:

- Is the brand selection wide enough?
- Does any brand have the features I want?
- Is the price fair?
- Is the salesperson helpful, pleasant, and honest?
- Is there a warranty and good follow-up service?

John Smith wants the marketplace to provide quality products at reasonable prices at convenient locations. The marketing system can make a great difference to people's satisfaction as buyers.

THE SELLER. Bill Thompson is the marketing manager of a company that manufactures stereo equipment. To do his job well, he must decide on a number of issues:

- What features do consumers want in stereo equipment?
- Which consumer groups and needs should my company try to satisfy?
- How should the product be designed and priced?

- What guarantees and services should we offer?
- Which wholesalers and retailers should we use?
- What advertising, personal selling, sales promotion, and publicity would help sell this product?

The seller faces several challenging decisions in preparing an offer for the market. The market is very demanding. The seller must apply modern marketing thinking to develop an offer that attracts and satisfies customers.

THE CITIZEN.   Jane Adams, a state senator, has a special interest in the marketing activities of business. As a legislator representing the citizens, she is concerned with the following questions:

- Are manufacturers making safe and reliable products?
- Are they describing their products accurately in their ads and packaging?
- Is competition working in this market to offer a reasonable range of quality and price choices?
- Are the retailers and service people treating consumers fairly?
- Are manufacturing and packaging activities hurting the environment?

Jane Adams acts as a watchdog of consumer interests and favors consumer education, information, and protection. The marketing system has a major impact on the quality of life, and legislators want to make the system work as well as possible.

Marketing affects so many people in so many ways that it inevitably stirs controversy. Some people intensely dislike modern marketing activity, charging it with ruining the environment, bombarding the public with inane ads, creating unnecessary wants, teaching greed to youngsters, and committing several other sins. Consider the following:

For the past 6,000 years the field of marketing has been thought of as made up of fast-buck artists, con-men, wheeler-dealers, and shoddy-goods distributors. Too many of us have been "taken" by the tout or con-men; and all of us at times have been prodded into buying all sorts of "things" we really did not need, and which we found later on we did not even want.[16]

What does a man need—really need? A few pounds of food each day, heat and shelter, six feet to lie down in—and some form of working activity that will yield a sense of accomplishment. That's all—in a material sense. And we know it. But we are brainwashed by our economic system until we end up in a tomb beneath a pyramid of time payments, mortgages, preposterous gadgetry, playthings that divert our attention from the sheer idiocy of the charade.[17]

Others vigorously defend marketing. Consider the following:

Aggressive marketing policies and practices have been largely responsible for the high material standard of living in America. Today through mass, low-cost marketing we enjoy products which once were considered luxuries, and which still are so classified in many foreign countries.[18]

Advertising nourishes the consuming power of men. It creates wants for a better standard of living. It sets up before a man the goal of a better home, better clothing, better food for himself and his family. It spurs individual exertion and greater production. It brings together in fertile union those things which otherwise would not have been met.[19]

What should society seek from its marketing system? The question is timely because various governments are increasingly regulating the marketing activities of firms. Some government interventions could be quite extreme:

Some government officials in India would like to ban the branding of sugar, soap, tea, rice, and other staples. They hold that branding, packaging, and advertising push up consumer prices.

Some government officials in the Philippines favor socialized pricing, namely, holding down the price of staples through price control.

Some government officials in Norway advocate banning certain "luxury" goods, such as private swimming pools, tennis courts, airplanes, and luxury automobiles. They think Norway's resources are too limited to use for these purposes. These officials favor "collective consumption" of expensive goods and services.

The Federal Trade Commission introduced three measures in the early 1970s to promote "truth in advertising." Advertising substantiation requires firms to stand ready to provide documentary evidence backing any claim they make in an ad. Corrective advertising requires a firm found guilty of a false claim to spend 25% of its advertising budget on a corrective message. Counter advertising encourages groups that oppose a product (such as an antismoking group) to have easy access to the media to present their opinion.

The possible and actual increase in marketing regulation throughout the world raises a basic question: What is the proper goal of a marketing system? Four alternative goals have been suggested: maximize consumption, maximize consumer satisfaction, maximize choice, and maximize life quality.

Maximize Consumption Many business executives believe that marketing's job should be to aid and stimulate maximum consumption, which will in turn create maximum production, employment, and wealth. This view comes across in typical headlines: "Wrigley Seeks Ways to Get People to Chew More Gum"; "Opticians Introduce Fashion in Glasses to Stimulate Demand"; "Steel Industry Maps Strategy to Expand Sales"; "Car Manufacturers Try to Hype Sales."

The underlying assumption is that the more people buy and consume, the happier they are. "More is better" is the war cry. Yet some people doubt that increased material goods mean more happiness. Their philosophy is "less is more" and "small is beautiful."

Maximize Consumer Satisfaction Another view holds that the goal of the marketing system is to maximize consumer satisfaction, not consumption. Chewing more gum or owning more clothes counts only if this results in more consumer satisfaction.

Unfortunately, consumer satisfaction is difficult to measure. First, no economist has figured out how to measure the total satisfaction created by a particular product or marketing activity. Second, the direct satisfaction that individual consumers obtain from particular "goods" fails to take into account the "bads," such as pollution and environmental damage. Third, the satisfaction that people experience when consuming certain goods, such as status goods, depends precisely on how few other people have these goods. Thus it is difficult to evaluate a marketing system in terms of how much satisfaction it delivers to its citizens.

Maximize Choice Some marketers believe that the goal of a marketing system should be to maximize product variety and consumer choice. The system would enable consumers to find those goods that precisely satisfy their tastes. Consumers would be able to maximize their life-styles and, therefore, their satisfaction.

Maximizing consumer choice, unfortunately, comes at a cost. First, goods and services will be more expensive, since the great variety will increase production and inventory costs. Higher prices will reduce the consumers' real income and consumption. Second, the increase in product variety will require more time and effort by consumers in learning about and evaluating the different products. Third, more products will not necessarily increase consumers' *real choice*. There are many brands of beer in the United States and most of them taste the same. When a product category contains many brands with few differences, this is called *brand proliferation* and the consumer faces *false choice*. Finally, great product variety is not always welcomed by all consumers. Some consumers feel that there is *overchoice* in certain product categories, which causes frustration and anxiety.

Maximize Life Quality Many people believe that the goal of a marketing system should be to improve the "quality of life." The quality of life consists of (1) the quality, quantity, range, accessibility, and cost of goods; (2) the quality of the physical environment; and (3) the quality of the cultural environment. They would judge marketing systems not solely by the amount of direct consumer satisfaction that is created but also by the impact of marketing activity on the quality of the physical and cultural environment. Most people would agree that the quality of life is a worthwhile goal for the marketing system, but they recognize that it is not easy to measure and is subject to conflicting interpretations.

The Rapid Adoption of Marketing

Most people think that marketing is carried on only in large companies operating in capitalistic countries. The truth is that marketing is carried on within and outside the business sector in all kinds of countries.

In the Business Sector In the business sector, different companies adopted marketing at different times. General Electric, General Motors, Sears, Procter & Gamble, and Coca-Cola saw marketing's potential almost immediately. Marketing spread most rapidly in consumer packaged-goods companies, consumer durables companies, and industrial equipment companies—in that order. Producers of such commodities as steel, chemicals, and paper adopted marketing later, and many still have a long way to go. Within the past decade, consumer service firms, especially airlines and banks, have moved toward modern marketing. Airlines began to study travelers' attitudes toward different service features: schedule frequency, baggage handling, in-flight service, friendliness, seat comfort. They shed the notion that they were in the air carrier business and realized that they were in the total travel business. Bankers initially resisted marketing but are now embracing it enthusiastically. Marketing is also beginning to attract the interest of insurance and stock brokerage companies, although they have a long way to go in applying marketing effectively.

The latest business groups to take an interest in marketing are professionals, such as lawyers, accountants, physicians, and architects. Professional societies have, until recently, prohibited their members from engaging in price competition, client solicitation, and advertising. The U.S. antitrust division recently ruled that these restraints are illegal. Accountants, lawyers, and other professional groups are now allowed to advertise and to price aggressively.

Consumer service firms, such as banks, have enthusiastically adopted marketing.

©1983, The First National Bank of Chicago, Member F.D.I.C. Courtesy Foote, Cone & Belding.

In the International Sector Marketing is practiced not only in the United States but in the rest of the world. In fact, several European and Japanese multinationals—companies like Nestlé, Siemens, Toyota, and Sony—have in many cases outperformed their U.S. competitors.[20] Multinationals have introduced and spread modern marketing practices throughout the world. As a result, management in smaller companies is beginning to ask: What is marketing? How does it differ from plain selling? How can we introduce marketing into the firm? Will it make a difference?

In socialist countries, marketing has traditionally had a bad name. However, various functions of marketing, such as marketing research, branding, advertising, and sales promotion, are now spreading rapidly. In the USSR there are now over one hundred state-operated advertising agencies and marketing research firms.[21] Several companies in Poland and Hungary have marketing departments, and several socialist universities teach marketing.

In the Nonprofit Sector Marketing is currently attracting the interest of nonprofit organizations such as colleges, hospitals, police departments, museums, and symphonies. Consider the following developments:

> More than 170 private colleges have closed their doors since 1965, unable to attract enough students or funds or both. Tuition at the top private universities is now over $8,000. If college costs continue to climb at the current rate, the parents of a child born today will have to save $83,000 to pay for a bachelor's degree at one of the top private colleges.[22]

> Hospital costs continue to soar, leading to daily room rates in excess of $300 at some large hospitals. Many hospitals are experiencing underutilization, particularly in the maternity and pediatrics sections. Some experts have predicted the closing of 1,400 to 1,500 hospitals in the next ten years.

> The Catholic Church drew as many as 55% of all adult Catholics under thirty years of age to church in a typical week in 1966. By 1975 the figure had fallen to 39%, and further declines in weekly attendance are expected.

> Many performing arts groups cannot attract enough audiences. Even those that have seasonal sellouts, such as the Lyric Opera Company of Chicago, face huge operating deficits at the end of the year.

> Many flourishing nonprofit organizations of yesteryear—the YMCA, Salvation Army, Girl Scouts, and Women's Christian Temperance Union—are losing members and failing to attract enough financial support.

These organizations have marketplace problems. Their administrators are struggling to keep them alive in the face of changing consumer attitudes and diminishing financial resources. Many institutions have turned to marketing as a possible answer to their problems. As a sign of the times, the Evanston Hospital of Evanston, Illinois, appointed a vice-president of marketing to develop and promote its hospital services in the community and to develop plans to attract more patients, physicians, and nurses.

U.S. government agencies are showing an increased interest in marketing. The U.S. Postal Service and Amtrak have developed marketing plans for their respective operations. The U.S. Army has a marketing plan to attract recruits and is one of the top advertising spenders in the country. Other government agencies are now marketing energy conservation, antismoking, and other public causes.

Plan of the Book

The next two chapters will elaborate on the themes and principles of marketing introduced in this chapter. Chapter 2, "The Marketing Management Process," provides an overview of the company marketing process, consisting of analyzing market opportunities, selecting target markets, developing the marketing mix, and managing the marketing effort. Chapter 3 discusses the importance of marketing research and information as the key step in knowing customers and how to satisfy their needs.

Chapters 4, 5, and 6 look at the changing marketing environment and the key characteristics of consumer and organizational markets. These are studied by the firm to identify attractive market opportunities.

Chapter 7 describes the art of selecting appropriate markets for the company to serve. This is done through segmenting and targeting markets and positioning the company's products in its markets.

Chapters 8 through 16 examine the major marketing activities of the firm, specifically designing, pricing, placing, and promoting products and services. We will look at the various concepts and techniques that marketing managers use to develop attractive products and bring them to the attention of the market.

Chapter 17 describes how these separate marketing activities are integrated into companywide plans, using a marketing control system to make sure that the organization's goals are being achieved.

Chapters 18 and 19 examine topics of high current interest, specifically international marketing and services and nonprofit marketing. The last chapter, "Marketing and Society," returns us to the basic question of the role and purpose of the marketing system in society, its contributions, and its possible deficiencies.

At the end of the book are two appendixes. The first shows the marketing arithmetic used by marketing managers to guide their calculations. The second discusses various marketing careers and describes how students can apply marketing principles in the search for a desirable job.

Summary

Marketing touches everyone's life. It is the means by which the products and services that create a standard of living are developed and delivered to a people. Marketing involves a large number of activities, including marketing research, product development, distribution, pricing, advertising, and personal selling. Many people confuse marketing with selling, whereas marketing actually combines several activities designed to sense, serve, and satisfy consumer needs while meeting the goals of the organization. Marketing occurs long before and after the selling event.

Marketing is human activity directed at satisfying needs and wants through exchange processes. The key concepts in the study of marketing are needs, wants, demands, products, exchange, transactions, and markets.

Marketing management is the analysis, planning, implementation, and control of programs designed to create, build, and maintain beneficial exchanges with target buyers for the purpose of achieving organizational objectives. Marketers must be good at managing the level, timing, and composition of demand, since demand can be at variance with what the organization wants.

Marketing management can be conducted under five different marketing philosophies. The production concept holds that consumers will favor products that are available at low cost, and therefore management's task is to improve production efficiency and bring down prices. The product concept holds that consumers favor quality products, and therefore little promotional effort is required. The selling concept holds that consumers will not buy enough of the company's products unless they are stimulated through a substantial selling and promotion effort. The marketing concept holds that a company should research the needs and wants of a well-defined target market and deliver the desired satisfactions. The societal marketing concept holds that the company should generate customer satisfaction and long-run consumer and societal well-being as the key to achieving organizational goals.

Marketing practices have a major impact on people in their roles as buyers, sellers, and citizens. Different goals have been proposed for a marketing system, such as maximizing consumption, or consumer satisfaction, or consumer choice, or life quality. Many people believe that marketing's goal should be to enhance the quality of life and that the means should be the societal marketing concept.

Interest in marketing is intensifying as more organizations in the business sector, in the international sector, and in the nonprofit sector recognize how marketing contributes to improved performance in the marketplace.

Questions for Discussion

1. The historian Arnold Toynbee has criticized marketing practice in America, saying that American consumers are being manipulated into purchasing products that aren't required to satisfy the "minimum material requirements of life or genuine wants." What is your position? Defend it.
2. How does marketing differ from selling? Would you rather be an expert marketer or an expert seller of yourself when you are looking for a job after graduation? Explain.
3. You are planning to go to a fast-food franchise for lunch. Apply the notions of products, exchange transactions, and a market to this situation.
4. Although McDonald's Corporation has been praised as being a prime practitioner of the marketing concept, it has also been criticized for practicing a product orientation. What might have stimulated this criticism?
5. Procter & Gamble's success is often credited to the company's ability to be a good "listener." How does this relate to the marketing concept?
6. How can the marketing management philosophies of the product concept and production concept be contrasted? Give an example of each.

7. Why has the societal marketing concept superseded the marketing concept for some organizations?
8. How can marketing have an impact on each of the three aspects of the quality of life mentioned? Can you think of other quality-of-life dimensions? How might marketing affect these?
9. Why has marketing been embraced by many nonprofit organizations in recent years? Elaborate on a specific example.

Key Terms in Chapter 1

Demands   Human wants that are backed by purchasing power.

Exchange   The act of obtaining a desired object from someone by offering something in return.

Human need   A person's feeling of deprivation.

Human want   The form that a human need takes as shaped by a person's culture and individuality.

Market   The set of actual and potential buyers of a product.

Marketing   Human activity directed at satisfying needs and wants through exchange processes.

Marketing concept   The idea that the key to achieving organizational goals consists in determining the needs and wants of target markets and delivering the desired satisfactions more effectively and efficiently than competitors.

Marketing management   The analysis, planning, implementation, and control of programs designed to create, build, and maintain beneficial exchanges with target buyers for the purpose of achieving organizational objectives.

Marketing manager   An employee of a company who is involved in analysis, planning, implementation, and/or control activities.

Product   Anything that can be offered to a market for attention, acquisition, use, or consumption that might satisfy a want or need.

Product concept   The idea that consumers will favor those products that offer the most quality, performance, and features, and therefore the organization should devote its energy to making continuous product improvements.

Production concept   The idea that consumers will favor those products that are available and highly affordable, and therefore management should concentrate on improving production and distribution efficiency.

Selling concept   The idea that consumers will not buy enough of the organization's products unless the organization undertakes a substantial selling and promotion effort.

Societal marketing concept   The idea that the organization's task is to determine the needs, wants, and interests of target markets and to deliver the desired satisfactions more effectively and efficiently than competitors in a way that preserves or enhances the consumer's and the society's well-being.

Transaction   A trade between two parties that involves at least two things of value, agreed-upon conditions, a time of agreement, and a place of agreement.

Transactional efficiency   The degree to which a volume of exchanges can be accomplished with the fewest possible transactions.

Cases for Chapter 1

Case 1   Sony Corporation: Walkman (p. 493)

Do American consumers need, want, or demand the Walkman? How can Sony create a demand for the Walkman among American consumers? This case looks at these points.

Case 2   Minnetonka, Inc.: ShowerMate™ (p. 494)

Can Minnetonka create enough demand for ShowerMate, a new product with many competitors? This case considers that question.

Chapter 2

The Marketing Management Process

Objectives

After reading this chapter, you should be able to:

1. Discuss how organizations look for new marketing opportunities
2. Explain why organizations segment markets.
3. Define marketing mix and list the "four *P*'s" of marketing.
4. Compare the five ways of organizing the marketing department.

Before 1970, Miller Brewing Company of Milwaukee stood as a stodgy seventh-place brewer with a 4% market share and flat sales. Meanwhile, Anheuser-Busch's and Schlitz's sales were growing 10% a year, twice the industry's overall growth rate. Then Philip Morris, flush with cash from its successful tobacco business, decided to buy Miller as an entry into the beer market. It put its marketing muscle behind flabby Miller, took several new initiatives, and propelled Miller, in the course of five years, into the number-two spot. And by 1981, Miller held 22% of the beer market, short of Anheuser-Busch's 29%, but far ahead of third-place Schlitz's 8%. How did Philip Morris create this modern marketing miracle?

Essentially, Philip Morris departed from the traditional approach to beer marketing, namely, working hard on production efficiency and price promotions. Philip Morris brought in classic consumer marketing techniques pioneered by Procter & Gamble and used by Philip Morris to win the number-two position in the tobacco industry and manage the most successful cigarette brand in history, Marlboro. The approach calls for studying consumer needs and wants, dividing the market into segments, identifying the best opportunity segments, producing products and packages specifically for these segments, and spending heavily to advertise and promote the new products. "Until Miller came along, the brewers operated as if there was a homogeneous market for beer that could be served by one product in one package," according to Robert S. Weinberg, a former executive with Anheuser-Busch.

Philip Morris's first step was to reposition Miller High Life, Miller's only product. Billed as the "champagne of beers," Miller High Life attracted mostly women and upper-income consumers who were not big beer drinkers. The Philip Morris executives commissioned marketing research and discovered that 30% of the beer drinkers consume 80% of the beer. Miller studied the characteristics of the six-pack-a-day beer drinkers—their demographic, psychological, and media profiles—and decided to develop a more "macho image" for Miller High Life. Its ads showed oil drillers drinking this beer after a major oil blowout, and young people drinking while riding dune buggies. The ad pitch was, "If you've got the time, we've got the beer," and this campaign ran successfully for seven years.

Then Miller began to open new market segments. It noted that diet-conscious women and older people thought the standard twelve-ounce bottle of beer was too much to consume. Miller introduced the "pony-size" seven-ounce bottle, and it was a great success.

This was nothing compared with its launch in 1975 of its lower-calorie beer called Lite. Lite is the most successful new beer introduced in the United States since 1900. Other low-cal beers had been marketed unsuccessfully, largely because they were promoted as diet drinks to diet-conscious consumers who do not drink much beer anyway. As a result, low-cal beers acquired a sissy image. Miller positioned Lite not as a low-calorie beer but as a less-filling beer for "real" beer drinkers. Sports personalities were featured who stated that because Lite had one-third fewer calories, they could drink more beer without feeling so filled. The advertising campaign has become one of the most popular and successful ones on television. Even the packaging projected a masculine appeal and looked "beery."

Miller next turned to attack Anheuser-Busch's most profitable beer, Michelob, by launching its own superpremium beer, Löwenbräu, through an agreement with the German company. Miller brews Löwenbräu in the United States and prices it higher than Michelob. It is positioned as a beer for "good friends" during special times when buyers should "let it be Löwenbräu." Löwenbräu achieved good success as a superpremium beer.

Because of its massive advertising expenditures, Miller's unprecedented growth in market share has not produced a comparable growth in profits. But Philip Morris's attitude is that it is in the beer market for the long run and could forgo short-run profits in order to reach the number-two position from which it can make large profits in the long run. Its clear target is Anheuser-Busch, which has been using the time to fine-tune its own marketing management process so that it can defend its championship title against Miller.[1]

"Lite sure tastes great."

"Red" Auerbach
Legendary Coach

One of the popular and successful advertisements for Miller Lite Beer.
Courtesy Miller Brewing Company and Backer & Spielvogel, Inc.

Philip Morris acquired the Miller Brewing Company and converted it from a stodgy production-oriented company to a highly successful marketing-oriented company. This chapter presents an overview of how successful marketing-oriented companies manage their marketing activities.

Every company operates in a complex and changing marketing environment. If the company is to survive, it must produce and offer something of value to some customer group in its environment. Through exchange, it gets back the revenue and resources it needs to survive.

The company must make sure that its objectives and product lines remain relevant to the market. Alert companies will periodically reexamine their objectives, strategies, and tactics. They will rely on marketing as the main system for monitoring and adapting to the changing marketplace. Marketing is not simply some advertising and sales-force activity but rather a whole process for matching the company to its best market opportunities. We define marketing management process as follows:

The **marketing management process** consists of (1) analyzing market opportunities, (2) selecting target markets, (3) developing the marketing mix, and (4) managing the marketing effort.

These steps are listed in figure 2-1, along with the numbers of the chapters dealing with each step. This chapter surveys the whole process.

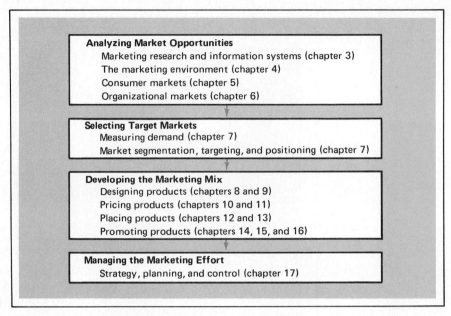

FIGURE 2-1

The Marketing
Management Process

Analyzing Market Opportunities

Every company needs to be able to identify new market opportunities. No company can depend on its present products and markets to last forever. We no longer hear about horse-drawn carriages, buggy whips, slide rules, gas lamps— all the manufacturers either went out of business or were smart enough to switch to new businesses. Many companies will testify that much of their current sales and profits comes from products they did not even produce or sell five years ago.

Companies may think that they have few opportunities, but this is only a failure to think strategically about what business they are in and what strengths they have. Every company faces, in fact, many market opportunities.

Let us test this by looking at a well-known company, Helene Curtis:

Helene Curtis Industries is a Chicago manufacturer of toiletries and other products. Founded over fifty years ago, the company's sales in 1981 were $163 million. Helene Curtis operates four divisions, each manufacturing several products: Consumer Products Division (shampoos, conditioners, skin-care lotions); Professional Division (shampoos, appliances); International Division; and Protective Treatments Division (sealants and adhesives).

Suppose Helene Curtis is seeking new market opportunities. How might it identify new opportunities and evaluate them?

FIGURE 2-2

Identifying New Markets through the Product/Market Expansion Grid

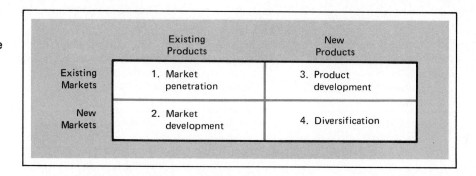

	Existing Products	New Products
Existing Markets	1. Market penetration	3. Product development
New Markets	2. Market development	4. Diversification

Identifying New Markets

Organizations can search for new opportunities casually or systematically. Many organizations find new ideas by simply keeping their ears and eyes open to the changing marketplace. Company executives read newspapers, attend trade shows, examine competitors' products, and gather market intelligence in other ways. Many ideas can be picked up by using informal methods.

Other organizations use formal methods of identifying new markets. One useful device is a *product/market expansion grid.*[2] This grid is shown in figure 2-2 and will be applied to Helene Curtis's shampoo products.

1. **MARKET PENETRATION.** First, the shampoo product manager at Helene Curtis considers whether the company's major brand, Suave, can achieve deeper *market penetration*—that is, more sales to its present target group of buyers—without changing the product in any way. The company would work with *existing products* in *existing markets*. Here a number of strategies can be tried, including cutting the list price of Suave shampoo, increasing the advertising budget, improving the advertising message, getting Suave into more stores, obtaining better shelf positions for Suave, and so on. Basically, the sham-

Helene Curtis followed product development strategies to create a whole range of Suave hair care and toiletry products.

Courtesy Helene Curtis Co.

Exhibit **2-1**

Video Games—An Attractive Industry But Not for Everyone

One of the fastest-growing U.S. industries is video games. Before 1977, lovers of action games had to go to pinball parlors or buy and hook up an Odyssey or Magnavox console to their television set, with one or a few built-in games. Atari introduced the first cartridge-driven games in 1977. Game lovers could now buy a programmable console to hook up to their television sets and choose from a large number of game cartridges bearing such names as Space Invaders, Asteroids, Pac-Man, and Crazy Climbers. The console sold for $150 and the game cartridges for $15 to $30. Sales of the new games took off in 1979 at a fantastic rate. By 1981, Atari, the industry leader, had sold more than 5 million consoles. Although only 8.5% of U.S. households have bought video games, industry experts are forecasting a 50% household penetration by 1985. And the overseas market is just opening up.

Atari dominates the game console market, with a 75% share, followed by Mattel Inc.'s Intellivision (15%), Odyssey (9%), and Astrovision (1%). Atari also dominates the game cartridge market, but a host of imitators have rushed in to design game cartridges that are compatible with Atari or Intellivision consoles. The most successful new game cartridge company is Activision, formed by four former software designers who defected from Atari. In less than two years, Activision sales reached $50 million, more than sixty times the company's original investment. At least a dozen other companies displayed new game cartridges at a recent consumer electronics trade show.

poo manager would like to attract customers of other brands to Suave while not losing any current Suave customers.

2. **MARKET DEVELOPMENT.** Second, the shampoo manager tries to identify *new markets* for Suave, the *existing product*. The manager reviews *demographic markets*—infants, preschoolers, teenagers, young adults, senior citizens—to see if any of these groups can be encouraged to switch to or buy more of its shampoo. Next, the manager reviews *institutional markets*—health clubs, beauty shops, hospitals—to see if sales to these buyers can be increased. Then the manager reviews *geographic markets*—France, Thailand, India—to see if these markets can be developed. All of these represent market development strategies.

3. **PRODUCT DEVELOPMENT.** Third, the shampoo manager might consider offering *new products* to current customers in *existing markets*. Suave shampoo

Atari executives are busily planning their marketing strategy for the next several years. One of their main concerns is Intellivision's attack strategy, which is to offer consumers a console and games that are far more sophisticated in graphics and sound effects, albeit at a higher console price of $250. In its advertising, Intellivision has positioned itself as the "Cadillac" product that costs more and delivers more. Atari's counterattack has been to use product development strategies, such as launching a Super Game console for $349 that it hopes will upstage Intellivision and destroy its "Cadillac" position. Mattel, however, plans to counter the counterattack with a voice synthesis unit that will turn Intellivision into a "talking game."

Atari also has to deal with industry experts' prediction that video-game console sales will taper off in a few years as more people acquire personal home computers. These computers will permit more sophisticated game playing as well as many other activities. Atari, fortunately, also operates a computer products division. According to one observer, "Over time, computers will replace many video games, and Atari is the only one to realize that by constantly moving to upgrade its computer business."

Clearly, Atari has found a home in an attractive industry. Whether this industry is an attractive opportunity for other companies depends on the objectives, resources, and differential advantages they can bring to this industry.

Source: Written by the author based on "New Video-Game Makers Jump into Fight for a Share of the Booming Home Market," *Wall Street Journal,* January 27, 1981, and other sources.

could be offered in new sizes, or with new scents or ingredients, or in new packaging, all representing possible product modifications. Helene Curtis could also launch one or more new brands of shampoo to appeal to different shampoo users. Helene Curtis could launch other hair-care products—hair conditioners, hair dressings—that its current customers might buy. All of these represent product development strategies.

4. DIVERSIFICATION. Fourth, Helen Curtis faces a whole set of *diversification* opportunities by offering *new products* in *new markets.* It could start or acquire businesses lying entirely outside of its current products and markets. It could consider entering such "hot" industries as video games (see exhibit 2-1), word processing equipment, personal computers, and day-care centers. Some companies try to identify the most attractive emerging industries. They feel that half the secret of success is to enter attractive industries instead of trying to be efficient in an unattractive industry.

Evaluating Marketing Opportunities It is one thing to identify opportunities and another to determine which opportunities are right for the company. We define company marketing opportunity as follows:

> A **company marketing opportunity** is an attractive arena for company marketing action in which a particular company would enjoy a competitive advantage.

For example, video games are an attractive industry, but we instinctively sense that they would not be right for Helene Curtis. Why? The answer is suggested in figure 2-3. A marketing opportunity must fit the company's objectives and resources. Let us consider each in turn.

FIGURE 2-3

Evaluating a Market Opportunity in Terms of the Company's Objectives and Resources

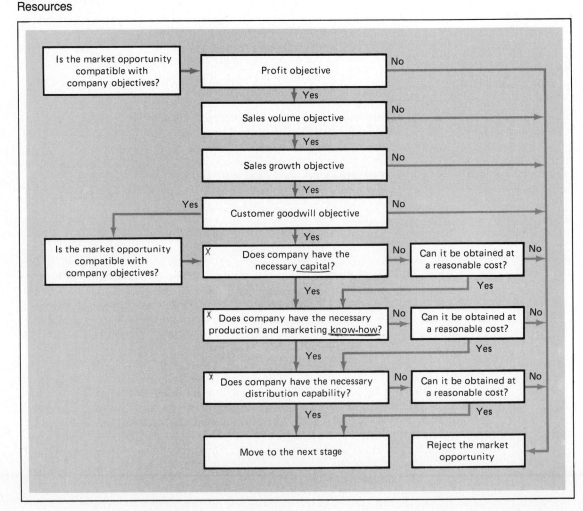

COMPANY OBJECTIVES.   Every company pursues a set of objectives. Helene Curtis, for example, primarily operates a hair-care business and seeks a high level of profits, sales, sales growth, and customer goodwill. Helene Curtis would probably decide that its objectives alone rule out the video-game industry. Sales and profits could be uncertain. Moreover, if Helene Curtis's customers view cosmetics and video games as being incompatible, goodwill could be diluted by this move.

COMPANY RESOURCES.   Even if the video-game industry fit in with Helene Curtis's objectives, Helene Curtis would probably lack the resources necessary to succeed in this industry. Each industry has certain *success requirements*. The video-game industry requires a great deal of capital, technical know-how, and effective distribution channels, all of which Helene Curtis would lack. And, while Helene Curtis could buy an existing video-game company, its present resources and experience could not help that company.

Selecting Target Markets

The process of identifying and evaluating market opportunities normally produces many new ideas. Often the company's real task is to choose the best ideas among several good ones—that is, ideas that match the company's objectives and resources.

Suppose Helene Curtis evaluated a number of market opportunities and found that the "headache pain relief" market was one of the most attractive opportunities. Helene Curtis executives would then feel that the introduction of a pain reliever conformed closely to the company's objectives and resources. This type of product would relate well to the company's existing marketing strengths—a strong sales force and distribution network and much experience in the promotion of consumer packaged goods.

More specifically, Helene Curtis must believe that it can work effectively with the important people in the pain reliever market. Helene Curtis must believe that it can establish good relations with *suppliers* of the basic chemicals, equipment, and other resources needed to make a pain reliever. It must believe that it has strong relationships with the main *marketing intermediaries* who will carry its pain reliever to customers. It must believe that it can develop a distinctive and attractive pain reliever in relation to the *competitors*. And it must believe that entry into this industry will not offend the public.

Each opportunity must also be studied in terms of the size and nature of the market. This involves four steps: *demand measurement and forecasting, market segmentation, market targeting,* and *market positioning.*

Demand Measurement and Forecasting   Now that Helene Curtis is thinking of introducing a pain reliever, it would want to make a more careful estimate of the current and future size of this market. To estimate current market size, Helene Curtis would identify all the products selling in this market—Bayer, Excedrin, Anacin, Bufferin, Tylenol, and so on—and estimate their current sales.

Equally important is the future growth of the "headache pain relief" market. Companies want to enter growing markets. The "headache pain relief" market's past growth rate has been strong, but what can be said of its future growth rate? Helene Curtis's marketing information specialists will have to look at the factors and trends that influence the pain reliever market and make forecasts about future growth.

Market Segmentation Suppose the demand forecast looks good. Helene Curtis now has to decide how to enter the market. The market consists of many types of customers, products, and needs. Consumer groups can be formed on the basis of geographic factors (regions, cities), demographic factors (sex, age, income, education), sociographic factors (social classes, life-styles), and behavior (purchase occasions, benefits sought, usage rates).

The process of classifying customers into groups with different needs, characteristics, and/or behavior is called market segmentation.

Not all ways of segmenting the market are equally useful. Distinguishing between male and female users of pain relievers, for example, is unnecessary if both respond the same way to marketing stimuli.

A market segment consists of consumers who respond in a similar way to a given set of marketing stimuli.

Consumers who choose the strongest pain reliever regardless of its price constitute a market segment; another market segment would be consumers who care mainly about price. It is difficult for one brand of pain reliever to be the first choice of every consumer. Companies are wise to focus their efforts on meeting the distinct needs of one or more market segments. Each target market segment should be profiled by its various factors so that its attractiveness as a company marketing opportunity can be evaluated.

Market Targeting A company can choose to enter one or more segments of a given market. Assume that the pain reliever market can be subdivided into three customer wants (W1: speedy relief; W2: long-lasting relief; and W3: gentle relief) and three customer groups (G1: young people; G2: middle-aged people; and G3: elderly people). By crossing these wants and groups, we can distinguish nine possible market segments. Helene Curtis can choose to enter this market in one of five ways, which are shown in figure 2-4 and listed below:

1. *Concentrating on a single segment:* The company can decide to serve only one segment of the market, here making a *long-lasting pain reliever* for *middle-aged adults* (see figure 2-4a).
2. *Specializing on a customer want:* The company can specialize in meeting a particular customer want, here making *long-lasting pain relievers* for *all types of buyers* (see figure 2-4b).

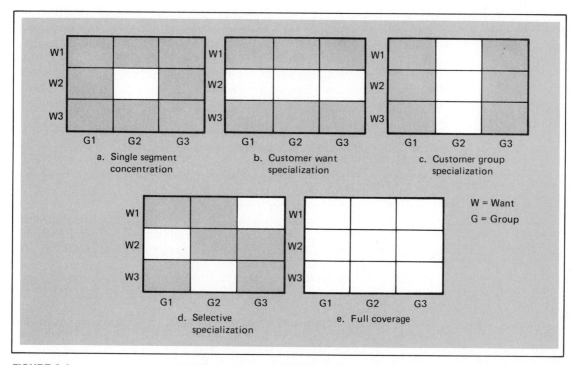

a. Single segment concentration

b. Customer want specialization

c. Customer group specialization

d. Selective specialization

e. Full coverage

W = Want
G = Group

FIGURE 2-4

Five Patterns of Market Coverage

Source: Adapted from Derek F. Abell, *Defining the Business: The Starting Point of Strategic Planning* (Englewood Cliffs, N.J.: Prentice-Hall, 1980), chap. 8.

3. *Specializing on a customer group:* The company can decide to make *all types of pain relievers* needed by a particular customer group, here *middle-aged adults* (see figure 2-4c).
4. *Serving some unrelated segments:* The company can decide to serve *several market segments* that have little relation to each other except that each provides an individually attractive opportunity (see figure 2-4d).
5. *Covering the entire market:* The company can decide to make a *complete range of pain relievers* to serve *all the market segments* (see figure 2-4e).

Most companies enter a new market by serving a single segment, and if this proves successful, they add segments. The sequence of market segments to enter should be thought through in terms of a grand plan. Japanese companies provide a good example of careful planning of market entry and domination. They enter a neglected part of the market, build a name by satisfying the customers, and then spread to other segments. This marketing formula has won them impressive global market shares in autos, cameras, watches, consumer electronics, steel, shipbuilding, and so on.

Large companies ultimately seek full market coverage. They want to be the "General Motors" of their industry. GM says that it makes a car for every "person, purse, and personality." The leading company would normally present different offers to different market segments or would otherwise risk being outperformed in certain segments by companies that concentrate on satisfying those segments.

Market Positioning Suppose Helene Curtis decides to go after the "heavy-user, older-adult market" for pain relievers. It would then need to identify all the products and brands currently serving customers in this market segment. And it would have to identify what customers in this market segment are looking for in pain relievers.

The marketer recognizes that the current brands differ in how they perform, how they are advertised, their prices, and so on. If Helene Curtis tried to offer a pain reliever exactly like one already on the market, there would be no reason for consumers to buy it.

Every product is a bundle of perceived attributes. For example, Excedrin aspirin is seen as a fast-acting, stomach-ungentle pain reliever; Tylenol is seen as a slower-acting, stomach-gentle pain reliever. One way of understanding why consumers buy one rather than the other is to compare where they stand on the key attributes used by consumers in making their choice. The results can be shown on a *product position map* (see figure 2-5a).[3]

A number of things can be observed in this map. First, it consists of only two attributes, gentleness and effectiveness, out of many other possibilities (such as costliness, riskiness). These were chosen because consumers say that these are the most important attributes.

Second, the attributes are numerically rated, each on a five-point scale. Excedrin, for example, rates a 4 on effectiveness (good effectiveness) and a 1 on gentleness (low gentleness).

Third, the brands are positioned according to how consumers perceive them, rather than by how they really are. Excedrin may be ungentle, but what counts is how buyers perceive Excedrin. If desired, the brands could also be plotted on another map according to their objective characteristics.

Fourth, the closer any two brands are in the product position map, the more they are seen by consumers as satisfying the same need. We would expect more

FIGURE 2-5

Maps Showing Product Positions and Consumer Preferences

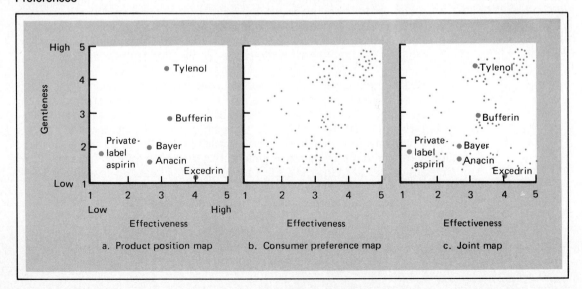

a. Product position map   b. Consumer preference map   c. Joint map

Knowing how customers perceive these pain relievers could help Helene Curtis develop a distinct position for a new product.
Marc Anderson

consumer switching to occur between Bayer and Bufferin than between Excedrin and Tylenol.

The company must now figure out what consumers want with respect to the major attributes. Consumers can be asked to describe the amount of effectiveness, gentleness, cost, speediness, and so on, that they want and would pay for in a pain reliever. Each consumer's ideal combination of attributes can be represented as a point in the same type of map shown earlier, now called a *consumer preference map.* Figure 2-5b shows a possible distribution of preferences for the two pain reliever attributes.

The marketer then combines the product position map and the consumer preference map into the *joint map* shown in figure 2-5c. A clear finding is that many consumers prefer and would be willing to pay for a pain reliever that combines high gentleness and high effectiveness (upper right corner), although no brand is perceived to offer both at the present time.

Helene Curtis can decide to go after this opportunity. To succeed, two things are necessary. First, the company must be able to manufacture a product that buyers of pain relievers view as gentle and effective. Perhaps competitors have not introduced a gentle and effective pain reliever because they cannot find a way to produce it. Second, the company must be able to offer this product at a price that the market is willing to pay. If the cost of manufacture is extremely high, then the product may be priced out of the market. But if these conditions can be fulfilled, the company will serve the market well and make a profit. The company has discovered an area of unsatisfied customer want and can try to satisfy it.

Suppose Helene Curtis cannot go after the opportunity, but decides to go after Tylenol. It can position its brand as the "Cadillac brand" by claiming higher effectiveness than Tylenol and charging the higher price. Or it can position its brand as the "gentlest brand" by showing that it has the lowest record of stomach upsets of any brand. Helene Curtis can position its brand on a large number of possible attributes. The new brand should have a set of attributes that enough customers consider important, desirable, and insufficiently supplied by competing brands.

> **Market positioning** is arranging for a product to occupy a clear, distinctive, and desirable place in the market and in the minds of target customers.

Developing the Marketing Mix

Once the company has decided how to position its product, it is then ready to begin planning the details of the marketing mix. Marketing mix is one of the major concepts in modern marketing. We define it as follows:

> **Marketing mix** is the set of controllable marketing variables that the firm blends to produce the response it wants in the target market.

The marketing mix consists of everything the firm can do to influence the demand for its product. The many possibilities can be collected into four groups of vari-

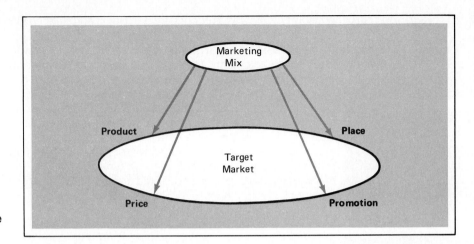

FIGURE 2-6

The Four *P*'s of the Marketing Mix

ables known as the "four *P*'s"; *product, price, place,* and *promotion.*[4] The particular marketing variables under each *P* will be listed and discussed in detail in chapters 8 through 16.

Product stands for the "goods-and-service" combination that the company offers to the target market. Thus Helene Curtis's new pain relief "product" might consist of fifty white tablets packaged in a dark-green bottle with a child-proof cap and a shelf life of three years, bearing the brand name "Relief" and offered with a money-back guarantee if the customer is not satisfied.

Price stands for the amount of money that customers have to pay to obtain the product. Helene Curtis suggests retail and wholesale prices, discounts, allowances, and credit terms. Its "price" has to match the perceived value of the offer, or else buyers will buy competing products.

Place stands for the various activities that make the product available to target consumers. Thus Helene Curtis chooses wholesalers and retailers, motivates them to give the product good attention and exposure, checks on stock, and arranges efficient transportation and storage of the product.

Promotion stands for the various activities undertaken by the company to communicate the merits of its product and to persuade target customers to buy it. Thus Helene Curtis buys advertising, employs salespeople, sets up sales promotions, and arranges publicity for its product.

These marketing mix decisions are heavily influenced by the company's market positioning decision. Suppose Helene Curtis decided to come out with a "Cadillac brand" for the high-gentleness market segment. This positioning decision suggests that Helene Curtis's brand must be at least as gentle as Tylenol, if not more gentle. It must use high-quality packaging, and the brand must be offered to the market in several sizes. The price should be higher than Tylenol's. The product should be sold in quality retail stores. The advertising budget should be large. The ads should show well-to-do users who want the best available pain reliever. The brand should avoid price cutting or promotions that would cheapen its image. Thus we can see that the market positioning decision provides the basis for designing a coordinated marketing mix.

Managing the Marketing Effort

All the work of analyzing market opportunities, selecting target markets, and developing and executing the marketing mix requires supporting marketing management systems. Specifically, the company needs a marketing information system, marketing planning system, marketing organization system, and marketing control system. We will describe the marketing information system in chapter 3. Here we will briefly describe the other three systems.

Marketing Planning System Every company must look ahead to see where it wants to go and how it will get there. Its future should not be left to chance. To do this, companies use two systems—a strategic planning system and a marketing planning system.

Strategic planning systems assume that every company consists of several businesses. For example, Helene Curtis's businesses are toiletries, beauty shop equipment and supplies, and sealants and adhesives. Each business consists of several products; thus toiletries at Helene Curtis include shampoos, conditioners, and skin-care lotions.

Not all of these businesses or products are equally attractive. Some businesses are growing, others are stable, and still others are declining. Now if Helene Curtis consisted of only declining businesses, it would be in serious trouble. Helene Curtis must make sure that it starts enough new promising businesses (or products) to keep the company growing. Helene Curtis must also know how to divide its scarce resources among its current businesses. It would be a mistake to use its money to prop up losing businesses while starving the more promising businesses. The purpose of a strategic planning system is to make sure the company finds and develops strong businesses and phases down or phases out its weaker businesses.

Marketing planning describes the act of planning for each individual business, product, or brand within the company. Presumably the company already decided what to do with each business through its strategic planning system. A detailed marketing plan is now needed for each business. For example, suppose Helene Curtis decides that Suave shampoo should be marketed further because of its strong growth potential. Then the company will develop a marketing plan to carry out Suave's growth objective.

The company will actually prepare two marketing plans, a long-range plan and an annual plan. The manager will first prepare a five-year plan for Suave that describes the major factors and forces affecting this market over the next five years, the five-year objectives, the major strategies that will be used to build the brand's market share and profits, the capital required, and the profits expected. This five-year plan would be reviewed and updated each year, so that there would always be a current five-year plan.

The annual plan is then prepared, and it represents a detailed version of the first year of the five-year plan. The annual plan describes the current marketing situation, the current threats and opportunities, the objectives and issues facing the product or brand, the marketing strategy for the year, the action program, budgets, and controls. This plan becomes the basis for coordinating all the activities—production, marketing, financial—to meet the product's objectives. Marketing strategy and planning are discussed further in chapter 17.

Marketing Organization System The company must design a marketing organization that is capable of carrying out the necessary marketing work, including planning. If the company is very small, one person might end up doing all the marketing tasks: marketing research, selling, advertising, customer servicing, and so on. This person might be called the sales manager, marketing manager, or marketing director. If the company is large, several marketing specialists will be available. Thus Helene Curtis has salespeople, sales managers, marketing researchers, advertising personnel, product and brand managers, market segment managers, and customer service personnel. The marketing functions will be directed by the marketing department.

WAYS OF ORGANIZING THE MARKETING DEPARTMENT. Modern marketing departments can be arranged in several ways. A company will set up its marketing department in the way that best helps it meet its marketing objectives.

Functional Organization. The most common form of marketing organization is the **functional organization**. Marketing specialists are in charge of different marketing activities, or functions. They report to a marketing vice-president, who coordinates their activities. Figure 2-7 shows five specialists: marketing administration manager, advertising and sales promotion manager, sales manager, marketing research manager, and new-products manager. There may be other specialists, including a customer service manager, a marketing planning manager, and a physical distribution manager.

The main advantage of a functional organization is that it is simple to administer. On the other hand, this form is less and less effective as the company's products and markets grow. It becomes difficult to make plans for each market or product and to coordinate all of the company's marketing activities.

Geographic Organization. A company selling throughout the country often creates a **geographic organization** for its sales force. Figure 2-8 shows 1 national sales manager, 4 regional sales managers, 24 zone sales managers, 192 district sales managers, and 1,920 sales representatives. Geographic organization allows sales representatives to settle in a territory, get to know their customers, and work effectively with a minimum of travel time and cost.

FIGURE 2-7

Functional Organization

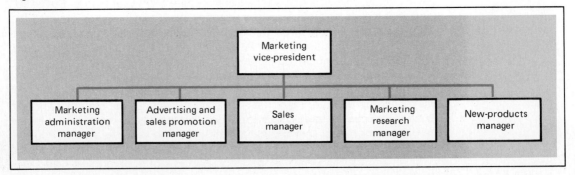

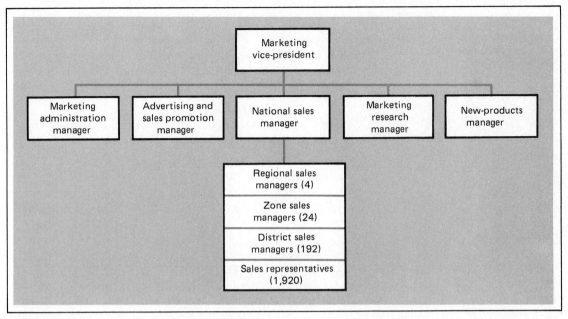

Geographic
Organization

Product Management Organization. Companies producing a variety of products and/or brands often establish a product or brand management organization. The **product management organization** does not replace the functional organization but serves as another layer of management. The product management organization is headed by a products manager, who supervises several product groups managers, who supervise product managers in charge of specific products (see figure 2-9). Product managers themselves develop product plans, see that they are carried out, watch the results, and revise the plans, if necessary.

A product management organization makes sense if the products are quite different and/or if the sheer number of products is beyond the capacity of a functional marketing organization to handle.

Product management first appeared in the Procter & Gamble Company in 1927. A new company soap, Camay, was not doing well, and one of the young executives, Neil H. McElroy (later president of P&G), was assigned to give his exclusive attention to developing and promoting this product. He did this successfully, and the company soon added other product managers.

Since then, many firms, especially in the food, soap, toiletries, and chemical industries, have established product management organizations. General Foods, for example, uses a product management organization in its Post Division. There are separate product group managers in charge of cereals, pet food, and beverages. Within the cereal product group, there are separate product managers for nutritional cereals, children's presweetened cereals, family cereals, and miscellaneous cereals. In turn, the nutritional cereal product manager supervises brand managers.[5]

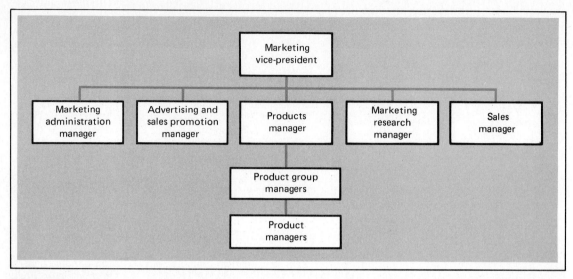

FIGURE 2-9

Product Management
Organization

Product management organization has several advantages. First, the product manager coordinates the whole marketing mix for the product. Second, the product manager can react more quickly to problems in the marketplace than can individual specialists. Third, smaller brands are less neglected because they have their own product manager. Fourth, product management is an excellent training ground for young executives, for it involves them in almost every area of company operations.

But a price is paid for these advantages. First, product management creates some conflict and frustration.[6] Product managers are often not given enough authority to carry out their responsibilities effectively. Second, product managers become experts in their product but rarely become experts in any functions. Third, the product management system often turns out to be more expensive than anticipated due to higher payroll costs.

Market Management Organization.   Many companies will sell a product line to different types of markets. For example, Smith-Corona sells its electric typewriters to consumer, business, and government markets. U.S. Steel sells its steel to the railroad, construction, and public utility industries. When the different markets have different buying habits or product preferences, a market management organization is desirable.

A **market management organization** is similar to the product management organization shown in figure 2-9. A market manager supervises several market managers. Market managers are responsible for developing long-range and annual plans for the sales and profits in their markets. They have to coax help from marketing research, advertising, sales, and other specialists. This system's main advantage is that the company is organized around the needs of specific customer segments.

Many companies are reorganizing along market lines. Xerox has converted from geographic selling to selling by industry. The Heinz Company split its marketing organization into three groups: groceries, commercial restaurants, and institutions. Each group contains further market specialists. For example, the institutional division contains separate market specialists who plan for schools, colleges, hospitals, and prisons.

Product Management/Market Management Organization. Companies that produce many products that sell in many markets face a problem. They could use a product management system, which requires product managers to be familiar with highly different markets. Or they could use a market management system, which means that market managers would have to be familiar with highly different products bought by their markets. Or they could install both product and market managers, that is, a **matrix organization**.

Exhibit **2-2**

Du Pont's Product Management/Market Management System

Du Pont's textile fibers division consists of both product managers and market managers:

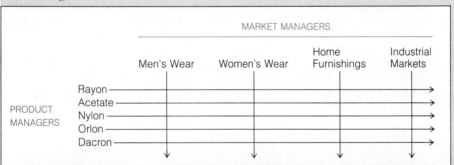

The product managers have the responsibility for planning the sales and profits of their respective fibers. These managers are focusing primarily on the short-run performance and uses of their fiber. Their job is to contact each market manager and ask for an estimate of how much material can be sold in each market. The market managers, on the other hand, have the responsibility for developing profitable markets for existing and potential Du Pont fibers. They take a long view of market needs and care more about evolving the right products for their market than pushing specific fibers. In preparing their market plan, they contact each product manager to learn about planned prices and availabilities of different materials. The final sales forecasts of the market managers and the product managers should add up to the same grand total.

The problem, however, is that this system is costly and creates conflict. Here are two of the many conflicts:

1. How should the sales force be organized? In the Du Pont example in exhibit 2-2, should there be separate sales forces for rayon, nylon, and each of the other fibers? Or should the sales force be organized according to men's wear, women's wear, and other markets? Or should the sales force not be specialized?
2. Who should set the prices for a particular product/market? In the Du Pont example, should the nylon product manager have final authority for setting nylon prices in all markets? What happens if the men's wear market manager feels that nylon will lose out in this market unless special price concessions are made on nylon?

Most managers feel that only the more important products and markets would justify separate managers. Some are not upset about the conflicts and cost and believe that the benefits of matrix organization outweigh the costs.[7]

Marketing Control System

Many surprises are likely to occur as marketing plans are being implemented. The company needs control procedures to make sure that the marketing objectives will be achieved. Three types of marketing control can be distinguished: *annual plan control, profitability control,* and *strategic control.* Annual plan control is the task of making sure that the company is achieving the sales, profits, and other goals that it established in its annual plan. Profitability control is the periodic analysis of the actual profitability of different products, customer groups, trade channels, and order sizes. A company might also make marketing efficiency studies to look at how various marketing activities can be carried on more efficiently. Strategic control involves stepping back from time to time and critically examining the company's overall approach to the marketplace. The marketing control system will be discussed further in chapter 17.

A Review of the Marketing Management Process

Figure 2-10 summarizes the entire company marketing management process and the forces influencing the setting of company marketing strategy. The target customers are in the center, and the company focuses its efforts on serving and satisfying them. The company develops a marketing mix made up of the factors under its control, the four *P*'s—product, price, place, and promotion. To arrive at its marketing mix, the company manages four systems: a marketing information system, a marketing planning system, a marketing organization system, and a marketing control system. These systems are interrelated in that marketing information is needed to develop marketing plans, which in turn are carried out by the marketing organization, the results of which are reviewed and controlled.

Through those systems, the company monitors and adapts to the marketing environment. The company adapts to its microenvironment consisting of marketing intermediaries, suppliers, competitors, and publics. And it adapts to the

uncontrollable Variables

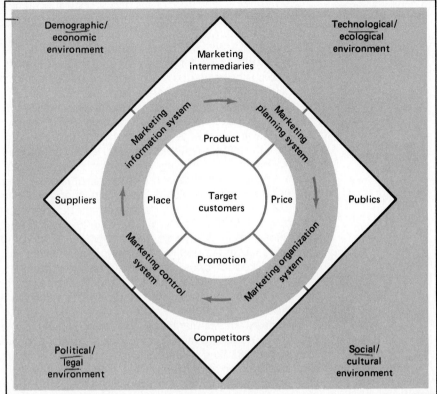

FIGURE 2-10

Factors Influencing Company Marketing Strategy

macroenvironment consisting of demographic/economic forces, political/legal forces, technological/ecological forces, and social/cultural forces. The company takes into account the actors and forces in the marketing environment in developing and positioning its offer to the target market.

Summary

Every company needs to manage its marketing activities effectively. Specifically, the company needs to know how to analyze its market opportunities, select appropriate target markets, develop an effective marketing mix, and manage the marketing effort effectively. These steps make up the marketing management process.

Analyzing market opportunities is the starting point of marketing activity. Management needs to know how to identify and evaluate market opportunities. Management can identify market opportunities by working with the product/market expansion grid and paying attention to attractive new industries. Each opportunity must be evaluated as to whether it fits the company's objectives and can be handled with the company's resources.

Market opportunity analysis should reveal a number of attractive market opportunities. Each market opportunity will require deeper study before it can be selected as a target market. The company will want to make a more careful estimate of current and future demand to make sure that the opportunity is sufficiently attractive. If it is, the next step involves market segmentation to identify those customer groups and needs that the company can best serve. A market segment consists of consumers who react in a similar way to a given set of marketing stimuli. The company might choose to serve one or more market segments. For each target market segment, the company has to determine what position it wants in that segment. It should study the positions of the competing brands in the target market with respect to the attributes that the consumers think are important. The company should also study the amount of demand for different possible combinations of product attributes. Then it should determine whether it wants to develop a brand to meet an unfilled need or a brand similar to an existing brand. In the latter case, it must be prepared to fight that competing brand by establishing some difference in the customer's mind.

Once the company has decided on its market positioning, it develops a marketing mix to support its positioning. The marketing mix is a blending of the four P's—product, price, place, and promotion. The company has to decide on its total marketing budget, how the budget will be allocated to the major marketing mix categories, and how the budget within each marketing category will be allocated.

To carry out this marketing work, the company has to develop a marketing information system, a marketing planning system, a marketing organization system, and a marketing control system. The marketing planning system consists of a strategic planning system and a marketing planning system. The strategic planning system focuses on designing a robust company made up of at least some growing businesses to compensate for those that might be declining. The marketing planning system develops long-range and annual marketing plans for specific businesses, products, and brands that carry out the mission assigned as a result of strategic planning.

Modern marketing departments are organized in a number of ways. The most common form is the functional organization, in which marketing functions are headed by separate managers reporting to the marketing vice-president. A geographic organization allows sales representatives to concentrate in a specific geographic market. Another form is the product management organization, in which products are assigned to products managers who work with functional specialists to develop and achieve their plans. Another form is the market management organization, in which major markets are assigned to market managers who work with functional specialists to develop and achieve their plans. Some large companies use a product management/market management organization.

Questions for Discussion

1. In 1978 the chairman of AT&T went on intracompany TV to announce to every employee that "we will become a marketing company." What do you think he meant by that, and what company changes may be necessary for this to occur?

2. It has been reported that some Japanese manufacturers of specialized audio equipment are experiencing lagging sales and increased competition. Using the product/market expansion grid shown in figure 2-2, what strategies might these companies pursue?
3. Manufacturers of paraffin candles, if asked one hundred years ago what business they were in, would have said, "We make paraffin candles." If they had been market-oriented, what would they have said?
4. Describe the four major steps in the marketing management process in relation to a service of your choice.
5. It is argued that the success of L'eggs panty hose is due to the company's understanding of the marketing mix factors. Discuss the important marketing mix variables as they relate to L'eggs.
6. If managers do a good job of planning and control, they will be properly accomplishing the managing of the marketing effort step in the marketing process. Comment.

Key Terms in Chapter 2

Company marketing opportunity An attractive arena for company marketing action in which a particular company would enjoy a competitive advantage.

Functional organization A group of marketing specialists who are in charge of different marketing activities and who report to a marketing vice-president.

Geographic organization Organizing a company's national sales force along geographic lines.

Market management organization A form of marketing organization in which major markets are the responsibility of market managers, who work with various functional specialists in the company to develop their plans for the market.

Marketing management process A procedure that consists of (1) analyzing market opportunities, (2) selecting target markets, (3) developing the marketing mix, and (4) managing the marketing effort.

Marketing mix The set of controllable variables that the firm blends to produce the response it wants in the target market.

Market positioning Arranging for a product to occupy a clear, distinctive, and desirable place in the market and in the minds of target customers.

Market segment Consumers who respond in a similar way to a given set of marketing stimuli.

Market segmentation The process of classifying customers into groups with different needs, characteristics, and/or behavior.

Matrix organization A marketing organization that uses both product managers and market managers.

Product management organization A form of marketing organization in which products are the responsibility of product managers, who work with the various functional specialists in the company to develop and achieve their plans for the product.

Cases for Chapter 2

Case 1 Sony Corporation: Walkman (p. 493)

How does Sony develop and carry out a marketing plan for the Walkman? The material in the chapter helps answer this question.

Case 2 Minnetonka, Inc.: ShowerMate™ (p. 494)

Is ShowerMate a good opportunity for Minnetonka? Can it be successfully marketed? This case suggests some answers.

Chapter 3

Marketing Research and Information Systems

Objectives

After reading this chapter, you should be able to:

1. Discuss the importance of information to a company.
2. Describe the parts of a marketing information system.
3. List the steps in the marketing research process.
4. Compare the advantages and disadvantages of the various methods of collecting information.

Agree Shampoo and Agree Creme Rinse, made by Johnson Wax, have been two of the most successful new personal-care products. For Fred Nordeen and Neil DeClerk of Johnson Wax, the success of these two products represented almost a decade of hard work—otherwise known as marketing research. The two researchers had begun the project back in 1970 when Johnson Wax wanted to develop a new women's hair care product.

Nordeen and DeClerk began the project by sending out hair care questionnaires to a large number of women across the country. The researchers were hoping to learn about women's hair care habits, their hair problems, what kinds of new products could solve these problems, and which group could benefit most from these new products.

The responses to the questionnaire showed that, in general, women felt that their main hair problem was oiliness. Teenage girls were particularly concerned about oiliness and said they shampooed frequently because of it. Survey responses also showed that teenage girls were more likely to try new products than were older women. These results gave Nordeen and DeClerk enough information to decide that the problem they wanted their hair care product to solve was oiliness. They also decided that their target group for this product was teenage girls.

The Johnson Wax research and development department was given the task of creating an oil-free shampoo and creme rinse to be put on the market together. The shampoo team ran into difficulties, though, so that the creme rinse was ready for marketing first. Ad writers went to work on developing a simple message for creme rinse television commercials to be aimed at teenagers. After testing commercials on potential Agree users, Nordeen and DeClerk decided on the slogan "Helps stop 'the greasies'—between shampoos."

When the shampoo was finally ready, the creme rinse had been on the market several months, and consumers were already familiar with the name and slogan. But before they could put the shampoo on store shelves, the researchers conducted a number of tests to find out how it would sell. Some of these tests involved blind comparisons of Agree Shampoo and competing brands. Participants received Agree and another brand (without their labels), used them for two weeks each, and then reported their preference to telephone interviewers. Nordeen and DeClerk also conducted extended-use studies in Fresno, California, and South Bend, Indiana. In these tests, the researchers gave Agree Shampoo (with its label this time) to women who had seen it advertised and were interested in buying it. Every four weeks for the next four months, the women rated the shampoo on a list of traits and decided whether they wanted to continue using Agree. Most participants in these studies liked the product, even in comparison with other brands.

Another marketing research issue, besides whether consumers would find the product satisfactory, was whether Johnson Wax could convince them to buy it through a marketing plan. To determine the effectiveness of the company's national marketing plan, Nordeen and DeClerk scaled it down to fit two test markets: Fresno and South Bend. This test involved putting the same Agree ads on local television and showing them with the frequency that had been planned for the national campaign. Ads were placed in local newspapers. The company also sent promotional mailings to local households in numbers that corresponded to those planned for the country as a whole. To measure the marketing plan's success, Nordeen and DeClerk received counts of Agree sales from individual stores in Fresno and South Bend.

According to Nordeen and DeClerk, almost ten years of marketing research was responsible for the present success of the two Agree products.[1]

In carrying out marketing analysis, planning, implementation, and control, marketing managers need information at almost every turn. They need information about customers, competitors, dealers, and other forces in the marketplace. This chapter looks at how information is gathered and how it is organized in a useful way.

The Concept of a Marketing Information System

During the nineteenth century, most companies were small and knew their customers firsthand. Managers picked up marketing information by being around people, observing them, and asking questions.

In this century, three trends have increased the need for more and better marketing information.

1. *From local to national marketing.* As a company expands its market area, its managers no longer know all customers directly. It needs to develop other ways of gathering marketing information.
2. *From buyer needs to buyer wants.* As buyers' incomes increase, they become more selective in their choice of goods. Sellers find it harder to predict buyers' response to different features, styles, and other attributes, and they turn to marketing research.
3. *From price to nonprice competition.* As sellers increase their use of nonprice marketing tools, such as branding, product differentiation, advertising, and sales promotion, they need information on how the market responds to the tools.

Although sellers always need more marketing information, the supply never seems sufficient. Marketers complain that they cannot gather enough of the accurate and useful information they need. To solve this problem, many companies are developing marketing information systems (MIS). We define a marketing information system as follows:[2]

A **marketing information system** is a continuing and interacting structure of people, equipment, and procedures to gather, sort, analyze, evaluate, and distribute pertinent, timely, and accurate information for use by marketing decision makers to improve their marketing planning, execution, and control.

The marketing information system concept is illustrated in figure 3-1. The box on the left lists the parts of the marketing environment that marketing manag-

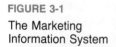

FIGURE 3-1

The Marketing Information System

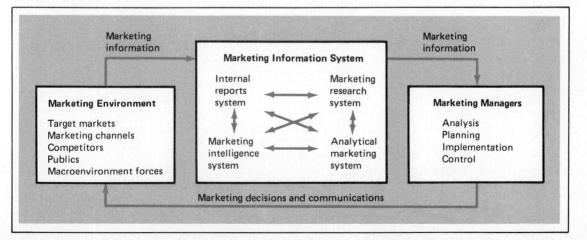

ers must watch. Information is picked up and analyzed through four subsystems making up the marketing information system—the internal reports system, intelligence system, marketing research system, and analytical marketing system. The information flows to marketing managers to help them in their marketing analysis, planning, implementation, and control. Their marketing decisions and communications then flow back to the market.

We will now take a closer look at the four subsystems of the company's marketing information system.

Internal Reports System

All companies produce internal reports showing current sales, costs, inventories, cash flows, and accounts receivable and payable. The computer has permitted companies to build first-rate internal reports systems that can spread this information to all departments. Here are examples of three systems:

- *General Mills:* Managers in the Grocery Products Division of General Mills receive sales information daily. Zone, regional, and district sales managers start their day with a Teletype report on orders and shipments in their area the day before. The report also contains percentages to compare with target percentages and last year's percentages.
- *Schenley:* Managers at Schenley can retrieve, within seconds, current and past sales and inventory figures for any brand and package size for each of four hundred distributors. They can determine the areas where sales are lagging behind targets.
- *Mead Paper:* Mead sales representatives can obtain on-the-spot answers to customers' questions about paper availability by dialing Mead Paper's computer center. The computer determines whether paper is available at the nearest warehouse and when it can be shipped; if it is not in stock, the computer checks the inventory at other nearby warehouses until one is located. If the paper is nowhere in stock, the computer determines where and when the paper can be produced. The sales representative gets an answer in seconds and thus has an advantage over competitors.

The information collected should be able to help managers make their major decisions. For example, brand managers who are deciding on the advertising budget need to know how many people are already aware of the brand, the advertising budgets and strategies of competitors, the relative effectiveness of advertising in the promotional mix, and so on.

Marketing Intelligence System

The marketing intelligence system supplies executives with happenings data.

The **marketing intelligence system** is the set of sources and procedures by which executives obtain their everyday information about developments in the commercial environment.

Executives gather marketing intelligence by reading books, newspapers, and trade publications; talking to customers, suppliers, distributors, and other outsiders; and exchanging information with other managers and personnel within the company. Well-run companies take additional steps to improve the quality and quantity of marketing intelligence. First, they train and motivate the sales force to spot and report new developments. Sales representatives are the company's "eyes and ears." They are in an excellent position to pick up information missed by other means.

Second, the company motivates distributors, retailers, and other allies to pass along important intelligence. Some companies appoint specialists to gather marketing intelligence. They send out "ghost shoppers" to monitor the sales presentations of retail personnel. Much can be learned about competitors by (1) purchasing competitors' products; (2) attending "open houses" and trade shows; (3) reading competitors' published reports and attending stockholders' meetings; (4) talking to competitors' former employees and present employees, dealers, distributors, suppliers, and freight agents; (5) collecting competitors' ads; and (6) reading the *Wall Street Journal, New York Times,* and trade association papers.

Third, the company purchases information from outside intelligence suppliers. The A. C. Nielsen Company sells data on brand shares, retail prices, and percentage of stores stocking the item. Market Research Corporation of America sells reports on weekly movements of brand shares, sizes, prices, and deals. Clipping services are hired to report on competitors' ads, advertising expenditures, and media mixes.

Fourth, some companies establish an office to collect and circulate marketing intelligence. The staff scans major publications for relevant news and sends a news bulletin to marketing managers. It develops a file of relevant information. The staff assists managers in evaluating new information. These services greatly improve the quality of information available to marketing managers.

Marketing Research System

Marketing managers also need studies of specific situations. Consider the following:

- Playboy, Inc., would like to find out more about the incomes, education, and life-styles of the current readers of its magazine, their reading preferences, and their attitudes toward some possible changes in the magazine.
- Pacific Stereo operates a national chain of audio equipment stores. Management wants to study the market potential of some cities in the South as locations for new stores.
- Barat College in Lake Forest, Illinois, seeks to enroll high-school graduates who are above-average women. It needs to know what percentage of its target market has heard of Barat, what they know, how they heard about Barat, and how they feel about Barat. This information would help Barat improve its communications program.

In such situations, managers cannot wait for the information to arrive in bits and pieces. Each situation needs a formal study. Managers normally do not have the skill or time to obtain this information on their own. They need to commission formal marketing research. We define marketing research as follows:

Marketing research is the systematic design, collection, analysis, and reporting of data and findings relevant to a specific marketing situation facing the company.

Table 3-1

Types of Marketing Research Performed by 798 Companies

TYPE OF RESEARCH	PERCENT OF COMPANIES DOING RESEARCH
In Advertising:	
Customer motivation research	48
Copy research	49
Media research	61
Studies of ad effectiveness	67
In Business and Economics:	
Short-range forecasting	85
Long-range forecasting	82
Studies of business trends	86
Pricing studies	81
Plant and warehouse location studies	71
Product mix studies	51
Studies of international markets	51
Management information system	72
In Corporate Responsibilities:	
Consumer "right-to-know" studies	26
Ecological impact studies	33
Studies of legal restrictions in advertising and promotion	51
Studies of social values and policies	40
In Product Development:	
New-product acceptance and potential	84
Studies of competing products	85
Testing of products	75
Studies of package design	60
In Sales and Markets:	
Measuring market potentials	93
Analysis of market shares	92
Studies of market characteristics	93
Sales analysis	89
Establishing sales quotas and territories	75
Studies of distribution channels	69
Test marketing	54
Studies of promotion strategies	52

Source: Adapted from Dik Warren Twedt, ed., *1978 Survey of Marketing Research* (Chicago: American Marketing Association, 1978), p. 11.

A company can obtain marketing research in a number of ways. Small companies can ask students or professors at a local college to design and carry out the project, or they can hire a marketing research firm. Large companies—in fact, over 73% of them—have their own marketing research departments.[3] Marketing research departments consist of anywhere from one to several dozen researchers. The marketing research manager normally reports to the marketing vice-president and performs such roles as study director, administrator, company consultant, and advocate. The other marketing researchers include survey designers, statisticians, behavioral scientists, and model builders.

Marketing researchers have steadily expanded their activities (see table 3-1). The ten most common activities are studies of market characteristics, measurement of market potentials, market-share analysis, sales analysis, studies of business trends, competitive-product studies, short-range forecasting, new-product acceptance and potential, long-range forecasting, and pricing studies.

Analytical Marketing System

The analytical marketing system consists of advanced techniques for analyzing marketing data and problems. Companies such as Lever Brothers, General Electric, and RCA use analytical marketing systems extensively. Other companies may consider these approaches too technical or too academic.

An analytical marketing system is made up of a statistical bank and a model bank (see figure 3-2). *The statistical bank is a collection of advanced statistical procedures for learning more about the relationships within a set of data and their statistical reliability.* These procedures allow management to answer such questions as:

- What are the major variables affecting my sales and how important is each one?
- If I raised my price 10% and increased my advertising expenditures 20%, what would happen to sales?
- What are the best predictors of consumers who are likely to buy my brand versus my competitor's brand?
- What are the best variables for segmenting my market, and how many segments exist?

FIGURE 3-2

Analytical Marketing System

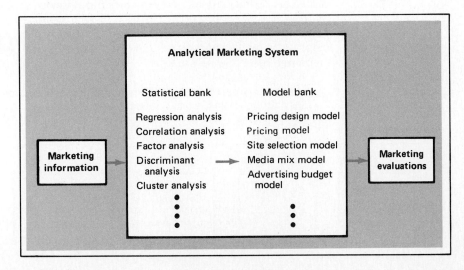

These statistical procedures are described in many standard sources.[4]

The model bank is a collection of mathematical models that will help market-ers make better marketing decisions. Each model consists of a set of interrelated variables that represent some real system, process, or outcome. These models can help answer the questions of what if and which is best. In the past twenty years, marketing scientists have developed a great number of models to help marketing executives do a better job of designing sales territories and sales call plans,[5] selecting sites for retail outlets,[6] developing optimal advertising media mixes,[7] and forecasting new-product sales.[8]

This concludes our review of the four major subsystems of a marketing information system. We will now examine the marketing research process.

The Marketing Research Process

To understand a company's customers, competitors, dealers, and so on, every marketer needs marketing research. A brand manager at a large company such as Procter & Gamble will commission three or four major marketing research studies annually. Marketing managers in smaller companies will order fewer marketing research studies. More and more nonprofit organizations are finding that they need marketing research. A hospital wants to know whether people in its service area have a positive attitude toward the hospital. A college wants to determine what kind of image it has among high-school counselors. A political organization wants to find out what voters think of the candidates.

Managers who use marketing research need to know enough about it so that they can get the right information at a reasonable cost. If they know nothing about marketing research, they may allow the wrong information to be collected, or it may be collected at great expense or interpreted incorrectly. They can work with highly experienced marketing researchers because it is in their own interests to produce information that leads to correct decisions. Equally important is that managers know enough about marketing research procedure to participate in its planning and subsequent interpretation. This section describes the five basic steps in the marketing research process (see figure 3-3). We will illustrate these steps with the following situation:

FIGURE 3-3

The Marketing Research Process

Some years ago, Allegheny Airlines was primarily a commuter airline serving the eastern United States. In the late 60s and the early 70s, however, Allegheny was able to expand its routes; mergers with two small airlines and

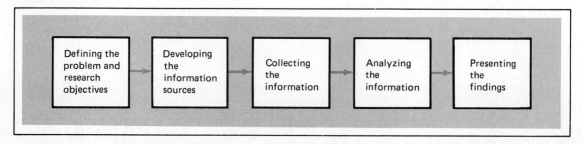

Defining the problem and research objectives → Developing the information sources → Collecting the information → Analyzing the information → Presenting the findings

deregulation of the airlines industry enabled Allegheny to fly to a total of 25 states, the District of Columbia, and parts of Canada. But its competitors, such as United, TWA, and American, were better known and preferred by air travelers. Allegheny needed a new advertising campaign to let people know about its expansion. To design the most effective campaign, though, the marketing department had to do extensive research to learn more about the airline market.

Defining the Problem and Research Objectives

The first step in research calls for the marketing manager and marketing researcher to define the problem carefully and agree on the research objectives. If the marketing manager tells the marketing researcher, "Go and gather data on the airline market," he or she is likely to be disappointed with the results. Hundreds of things can be researched about a market. If the research findings are to be useful, they must bear on a decision problem facing the company. Information is too costly to collect, and allowing the problem to be defined vaguely or incorrectly is wasteful. An old saying goes: A problem well defined is half solved.

The marketing manager and the marketing researcher in the Allegheny case agreed that the problem was that Allegheny did not attract as many passengers as desired. This led to two subproblems: (1) How do passengers choose their airline? and (2) How might more passengers be induced to fly Allegheny?

At this point, the managers need to set the research objectives. The objectives may be *exploratory*—that is, to gather some preliminary data to throw more light on the problem and possibly suggest some hypotheses. They may be *descriptive*—that is, to describe certain phenomena, such as how many people fly, or how many people have heard of Allegheny. Or they may be *causal*—that is, to test a hypothesis about some cause-and-effect relationship, such as a fare cut of $15 that would increase passenger traffic by at least 10%.

Developing the Information Sources

The second stage of research calls for determining the type of information needed and the most efficient ways to gather this information. A researcher can gather secondary data, primary data, or both.

Secondary data consist of information that already exists somewhere, having been collected for another purpose.

Primary data consist of originally collected information for the specific purpose at hand.

COLLECTING SECONDARY DATA. Researchers usually start their investigation by collecting secondary data. Figure 3-4 shows the many secondary data sources available, including internal sources (company profit and loss statements, sales call reports, prior research reports) and external sources (government publications, periodicals and books, and commercial services).[9]

In the case of the Allegheny project, the researchers could find a great deal of secondary data on the air travel market. For example, U.S. Civil Aeronautics Board publications provide data on the size, growth, and market shares of the various carriers. The Air Transport Association of America has conducted numerous studies on the characteristics, attitudes, and behavior of air travelers. Simi-

A. Internal Sources

Internal sources include company profit and loss statements, balance sheets, sales figures, sales call reports, invoices, inventory records, and prior research reports.

B. Government Publications

Statistical Abstract of the U.S. provides summary data on demographic, economic, social, and other aspects of the American economy and society.

County and City Data Book presents statistical information for counties, cities, and other geographic units on population, education, employment, total and median income, housing, bank deposits, retail sales, and so on.

U.S. Industrial Outlook provides projections of industrial activity by industry and includes data on production, sales, shipments, employment, and so on.

Marketing Information Guide provides a monthly annotated bibliography of marketing information.

Other government publications include the *Annual Survey of Manufacturers; Business Statistics; Census of Manufacturers; Census of Population; Census of Retail Trade, Wholesale Trade, and Selected Service Industries; Census of Transportation; Federal Reserve Bulletin; Monthly Labor Review; Survey of Current Business;* and *Vital Statistics Report.*

C. Periodicals and Books

Business Periodicals Index lists business articles appearing in a wide variety of business publications.

Standard and Poor's Industry Surveys provide updated statistics and analyses of industries.

Moody's Manuals provide financial data and names of executives in major companies.

Encyclopedia of Associations provides information on every major trade and professional association in the U.S.

Marketing journals include the *Journal of Marketing, Journal of Marketing Research,* and *Journal of Consumer Research.*

Useful trade magazines include *Advertising Age, Chain Store Age, Progressive Grocer, Sales and Marketing Management,* and *Stores.*

Useful general business magazines include *Business Week, Fortune, Forbes,* and *Harvard Business Review.*

D. Commercial Data

A. C. Nielsen Company provides data on products and brands sold through retail outlets, data on television audiences, magazine circulation data, and so on.

Market Research Corporation of America provides data on weekly family purchases of consumer products, data on home food consumption, and data on 6,000 retail, drug, and discount retailers in various geographic areas.

Selling Areas-Marketing, Inc., provides reports on warehouse withdrawals to food stores in selected market areas.

Simmons Market Research Bureau provides annual reports covering television markets, sporting goods, proprietary drugs, and so on, giving demographic data by sex, income, age, and brand preferences.

Other commercial research houses selling data to subscribers include the *Audit Bureau of Circulation, Audits and Surveys, Dun and Bradstreet, National Family Opinion, Standard Rate and Data Service,* and *Starch.*

FIGURE 3-4

Sources of Secondary Data

larly, various travel agencies have data that may reveal how air travelers choose their carriers.

Secondary data provide a starting point for research and offer the advantages of lower cost and quicker availability. However, the data needed by the researcher might not exist, or the existing data might be obsolete, inaccurate, incomplete, or unreliable. In this case, the researcher would have to resort to collecting primary data at greater cost and longer delay, but supposedly with more relevance and accuracy.

Researchers often find secondary data in a variety of external sources.
Teri Leigh Stratford

COLLECTING PRIMARY DATA.   Most marketing research projects involve collecting primary data. Some managers, unfortunately, collect primary data by dreaming up a few questions and finding some people to interview. Data gathered this way, however, might be useless or, even worse, misleading. Rather, a plan should be created for collecting primary data. Figure 3-5 shows a plan that calls for decisions on the research approaches, research instruments, sampling plan, and contact methods.

Research Approaches.   Primary data can be collected in three broad ways, namely, observation, experiments, and surveys.

One way that the researcher can gather primary data is by *observation* — observing people and settings. Allegheny researchers might linger around airports, airline offices, and travel agencies to hear how travelers talk about the different carriers and how agents handle flight arrangements. The researchers could fly on Allegheny's and competitors' planes to observe the quality of in-flight service and hear consumer reactions. Their observations might yield some useful hypotheses that Allegheny could evaluate.

Another way is by *experiments.* Experimental research calls for selecting matched groups of subjects, giving them different treatments, controlling variables, and checking on whether observed differences are significant. The purpose of experimental research is to see cause-and-effect relationships by eliminating competing explanations of the observed findings.

Allegheny researchers might use experimental research to answer such questions as the following:

- Would creating a new image lead to more positive passenger feelings for Allegheny?
- What effect would superior food service have on repeat business?
- Which advertising approach—testimonial or slice-of-life advertising— would have the greater effect on Allegheny's sales?
- How much more business would be obtained if children were allowed to fly free when accompanying their parents?

Let us apply the experimental method to the second question and select three similar Allegheny routes where about 20% of the air travelers say they

FIGURE 3-5
A Plan for Primary Data Collection

Research approaches	Observation	Experiment	Surveys
Research instruments	Questionnaire	Mechanical instruments	
Sampling plan	Sampling unit	Sample size	Sampling procedure
Contact methods	Telephone	Mail	Personal

prefer Allegheny. Suppose Allegheny served standard "airlines food" hot meals on the first route, cold sandwiches on the second route, and specially prepared deluxe meals on the third route. If the food makes no difference, we should still find that about 20% of the air travelers along each route prefer Allegheny. Suppose, however, that at the end of the period, 20% of the air travelers on the standard hot-meal route prefer Allegheny, 10% on the cold-sandwiches route prefer Allegheny, and 30% on the deluxe-meal route prefer Allegheny. We would guess that better hot food increases passenger interest and cold food decreases passenger interest. We must check, however, to make sure that the sample size is adequate and that other hypotheses could not explain the same results. For example, if the airline crews on the deluxe-meal route are friendlier, then their friendliness more than the food may have influenced passenger satisfaction. Maybe better food is not needed as much as hiring and training friendlier personnel.

The experimental method supplies the most convincing data if the proper controls are exercised. To the extent that the design and execution of the experiment eliminate alternative hypotheses that might explain the same results, the research and marketing managers can have confidence in the conclusions.[10] (For another example of experimental research, see exhibit 3-1.)

Surveys stand midway between observation and experiments. While observation is best suited for exploratory research and experimentation for causal research, survey work is best suited for descriptive research. Companies undertake surveys to learn about people's knowledge, beliefs, preferences, satisfaction, and so on, and to measure their strength in the population. Thus Allegheny researchers might want to survey how many people know Allegheny, have flown it, prefer it, and so on. We will say more about survey research as we move to research instruments, sampling plan, and contact methods.

Research Instruments.   Marketing researchers have a choice of two main research instruments in collecting primary data—the questionnaire and mechanical devices.

The *questionnaire* is by far the most common instrument used in collecting primary data. Broadly speaking, a questionnaire consists of a set of questions presented to respondents for their answers. The questionnaire is very flexible in that there are many ways to ask questions. Questionnaires need to be carefully developed, tested, and debugged before they can be used on a large scale. We can usually spot several errors in a casually prepared questionnaire (see exhibit 3-2 on p. 68).

In preparing a questionnaire, the marketing researcher carefully chooses the questions to be asked, the form of the questions, the wording of the questions, and the sequencing of the questions.

A common type of error occurs in the questions to be asked, including questions that cannot be answered, would not be answered, or need not be answered, and omitting questions that should be answered. Each question should be checked to determine whether it contributes to the research objectives. Questions that are merely interesting should be dropped because they lengthen the time required and try the patience of respondents.

The form of the question can influence the response. Marketing researchers distinguish between closed-end and open-end questions. Closed-end questions

Exhibit 3-1

Why Did People Initially Resist Buying Instant Coffee?

An excellent example of experimental marketing research was conducted by Mason Haire to determine why homemakers resisted buying instant coffee when it was first introduced. Homemakers were heard to complain that it did not taste like real coffee. Yet in blindfold tests, many of these same homemakers could not distinguish between a cup of instant coffee and a cup of brewed coffee. This indicated that much of their resistance was psychological. Haire designed the following shopping lists, the only difference being that regular coffee was on one list and instant coffee on the other:

SHOPPING LIST 1	SHOPPING LIST 2
$1\frac{1}{2}$ lbs. of hamburger	$1\frac{1}{2}$ lbs. of hamburger
2 loaves of Wonder Bread	2 loaves of Wonder Bread
Bunch of carrots	Bunch of carrots
1 can Rumford's Baking Powder	1 can Rumford's Baking Powder
Nescafé Instant Coffee	1 lb. Maxwell House coffee (drip grind)
2 cans Del Monte peaches	2 cans Del Monte peaches
5 lbs. potatoes	5 lbs. potatoes

Homemakers were asked to guess the social and personal characteristics of the person whose shopping list they saw. The comments were pretty much the same with one significant difference: A higher proportion of the homemakers whose list mentioned instant coffee described the person as "lazy, a spendthrift, a poor spouse, and failing to plan well for the family." These people were attributing to the fictional homemaker their own anxieties and negative images about instant coffee. The instant-coffee company now knew the nature of the resistance and developed a campaign to change the image of homemakers who serve instant coffee.

Source: Mason Haire, "Projective Techniques in Marketing Research," *Journal of Marketing*, April 1950, pp. 649–56. Reprinted by permission of the American Marketing Association.

include all the possible answers, and respondents make a choice among them. Figure 3-6 shows the most common forms of closed-end questions.

Open-end questions allow respondents to answer in their own words. The questions take various forms; the main ones are shown in figure 3-6. Generally speaking, open-end questions often reveal more because respondents are not limited in their answers. Open-end questions are especially useful in the exploratory stage of research where the investigator is trying to determine how people think and is not measuring how many people think in a certain way. Closed-end questions, on the other hand, provide answers that are easier to interpret and tabulate.

Closed-End Questions		
Name	**Description**	**Example**
Dichotomous	A question offering two answer choices.	"In arranging this trip, did you personally phone Allegheny?" Yes ☐ No ☐
Multiple choice	A question offering three or more answer choices.	"With whom are you traveling on this flight?" No one ☐ Children only ☐ Spouse ☐ Business associates/friends/relatives ☐ Spouse and children ☐ An organized tour group ☐
Likert scale	A statement where respondent shows the amount of agreement/disagreement.	"Small airlines generally give better service than large ones." Strongly disagree 1 ☐ Disagree 2 ☐ Neither agree nor disagree 3 ☐ Agree 4 ☐ Strongly agree 5 ☐
Semantic differential	A scale is inscribed between two bipolar words, and the respondent selects the point that represents the direction and intensity of his or her feelings.	*Allegheny Airlines* Large [X] Small Experienced [X] Inexperienced Modern [X] Old-fashioned
Importance scale	A scale that rates the importance of some attribute from "not at all important" to "extremely important."	"Airline food service to me is:" Extremely important 1 Very important 2 Somewhat important 3 Not very important 4 Not at all important 5
Rating scale	A scale that rates some attribute from "poor" to "excellent."	"Allegheny's food service is:" Excellent 1 Very good 2 Good 3 Fair 4 Poor 5

FIGURE 3-6

Types of Questions

Care should be used in the wording of questions. The researcher should use simple, direct, unbiased wording. The questions should be tested before they are widely used.

Care should also be used in the sequencing of questions. The lead question should create interest if possible. Difficult or personal questions should be asked toward the end of the interview so that respondents do not become defensive. The questions should come up in a logical order. Questions that classify the respondent are put last because they are more personal and less interesting to the respondent.

Although questionnaires are the most common research instrument, *mechanical instruments* are also used in marketing research. Galvanometers are used to measure the strength of a subject's interest or emotions aroused by exposure to a specific ad or picture. The galvanometer picks up the minute degree of sweating that accompanies emotional arousal. The tachistoscope is a device that flashes an ad to a subject with an exposure interval that may range

Open-End Questions		
Name	**Description**	**Example**
Completely unstructured	A question that respondents can answer in an almost unlimited number of ways.	"What is your opinion of Allegheny Airlines?"
Word association	Words are presented, one at a time, and respondents mention the first word that comes to mind.	"What is the first word that comes to your mind when you hear the following?" Airline _____ Travel_____ Allegheny_____
Sentence completion	Incomplete sentences are presented, one at a time, and respondents complete the sentence.	"When I choose an airline, the most important consideration in my decision is _____ _____ .
Story completion	An incomplete story is presented, and respondents are asked to complete it.	"I flew Allegheny a few days ago. They gave me a cold sandwich to eat. This aroused in me the following thoughts and feelings." Now complete the story.
Picture completion	A picture of two characters is presented, with one making a statement. Respondents are asked to identify with the other and fill in the empty balloon.	 Fill in the empty balloon.
Thematic Apperception Tests (TAT)	A picture is presented, and respondents are asked to make up a story about what they think is happening or may happen in the picture.	Make up a story about what you see.

from less than one-hundredth of a second to several seconds. After each exposure, respondents describe everything they recall. Eye cameras are used to study respondents' eye movements to determine at what points their eyes land first, how long they linger on a given item, and so on. The audiometer is an electronic device that is attached to television sets in participating homes to record when the set is on and to which channel it is tuned.[11]

Sampling Plan. A sample is the segment of the population selected to represent the population as a whole. Marketing researchers must develop a sampling plan that will help them find the appropriate sample for their research. This involves three decisions. First, who is to be surveyed? This is not always obvious. In the Allegheny survey, should the sample be made up of business people, secretaries, vacationers, or some combination of these? The researcher must decide what information is needed and who is most likely to have it.

Second, how many people should be surveyed? Large samples are more

Exhibit **3-2**

A "Questionable" Questionnaire

Suppose the following questionnaire had been prepared by a summer camp director to be used in interviewing parents of prospective campers. How do you feel about each question?

1. What is your income to the nearest hundred dollars?

> People don't necessarily know their income to the nearest hundred dollars nor do they want to reveal their income that closely. Furthermore, a questionnaire should never open with such a personal question.

2. Are you a strong or weak supporter of overnight summer camping for your children?

> What do "strong" and "weak" mean?

3. Do your children behave themselves well in a summer camp? Yes ( ) No ( )

> "Behave" is a relative term. Besides, will people want to answer this? Furthermore, is "yes" or "no" the best way to allow a response to the question? Why is the question being asked in the first place?

4. How many camps mailed literature to you last April? This April?

> Who can remember this?

5. What are the most salient and determinant attributes in your evaluation of summer camps?

> What are "salience" and "determinant attributes"? Don't use big words.

6. Do you think it is right to deprive your child of the opportunity to grow into a mature person through the experience of summer camping?

> Loaded question. How can one answer "yes," given the bias?

reliable than small samples, but a researcher does not have to survey more than 1% of the population to get accurate answers.

Third, how should the people in the sample be chosen? They may be chosen at random. They may be chosen because they belong to a certain group or category, such as an age group or a resident of a certain area. Or they may be chosen because the researcher feels they may be good sources of information.

Contact Methods. This answers the question, How should the members of the sample be contacted? The choices are by telephone, mail, or personal interviews.

Telephone interviewing is the best method for gathering information quickly. The interviewer is also able to clarify questions if they are not understood. The two main drawbacks are that only people with telephones can be interviewed and that only short, not too personal, interviews can be carried out.

The *mail questionnaire* may be the best method for reaching persons who will not give personal interviews or who may be biased by interviewers. However, mail questionnaires require simple and clearly worded questions, and the return rate is usually low or slow, or both.

Personal interviewing is the most versatile of the three methods. The interviewer can ask more questions and can supplement the interview with personal observations. Personal interviewing is the most expensive method and requires more administrative planning and supervision.

Personal interviewing takes two forms, individual and group interviewing. *Individual interviewing* involves calling on people either in their home or office, or talking to them on the street. The interviewer must gain their cooperation, and the time involved can range from a few minutes to several hours. Sometimes a small payment or incentive is presented to the person in appreciation of his or her time.

Group interviewing consists of inviting from six to ten persons to gather for a few hours with a trained interviewer to discuss a product, service, organization, or other marketing topic. The interviewer needs good qualifications, such as

Personal interviewing allows the interviewer to observe the respondent, as well as ask questions.

Courtesy Burke Marketing Services, Inc.

A marketing research team is taping and observing a group interview.

Courtesy Burgoyne, Inc.

objectivity, knowledge of the subject matter and industry to be discussed, and some understanding of group dynamics and consumer behavior. Otherwise, the results can be worthless or misleading. The participants are normally paid a small sum for attending. The meeting is typically held in pleasant surroundings (a home, for example), and refreshments are served to emphasize the informality. The group interviewer starts with a broad question, such as "How do you feel when you are about to fly on an airplane?" Questions then move to how people feel about preflight, in-flight, and postflight services, and finally to how people feel about Allegheny and each of its competitors. The interviewer encourages free and easy discussion among the participants, hoping that the group dynamics will bring out actual feelings and thoughts. The comments are recorded through note-taking or tape recording and are subsequently studied to understand the consumers' buying process. Group interviewing is becoming one of the major marketing research tools for gaining insight into consumer thoughts and feelings.[12]

Collecting the Information

After developing the research design, the researcher must collect the data. This step is generally the most expensive and the most liable to error. In the case of surveys, four major problems arise. Some respondents will not be in their home or office and must be recontacted. Other respondents may refuse to cooperate. Still others may give biased or dishonest answers. Finally, some interviewers will occasionally be biased or dishonest.

In the case of experiments, the researchers have to worry about matching the experimental and control groups, not influencing the participants by their presence, administering the treatments in a uniform way, and controlling for other factors.

Analyzing the Information

The next step in the marketing research process is to sort out the important information and findings from the data. The researcher puts the data in the form of tables. He or she then develops or computes such statistics as frequency distributions, averages, and measures of dispersion. The researcher then attempts to apply some of the advanced statistical techniques and decision models in the analytical marketing system in the hope of discovering additional information.

Presenting the Findings

The researcher should not try to overwhelm marketing managers with numbers and fancy statistical techniques—this will lose them. The researcher should present major findings that are useful in the major marketing decisions facing management. The study is useful when it reduces the amount of uncertainty facing marketing executives. This is what happened in the Allegheny case:

Allegheny's marketing researchers found that most people still thought of the airline as a very small one, even though it had become the sixth largest in the country. The worst part of it was that travelers preferred big airlines to small ones, believing that the bigger airlines were safer, used more experienced pilots, and were more dependable. In response to these findings, Allegheny launched an advertising campaign to convince people that, like Pan Am, TWA, and American,

Good marketing research helped USAir create a new image and increase business.

Marc Anderson

Allegheny was a "big" airline. Television, newspaper, and magazine ads carried such messages as:

- It takes a big airline to fly over a million more passengers a year than Pan Am.
- It takes a big airline to operate more daily flights than TWA.
- It takes a big airline to fly to more American cities than American.

The Allegheny researchers also found out that part of the airline's problem was its name. In its days as a commuter airline, Allegheny had been nicknamed "Agony Airlines" because back then it had used small planes that flew through bad weather, rather than jets that can fly above it. The small plane resulted in many bumpy rides and late arrivals. Also, the name linked the airline with a small region of the United States, while it now flew to many parts of the country. The solution to the problem was to change the airline's name to USAir. The new name sounded like a "big" airline and reminded travelers of the company's national routes.

USAir's business has continued to grow. After the advertising campaign, a larger number of families and vacationers began to use the airline, rather than just business people. The marketing research and resulting advertising campaign were successful in making the airline better known and more widely used.[13]

Summary

In carrying out their marketing responsibilities, marketing managers need a great deal of information. Too often, such information is not available, comes too late, or cannot be trusted. An increasing number of companies have become aware of these information deficiencies and are taking steps to improve their marketing information systems.

A well-designed marketing information system consists of four subsystems. The first is the internal reports system, which provides current data on sales, costs, inventories, cash flows, and accounts receivable and payable. Many companies have developed advanced computer-based internal reports systems that provide more comprehensive information and also get it faster. The second is the marketing intelligence system, which supplies marketing executives with everyday information about developments in the commercial environment. Here a well-trained sales force, special marketing intelligence personnel, purchase data from syndicated sources, and an intelligence office can improve the marketing intelligence available to company executives. The third system is marketing research, which involves collecting information that is relevant to a specific marketing problem facing the company. Three-fourths of all large companies operate marketing research departments. The fourth system is the analytical marketing system, which consists of advanced statistical procedures and models to help marketers make better marketing decisions. A growing number of companies are building statistical and model banks to improve their analytical capabilities.

Marketing managers will work with professional marketing researchers to design needed studies. Marketing research involves a five-step procedure. The first step consists of carefully defining the problem and setting the research objectives. The second step consists of developing a plan for collecting data from primary and secondary sources. Primary data collection calls for choosing a research approach (observation, experimentation, survey), developing a research instrument (questionnaire, mechanical instruments), formulating a sampling plan (sample unit, sample size, sampling procedure), and choosing a contact method (telephone, mail, personal). The third step consists of collecting the information through fieldwork or laboratory work. The fourth step consists of analyzing the information to find averages, variables, and various relationships in the data. The fifth step consists of presenting the main findings to the marketing managers so that they can make better decisions.

Questions for Discussion

1. What might some research tasks be for the following areas: distribution decisions, product decisions, advertising decisions, personal-selling decisions, pricing decisions?
2. In several test communities in the United States, it is possible to scan a consumer's purchases at a grocery checkout counter, beam customer-tailored commercials into the consumer's home via split cable TV, and determine if he or she later changed from buying brand A to brand B after having seen the commercials. Consumers volunteer for participation in this test. The ACLU (American Civil Liberties Union) claims that this is an invasion of privacy; marketers claim that it will revolutionize the marketing research business. What do you think?
3. How does a marketing information system differ from a marketing intelligence system?

4. What is the main objective of the marketing research system at Prentice-Hall (the publishers of this book)?
5. Briefly describe the meaning of analytical marketing system. Do you feel that a men's clothing store in a small town would use this type of system? Why?
6. Once the research objectives and the problem have been defined, the researcher is then ready to begin the formal survey of people. Comment.
7. Which type of research would be the most appropriate in the following situations and why?
    a. Post cereals wants to investigate the effect that children have on the actual purchase of its products.
    b. Your college bookstore wants to gather some preliminary information as to how students feel about the merchandise and service provided by the bookstore.
    c. McDonald's is considering locating a new outlet in a fast-growing suburb.
    d. Gillette wants to test the effect of two new advertising themes for its Right Guard lime stick deodorant sales in two cities.
8. The president of a campus organization to which you belong has asked you to conduct a marketing research project on why membership is declining. Discuss how you would apply the steps in the marketing research procedure to this project.
9. List some internal company or environmental factors that would call for more marketing research by a company.

Key Terms in Chapter 3

Marketing information system A continuing and interacting structure of people, equipment, and procedures to gather, sort, analyze, evaluate, and distribute pertinent, timely, and accurate information for use by marketing decision makers to improve their marketing planning, execution, and control.

Marketing intelligence system The set of sources and procedures by which executives obtain their everyday information about developments in the commercial environment.

Marketing research The systematic design, collection, analysis, and reporting of data and findings relevant to a specific marketing situation facing the company.

Primary data Data that consist of originally collected information for the purpose at hand.

Sample The segment of the population selected to represent the population as a whole.

Secondary data Data that consist of information already existing somewhere, having been collected for another purpose.

Case for Chapter 3

Case 2   Minnetonka, Inc.: ShowerMate™ (p. 494)
Marketing research played a major role in the development of ShowerMate. How could Minnetonka develop information about this market? This case helps answer that question.

Chapter 4

The Marketing Environment

Objectives

After reading this chapter, you should be able to:

1. List the forces in a company's micro- and macro-environments.
2. Explain why marketers respond to demographic changes.
3. Name the major regulations affecting marketing.
4. Discuss how the cultural environment influences people's buying patterns.

The CBS Cable channel designed its programs for television viewers who would rather watch the Royal Shakespeare Company's *Macbeth* than *Love Boat*. CBS Cable believed that a schedule of high-quality plays, concerts, operas, dance, and other arts programs would attract a modest but loyal group of viewers looking for an alternative to network programs. This audience, though small, would also be an affluent one that would attract advertisers, CBS reasoned.

Among the cable channel's presentations were musical programs like a Count Basie concert, dramas starring renowned actors such as Peter O'Toole and Liv Ullmann, and interviews with such notable people as writer John Irving and film director Louis Malle. CBS Cable's specialty was its dance programs, which featured modern choreographers, such as Twyla Tharp. Critics gave CBS Cable's programs glowing praise. The channel was also enthusiastically received by the arts community, who welcomed the television exposure and the opportunity to expand their audiences. Then one year after it began, CBS Cable announced that it would cease broadcasting. The channel was a financial failure; at last count, the venture had lost over $30 million.

The reasons for CBS Cable's failure had nothing to do with the quality of its programs. Audiences were generally impressed with the unusually fine presentations. The channel's failure was due to several factors outside its control. The main one was that CBS Cable had expected strong financial support from advertisers that never materialized. Because the cable channel appeared during a recession, most companies had fewer advertising dollars to spend and were spending very cautiously. Adding to advertisers' reluctance was the fact that in cable television there is no viewer poll comparable to the Nielsen ratings of network television. Advertisers felt that to sponsor programs with an unknown number of viewers was too big a risk.

Another major problem for CBS Cable was that there were several other cable channels with similar programming competing for the same limited number of viewers. At that time, one competitor was ABC ARTS, another was a station called Bravo, and a third was The Entertainment Channel. Bravo and The Entertainment Channel, both commercial-free, were supported by subscription fees that audiences paid in addition to a monthly charge for cable service. Like CBS Cable, though, ABC ARTS was vying for advertisers' support. At one time, CBS Cable considered becoming a subscriber-supported station. However, most cable-equipped homes already had at least one station subscription, either another arts channel or one of the movie channels like Home Box Office. Analysts at CBS Cable felt that, due to the recession, too small a portion of their audience would pay for an additional subscription. Small audiences and few advertisers, then, were split between too many channels.

Competition with other channels also increased operating costs. As several channels competed for desirable dramas, ballets, and other possible programs, the cost of obtaining the rights rose. Because of this increasing expense, CBS Cable began to produce its own material, also a costly venture. The channel's original productions, like its other programs, were of high quality and lavishly produced. But often audiences had other attractive choices, sometimes even outside the television medium. For example, the channel presented its own expensive production of *The Pirates of Penzance* just prior to the release of a movie version starring Linda Ronstadt. So despite their quality and cost, CBS Cable's original programs did not increase advertiser and audience support.

The fate of CBS Cable appears to have been doomed by external forces. The audience to which the channel introduced its arts programs was receptive, but other factors in the marketing environment, such as the economy and the number of competitors, had more impact on the channel. Entrepreneurs in the cable television market have to watch more than their own programs; they also have to keep an eye on a host of other conditions in the marketing environment that may affect their survival.[1]

Clearly, the cable television industry depends not only on the marketing mixes used by various companies but also on trends and developments in the marketing environment. The marketing environment represents the set of "noncontrollable" forces to which the companies must adapt their marketing mix. We define a company's marketing environment as follows:

A **company's marketing environment** consists of the actors and forces that are outside the firm and that affect the marketing management's ability to develop and maintain successful transactions with its target customers.

The marketing environment deeply affects the company because it is changing, limiting, and uncertain. Instead of changing slowly and predictably, it is capable of producing major surprises and shocks. Which oil companies in 1971 would have predicted the end of cheap energy in the years that followed? How many managers at Gerber Foods foresaw the end of the "baby boom"? Which auto companies foresaw the tremendous impact Ralph Nader and consumers would have on their business decisions? The firm must use its marketing research and marketing intelligence capabilities to monitor the changing environment.

The marketing environment is made up of a microenvironment and a macroenvironment. The **microenvironment** consists of the forces close to the company that affect its ability to serve its customers, namely, the company suppliers, marketing intermediaries, customers, competitors, and publics. The **macroenvironment** consists of the larger societal forces that affect the microenvironment, such as the demographic, economic, natural, technological, political, and cultural forces. We will first examine the company's microenvironment and then its macroenvironment.

Forces in the Company's Microenvironment

Every company's primary goal is to make a profit. The job of marketing management is to make attractive products for its target markets. Marketing management's success, however, will be affected by the rest of the company, middlemen, competitors, and various publics. These forces in the company's microenvironment are shown in figure 4-1. Marketing managers cannot simply

FIGURE 4-1

Major Forces in the Company's Microenvironment

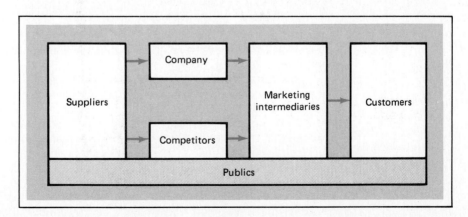

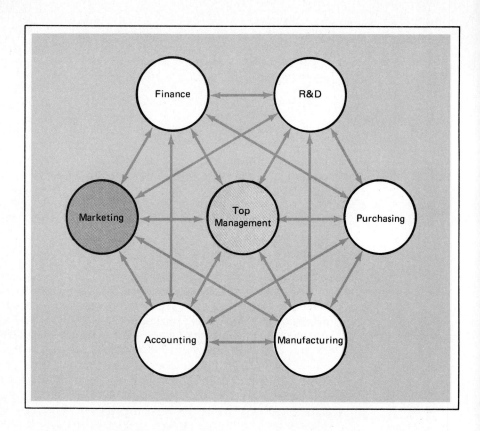

FIGURE 4-2

A Company's
Microenvironment

focus on the target market's needs, but they must be conscious of all forces in the microenvironment in which the company operates. We will now look at these forces. We will illustrate the role and impact of these forces by referring to the Schwinn Bicycle Company of Chicago, a major U.S. producer of bicycles.

The Company Marketing management at Schwinn, in making marketing plans, must take into account the other groups in the company, such as top management, finance, research and development (R&D), purchasing, manufacturing, and accounting. All of these groups form a company's microenvironment for the marketing planners (see figure 4-2).

Top management at Schwinn consists of the bicycle division's general manager, the executive committee, the chief executive officer, the chairman of the board, and the board of directors. These higher levels of management set the company's objectives, broad strategies, and policies. Marketing managers must make decisions within the plans made by top management. Furthermore, their marketing proposals must be approved by top management.

Marketing managers must also work closely with other departments. Finance is concerned with the availability and use of funds to carry out the marketing plan. R&D focuses on the technical problems of designing safe and attractive bicycles and developing efficient methods of producing them. Purchasing worries about getting sufficient supplies to produce the bicycles. Manufacturing is responsible for producing the desired number of bicycles. Accounting has to watch revenues and costs to help marketing know how well it is achieving its objectives. All of these departments have an impact on the marketing department's plans and actions.

Suppliers

Suppliers are business firms and individuals who provide resources needed by the company and its competitors to produce the particular goods and services. For example, Schwinn must buy steel, aluminum, rubber tires, gears, seats, and other materials to produce bicycles. In addition, it must buy labor, equipment, fuel, electricity, computers, and the other things it needs to carry out its business.

Developments in the "supplier" environment can seriously affect marketing. Marketing managers need to watch the prices of the supplies, since rising supply costs may force price increases on the bicycles. Shortages, labor strikes, and other events can interfere with the availability of supplies and with the fulfillment of delivery of bicycles to customers. This can lose sales in the short run and damage customer goodwill in the long run.

Marketing Intermediaries

Marketing intermediaries are firms that aid the company in promoting, selling, and distributing its goods to customers. They include middlemen, physical distribution firms, marketing service agencies, and financial intermediaries.

MIDDLEMEN. Middlemen are business firms that help the company find customers and/or close sales with them. Why does Schwinn use middlemen at all? The answer is that middlemen help produce **place time**, and **possession utility** for the customer more cheaply than Schwinn can by itself. Middlemen create place utility by stocking bicycles where customers are located. They create time utility by showing and delivering bicycles when the consumers want to buy them. They create possession utility by selling and transferring titles to the buyers. Schwinn would have to finance, establish, and operate a major system of national

The forces in Schwinn's microenvironment affect the marketing of its bicycles.
Courtesy Schwinn Bicycle Co.

outlets if it wanted to create place, time, and possession utility on its own. Schwinn finds it better to work through a system of independent middlemen.

Selecting and working with middlemen, however, is not a simple task. No longer does the manufacturer face many small independent middlemen from which to choose, but rather large and growing middlemen organizations. More and more bicycles are being sold through large corporate chains (such as Sears and K mart) and large wholesalers, retailers, and franchises. These groups have great power either to dictate terms or to shut the manufacturer out of some large-volume markets. Manufacturers must work hard to get "shelf space." In addition, they have to choose their middlemen carefully, because working with some channels keeps them from working with others.

i.e. National Freight Federal Express

PHYSICAL DISTRIBUTION FIRMS. Physical distribution firms assist the company in stocking and moving goods from their origin to their destination. Warehouses are firms that store and protect goods before they move to the next destination. Transportation firms consist of railroads, truckers, airlines, barges, and other freight-handling companies that move goods from one location to another. A company has to decide on the most economical means of shipment, balancing such considerations as cost, delivery, speed, and safety.

MARKETING SERVICES AGENCIES. Marketing services agencies—marketing research firms, advertising agencies, media firms, and marketing consulting firms—assist the company in targeting and promoting its products to the right markets. The company must decide whether to hire these services or do them themselves. When it decides to hire, it must carefully choose whom to hire, since these firms vary in their creativity, quality, service, and price. The company has to review the performance of these firms periodically and consider replacing those that no longer perform adequately.

FINANCIAL INTERMEDIARIES. Financial intermediaries include banks, credit companies, insurance companies, and other companies that help finance transactions and/or insure risk associated with the buying and selling of goods. Most firms and customers depend on financial intermediaries to finance their transactions. The company's marketing performance can be seriously affected by rising credit costs or limited credit, or both. For this reason, the company has to develop strong relationships with critical financial institutions.

Customers The company needs to study its customers closely. The company can operate in five types of customer markets, which are shown in figure 4-3 and defined below:

1. *Consumer markets:* individuals and households that buy goods and services for personal consumption
2. *Producer markets:* organizations that buy goods and services for their production process
3. *Reseller markets:* organizations that buy goods and services in order to resell them at a profit
4. *Government markets:* government agencies that buy goods and services either to produce public services or to transfer these goods and services to others who need them

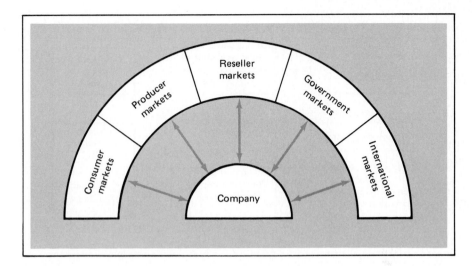

FIGURE 4-3

Basic Types of
Customer Markets

5. *International markets:* buyers found abroad, including foreign consumers, producers, resellers, and governments

Schwinn sells bicycles in all of these markets. It sells some bicycles directly to consumers through factory or retail outlets. It sells bicycles to producers who use them in their operations to deliver goods or ride around the plant. It sells bicycles to bicycle wholesalers and retailers, who resell them to consumer and producer markets. It could sell bicycles to government agencies. And it sells bicycles to foreign consumers, producers, resellers, and governments. Each market type has particular characteristics that call for careful study by the seller (see chapters 5 and 6).

Competitors Every company faces a wide range of competitors. Suppose Schwinn's marketing vice-president wants to identify Schwinn's competitors. The best way to do this is to research how people make bicycle-buying decisions. The researcher can interview John Adams, a college freshman who is planning to spend some money (see figure 4-4). John is considering several possibilities, including buying a transportation vehicle, a stereo system, or a trip to Europe. These are *desire competitors,* namely, the desires that the consumer might want to satisfy. Suppose John decides that he really needs better transportation. Among the possibilities are buying a car, a motorcycle, or a bicycle. These are *generic competitors,* namely, other basic ways in which the buyer can satisfy a particular desire. If buying a bicycle turns out to be the most attractive alternative, John will next think about what type of bicycle to buy. This leads to a set of *product form competitors,* namely, other product forms that can satisfy the buyer's particular desire. Here, the product forms are three-speed, five-speed, or ten-speed bicycles. John may decide on a ten-speed bicycle, in which case he will want to examine several *brand competitors.* These are other brands that can satisfy the same desire, namely, Raleigh, Sears, Azuki, and Gitane.

Understanding how consumers make decisions can help Schwinn's market-

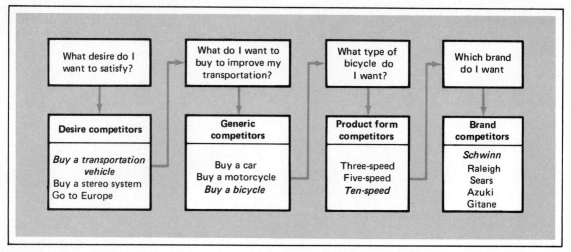

FIGURE 4-4

Four Basic Types of
Competitors

ing vice-president determine all the competitors standing in the way of selling more Schwinn bicycles. The manager will want to watch all four types of competitors, paying the most attention to the brand competitors because they are actively competing with Schwinn for sales.

Publics The company's marketing environment also includes various publics. We define public as follows:

> A **public** is any group that has an actual or potential interest in or impact on an organization's ability to achieve its objectives.

A public can help or hurt a company's effort to serve its markets. A *welcome public* is one whose interest in the company is very helpful (such as donors). A *sought public* is one whose interest the company seeks but does not necessarily obtain (such as mass media). An *unwelcome public* is one whose interest the company shuns but has to endure (such as a consumer boycott group).

A company can prepare marketing plans for its major publics as well as its customer markets. Suppose the company wants some response from a particular public, such as its goodwill, favorable word of mouth, or donations of time or money. The company would have to design a product that is attractive to this public.

Every company is surrounded by seven types of publics (see figure 4-5):

1. *Financial publics*. Financial publics influence the company's ability to obtain funds. Banks, investment houses, stock brokerage firms, and stockholders are the major financial publics. Schwinn seeks the goodwill of these groups by issuing annual reports, answering financial questions, and satisfying the financial community that it is in good financial shape.
2. *Media publics*. Media publics are organizations that carry news, features, and editorial opinions—specifically, newspapers, magazines, and radio

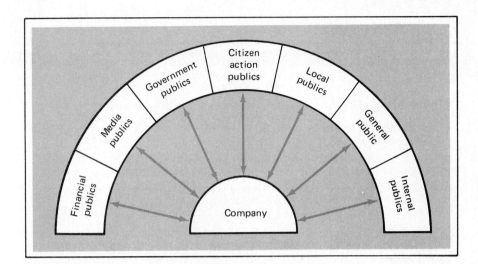

FIGURE 4-5

Types of Publics

and television stations. Schwinn is interested in getting more and better media coverage, perhaps in the form of stories on bicycling as good exercise or on Schwinn's charitable activities.

3. *Government publics.* Management must take government developments into account. Schwinn's marketers must respond to the issues of product safety, truth in advertising, dealers' rights, and so on. Schwinn must consider joining with other bicycle manufacturers to lobby for more favorable laws.

4. *Citizen action publics.* A company's marketing decisions may be questioned by consumer organizations, environmental groups, minority groups, and others. For example, parents are lobbying for more safety features in bicycles. Schwinn has the opportunity to be the leader in product safety design. Schwinn's public relations department can help it stay in touch with consumer groups. (See exhibit 4-1 for another example.)

5. *Local publics.* Every company comes into contact with local publics, such as neighborhood residents and community organizations. Large companies usually appoint a community relations officer to deal with the community, attend meetings, answer questions, and make contributions to worthwhile causes.

6. *General public.* A company needs to be concerned about the general public's attitude toward its products and activities. Although the general public does not act in an organized way toward the company, the public's image of the company affects its business. To build a strong "corporate citizen" image, Schwinn will lend its officers to community fund drives, make substantial contributions to charity, and set up systems for handling consumer complaints.

7. *Internal publics.* A company's internal publics include blue-collar workers, white-collar workers, volunteers, managers, and the board of directors. Large companies develop newsletters and other forms of communication to inform and motivate their internal publics. When employees feel good about their company, this positive attitude spills over to the other publics.

Exhibit **4-1**

Citizen Action Group Calls for Boycott of Nestlé Products

Even the most respected marketing company can wake up one day and find one of its products under attack by a citizen action group that thinks the company is acting irresponsibly. In fact, the attacking group is likely to call for a boycott of all the company's products, even though only one is under criticism. The publicity resulting from such boycott efforts can damage the goodwill a company had taken years to build.

Nestlé was singled out as such a target in 1978. Nestlé, the Swiss-based company that makes such well-known products as Nestlé Crunch bars, Taster's Choice coffee, and Stouffer's frozen foods, also produces infant baby formula.

The group accusing Nestlé is known as INFACT (Infant Formula Action Coalition). It claims that Nestlé is aggressively marketing infant milk formula to Third-World mothers who do not know how to use this product properly. Mothers using the formula often mix it with contaminated water, store it in improperly cleaned bottles, and frequently are unable to keep it refrigerated. This has resulted in infant illness and some infant deaths.

INFACT called for a worldwide boycott of all Nestlé products. Its mail campaign urges "more people have to know" and asks for financial support to bring the message to more people. The INFACT letter names all the brands owned by Nestlé that consumers should boycott.

Nestlé claims that it has handled the infant formula marketing responsibly and that infant formula is often the best food for infants under certain conditions. Nevertheless, Nestlé has been uncomfortable about the bad publicity. In March of 1982, Nestlé agreed to comply with the provisions of a new United Nations health code aimed at encouraging breast-feeding. The code outlaws advertising infant formula, distributing free samples, and paying commissions to salespeople.

Forces in the Company's Macroenvironment

The company and its suppliers, marketing intermediaries, customers, competitors, and publics all operate in a larger macroenvironment of forces that shape opportunities and pose threats to the company. These forces represent "uncontrollables," which the company must monitor and respond to. The macroenvironment consists of the six major forces shown in figure 4-6. The remaining sections of this chapter will examine these forces and show how they affect a company's marketing plans.

FIGURE 4-6

Major Forces in the Company's Macroenvironment

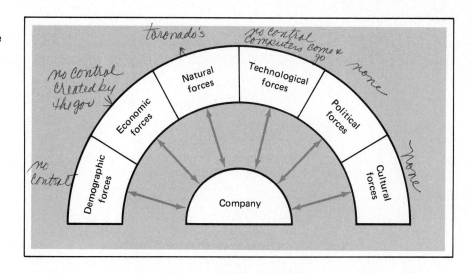

(handwritten annotations on figure: "toronado's", "no control created by the gov", "no control", "no control computers come + go", "none", "none")

Demographic Environment

Demography is the study of human populations in respect to size, density, and so on. The demographic environment is of major interest to marketers because people make up markets. The most important demographic trends are described here.

WORLDWIDE EXPLOSIVE POPULATION GROWTH. The world population is experiencing "explosive" growth. It totaled 4.5 billion in 1981 and is growing at a rate of 2% per year. At this rate, the world population will double in thirty-three years.[2]

The population explosion has become a major concern of many governments and groups throughout the world. First, the earth's resources may not be able to support this much human life, particularly at the high standards of living that most people seek. Second, the population growth is highest in countries and communities that can least afford it.

Population growth means growing human needs that business has to meet. It means growing markets if there is sufficient purchasing power. But if there is insufficient purchasing power, it means recession and shrinking markets.

SLOWDOWN IN U.S. BIRTHRATE. A "birth dearth" has replaced the former "baby boom" in the United States. The U.S. population stood at 234 million on July 1, 1983. It is projected to reach 260 million by the year 2000. Yet despite the increase in the number of people, the rate of population growth has slowed considerably since the 1950s. The annual number of births peaked at 4.3 million in 1957, and by the mid-1970s had fallen to under 3.2 million. Recently there has been a slight gain to 3.6 million births. During this decade the population is expected to grow by less than 1% per year. Factors contributing to smaller families are (1) the desire to improve personal living standards, (2) the increasing desire of women to work outside the home, and (3) the more effective use of birth control.

FIGURE 4-7
Projected Age-Group
Shifts, 1980–1990

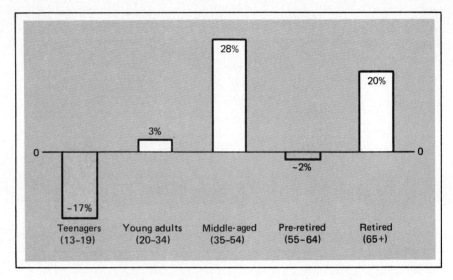

The declining birthrate is a threat to some industries, a boon to others. It has created sleepless nights for executives in such businesses as children's toys, clothes, furniture, and food. For many years the Gerber Company advertised "Babies are our business—our only business" but quietly dropped this slogan some time ago. Gerber now sells life insurance to older folks, using the theme "Gerber now babies the over-50's." Johnson & Johnson responded by persuading adults to use the company's baby powder, baby oil, and baby hair shampoo. Meanwhile, industries such as hotels, airlines, and restaurants have benefited from the fact that young couples have more leisure time and income.

AGING OF U.S. POPULATION. The current generation is living longer, as witnessed by a declining death rate. Average life expectancy is 73 years, a 24-year increase since 1900. The life expectancy for males is 69 and for females, 77. The rise in life expectancy and the declining birthrate are producing an aging U.S. population. The U.S. median age is now 30 and is expected to reach 35 by the year 2000.

Age-group populations show different rates of growth (see figure 4-7). The number of teenagers will decrease by 17%, or 4.6 million, in the 1980–90 decade. This suggests a slowdown in the sales growth for motorcycles, baseball and football equipment, denim clothing, records, and college educations.

The 20–34 age group will undergo a modest increase of 3% during this decade. Marketers who sell to this group—furniture manufacturers, vacation planners, life insurance companies, tennis and ski equipment manufacturers—will have to suggest more uses for these products to this group, since the number of users will not increase substantially.

The 35–54 age group will undergo the greatest increase of all age groups in the 1980–90 decade, namely, 28%. Members of this group are well established in their occupations and are a major market for large homes, new cars, and clothing.

The 55–64 age group will shrink by 2% during this decade. These "empty-nesters," whose children have left home, will have more time and income than formerly. This group is a major market for eating out, travel, expensive clothes, and golf and other forms of recreation.

The over-65 age group will show the second-largest increase in the 1980–90 decade, up by 20%. This group has a growing demand for retirement homes and communities, campers, quieter forms of recreation (fishing, golf), single-portion food packaging, and medical goods and services (medicine, eyeglasses, canes, hearing aids, and convalescent homes). This group is also becoming more self-centered, more active, and more leisure-oriented than the comparable group in past generations. They tend to spend more money on themselves, not worrying about leaving money to their children.

Companies that sold primarily to the youth market have responded to the graying of America by repositioning their products or introducing new ones. In addition to Johnson & Johnson's persuading adults to use its baby powder, oil, and shampoo and Gerber's selling life insurance to older people, Wrigley has introduced a stick-proof gum called Freedent for people who wear dentures. And Helena Rubenstein produces a line of skin-care products for women over 50.

THE CHANGING AMERICAN FAMILY. The American ideal of the two-children, two-car suburban family has been losing some of its luster. Several forces are changing the American family. First, people are marrying later. The average age of couples marrying for the first time has been rising over the years and now stands at 23.4 years for males and 21.6 for females. This trend is expected to continue through the 1980s. This will slow down the sales of engagement and wedding rings, bridal outfits, and life insurance.

Second, couples are having fewer children. Additionally, the newly married are also delaying childbearing longer. This means a slowed-down demand for baby food, toys, children's clothes, and other children's goods and services.

Third, about 50% of the marriages in the United States end in divorce. This has created over a million single-parent families and the need for additional housing units, furniture, appliances, and other household products.

As more married women enter the labor force, more husbands take on domestic responsibilities, including shopping for food and household goods.
Teri Leigh Stratford

Fourth, 51% of all married women are in the labor force. Working women are a market for better clothing, day-care services, home-cleaning services, and more frozen dinners. The growing number of working women means less viewing of television soap operas and less reading of domestic women's magazines. Their incomes contribute 40% of the household's income and influence the purchase of higher-quality goods and services. Marketers of tires, automobiles, insurance, and travel service are increasingly directing their advertising to working women. All of this is accompanied by a shift in the traditional roles and values of husbands and wives, with the husband assuming more domestic functions, such as shopping and child care. As a result, husbands are becoming more of a target market for food and household appliance manufacturers and retailers.[3]

Fifth, many young adults leave home early and move into apartments. In addition, many divorced and widowed people live alone. In the United States, more than 19 million people live alone (23% of all households). This group needs smaller apartments; inexpensive and smaller appliances, furniture, and furnishings; and food that is packaged in smaller sizes. Singles are also a market for various services that enable singles to meet each other, such as singles bars, tours, and cruises.

GEOGRAPHIC SHIFTS IN POPULATION. Americans are a mobile people, with approximately one out of five, or 42 million Americans, moving each year. Many of them are moving out of the Northeast and going to the Sun Belt states. Figure 4-8 shows which states have the fastest-growing populations. The move to the Sun Belt states will lessen the demand for warm clothing and home heating equipment and increase the demand for air conditioning.

Many of them have also moved from rural to urban areas. Cities show a faster pace of living, more commuting, higher incomes, and greater variety of goods and services than can be found in the small towns and rural areas that dot America. The largest cities, such as New York, Chicago, and San Francisco,

Table 4-1

The Top 20 SMA Markets in the United States

RANK	SMA	POPULATION	RANK	SMA	POPULATION
1	New York, N.Y.	9,120,000	11	Nassau-Suffolk, N.Y.	2,606,000
2	Los Angeles-Long Beach,		12	St. Louis, Mo.	2,356,000
	Calif.	7,478,000	13	Pittsburgh, Pa.	2,264,000
3	Chicago, Ill.	7,104,000	14	Baltimore, Md.	2,174,000
4	Philadelphia, Pa.	4,717,000	15	Minneapolis-St. Paul, Minn.	2,114,000
5	Detroit, Mich.	4,353,000	16	Atlanta, Ga.	2,030,000
6	San Francisco-Oakland, Calif.	3,251,000	17	Newark, N.J.	1,966,000
7	Washington, D.C.	3,061,000	18	Anaheim-Santa Ana-Garden	
8	Dallas-Fort Worth, Tex.	2,975,000		Grove, Calif.	1,933,000
9	Houston, Tex.	2,905,000	19	Cleveland, Ohio	1,899,000
10	Boston, Mass.	2,763,000	20	San Diego, Calif.	1,862,000

Source: *Statistical Abstract of the United States, 1982–83.*

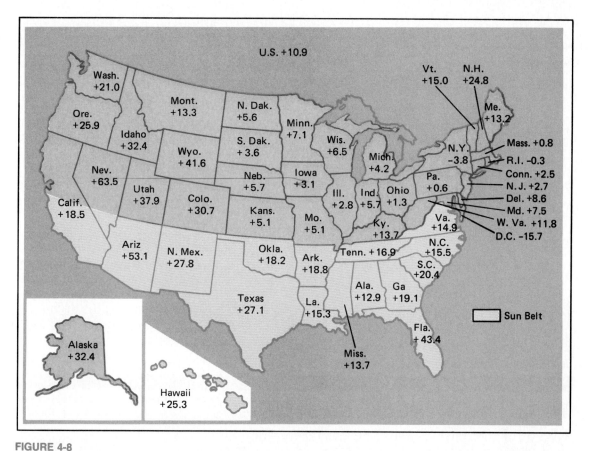

U.S. +10.9

Wash. +21.0
Ore. +25.9
Idaho +32.4
Mont. +13.3
N. Dak. +5.6
Minn. +7.1
Wis. +6.5
Vt. +15.0
N.H. +24.8
Me. +13.2
Mass. +0.8
R.I. −0.3
S. Dak. +3.6
Mich. +4.2
N.Y. −3.8
Conn. +2.5
N.J. +2.7
Nev. +63.5
Wyo. +41.6
Neb. +5.7
Iowa +3.1
Pa. +0.6
Del. +8.6
Md. +7.5
Calif. +18.5
Utah +37.9
Colo. +30.7
Kans. +5.1
Mo. +5.1
Ill. +2.8
Ind. +5.7
Ohio +1.3
Ky. +13.7
Va. +14.9
W. Va. +11.8
D.C. −15.7
Ariz +53.1
N. Mex. +27.8
Okla. +18.2
Ark. +18.8
Tenn. +16.9
N.C. +15.5
S.C. +20.4
Texas +27.1
La. +15.3
Ala. +12.9
Ga +19.1
Sun Belt
Fla. +43.4
Miss. +13.7
Alaska +32.4
Hawaii +25.3

FIGURE 4-8

Where the Population Moved, 1970–1980 (% Resident Population Gains)

Source: *Information Please Almanac, 1982* (New York: Simon & Schuster, 1981), p. 755

account for most of the sales of expensive furs, perfumes, luggage, and works of art. These cities also support the opera, ballet, and other forms of "high culture." Recently, however, there has been a slight shift of population back to small towns and rural areas.

Not all people have stayed in the cities. Cities have become surrounded by suburbs, and these suburbs in turn by "exurbs." The U.S. Census Bureau has created a separate population classification for sprawling urban concentrations, called Standard Metropolitan Areas (SMAs).[4] About 75% of the nation's population live in the 323 Standard Metropolitan Areas, and these SMAs constitute the primary market focus of firms. The top twenty SMA markets are listed in table 4-1. (Also see figure 4-8.)

About 60% of the total population, or 39% of the metropolitan population, live in suburbs. Suburbs are characterized by more casual, outdoor living, greater neighborhood interaction, higher incomes, and younger families. Suburbanites buy station wagons, home workshop equipment, garden furniture, lawn and gardening tools and supplies, and outdoor cooking equipment. Retailers have acknowledged the suburbs by building branch department stores and suburban shopping centers.

A BETTER-EDUCATED AND INCREASING WHITE-COLLAR POPULATION. Almost 44 million Americans (19% of the population) will have attended or graduated from college by 1985. The rising number of educated people will increase the demand for quality products, books, magazines, and travel. It suggests a decline in television viewing because college-educated consumers watch TV less than does the population at large.

In 1982 the total labor force consisted of 112 million people. Between 1960 and 1980, the number of white-collar workers rose from 43% to 51%, blue-collar workers declined from 37% to 33%, service workers stayed steady at 13%, and farm workers declined from 8% to 3%. For the 1980s, the U.S. Bureau of Labor Statistics predicts the most growth in the following occupational categories: engineering, science, medicine, computers, social science, buying, selling, secretarial, construction, refrigeration, health service, personal service, and protection. (For another labor force trend, see exhibit 4-2.)

These demographic trends are highly reliable for the short and intermediate run. Companies can list the major demographic trends and spell out what the trends mean for them. This is done in table 4-2 for three industries. In the case of airlines, for example, each population trend is expected to have a positive sales and profit impact.

Exhibit 4-2

The Night Frontier—A New Opportunity for Marketers

Professor Murray Melbin proposed the thesis that America's new frontier is not located in space but in time. More and more people are awake at all hours of the night, particularly in cities. Melbin's statistics bear this out. Approximately 13.5 million people—18% of the labor force—worked full- or part-time night shifts in 1977. In 1929, none of Boston's radio stations operated at night; in 1974, 57% of them broadcast twenty-four hours a day. The proportion of U.S. households tuned in to television between 1:00 A.M. and 7:00 A.M. increased from 4.4% in 1973 to 5.8% in 1977.

Night people create new markets. Dining places stay open late. Convenience stores, which used to stay open sixteen hours a day, now in most cases stay open twenty-four hours a day and do 20% of their business between midnight and 7:00 A.M. From 1973 to 1977, nighttime business calls in the Bell System increased by more than 50%. The city of Baltimore has successfully sponsored a postmidnight tour of the city called the "Insomniacs Tour." Triton Community College in Elk Grove, Illinois, offers midnight classes; its main problem is getting teachers, not students. We may soon see some department stores and boutiques staying open all night as the number of night people keeps increasing.

Source: Adapted from Murray Melbin, "Night as Frontier," *American Sociological Review*, February 1978, pp. 3–22.

Table 4-2			
The Effect of the Changing Population Mix on Three Industries			
TRENDS	AIRLINES	APPAREL	CONSUMER ELECTRONICS
Baby boom generation matures	Many will have more money for travel as they get older. ✔✔✔	Will spend more on clothes as they age; shift from casual to higher quality. ✔✔✔	Rising incomes provide means to buy better-quality stereos, TVs, and so on. ✔✔
More elderly persons	They have the time to travel but inflation may rob them of the means. ✔	Older people spend less on clothing.	Little demand from this group; often forced to make do with older products.
More working women	Second income allows more females to take trips; more single women have money. ✔✔✔	Career women need more clothing and have the money to buy it. ✔✔✔	Can buy more and higher-priced merchandise. ✔✔
Smaller family units	More disposable income per member; more economical to fly than drive. ✔✔	A shift toward higher-quality, higher-margin merchandise. ✔✔	More income per capita; electronic entertainment replaces family activities. ✔✔

Note: ✔✔✔ = Very positive   ✔✔ = Positive   ✔ = Mildly positive

Source: From *The Outlook,* March 26, 1979. Copyright © 1979 by Standard & Poor's. Reprinted by permission.

Economic Environment

Markets require purchasing power as well as people. Total purchasing power is related to current income, prices, savings, and credit availability. An economic recession, high unemployment, and the rising cost of credit all affect purchasing power.

In response to economic conditions, many Americans have turned to more cautious buying. They are buying more "store brands" and fewer "national brands" to save money. Many companies have introduced economy versions of their products and have turned to price appeals in their advertising messages. Some consumers have postponed their purchase of durable goods, and other consumers have made a purchase out of fear that prices will be 10% higher next year. Many families have begun to feel that a large home, two cars, foreign travel, and private higher education are now beyond their reach. At the same time, the percentage of income spent in various categories, such as food and clothing, has shifted, as can be seen in table 4-3.

Marketers should pay attention to income distribution as well. Income distribution in the United States is still pronouncedly skewed. At the top are upper-class consumers, whose expenditure patterns have not been affected by current economic events and who are a major market for luxury goods (Rolls Royces starting at $100,000) and services (round-the-world cruises starting at $10,000).

Table 4-3

Percentage Distribution of Consumption Expenditures, 1960, 1970, and 1980

EXPENDITURE	1960	1970	1980
Food, beverages, tobacco	27.1%	23.8%	21.9%
Housing	14.8	15.2	16.3
Household operations	14.2	14.2	13.7
Transportation	13.1	12.6	14.5
Medical-care expenses	7.2	8.1	9.9
Clothing, accessories, jewelry	9.9	9.0	7.4
Recreation	5.5	6.6	6.4
Personal business	4.4	5.1	5.4
Personal care	1.6	1.8	1.4
Other	3.3	3.7	3.2

Sources: *The National Income and Product Accounts of the United States, 1929–1974* (Washington, D.C.: U.S. Bureau of Economic Analysis); and *Survey of Current Business*.

There is a comfortable middle class that exercises some expenditure restraint but is able to afford expensive clothes, antiques, and a small boat or second home. The working class must stick close to the basics of food, clothing, and shelter and must try hard to save. Finally, the underclass (persons on welfare) and many retirees have to count their pennies when making purchases of even the most basic kind.

Marketers also have to take geographic income variations into account. A city like Houston is growing at a fast rate while Detroit is languishing. Marketers must focus their efforts on the areas of greatest opportunity.

Natural Environment The 1960s witnessed a growing public concern over whether the natural environment was being damaged by the industrial activities of modern nations. Rachel Carson, in *Silent Spring,*[5] pointed out the environmental damage to water, earth, and air caused by industrial activity of certain kinds. Watchdog groups, such as the Sierra Club and Friends of the Earth, sprang up, and concerned legislators proposed various measures to protect the environment. Changes in the environment affect the products that companies make and market.

SHORTAGES OF CERTAIN RAW MATERIALS. Air and water may seem to be infinite resources, but some groups see a long-run danger. Environmental groups have lobbied for a ban on the sale of certain propellants in aerosol cans because of their potential damage to the ozone layer of air. Water is already a problem in some parts of the world.

Renewable resources, such as forests and food, have to be used wisely. Companies in the forestry business are required to reforest timberlands in order to protect the soil and to ensure a sufficient level of wood supplies to meet future demand. Food supply can be a major problem in that the amount of farmland is limited, and more and more land is being developed for housing and commercial use.

Nonrenewable resources, such as oil, coal, and various minerals, pose a serious problem:

> It would appear at present that the quantities of platinum, gold, zinc, and lead are not sufficient to meet demands . . . silver, tin, and uranium may be in short supply even at higher prices by the turn of the century. By the year 2050, several more minerals may be exhausted if the current rate of consumption continues.[6]

Firms using scarce minerals may find it more difficult and expensive to do business, even if the materials remain available. They may not find it easy to pass these cost increases on to the consumer. Firms engaged in research and development and in exploration can help to relieve the problem by developing valuable new sources and materials.

INCREASED COST OF ENERGY.   One nonrenewable resource, oil, has created the most serious problem for future economic growth. The major industrial economies of the world are heavily dependent on oil, and until economical substitute forms of energy can be developed, oil will continue to dominate the world political and economic picture. The high price of oil (up from $2.23 per barrel in 1970 to $34.00 per barrel in 1982) has created a frantic search for alternative forms of energy. Coal is again popular, and companies are searching for practical means to harness solar, nuclear, wind, and other forms of energy. In the solar energy field alone, hundreds of firms are putting out products to harness solar energy for heating homes and other uses.[7]

INCREASED LEVELS OF POLLUTION.   Industry will almost always damage the quality of the natural environment. Consider the disposal of chemical and nuclear wastes, the dangerous mercury levels in the ocean, the quantity of DDT and other chemical pollutants in soils and food supplies, and the littering of the environment with nonbiodegradable bottles, plastics, and other packaging materials.

The public's concern creates a marketing opportunity for alert companies. It creates a large market for pollution control solutions, such as scrubbers and recycling centers. It leads to a search for alternative ways to produce and package goods that do not cause environmental damage.[8]

STRONG GOVERNMENT INTERVENTION IN NATURAL RESOURCE MANAGEMENT.   Marketing management needs to pay attention to the natural environment in terms of obtaining needed resources and avoiding damage to the natural environment. Business can expect strong controls from both government and pressure groups. Instead of opposing all forms of regulation, business should help develop acceptable solutions to the material and energy problems facing the nation.

Technological Environment The most dramatic force shaping people's destiny is technology. Technology has released such wonders as penicillin, open-heart surgery, and birth-control pills. It has released such horrors as the hydrogen bomb, nerve gas, and the submachine gun. It has released such mixed blessings as the automobile, television, and white bread. One's attitude toward technology depends on whether one is more impressed with its wonders or with its blunders.

Every new technology takes the place of previous technology. Transistors hurt the vacuum-tube industry, photocopiers hurt the carbon-paper business, automobiles hurt the railroads, and television hurt the movies. Instead of the older industries transforming into the new, they fought or ignored them, and their businesses declined.

Each technology creates major long-run consequences that are not always foreseeable. Contraceptives, for example, led to smaller families, more working wives, and larger discretionary incomes—resulting in higher spending for vacation travel, durables, and other things.

The marketer should watch the following trends in technology.

FASTER PACE OF TECHNOLOGICAL CHANGE. Many of today's common products were not available even one hundred years ago. Abraham Lincoln did not know of automobiles, airplanes, phonographs, radios, or electric lights. Woodrow Wilson did not know of television sets, aerosol cans, home freezers, automatic dishwashers, room air conditioners, antibiotics, or electronic computers. Franklin Delano Roosevelt did not know of photocopiers, synthetic detergents, tape recorders, birth-control pills, or earth satellites. And John Kennedy did not know of personal computers, digital wristwatches, videorecorders, or word processors.

Robots assembling cars at a Ford Motor Company plant. New technologies are revolutionizing our production processes.
Courtesy Ford Motor Co.

Alvin Toffler, in his book *Future Shock,* sees a faster growth in the invention, exploitation, and diffusion of new technologies.[9] More ideas are being worked on; the time lag between new ideas and their successful implementation is decreasing rapidly; and the time between introduction and peak production is shortening considerably. Ninety percent of all the scientists who ever lived are alive today, and technology feeds upon itself.

UNLIMITED OPPORTUNITIES. Scientists today are working on a startling range of new technologies that will revolutionize our products and production processes. The most exciting work is being done in biotechnology, solid-state electronics, robotics, and materials science.[10] Scientists today are working on the following promising new products and services:

- Practical solar energy
- Cancer cures
- Chemical control of mental health
- Lung and liver cures
- Desalinization of seawater

- Commercial space shuttle
- Household robots that do cooking and cleaning
- Nonfattening, tasty, nutritious foods

- Happiness pills
- Electric cars
- Electronic anesthetic for pain killing
- Totally safe and effective contraceptive

In addition, scientists speculate on fantasy products, such as small flying cars, single-person rocket belts, space colonies, and human clones. The challenge in each case is not only technical but commercial, namely, to develop practical, affordable versions of these products.

HIGH R&D BUDGETS.   The United States leads the world in research and development spending. In 1981, R&D expenditures exceeded $68 billion and are expected to increase an average of 3% annually during this decade.

The five industries spending the most R&D money are aircraft and missiles, electrical equipment and communication, chemicals and allied products, machinery, and motor vehicles and other transportation. The industries spending the least R&D money are lumber, wood products, furniture, textiles, apparel, and paper and allied products. Industries in the top range spend between 5% and 10% of their sales dollar on R&D, and those in the lowest range spend less than 1% of their sales dollar. The average company spends about 2% of its sales dollar on R&D.

CONCENTRATION ON MINOR IMPROVEMENTS.   Many companies are making minor product improvements instead of gambling on major discoveries. Even basic research companies like Du Pont, Bell Laboratories, and Pfizer are proceeding cautiously. Most companies are content to put their money into copying competitors' products and making minor feature and style improvements. Much of the research is defensive rather than offensive.

INCREASED REGULATION OF TECHNOLOGICAL CHANGE.   The public needs to know that new products are safe. Government agencies investigate and ban potentially unsafe products. The federal Food and Drug Administration has issued elaborate regulations on testing new drugs, resulting in much higher industry research costs and lengthening of the time between idea and introduction from five to about nine years. Safety and health regulations have also increased in the areas of food, cars, clothing, electrical appliances, and construction. Marketers must be aware of these regulations when proposing, developing, and launching new products.

Technological change faces opposition from those who see it as threatening nature, privacy, simplicity, and even the human race. Various groups have opposed the construction of nuclear plants, high-rise buildings, and recreational facilities in national parks.

Marketers need to understand the changing technological environment and how new technologies can serve human needs. They need to work closely with R&D people to encourage more market-oriented research. They must be alert to possible negative aspects of any new ideas that might harm the users and bring about distrust and opposition.

Political Environment   Marketing decisions are highly affected by developments in the political environment. This environment is made up of laws, government agencies, and pressure groups that influence and limit various organizations and individuals in society.

LEGISLATION REGULATING BUSINESS. Legislation regulating business has steadily increased over the years. This legislation has been enacted for a number of reasons. The first is to protect companies from each other. Business executives all praise competition but try to neutralize it when it touches them. If threatened, they show their teeth:

> ReaLemon Foods, a subsidiary of Borden, held approximately 90% of the reconstituted lemon juice market until 1970. Fearing antitrust action, ReaLemon began to allow companies on the West Coast and in the Chicago area to make inroads. By 1972, however, a Chicago competitor, Golden Crown Citrus Corporation, had captured a share that ReaLemon considered too large. ReaLemon went on the offensive, and, in 1974, the Federal Trade Commission filed a complaint charging ReaLemon with predatory pricing and sales tactics.[11]

So laws are passed to define and prevent unfair competition. These laws are enforced by the Federal Trade Commission and the Antitrust Division of the attorney general's office.

The second purpose of government regulation is to protect consumers from unfair business practices. Some firms, if left alone, would make bad products, tell lies in their advertising, and deceive through their packaging and pricing. Unfair consumer practices have been defined and are enforced by various agencies. Many managers see purple with each new consumer law, and yet a few have said that "consumerism may be the best thing that has happened . . . in the past 20 years."[12] (See chapter 20 for more on consumerism.)

The third purpose of government regulation is to protect the larger interests of society against unbridled business behavior. Business activity does not always create a better quality of life. As the environment deteriorates, new laws and their enforcement will continue or increase. Business executives have to watch these developments in planning their products and marketing programs.

The marketing executive needs a good working knowledge of the major laws protecting competition, consumers, and the larger interests of society. The main federal laws are listed in table 4-4. The earlier laws dealt mainly with protecting competition, and the later laws with protecting consumers. Marketing executives should know these federal laws. And they should know the state and local laws that affect their local marketing activity.

CHANGING GOVERNMENT AGENCY ENFORCEMENT. To enforce the laws, Congress established several federal regulatory agencies—the Federal Trade Commission, the Food and Drug Administration, the Interstate Commerce Commission, the Federal Communications Commission, the Federal Power Commission, the Civil Aeronautics Board, the Consumer Products Safety Commission, the Environmental Protection Agency, and the Office of Consumer Affairs. These agencies can have a major impact on a company's marketing performance. Government agencies have some discretion in enforcing the laws. From time to time, they appear to be overzealous and unpredictable. The agencies are dominated by lawyers and economists, who often lack a practical sense of how business and marketing works. In recent years the Federal Trade Commission has added staff marketing experts to better understand the complex issues. The degree of enforcement appears to be moderating under President Reagan, with a strong trend toward deregulation.[13]

Remember these laws

any deception via advertising can be protected by the FTCA

not good for international

Table 4-4

Milestone U.S. Legislation Affecting Marketing

THE LAW	WHAT THE LAW DID
Sherman Antitrust Act (1890)	Prohibited (a) "monopolies or attempts to monopolize" and (b) "contracts, combinations, or conspiracies in restraint of trade" in interstate and foreign commerce.
Federal Food and Drug Act (1906)	Forbid the manufacture, sale, or transport of adulterated or fraudulently labeled foods and drugs in interstate commerce. Supplanted by the Food, Drug, and Cosmetic Act, 1938; amended by Food Additives Amendment in 1958 and the Kefauver-Harris Amendment in 1962. The 1962 amendment dealt with pretesting of drugs for safety and effectiveness and labeling of drugs by generic name.
Meat Inspection Act (1906)	Provided for the enforcement of sanitary regulations in meat-packing establishments and for federal inspection of all companies selling meats in interstate commerce.
Federal Trade Commission Act (1914)	Established the commission, a body of specialists with broad powers to investigate and to issue cease and desist orders to enforce Section 5, which declared that "unfair methods of competition in commerce are unlawful."
Clayton Act (1914)	Supplemented the Sherman Act by prohibiting certain specific practices (certain types of price discrimination, tying clauses and exclusive dealing, intercorporate stockholdings, and interlocking directorates) "where the effect . . . may be to substantially lessen competition or tend to create a monopoly in any line of commerce." Provided that violating corporate officials can be held individually responsible; exempted labor and agricultural organizations from its provisions.
Robinson-Patman Act (1936)	Amended the Clayton Act. Added the phrase "to injure, destroy, or prevent competition." Defined price discrimination as unlawful (subject to certain defenses) and provided the FTC with the right to establish limits on quantity discounts, to forbid brokerage allowances except to independent brokers, and to prohibit promotional allowances or the furnishing of services or facilities except where made available to all "on proportionately equal terms."
Miller-Tydings Act (1937)	Amended the Sherman Act to exempt interstate fair-trade (price fixing) agreements from antitrust prosecution. (The McGuire Act, 1952, reinstated the legality of the nonsigner clause.)
Wheeler-Lea Act (1938)	Prohibited unfair and deceptive acts and practices regardless of whether competition is injured; placed advertising of foods and drugs under FTC jurisdiction.
Antimerger Act (1950)	Amended Section 7 of the Clayton Act by broadening the power to prevent intercorporate acquisitions where the acquisition may have a substantially adverse effect on competition.

(continued)

Table 4-4 (continued)

Milestone U.S. Legislation Affecting Marketing

THE LAW	WHAT THE LAW DID
Automobile Information Disclosure Act (1958)	Prohibited car dealers from inflating the factory price of new cars.
National Traffic and Motor Vehicle Safety Act (1966)	Provided for the creation of compulsory safety standards for automobiles and tires.
Fair Packaging and Labeling Act (1966)	Provided for the regulation of the packaging and labeling of consumer goods. Required manufacturers to state what the package contained, who made it, and how much it contained. Permitted industries' voluntary adoption of uniform packaging standards.
Child Protection Act (1966)	Banned sale of hazardous toys and articles. Amended in 1969 to include articles that pose electrical, mechanical, or thermal hazards.
Federal Cigarette Labeling and Advertising Act (1967)	Required that cigarette packages contain the following statement: "Warning: The Surgeon General Has Determined That Cigarette Smoking Is Dangerous to Your Health."
Truth-in-Lending Act (1968)	Required lenders to state the true costs of a credit transaction, outlawed the use of actual or threatened violence in collecting loans, and restricted the amount of garnishments. Established a National Commission on Consumer Finance.
National Environmental Policy Act (1969)	Established a national policy on the environment and provided for the establishment of the Council on Environmental Quality. The Environmental Protection Agency was established by Reorganization Plan No. 3 of 1970.
Fair Credit Reporting Act (1970)	Ensured that a consumer's credit report would contain only accurate, relevant, and recent information and would be confidential unless requested for an appropriate reason by a proper party.
Consumer Product Safety Act (1972)	Established the Consumer Product Safety Commission and authorized it to set safety standards for consumer products as well as exact penalties for failure to uphold the standards.
Consumer Goods Pricing Act (1975)	Prohibited the use of price maintenance agreements among manufacturers and resellers in interstate commerce.
Magnuson-Moss Warranty/FTC Improvement Act (1975)	Authorized the FTC to determine rules concerning consumer warranties and provided for consumer access to means of redress, such as the "class action" suit. Also expanded FTC regulatory powers over unfair or deceptive acts or practices.
Equal Credit Opportunity Act (1975)	Prohibited the discrimination of a credit transaction because of sex, marital status, race, national origin, religion, age, or receipt of public assistance.
Fair Debt Collection Practice Act (1978)	Made it illegal to harass or abuse any person and make false statements or use unfair methods when collecting a debt.

GROWTH OF PUBLIC INTEREST GROUPS. The number and power of public interest groups have increased during the past two decades. The most successful is Ralph Nader's Public Citizen group, which watchdogs consumer interests. Nader made consumerism a major social force, first with his successful attack on unsafe automobiles (resulting in the passage of the National Traffic and Motor Vehicle Safety Act of 1966), and then through investigations of meat processing (resulting in the passage of the Wholesome Meat Act of 1967), consumer credit, auto repairs, insurance, and X-ray equipment. Hundreds of other consumer interest groups—private and governmental—operate at the national, state, and local levels. Other groups that marketers need to consider are those seeking to protect the environment (Sierra Club, Environmental Defense), advance the "rights" of women, blacks, and senior citizens, and so on.

Cultural Environment   People grow up in a particular society that shapes their basic beliefs, values, and norms. They absorb, almost unconsciously, a world view that defines their relationship to themselves and others. The following cultural characteristics can affect marketing decision making.

HIGH PERSISTENCE OF CORE CULTURAL VALUES. People in a given society hold many beliefs and values. Their core beliefs and values have a high degree of persistence. For example, most Americans believe in working, getting married, giving to charity, and being honest. These beliefs shape and affect more specific attitudes and behaviors found in everyday life. Core beliefs and values are passed on from parents to children and are reinforced by society's major institutions—schools, churches, business, and government.

People's secondary beliefs and values are more open to change. Believing in the institution of marriage is a core belief; believing that people ought to get married early is a secondary belief. Supporters of family planning could argue more effectively that people should get married later than that they should not get married at all. Marketers have some chance of changing secondary values but little chance of changing core values.

Teenagers form a subculture with distinct needs and buying patterns.
Ken Karp

within our culture we have subcultures

CULTURE'S SUBCULTURES. Each society contains subcultures, that is, groups of people with shared value systems emerging from their common life experiences or circumstances. Episcopalians, teenagers, and Hell's Angels all represent separate subcultures whose members share common beliefs, preferences, and behaviors. Marketers can choose a subculture as a target market on the basis of its needs and buying patterns.

TIME SHIFTS OF SECONDARY CULTURAL VALUES. Although core values are fairly persistent, cultural swings do take place. Consider the impact of the hippies, the Beatles, Elvis Presley, and other culture heroes on young people's hairstyles, clothing, and sexual norms. Marketers have a keen interest in anticipating cultural shifts in order to spot new marketing opportunities or threats. For example, the percentage of people who value physical fitness and well-being has been going up steadily over the years, especially in the under-thirty group, the young women and upscale group, and people living in the West. Marketers will want to cater to this trend with appropriate products and communication appeals.

The major cultural values of a society are expressed in people's relationship to themselves, others, institutions, society, nature, and the universe.

People's relation to themselves. People vary in their relative emphasis on self-gratification versus serving others. Many people today focus on self-gratification. Some are pleasure-seekers, wanting fun, change, and escape. Others seek self-realization by joining therapeutic or religious groups.

The marketing implications of a "me-society" are many. People use products, brands, and services as a means of self-expression. They buy their "dream cars" and "dream vacations." They spend more time in the outdoors in health activities (jogging, tennis), in introspection, and in arts and crafts. The leisure industry (camping, boating, arts and crafts, sports) faces good growth prospects in a society where people seek self-fulfillment.

People's relation to others. People choose different degrees of sociability, from the hermit who avoids others to the gregarious person who only feels happy and alive in the company of others. A recent Doyle Dane Bernbach survey showed a widespread concern among adults about social isolation and a strong desire for human contact.[14] This suggests a bright future for "social support" products and services that enhance direct communication between human beings, such as health clubs, vacations, and games. It also suggests a growing market for "social surrogates," things that allow a person who is alone to feel that he or she isn't alone, such as home video games and computers.

People's relation to institutions. People vary in their attitudes toward corporations, government agencies, trade unions, universities, and other institutions. Most people accept these institutions, although some people are highly critical of certain ones. By and large, people are willing to work for major institutions and expect them to carry out society's work. There is, however, a decline in institutional loyalty. People are giving a little less to these institutions and are trusting them less. The work ethic is eroding.

Several marketing implications follow. Companies need to find new ways to win consumer confidence. They need to review their advertising communications to make sure that their messages are honest. They need to review their various activities to make sure that they are coming across as "good corporate citizens."

People's relation to society.   People vary in their attitudes toward their society, from patriots who defend it, to reformers who want to change it, to discontents who want to leave it. The trend is toward declining patriotism and stronger criticism as to where the country is going. People's orientation to their society will influence their consumption patterns, levels of savings, and attitudes toward the marketplace.

People's relation to nature.   People vary in their attitudes toward the natural world. Some feel ruled by it, others are in harmony with it, and still others seek to master it. A long-term trend has been people's growing mastery over nature through technology and their belief that nature is bountiful. More recently, however, people have become aware of nature's fragility and limited supplies. People recognize that nature can be destroyed or spoiled by human activities.

People's love of nature is leading to more camping, hiking, boating, and fishing. Business has responded with hiking gear, tenting equipment, and other supplies for nature enthusiasts. Tour operators are packaging more tours to wilderness areas. Food producers have found growing markets for "natural" products such as natural cereal, natural ice cream, and health foods. Companies are using natural backgrounds in advertising their products.

People's relation to the universe.   People vary in their beliefs about the origin of the universe and their place in it. Most Americans are monotheistic, although their religious conviction and practice have been waning through the years. Church attendance has been falling steadily, with the exception of certain evangelical movements reaching out to bring people back to organized religion. Some of the religious impulse has not been lost but has been redirected to a growing interest in Eastern religions, mysticism, and the occult.

As people lose their religious orientation, they seek to enjoy their life on earth as fully as possible. They seek goods and experiences that offer fun and pleasure. In the meantime, religious institutions start turning to marketers for help in reworking their appeals so that they can compete with the secular attractions of modern society.

The long-range trends in cultural values are summarized in table 4-5.

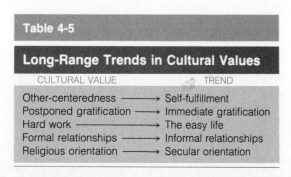

Table 4-5

Long-Range Trends in Cultural Values

CULTURAL VALUE	TREND
Other-centeredness ⟶	Self-fulfillment
Postponed gratification ⟶	Immediate gratification
Hard work ⟶	The easy life
Formal relationships ⟶	Informal relationships
Religious orientation ⟶	Secular orientation

Summary

The marketing environment includes those places where the company must start in searching for opportunities and in monitoring threats. It consists of all the forces that affect the company's ability to develop and maintain transactions with a target market. The company's marketing environment consists of a micro-environment and a macroenvironment.

The first force in the microenvironment is the company—its several departments and management levels—as it affects marketing management's decision making. The second force consists of the firms and individuals who produce the goods and services needed by the company, specifically, the suppliers. The third force consists of the marketing intermediaries (middlemen, physical distribution companies, marketing services agencies, and financial intermediaries). The fourth force consists of the five types of customer markets: consumer, producer, reseller, government, and international markets. The fifth force consists of the range of competitors facing any company: desire competitors, generic competitors, product form competitors, and brand competitors. The sixth force consists of all the publics that have an actual or potential interest in or impact on an organization's ability to achieve its objectives: financial, media, government, citizen action, and local, general, and internal publics.

The macroenvironment includes the major forces impinging on the company: demographic, economic, natural, technological, political, and cultural.

The demographic environment shows a worldwide explosive population growth, a U.S. birthrate slowdown, an aging U.S. population, a changing American family, geographic population shifts, and a better-educated and increasing white-collar population. The economic environment shows that due to conditions such as the recession, high unemployment, and high interest rates, many Americans are buying more cautiously. The natural environment shows shortages of certain raw materials, increased energy costs, increased pollution levels, and increasing government intervention in natural resource management. The technological environment shows faster technological change, unlimited opportunities, high R&D budgets, concentration on minor improvements, and increased regulation of technological change. The political environment shows business regulation, strong government agency enforcement, and the growth of public interest groups. The cultural environment shows long-run trends toward self-fulfillment, immediate gratification, the easy life, informal relationships, and a more secular orientation.

Questions for Discussion

1. You are the vice-president of marketing for Walt Disney Productions. Given the changes taking place in the demographic, economic, technological, and cultural environments, what plans would you make to ensure the company's success in the next decade?
2. A major alcoholic-beverage marketer is considering introducing an "adult" soft drink that would be a socially acceptable substitute for alcohol. What cultural factors could influence the introduction decision and marketing mix?

3. Life-style studies conducted from 1975 to 1979 showed a positive trend in the attitude that "meal preparation should take as little time as possible." How would this affect the sales of frozen vegetables?
4. Describe the marketing channel firms that Procter & Gamble might use in marketing a new brand of laundry detergent.
5. Compare and contrast the consumer, industrial, and reseller markets, using automobiles as an illustration.
6. Discuss the four types of competitors that someone planning to open a new pizza parlor near your campus must understand.
7. How do publics differ from consumers? Explain by using a specific example.
8. It is the year A.D. 2000. The price of gasoline is $4 per gallon, the price of hamburger is $6 per pound, the average home costs $200,000, and the annual rate of inflation has been 10% for the past twenty years. Given this economic information, what might you speculate the market size or potential for luxury products would be?
9. The political environment has become increasingly active. How have Ralph Nader, the FTC, and the actions of Congress affected marketing decision making in recent years?

Key Terms in Chapter 4

Company's marketing environment   The actors and forces that are outside the firm and that affect the marketing management's ability to develop and maintain successful transactions with its target customers.

Demography   The study of human populations in respect to characteristics such as size and density.

Macroenvironment   The larger societal forces that affect the microenvironment, such as the demographic, economic, natural, technological, political, and cultural forces.

Marketing intermediaries   Firms that aid the company in promoting, selling, and distributing its goods to customers, including middlemen, physical distribution firms, marketing services agencies, and financial intermediaries.

Microenvironment   The forces close to the company that affect its ability to serve its customers, namely, the company, marketing intermediaries, customers, competitors, and publics.

Place utility   Positioning a product in a location that is accessible to customers.

Possession utility   Making products available to consumers when they want to use them.

Public   Any group that has an actual or potential interest in or impact on an organization's ability to achieve its objectives.

Suppliers   Business firms and individuals who provide resources needed by the company and its competitors to produce the particular goods and services.

Time utility   The showing and delivering of a product at the time customers want to buy it.

Cases for Chapter 4

Case 3   Great Waters of France, Inc.: Perrier (p. 495)

What factors in the marketing environment led to the great success of Perrier? How does a changing environment affect a product? This case considers these questions.

Case 12   Fotomat Corporation (p. 508)

The marketing environment helped make Fotomat a success. Now a changing environment is creating major problems. This case looks at the forces affecting Fotomat.

Chapter 5

Consumer Markets and Consumer Buyer Behavior

Objectives

After reading this chapter, you should be able to:

1. Discuss the relationship between marketing stimuli and consumer response.
2. Name the four major factors that influence consumer buying behavior.
3. List the stages in the buyer decision process.
4. Describe the adoption process for new products.

The giant Du Pont Company of Wilmington, Delaware, was sure that it had a winner in its new Corfam "leather" for men's and women's shoes. Du Pont had been searching for a leather substitute since the 1930s, knowing that leather would one day be in short supply. In 1955 the company's scientists successfully synthesized a material called Corfam that had the necessary properties for a shoe material: permeability, strength, flexibility, and durability. A pilot plant was set up in 1958 to produce the new material for consumer evaluation. In 1959, following enthusiastic consumer response, Du Pont built a larger plant that started production of Corfam in 1961. Du Pont's total investment was $25 million.

The company selected seventeen top women's shoemakers and fifteen top men's shoemakers who agreed to buy the material from Du Pont and incorporate it in attractive shoe styles. Du Pont set a high price for Corfam because it felt that Corfam offered certain superior quality over leather, such as greater durability and ease of care. The material would be used in high-priced shoes to give consumers confidence in its quality, and Du Pont would consider penetrating the lower-priced shoe market at a later date.

The manufacturers' shoes featuring Corfam were launched at the 1963 National Shoe Fair, and many shoe retailers placed orders. Du Pont created a merchandising team to visit retail shoe stores to train salesmen in selling Corfam shoes. Du Pont created point-of-sale materials, window displays, and national advertising of Corfam at an initial cost of $2 million.

Du Pont was highly pleased with the results. One million pairs of Corfam shoes were bought by consumers in 1964; 5 million in 1965; and 15 million in 1966. But in 1967, Corfam shoe sales began to slip. What happened?

There was a disturbingly low rate of rebuying by former Corfam shoe purchasers. Du Pont had not done a sufficient job of analyzing the consumer shoe market and consumer shoe-buying behavior to catch a number of nuances in time. For example:

1. Corfam shoes were promoted as having high durability and ease of care. But high-priced shoe buyers were not primarily motivated by these factors in their choice of shoes.
2. Corfam was promoted as "breathing" the same as leather. But many Corfam shoe buyers found the shoes unusually warm.
3. Corfam was promoted as a material that did not stretch so that its fit would be right the first time. But many consumers bought a tight-fitting size thinking that it would stretch.
4. Consumers chose shoes for their style, not material. They never achieved enough interest in Corfam to ask the retailer if they could see the Corfam shoes.
5. Corfam might have gone over much better had it been used in domestic low-priced shoes. High-quality shoe buyers were increasingly shifting their purchases to imported high-styled leather shoes from Italy and elsewhere.

By 1971, Du Pont found the situation desperate and decided to stop its production of Corfam material for shoes. It incurred a loss of $100 million in one of the most expensive product failures in history.[1]

The story of Du Pont and Corfam suggests that there are many factors that control how people decide what to buy. Buying behavior is never simple. Yet understanding it is the essential task of marketing management under the marketing concept.

This chapter will explore the dynamics of the consumer market.

The **consumer market** consists of all the individuals and households who buy or acquire goods and services for personal consumption.

In 1981, the American consumer market consisted of 230 million persons who annually consume about $1.8 trillion worth of goods and services—the equivalent of $7,826 worth for every man, woman, and child. Each year this market grows by several million persons and over $100 billion, representing one of the most lucrative consumer markets in the world.[2] Figure 5-1 shows the annual food consumption of a family of four.

Consumers vary tremendously in their ages, incomes, educational levels,

mobility patterns, and tastes. Marketers have found it worthwhile to identify different consumer groups and develop products and services tailored to their needs. If a market segment is large enough, some companies may set up special marketing programs to serve this market. Here are two examples of special consumer groups:

- *Black consumers:* An important group in the United States are the 28 million black Americans with an aggregate personal income of over $100 billion. According to several research studies, blacks spend proportionately more than whites on clothing, personal care, home furnishings, alcohol, and tobacco and proportionately less on medical care, food, transportation, education, and utilities. Blacks do less "shopping around" than whites and patronize neighborhood and discount stores more. Blacks listen to radio more than whites, although they are less likely to listen to FM. Some companies run special marketing programs for black consumers. They advertise in *Ebony* and *Jet,* use blacks in commercials, and develop distinctive products (such as black cosmetics), packaging, and appeals. At the same time, these companies recognize that the black market contains several subsegments that may warrant different marketing approaches.[3]
- *Young adult consumers:* This market consists of 30 million persons between the ages of 18 and 24. The young adult market consists of three subgroups: college students, young singles, and young marrieds. Young adults spend disproportionately on books, records, stereo equipment, cameras, fashion clothing, hair driers, and personal-care and grooming products. They generally show low brand loyalty and high interest in new products. Young adults are an attractive market for several reasons: (1) they are receptive to trying new products, (2) they are more oriented toward spending than saving, and (3) they will be buying products for a longer time.[4]

Other consumer submarkets—the elderly,[5] women,[6] Spanish-Americans[7]

—could be similarly researched to see if tailored marketing programs would make competitive sense.

The 230 million American consumers buy an incredible variety of goods and services. We will now look at how consumers make their purchase choices among these goods.

A Model of Consumer Behavior

In earlier times, marketers could understand their consumers through the daily experience of selling to them. But the growth in the size of firms and markets has removed many marketing decision makers from direct contact with their customers. Increasingly, managers have had to turn to consumer research. They are spending more money than ever to study consumers, trying to learn: Who buys? How do they buy? When do they buy? Where do they buy? Why do they buy?

Of central interest is the question, How do consumers respond to various marketing stimuli that the company might arrange? The company that really understands how consumers will respond to different product features, prices, advertising appeals, and so on, will have an enormous advantage over its competitors. Therefore, companies and academics have invested much energy in researching the relationship between marketing stimuli and consumer response. Their starting point is the simple model shown in figure 5-2. This figure shows marketing and other stimuli entering the buyer's "black box" and producing certain responses.

This model is shown in more detail in figure 5-3. The stimuli on the left of the figure are of two types. Marketing stimuli consist of the four *P*'s: product, price, place, and promotion. Other stimuli consist of major forces and events in the buyer's environment: economic, technological, political, and cultural. All these stimuli pass through the buyer's black box and produce a set of observable buyer responses shown on the right: product choice, brand choice, dealer choice, purchase timing, and purchase amount.

The marketer's task is to understand what happens in the buyer's black box between the stimuli and the responses. The black box has two parts. First, the buyer's characteristics have a major influence on how he or she perceives and reacts to the stimuli. Second, the buyer's decision process influences the outcome. This chapter looks at these two parts to try to understand buyer behavior.

FIGURE 5-2

Simple Model of
Buyer Behavior

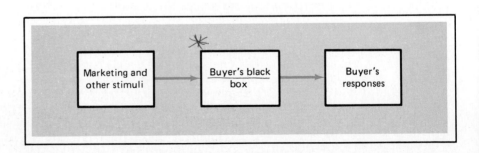

FIGURE 5-3

Detailed Model of
Buyer Behavior

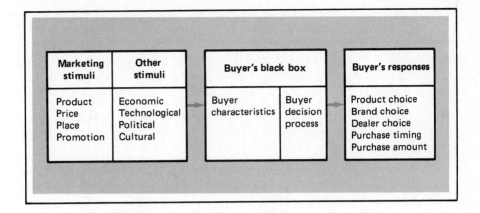

Buyer Characteristics

Consumers do not make their decisions in a vacuum. Their purchases are highly influenced by cultural, social, personal, and psychological characteristics (see figure 5-4). For the most part, they are "noncontrollable" by the marketer but must be taken into account. We want to examine the influence of each on a buyer's

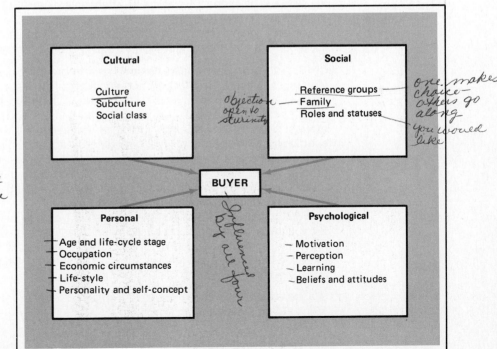

FIGURE 5-4

Characteristics
Influencing Buyer
Behavior

behavior. We will illustrate these characteristics for the case of a hypothetical consumer named Betty Smith:

> Betty Smith is a married college graduate who works as a brand manager in a leading consumer packaged-goods company. She is currently interested in finding a new leisure time activity that will offer some contrast to her working day. This need has led her to consider buying a camera and taking up photography. Many characteristics in her background will influence the way she goes about looking at cameras and choosing a brand.

Cultural Factors

Cultural factors exert the broadest and deepest influence on consumer behavior. We will look at the role played by the buyer's culture, subculture, and social class.

CULTURE.   Culture is the most basic cause of a person's wants and behavior. Human behavior is largely learned. The child growing up in a society learns a basic set of values, perceptions, preferences, and behaviors through a process of socialization involving the family and other key institutions. Thus a child growing up in America learns or is exposed to the following values: achievement and success, activity, efficiency and practicality, progress, material comfort, individualism, freedom, external comfort, humanitarianism, and youthfulness.[8]

Betty Smith's interest in cameras is a result of being raised in a modern society where camera technology and a whole set of consumer learnings and values have developed. Betty knows what cameras are. She knows how to read instructions on how to operate cameras, and her society has accepted the idea of women photographers. In another culture, say a remote tribe in central Australia, a camera may mean nothing. It may simply be a curiosity.

SUBCULTURE.   Each culture contains smaller groups, or subcultures, that provide more specific identification and socialization for its members. Nationality groups, such as the Irish, Polish, Italians, and Puerto Ricans, are found within large communities and exhibit distinct ethnic tastes and interests. Religious groups, such as the Catholics, Mormons, Presbyterians, and Jews, represent subcultures with specific cultural preferences and taboos. Racial groups, such as the blacks and Orientals, have distinct cultural styles and attitudes. Geographic areas, such as the Deep South, California, and New England, have distinct subcultures with characteristic life-styles. Exhibit 5-1 describes several geographic differences in product choice.

Betty Smith's interest in various goods will be influenced by her nationality, religion, race, and geographic background. These factors will influence her food preferences, clothing choices, recreation, and career goals. Her subculture may influence her interest in cameras. Subcultures attach different meanings to picture taking, and this could influence her interest.

SOCIAL CLASS.   Within almost every society, there are various social classes, which we define as follows:

> **Social classes** are relatively lasting groups in a society that are hierarchically ordered and whose members share similar values, interests, and behavior.

Table 5-1

Characteristics of the Six Major American Social Classes

SOCIAL CLASS	CHARACTERISTICS
Upper Uppers (less than 1%)	The social elite with family background, living on inherited wealth Give money to charity, have more than one home, send children to private schools, are not interested in ostentation Serve as reference group for other classes Market for jewelry, antiques, homes, vacations
Lower Uppers (about 2%)	Professionals or business people who earn high incomes through exceptional ability Active in social and civic affairs, seek social status and spend ostentatiously Want to become upper-upper Market for expensive homes, yachts, swimming pools, automobiles
Upper Middles (12%)	Career-oriented professionals, managers, and business people Concerned with education, ideas, culture, and civic activities Market for good homes, furniture, clothing, and appliances
Lower Middles (30%)	White-collar workers, small-business people, "aristocratic blue-collar workers" (plumbers, factory supervisors) Concerned with culturally defined rules and standards and with respectability Market for do-it-yourself items, home furnishings, conservative clothing
Upper Lowers (35%)	Blue-collar workers, skilled and semiskilled factory workers Concerned with well-defined sex roles, maintaining secure position within society Market for sports equipment, beer, homemaking items
Lower Lowers (20%)	Unskilled laborers, those on welfare Market for food, television sets, used cars

In the United States, social scientists have identified the six social classes shown in table 5-1.

Social classes have several characteristics: (1) persons within a given social class tend to behave alike; (2) persons are ranked as occupying a higher or lower position according to their social class; (3) social class is not indicated by any single variable but is based on one's occupation, income, wealth, education, value orientation, and so on; and (4) individuals are able to move into a higher social class or drop into a lower one.

Exhibit **5-1**

Where You Live Affects What You Buy

If you're a New York City resident, you're more likely to drink vermouth than you would be if you lived in St. Louis. That's what Mediamark, a marketing research firm, found out from an extensive survey of the geographic buying patterns in ten large American cities: New York, Los Angeles, Chicago, Philadelphia, San Francisco, Boston, Detroit, Washington, D.C., Cleveland, and St. Louis.

The purpose of the study was to provide information to the broadcasting networks, dependent on advertising revenue, about regional consumer behavior. One-third of the nation's population lives in the ten cities that were the focus of the study, and the major broadcasting networks also own and operate television stations in them. Mediamark's study showed that consumers had regional preferences even for products expected to have uniform buying strength across the country. Regional preference for different alcoholic beverages was one unexpected finding of the study, as was the finding that people in different cities prefer different forms of investment.

One surprising finding is that people in different parts of the country use different nonprescription drugs. The figure for Washington, D.C., consumers' use of sleeping pills is 122, somewhat above the national average of 100, while in Cleveland, the figure is 64, well below average. In St. Louis, the use of laxatives is slightly higher than average and measures 112, while in Boston, laxative use measures only 60. In the alcoholic beverages category, Los Angeles consumers show a strong preference for tequila at a figure of 274, while New Yorkers' purchasing habits show a much weaker liking for the drink at the figure of 49.

Personal investments are another area of unexpected regional difference, and Washington, D.C., residents have a particularly distinctive pattern in this category. The study shows that while Los Angeles residents overwhelmingly prefer U.S. Treasury notes (338), Washington residents do not (13); while people in Detroit prefer to invest in common stock (204), Washington residents feel otherwise (50). People who live in Washington, it seems, choose more often to invest in gold, precious metals, or gems (280) as compared to Chicago and St. Louis residents, who choose this form of investment less frequently (40).

The Mediamark study shows that consumer behavior is often affected by region. Sometimes the reasons for geographic differences are clear: We would not expect Detroit residents, who are likely to have a personal connection to the American auto industry, to buy many Japanese Datsuns. In fact, they don't; Detroit residents' preference for Datsuns measures expectedly low at 25. Other regional preferences aren't as easy to explain.

Source: Adapted from Eugene Carlson, "Where You Live Often Affects the Kinds of Goods You Buy," *Wall Street Journal*, September 14, 1982, p. 35.

Social classes show distinct product and brand preferences in such areas as clothing, home furnishings, leisure activity, and automobiles. Some marketers will focus their effort on one social class. The target social class suggests the type of store to sell in, the kind of media to advertise in, and the type of advertising message.

Betty Smith may have come from a higher social-class background. In this case, her family probably owned an expensive camera and may have dabbled in photography. The fact that she is thinking about "going professional" is also in line with a higher social-class background.

Social Factors A consumer's behavior is also influenced by social factors, such as the consumer's reference groups, family, and social roles and statuses.

REFERENCE GROUPS. A person's behavior is strongly influenced by many groups.

> A person's **reference groups** are those groups that have a direct (face-to-face) or indirect influence on the person's attitudes or behavior.

Groups having a direct influence on a person are called membership groups. These are groups to which the person belongs and interacts. Some are primary groups with whom there is fairly continuous interaction, such as family, friends, neighbors, and co-workers. Primary groups tend to be informal. The person also belongs to secondary groups, which tend to be more formal and where there is less continuous interaction. They include social organizations, such as religious organizations, professional associations, and trade unions.

Reference groups have a significant influence on a person's norms, life-style, and buying behavior.
Ray Ellis, Photo Researchers, Inc.

People are also influenced by groups to which they do not belong. An aspirational group is one to which the individual wishes or aspires to belong. For example, a teenage football player may hope to play someday for the Dallas Cowboys, and he identifies with this group although there is no face-to-face contact. A dissociative group is one whose values or behavior an individual rejects. The same teenager may want to avoid any relationship with the Hare Krishna cult.

Marketers try to identify the reference groups of the particular target market they are selling to. People are significantly influenced by their reference groups in at least three ways. Reference groups expose a person to new behaviors and life-styles. They also influence the person's attitudes and self-concept because he or she normally desires to "fit in." And they create pressures for conformity that may affect the person's actual product and brand choices (see exhibit 5-2).

Group influence tends to be strong when the product is visible to others whom the buyer respects. Betty Smith's decision to buy a camera and her brand choice may be strongly influenced by some of her groups. Friends who belong to a photography club may influence her to buy a good camera. The more cohesive the group, the more effective its communication process; and the higher the person esteems it, the more influential it will be in shaping the person's product and brand choices.

FAMILY.   Members of the buyer's family can exercise a strong influence on the buyer's behavior. The *family of orientation* consists of one's parents. From parents a person acquires an orientation toward religion, politics, and economics and a sense of personal ambition, self-worth, and love. Even if the buyer no longer interacts very much with his or her parents, the parents' influence on the buyer's unconscious behavior can be significant. In countries where parents continue to live with their children, their influence can be crucial.

A more direct influence on everyday buying behavior is one's *family of procreation,* namely, one's spouse and children. The family is the most important consumer-buying organization in society, and it has been researched extensively.[9] Marketers are interested in the roles and influence of the husband, wife, and children on the purchase of a large variety of products and services.

Husband-wife involvement varies widely by product category. The wife has traditionally been the main buyer for the family, especially in the areas of food, sundries, and staple clothing items. This is changing with the increased number of working wives and the willingness of husbands to do more of the family buying. Marketers of basic products would therefore be making a mistake to continue to think of women as the main or only purchasers of their products.

In the case of expensive products and services, husbands and wives make a joint decision. The marketer needs to determine which member normally has the greater influence on the purchase of a particular product or service. Either the husband is more dominant, or the wife, or they have equal influence. The following products and services fall under each:

- Husband-dominant: life insurance, automobiles, television
- Wife-dominant: washing machines, carpeting, non-living-room furniture, kitchenware
- Equal: living-room furniture, vacation, housing, outside entertainment

Exhibit 5-2

Home-Party Selling—Using Reference Groups to Sell

An increasingly popular form of nonstore selling involves throwing sales parties in homes and inviting friends and acquaintances to see merchandise demonstrated. Companies such as Mary Kay Cosmetics and Tupperware Home Parties are masters at this form of selling and have enjoyed great growth in sales and profits. Here is how home-party selling works.

A Mary Kay "beauty consultant" (of which there are 46,000) will ask different neighbors to hold small beauty shows in their homes. The neighbor will invite her friends for a few hours of informal socializing and refreshment. Within this congenial atmosphere, the Mary Kay consultant will give a two-hour beauty plan and free makeup lessons to the guests, hoping that the majority of the guests will buy some of the cosmetics just demonstrated. The hostess receives a commission of approximately 15% on sales plus a discount on personal purchases. About 60% of the guests are likely to purchase something, partly because they want to look good in the other women's eyes.

Courtesy Mary Kay Cosmetics, Inc.

Home-party selling is being used to sell cosmetics, cookware, household products, dresses, shoes, and lingerie. Tupperware Home Parties, now thirty-two years old, handles 140 different products, has eighty thousand independent salespeople, and has annual sales of approximately $200 million. Mary Kay Cosmetics, now twenty-two years old, uses a highly motivational approach, rewarding its saleswomen for recruiting new consultants—called "offspring"—and honoring the top saleswomen at the annual convention by naming them Queens of Personal Sales and giving them a pink Cadillac to drive for an entire year. Mary Kay's enterprise depends on her sharp understanding of Middle American women and how they can influence each other in the buying process.

Sources: See "The Mary Kay Way," *Newsweek*, May 7, 1979, p. 75; and David D. Seltz, "The Party-Plan Concept," in *Handbook of Innovative Marketing Techniques* (Reading, Mass.: Addison-Wesley, 1981), pp. 3–11.

In the case of Betty Smith's purchase of a camera, her husband will play an influencer role. He may have an opinion about her buying a camera and the kind of camera to buy. At the same time, she will be the primary decider, purchaser, and user.

ROLES AND STATUSES. A person participates in many groups—family, clubs, organizations. The person's position in each group can be defined in terms of *role* and *status*. With her parents, Betty Smith plays the role of daughter; in her family, she plays the role of wife; in her company, she plays the role of brand manager. A role consists of the activities that a person is expected to perform according to the people around him or her. Each of Betty's roles will influence some of her buying behavior.

Each role carries a status reflecting the general esteem accorded to it by society. The role of brand manager has more status in this society than the role of daughter. As a brand manager, Betty will buy the kind of clothing that reflects her role and status.

People often choose products to communicate their status in society. Thus company presidents will drive Mercedes and Cadillac automobiles, wear expensive, finely tailored suits, and drink Cutty Sark Scotch. Marketers are aware of products' potential for becoming status symbols. However, status symbols vary not only for different social classes but also geographically. Status symbols that are "in" in New York are jogging to work, fish and fowl, and cosmetic surgery for men; in Chicago, buying through catalogs, croissants and tacos, and telephones in cars; in Houston, elegant parties, caviar, and the "preppy" look; and in San Francisco, skydiving, freshly made pasta, and Izod shirts.[10]

Personal Factors A buyer's decisions are also influenced by personal outward characteristics, notably the buyer's age and life-cycle stage, occupation, economic circumstances, life-style, and personality and self-concept.

AGE AND LIFE-CYCLE STAGE. People change the goods and services they buy over their lifetime. They eat baby food in the early years, most foods in the growing and mature years, and special diets in the later years. People's taste in clothes, furniture, and recreation is also age-related.

Consumption is also shaped by the stage of the family life cycle. Nine stages of the family life cycle are listed in table 5-2 along with the financial situation and typical product interests of each group. Marketers often define their target markets in terms of their life-cycle stage and develop appropriate products and marketing plans.

Some recent work has identified psychological life-cycle stages. Adults experience certain passages or transformations as they go through life.[11] Thus Betty Smith may move from being a satisfied brand manager and wife to being an unsatisfied person searching for a new way to self-fulfillment. This may have stimulated her strong interest in photography. Marketers should pay attention to the changing consumption interests that might be associated with these adult passages.

OCCUPATION. A person's occupation has an influence on the goods and services bought. A blue-collar worker may buy work clothes, work shoes, lunch boxes, and bowling equipment. A company president may buy expensive blue serge suits, air travel, country club membership, and a large sailboat. Marketers try to identify the occupational groups that have an above-average interest in their products and services. A company can even specialize in producing products needed by a particular occupational group.

ECONOMIC CIRCUMSTANCES. A person's economic circumstances will greatly affect product choice. People's economic circumstances consist of their spendable income, savings and assets, borrowing power, and attitude toward

Table 5-2

An Overview of the Family Life Cycle and Buying Behavior

STAGE IN FAMILY LIFE CYCLE	BUYING OR BEHAVIORAL PATTERN
1. Bachelor stage: Young single people not living at home	Few financial burdens. Fashion opinion leaders. Recreation-oriented. Buy: basic kitchen equipment, basic furniture, cars, equipment for the mating game, vacations.
2. Newly married couples: Young, no children	Better off financially than they will be in near future. Highest purchase rate and highest average purchase of durables. Buy: cars, refrigerators, stoves, sensible and durable furniture, vacations.
3. Full nest I: Youngest child under six	Home purchasing at peak. Liquid assets low. *cash* Dissatisfied with financial position and amount of money saved. Interested in new products. Like advertised products. Buy: washers, dryers, TV, baby food, cough medicines, vitamins, dolls, wagons, sleds, skates.
4. Full nest II: Youngest child six or over	Financial position better. Some wives work. Less influenced by advertising. Buy larger-sized packages, multiple-unit deals. Buy: many foods, cleaning materials, bicycles, music lessons, pianos.
5. Full nest III: Older married couples with dependent children	Financial position still better. More wives work. Some children get jobs. Hard to influence with advertising. High average purchase of durables. Buy: new, more tasteful furniture, auto travel, nonnecessary appliances, boats, dental services, magazines.
6. Empty nest I: Older married couples, no children living with them, head in labor force	Home ownership at peak. Most satisfied with financial position and money saved. Interested in travel, recreation, self-education. Make gifts and contributions. Not interested in new products. Buy: vacations, luxuries, home improvements.
7. Empty nest II: Older married couples, no children living at home, head retired	Drastic cut in income. Keep home. Buy: medical appliances, medical-care products that aid health, sleep, and digestion.
8. Solitary survivor, in labor force	Income still good but likely to sell home.
9. Solitary survivor, retired	Same medical and product needs as other retired group; drastic cut in income. Special need for attention, affection, and security.

Sources: William D. Wells and George Gubar, "Life Cycle Concepts in Marketing Research," *Journal of Marketing Research*, November 1966, p. 362. Also see Patrick E. Murphy and William A. Staples, "A Modernized Family Life Cycle," *Journal of Consumer Research*, June 1979, pp. 12–22.

spending versus saving. Thus Betty Smith can consider buying an expensive Nikon if she has enough spendable income, savings, or borrowing power and she prefers spending to saving. Marketers of income-sensitive goods pay continuous attention to trends in personal income, savings, and interest rates. If economic indicators point to a recession, marketers can take steps to redesign, reposition, and reprice their product, reduce their production and inventories, and do other things to protect themselves financially.

LIFE-STYLE.   People coming from the same subculture, social class, and even occupations may have quite different life-styles. Betty Smith, for example, can choose to live like a capable homemaker, a career woman, or a free spirit. She plays several roles, and her way of reconciling them expresses her life-style. If she becomes a professional photographer, this has further life-style implications, such as keeping odd hours and doing a considerable amount of traveling.

> A person's **life-style** refers to the person's pattern of living in the world as expressed in his or her activities, interests, and opinions.

A person's life-style portrays the "whole person" in interaction with his or her environment. It captures something more than the person's social class or personality alone. If we know what social class someone belongs to, we can infer several things about that person's likely behavior but fail to see him or her as an individual. If we know what kind of personality someone has, we can infer several things about that person's distinguishing psychological characteristics but not much about his or her activities, interests, and opinions. It is the life-style that profiles a whole person's pattern of acting and interacting in the world.

In preparing a marketing strategy for a product, the marketer will search for relationships between a product or brand and a certain life-style. A yogurt manufacturer may find that many heavy male users of yogurt are successful professionals. The marketer may then aim the brand more clearly at this life-style:

> He's a bachelor . . . lives in one of those modern high-rise apartments and the rooms are brightly colored. He has modern, expensive furniture, but not Danish modern. He buys his clothes at Brooks Brothers. He owns a good hi-fi. He skis. He has a sailboat. He eats Limburger and any other prestige cheese with his beer. He likes and cooks a lot of steak and would have a filet mignon for company. His liquor cabinet has Jack Daniels bourbon, Beefeater gin, and a good Scotch.[12]

Advertising copywriters can then create advertising aimed at this life-style.

PERSONALITY AND SELF-CONCEPT.   Each person has a distinct personality that will influence his or her buying behavior.

> By **personality** we mean a person's distinguishing psychological characteristics that lead to relatively consistent and enduring responses to his or her environment.

A person's personality is usually described in terms of such traits as the following:[13]

- Self-confidence
- Dominance
- Autonomy
- Change
- Deference

- Ascendancy
- Sociability
- Defensiveness
- Affiliation
- Aggressiveness

- Emotional stability
- Achievement
- Order
- Adaptability

Personality can be useful in analyzing consumer behavior if relationships exist between certain personality types and product or brand choices. For example, a beer company may discover that many heavy beer drinkers are high on sociability and aggressiveness. This suggests a possible brand image for the beer and the kinds of people to show in the advertising.

Many marketers use a concept related to personality—a person's self-concept (also called self-image). All of us carry around a complex mental picture of ourselves. For example, Betty Smith may see herself as being extroverted, creative, and active. To that extent, she will favor a camera that projects the same qualities. If the Nikon is promoted as a camera for extroverted, creative, and active people, then its brand image will match her self-image. Marketers should try to develop brand images that match the self-image of the target market.[14]

Psychological Factors A person's buying choices are also influenced by four major psychological factors—motivation, perception, learning, and beliefs and attitudes.

MOTIVATION. We saw that Betty Smith became interested in buying a camera. Why? What is she really seeking? What need is she trying to satisfy?

A person has many needs at any point in time. Some needs are biogenic. They arise from physiological states of tension, such as hunger, thirst, discomfort. Other needs are psychogenic. They arise from psychological states of tension, such as the need for recognition, esteem, or belonging. Most of these needs will not be intense enough to motivate the person to act at a given point in time. A need becomes a motive when it is aroused to a sufficient level of intensity.

> A **motive** (or drive) is a need that is sufficiently pressing to direct a person to seek satisfaction of the need.

Satisfying the need reduces the felt tension.

Psychologists have developed theories of human motivation. Two of the most popular—the theories of Sigmund Freud and Abraham Maslow—carry quite different implications for consumer analysis and marketing.

Freud's theory of motivation. Freud assumed that people are largely unconscious about the real psychological forces shaping their behavior. He saw the person as growing up and repressing many urges. These urges are never eliminated or under perfect control; they emerge in dreams, in slips of the tongue, in neurotic and obsessive behavior, or ultimately in psychoses when the person's ego can no longer balance the impulsive power of the id with the oppressive power of the superego.

Thus a person does not fully understand his or her motivation. If Betty Smith wants to purchase an expensive camera, she may describe her motive as wanting a hobby or career. At a deeper level, she may be purchasing the camera to impress others with her creative talent. At a still deeper level, she may be buying the camera to feel young and independent again.

When Betty looks at a camera, she will react not only to the camera's performance but also to other cues. The camera's shape, size, weight, material, color, and case can all trigger certain emotions. A rugged-looking camera can arouse Betty's feelings about being independent, which she can either handle or avoid. In designing a camera, the manufacturer should be aware of the impact of its look and feel in triggering consumer emotions that can stimulate or inhibit purchase.

Motivation researchers have produced some interesting and occasionally odd hypotheses as to what may be in the buyer's mind regarding certain purchases. They have suggested that:

- Consumers resist prunes because they are wrinkled-looking and remind people of old age.
- Men smoke cigars as an adult version of thumb-sucking. They like their cigars to have a strong odor in order to prove their masculinity.
- Women prefer vegetable shortening to animal fats because the latter arouse a sense of guilt over killing animals.
- A woman is very serious when baking a cake because unconsciously she is going through the symbolic act of giving birth. She dislikes easy-to-use cake mixes because the easy life evokes a sense of guilt.

Maslow's theory of motivation.   Abraham Maslow sought to explain why people are driven by particular needs at particular times.[15] Why does one person spend considerable time and energy on personal safety and another on pursuing the esteem of others? His answer is that human needs are arranged in a hierarchy, from the most pressing to the least pressing. Maslow's hierarchy of needs is shown in figure 5-5. In their order of importance, they are physiological needs, safety needs, social needs, esteem needs, and self-actualization needs. A person will try to satisfy the most important needs first. When a person succeeds in satisfying an important need, it will cease being a motivator for the present time, and the person will be motivated to satisfy the next most important need.

For example, a starving man (need 1) will not take an interest in the latest happenings in the art world (need 5), nor in how he is seen or esteemed by others (need 3 or 4), nor even in whether he is breathing clean air (need 2). But as each important need is satisfied, the next most important need will come into play.

What light does Maslow's theory throw on Betty Smith's interest in buying a camera? We can guess that Betty has satisfied her physiological, safety, and social needs; they do not motivate her interest in cameras. Her camera interest might come from a strong need for more esteem from others, or it might come

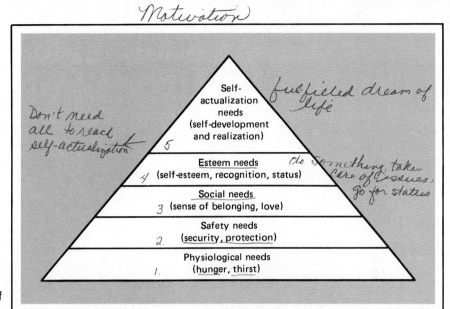

Motivation [handwritten]

Don't need all to reach self-actualization [handwritten]

fulfilled dream of life [handwritten]

do something, take care of issues, go for status [handwritten]

FIGURE 5-5

Maslow's Hierarchy of Needs

from a need for self-actualization. She wants to realize her potential as a creative person and express herself through photography.

PERCEPTION. A motivated person is ready to act. How the motivated person acts is influenced by his or her perception of the situation. Two people in the same motivated state and objective situation may act quite differently because they perceive the situation differently. Betty Smith might consider a fast-talking camera salesperson aggressive and insincere. Another camera buyer might consider the same salesperson intelligent and helpful.

Why do people have different perceptions of the same situation? All of us learn about a stimulus object through sensations, that is, the flow of information through our five senses: sight, hearing, smell, touch, and taste. However, each of us organizes and interprets this sensory information in an individual way.

> **Perception** can be defined as "the process by which an individual selects, organizes, and interprets information inputs to create a meaningful picture of the world."[16]

Perception depends not only on the character of the physical stimuli but also on the relation of the stimuli to the environment and to the individual.

People can emerge with different perceptions of the same stimulus because of three perceptual processes: selective exposure, selective distortion, and selective retention.

Selective exposure. People are exposed to a great number of stimuli every day of their lives. For example, the average person may be exposed to over fifteen hundred ads a day. It is impossible for a person to pay attention to all of these stimuli. Most of the stimuli will be screened out. The real challenge is to explain which stimuli people will notice.

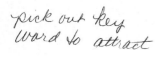

pick out key word to attract

1. People are more likely to notice stimuli that relate to a current need. Betty Smith will notice all kinds of ads about cameras because she is motivated to buy one; she will probably not notice ads about stereo equipment.
2. People are more likely to notice stimuli that they anticipate. Betty Smith is more likely to notice cameras in the camera store than a line of radios also carried by the store, because she did not expect the store to carry radios.
3. People are more likely to notice stimuli whose deviation is large in relation to the normal size of the stimuli. Betty Smith is more likely to notice an ad offering $100 off the list price of a Nikon than one offering $5 off the list price.[17]

Selective exposure means that marketers have to work especially hard to attract the consumer's attention. Their message will be lost on most people who are not in the market for the product. Even people who are in the market may not notice the message until it stands out from the surrounding sea of stimuli. Ads are more likely to be noticed if they are larger in size, or in color where most ads are black and white, or are novel and provide contrast.

Courtesy Nikon, Inc.

Selective distortion. Even stimuli that consumers notice do not necessarily come across in the intended way. Each person attempts to fit incoming information into his or her existing opinion. Selective distortion describes the tendency of people to twist information into personal meanings. Thus Betty Smith may hear the salesperson mention some good and bad points about a competing camera brand. Since she already has a strong leaning toward Nikon, she is likely to distort the points in order to conclude that Nikon is the better camera. People tend to interpret information in a way that will support rather than challenge their preconceived ideas or opinions.

Selective retention. People will forget much that they learn. They will tend to retain information that supports their attitudes and beliefs. Because of selective retention, Betty is likely to remember good points mentioned about the Nikon and forget good points mentioned about competing cameras. She remembers Nikon's good points because she "rehearses" them more whenever she thinks about choosing a camera.

These three perceptual factors—selective exposure, distortion, and retention—mean that marketers have to work hard to get their messages through. This explains why marketers use so much drama and repetition in sending messages to their markets.

LEARNING. When people act, they learn.

Learning describes changes in an individual's behavior resulting from experience.

Most human behavior is learned. Learning theorists say that a person's learning is produced through the interplay of drives, stimuli, cues, responses, and reinforcement.

We saw that Betty Smith has a drive toward self-actualization. Drive is defined as a strong internal stimulus-impelling action. Her drive becomes a motive when it is directed toward a particular drive-reducing stimulus object, in this case a camera. Betty's response to the idea of buying a camera is conditioned by the surrounding cues. Cues are minor stimuli that determine when, where, and how the person responds. Seeing cameras in a shop window, hearing of a special sales price, and being encouraged by her husband are all cues that can influence Betty's response to the impulse to buy a camera.

Suppose Betty buys the camera. If the experience is rewarding, the probability is that she will use the camera more and more. Her response to cameras will be reinforced.

Later on, Betty may want to buy binoculars. She notices several brands, including one by Nikon. Since she knows that Nikon makes good cameras, she infers that Nikon also makes good binoculars. She is generalizing her response to similar stimuli.

The opposite of generalization is discrimination. When Betty examines binoculars made by Olympus, she sees that they are lighter and more compact than Nikon's binoculars. Discrimination means that she has learned to recognize differences in sets of stimuli and can adjust her response accordingly.

BELIEFS AND ATTITUDES.   Through acting and learning, people acquire their beliefs and attitudes. These in turn influence their buying behavior.

A **belief** is a descriptive thought that a person holds about something.

Betty Smith may believe that a Nikon takes great pictures, stands up well under rugged usage, and costs $550. These beliefs may be based on real knowledge, opinion, or faith. They may or may not carry an emotional charge. For example, Betty Smith's belief that a Nikon camera is heavy may or may not matter in her decision.

Manufacturers, of course, are very interested in the beliefs that people carry in their head about specific products and services. These beliefs make up product and brand images, and people act on their beliefs. If some of the beliefs are wrong and inhibit purchase, the manufacturer would want to launch a campaign to correct these beliefs.

People have attitudes regarding almost everything: religion, politics, clothes, music, food, and so on.

An **attitude** describes a person's enduring favorable or unfavorable cognitive evaluations, emotional feelings, and action tendencies toward some object or idea.[18] *or person.*

Attitudes put people in a frame of mind to like or dislike things, to move toward or away from them. Thus Betty Smith may hold such attitudes as "Buy the best," "The Japanese make the best products in the world," and "Creativity and self-expression are among the most important things in life." The Nikon camera is therefore important to Betty because it fits well into her preexisting attitudes. A company would benefit greatly from researching the various attitudes people have that might affect the sale of its product.

*attitude
against a
bad product,
store, or people*

Attitudes lead people to behave in a fairly consistent way toward similar objects. People do not have to interpret and react to everything in a fresh way. Attitudes economize on energy and thought. For this very reason, attitudes are very difficult to change. A person's various attitudes settle into a coherent pattern, and to change one may require difficult adjustments in many other attitudes.

Thus a company would be well advised to fit its products into existing attitudes, rather than to try to change people's attitudes. There are exceptions, of course, where the great cost of trying to change attitudes may pay off.

> Honda entered the U.S. motorcycle market facing a major decision. It could either sell its motorcycles to a small number of people already interested in motorcycles or try to increase the number interested in motorcycles. The latter would be more expensive because many people had negative attitudes toward motorcycles. They associated motorcycles with black leather jackets, switchblades, and crime. Honda took the second course and launched a major campaign based on the theme "You meet the nicest people on a Honda." Its campaign worked, and many people adopted a new attitude toward motorcycles.

We can now appreciate the many forces acting on consumer behavior. The person's choice is the result of the complex interplay of cultural, social, personal, and psychological factors. Many of these factors cannot be influenced by the marketer. However, they are useful in identifying the buyers who may be more interested in the product. Other factors are subject to marketer influence and clue the marketer on how to develop the product, price, place, and promotion to attract strong consumer response.

The Buyer Decision Process

We are now ready to examine the stages that the buyer passes through to reach a buying decision and outcome. The model in figure 5-6 shows the consumer as passing through five stages: problem recognition, information search, evaluation of alternatives, purchase decision, and postpurchase behavior. This model emphasizes that the buying process starts long before the actual purchase and has consequences long after the purchase. It encourages the marketer to focus on the entire buying process rather than only on the purchase decision.[19]

This model seems to imply that consumers pass through all five stages with every purchase they make. In more routine purchases, consumers skip or reverse some of these stages. Thus a woman buying her regular brand of toothpaste would recognize the problem and go right to the purchase decision, skipping information search and evaluation. However, we will use the model in figure 5-6 because it shows the full range of considerations that arise when a consumer faces a new purchase situation, especially one involving extensive problem solving.

We will follow Betty Smith and try to understand how she became interested in buying an expensive camera and the stages she went through to make the final choice.

Problem Recognition The buying process starts with the buyer recognizing a problem or need. The buyer senses a difference between his or her actual state and a desired state. The need can be triggered by internal stimuli. One of the person's normal needs—hunger, thirst, sex—rises to a threshold level and becomes a drive. From previous experience, the person has learned how to cope with this drive and is motivated toward a class of objects that he or she knows will satisfy this drive.

Or a need can be aroused by external stimuli. A woman passes a bakery and the sight of freshly baked bread stimulates her hunger; she admires a neighbor's new car; or she watches a television commercial for a Jamaican vacation. All of these can lead her to recognize a problem or need.

The marketer at this stage needs to determine the circumstances that usually trigger recognition of a problem. The marketer should find out (a) what kinds of felt needs or problems arose, (b) what brought them about, and (c) how they led to this particular product.

Betty Smith might answer that she felt a need for a new hobby. This happened when her "busy season" at work slowed down, and she was led to think of cameras as a result of a friend talking to her about photography. By gathering such information, the marketer will have a chance to identify the more frequent stimuli that attract interest in the product. The marketer can then develop marketing plans that use these stimuli.

Information Search An aroused consumer may or may not search for more information. If the consumer's drive is strong and a product that will satisfy the drive is near at hand, the consumer is likely to buy it then. If not, the consumer's need may simply be stored in memory. The consumer may stop searching, do a little more searching, or actively search for information bearing on the need.

At a mild level, the searcher may simply have heightened attention. Here Betty Smith simply becomes more receptive to information about cameras. She pays attention to camera ads, cameras used by friends, and camera conversations.

Or Betty may go into active information search, where she will look for reading material, phone friends, and engage in other search activities to gather product information. How much search she undertakes will depend on the strength of her drive, the amount of information she initially has, the ease of obtaining additional information, the value she places on additional information, and the satisfaction she gets from the search.

FIGURE 5-6

The Buyer Decision Process

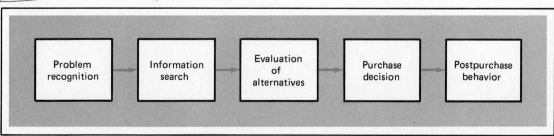

An advertisement can lead a consumer to recognize a need.

Teri Leigh Stratford

When searching for information, the consumer may turn to:

- Personal sources (family, friends, neighbors, acquaintances)
- Commercial sources (advertising, salespeople, dealers, packaging, displays)
- Public sources (mass media, consumer-rating organizations)
- Experiential sources (handling, examining, using the product)

The relative influence of these information sources varies with the product category and the buyer's characteristics. Generally speaking, the consumer receives the most information about a product from commercial sources, that is, marketer-dominated sources. The most effective sources, however, are personal. Each source may have a different influence on the buying decision. Commercial information normally informs. Personal sources legitimize and/or evaluate the information. For example, doctors generally learn of new drugs from commercial sources but turn to other doctors when evaluating information.

As a result of gathering information, consumers increase their awareness of the available brands and their features. Before looking for information, Betty Smith knew only a few camera brands out of the *total set* of available cameras shown at the far left in figure 5-7. The camera brands she knew constituted her *awareness set.* The incoming information increased her awareness set, and further information helped her eliminate certain brands from consideration. The remaining brands that fitted her buying criteria constituted her *choice set.* Her final decision will be made from this set.[20]

In practical terms, a company must design its marketing mix to get its brand into the prospect's awareness set and choice set. If its brand fails to get into these sets, the company has lost its opportunity to sell to the customer. The company must go further and learn which other brands remain in the consumer's choice set, so that it knows its competition and can plan its appeals.

As for the sources of the information used by the consumer, the marketer

FIGURE 5-7

Successive Sets Involved in Consumer Decision Making

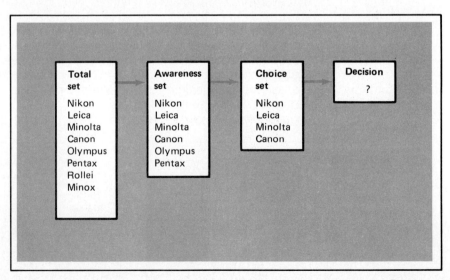

should identify them carefully and then determine their relevant importance as sources of information. Consumers should be asked how they first heard about the brand, what other information they had, and the relative importance that could be attributed to each of the different information sources. The marketer will find this information critical in preparing effective communication to the target market.

Evaluation of Alternatives We have seen how the consumer uses information to arrive at a set of final brand choices. The question is, How does the consumer choose among the alternative brands in the choice set? The marketer needs to know how the consumer evaluates information to arrive at brand choices. Unfortunately there is no simple and single evaluation process used by all consumers, or even by one consumer in all buying situations. There are several evaluation processes.

Certain basic concepts help throw light on consumer evaluation processes. The first concept is that of *product attributes.* We assume that each consumer sees a given product as a bundle of attributes. The following attributes are of interest to buyers in some familiar product classes:

- Cameras: picture sharpness, camera speeds, camera size, price
- Hotels: location, cleanliness, atmosphere, cost
- Mouthwash: color, effectiveness, price, taste/flavor
- Bras: comfort, fit, life, price, style
- Lipstick: color, container, creaminess, prestige factor, taste/flavor
- Tires: safety, tread life, ride quality, price

While the above traits are of normal interest, consumers will vary as to which they consider relevant. Consumers will pay the most attention to those attributes that are connected with their needs.

Second, the consumer is likely to attach different *importance weights* to the relevant attributes. A distinction can be drawn between the importance of an attribute and its salience, or prominence.[21] *Salient attributes* are those that come to the consumer's mind when he or she is asked to think of a product's qualities. The marketer must not conclude that these are necessarily the most important attributes. Some of them may be salient because the consumer has just been exposed to a commercial message mentioning them or has had a problem involving them, hence making these attributes "top-of-the-mind." Furthermore, there may be more important attributes, but the consumer just forgot to mention them.

Third, the consumer is likely to develop a set of *brand beliefs* about where each brand stands on each attribute. The set of beliefs held about a particular brand is known as the *brand image.* The consumer's beliefs may vary from the true attributes due to his or her particular experience and the effect of selective perception, selective distortion, and selective retention.

Fourth, the consumer is assumed to have a *utility function* for each attribute. The utility function describes how satisfied the consumer expects to be with each attribute. For example, Betty Smith may expect her satisfaction from a camera to increase with the speed of its lens; to peak with a medium-weight camera as opposed to a very light or very heavy one; to be higher for a 35-mm camera than for a 135-mm camera. If we combine the attribute levels where the utilities are highest, they make up Betty's ideal camera. The camera would also be her preferred camera if it were available and affordable.

Fifth, the consumer arrives at attitudes toward the brand alternatives through some *evaluation procedure.* Consumers have different ways to make choices among brands.[22]

Purchase Decision The evaluation stage leads consumers to rank objects in the choice set. They will form a purchase intention. Generally, consumers will buy the most preferred object. However, two factors can intervene between the purchase intention and the purchase decision. These factors are shown in figure 5-8.[23]

The first is the attitudes of others. Suppose Betty Smith's husband strongly feels that Betty should buy the least expensive camera to keep down expenses. As a result, Betty's purchase probability for the more expensive camera of her choice will be somewhat reduced. The extent to which another person's attitude will change one's preferred alternative depends on two things: (1) the intensity of the other person's negative attitude toward the consumer's preferred alternative and (2) the consumer's motivation to comply with the other person's wishes.[24] The more negative or positive the other person and the closer the other person is to the consumer, the more the consumer will revise upward or downward his or her purchase intention.

Purchase intention is also influenced by unanticipated situational factors. The consumer forms a purchase intention on the basis of such factors as expected family income, expected price, and expected benefits from the product. When the consumer is about to act, unanticipated situational factors may erupt to change the purchase intention. Betty Smith may lose her job, some other purchase may become more urgent, or a friend may report being disappointed in that camera.

Postpurchase Behavior After purchasing a product the consumer will be satisfied or dissatisfied. The consumer will also follow some postpurchase behavior of interest to the marketer. The marketer's job does not end when the product is bought but continues into the postpurchase period.

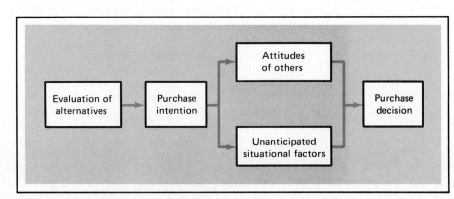

FIGURE 5-8

Factors That Keep a Purchase Intention from Becoming a Purchase Decision

Exhibit **5-3**

What Makes a Restaurant Successful?

If you were opening a restaurant, you would want to attract as many customers as possible. Besides the menu, your main considerations would probably be the restaurant's location and its prices. You might expect that the best location would be nearest to potential customers and that the lowest prices would bring in the most people. Recently a psychologist conducted a study of how people choose restaurants.

Contrary to what you might expect, people going out to dinner tend to choose restaurants that require a bit of travel. New Yorkers who live on the city's Upper West Side, for example, believe that the best restaurants are downtown in Greenwich Village; many Village residents think the Upper East Side restaurants have the best food; Upper East Siders often prefer to dine on the Upper West Side. Residents of cities across the country—Miami, Dallas, and Los Angeles—agree that the best eating places are elsewhere.

Location is important in another way, too. Once a restaurant in an area becomes successful, people tend to believe that other eating places nearby must also be good. Restaurants that happen to be in the same neighborhood benefit from each other's success.

The study also looked at how people choose restaurants when they are on their way to some other activity. Specifically, this study focused on theatergoers who often eat out before attending a performance. In this situation, price was one of the most important factors in restaurant choice. Despite what you might think, moderate-priced places—not high-priced or low-priced places—are most attractive to theatergoers. This group likes to stay away from high-priced restaurants where they feel a meal may be too complicated or too large and might cause them to be late or to fall asleep during the show. Low-priced restaurants, theatergoers feel, will ruin the mood of their evening. So as a savings after buying expensive tickets, to eat well without overeating, and to stay in a festive spirit, theatergoers prefer moderate-priced restaurants. Location is also important to this group. Since theatergoers are concerned about being on time for the performance, convenience to the theater makes a restaurant a more likely choice.

The effects of a restaurant's location and prices aren't always straightforward. A somewhat distant location can work in favor of a restaurant, when dining is to be the main activity of an evening, or against it, when eating is the prelude to another activity. Low price can also be a negative factor when it seems to make an occasion less festive. Depending on the circumstances, people use different factors to decide whether or not to become patrons of a restaurant.

Source: Adapted from Srully Blotnick, "Crowds Passing in the Night," *Forbes*, February 18, 1980, p. 180.

Monitoring postpurchase satisfaction can help companies improve the performance of their products.

Anita Duncan

POSTPURCHASE SATISFACTION. What determines whether the buyer is highly satisfied, somewhat satisfied, somewhat dissatisfied, or highly dissatisfied with a purchase? The answer lies in the relationship between the consumer's expectations and the product's perceived performance.[25] If the product matches expectations, the consumer is satisfied; if it exceeds them, the consumer is highly satisfied; if it falls short, the consumer is dissatisfied.

Consumers form their expectations on the basis of messages they receive from sellers, friends, and other information sources. If the seller exaggerates the product's performance, consumers will have too high expectations, which lead to dissatisfaction. The larger the gap between expectations and performance, the greater the consumer's dissatisfaction.

This suggests that the seller should make product claims that faithfully represent the product's likely performance so that buyers are satisfied. Some sellers might even understate performance levels so that consumers have higher than expected satisfaction with the product.

POSTPURCHASE ACTIONS. The consumer's satisfaction or dissatisfaction with a product will feed back on subsequent behavior. If the consumer is satisfied, then he or she will probably purchase the product on the next occasion. The satisfied consumer will also tend to say good things about the product to others. According to marketers: "Our best advertisement is a satisfied customer."

A dissatisfied consumer responds differently. He or she may abandon or return the product, or may try to find some good information about the purchase. In the case of Betty Smith, she may return the camera or she may seek information that will make her feel better about the camera.

Dissatisfied consumers have a choice between taking and not taking any action. Some actions include complaining to the company, going to a lawyer, or complaining to other groups that might help the buyer get satisfaction. Or the buyer may simply stop buying the product and/or bad-mouth it to friends and others. In all these cases, the seller loses something in having done a poor job of satisfying the customer.

A FINAL STEP. There is one more step in the postpurchase behavior of buyers that sellers should watch, namely, what the buyers ultimately do with the product. The major possibilities are shown in figure 5-9. If consumers use the product to serve a new purpose, this should interest the seller because this purpose can be advertised. If consumers store the product and make little use or get rid of it, this indicates that the product is not very satisfying and word-of-mouth recommendations would not be strong. Of equal interest is how consumers ultimately dispose of the product. If they sell or trade the product, this will reduce new product sales. All said, the seller needs to study how the product is used and disposed of for clues as to possible problems and opportunities.

Understanding the consumer's needs and buying process is the foundation of successful marketing. By understanding how buyers go through problem recognition, information search, evaluation of alternatives, the purchase decision, and postpurchase behavior, the marketer can pick up many clues as to how to meet the buyer's needs. By understanding the various participants in the

FIGURE 5-9

How Customers Use and/or Dispose of Products

Source: Jacob Jacoby, Carol K. Berning, and Thomas F. Dietvorst, "What about Disposition?" *Journal of Marketing*, July 1977, p. 23. Reprinted by permission.

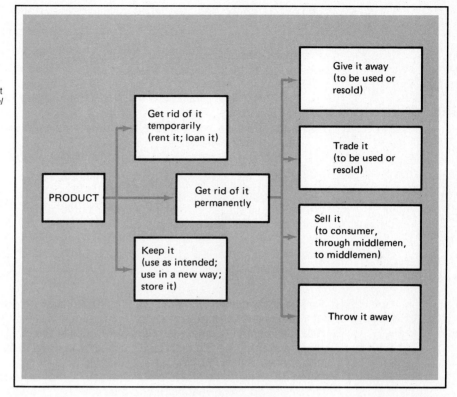

buying process and the major influences on their buying behavior, the marketer can develop an effective marketing program to support an attractive offer to the target market.

Buyer Decision Processes

We have looked at the stages through which buyers go in trying to satisfy a need. Buyers may pass quickly or slowly through these stages, and some of the stages may even be reversed.[26] Much depends on the nature of the buyer, the product, and the buying situation.

We are now going to look at how buyers approach the purchase of new products. We define *new product* as a good, service, or idea that is perceived by some potential customers as new. The new product may have been around for awhile, but our interest is in how consumers learn about products for the first time and make decisions on whether to adopt them. We define *adoption process* as "the mental process through which an individual passes from first hearing about an innovation to final adoption."[27] We define *adoption* as the decision by an individual to become a regular user of the product.

Stages in the Adoption Process

Consumers go through five stages in the process of adopting a new product:

1. *Awareness:* The consumer becomes aware of the innovation but lacks information about it.
2. *Interest:* The consumer is stimulated to seek information about the innovation.
3. *Evaluation:* The consumer considers whether it would make sense to try the innovation.
4. *Trial:* The consumer tries the innovation on a small scale to improve his or her estimate of its value.
5. *Adoption:* The consumer decides to make full and regular use of the innovation.

This suggests that the innovator should think about how to move consumers through these stages. A manufacturer of electric dishwashers may discover that many consumers are in the interest stage; they do not move to the trial stage because of their uncertainty and the large investment. But these same consumers would be willing to use an electric dishwasher on a trial basis for a small fee. The manufacturer should consider offering a trial-use plan with option to buy.

Individual Differences in Innovativeness

People differ markedly in their readiness to try new products. A person's innovativeness is "the degree to which an individual is relatively earlier in adopting new ideas than the other members of his social system." In each product area, there are apt to be pioneers and early adopters. Some women are the first to adopt new clothing fashions or new appliances, such as the microwave oven; some doctors are the first to prescribe new medicines;[28] and some farmers are the first to adopt new farming methods.[29]

And other individuals adopt new products much later. This has led to a classification of people into the adopter categories shown in figure 5-10. After a slow start, an increasing number of people adopt the innovation, the number reaches a peak, and then it diminishes as fewer nonadopters remain. Innovators are defined as the first 25% of the buyers to adopt a new idea; the early adopters are the next 13.5% who adopt the new idea; and so forth.

Rogers sees the five adopter groups as differing in values. Innovators are venturesome; they try new ideas at some risk. Early adopters are guided by respect; they are opinion leaders in their community and adopt new ideas early but carefully. The early majority are deliberate; they adopt new ideas before the average person, although they are rarely leaders. The late majority are skeptical; they adopt an innovation only after a majority of people have tried it. Finally, laggards are tradition-bound; they are suspicious of changes, mix with other tradition-bound people, and adopt the innovation only because it has now taken on a measure of tradition in itself.

Role of Personal Influence

Personal influence plays a major role in the adoption of new products. Personal influence describes the effect of product statements made by one person on another's attitude or probability of purchase. According to Katz and Lazarsfeld:

About half of the women in our sample reported that they had recently made some change from a product or brand to which they were accustomed to

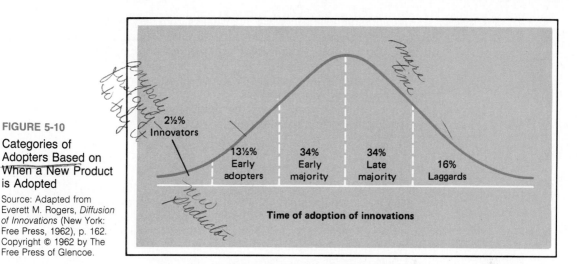

FIGURE 5-10

Categories of Adopters Based on When a New Product is Adopted

Source: Adapted from Everett M. Rogers, *Diffusion of Innovations* (New York: Free Press, 1962), p. 162. Copyright © 1962 by The Free Press of Glencoe.

something new. The fact that one-third of these changes involved personal influences indicates that there is also considerable traffic in marketing advice. Women consult each other for opinions about new products, about the quality of different brands, about shopping economies and the like.[30]

Although personal influence is an important factor, its significance is greater in some situations and for some individuals than for others. Personal influence is more important in the evaluation stage of the adoption process than in the other stages. It has more influence on later adopters than early adopters. And it is more important in risky situations than in safe situations.

Influence of Product Characteristics on the Rate of Adoption

The characteristics of the innovation affect its rate of adoption. Some products catch on almost overnight (such as Frisbees), while others take a long time to gain acceptance (such as diesel-engined cars). Five characteristics are especially important in influencing an innovation's rate of adoption. We will consider the characteristics in relation to the adoption rate of personal computers for home use.

The first characteristic is the innovation's *relative advantage*—the degree to which it appears superior to existing products. The greater the perceived relative advantages of using personal computers, say in preparing income taxes and keeping financial records, the sooner personal computers will be adopted.

The second characteristic is the innovation's *compatibility*—the degree to which it matches the values and experiences of the individuals in the community. Personal computers, for example, are highly compatible with the life-styles found in upper-middle-class homes.

The third characteristic is the innovation's *complexity*—the degree to which it is relatively difficult to understand or use. Personal computers are complex and will therefore take a longer time to penetrate the U.S. home market.

The fourth characteristic is the innovation's *divisibility*—the degree to which it may be tried on a limited basis. If people can rent personal computers with an option to buy, their rate of adoption will increase.

The fifth characteristic is the innovation's *communicability*—the degree to which the results can be seen or described to others. Because personal computers lend themselves to demonstration and description, this will help them diffuse faster into the social system.

Other characteristics influence the rate of adoption, such as initial costs, ongoing costs, risk and uncertainty, scientific credibility, and social approval. The new-product marketer has to research all these factors and give the key ones maximum attention in developing the new-product and marketing program.

Summary

Markets have to be understood before marketing plans can be developed. The consumer market buys goods and services for personal consumption. The market consists of many submarkets, such as black consumers, young adult consumers, and elderly consumers.

A buyer's behavior is influenced by four major factors: cultural (culture, subculture, and social class); social (reference groups, family, and roles and statuses); personal (age and life-cycle stage, occupation, economic circumstances, life-style, and personality and self-concept); and psychological (motivation, perception, learning, and beliefs and attitudes). All of these provide clues as to how to reach and serve the buyer more effectively.

Before planning its marketing, a company needs to identify its target consumers and the type of decision process they go through. When buying something, a buyer goes through a decision process consisting of problem recognition, information search, evaluation of alternatives, purchase decision, and postpurchase behavior. The marketer's job is to understand the various participants in the buying process and the major influences on buying behavior. This understanding allows the marketer to develop a significant and effective marketing program for the target market.

With regard to new products, consumers respond at different rates, depending on the consumer's characteristics and the product's characteristics. Manufacturers try to bring their new products to the attention of potential early adopters, particularly those who are opinion leaders.

Questions for Discussion

1. The Mondavi Winery of California has introduced a six-pack of 6.3-ounce cans of Chablis, with future plans to introduce six-packs of rosé, Burgundy, and other varieties of wine. Based on your knowledge of cultural, social, personal, and psychological variables influencing consumer behavior, what factors would work for or against the success of such a product?
2. Using automobile ads as examples, show how car advertising stresses one or more of the major factors influencing consumer behavior.
3. In 1982, Seven-Up ran ads with the theme "crisp and clean with no caffeine." What consumer behavior factors were considered in the decision to run this ad?
4. Discuss the influence of cultural characteristics (culture, subculture, and social class) on the choice of department stores to shop in.

5. Discuss the level of Maslow's hierarchy of needs that marketers of the following products are attempting to satisfy: (a) smoke detectors, (b) Bell Telephone long-distance dialing, (c) Seagram's VO, (d) life insurance, and (e) transcendental meditation.
6. A shopper is at the evaluation of alternatives stage of the buyer decision process when considering the choice of a supermarket in which to do "routine" shopping. What factors do you believe most consumers would consider "very important" in their choice of a supermarket? (List these factors in the order of their importance.)
7. If you were given the task of developing a model of consumer behavior, what variables and/or relationships would you add to those discussed in this chapter?
8. Relate the stages of the consumer buying process to your latest purchase of a pair of shoes.
9. Why is the postpurchase behavior stage included in the model of the buying process?

Key Terms in Chapter 5

Attitude A person's enduring favorable or unfavorable cognitive evaluations, emotional feelings, and action tendencies toward some object or idea.

Belief A descriptive thought that a person holds about something.

Consumer market All the individuals and households who buy or acquire goods and services for personal consumption.

Learning Changes in an individual's behavior resulting from experience.

Life-style A person's pattern of living in the world as expressed in his or her activities, interests, and opinions.

Motive A need that is sufficiently pressing to direct a person to seek a way to satisfy it.

Perception "The process by which an individual selects, organizes, and interprets information inputs to create a meaningful picture of the world."

Personality A person's distinguishing psychological characteristics that lead to relatively consistent and enduring responses to his or her environment.

Reference group A group that has a direct (face-to-face) or indirect influence on a person's attitudes or behavior.

Social class A relatively lasting group whose members share similar values, interests, and behavior; exists in a hierarchically ordered society.

Cases for Chapter 5

Case 3 Great Waters of France, Inc.: Perrier (p. 495)
What factors led consumers to buy an expensive French sparkling mineral water? The chapter provides many answers to this question.

Case 4 Levi Strauss & Co. (p. 496)
Changing factors in consumer behavior led Levi Strauss to reevaluate its marketing plan. This case looks at these factors.

Chapter 6

Organizational Markets and Organizational Buyer Behavior

Objectives

After reading this chapter, you should be able to:

1. Discuss how organizational marketing differs from consumer marketing.
2. Describe the major factors that influence organizational buyers.
3. List and define the steps in the industrial buying decision process.
4. Explain how government buyers make their decisions.

Colleges not only have to teach their students but also have to feed them. Colleges have two options. They can set up their own food service operations by hiring a staff, buying food daily, and carrying out the cleanup operations. Or they can contract for the services of a food service company. Today over 31,000 schools and colleges across the nation have adopted the latter option. They have engaged the services of one of the 150 food service companies that stand ready to develop menus, cook, and do the cleanup.

Those involved in the selection of the food service company may be the college's purchasing department, some student representatives, the business manager, and even the college president. They seek a contract that will provide students with several food choices, second and third helpings, and a reasonable amount of meat in relation to poultry and pasta, all at a cost not to exceed so many dollars per student. They examine each major food service company's reputation for food quality, service, and reliability before making a choice. On the other hand, the food service companies, who want the contracts, are becoming more demanding. They are shifting away from fixed-fee contracts to contracts with escalator clauses. Sometimes they underbid other bidders, get the contract, and subsequently raise the price or cut the quality or quantity of food or service under the pressure of spiraling costs.

The more progressive food service companies keep searching for ways to lower their costs in order to be low bidders. The largest institutional feeder, ARA Food Services Company, has developed a computerized food-purchasing, production, and service system that includes portion control and predicts how students will choose from a multiple-choice menu. Saga Corporation is running a waste education campaign directed at students who leave much of the food on their plates. Both are trying to help their buyers—the colleges—cut down on their costs so that the colleges will continue to favor these suppliers.[1]

Companies that sell to other organizations, such as manufacturers, wholesalers, retailers, and the government, must do their best to understand buyers' needs, resources, policies, and buying procedures. They must take into account several considerations not normally found in consumer marketing:

1. Organizations buy goods and services for the purpose of making profits, reducing costs, serving their internal clientele's needs, and meeting social and legal obligations.
2. More people tend to participate formally in organizational buying decisions than in consumer buying decisions. The decision participants usually have different responsibilities within the organization and apply different criteria to the purchase decision.
3. Purchasing agents must follow formal policies, limits, and requirements established by their organizations.
4. The methods of buying, such as requests for quotations, proposals, and purchase contracts, add another dimension not typically found in consumer buying.

Organizations are a vast market for raw materials, manufactured parts, installations, accessory equipment, supplies, and business services. Table 6-1 shows that more than 14 million organizations buy goods and services.

Table 6-1

Number and Kinds of Organizational Buyers

KINDS OF ORGANIZATIONAL BUYERS	NUMBER
Services	4,495,000
Agriculture, forestry, and fisheries	3,471,000
Retailers	2,664,000
Construction	1,423,000
Wholesalers	613,000
Manufacturers	503,000
Government units	82,688
Others	2,796,000
Total	16,047,688

Source: *Statistical Abstract of the United States, 1982–83*

Organizational buying is "the decision-making process by which formal organizations establish the need for purchased products and services, and identify, evaluate, and choose among alternative brands and suppliers."[2]

In this chapter we will look at three organizational markets: industrial markets, reseller markets, and government markets. For each market, we will look at the following:

1. Who is in the market?
2. What buying decisions do the buyers make?
3. Who participates in the buying process?
4. What are the major influences on the buyers?
5. How do the buyers make their buying decisions?

The Industrial Market

Who Is in the Industrial Market? The first organizational market is the industrial market, which we define as follows:

some products can be industrial and consumer

The **industrial market** is made up of all the individuals and organizations who buy goods and services that enter into the production of other products or services that are sold, rented, or supplied to others.

sells to other wholesalers to produce products

The major types of industries making up the industrial market are (1) agriculture, forestry, and fisheries; (2) mining; (3) manufacturing; (4) construction; (5) transportation; (6) communication; (7) public utilities; (8) banking, finance, and insurance; and (9) services.

More dollars and items are involved in sales to industrial buyers than to consumers. To produce and sell a simple pair of shoes, hide dealers must sell hides to tanners, who sell leather to shoe manufacturers, who sell shoes to wholesalers, who in turn sell shoes to retailers, who finally sell them to consumers. Each party in the chain of production and distribution has to buy many other goods and services as well. Figure 6-1 illustrates the substantial number of transactions involved in producing and selling a pair of shoes.

Industrial markets have certain characteristics that contrast sharply with consumer markets. These characteristics are described below.

THERE ARE FEWER BUYERS. The industrial marketer normally deals with far fewer buyers than does the consumer marketer. For example, the Goodyear Tire Company sells tires both to industry and to consumers. Its fate in the industrial market critically depends on getting an order from one of the big three automakers. But when Goodyear sells replacement tires to consumers, it has a potential market of owners of 105 million American automobiles currently in use.

THE FEWER BUYERS ARE LARGER BUYERS. Even in industries with many producers, a few large buyers normally account for most of the purchasing. In such industries as motor vehicles, telephone and telegraph, cigarettes, aircraft

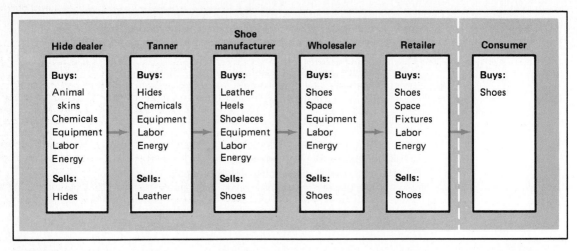

Hide dealer	Tanner	Shoe manufacturer	Wholesaler	Retailer	Consumer
Buys:	**Buys:**	**Buys:**	**Buys:**	**Buys:**	**Buys:**
Animal skins	Hides	Leather	Shoes	Shoes	Shoes
Chemicals	Chemicals	Heels	Space	Space	
Equipment	Equipment	Shoelaces	Equipment	Fixtures	
Labor	Labor	Equipment	Labor	Labor	
Energy	Energy	Labor	Energy	Energy	
		Energy			
Sells:	**Sells:**	**Sells:**	**Sells:**	**Sells:**	
Hides	Leather	Shoes	Shoes	Shoes	

FIGURE 6-1

Transactions Involved in Producing and Distributing a Pair of Shoes

Industrial buyers purchase the raw materials, such as the lumber for this plant, that companies use to make other products.

Courtesy ITT

engines and engine parts, and organic fibers, the top four manufacturers account for over 70% of total production. They will thus buy most of the supplies for industry as a whole.

THE BUYERS ARE GEOGRAPHICALLY CONCENTRATED. More than half of the nation's industrial buyers are concentrated in seven states: New York, California, Pennsylvania, Illinois, Ohio, New Jersey, and Michigan. Such industries as petroleum, rubber, and steel show even greater geographic concentration. Most agricultural output comes from a relatively few states. This geographic concentration of producers helps to reduce the costs of selling to them. Industrial marketers will want to watch any tendencies toward or away from further geographic concentration.

INDUSTRIAL DEMAND IS BASED ON CONSUMER DEMAND. The demand for industrial goods ultimately comes from the demand for consumer goods. Thus animal hides are purchased because consumers buy shoes, purses, and other leather goods. If the demand for these consumer goods slackens, so will the demand for all the industrial goods entering into their production.

INDUSTRIAL DEMAND IS INELASTIC. The total demand (as opposed to individual firm demand) for many industrial goods and services shows low price elasticity; that is, the total demand is not much affected by price changes. Shoe manufacturers are not going to buy a great deal more leather if the price of leather falls, nor are they going to buy much less leather if the price of leather rises. Demand is especially inelastic in the short run because producers cannot make many changes in their production methods. At the same time, producers will use price to decide which supplier to buy from, although it will have less effect on the amount bought.

INDUSTRIAL DEMAND CHANGES RAPIDLY. The demand for industrial goods and services tends to change more rapidly than that for consumer goods and services. This is especially true of the demand for new plant and equipment. A given percentage increase in consumer demand can lead to a much larger percentage increase in the demand for plant and equipment necessary to produce the additional output. Sometimes a rise of only 10% in consumer demand can cause as much as a 200% rise in industrial demand in the next period. This phenomenon has led many industrial marketers to diversify their product lines to achieve some balance over the business cycle.

INDUSTRIAL BUYERS ARE PROFESSIONALS. Industrial goods are purchased by professionally trained purchasing agents who spend their work lives learning how to buy better. Many belong to the National Association of Purchasing Agents, which seeks to improve the effectiveness and status of professional buyers. Consumers, on the other hand, are less trained in the art of careful buying. The more complex the industrial purchase, the more likely that several persons will participate in the decision-making process. Buying committees made up of technical experts and top management are common in the purchase of major goods. This means that companies that sell to industry have to hire well-trained sales representatives to deal with the well-trained buyers. Although advertising, sales promotion, and publicity play a major role in the industrial promotional mix, personal selling is the main selling tool.

What Buying Decisions Do Industrial Buyers Make? The industrial buyer faces a whole set of decisions in making a purchase. The number of decisions depends on the type of buying situation.

MAJOR TYPES OF BUYING SITUATIONS. There are three major types of buying situations.[3] At one extreme is the straight rebuy, which is a fairly routine decision; at the other extreme is the new task, which may call for thorough research; in the middle is the modified rebuy, which requires some research. Examples of each of these situations are shown in figure 6-2.

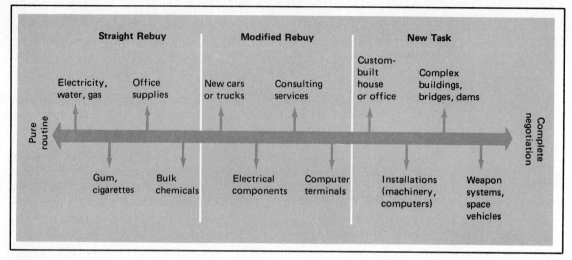

FIGURE 6-2

Three Types of
Industrial Buying
Situations

Source: From *Marketing
Principles,* by Ben M. Enis.
Copyright © 1980 by Scott,
Foresman and Company.
Reprinted by permission.

Straight rebuy. The straight rebuy describes the buying situation where the buyer reorders something without any modifications. Regular office supplies, for example, are often handled this way. This situation is usually handled on a routine basis by the purchasing department. The buyer chooses from suppliers on its list, giving weight to its past buying satisfaction with the various suppliers. The "in" suppliers make an effort to maintain product and service quality. They often propose automatic reordering systems so that the purchasing agent will save reordering time. The "out" suppliers attempt to offer something new or exploit dissatisfaction so that the buyer will consider them. They try to get their foot in the door with a small order and then enlarge their "purchase share" over time.

Modified rebuy. The modified rebuy describes the situation where the buyer wants to modify product specifications, prices, other terms, or suppliers. New equipment or parts are often handled this way. The modified rebuy usually expands the number of decision participants. The in suppliers become nervous and have to put their best foot forward to protect the account. The out suppliers see it as an opportunity to make a better offer to gain some new business.

New task. The new task faces a company buying a product or service for the first time. A company installing its first computer system or building a new factory is in this situation. The greater the cost and/or risk, the larger the number of decision participants and the greater their information seeking. The new-task situation is the marketer's greatest opportunity and challenge. The marketer not only tries to reach as many key buying influences as possible but also provides information and assistance. Because of the complicated selling involved in the new task, many companies use a special sales force, called a *missionary sales force,* made up of their best salespeople.

MAJOR SUBDIVISIONS INVOLVED IN THE BUYING DECISION. The number of decisions that the buyer has to make is the smallest in the straight rebuy and the largest in the new-task situation. In the new-task situation, the buyer has to determine (1) product specifications, (2) price limits, (3) delivery time and terms, (4) service terms, (5) payment terms, (6) order quantities, (7) acceptable suppliers, and (8) the selected supplier. Different decision participants influence each decision, and the order in which the decisions are made varies.

THE ROLE OF SYSTEMS BUYING AND SELLING. Many buyers prefer to buy a whole solution to their problem and not make all the separate decisions involved. This is called *systems buying,* and it began with government practices in buying major weapons and communication systems. Instead of purchasing and putting all the components together, the government would solicit bids from prime contractors who would assemble the package or system. The winning prime contractor would be responsible for bidding and assembling the subcomponents.

Sellers have increasingly recognized that buyers like to purchase in this way and have adopted the practice of *systems selling* as a marketing tool. Systems selling has two parts. First, the supplier sells a group of interlocking products. For example, the supplier sells not only glue but glue applicators and dryers as well. Second, the supplier sells a system of production, inventory control, distribution, and other services to meet the buyer's need for a smooth-running operation. Systems selling is a key industrial marketing strategy for winning and holding accounts. For an example of a successful system, see exhibit 6-1.

Who Participates in the Industrial Buying Process? Who does the buying of the hundreds of billions of dollars of goods and services needed by the industrial market? It can range from one or a few purchasing agents to large purchasing departments headed by a vice-president of purchasing. In some cases, purchasing executives make the entire decision as to product specifications and suppliers; in other cases, they are responsible for supplier selections only; and in still other cases, they only place the order. They typically make decisions on smaller items and carry out the wishes of others on major capital items.

Webster and Wind call the decision-making unit of a buying organization the *buying center,* defined as "all those individuals and groups who participate in the purchasing decision-making process, who share some common goals and the risks arising from the decisions."[4]

The buying center includes all members of the organization who play any role in the purchase decision process.[5] This includes the actual users of the product, all those who influence the buying decision, the purchasing agents, the decision makers, and the people who control the information about the purchase.

Within any organization, the size and composition of the buying center will vary for different classes of products. More decision participants will be involved in buying a computer than in buying paper clips. The industrial marketer has to figure out: Who are the major decision participants? In what decisions do they exercise influence? What is their relative degree of influence? And what evaluation criteria does each decision participant use? Consider the following example:

The American Hospital Supply Corporation sells nonwoven disposable surgical gowns to hospitals. It tries to identify the hospital personnel who par-

Exhibit **6-1**

Standard Register's Success at Selling Business Forms

The Standard Register Company is not number one in making business forms for other companies; it hovers around the number two and three positions. But Standard Register has such consistently high sales that many people consider the company the leader in many business forms marketing areas.

The company's customers include 26,000 businesses of all types and sizes. The smallest companies buy only one kind of form in modest quantities; the company's one hundred largest accounts spend over $100 million per year on Standard's forms. The company sells these customers business forms for virtually every printed-products use: W-2 forms; forms for purchasing and billing; forms that can be used with computers, typewriters, and accounting machines; single-copy forms, multiple-copy forms (with and without carbon paper), and pressure-sensitive labels. The company's success is based on its ability to match its products and services to its customers needs.

One of Standard Register's methods that attracts customers is its team-selling approach. In this system, a senior and a junior sales representative share large accounts. Team-selling ensures that if one sales representative is ill or leaves the job, there is still another one who is thoroughly familiar with the account. Another advantage is that more frequent contact is possible between the Standard representatives and the customer. Standard has found that sales usually increase under the team-selling system and that customers enjoy the extra service. One customer, American Heritage Life, reports that a sales representative visits about twice a week; another customer

ticipate in this buying decision. The decision participants turn out to be (1) the vice-president of purchasing, (2) the operating room administrator, and (3) the surgeons. Each party plays a different role. The vice-president of purchasing analyzes whether the hospital should buy disposable gowns or reusable gowns. If the findings favor disposable gowns, then the operating room administrator compares various competitors' products and prices and makes a choice. This administrator considers the gown's absorbency, antiseptic quality, design, and cost and normally buys the brand that meets the functional requirements at the lowest cost. Finally, surgeons influence the decision retroactively by reporting their satisfaction or dissatisfaction with the particular brand.

reports a minimum of three visits weekly. Both customers feel that the attention Standard gives them is one of its strong points.

Standard is also known among the organizations it serves for having a particularly efficient and individualized forms management program. The system is designed to save money for each organization, to provide forms that meet its needs, and to ensure that necessary forms are always available. To keep costs down, the company modifies existing forms whenever possible, rather than designing entirely new forms. Standard also maintains a current inventory of all the forms that are stored or on order for each organization. To meet the demands of each customer's business, Standard designs individual ordering systems to be as efficient and economical as possible. Recently, Standard advertised its forms-management program in a national, widely read magazine (*Business Week*), rather than an industry publication, to reach a larger number of businesses.

The company has also chosen to concentrate considerable marketing efforts on hospitals, an industry that spends especially large amounts on forms. To attract health care organizations as customers, Standard advertises in hospital publications. Advertisements stress the fact that Standard can help increase hospital efficiency by reducing paperwork. Teams of salespeople trained to specialize in this area learn medical terms, hospital management structure, and some ways to cut down on paperwork. Standard now claims between 15% and 20% of the health care market, in comparison to its 7% share of the total business forms market.

Source: Rayna Skolnick, "Standard Register Sells in Top Form," *Sales and Marketing Management,* October 11, 1982, pp. 49–52.

What Are the Major Influences on Industrial Buyers? Industrial buyers are subject to many influences when they make their buying decisions. Some marketers assume that the major influences are economic. They see the buyers as favoring the supplier who offers the minimum price, or best product, or most service. This view suggests that industrial marketers should concentrate on offering strong economic benefits to buyers.

Other marketers see the company's purchasing agents responding to personal motives, seeking favors, or attention, or risk reduction. A study of purchasing agents in ten large companies concluded:

Corporate decision-makers remain human after they enter the office. They respond to "image"; they buy from companies to which they feel "close"; they favor suppliers who show them respect and personal consideration, and who do extra things "for them"; they "over-react" to real or imagined slights, tending to reject companies which fail to respond or delay in submitting requested bids.[6]

This view suggests that industrial marketers should concentrate mostly on the human and social factors in the buying situation.

Purchasing agents actually respond to both economic and personal factors. Where there is substantial similarity in supplier offers, they have little basis for rational choice. Since purchasing agents can meet organizational goals with any supplier, they can bring in personal factors. On the other hand, where competing products differ substantially, purchasing agents are more accountable for their choice and pay more attention to economic factors.

The various influences on purchasing agents—environmental, organizational, interpersonal, and individual—are listed in figure 6-3 and are described below.[7]

ENVIRONMENTAL FACTORS. Industrial buyers are heavily influenced by factors in the current and expected economic environment, such as the level of primary demand, the economic outlook, and the cost of money. As the level of economic uncertainty rises, industrial buyers cease making new investments in

FIGURE 6-3
Major Influences on Industrial Buying Behavior

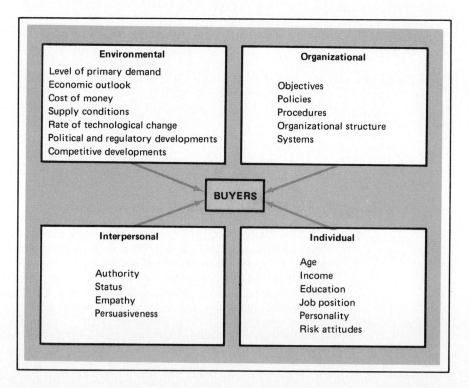

Environmental	Organizational
Level of primary demand	
Economic outlook	Objectives
Cost of money	Policies
Supply conditions	Procedures
Rate of technological change	Organizational structure
Political and regulatory developments	Systems
Competitive developments	

BUYERS

Interpersonal	Individual
	Age
Authority	Income
Status	Education
Empathy	Job position
Persuasiveness	Personality
	Risk attitudes

plant and equipment and attempt to reduce their inventories. An increasingly important environmental factor is imminent shortages in key materials. Companies are showing a greater willingness to buy and hold larger inventories of scarce materials. Industrial buyers are also affected by technological, political, and competitive developments in the environment. The industrial marketer has to monitor the same factors, determine how they will affect the buyer, and try to turn these problems into opportunities.

ORGANIZATIONAL FACTORS. Each buying organization has its own objectives, policies, procedures, organizational structure, and systems, which the industrial marketer should get to know. Such questions arise as: How many people are involved in the buying decision? Who are they? What are their evaluative criteria? What are the company's policies and constraints on the purchasing agents?

INTERPERSONAL FACTORS. The buying center usually includes several participants with different statuses, authority, empathy, and persuasiveness. Industrial marketers are not likely to know what kind of group dynamics will take place during the buying process, although whatever information they can discover about the personalities and interpersonal factors will be useful.

INDIVIDUAL FACTORS. Each participant in the buying decision process brings in personal motivations, perceptions, and preferences. These are influenced by the participant's age, income, education, job position, personality, and attitudes toward risk. Purchasing agents definitely exhibit different buying styles. Some of the younger, higher-educated purchasing agents are "computer freaks" and make rigorous analyses of competitive proposals before choosing a supplier. Others are "tough guys" from the old school and play suppliers off against each other. Industrial marketers must know their customers and adapt their tactics to specific environmental, organizational, interpersonal, and individual influences on the buying situation.

How Do Industrial Buyers Make Their Buying Decisions? We now come to the issue of how industrial buyers move through the buying decision process. This process is similar to the consumer buyer decision process described in chapter 5, but it has a few more steps:[8]

1. Problem recognition
2. General need description
3. Product specification
4. Supplier search

5. Proposal solicitation
6. Supplier selection
7. Order routine specification
8. Performance review

All eight stages apply to a new-task buying situation, but not all apply in the other types of buying situations. We will describe these steps for the typical new-task buying situation.

PROBLEM RECOGNITION. The buying process begins when someone in the company recognizes a problem or need that can be met by acquiring a product or a service. Problem recognition can occur as a result of internal or external stimuli. Internally, the most common events leading to problem recognition are the following:

- The company decides to launch a new product and needs new equipment and materials to produce this product.
- A machine breaks down and requires replacement or new parts.
- Some purchased material turns out to be unsatisfactory, and the company searches for another supplier.
- A purchasing agent senses an opportunity to obtain better prices or quality.

Externally, the purchasing agent may get some new ideas at a trade show, or see an ad, or receive a call from a sales representative who offers a better product or a lower price.

GENERAL NEED DESCRIPTION. Having recognized a need, the purchasing agent proceeds to determine the general characteristics and quantity of the needed item. For standard items, this is not much of a problem. For complex items, a purchasing agent will work with others in the buying center—engineers, users, and so on—to define the general characteristics. They will want to rank the importance of reliability, durability, price, and other attributes desired in the item.

The industrial marketer can help the buying company in this phase. Often the purchasing agent is not aware of the value of different product characteristics. An alert marketer can help the purchasing agent define the company's needs.

PRODUCT SPECIFICATION. The buying organization now proceeds to develop the item's technical specifications. A value analysis engineering team will be put to work on the problem. *Value analysis,* which General Electric pioneered in the late forties, *is an approach to cost reduction in which components are carefully studied to determine if they can be redesigned or standardized or made by cheaper methods of production.* The team will examine the expensive components of a given product. They will also look for product components that are overdesigned, which will make the component last longer than the product itself. The team will decide on the best product characteristics and specify them accordingly. The following are the major questions that are raised in the value analysis:[9]

1. Does the use of the item contribute value?
2. Is its cost proportionate to its usefulness?
3. Does it need all its features?
4. Is there anything better for its intended use?
5. Can a usable part be made by a lower cost method?
6. Can a standard product be found that will be usable?
7. Is the product made on proper tooling, considering the quantities that are used?
8. Do material, labor, overhead, and profit total its cost?
9. Will another dependable supplier provide it for less?
10. Is anyone buying it for less?

When companies advertise to other companies, they point out how they can solve problems for that company.

Courtesy of Emery Worldwide in association with Benton & Bowles, Inc.

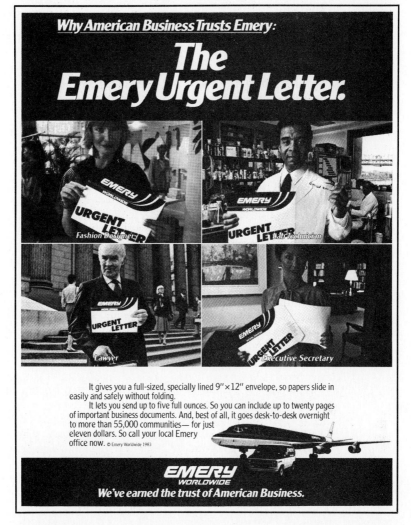

Sellers can also use value analysis as a tool for making a sale. By demonstrating a better way to make an object, an outside seller can turn a straight rebuy situation into a new-task situation in which his or her company has a chance for business.

SUPPLIER SEARCH. The purchasing agent now tries to identify the most appropriate suppliers. The purchasing agent can examine trade directories, do a computer search, or phone other companies for recommendations. Some of the suppliers will be dropped from consideration because they are not large enough to supply the needed quantity or because they have a poor reputation for delivery and service. The purchasing agent will end up with a small list of qualified suppliers. The newer the buying task, and the more complex and expensive the item, the greater amount of time spent in searching for qualified suppliers.

PROPOSAL SOLICITATION. The purchasing agent will now invite qualified suppliers to submit proposals. Some suppliers will only send a catalog or a sales representative. Where the item is complex or expensive, the purchasing agent will require detailed written proposals from each potential supplier. The purchasing agent will review the remaining suppliers when they make their formal presentations.

SUPPLIER SELECTION. In this stage, the members of the buying center will review the proposals and move toward supplier selection. They will consider not only the technical competence of the various suppliers but also their ability to deliver the item on time and provide necessary services. The buying center will often draw up a list of the desired supplier attributes and their relative importance. For example, in selecting a chemical supplier, a buying center listed the following attributes in their order of importance:

1. Technical support service
2. Prompt delivery
3. Quick response to customer needs
4. Product quality
5. Supplier reputation
6. Product price
7. Complete product line
8. Sales representatives' caliber
9. Extension of credit
10. Personal relationships
11. Literature and manuals

The members of the buying center will rate the suppliers against these attributes and will identify the most attractive suppliers.

The purchasing agent may attempt to negotiate with the preferred suppliers for better prices and terms before making the final selections. In the end, they may select a single supplier or a few suppliers. Many purchasing agents prefer to have many sources of supply; then they will not be totally dependent on one supplier in case something goes wrong, and they will be able to compare the prices and performance of the various suppliers.

ORDER ROUTINE SPECIFICATION. The purchasing agent now prepares the final purchase order for the chosen supplier(s), listing the technical specifications, quantity needed, expected time of delivery, return policies, warranties, and so on. In the case of MRO items (*m*aintenance, *r*epair, and *o*perating items), purchasing agents are increasingly moving toward blanket contracts rather than periodic purchase orders. Writing a new purchase order each time stock is needed is expensive. Nor does the purchasing agent want to write fewer and larger purchase orders because this means carrying more inventory. A blanket contract establishes a long-term relationship where the supplier promises to resupply the company as needed on agreed price terms over a specified period of time. The stock is held by the seller, hence the name "stockless purchase plan." The company's computer automatically prints out or teletypes an order to the seller when the stock is needed. Blanket contracting leads to more single-source buying and the buying of more items from that single source. This locks the supplier in tighter with the company and makes it difficult for other suppliers to break in unless the company becomes dissatisfied with the supplier's prices or service.[10]

PERFORMANCE REVIEW.   In this stage, the purchasing agent reviews the performance of the particular supplier(s). The purchasing agent may contact users and ask them to rate their satisfaction. The performance review may lead the purchasing agent to continue, modify, or drop the supplier. The supplier's job is to make sure that the buyer is receiving the expected satisfaction.

We have described the buying stages that would operate in a new-task buying situation. In the modified rebuy or straight rebuy situation, some of these stages would be compressed or bypassed. In some situations, steps may be added. The industrial marketer needs to look at each situation individually.

Thus we see that industrial marketing is a challenging area. The key step is to know the customer's needs and buying procedures. With this knowledge, the industrial marketer can design an effective marketing plan for selling and servicing the customer.

The Reseller Market

Who Is in the Reseller Market? The second organizational market is the reseller market, which we define as follows:

> The **reseller market** consists of all the individuals and organizations who acquire goods for the purpose of reselling or renting them to others at a profit.

The reseller market includes over 383,000 wholesaling firms employing 3,775,000 people, and 1,567,000 retailing firms employing 15,898,000 people. We will discuss wholesalers and retailers in detail in chapter 13, but will look at some of their characteristics now.

Resellers purchase both goods for resale and goods and services for conducting their operations. The latter are bought by resellers in their role as producers. We will confine the discussion here to the goods they purchase for resale.

Resellers handle a vast variety of products for resale, except the few classes of goods that producers sell directly to final customers. The excluded class includes heavy or complex machinery, custom-made products, and products sold on a direct-mail or a door-to-door basis. With these exceptions, most products are sold first to resellers, who then sell them to the final consumers.

What Buying Decisions Do Resellers Make? Like other organizations, resellers must decide which suppliers to buy from and what prices and terms to negotiate. Resellers, however, must also decide what assortment of goods to carry. This is their most important decision, because it determines their position in the marketplace.

Resellers can carry an *exclusive assortment,* the products of only one producer. They can carry a *deep assortment,* many types of similar products from many producers. They can carry a *broad assortment,* several related product lines. Or they can carry a *scrambled assortment,* many unrelated product lines. Thus a camera store might carry only Kodak cameras (exclusive assortment); many brands of cameras (deep assortment); cameras, tape recorders, radios, and stereophonic equipment (broad assortment); or the last plus stoves and refrigerators (scrambled assortment). The reseller's chosen assortment will influence its customer mix, marketing mix, and supplier mix.

Who Participates in the Reseller Buying Process? Who does the buying for wholesale and retail organizations? In small mom-and-pop firms, the owner usually selects and buys the products. In large firms, buying is a specialized function and full-time job. Buying is carried out in different ways by department stores, supermarkets, drug wholesalers, and so on, and differences can even be found within each type of enterprise. Consider supermarkets. In the corporate headquarters of a supermarket chain, specialist buyers will have the responsibility for developing brand assortments and listening to new-brand presentations made by salespeople. But the manager of a single store in the chain may reject a product and refuse to sell it. And the manager may choose to offer other new products.

How Do Resellers Make Their Buying Decisions? Resellers are influenced by the same factors—environmental, organizational, interpersonal, and individual—shown in figure 6-3. For new items, resellers use roughly the same buying process described for the industrial buyer. For standard items, resellers simply reorder goods when the inventory gets low. The orders are placed with the same suppliers as long as their terms, goods, and services are satisfactory.

The Government Market *stay away from it*

Who Is in the Government Market? The third organizational market is the government market, which we define as follows:

> The **government market** consists of government units—federal, state, and local—that purchase or rent goods for carrying out the main functions of government.

In 1979, government units purchased $476 billion of products and services, or 20% of the gross national product, making government the nation's largest customer. The federal government accounts for approximately 35% of the total spent by government at all levels.

What Buying Decisions Do Government Buyers Make? Government buying is based on acquiring products and services that the voters establish as necessary to carry out public objectives. Government agencies buy an amazing range of products and services. They buy bombers, sculpture, chalkboards, furniture, toiletries, clothing, materials-handling equipment, fire engines, mobile equipment, and fuel. In 1980, the federal, state, and local government units spent approximately $143 billion for education, $149 billion for defense, $64 billion for public welfare, $44 billion for health and hospitals, $33 billion for highways, $35 billion for natural resources, and smaller sums for postal service, space research, and housing and urban renewal. No wonder the government represents a huge market for any producer or reseller.

Each product that the government buys requires further decisions on how much to buy, where to buy it, how much to pay, and what services to require. These decisions are made on the basis of trying to minimize taxpayer cost. Normally government buyers will favor the lowest-cost bidders that can meet the stated specifications.

Who Participates in the Government Buying Process?

Who does the buying of the $476 billion of goods and services? Government buying organizations are found at the federal, state, and local levels. The federal level is the largest, and its buying units operate in the civilian and military sectors. The federal civilian buying establishment consists of seven categories: departments (Commerce), administration (General Services Administration), agencies (Federal Aviation Agency), boards (Railroad Retirement Board), commissions (Federal Communications Commission), the executive office (Bureau of the Budget), and miscellaneous (Tennessee Valley Authority). "No single federal agency contracts for all the government's requirements and no single buyer in any agency purchases all that agency's needs for any single item of supplies, equipment or services."[11] Many agencies control a substantial percentage of their own buying, particularly for industrial products and specialized equipment. At the same time, the General Services Administration plays a major role in centralizing the procurement of commonly used items in the civilian sector (office

Executives at Lockheed are displaying a product to Defense Department buyers.

Lockheed-California Company, Office of Public Information

furniture and equipment, vehicles, fuel, and so on) and in developing standardized buying procedures for the other agencies.

Federal military buying is carried out by the Defense Department largely through the Defense Supply Agency and the army, navy, and air force. The Defense Supply Agency was set up in 1961 to procure and distribute supplies used by all military services in an effort to reduce costly duplication. It operates six supply centers, which specialize in construction, electronics, fuel, personnel support, industrial, and general supplies. The trend has been toward "single managers" for major product classifications. Each service branch procures equipment and supplies in line with its own mission; for example, the Army Department operates offices for acquiring its own matériel, vehicles, medical supplies and services, and weaponry.

State and local buying agencies include school districts, highway departments, hospitals, housing agencies, and many others. Each has its own buying procedures that suppliers have to master.

What Are the Major Influences on Government Buyers? Government buyers are influenced by environmental, organizational, interpersonal, and individual factors. A unique thing about government buying is that it is carefully monitored by outside publics. One watchdog is Congress, and certain members of congress have made a career out of exposing government extravagance and waste. Another watchdog is the Bureau of the Budget, which checks on government spending and seeks to improve spending efficiency. Many private watchdog groups also watch government agencies to monitor how they spend the public's money.

Because spending decisions are subject to public review, government organizations get involved in considerable paperwork. Elaborate forms must be filled out and signed before purchases are approved. The level of bureaucracy is high, and marketers have to find a way to cut through the red tape.

Noneconomic criteria are playing a growing role in government buying. Sometimes government buyers are asked to favor minority business firms, small-business firms, and business firms that avoid racial, sex, or age discrimination. Suppliers need to keep these factors in mind when deciding whether to go after government business.

How Do Government Buyers Make Their Buying Decisions? Government buying practices often seem complex and frustrating to suppliers. In a recent survey, suppliers registered a variety of complaints about government purchasing procedures. These included excessive paperwork, bureaucracy, needless regulations, emphasis on low bid prices, decision-making delays, frequent shifts in procurement personnel, and excessive policy changes.[12] Yet the ins and outs of selling to the government can be mastered in a short time. The government is generally helpful in spreading information about its buying needs and procedures. Government is often as anxious to attract new suppliers as the suppliers are to find customers. For example, the Small Business Administration prints a booklet entitled *U.S. Government Purchasing, Specifications, and Sales Directory,* which lists thousands of items most frequently purchased by the government and is cross-referenced by the agencies most frequently buying them.

The Government Printing Office issues the *Commerce Business Daily,* which lists current defense procurements estimated to exceed $10,000 and civilian agency procurements expected to exceed $5,000, as well as recent contract awards that can provide leads to subcontracting markets. The General Services Administration operates Business Service Centers in several major cities, whose staff provides a complete education on the way government agencies buy and the steps that suppliers should follow. Various trade magazines and associations provide information on how to reach schools, hospitals, highway departments, and other government agencies.

Government buying procedures fall into two types: the open bid and the negotiated contract. Open-bid buying means that the government procuring office invites bids from qualified suppliers for carefully described items, generally awarding a contract to the lowest bidder. The supplier must consider whether it can meet the specifications and accept the terms. For commodities and standard items, such as fuel or school supplies, the specifications are not a hurdle. However, specifications may be a hurdle for nonstandard items. The government procurement office is usually required to award the contract to the lowest bidder on a winner-take-all basis. In some cases, allowance is made for the supplier's superior product or reputation for completing contracts.

In negotiated-contract buying, the agency works with one or more companies and directly negotiates a contract with one of them covering the project and terms. This occurs primarily in connection with complex projects, often involving major research and development cost and risk and/or where there is little effective competition. Contract performance is open to review and renegotiation if the supplier's profits seem excessive.

Many companies that sell to the government have not shown a marketing orientation—for a number of reasons. Total government spending is determined by elected officials rather than by marketing effort to develop this market. The government's buying policies have emphasized price, leading the suppliers to invest all their effort in a technological orientation to bring their costs down. Where the product's characteristics are carefully specified, product differentiation is not a marketing factor. Nor is advertising or personal selling of much consequence in winning bids on an open-bid basis.

More companies are now establishing separate marketing departments to guide government-directed marketing efforts. J. I. Case, Eastman Kodak, and Goodyear are examples. These companies want to coordinate bids and prepare them more scientifically, to propose projects to meet government needs rather than just respond to government initiatives, to gather competitive intelligence, and to prepare stronger communications to describe the company's competence.

Summary

The organizational market consists of all the individuals and organizations that buy goods for purposes of further production, resale, or redistribution. Organizations are a market for raw materials, manufactured parts, installations, accessory equipment, and supplies and services.

The industrial market is made up of all the individuals and organizations who buy goods and services for the purpose of increasing sales, cutting costs, or meeting social and legal requirements. Compared with the consumer market, the industrial market consists of fewer buyers, larger buyers, and more geographically concentrated buyers; the demand is based on consumer demand, is inelastic, and changes rapidly; and the purchasing is done by professionals. Industrial buyers make decisions that vary with the buying situation. There are three major types of buying situations: the straight rebuy, the modified rebuy, and the new task. The decision-making unit of a buying organization—the buying center—consists of those who play a role in the purchase decision process. This includes the users of the product, those who influence the buying decision, the purchasing agents, the decision makers, and those who control the information about the purchase. The industrial marketer needs to know: Who are the major decision participants? In what decisions do they exercise influence? What is their relative degree of influence? What evaluation criteria does each decision participant use? The industrial marketer also needs to understand the major environmental, organizational, interpersonal, and individual factors operating in the buying process. The buying process itself consists of eight stages: problem recognition, general need description, product specification, supplier search, proposal solicitation, supplier selection, order routine specification, and performance review. As industrial buyers become more sophisticated, industrial marketers must upgrade their marketing capabilities.

The reseller market consists of individuals and organizations who acquire and resell goods produced by others. Resellers have to decide on their suppliers, prices, terms, and assortment. In small wholesale and retail organizations, buying may be carried on by one or a few individuals; in large organizations, by an entire purchasing department. With new items, resellers go through a buying process similar to the one shown for industrial buyers; with standard items, the buying process consists of routines for reordering and renegotiating contracts.

The government market is a vast one that annually spends more than $476 billion for products and services—for defense, education, public welfare, and other public needs. Government buying practices are highly specialized and specified, with open bidding and/or negotiated contracts characterizing most of the buying. Government buyers operate under the watchful eye of Congress, the Bureau of the Budget, and several private watchdog groups. Hence they tend to fill out more forms, need more signatures, and respond more slowly when placing orders.

Questions for Discussion

1. Discuss into which of the major types of buying situations you would classify the following: (a) United Airlines' purchase of an additional DC-10, (b) Caterpillar's purchase of diesel engine parts, and (c) Pacific Power and Electric's purchase of solar energy panels.
2. How would the participants in the industrial buying decision process differ between a small machine tool shop and the U.S. Steel Corporation?

3. Discuss the major environmental factors that would influence Greyhound's purchase of buses.
4. Apply the industrial buying decision process to a farmer seeking to buy a large tractor.
5. How do the two major types of resellers differ in the way they make their buying decisions?
6. The government market is not a significant one for most products. Comment.
7. How do the buying influences on the government buyer differ from those on the industrial or reseller buyer?
8. Companies are searching for "more able" purchasing agents. What kinds of abilities should a modern purchasing agent have?

Key Terms in Chapter 6

Government market   Government units—federal, state, and local—that purchase or rent goods for carrying out the main functions of government.

Industrial market   All the individuals and organizations who buy goods and services that enter into the production of other products or services that are sold, rented, or supplied to others.

Organizational buying   "The decision-making process by which formal organizations establish the need for purchased products and services, and identify, evaluate, and choose among alternative brands and suppliers."

Purchasing agents   Professionally trained buyers of industrial goods.

Reseller market   All the individuals and organizations who acquire goods for the purpose of reselling or renting them to others at a profit.

Cases for Chapter 6

Case 4   Levi Strauss & Co. (p. 496)

A new marketing plan led to changes in the reseller market. This case evaluates these changes from both the company's and the reseller's points of view.

Case 6   American Cyanamid Co. (p. 499)

How does a company move a product into organizational markets? This case suggests some strategies.

Chapter **7**

Market Segmentation, Targeting, and Positioning

Objectives

After reading this chapter, you should be able to:

1. Define market segmentation, market targeting, and market positioning.
2. List the bases for segmenting consumer and industrial markets.
3. Explain how companies choose a market-coverage strategy.
4. Describe how a company chooses a position for a new product.

These days soft-drink manufacturers seem to have a product for everyone: There are the standard colas; sugar-free colas; sugared colas without caffeine; sugar-free, caffeine-free colas; and noncola soft drinks with or without sugar, sometimes also with or without caffeine. The Coca-Cola Company, PepsiCo Inc., and other makers of soft drinks are now operating under a policy of market segmentation, developing new products to meet the wishes of specific groups of consumers.

The earliest successful sugar-free cola was Diet Rite, manufactured by Royal Crown beginning in 1962. The following year Coca-Cola, noting RC's success in the area, introduced its own diet cola, Tab. PepsiCo entered the diet cola market in 1964 with Diet Pepsi. Almost immediately, Coca-Cola's and PepsiCo's products took over as the two top-selling diet soft drinks. Diet Rite, Tab, and Diet Pepsi were all aimed at the weight-conscious female market segment.

In the early 1970s, soft drinks had long been favorite beverages for the large segment of young people born during the post–World War II baby boom. Soft-drink sales were increasing at the rate of 10% a year. As this segment has gotten older, however, health and diet have become two of its main concerns. Many people have given up sugared and caffeinated soft drinks, such as Coke and Pepsi, believing them to be unhealthy or fattening, or both. While soft-drink sales were still increasing, growth had slowed to 2% by 1982.

The Coca-Cola Company had an additional problem: Coke had always been the number-one soft drink, but Pepsi was starting to catch up. While the overall growth rate in the soft-drink industry had been sluggish, diet-drink sales increased over 10% between 1981 and 1982. Coca-Cola saw the diet market as an area with strong potential for expansion. To strengthen its top position, the company developed a new product, diet Coke, aimed at weight-conscious men. This new product became "the hottest-selling soft drink in the shortest amount of time ever," according to one beverage industry expert. Pepsi responded quickly by repositioning its lemon-flavored diet cola, Pepsi Light, to appeal to the same market segment—men cutting back on calories. Both companies continued to market their original diet drinks, Tab and Diet Pepsi, for women.

Meanwhile, soft-drink manufacturers were developing a caffeine-free market. A growing concern among health-conscious consumers was that the caffeine in soft drinks had negative physical effects. For this group of consumers, RC had introduced a caffeine-free cola in 1980. Philip Morris Inc. picked up the idea and repositioned its biggest seller, 7Up, to attract the caffeine-free market. In addition, Philip Morris created a new drink, Like, a caffeine-free cola. Not wanting to miss out on a growing market, PepsiCo introduced two new colas in 1982: Pepsi-free, a decaffeinated cola, and Sugar-free Pepsi-free, a decaffeinated, sugar-free cola. Other companies, such as Dr Pepper, have produced their own decaffeinated drinks so that now there are about 20 on the market.

Coca-Cola was one of the last companies to enter the decaffeinated market. Its reluctance was due to the fact that most of its past business success was based on caffeinated drinks, and Coca-Cola didn't want to bring out new products that might damage older ones. Other companies' success in the caffeine-free market, however, convinced Coca-Cola to put out a decaffeinated version of each of its colas—Coke, Tab, and diet Coke—in 1983.

Both Coca-Cola's and PepsiCo's executives plan to continue the market segmentation strategy in developing new products. Brian Dyson, president of Coca-Cola USA, says that his company will "probably go after smaller segments than we have in the past, maybe bringing out juice-based drinks or noncarbonated ones, or even getting into the area of nutritive beverages." PepsiCo's Roger Enrico stresses demographic trends as the impetus for new products, "because as the population ages the needs and wants will change, and that will give us the keys to segmentation."[1]

Every company recognizes that it cannot appeal to all buyers. The buyers are too numerous, widely scattered, and varied in their buying needs and buying practices. Some companies will be in the best position to serve particular parts, or segments, of the market. Each company has to identify the most attractive segments of the market that it can serve effectively.

PepsiCo uses the New York Giants defensive team to emphasize that Pepsi Light is for diet-conscious men.

Reproduced courtesy of © PepsiCo, Inc. 1983, owner of registered trademarks Pepsi Light and Pepsi-Cola Light.

Sellers have not always tried to do this. Their thinking has passed through three stages:

- *Mass marketing:* In mass marketing, the seller mass-produces, mass-distributes, and mass-promotes one product to all buyers. At one time Coca-Cola produced only one drink for the whole market, hoping it would appeal to everyone. The argument for mass marketing is that it should lead to the lowest costs and prices and create the largest potential market.
- *Product-differentiated marketing:* Here the seller produces two or more products that exhibit different features, styles, quality, sizes, and so on. Today Coca-Cola produces several soft drinks packaged in different sizes and containers. They are designed to offer variety to buyers rather than appeal to different market segments.
- *Target marketing:* Here the seller distinguishes between market segments, selects one or more of these segments, and develops products and marketing mixes tailored to each segment. For example, Coca-Cola developed Tab to meet the needs of diet-conscious drinkers.

Today's companies are moving away from mass marketing and product-differentiated marketing toward target marketing. Target marketing helps sellers identify marketing opportunities better. The sellers can develop the right product for each target market. They can adjust their prices, distribution channels, and advertising to reach the target market efficiently. Instead of scattering their marketing effort ("shotgun" approach), they can focus it on the buyers who have the greater purchase interest ("rifle" approach).

Market Segmentation	Market Targeting	Market Positioning
1. Identify ways to segment the market 2. Develop profiles of resulting segments	3. Evaluate attractiveness of segments 4. Select the target segment(s)	5. Develop positioning for each target segment 6. Develop marketing mix for each target segment

FIGURE 7-1

Steps in Target Marketing

Target marketing calls for three major steps (see figure 7-1):

First, **market segmentation**—the act of dividing a market into distinct groups of buyers who might need separate products and/or marketing mixes. The company identifies different ways to segment the market, develops profiles of the resulting market segments, and evaluates each segment's attractiveness.

Second, **market targeting**—the act of evaluating and selecting one or more of the market segments to enter.

Third, **market positioning**—the act of creating a competitive positioning for the product and a detailed marketing mix.

This chapter will describe the principles of market segmentation, market targeting, and market positioning.

Market Segmentation *Like a pie into segments*

Markets consist of buyers, and buyers differ in one or more respects. They may differ in their wants, resources, geographic locations, buying attitudes, and buying practices. Any of these variables can be used to segment a market.

The General Approach to Segmenting a Market

Figure 7-2a shows a market of six buyers. Each buyer is potentially a separate market because of unique needs and wants. Ideally, a seller might design a separate marketing program for each buyer. For example, airframe producers such as Boeing and McDonnell-Douglas face only a few buyers and treat them as separate markets. This ultimate degree of market segmentation is illustrated in figure 7-2b.

Most sellers will not find it worthwhile to customize their product to satisfy each specific buyer. Instead, the seller identifies broad classes of buyers who differ in their product requirements and/or marketing responses. For example, the seller may discover that income groups differ in their wants. In figure 7-2c, a number (1, 2, or 3) is used to identify each buyer's income class. Lines are drawn around buyers in the same income class. Segmentation by income results in three segments, the most numerous segment being income class 1.

On the other hand, the seller may find strong differences between younger and older buyers. In figure 7-2d, a letter (*a* or *b*) is used to indicate each buyer's age. Segmentation by age group results in two segments, each with three buyers.

Now income and age may both count heavily in influencing the buyer's behavior toward the product. In this case, the market can be divided into five segments: 1*a*, 1*b*, 2*b*, 3*a*, and 3*b*. Figure 7-2e shows that segment 1*a* contains two buyers and the other segments contain one buyer. As a market is segmented using more characteristics, each segment is more precise, but the number of segments grows and the population in each segment drops.

Bases for Segmenting Consumer Markets There is no single way to segment a market. A marketer has to try different segmentation variables, singly and in combination, hoping to find a useful way to view the market structure. Here we will look at the major geographic, demographic, psychographic, and behavioristic variables used in segmenting consumer markets (see table 7-1).

GEOGRAPHIC SEGMENTATION. Geographic segmentation calls for dividing the market into different geographic units, such as nations, states, regions, counties, cities, or neighborhoods. The company may decide to (1) operate in one or a few geographic areas or (2) operate in all areas but pay attention to variations in geographic needs and preferences. For example, General Foods' Maxwell House ground coffee is sold nationally but is flavored regionally. People in the West prefer stronger coffee than people in the East.

FIGURE 7-2

Different Segmentations of a Market

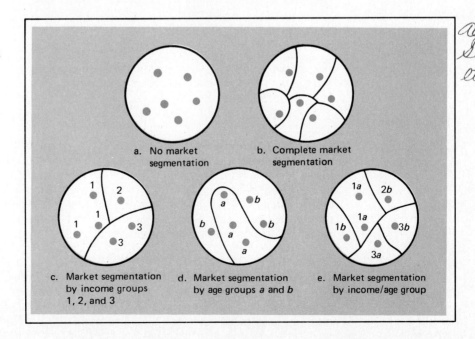

a. No market segmentation

b. Complete market segmentation

c. Market segmentation by income groups 1, 2, and 3

d. Market segmentation by age groups *a* and *b*

e. Market segmentation by income/age group

Table 7-1	

Some Variables Used to Segment Consumer Markets	
VARIABLE	TYPICAL BREAKDOWNS
Geographic:	
Region	Pacific, Mountain, West North Central, West South Central, East North Central, East South Central, South Atlantic, Middle Atlantic, New England
County size	A, B, C, D
City or SMA size	Under 5,000; 5,000–20,000; 20,000–50,000; 50,000–100,000; 100,000–250,000; 250,000–500,000; 500,000–1,000,000; 1,000,000–4,000,000; 4,000,000 and over
Density	Urban, suburban, rural
Climate	Northern, southern
Psychographic:	
Social class	Lower lowers, upper lowers, lower middles, upper middles, lower uppers, upper uppers
Life-style	Straights, swingers, longhairs
Personality	Compulsive, gregarious, authoritarian, ambitious
Behavioristic:	
Purchase occasion	Regular occasion, special occasion
Benefits sought	Quality, service, economy
User status	Nonuser, ex-user, potential user, first-time user, regular user
Usage rate	Light user, medium user, heavy user
Loyalty status	None, medium, strong, absolute

Some companies even subdivide major cities into smaller geographic areas. R. J. Reynolds Company has subdivided Chicago into three distinct submarkets.[2] In the North Shore area, Reynolds promotes its low-tar brands because residents are better educated and more knowledgeable and concerned about health. In the conservative, blue-collar Southeast area, Reynolds promotes Winston. In the South side, Reynolds promotes the high menthol content of Salem, using the black press and billboards heavily.

DEMOGRAPHIC SEGMENTATION. Demographic segmentation consists of dividing the market into groups on the basis of demographic variables, such as age, sex, family size, family life cycle, income, occupation, education, religion, race, and nationality. Demographic variables are the most popular bases for distinguishing customer groups. One reason is that consumer wants, prefer-

VARIABLE	TYPICAL BREAKDOWNS
Readiness stage	Unaware, aware, informed, interested, desirous, intending to buy
Attitude toward product	Enthusiastic, positive, indifferent, negative, hostile
Demographic:	
Age	Under 6, 6–11, 12–19, 20–34, 35–49, 50–64, 65+
Sex	Male, female
Family size	1–2, 3–4, 5+
Family life cycle	Young, single; young, married, no children; young, married, youngest child under 6; young, married, youngest child 6 or over; older, married, with children; older, married, no children under 18; older, single; other
Income	Under $2,500; $2,500–$5,000; $5,000–$7,500; $7,500–$10,000; $10,000–$15,000; $15,000–$20,000; $20,000–$30,000; $30,000–$50,000; $50,000 and over
Occupation	Professional and technical; managers, officials, and proprietors; clerical, sales; artisans, supervisors; operatives; farmers; retired; students; homemakers; unemployed
Education	Grade school or less; some high school; high school graduate; some college; college graduate
Religion	Catholic, Protestant, Jewish, other
Race	White, black, Oriental
Nationality	American, British, French, German, Scandinavian, Italian, Latin American, Middle Eastern, Japanese

ences, and usage rates are often highly associated with demographic variables. Another is that demographic variables are easier to measure than most other types of variables. Even when the target market is described in nondemographic terms (say, a personality type), the link back to demographic characteristics is necessary.

Here we will illustrate how certain demographic variables have been applied to market segmentation.

Age and life-cycle stage. Consumer wants and capacities change with age. Even children who are six months old differ from children who are three months old in their consumption potential. Alabe Products, a toy manufacturer, realized this and designed twelve different toys to be used by babies sequentially as they move from the age of three months to one year. Crib Jiminy is to be used when babies begin to reach for things, Talky Rattle when they first grasp things, and so on.[3] This segmentation strategy means that parents and gift givers can more easily find the appropriate toy by simply considering the baby's age.

General Foods has applied the same strategy to dog food. Many dog owners think of their dog as a family member whose food needs change with age. So General Foods formulated four types of canned dog food: Cycle 1 for puppies, Cycle 2 for young dogs, Cycle 3 for overweight dogs, and Cycle 4 for older dogs. General Foods managed to gain a large market share through this creative segmentation strategy.[4]

Nevertheless, age and life cycle can be tricky variables. For example, the Ford Motor Company used the buyers' age in developing the target market for its Mustang automobile. The car was designed to appeal to young people who wanted an inexpensive sporty automobile. But Ford found that the car was being purchased by all age groups. It then realized that its target market was not the chronologically young but the psychologically young.

Sex. Sex segmentation has long been applied in clothing, hairdressings, cosmetics, and magazines. Occasionally other marketers will notice an opportunity for sex segmentation. The cigarette market provides an excellent example. Most cigarette brands are smoked by men and women alike. Increasingly, however, feminine brands, such as Virginia Slims, have been introduced accompanied by appropriate flavor, packaging, and advertising cues to reinforce the female image. Today it is as unlikely to see men smoking Virginia Slims as it is to see women smoking Marlboros. Another industry that is beginning to recognize the potential for sex segmentation is the automobile industry. In the past, cars were designed to appeal to male and female family members. With more working women and women car owners, however, some manufacturers are studying the opportunity to design "feminine" cars for women drivers.

Income. Income segmentation is another long-standing practice in such product and service categories as automobiles, boats, clothing, cosmetics, and travel. Other industries occasionally recognize its possibilities. For example, Suntory, the Japanese liquor company, introduced a Scotch selling for $75 to attract drinkers who want the very best.

At the same time, income does not always predict the customers for a given product. One would think that blue-collar workers would buy Chevrolets and managers would buy Cadillacs. Yet many Chevrolets are bought by managers (often as a second car), and some Cadillacs are bought by blue-collar workers (such as high-paid plumbers and carpenters). Blue-collar workers were among the first purchasers of color television sets; it was cheaper for them to buy these sets than to go out to movies and restaurants.

Segmenting by more than one demographic variable. Most companies will segment a market by combining two or more demographic variables. The Charles Home for the Blind (name disguised) serves the needs of blind persons for care, psychological counseling, and vocational training. However, it is not able to serve all types of blind people because of limited facilities. A multiple segmentation of blind people is shown in figure 7-3, where they are distinguished

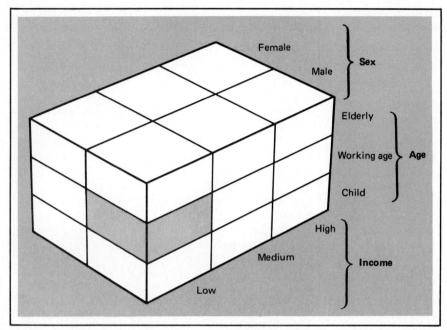

FIGURE 7-3
Segmentation of Blind People by Three Demographic Variables

according to age, sex, and income. The Charles Home has chosen to serve low-income males of working age. It feels that it can do the best job for this group.

PSYCHOGRAPHIC SEGMENTATION. In psychographic segmentation, buyers are divided into different groups on the basis of their social class, life-style, and/or personality characteristics. People within the same demographic group can exhibit very different psychographic profiles.

Social class. We described the six American social classes in chapter 5 (p. 111) and showed that social class has a strong influence on a person's preferences in cars, clothes, home furnishings, leisure activities, reading habits, retailers, and so on. Many companies design products and/or services for specific social classes, building in those features that appeal to the target social class.

Life-style. We saw in chapter 5 that people's interest in various goods is influenced by their life-styles. Marketers of various products and brands are increasingly segmenting their markets by consumer life-styles. For example, a manufacturer of men's blue jeans will want to design jeans for a specific male group: the "active achiever," the "self-indulgent pleasure seeker," the "traditional homebody," the "blue-collar outdoorsman," the "business leader," or the "successful traditionalist."[5] Each group would require different jeans designs, prices, advertising copy, outlets, and so on. Unless the company states which life-style group it is aiming at, its jeans may not appeal to any male group in particular.

In this advertise-
ment, Nabisco is
positioning
Shredded Wheat as a
natural, good-for-
you food to appeal
to health-conscious
consumers.
Courtesy Nabisco Brands,
Inc.

Personality. Marketers have also used personality variables to segment markets. They give their products personalities that correspond to consumer personalities. In the late fifties, Fords and Chevrolets were promoted as having different personalities. Ford buyers were thought to be "independent, impulsive, masculine, alert to change, and self-confident, while Chevrolet owners are conservative, thrifty, prestige-conscious, less masculine, and seeking to avoid extremes."[6] Evans investigated whether this was true by subjecting Ford and Chevrolet owners to a standard personality test, which measured needs for achievement, dominance, change, aggression, and so on. Except for a slightly higher score on dominance, Ford owners' scores were not significantly different from those of Chevrolet owners. Evans concluded that the overlapping of scores showed that personality discrimination is almost impossible. Later studies occasionally turned up personality differences. Westfall found some evidence of personality differences between the owners of convertibles and nonconvertibles, the former appearing to be more active, impulsive, and sociable.[7] Shirley Young, the director of research for a leading advertising agency, reported developing successful market segmentation strategies based on personality traits in such product categories as women's cosmetics, cigarettes, insurance, and liquor.[8] Ackoff and Emshoff were able to identify four drinker-personality types (see table 7-2) and help Anheuser-Busch develop specific advertising campaigns to reach them.[9]

Table 7-2

Drinker-Personality Segmentation

TYPE OF DRINKER	PERSONALITY TYPE	DRINKING PATTERN
Social drinker	Driven by his own needs, particularly to achieve, and attempts to manipulate others to get what he wants. Driven by a desire to get ahead. Usually a younger person.	Controlled drinker who may sometimes become high or drunk but is unlikely to be an alcoholic. Drinks primarily on weekends, holidays, and vacations, usually in a social setting with friends. Drinking is seen as a way to gain social acceptance.
Reparative drinker	Sensitive and responsive to the needs of others and adapts to their needs by sacrificing his own aspirations. Usually middle-aged.	Controlled drinker who infrequently becomes high or drunk. Drinks primarily at the end of the workday, usually with a few close friends. Views drinking as a reward for sacrifices made for others.
Oceanic drinker	Sensitive to the needs of others. Often a failure who blames himself for his nonachievement.	Drinks heavily, especially when under pressure to achieve. At times shows a lack of control over his drinking and is likely to become high, drunk, and even alcoholic. Drinking is a form of escape.
Indulgent drinker	Generally insensitive to others and places the blame for his failures on others' lack of sensitivity to him.	Like the oceanic drinker, he drinks heavily, often becomes high, drunk, or alcoholic. Drinks as a form of escape.

Source: Adapted from Russell L. Ackoff and James R. Emshoff, "Advertising Research at Anheuser-Busch, Inc. (1968–74)," *Sloan Management Review,* Spring 1975, pp. 1–15.

A well-known campaign promotes orange juice for other occasions, not just for breakfast.

Courtesy Florida
Department of Citrus

BEHAVIORISTIC SEGMENTATION.   In behavioristic segmentation, buyers are divided into groups on the basis of their knowledge, attitude, use, or response to a product. Many marketers believe that behavioristic variables are the best starting point for constructing market segments.

Occasions.   Buyers can be distinguished according to occasions when they get the idea, make a purchase, or use a product. For example, air travel is triggered by occasions related to business, vacation, or family. An airline can specialize in serving people for whom one of these occasions dominates. Thus charter airlines serve people whose vacation includes flying somewhere.

Occasion segmentation can help firms build up product usage. For example, orange juice is most commonly consumed at breakfast. An orange juice company can try to promote drinking orange juice at lunch or dinner. Certain holidays—Mother's Day and Father's Day, for example—were promoted partly to increase the sale of candy and flowers. The Curtis Candy Company promoted the "trick-or-treat" custom at Halloween, with every home ready to dispense candy to eager little callers knocking at its door.

Benefits sought.   A powerful form of segmentation is to classify buyers according to the different benefits that they seek from the product. Yankelovich applied benefit segmentation to the purchase of watches. He found that "approximately 23 percent of the buyers bought for lowest price, another 46 percent bought for durability and general product quality, and 31 percent bought watches as symbols of some important occasion."[10] The better-known watch companies at the time focused almost exclusively on the third segment by producing expensive watches, stressing prestige, and selling through jewelry stores. The U.S. Time Company decided to focus on the first two segments by creating Timex watches and selling them through mass merchandisers. This segmentation strategy led to its becoming the world's largest watch company.

Benefit segmentation requires determining the major benefits that people look for in the product class, the kinds of people who look for each benefit, and the major brands that deliver each benefit. One of the most successful benefit segmentations was reported by Haley, who studied the toothpaste market (see table 7-3). Haley's research uncovered four benefit segments: economy, medicinal, cosmetic, and taste. Each segment had particular demographic, behavioristic, and psychographic characteristics. For example, decay prevention seekers had large families, were heavy toothpaste users, and were conservative. Each segment also favored certain brands. A toothpaste company can use these results to clarify which benefit segment it is appealing to, its characteristics, and the major competitive brands. The company can also search for a new benefit and launch a brand that delivers this benefit.

User status. Many markets can be segmented into nonusers, ex-users, potential users, first-time users, and regular users of a product. Large companies looking for a high market share are particularly interested in attracting potential users, while smaller firms will try to attract regular users to their brand. Potential users and regular users require different kinds of marketing appeals.

Social marketing agencies pay close attention to user status. Drug rehabilitation agencies sponsor rehabilitation programs to help regular users quit the habit. They sponsor talks by ex-users to discourage young people (nonusers) from trying drugs.

Table 7-3

Benefit Segmentation of the Toothpaste Market

BENEFIT SEGMENTS	DEMOGRAPHICS	BEHAVIORISTICS	PSYCHOGRAPHICS	FAVORED BRANDS
Economy (low price)	Men	Heavy users	High autonomy, value-oriented	Brand on sale
Medicinal (decay prevention)	Large families	Heavy users	Hypochondriac, conservative	Crest
Cosmetic (bright teeth)	Teens, young adults	Smokers	High sociability, active	Macleans, Ultra Brite
Taste (good tasting)	Children	Spearmint lovers	High self-involvement, hedonistic	Colgate, Aim

Source: Adapted from Russell J. Haley, "Benefit Segmentation: A Decision Oriented Research Tool," *Journal of Marketing*, July 1963, pp. 30–35.

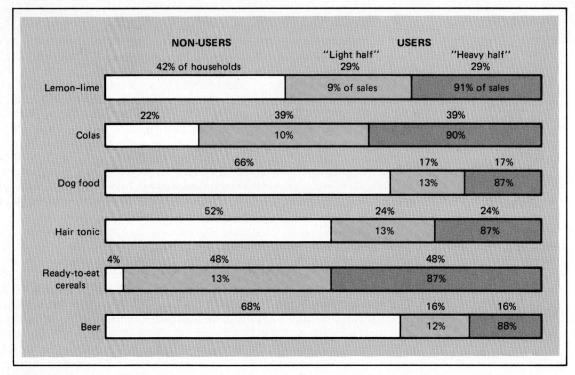

FIGURE 7-4

Segmentation by Usage Rate in Several Product Categories

Source: Dik Warren Twedt, "How Important to Marketing Strategy Is the Heavy User?" *Journal of Marketing,* January 1964, p. 72. Reprinted by permission.

Usage rate. Markets can also be segmented into light-, medium-, and heavy-user groups of the product. Heavy users are often a small percentage of the market but account for a high percentage of total consumption. Some data on usage rates for popular consumer products are shown in figure 7-4. Using beer as an example, the chart shows that 68% of those questioned did not drink beer. The 32% who did were divided into two groups. The lower 16% were light users and accounted for only 12% of total beer consumption. The heavy half accounted for 88% of the total consumption—that is, for over seven times as much consumption as the light users. Clearly a beer company would prefer to attract one heavy user to its brand over several light users. Most beer companies target the heavy beer drinker, using appeals such as Schaefer's, "One beer to have when you're having more than one."

The heavy users of a product often have common demographics, psychographics, and media habits. In the case of heavy beer drinkers, their profile shows that more of them are in the working class compared with light beer drinkers and that they fall between the ages of 25 and 50 (instead of under 25 and over 50), watch television more than three and one-half hours per day (instead of under two hours), and prefer to watch sports programs.[11] Profiles like this assist the marketer in developing price, message, and media strategies.

Social marketing agencies often face a heavy-user dilemma. A family planning agency would normally target families who would have the most children, but these families are also the most resistant to birth-control messages. The National Safety Council would target unsafe drivers, but these drivers are the most resistant to safe-driving appeals. The agencies must consider whether to go after a few high-resistant heavy offenders or many less-resistant light offenders.

Loyalty status. A market can also be segmented by consumer loyalty patterns. Consumers can be loyal to brands (Schlitz), stores (Sears), and other entities. We will deal here with brand loyalty. Suppose there are five brands: A, B, C, D, and E. Buyers can be divided into four groups according to their loyalty status:[12]

- *Hard-core loyals:* Consumers who buy one brand all the time. Thus a buying pattern of A, A, A, A, A, A represents a consumer with undivided loyalty to brand A.
- *Soft-core loyals:* Consumers who are loyal to two or three brands. The buying pattern A, A, B, B, A, B represents a consumer with a divided loyalty between A and B.
- *Shifting loyals:* Consumers who shift from favoring one brand to another. The buying pattern A, A, A, B, B, B would suggest a consumer who is shifting brand loyalty from A to B.
- *Switchers:* Consumers who show no loyalty to any brand. The buying pattern A, C, E, B, D, B would suggest a nonloyal consumer who either buys the brand on sale or wants something different.

Each market is made up of different numbers of the four types of buyers. A brand-loyal market is one with a high percentage of the buyers showing hard-core brand loyalty. Thus the toothpaste market and the beer market seem to be fairly high brand-loyal markets. Companies selling in a brand-loyal market have a hard time gaining more market share, and companies trying to enter such a market have a hard time getting in.

A company can learn a great deal by analyzing loyalty patterns in its market. It should study the characteristics of its own hard-core loyals. Colgate finds that its hard-core loyals are more middle class, have larger families, and are more health conscious. This pinpoints the target market for Colgate.

By studying its soft-core loyals, the company can pinpoint which brands are most competitive with its own. If many Colgate buyers also buy Crest, Colgate can attempt to improve its positioning against Crest, possibly by using direct comparison advertising.

By looking at customers who are shifting away from its brand, the company can learn about its marketing weaknesses. As for nonloyals, the company can attract them by putting its brand on sale.

The company should be aware that what appear to be brand-loyal purchase patterns may reflect habit, indifference, a low price, or the nonavailability of other brands. The concept of brand loyalty has some ambiguities and must be used carefully.

Buyer readiness stage. At any time, people are in different stages of readiness to buy a product. Some people are unaware of the product; some are aware; some are informed; some are interested; some are desirous; and some intend to buy. The relative numbers make a big difference in designing the marketing program. Suppose a health agency wants women to take an annual Pap test to detect cervical cancer. At the beginning, most women may not be aware of the Pap test. The marketing effort should go into high awareness-building advertising using a simple message. If successful, the advertising should dramatize the benefits of the Pap test and the risks of not taking it, in order to move more women into the stage of desire. Facilities should be readied for handling the large number of women who may be motivated to take the examination. In general, the marketing program must be adjusted to the changing distribution of buyer readiness.

Attitude. People in a market can be enthusiastic, positive, indifferent, negative, or hostile about a product. Door-to-door workers in a political campaign use the voter's attitude to determine how much time to spend with the voter. They thank enthusiastic voters and remind them to vote; they spend no time trying to change the attitudes of negative and hostile voters. They reinforce those who are positively disposed and try to win the vote of the indifferent voters. To the extent that attitudes correspond with demographic variables, the organization can increase its efficiency in reaching the best prospects.[13]

Exhibit 7-1 presents a profile of one segment of the consumer market.

Bases for Segmenting Industrial Markets

Industrial markets can be segmented with many of the same variables used in consumer market segmentation. Industrial buyers can be segmented geographically and by several behavioristic variables: benefits sought, user status, usage rate, loyalty status, readiness stage, and attitudes.

A common way to segment industrial markets is by end users. Different end users often seek different benefits and can be approached with different marketing mixes. Consider the transistor market:

The market for transistors consists of three submarkets: military, industrial, and commercial.

The military buyer attaches great importance to the product's quality and availability. Firms selling transistors to the military market must make a considerable investment in R&D, use sales representatives who know military buying procedures, and specialize in limited-line products.

Industrial buyers, such as computer manufacturers, look for high quality and good service. Price is not critical unless it becomes exorbitant. In this market, transistor manufacturers make a modest investment in R&D, use sales representatives who have technical product knowledge, and offer a broad line.

Commercial buyers, such as pocket-radio manufacturers, buy their components largely on price and delivery. Transistor manufacturers selling in this market need little or no R&D effort, use aggressive sales representatives who are nontechnical, and offer the most common lines that can be mass-produced.

Exhibit **7-1**

A Profile of the College-Student Market Segment

A recent study examined the spending habits and characteristics of a particular market segment—college students.

Among the spending habits investigated in this research were food and drink purchasing. Drink consumption is particularly high in this group. Preferred beverages are orange juice, milk, and soft drinks in the non-alcoholic category. Beer and wine are also group favorites, and drinkers of the stronger alcoholic beverages prefer rum. Students' food purchases commonly included snack items in addition to staples. College students make an average of seven monthly shopping trips, and 76% of the group patronize supermarkets.

Personal care items are quite popular in this market segment, with 81% of the females purchasing hair conditioners and 80% purchasing cosmetics. Also popular are shaving creams and face soaps.

The best means of communicating with this group is through college newspapers; 87% reported reading college newspapers regularly. Radio and television were less effective. Many students use coupons, rebate offers on items they purchase, or free samples.

College students are currently spending at the highest level ever recorded for the group. After room, board, and tuition expenses, the average student spends an additional $224 per month. Generally, students work to earn this money. Most of it is spent on entertainment, food, drink, and personal care products. Additionally, 59% of college students own an automobile, and 91% expect to buy an automobile in the near future.

Finally, 89% of college students have a checking account, 64% a savings account, and 19% a Visa credit card.

Source: Based on "Report Examines Media Habits of College Students," *Marketing News*, November 12, 1982.

Customer size is another industrial segmentation variable. Many companies set up separate systems for dealing with major and minor customers. For example, Steelcase, a major manufacturer of office furniture, divides its customers into two groups:

- *Major accounts:* Accounts such as IBM, Prudential, and Standard Oil are handled by national account managers working with field district managers.
- *Dealer accounts:* Smaller accounts are handled by field sales personnel working with franchised dealers who sell Steelcase products.

Industrial companies typically define their target market opportunities by applying several of these segmentation variables at the same time.

After segment, identify target ie. newly married couple

Market Targeting

design plan, mix

Marketing segmentation reveals the market segment opportunities facing the firm. The firm now has to decide on (1) how many segments to cover and (2) how to identify the best segments. We will look at each decision in turn.

Three Market-Coverage Alternatives   The firm can adopt one of three market-coverage strategies: undifferentiated marketing, differentiated marketing, and concentrated marketing. These strategies are illustrated in figure 7-5 and discussed below.

UNDIFFERENTIATED MARKETING.   The firm might decide to ignore market segment differences and go after the whole market with one market offer.[14] It focuses on what is common in the needs of consumers rather than on what is different. It designs a product and a marketing program that will appeal to the broadest number of buyers. It relies on mass distribution and mass advertising.

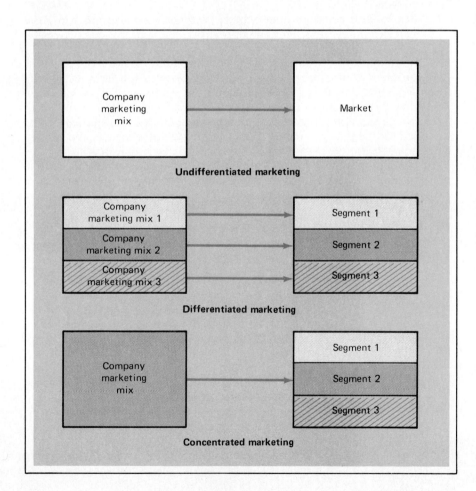

FIGURE 7-5

Three Alternative Market-Coverage Strategies

It aims to give the product a superior image in people's minds. An example of undifferentiated marketing is the Hershey Company's marketing some years ago of only one chocolate candy bar for everyone.

Undifferentiated marketing is economical. Production, inventory, and transportation costs are low. The undifferentiated advertising program keeps down advertising costs. The absence of segment marketing research and planning lowers the costs of marketing research and product management.

The firm that uses undifferentiated marketing typically develops a product aimed at the largest segments in the market. When several firms do this, the result is intense competition for the largest segments and less satisfaction for the smaller ones. Thus the American auto industry for a long time produced only large automobiles. The result is that the larger segments may be less profitable because of heavy competition.

DIFFERENTIATED MARKETING. Here the firm decides to operate in several segments of the market and designs separate offers to each. Thus General Motors tries to produce a car for every "purse, purpose, and personality." By offering various products, it hopes to attain higher sales and a deeper position within each market segment. It hopes that obtaining a stronger position in several segments will strengthen the consumers' overall identification of the company with the product category. Furthermore, it hopes for greater repeat purchasing because the firm's product matches the customer's desire rather than the other way around.

A growing number of firms have adopted differentiated marketing. Here is an excellent example.[15]

> Edison Brothers operates nine hundred shoe stores that fall into four different chain categories, each appealing to a different market segment. Chandler's sells higher-priced shoes. Baker's sells moderate-priced shoes. Burt's sells shoes for budget shoppers, and Wild Pair is oriented to the shopper who wants very stylized shoes. Within three blocks on State Street in Chicago are found Burt's, Chandler's, and Baker's. Putting the stores near each other does not hurt them because they are aimed at different segments of the women's shoe market. This strategy has made Edison Brothers the country's largest retailer of women's shoes.

Another example of differentiated marketing is shown in exhibit 7-2.

General Motors' Chevrolet Citation and Chevrolet Corvette are aimed at market segments with quite different purses and personalities.
Photos courtesy Chevrolet Public Relations

Exhibit **7-2**

With 1,134 Editions, Farm Journal Targets Its Readers

Hog farmers don't want to hear about calves growing fat on "souped-up alfalfa." And cattlemen don't care that sows farrow sooner when the lights are on.

Such simple truths of rural life have helped make the *Farm Journal* the nation's largest farm publication and one of the most elaborate magazines of any kind. Its February issue, for instance, will be printed in 1,134 versions to suit the very particular tastes of its one million subscribers.

"Farmers are becoming more specialized, and the challenge of serving them is more and more difficult," says Dale E. Smith, president of the Philadelphia-based Farm Journal Inc. "You don't get very far with today's farmer unless you're talking about what he has on his farm."

To meet this need, the *Farm Journal* publishes supplements for five kinds of farmers—cotton, dairy, beef, hog, and livestock—and for 26 regions of the country. The Journal also has a "top producer" insert for farmers with sales exceeding $200,000 a year. About 20% of each issue's editorial content is the same coast to coast. The rest is some combination of the 32 supplements, depending on the subscriber's farm and location. All farmers pay the same $8 annual subscription rate for 14 issues.

Whatever their specialties, all subscribers get practical information. Recent articles debate whether to bury drip irrigation lines and discuss "precision placement" fertilization. Notes Mr. Smith, "A farmer doesn't pick up a farm magazine to be entertained."

Source: Jeffrey H. Birnbaum, "With 1,134 Editions, Farm Journal Labors to Please All of Its Readers," *Wall Street Journal*, January 21, 1983. Reprinted by permission. © Dow Jones & Company, Inc. All rights reserved.

CONCENTRATED MARKETING. Many firms see a third possibility that is especially appealing when company resources are limited. Instead of going after a small share of a large market, the firm goes after a large share of one or a few submarkets.

Several examples of concentrated marketing can be cited. Volkswagen has concentrated on the small-car market; Hewlett-Packard on the high-priced calculator market; and Richard D. Irwin on the economics and business textbook market. Through concentrated marketing the firm achieves a strong market position in the segments it serves, because of its greater knowledge of the segments' needs and its special reputation. Furthermore, it enjoys many operating economies because of specialization in production, distribution, and promotion.

At the same time, concentrated marketing involves higher than normal risks. The particular market segment can turn sour; for example, when young women suddenly stopped buying sportswear, it caused Bobbie Brooks's earnings to go deeply into the red. Or a competitor may decide to enter the same segment. For these reasons, many companies prefer to diversify in several market segments.

CHOOSING A MARKET-COVERAGE STRATEGY. The following factors need to be considered in choosing a market-coverage strategy:[16]

- *Company resources:* When the firm's resources are limited, concentrated marketing makes the most sense.
- *Product homogeneity:* Undifferentiated marketing is more suited for homogeneous products, such as grapefruit or steel. Products that are capable of design variation, such as cameras and automobiles, are more suited to differentiated or concentrated marketing.
- *Product stage in the life cycle:* When a firm introduces a new product, it is practical to launch only one version, and undifferentiated marketing or concentrated marketing makes the most sense.
- *Market homogeneity:* If buyers have the same tastes, buy the same amounts per period, and react the same way to marketing stimuli, undifferentiated marketing is appropriate.
- *Competitive marketing strategies:* When competitors segment the market, undifferentiated marketing can be suicidal. Conversely, when competitors practice undifferentiated marketing, a firm can gain by using differentiated or concentrated marketing.

Identifying Attractive Market Segments

Suppose the firm uses the preceding criteria for choosing a market-coverage strategy and decides on concentrated marketing. It must now identify the most attractive segment to enter. Consider the following situation:

> A successful manufacturer of snow-removal equipment is looking for a new product. Management reviews several opportunities and lands on the idea of producing snowmobiles. Management recognizes that it could manufacture any of three product types: gasoline, diesel, or electric. And it can design a snowmobile for any of three markets: consumer, industrial, or military. The nine product/market alternatives are shown in figure 7-6. Assuming that the company wants to focus initially on a single segment, management has to decide on which one.

FIGURE 7-6

Product/Market Grid for Snowmobiles

Products	Markets: Consumer	Industrial	Military
Gas-driven snowmobiles			
Diesel-driven snowmobiles			
Electric-driven snowmobiles			

The company needs to collect data on the nine market segments. The data would include current dollar sales, projected sales-growth rates, estimated profit margins, competitive intensity, marketing channel requirements, and so on. The best segment would have large current sales, a high growth rate, a high profit margin, weak competition, and simple marketing channel requirements. Usually no segment would excel in all of these dimensions, and trade-offs would have to be made.

After the company identifies the more objectively attractive segments, it must ask which segments fit its business strengths best. For example, the military market may be highly attractive, but the company may have had no experience selling to the military. On the other hand, it may have a lot of experience in selling to the consumer market. Thus the company seeks a segment that is attractive in itself and for which it has the necessary business strengths to succeed.

Market Positioning

reposition to new area ie. Arm + Hammer for deodorant swimming pools, debugging etc. bee stings Keep looking for new uses

Once a company decides on a segment to enter, it must then decide <u>how to enter it</u>. If it is an established <u>segment</u>, competitors already operate in this segment. Furthermore, the competitors have taken "positions" in this segment. The company has to identify the positions of existing competitors before deciding on its own positioning.

Suppose the company learns that snowmobile buyers in its target segment are primarily interested in two attributes: size and speed. Potential customers and dealers can be asked where they see competitors' snowmobiles along these dimensions. The findings are shown in the product position map in figure 7-7. Competitor A is seen as producing small/fast snowmobiles; B, medium-sized/medium-speed snowmobiles; C, small- to medium-sized/slow snowmobiles; and D, large/slow snowmobiles. The areas of the circles are proportional to the competitors' sales.[17]

Given these competitor positions, what position should the company seek? It has two choices. One is to position next to one of the existing competitors and fight for a market share. The management might do this if it feels that (1) it can build a superior snowmobile, (2) the market is large enough for two competitors,

Kawasaki News Bureau

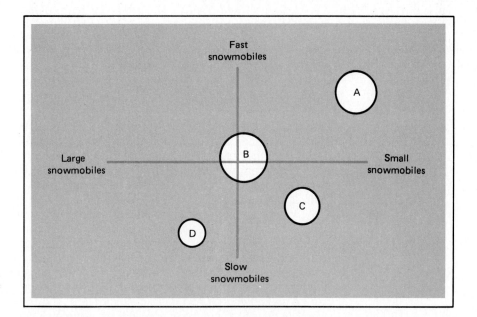

(3) the company has more resources than the competitor, and/or (4) this position is the most consistent with the company's business strengths.

The other choice is to develop a snowmobile that is not currently being offered to this market, such as a large/fast snowmobile (see empty northwest quadrant of figure 7-7). The company would win those customers seeking this type of snowmobile, since competitors are not offering it. But before making this decision, the management has to be sure that (1) it is technically feasible to build a large/fast snowmobile, (2) it is economically feasible to build a large/fast snowmobile at the planned price level, and (3) a sufficient number of buyers prefer a large/fast snowmobile. If the answers are all positive, the company has discovered a "hole" in the market and should move to fill it.

Suppose, however, management decides there is more profit potential and less risk in building a small/fast snowmobile to compete with competitor A. In this case, it would study A's snowmobile and seek a way to differentiate its offer in the eyes of potential buyers. It can develop its competitive positioning on product features, style, quality, price, and other dimensions.

Once management decides on its positioning strategy, it can turn to the task of developing its detailed marketing mix. If the company decides to take the high-price/high-quality position in this market segment, it must develop superior product features and quality, seek retailers who have an excellent reputation for service, develop advertising that appeals to affluent buyers, limit sales promotion to tasteful presentations, and so on.

The company's fundamental decision on which market segment to target determines its competitors. The company then makes a decision on competitive positioning. This decision, in turn, allows it to plan the details of its marketing mix. We can now focus on marketing mix planning, the subject of the next nine chapters of this book.

Summary

Sellers can take three approaches to a market. Mass marketing is the decision to mass-produce and mass-distribute one product and attempt to attract all kinds of buyers. Product differentiation is the decision to produce two or more products that have different features, styles, quality, sizes, and so on, in order to offer variety to the market and distinguish the seller's products from competitors' products. Target marketing is the decision to distinguish the different groups that make up a market and to develop appropriate products and marketing mixes for each target market. Sellers today are moving away from mass marketing and product differentiation toward target marketing because the latter is more helpful in spotting market opportunities and developing more effective products and marketing mixes.

The key steps in target marketing are market segmentation, market targeting, and market positioning. Market segmentation is the act of dividing a market into distinct groups of buyers who might need separate products and/or marketing mixes. The marketer tries different ways to find the best segmentation opportunities. For consumer marketing, the major segmentation variables are geographic, demographic, psychographic, and behavioristic. Industrial markets can be segmented by end user, customer size, and geographic location. The effectiveness of the segmentation analysis depends upon arriving at segments that are measurable, accessible, substantial, and actionable.

Next, the seller has to target the best market segment(s). The first decision is how many segments to cover. The seller can ignore segment differences (undifferentiated marketing), develop different market offers for several segments (differentiated marketing), or go after one or a few market segments (concentrated marketing). Much depends on a company's resources, product and market homogeneity, product life-cycle stage, and competitive marketing strategies.

If the company decides to enter one segment, which one should it be? Market segments can be evaluated on their intrinsic attractiveness and on company business strengths needed to succeed in that market segment.

Market selection then defines the company's competitors and positioning possibilities. The company researches the competitors' positions and decides whether to take a position similar to that of some competitor or go after a hole in the market. If the company positions itself near another competitor, it must seek further differentiation through product features and price/quality differences. Its decision on positioning will then enable it to take the next step, namely, planning the details of the marketing mix.

Questions for Discussion

1. When the Cadillac Cimarron was introduced, Cadillac officials said that even if they sold every car, they would consider the Cimarron a disaster if it had been sold only to traditional customers. The Cadillac merchandising director said: "Our salespeople will tell some buyers, 'This car isn't for you.'" Explain this sales rationale in terms of market segmentation.

2. What three stages do sellers move through in their approach to a market? Relate these to the Ford Motor Company.
3. After the market segmentation process has been completed, the organization should begin developing the marketing mix factors. Comment.
4. Besides age and sex, what other demographic segmentation variables are used by the brewery industry? Explain. Also, identify major benefit segments in the beer market.
5. If you were a manager of a mass transit company, how would you use benefit segmentation to appeal to potential riders?
6. Give specific examples of marketers who have been successful in segmenting their markets on each of the following bases: low price, high quality, and service.
7. Has Wendy's International hamburger chain met the requirements for effective segmentation? Why?
8. Differentiated marketing is always the best approach to target marketing. Comment.
9. If Levi's were considering adding a new line of women's skirts for casual wear, how would it go about the market segmentation and target marketing process?

Key Terms in Chapter 7

Concentrated marketing Focusing marketing efforts on a large share of one or a few submarkets, rather than going after a small share of a large market.

Differentiated marketing Operating in several segments of the market and designing separate offers for each.

Market positioning The act of creating a competitive positioning for the product and a detailed marketing mix.

Market segmentation The act of dividing a market into distinct groups of buyers who might need separate products and/or marketing mixes.

Market targeting The act of evaluating and selecting the market segments to enter.

Mass marketing Mass production, mass distribution, and mass promotion of one product to all buyers.

Product-differentiated marketing Producing two or more products that exhibit different features, styles, quality, sizes, and so on.

Target marketing Distinguishing between market segments, selecting one or more of these segments, and developing products and marketing mixes for each.

Undifferentiated marketing Going after the whole market with one market offer, rather than focusing on one segment.

Cases for Chapter 7

Case 5   Maytag Co: Microwave Ovens (p. 498)

What market segment would be interested in a Maytag microwave oven? How could Maytag position its microwave oven against competitors' microwave ovens? This case looks at these questions.

Case 6   American Cyanamid Co. (p. 499)

What organizational target markets would be interested in the Cyalume light stick? This case suggests answers to that question.

Chapter 8

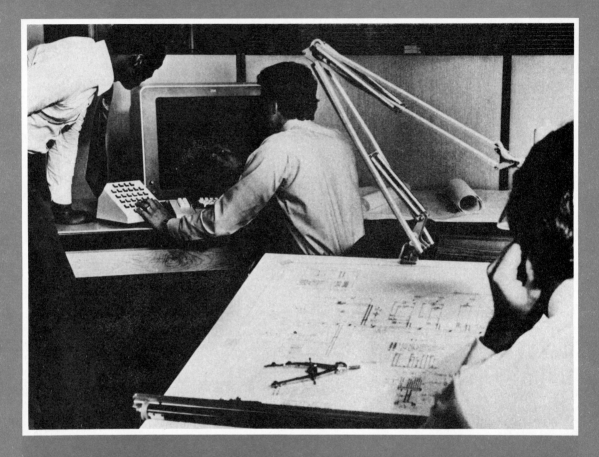

Designing Products: Products, Brands, Packaging, and Services

Objectives

After reading this chapter, you should be able to:

1. Define product and the major classifications of products.
2. Explain why companies use brands.
3. Describe the roles of a product's packaging and label.
4. Discuss how companies develop product lines.

When is a lipstick more than a lipstick? When an Avon lady sits in your living room and sells it to you! The world's largest seller of cosmetics knows that when the customer buys lipstick, she is buying more than lip color. No doubt a crucial element of Avon's success is a high-quality product. But why buy Avon and not Revlon, which also makes a high-quality product?

The Avon lady is one of the reasons. The Avon lady brings to the buyer many benefits: convenience, a break from routine, conversation, personal attention, help on how to look better, and even a friend. Avon's product is all of these things, and no other major cosmetics firm makes a similar offer. Avon markets its wares through an army of 680,000 Avon representatives who call on over 85 million households in the United States and seventeen other countries. Most reps are married women who work part time to supplement their husband's income. They sell their products to other homemakers whose needs they understand. Suburban homemakers in the middle-income bracket are the majority of Avon's customers.

Avon maintains strong morale among its sales force through sales training, sales meetings to demonstrate new products, and internal incentive programs, such as prizes and contests. The sales force is organized into five levels. A general manager oversees two regional managers. Each regional manager supervises eight divisional managers, each of whom supervises eighteen district managers. A district manager is responsible for recruiting, training, and supervising approximately 150 Avon representatives.

Courtesy Avon

The typical Avon representative works fifteen hours a week and earns about $1,400 a year, before expenses, on about $3,500 of sales. She gets a commission varying between 25% and 40% and also receives a flat fee of $7.50 for each new Avon representative she recruits. There is a great turnover of salespeople because many Avon representatives work until they can accumulate enough cash to make some major purchase.

Avon's product line is highly diversified—thirteen hundred products, including cosmetics, jewelry, and household items. If a customer says that she uses Revlon lipstick, the representative can turn to jewelry or household items and make a sale. A strong purchase incentive is the Avon money-back guarantee if the customer is not satisfied with the product.

Avon supplies its salespeople with a handsome color catalog. The customer can browse this catalog, which lists a few hundred products. The company also runs specials throughout the year to stimulate sales and reduce inventories.

One of the most interesting Avon features is the packaging. The packages are attractive and often double as reusable containers, such as mugs or salt and pepper shakers. Many Avon containers have become collector's items. Packaging is so important that Avon redesigns its packaging for over one-third of its products each year. Avon's salespeople provide continuous feedback to Avon's management about customer satisfaction, complaints, and needs. And when Avon tests new products, they are first tested with Avon's own representatives before being sold to customers.

Clearly, a lipstick is more than a lipstick when Avon sells it. Avon's exceptional success in the rough-and-tumble cosmetics world is based on developing an innovative product concept. Constructing an effective product concept is the first step in marketing mix planning.

This chapter begins with the question, What is a product? It turns out that "product" is a complex concept that has to be carefully defined. We will then look at ways to classify the multitude of products found in consumer and industrial markets, hoping to find links between appropriate marketing strategies and types of products. Next, we will recognize that each product can be turned into a brand, which involves several decisions. The product can also be packaged and labeled, and, in addition, various customer services can be offered. Finally, we will move from decisions about individual products to decisions the company must make in building its product lines and product mixes.

What Is a Product?

A Wilson tennis racquet, a Vidal Sassoon haircut, a Rolling Stones concert, a Club Med vacation, a two-ton stake truck, Head skis, and a telephone answering service are all products. We define product as follows:

A **product** is anything that can be offered to a market for attention, acquisition, use, or consumption that might satisfy a want or need. It includes physical objects, services, persons, places, organizations, and ideas.

We also need to define product item:

A **product item** is a distinct unit that is distinguishable by size, price, appearance, or some other attribute. Toothpaste, for example, is a product. A $1.29 tube of Colgate Winter-Fresh Gel is a product item.[1]

Core, Actual, and Augmented Products

In developing a product, the product planner needs to think about the product on three levels. The most fundamental level is the *core product,* which answers the question, What is the buyer really buying? Every product is really the packaging of a problem-solving service. A woman buying lipstick is not simply buying lip color. Charles Revson of Revlon, Inc., recognized this early: "In the factory, we make cosmetics; in the store, we sell hope." Theodore Levitt pointed out that "purchasing agents do not buy quarter-inch drills; they buy quarter-inch holes." And supersalesman Elmer Wheeler would say, "Don't sell the steak—sell the sizzle." The marketer's job is to uncover the needs hiding under every product and to sell benefits, not features. The core product stands at the center of the total product, as illustrated in figure 8-1.

The product planner has to turn the core product into an *actual product.* Lipsticks, computers, educational seminars, and political candidates are all actual products. Actual products may have as many as five characteristics: a quality level, features, styling, a brand name, and packaging.

Finally, the product planner may offer additional services and benefits that make up an *augmented product.* Avon's augmented product includes personal attention, delivery, money-back guarantee, and so on. IBM's success is partly traceable to skillful augmentation of its actual product—the computer. While its competitors were busy selling computer features to buyers, IBM recognized that customers were more interested in solutions, not hardware. Customers wanted instruction, canned software programs, programming services, quick repairs, guarantees, and so on. IBM sold a system, not just a computer.[2]

Product augmentation leads the marketer to look at the buyer's total consumption system: "The way a purchaser of a product performs the total task of whatever it is that he or she is trying to accomplish when using the product."[3] In this way, the marketer will recognize many opportunities for augmenting its offer in a competitively effective way. According to Levitt:

The *new* competition is not between what companies produce in their factories, but between what they add to their factory output in the form of packaging, services, advertising, customer advice, financing, delivery arrangements, warehousing, and other things that people value.[4]

A firm should search for satisfactory ways to augment its product offer.

FIGURE 8-1

Three Levels of
Product

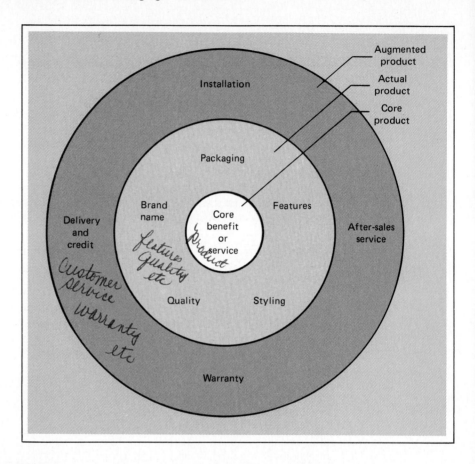

Product Classifications

In seeking marketing strategies for individual products, marketers have developed several product classifications based on product characteristics.

**Durable
Goods,
Nondurable
Goods, and
Services**

Products can be classified into three groups according to their durability or tangibility:[5]

Durable goods are tangible goods that normally survive many uses. Examples include refrigerators, machine tools, and clothing.

Nondurable goods are tangible goods that normally are consumed in one or a few uses. Examples include beer, soap, and salt.

Services are activities, benefits, or satisfactions that are offered for sale. Examples include haircuts and repairs.

(Because of the growing importance of services in our society, their marketing will be examined in chapter 19.)

Consumer Goods Classification

Consumers buy a vast number of goods. A useful way to classify these goods is on the basis of consumer shopping habits. We can distinguish among convenience, shopping, specialty, and unsought goods (see figure 8-2).[6]

Cheap & frequently

Convenience goods are goods that the customer usually purchases frequently, immediately, and with the minimum of effort in comparison buying. Examples include tobacco products, soap, and newspapers. *bread milk*

Convenience goods can be further divided into staples, impulse goods, and emergency goods. *Staples* are goods that consumers purchase on a regular basis. For example, one buyer might routinely purchase Heinz ketchup, Crest toothpaste, and Ritz crackers. *Impulse goods* are purchased without any planning or searching. These goods are normally available in many places because consumers seldom look specifically for them. Thus candy bars and magazines are placed next to checkout counters because shoppers may not have thought of buying them. *Emergency goods* are purchased when a need is urgent—umbrellas during a rainstorm, boots and shovels during the first winter snowstorm. Manufacturers of emergency goods will place them in many outlets to avoid losing the sale when the customer needs these goods.

shop around for car, tv

Shopping goods are goods that the customer, in the process of selection and purchase, characteristically compares on such bases as suitability, quality, price, and style. Examples include furniture, clothing, used cars, and major appliances.

Shopping goods can be divided into *like* and *unlike goods*. The buyer sees like shopping goods as being similar in quality but different enough in price to justify shopping comparisons. The seller has to "talk price" with the buyer. But in shopping for clothing, furniture, and more unlike goods, product features are often more important to the consumer than the price. If the buyer wants a pin-striped suit, the cut, fit, and look are likely to be more important than small price differences. The seller of unlike shopping goods must therefore carry a wide assortment to satisfy individual tastes and must have well-trained sales personnel to provide information and advice to customers.

Specialty goods are goods with unique characteristics and/or brand identification for which a significant group of buyers is habitually willing to make a special purchase effort. Examples include specific brands and types

FIGURE 8-2

Classification of Consumer Goods

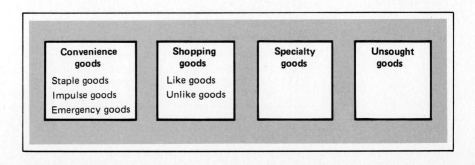

Convenience goods	Shopping goods	Specialty goods	Unsought goods
Staple goods	Like goods		
Impulse goods	Unlike goods		
Emergency goods			

[handwritten marginalia: go out of your way to buy the product]

of fancy goods, cars, stereo components, photographic equipment, and men's suits.

A Mercedes, for example, is a specialty good because buyers are willing to travel a great distance to buy a Mercedes. Specialty goods do not involve the buyer's making comparisons; the buyer only invests time to reach the dealers carrying the wanted products. The dealers do not need convenient locations; however, they must let prospective buyers know their locations.

[handwritten marginalia: dormant desire that needs to be stimulated]

Unsought goods are goods that the consumer does not know about or knows about but does not normally think of buying. New products such as smoke detectors and food processors are unsought goods until the consumer is made aware of them through advertising. The classic examples of known but unsought goods are life insurance, cemetery plots, gravestones, and encyclopedias.

By their very nature, unsought goods require a lot of marketing effort in the form of advertising and personal selling. Some of the most sophisticated personal-selling techniques have developed out of the challenge of selling unsought goods.

Industrial Goods Classification

Organizations buy a vast variety of goods and services. Industrial goods can be classified in terms of how they enter the production process and their relative costliness. We can distinguish three groups: materials and parts, capital items, and supplies and services (see figure 8-3).

[handwritten marginalia: designs marketing mix]

Materials and parts are goods that enter the manufacturer's product completely. They fall into two classes: raw materials and manufactured materials and parts.

Raw materials include farm products (such as wheat, cotton, livestock, fruits and vegetables) and natural products (such as fish, lumber, crude petroleum, iron ore). Each is marketed somewhat differently. Farm products are supplied by many small producers, who turn them over to marketing intermediaries, who

FIGURE 8-3

Classification of Industrial Goods

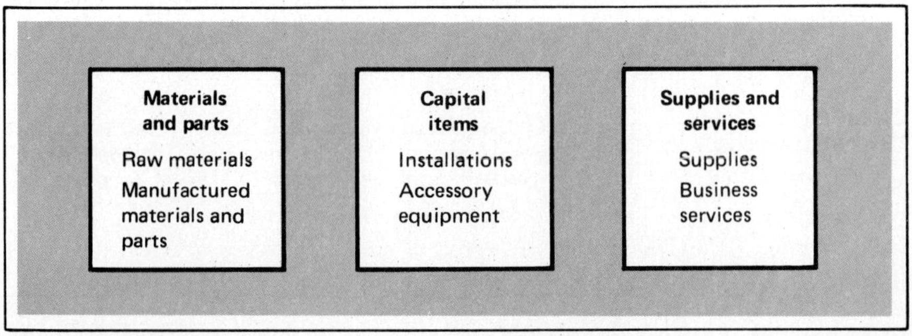

Materials and parts	Capital items	Supplies and services
Raw materials	Installations	Supplies
Manufactured materials and parts	Accessory equipment	Business services

provide assembly, grading, storage, transportation, and selling services. The supply of farm products is somewhat expandable in the long run, but not in the short run. Farm products are perishable and their seasonal nature gives rise to special marketing practices. They are rarely advertised and promoted, but from time to time, producers will launch campaigns to promote the consumption of their product—such as potatoes, prunes, or milk. And some producers even brand their product—such as Sunkist oranges and Chiquita bananas.

Natural products are highly limited in supply. They usually have great bulk and low unit value and require substantial transportation in moving them from producer to user. There are fewer and larger producers, who tend to market them directly to industrial users. Because the users depend on these materials, long-term supply contracts are common. The likeness of natural materials limits the amount of promotional activity. Price and supplier reliability are the major factors influencing the selection of suppliers.

Manufactured materials and parts are either component materials (such as iron, yarn, cement, wires) or component parts (such as small motors, tires, castings). Component materials are usually used further—for example, pig iron is made into steel and yarn is woven into cloth. The likeness of component materials usually means that price and supplier reliability are the most important purchase factors. Component parts enter the finished product completely with no further change in form, as when small motors are put into vacuum cleaners and tires are added on automobiles. Most manufactured materials and parts are sold directly to industrial users, with orders often placed a year or more in advance. Price and service are the major marketing considerations, and branding and advertising tend to be less important.

Capital items are goods that enter the finished product partly. They include two groups: installations and accessory equipment.

Installations consist of buildings (such as factories and offices) and fixed equipment (such as generators, drill presses, computers, elevators). Installations are major purchases. They are usually bought directly from the producer. The producers use a top-notch sales force, which often includes sales engineers. The producers have to be willing to design to specification and to supply postsale services. Advertising is used but is much less important than personal selling.

Accessory equipment comprises portable factory equipment and tools (such as hand tools, lift trucks) and office equipment (such as typewriters, desks). These types of equipment do not become part of the finished product. They simply aid in the production process. They have a shorter life than installations but a longer life than operating supplies. Some accessory equipment manufacturers sell directly to customers. More often they use middlemen because the market is geographically dispersed, the buyers are numerous, and the orders are small. Quality, features, price, and service are major considerations in supplier selection. The sales force tends to be more important than advertising, although the latter can be used effectively.

Supplies and services are items that do not enter the finished product at all.

Supplies are of two kinds: operating supplies (such as lubricants, coal, typing paper, pencils) and maintenance and repair items (such as paint, nails, brooms). Supplies are the equivalent of convenience goods in the industrial field because they are usually purchased with minimum effort on a straight rebuy basis. They are normally marketed through intermediaries because of the great number of customers, their geographic dispersion, and the low unit value of these goods. Price and service are important considerations because suppliers are quite standardized and brand preference is not high.

Business services include maintenance and repair services (such as window cleaning, typewriter repair) and business advisory services (such as legal, management consulting, advertising). Maintenance and repair services are usually supplied under contract. Maintenance services are often provided by small producers, and repair services are often available from the manufacturers of the original equipment. Business advisory services are normally new-task-buying situations, and the industrial buyer will choose the supplier on the basis of the supplier's reputation and personnel.

Thus we see that a product's characteristics will have a major influence on marketing strategy. At the same time, marketing strategy will also depend on such factors as the number of competitors, the degree of market segmentation, and the condition of the economy.

Brand Decisions

In developing a marketing strategy for individual products, the seller has to make decisions about branding. Branding can add value to a product and is therefore an important aspect of product strategy.

First, we should become familiar with the language of branding. Here are some key definitions:[7]

Brand is a name, term, sign, symbol, or design, or a combination of them, which is intended to identify the goods or services of one seller or group of sellers and to differentiate them from those of competitors.

Brand name is that part of a brand which can be vocalized—the utterable. Examples are Avon, Chevrolet, Disneyland, American Express, and UCLA.

Brand mark is that part of a brand which can be recognized but is not utterable, such as a symbol, design, or distinctive coloring or lettering. Examples are the Playboy bunny and the Metro-Goldwyn-Mayer lion.

Trademark is a brand or a part of a brand that is given legal protection. A trademark protects the seller's exclusive rights to use the brand name and/or brand mark.

Copyright is the exclusive right to reproduce, publish, and sell the matter and form of a literary, musical, or artistic work.

Here are some well-known brand marks.

Whirlpool brand mark used with permission of Whirlpool Corporation; Volkswagen brand mark used with permission of Volkswagen of America, Inc.

Branding Decision

The first decision is whether the company should put a brand name on its product. Historically, most products went unbranded. Producers and middlemen sold their goods directly out of barrels, bins, and cases, without any supplier identification. In the United States, the earliest brand promoters were the patent medicine makers. The real growth of product branding occurred after the Civil War with the growth of national firms and national advertising media. Some of the early brands still survive, such as Borden's Condensed Milk, Quaker Oats, Vaseline, and Ivory Soap.

Branding has grown so strong that today hardly anything goes unbranded. Salt is packaged in distinctive manufacturers' containers, oranges are stamped with growers' names, common nuts and bolts are packaged in cellophane with a distributor's label, and automobile components—spark plugs, tires, filters—bear brand names that differ from those of the automakers. Even chicken has been branded successfully:[8]

> Frank Perdue of Perdue Farms, Salisbury, Maryland, has converted a basic agricultural commodity into a branded product. Many consumers on the East Coast insist on a Perdue chicken. Perdue spends about $1 million annually on television and radio commercials where he touts the merits of his chickens. His theme is "It takes a tough man to make a tender chicken," and he offers a money-back guarantee to dissatisfied customers.

Recently there has been a return to "no branding" of certain staple consumer goods and pharmaceuticals. These "generics" are plainly packaged with no producer identification (see exhibit 8-1). The intent of generics is to bring down the cost to the consumer by saving on packaging and advertising. Thus the issue of branding versus no branding is very much alive today.

Brand Sponsor Decision

In deciding to brand a product, the producer has three options. The product may be launched as a manufacturer's brand (also called a national brand). Or the manufacturer may sell the product to middlemen who put on a private brand (also called middlemen brand, distributor brand, or dealer brand). Or the manufacturer may make some products to sell under its own name and some that are to be sold under private labels. Kellogg's, International Harvester, and IBM produce virtually all of their output under their own brand names. Warwick Electronics produces virtually all of its output under various distributors' names, such as Sears. Whirlpool makes products both under its own name and under distributors' names.

Manufacturers' brands tend to dominate the American scene. Consider such well-known brands as Campbell's soup and Heinz ketchup. In recent times, however, large retailers and wholesalers have developed their own brands. The private-label tires of Sears and J. C. Penney are as well known today as are the manufacturers' brands of Goodyear, Goodrich, and Firestone. Sears has created several names—Diehard batteries, Craftsman tools, Kenmore appliances—that consumers look for and demand; over 90% of Sears's products are sold under its own labels. A&P has created different private labels for its canned goods, and they account for over 25% of its sales. An increasing number of department stores, service stations, clothiers, drugstores, and appliance dealers are launching private labels.

Exhibit **8-1**

A Food Chain Adds a Generic Line of Items

In late 1978, Dominick's Finer Foods, a large Chicago-based supermarket chain, introduced a forty-item "generic" line. Generics are unbranded, plainly packaged, less expensive versions of common products purchased in supermarkets, such as spaghetti, paper towels, and peaches. They offer standard or lower quality at a price that may be as much as 30% lower than that of nationally advertised brands and 15% lower than that of private labels. The lower price is made possible by lower-quality ingredients, lower-cost labeling and packaging, and minimal advertising.

A year earlier the Jewel Food Stores, another large Chicago-based chain, had introduced a forty-item generic line, which has now been expanded to 140 generics and accounts for approximately 4% of Jewel's sales. Jewel's success with generics forced Dominick's hand.

The price savings of generics have strong pocketbook appeal to American consumers in this age of high inflation. A Nielsen survey indicated that 59% of shoppers are aware of generic products. Of those aware, 44% have already purchased them, and 70% would purchase them again. Demographic profiles of consumers who purchase generics reveal large families, high income, college education, and an average age bracket of 35 to 45.

Four out of five shoppers believe that the lower prices result from the reduced advertising expenditures and the simple packaging. Only one out of five shoppers believes that the lower cost is related to lower quality. Yet lower quality is one of the major factors. For example, the paper towels may be less absorbent, and the detergent may lack perfume. Yet consumers are impressed by the savings, and generics, such as paper products, peanut butter, preserves, canned vegetables, and tomato products, have especially won their acceptance. The smallest impact has been in household product categories, such as detergents, fabric softeners, and liquid bleach.

The group most threatened by generics are those national brand companies that produce the weaker brands. Why pay 30% more for a branded item when its quality is not noticeably different from that of its generic cousin?

Sources: Compiled by the author from miscellaneous sources, including "Generic Groceries Keep Adding Market Share," *Marketing News,* February 23, 1979, p. 16; George Lazarus, "Generic Label Carving Place on Grocery Shelf," *Chicago Tribune,* May 9, 1979, Business section; and "Buyers Mix Generics, Quality," *Advertising Age,* August 20, 1979, p. 3.

Brand Quality Decision In developing a brand, the producer has to choose a quality level and other attributes that will support the brand's position in the target market. Quality is one of the marketer's major positioning tools. Quality stands for the rated ability of the brand to perform its functions. Quality includes the product's durability, reliability, precision, ease of operation and repair, and other valued attributes. Some of these attributes can be measured objectively. From a marketing point of view, quality should be measured in terms of buyèrs' perceptions of quality.

The theme of quality is now attracting stronger interest among consumers and companies. American consumers have been impressed with the product quality found in Japanese automobiles and electronics and in European automobiles, clothing, and food. Many consumers are favoring apparel that lasts and stays in style longer, instead of trendy clothes. They are showing more interest in fresh and nutritious foods, cheeses, and gourmet items, and less interest in soft drinks, sweets, and TV dinners. A number of companies are catering to this growing interest in quality, but much more can be done.[9]

Family Brand Decision Producers who brand their product will face several more choices. At least four brand-name strategies can be distinguished:

1. *Individual brand names:* This policy is followed by Procter & Gamble (Tide, Bold, Dash, Cheer, Gain, Oxydol, Duz) and Genesco, Inc. (Jarman, Mademoiselle, Johnson & Murphy, and Cover Girl).
2. *A blanket family name for all products:* This policy is followed by Heinz and General Electric.
3. *Separate family names for all products:* This policy is followed by Sears (Kenmore for appliances, Kerrybrook for women's clothing, and Homart for major home installations).
4. *Company trade name combined with individual product names:* This policy is followed by Kellogg's (Kellogg's Rice Krispies and Kellogg's Raisin Bran).

What are the advantages of an individual brand-name strategy? A major advantage is that the company does not tie its reputation to one product's acceptance. If one product fails, it does not hurt the company's name.

Using a blanket family name for all products also has some advantages. The cost of introducing the product will be less, because there is no need for heavy

Kellogg's uses a family brand strategy that combines its own name with that of each individual cereal.
©1983 Kellogg Company

Exhibit **8-2**

What's in a Name? Lots if the Name Is Jell-O!

Several years ago marketers at General Foods became concerned about the slowed growth in the sales of both their Jell-O gelatin and Jell-O pudding products. One explanation for the slowed growth was that consumers had less time for making desserts; another was that people had become more concerned about their weight and didn't want to add the extra calories that desserts contain.

General Foods came up with solutions to both these problems in a new product called Jell-O Pudding Pops. The product is a frozen pudding on a stick available in chocolate, vanilla, and banana flavors. Because no preparation time is required, the dessert is convenient for consumers who wouldn't have time to prepare a pudding or gelatin. For those counting calories, this product contains almost 60% fewer calories than an ice-cream bar of the same size.

The Jell-O brand name is an additional attraction for consumers, as it is an already familiar one. To stress this familiarity, General Foods has used Bill Cosby, a personality associated with other Jell-O products, in its TV and magazine advertisements for Pudding Pops. A number of other companies have tried to develop similar pops. According to one competitor, the Jell-O product will be superior to most others because it is backed by extensive experience with pudding. General Foods believes that consumers will also view the product as superior because of the other products connected with its brand name. The Jell-O name has given General Foods an entry into an entirely new area of business: frozen confections.

Advertising and promoting Pudding Pops has cost $25 million. But this expense has produced big profits. In the product's first year, sales totaled $65 million. So successful is the product that General Foods plans to use its valuable name on other frozen desserts, including Gelatin Pops, whipped frozen gelatin on a stick. Not only has the Jell-O name helped the success of a new product, but Pudding Pops have also revitalized General Foods's Jell-O brand.

Source: Based on "General Foods Gets a Winner with Its Jell-O Pudding Pops," *Wall Street Journal*, March 10, 1983, p. 33.

advertising expenditures to create brand-name recognition and preference. Furthermore, sales will be strong if the manufacturer's name is good. Thus Campbell's introduces new soups under its brand name with extreme simplicity and instant recognition. General Foods is using its Jell-O brand to introduce new products, as can be seen in exhibit 8-2.

Where a company produces quite different products, it may not be appropriate to use one blanket family name. Swift & Company developed separate family names for its hams (Premium) and fertilizers (Vigoro). When Mead Johnson developed a diet supplement for *gaining* weight, it created a new family name, Nutriment, to avoid confusion with its family brand for weight-*reducing* products, Metrecal. Companies will often invent different family brand names for different quality lines within the same product class. Thus A&P sells a first-grade, second-grade, and third-grade set of brands—Ann Page, Sultana, and Iona, respectively.

Finally, some manufacturers want to associate their company name along with an individual brand name for each product. The company name legitimizes, and the individual name individualizes, the new product. Thus *Quaker Oats* in the product name Quaker Oats Cap'n Crunch taps the company's reputation in the breakfast cereal field, and *Cap'n Crunch* individualizes and dramatizes the new product.

The brand name should not be chosen casually but should help to reinforce the product concept. Among the desirable qualities for a brand name are: (1) It should suggest something about the product's benefits. Examples: Coldspot, Beautyrest, Craftsman, Accutron. (2) It should suggest product qualities such as action or color. Examples: Duz, Sunkist, Spic and Span, Firebird. (3) It should be easy to pronounce, recognize, and remember. Short names help. Examples: Tide, Crest, Puffs. (4) It should be distinctive. Examples: Mustang, Kodak, Exxon.

Many firms strive to build a unique brand name that will eventually become identified with the product category. Such brand names as Frigidaire, Kleenex, Levi's, Jell-O, Scotch tape, and Xerox have succeeded in this way. However, their very success may threaten the exclusive rights to the name. Cellophane and shredded wheat are now names in the common domain.

Brand Extension Decision

A successful brand name can be extended. We define brand extension strategy as follows:

A **brand extension strategy** is any effort to use a successful brand name to launch product modifications or new products.

After Quaker Oats's success with Cap'n Crunch dry breakfast cereal, it used the brand name and cartoon character to launch a line of ice-cream bars, T-shirts, and other products. Armour used its Dial brand name to launch a variety of new products that would not easily have obtained distribution without the strength of the Dial name. Honda Motor Company used its name to launch its new power lawn mower. Brand extension saves the producer the high cost of promoting new names and creates instant brand recognition of the new product. At the same time, if the new product fails to satisfy, it may hurt consumers' attitudes toward the other products carrying the same brand name.[10]

Multibrand Decision

Multibrand strategy is the seller's development of two or more brands in the same product category. This marketing practice was pioneered by P&G when it introduced Cheer detergent as a competitor for its already successful Tide. Although Tide's sales dropped slightly, the combined sales of Cheer and Tide were higher. P&G now produces eight detergent brands.

Manufacturers adopt multibrand strategies for several reasons. First, manufacturers can gain more shelf space in stores to hold their products. Second, few consumers are so loyal to a brand that they will not try another. The only way to capture the "brand switcher" is to offer several brands. Third, creating new brands develops excitement and efficiency within the manufacturer's organization. Managers in P&G and General Motors compete to outperform each other. Fourth, a multibrand strategy positions the different benefits and appeals, and each brand can attract a separate following.[11]

Important

Packaging Decisions

Make lousy product look good

Many physical products offered to the market have to be packaged. Packaging can play a minor role (such as inexpensive hardware items) or a major role (such as cosmetics). Some packages—such as the Coca-Cola bottle and the L'eggs container—are world famous. Many marketers have called packaging a fifth *P*, along with price, product, place, and promotion. Most marketers, however, treat packaging as an element of product strategy.

Packaging is the activities of designing and producing the container or wrapper for a product.

The container or wrapper is called the package. The package may include up to three levels of material. The primary package is the product's immediate container. Thus the bottle holding Old Spice After-Shave Lotion is the primary package. The secondary package refers to the material that protects the primary package and which is discarded when the product is about to be used. Thus the cardboard box containing the bottle of after-shave lotion is a secondary package

Simple, classic, and attractive packaging helps create an image for a line of cosmetics.

and provides additional protection and promotion opportunity. The shipping package refers to packaging necessary for storage, identification, or transportation. Thus a corrugated box carrying six dozen bottles of Old Spice After-Shave Lotion is a shipping package. Finally, labeling is part of packaging and consists of printed information appearing on or with the package that describes the product.

Packages go back to the dawn of history. Primitive peoples used animal skins and grass baskets to carry wild berries and other fruit from the forests to their caves. Eight thousand years ago the Chinese developed a variety of earthenware containers for holding solid and liquid objects. The ancient Egyptians developed glass containers for holding liquids. By the Middle Ages, packaging materials included leather, cloth, wood, stone, earthenware, and glass. For centuries, packaging was provided to hold, protect, and transport goods.

In recent times, packaging has become a strong marketing tool. Well-designed packages can create convenience value for consumers and promotional value for producers. Various factors have contributed to packaging's growing use as a marketing tool:

1. *Self-service.* An increasing number of products are sold on a self-service basis in supermarkets and discount houses. The package must now perform many of the sales tasks. It must attract attention, describe the product's features, give the consumer confidence, and make a favorable impression.
2. *Consumer affluence.* Rising consumer affluence means that consumers are willing to pay a little more for the convenience, appearance, dependability, and prestige of better packages.
3. *Company and brand image.* Companies are recognizing the power of well-designed packages to contribute to instant consumer recognition of the company or brand. Every film buyer immediately recognizes the familiar yellow packaging of Kodak film.
4. *Innovational opportunity.* Innovative packaging can bring large benefits to producers. Uneeda Biscuit's innovation in 1899 of a stay-fresh unit package (paperboard, inner paper wrap, and paper overwrap) helped to prolong the shelf life of crackers better than the old cracker boxes, bins, and barrels could. Kraft's development of processed cheese in tins extended cheese's shelf life and earned Kraft a reputation for reliability. Today Kraft is testing retort pouches, which are foil-and-plastic containers, as a successor to cans. The first companies to put their soft drinks in pop-top cans and their liquid sprays in aerosol containers attracted many new customers. Now wine makers are experimenting with pop-top cans and bag-in-the-carton forms of packaging.

Developing an effective package for a new product requires a large number of decisions. The first task is to establish a packaging concept. The packaging concept is a definition of what the package should basically be or do for the particular product. Should the main function(s) of the package be to offer superior product protection, introduce a novel dispensing method, suggest certain qualities about the product or the company, or something else?

General Foods developed a new dog-food product in the form of meatlike patties. Management decided that the unique and palatable appearance of these patties demanded maximum visibility. Visibility was defined as the basic packaging concept, and management considered alternatives in this light. It finally narrowed down the choice to a tray with a film covering.[12]

Decisions must be made on further elements of package design—size, shape, materials, color, text, and brand mark. Decisions must be made between much text and little text, between cellophane and other transparent films, between a plastic tray and a laminated tray, and so on. The various packaging elements must be coordinated. Size suggests certain things about materials, colors, and so forth. The packaging elements must also be coordinated with decisions on pricing, advertising, and other marketing elements.

After the packaging has been designed, it must be put through a number of tests. Engineering tests are conducted to ensure that the package stands up under normal conditions; visual tests, to ensure that the script is legible and the colors coordinated; dealer tests, to ensure that dealers find the package attractive and easy to handle; and consumer tests, to ensure favorable consumer response.

In spite of these precautions, a packaging design occasionally gets through with some basic flaw:

> Sizzl-Spray, a pressurized can of barbeque sauce developed by Heublein, . . . had a potential packaging disaster that was discovered in the market tests. . . . "We thought we had a good can, but fortunately we first test marketed the product in stores in Texas and California. It appears as soon as the cans got warm they began to explode. Because we hadn't gotten into national distribution, our loss was only $150,000 instead of a couple of million."[13]

Developing effective packaging for a new product may cost a few hundred thousand dollars and take from a few months to a year. The importance of packaging cannot be overemphasized, considering the several functions it performs in attracting and satisfying customers. Companies must pay attention, however, to the growing societal concerns about packaging and make decisions that serve society's interests as well as immediate customer and company objectives (see exhibit 8-3).

Labeling Decisions

Sellers will also design labels for their products, which may be a simple tag attached to the product or an elaborately designed graphic that is part of the package. The label might carry only the brand name or a great deal of information. Even if the seller prefers a simple label, the law may require additional information.

Labels perform several functions, and the seller has to decide which ones to

FIGURE 8-4

The Functions of Labels

This label identifies the product through the use of the well-known "V-8" brand name and promotes the product through its attractive graphic design. It also provides a list of ingredients, nutritional information, the name and address of the maker, instructions for use, and a guarantee.

Used by permission of Campbell Soup Company.

use. At the very least the label *identifies* the product or brand, such as the name Sunkist stamped on oranges. The label might also *grade* the product; thus canned peaches are grade-labeled A, B, and C. The label might *describe* several things about the product: who made it, where it was made, when it was made, its contents, how it is to be used, and how to use it safely. Finally, the label might *promote* the product through its attractive graphics. Some writers distinguish between identification labels, grade labels, descriptive labels, and promotional labels.

Labels of well-known brands seem old-fashioned after a while and need freshening up. The label on Ivory Soap has been redone eighteen times since the 1890s, with gradual changes in the letters' size and script. On the other hand, the label on Orange Crush soft drink was substantially changed when its competitors' labels began to picture fresh fruits and pull in more sales. Orange Crush developed a label with new symbols to suggest freshness and used stronger and deeper colors.

There has been a long history of legal concerns about labels. Labels could mislead customers or fail to describe important ingredients or fail to include sufficient safety warnings. As a result, several federal and state laws regulate labeling, the most prominent being the Fair Packaging and Labeling Act of 1966. Labeling practices have been affected in recent times by unit pricing (stating the price per unit of standard measure), open dating (stating the expected shelf life of the product), and nutritional labeling (stating the product's nutritional values). Sellers should make sure that their labels contain all the required information before launching new products.

Exhibit **8-3**

Packaging and Public Policy

Packaging is attracting more and more public attention. Marketers should heed the following issues in making their packaging decisions.

1. *Fair packaging and labeling.* The public is concerned about packaging and labeling that might be false and misleading. The Federal Trade Commission Act of 1914 held that false, misleading, or deceptive labels or packages would be considered unfair competition. Consumers have also been concerned about the confusing sizes and shapes of packages, which make price comparisons difficult. Congress passed the Fair Packaging and Labeling Act in 1966, which established mandatory labeling requirements, encouraged the adoption of additional voluntary industry-wide packaging standards, and empowered federal agencies to set packaging regulations in specific industries. The Food and Drug Administration has required processed-food producers to include nutritional labeling clearly stating the amounts of protein, fat, carbohydrates, and calories contained in the contents of the package, as well as vitamin and mineral content expressed as a percentage of the recommended daily allowance. Consumerists have lobbied for additional labeling legislation to require open dating (to describe the freshness of the product), unit pricing (to describe the cost of the item in some standard measurement unit), grade labeling (to rate the A, B, C quality level of certain consumer goods), and percentage labeling (to describe the percentage of each important ingredient).

2. *Excessive cost.* Critics have called packaging excessive in many cases,

Customer Service Decisions

Customer service is another element of product strategy. A company's product usually includes some services. The service can be a minor or a major part of the total product. In chapter 19, we discuss services as products themselves. Here we will discuss services attached to goods. The marketer faces three decisions with respect to customer services: (1) What customer services should be included? (2) What level of service should be offered? (3) In what forms should the services be provided?

The Service Mix Decision   The marketer needs to survey customers to identify the main services that might be offered and their relative importance. For example, Canadian buyers of industrial equipment ranked thirteen service elements in the following order of im-

charging that it raises prices. They point to secondary "throwaway" packaging and raise the question of its value to the consumer. They point to the fact that the package sometimes costs more than the contents; for example, Evian moisturizer consists of five ounces of natural spring water packaged in an aerosol spray selling for $5.50. Marketers retort that critics do not understand all the functions of the package and that marketers also want to keep packaging costs down.

3. *Scarce resource.* The growing concern over shortages of paper, aluminum, and other materials raises the question of whether industry should try harder to reduce its packaging. For example, the growth of nonreturnable glass containers has resulted in using up to seventeen times as much glass as compared to glass used in returnable containers. The throwaway bottle is also an energy waster, which can be ill-afforded in this time of high energy costs. Some states have passed laws prohibiting or taxing nonreturnable containers.

4. *Pollution.* As much as 40% of the total solid waste in this country is made up of discarded packages. Many packages end up in the form of broken bottles and bent cans littering the streets and countrysides. All of this packaging creates a major problem in solid waste disposal that is a huge consumer of labor and energy.

These questionable aspects of packaging have mobilized public interest in new packaging laws. Marketers must be equally concerned and must attempt to design ecological packages for their products.

portance: (1) delivery reliability, (2) prompt price quotation, (3) technical advice, (4) discounts, (5) after-sales service, (6) sales representation, (7) ease of contact, (8) replacement guarantee, (9) wide range of manufacturer, (10) pattern design, (11) credit, (12) test facilities, and (13) machining facilities.[14] These importance rankings suggest that in this market the seller should at least match competition on delivery reliability, prompt price quotation, technical advice, and other services deemed most important by customers.

But the issue of which services to offer is more subtle than this. A service can be highly important to customers and yet not determine supplier selection if all the suppliers offer the service at the same level. Consider the following example:

The Monsanto Company was seeking a way to improve its customer services mix. Customers were asked to rate Monsanto, Du Pont, and Union Carbide on several attributes. All three companies were seen by customers as offering high delivery reliability and having good sales representatives. However, none of them were viewed as rendering sufficient technical service.

Monsanto carried out a study to determine how important technical service is to chemical buyers and found out it had high importance. Monsanto then hired and trained additional technical people and launched a campaign describing itself as the leader in technical service. This gave Monsanto a different advantage in the minds of buyers seeking technical service.

The Service Level Decision Customers not only want certain services but also want them in the right amount and quality. If bank customers have to stand in long lines or confront frowning bank tellers, they might switch to another bank.

Companies need to check on their own and competitors' service levels in relation to customers' expectations. The company can spot service deficiencies through a number of devices: comparison shopping, periodic customer surveys, suggestion boxes, and complaint-handling systems. This helps the company know how it is doing and disappointed customers can get satisfaction.

The Service Form Decision Marketers must also decide on the forms in which to offer various services. The first question is, How should each service element be priced? Consider, for example, what Zenith should offer in repair services on its television sets. Zenith has three options:

1. It could offer free television repair service for a year with the sale of its set.
2. It could sell a service contract.
3. It could decide not to offer any repair services, leaving this to television repair specialists.

In addition, Zenith can provide repair services in three ways:

1. It could hire and train its own service repair people and locate them through the country.
2. It could make arrangements with distributors and dealers to provide the repair services.
3. It could leave it to independent companies to provide the necessary repair services.

For each service, various options exist. The company's decision depends on customers' preferences as well as competitors' strategies.

The Customer Service Department Given the importance of customer service as a competitive tool, many companies have established strong customer service departments, handling complaints and adjustments, credit, maintenance, technical service, and information.[15] Whirlpool, for example, has set up hot lines to handle consumer complaints. By keeping statistics on the types of complaints, the customer service department can press for desired changes in product design, quality control, high-pressure selling, and so on. It is less expensive to preserve the goodwill of existing customers than to attract new customers or woo back lost customers. Procter & Gamble lists a toll-free number on all of its products that customers can call for information and advice. All of these services should be coordinated and used as tools in creating customer satisfaction and loyalty.

Product Line Decisions

We have looked at product strategy decisions—branding, packaging, and services—at the level of the individual product. But product strategy also calls for building a product line. We define product line as follows:

> A **product line** is a group of products that are closely related, either because they function in a similar manner, are sold to the same customer groups, are marketed through the same types of outlets, or fall within a given price range.

Thus General Motors produces a line of cars, and Revlon produces a line of cosmetics.

Each product line needs a marketing strategy. Most companies assign a specific person to manage each product line. This person faces a number of tough decisions on product line length and product line featuring.

Product Line Length Decision Product line managers have to decide on product line length. The line is too short if the manager can increase profits by adding items; the line is too long if the manager can increase profits by dropping items.

The issue of product line length is influenced by company objectives. Companies that want to be known as full-line companies and/or are seeking a high market share and market growth will carry longer lines. They are less concerned when some items fail to contribute to profits. Companies that are keen on high profitability will carry shorter lines consisting of profitable items.

Product lines tend to lengthen over time.[16] A company can increase the length of its product line in two ways: by stretching its line and by filling its line.

PRODUCT LINE STRETCHING DECISION. Every company's product line covers a certain range of the total range of products offered by the industry as a whole. For example, BMW automobiles are located in the medium-high price range of the total automobile market. Line stretching occurs when a company lengthens its product line beyond its current range. The company can stretch its line downward, upward, or both ways.

Downward stretch. Many companies initially locate at the high end of the market and subsequently stretch their line downward. A company may stretch downward to deter or attack competitors or to enter faster-growing segments of the market.

One of the great miscalculations of several American companies has been their unwillingness to stretch downward into the lower end of their markets. General Motors resisted building smaller cars; Xerox, smaller copying machines; and Harley Davidson, smaller motorcycles. In all these cases, Japanese companies found a major opening and moved in quickly and successfully.

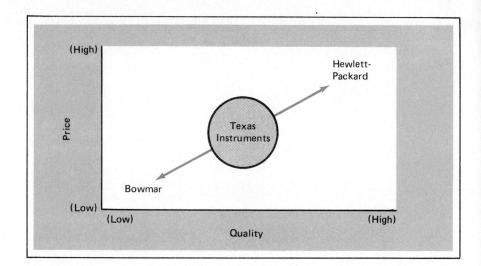

FIGURE 8-5

Two-Way Product
Line Stretch in the
Pocket Calculator
Market

Upward stretch. Companies at the lower end of the market may want to enter the higher end. They may be attracted by a faster growth rate or greater profits at the higher end, or they may simply want to position themselves as full-line manufacturers.

An upward stretch decision can be risky. The higher-end competitors not only are well entrenched but also may counterattack by entering the lower end of the market. Prospective customers may not believe that the newcomer can produce quality products. Finally, the company's sales representatives and distributors may lack the talent and training to serve the higher end of the market.

Two-way stretch. Companies in the middle range of the market may decide to stretch their line in both directions. Texas Instruments' strategy in the pocket calculator market illustrates this. Before Texas Instruments (TI) entered this market, the market was dominated primarily by Bowmar at the low-price/low-quality end and Hewlett-Packard at the high-price/high-quality end (see figure 8-5). TI introduced its first calculators in the medium-price/medium-quality end of the market. Gradually it added more machines at each end. It offered better calculators at the same price as, or at lower prices than, Bowmar, ultimately destroying it; and it designed high-quality calculators selling at lower prices than Hewlett-Packard calculators, taking away a good share of HP's sales at the high end. This two-way stretch won TI the market leadership in the pocket calculator market.

PRODUCT LINE FILLING DECISION. A product line can also be lengthened by adding more items within the present range of the line. There are several reasons for line filling: (1) reaching for extra profits, (2) trying to satisfy dealers who complain about missing items in the line, (3) trying to use excess production capacity, (4) trying to be the leading full-line company, and (5) trying to plug holes to keep out competitors.

Line filling is overdone if it results in cannibalization and customer confusion. The company needs to make sure that new product items are noticeably different from present items.

Product Mix Decisions

An organization with several product lines has a product mix. We define product mix as follows:[17]

A **product mix** is the set of all product lines and items that a particular seller offers for sale to buyers.

Avon's product mix consists of three major product lines: cosmetics, jewelry, and household items. Each product line consists of several sublines: For example, cosmetics breaks down into lipstick, rouge, powder, and so on. Each line and subline has many individual items.

Altogether, Avon's product mix includes 1,300 items. A large supermarket handles as many as 10,000 items; a typical K mart carries 15,000 items; and General Electric manufactures as many as 250,000 items.

A company's product mix can be described as having a certain width, length, depth, and consistency. These concepts are illustrated in figure 8-6 in connection with selected Procter & Gamble consumer products.

FIGURE 8-6

Product Mix Width and Product Line Length for Procter & Gamble Products

DETERGENTS	TOOTHPASTE	BAR SOAP	DEODORANTS	DISPOSABLE DIAPERS	COFFEE
Ivory Snow 1930	Gleem 1952	Ivory 1879	Secret 1956	Pampers 1961	Folger's 1963
Dreft 1933	Crest 1955	Camay 1927	Sure 1972	Luvs 1976	Instant
Tide 1946		Lava 1928			Folger's 1963
Joy 1949		Kirk's 1930			High Point
Cheer 1950		Zest 1952			Instant 1975
Oxydol 1952		Safeguard 1963			Folger's
Dash 1954		Coast 1974			Flaked
Cascade 1955					Coffee 1977
Duz 1956					
Ivory Liquid 1957					
Gain 1966					
Dawn 1972					
Era 1972					
Bold 3 1976					

Product mix width →

Product line length ↕

Exhibit **8-4**

Product Decisions and Public Policy

Marketing managers must heed various laws and regulations when making their product decisions. The main areas of product concern are as follows.

Product additions and deletions: Decisions to add product lines, particularly through acquisitions, may be prevented under the 1950 Kefauver-Celler Act if the effect threatens to lessen competition. Decisions to drop old products must be made with an awareness that the firm has legal obligations, written or implied, to its suppliers, dealers, and customers who have a stake in the discontinued product.

Patent protection: The firm must heed the U.S. patent laws in developing new products. The firm is prevented from designing a product that is "illegally similar" to another company's established product. An example is Polaroid's suit trying to prevent Kodak from selling its new instant picture camera on the grounds that it infringes on Polaroid's instant camera patents.

Product quality and safety: Manufacturers of foods, drugs, cosmetics, and certain fibers must comply with specific laws regarding product quality and safety. The Federal Food, Drug, and Cosmetic Act protects consumers from unsafe and tainted food, drugs, and cosmetics. Various acts provide for the inspection of sanitary conditions in the meat and poultry processing industries. Safety legislation has been passed to regulate the manufacture of fabrics, chemical substances, automobiles, toys, and drugs and poisons. The Consumer Product Safety Act of 1972 established a Consumer Product Safety Commission, which has the authority to ban or seize hazardous products and set severe penalties for violation of the law. If consumers have been injured by a product that has been defectively designed, they can sue manufacturers or dealers. Product liability suits are now occurring at the rate of over one million a year. This has resulted in a substantial increase in product recalls. General Motors spent $3.5 million on postage alone when it had to notify 6.5 million car owners of defective motor mounts.

Product warranties: Many manufacturers offer written product warranties to convince customers of their product's quality. But these warranties are often subject to certain qualifications and written in a language that the average consumer does not understand. Too often consumers learn that they are not entitled to services, repairs, and replacements that seem to be implied. To protect consumers, Congress passed the Magnuson-Moss Warranty/Federal Trade Commission Improvement Act in 1975. The act requires that full warranties meet certain minimum standards, including repair "within a reasonable time and without charge" or a replacement or full refund if the product does not work "after a reasonable number of attempts" at repair. Otherwise the company must make it clear that it is offering only a limited warranty. The law has led several manufacturers to switch from full to limited warranties and others to drop warranties altogether as a marketing tool.

Sources: Howard C. Sorenson, "Products Liability: The Consumer's Revolt," *Best's Review,* September 1974, p. 48; "Managing the Product Recall," *Business Week,* January 1975, pp. 46–48; Roger A. Kerin and Michael Harvey, "Contingency Planning for Product Recall," *MSU Business Topics,* Summer 1975, pp. 5–12; and "The Guesswork on Warranties," *Business Week,* July 14, 1975, p. 51.

The *width* of P&G's product mix refers to the number of different product lines the company carries. Figure 8-6 shows a product mix width of six lines. (In fact, P&G produces many additional lines, including mouthwashes, toilet tissue, and so on.)

The *length* of P&G's product mix refers to the total number of items in its product mix. In figure 8-6, it is thirty-one. The *depth* of P&G's product mix refers to the varieties that are offered of each product in the line. Thus if Crest comes in three sizes and two flavors (regular and mint), Crest has a depth of six.

The *consistency* of the product mix refers to how closely related the various product lines are in end use, production requirements, distribution channels, or in some other way. P&G's product lines are consistent as they are consumer goods that go through the same distribution channels. The lines are less consistent in terms of the different functions they perform for the buyers.

These four dimensions of the product mix help determine the company's product strategy. The company can increase its business in four ways. The company can add new product lines, thus widening its product mix. Or the company can lengthen its existing product lines to become a more full-line company. Or the company can add more product variations to each product and thus deepen its product mix. Finally, the company can pursue more product line consistency or less, depending upon whether it wants to have a strong reputation in a single field or participate in several fields.

Thus we see that product strategy is a multidimensional and complex subject calling for decisions about product mix, product line, branding, packaging, and services. These decisions must be made not only with a full understanding of consumer wants and competitors' strategies but also with increasing attention to public policy and legislation affecting product decisions (see exhibit 8-4).

Summary

Product is the first and most important element of the marketing mix. Product strategy calls for making coordinated decisions on product items, product lines, and product mixes.

Each product item offered to customers can be looked at on three levels. The core product is the essential service that the buyer is really buying. The actual product includes the features, styling, quality level, brand name, and packaging of the product offered for sale. The augmented product is the actual product plus the various services accompanying it, such as warranty, installation, service maintenance, and free delivery.

Several schemes have been proposed for classifying products. For example, all products can be classified according to their durability (nondurable goods, durable goods, and services). Consumer goods are usually classified according to consumer shopping habits (convenience, shopping, specialty, and unsought goods). Industrial goods are classified according to how they enter the production process (materials and parts, capital items, and supplies and services).

Companies have to develop brand policies for the product items in their lines. They must decide whether to brand at all, whether to do manufacturing or private branding, what quality they should build into the brand, whether to use family brand names or individual brand names, whether to extend the brand name to new products, and whether to put out several competing brands.

Physical products require packaging decisions that have to do with protection, economy, convenience, and promotion. Physical products also require labeling for identification and possible grading, description, and promotion of the product. U.S. laws require sellers to present certain minimum information on the label to inform and protect consumers.

Companies have to develop customer services that are desired by customers and effective against competitors. The company has to decide on the most important services to offer, the level at which each service should be provided, and the form of each service. The service mix can be coordinated by a customer service department that handles complaints and adjustments, credit, maintenance, technical service, and customer information.

Most companies produce not a single product but a product line. A product line is a group of products related in function, customer purchase needs, or distribution channels. Each product line requires a marketing strategy. Line stretching raises the question of whether a particular line should be extended downward, upward, or both ways. Line filling raises the question of whether additional items should be added within the present range of the line. Line featuring raises the question of which items to feature in promoting the line.

Product mix describes the set of product lines and items offered to customers by a particular seller. The product mix can be described as having a certain width, length, depth, and consistency. The four dimensions of the product mix are the tools for developing the company's product strategy.

Questions for Discussion

1. A Sony color TV would be grouped under which consumer product classification (convenience, shopping, specialty, or unsought goods)?
2. The latest buzzword on Madison Avenue is "brand personality," or how people feel about a brand rather than what the brand does. Timex wants to change its brand personality from useful to something else. What would you suggest, and how should Timex go about accomplishing the change in brand personality?
3. Relate the concepts of product mix, product line, and product item to General Motors.
4. Discuss the core, actual, and augmented product for your favorite brand of perfume or after-shave lotion.
5. In how many retail outlets must each type of consumer good (convenience, shopping, specialty, and unsought) be distributed in a particular geographic area? Explain why.
6. Industrial goods always become part of the finished product. Comment.
7. Who benefits from the use of brand names? Explain briefly.
8. Describe some of the service decisions that the following marketers must make: (a) women's dress shop, (b) savings and loan association, and (c) sporting goods store.

Key Terms in Chapter 8

Brand   A name, term, sign, symbol, or design, or a combination of them, which is intended to identify the goods or services of one seller or group of sellers and to differentiate them from those of competitors.

Brand extension strategy   Any effort to use a successful brand name to launch product modifications or new products.

Brand mark   That part of a brand which can be recognized but is not utterable, such as a symbol, design, or distinctive coloring or lettering.

Brand name   That part of a brand which can be vocalized.

Capital items   Goods that enter the finished product partly; they include two groups—installations and accessory equipment.

Convenience goods   Goods that the customer usually purchases frequently, immediately, and with the minimum of effort in comparison buying.

Copyright   The exclusive legal right to reproduce, publish, and sell the matter and form of a literary, musical, or artistic work.

Durable goods   Tangible goods that normally survive many uses.

Materials and parts   Goods that enter the manufacturer's product competely; they fall into two classes—raw materials and manufactured materials and parts.

Nondurable goods   Tangible goods that normally are consumed in one or a few uses.

Packaging   The activities of designing and producing the container or wrapper for a product.

Product   Anything that can be offered to a market for attention, acquisition, use, or consumption that might satisfy a want or need; includes physical objects, services, persons, places, organizations, and ideas.

Product item   A distinct unit that is distinguishable by size, price, appearance, or some other attribute.

Product line   A group of products that are closely related, either because they function in a similar manner, are sold to the same customer groups, are marketed through the same types of outlets, or fall within a given price range.

Product mix   The set of all product lines and items that a particular seller offers for sale to buyers.

Services   Activities, benefits, or satisfactions that are offered for sale.

Shopping goods   Goods that the customer, in the process of selection and purchase, characteristically compares on such bases as suitability, quality, price, and style.

Specialty goods   Goods with unique characteristics and/or brand identification for which a significant group of buyers is habitually willing to make a special purchase effort.

Supplies and services   Items that do not enter the finished product at all.

Trademark   A brand or part of a brand that is given legal protection; protects the seller's exclusive rights to use the brand name and/or brand mark.

Unsought goods   Goods that the consumer does not know about or knows about but does not normally think of buying.

Cases for Chapter 8

Case 7   Hanes Corporation: From L'eggs to Children's Books? (p. 501)
Can Hanes successfully extend its product mix to include children's books? The chapter provides several answers to this question.

Case 8   Kraft, Inc.: A La Carte Retort Pouch Foods (p. 501)
Will consumers and retailers accept a new kind of packaging? This case looks at factors that may affect the acceptance.

Chapter 9

Designing Products: New-Product Development and Product Life-Cycle Strategies

Objectives

After reading this chapter, you should be able to:

1. List and define the steps in new-product development.
2. Explain how companies decide which products to develop.
3. Follow a product through the stages in its life cycle.
4. Discuss how marketing strategies change during a product's life cycle.

In the mid-1950s, Procter & Gamble (P&G) learned that the old standard potato chip could stand improvement. Nobody had applied any new technology to potato chips in the roughly one hundred years they had been around, nor did P&G have a very clear-cut idea of what a better potato chip should be. But the company did know that consumers were not satisfied with potato chips the way they were.

P&G talked to a lot of potato chip eaters. The company found out from this market research that most users of potato chips were unhappy with one or more things. Specifically, consumers complained about the following: (1) Potato chips get stale too fast; (2) sometimes they're already stale when you buy them; (3) they should be crisper; (4) most always they're broken; (5) or burnt; (6) they taste too greasy; (7) the bags are hard to close; and (8) the bags are hard to store.

These eight complaints uncovered by consumer research became the starting point for P&G's research and development department. The department took more than a decade to develop Pringle's New-Fangled Potato Chips. It found a way to form dehydrated potatoes into potato tissue and to slice this tissue into chips of uniform size that can easily be stacked. The chips are vacuum-cooked and packaged in canisters resembling tennis ball cans.

In the fall of 1968, Pringle's were test-marketed in Evansville, Indiana, where they took a big 20% bite of the local potato chip market. P&G proceeded cautiously with market-by-market introductions. It finally achieved national distribution in 1975, with total sales hitting $100 million, or almost 10% of the potato chip market. It looked like P&G had another winner. P&G's development of the product over a period of twenty years—initial research to nationwide distribution— was finally paying off.

P&G was excited about the profit potential. Although its plant and equipment costs were higher than those of conventional chip makers, P&G distribution costs were lower. Where its competitors needed a costly sales force and truck fleet to hand-deliver a fresh product to grocery stores, Pringle's crushproof can and year-long shelf life allowed P&G to send its product through normal warehouse distribution channels with minimal breakage and shipping costs.

But Pringle's sales started to tumble in 1976 when they slipped to $90 million. A number of cracks began to appear in Pringle's picture. The public was growing increasingly diet conscious and turning to natural foods. To many people, Pringle's represented a plastic food, high in preservatives and additives without the natural good taste of fresh potato chips. One consumer complained that Pringle's tasted more like tennis balls than potato chips. This became the basis of a counterattack by the fresh potato chip makers, led by the Potato Chip Institute. They hammered away at Pringle's not being "the real thing," and even took P&G to court to try to stop Pringle's from calling itself a potato chip.

Also, some consumers thought Pringle's was too expensive. They didn't believe that P&G crammed as many chips into the Pringle's can as they got in competing potato chip bags. Many consumers turned back to fresh potato chips and bought Pringle's only on special occasions.

P&G's sales slipped to $80 million. But P&G wouldn't give up. It dug deep into its bag of marketing and technological tricks. Among the things it did was to change its advertising campaigns a number of times. The company sponsored ads showing that a can of Pringle's would fill a snack bowl as full as a bag of potato chips. Later it changed its processing formula so that it could advertise "no preservatives, no artificial ingredients."

In 1980, P&G launched a "new and improved" version of Pringle's in the hope of creating a new product life cycle. P&G believes that it has developed a "better-tasting" chip by adjusting the salt and cooking oil, thus overcoming one of the main obstacles. It offers the new and improved Pringle's in regular, light, and rippled varieties. It raised its advertising budget for the relaunch from $339,700 in 1980 to $8 million in 1981 and is using the campaign theme "I've got the fever for the flavor of new Pringle's." In the first three months, its share of the $2 billion potato chip market grew from 4.5% to 5.5%.

Procter & Gamble is true to its last name and is gambling that Pringle's will make it this time. Its losses of $200 million thus far do not daunt this patient marketer, who took ten years to develop Crest and several years to develop Head and Shoulders into successful products and never regretted it.[1]

A company has to be good at developing new products. It also has to be good at managing them in the face of changing tastes, technologies, and competition. Every product seems to go through a life cycle of four stages: introduction, growth, maturity, and decline.

The existence of a product life cycle means that the firm faces two major challenges. First, the firm must find new products to replace declining ones (the problem of new-product development). Second, the firm must know how to manage existing products effectively at each product life-cycle stage (the problem of product life-cycle strategies). Some companies concentrate on developing new products without skillfully managing their existing products. Other companies put their energy into managing current products and fail to develop enough new products on which to base their future. Companies need to strike a balance between these two extremes.

We will first look at the problem of developing new products and then the problem of managing them successfully over their life cycle.

New-Product Development Strategy

never get involved c̄ new products unless you do some research then test market

Given the rapid changes in tastes, technology, and competition, a company cannot rely only on its existing products. Customers want and expect new and improved products. Competition will do its best to provide them. Every company needs a new-product development program.

A company can obtain new products in two ways. One is through acquisition—by buying a whole company, a patent, or a license to produce someone else's product. The other is through new-product development—by setting up its own research and development department.

We will concentrate on new-product development. By "new products" we mean original products, product improvements, product modifications, and new brands that the firm develops through its own R&D efforts. We will also be concerned with whether the consumer sees the item as new.

Innovation can be very risky. Ford lost an estimated $350 million on its ill-fated Edsel (see exhibit 9-1); Du Pont lost an estimated $100 million on its synthetic leather called Corfam (see pp. 105–106); Xerox's venture into computers was a disaster; and the French Concorde aircraft will never recover its investment. Here are several consumer packaged-goods products, launched by sophisticated companies, that failed in the marketplace:

- Red Kettle soup (Campbell)
- Knorr soup (Best)
- Cue toothpaste (Colgate)
- Flavored ketchups (Hunt)
- Babyscott diapers (Scott)
- Nine Flags men's cologne (Gillette)
- Vim tablet detergent (Lever)
- Post dried fruit cereal (General Foods)
- Gablinger's beer (Rheingold)
- Resolve analgesic (Bristol-Myers)
- Mennen E deodorant (Mennen)

The famous Edsel—launched 1957, buried 1959—at a cost to Ford of $350 million.

Courtesy Ford Motor Company

One study found that the new-product failure rate was 40% for consumer products, 20% for industrial products, and 18% for services.[2] The failure rate for new consumer products is especially alarming.

Why do new products fail? There are several reasons. A high-level executive might push a favorite idea through in spite of negative marketing research findings. Or the idea is good, but the market size has been overestimated. Or the actual product has not been designed as well as it should have been. Or it has been incorrectly positioned in the market, has not been advertised effectively, or is overpriced. Sometimes the costs of product development are higher than expected, or the competitors fight back harder than expected.

Thus companies face a dilemma: They should develop new products, and yet the odds weigh heavily against their success. The answer partly lies in making sure the company is organized for handling new products. In addition, the new-product development groups must handle each step of the new-product development process carefully. The major new-product development steps are shown in figure 9-1 and described below.

FIGURE 9-1

Major Steps in New-Product Development

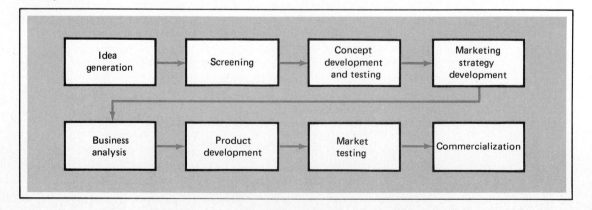

Exhibit **9-1**

One of the Costliest New-Product Failures in History: Ford's Edsel

One of the costliest new-product failures in history was Ford's Edsel automobile, introduced in 1957. The Ford Motor Company in the early fifties began to feel the need for adding a new automobile to its product line. At that time, Fords and Chevrolets each had 25% of the auto market. But there was a difference. Chevrolet car owners, when they became more prosperous, moved up to the Pontiac-Buick-Oldsmobile class. Ford owners, as they moved to higher-priced cars, also favored Pontiacs, Buicks, and Oldsmobiles. They did not find the higher-priced Ford Mercury appealing and could not afford the elegant Lincoln.

Ford needed to develop an attractive intermediate-priced car for upwardly mobile Ford and Chevrolet owners. Ford's marketing research indicated that the growing middle class would be buying better cars. Ford studied car owner demographics, desires, and preferences and set about designing a car that would appeal to these buyers. The car's design was kept top secret, although Ford ran publicity to excite the public about the coming of a new and unique car. Ford decided, at tremendous cost, to establish a separate dealer system for Edsel. Edsel was to be sold by Edsel dealers exclusively. The company also considered over six thousand possible names for the car, including several created by poet Marianne Moore, such as Bullet Cloisonne, Mongoose Civique, and Andante Con Motor. Ignoring all these names, the car was named Edsel in honor of Henry Ford's only son.

Ford launched the Edsel with great fanfare on September 4, 1957. On that day sixty-five hundred cars were purchased or ordered. That day belonged to Edsel, but it was the only day. Although over 2 million people went to look at the car in showrooms, few bought it. By January 1958, the exclusive dealerships were discontinued, and Ford created a new Mercury-Edsel-Lincoln Division. In November 1959 Ford stopped producing Edsels.

Why did the Edsel fail? First, many consumers did not find the car attractive. The front of the car carried vertical lines and the back carried horizontal lines, suggesting that two design teams went to work on opposite ends of the car. Furthermore, the front grill was peculiar looking and became the butt of many Freudian jokes. Second, Ford advertised the Edsel as being a new kind of car. However, consumers did not see it this way; it seemed like another medium-priced car. Ford got itself into trouble by overpromising. Third, in Ford's rush to produce the car, quality control was careless and many Edsels were "lemons."

Edsel's timing was also bad. Ford introduced the car in 1957 just as the economy started to dip into a major recession. People wanted cheaper cars and turned to the Volkswagen and American Motors' Rambler. There was a strong reaction against chrome and flashy cars like the Edsel. Yet nothing in the earlier research forecasted these changes in the economy and customer preferences. The Edsel was a victim of poor planning and timing, and this cost Ford $350 million.

Sources: Based on William H. Reynolds, "The Edsel Ten Years Later," *Business Horizons,* Fall 1967, pp. 39–46; and John Brooks, *The Fate of the Edsel and Other Business Adventures* (New York: Harper and Row, 1963).

Idea Generation

New-product development starts with the search for new-product ideas. The search should be systematic rather than haphazard. Otherwise the company will find scores of ideas, most of which will not be appropriate for its type of business. In one company a new product came all the way up for final approval after a research cost of more than a million dollars only to be killed by members of top management, who decided they did not want to get into that type of business.

Top management can avoid this by carefully defining its new-product development strategy. It should state what products and markets to emphasize. It should state what the company wants to accomplish with the new products, whether it is high cash flow, market-share domination, or some other objective. It should state the relative effort to be devoted to developing original products, modifying existing products, and imitating competitors' products.

There are many excellent sources for new-product ideas. Customers are the most logical starting point in the search for new-product ideas. Their needs and wants can be monitored through customer surveys, group discussions, and the letters and complaints that customers send in. Scientists are another source, as they may discover or identify new materials or features that can lead to original products or product improvements. Companies should also watch competitors' products to see which ones are attracting customers. The company's sales force and dealers are another good source of ideas because they are in daily contact with customers. Other idea sources are inventors, patent attorneys, university and commercial laboratories, industrial consultants, management consultants, advertising agencies, marketing research firms, trade associations, and industrial publications (see exhibit 9-2).

Screening

The purpose of idea generation is to create a large number of ideas. The purpose of the succeeding steps is to reduce the number of ideas. The first idea-reducing step is screening.

The purpose of screening is to spot and drop poor ideas as early as possible. Most companies require their executives to write up new-product ideas on a standard form that can be reviewed by a new-product committee. They describe the product, the target market, and the competition and make some rough guesses as to market size, product price, development time and costs, manufacturing costs, and rate of return.

Even if the idea looks good, the questions arise: Is it appropriate for the particular company? Does it mesh well with the company's objectives, strategies, and resources? Many companies have specific systems for rating and screening ideas.

Concept Development and Testing

Surviving ideas must now be developed into product concepts. It is important to distinguish between a product idea, a product concept, and a product image. A *product idea* is an idea for a possible product that the company can see itself offering to the market. A *product concept* is an elaborated version of the idea expressed in meaningful consumer terms. A *product image* is the particular picture that consumers acquire of an actual or potential product.

Exhibit 9-2

Wild New Ideas—Keep Them Coming!

There is no lack of wild ideas. Burt Shulman has invented a number of things in his spare time: a gadget that blows smoke away from the noses of people who use soldering guns; an alarm-clock radio that senses when it is going to snow or rain and wakens the sleeper earlier than usual; a tiny machine that improves the circulation of desk-bound executives by continuously moving their feet up and down; a device that permits motorists to breathe fresh air when they are caught in traffic jams; ultrasonic tweezers for the permanent removal of ingrown hairs; and a jogging machine strapped on the jogger's back to help the jogger run at twenty miles an hour. None of these, unfortunately, have been commercial successes.

Occasionally a wild idea works. Consider contact lenses for chickens! Robert Garrison invented them while working with the owner of a large chicken farm in Oregon. There were 470.8 million chickens in 1978, and the large farms had more than ten thousand birds each. Raising chickens for egg production is big business, and a device that saves chickens from pecking each other to death and makes them concentrate on eating and producing eggs is a needed product. The chicken's comb and the way it holds its head signal the pecking order. If chickens cannot see the combs, cannibalism among chickens is greatly reduced. When the birds wear contact lenses, their perception is reduced to twelve inches, and they cannot recognize the comb of another chicken. The lens also solves the problem of the most submissive birds having a hard time getting to the feeding trough. Since chicken farms already spend money debeaking birds in order to avoid cannibalism and debeaking often creates trauma, the expense of putting in lenses saves money in the long run.

Who knows what will be next? A contraceptive pet food to keep down cat population? Don't laugh. The Carnation Company of Los Angeles is working on it.

Sources: "Burt Shulman" is described in ". . . or Jogger Huff Puffing: It's a Gas," *Chicago Tribune*, January 7, 1979. "Contact lenses for chickens" is adapted from Darral G. Clarke, "Optical Distortion, Inc.," in *Problems in Marketing*, ed. Steven H. Star and Nancy Davis (New York: McGraw-Hill, 1977), pp. 530–50.

CONCEPT DEVELOPMENT. Suppose an automobile manufacturer discovers how to design an electric car that can go as fast as fifty miles an hour and as far as one hundred miles before needing to be recharged. The manufacturer estimates that the operating costs for an electric car will be about half as much as for a conventional car.

This is a product idea. Customers, however, do not buy a product idea; they buy a product concept. The marketer's task is to develop this product idea into some alternative product concepts, evaluate their relative attractiveness to customers, and choose the best one.

Among the product concepts that might be created for the electric car are the following:

- Concept 1: An inexpensive subcompact designed as a second family car to be used by the homemaker for short shopping trips. The car is ideal for loading groceries and transporting children, and it is easy to enter.
- Concept 2: A medium-cost, intermediate-sized car designed as an all-purpose family car.
- Concept 3: A medium-cost sporty compact appealing to young people.
- Concept 4: An inexpensive subcompact appealing to the conscientious citizen who wants basic transportation, low fuel cost, and low ecological pollution.

try test market basis

then follow the next 3

CONCEPT TESTING. Concept testing calls for testing these concepts with an appropriate group of target consumers. The consumers are presented with an elaborated version of each concept. Here is concept 1:

An efficient, fun-to-drive, electric-powered car in the subcompact class that seats four. Great for shopping trips and visits to friends. Costs half as much to operate as similar gasoline-driven cars. Goes up to fifty miles an hour and does not need to be recharged for one hundred miles. Priced at $6,000.

Consumers are asked to react to this concept with the following questions:

1. Is the concept of an electric car clear to you?
2. What do you see as distinct benefits of an electric car compared with a conventional car?
3. Do you find the claims about the electric car's performance believable?
4. Would an electric car meet a real need of yours?
5. What improvements can you suggest in various features of the electric car?
6. Who would be involved in a possible purchase decision and who would use the car?
7. What do you think the price of the electric car should be?
8. Would you prefer an electric car to a conventional car? For what uses?
9. Would you buy an electric car? (Definitely, probably, probably not, definitely not)

The consumers' responses will help the company determine which concept has the strongest appeal. For example, the last question goes after the consumers' intention to buy and usually reads: "Would you *definitely, probably, probably not, definitely not* buy this product?" Suppose 10% of the consumers said "definitely" and another 5% said "probably." The company would project these figures to the corresponding population size of this target group to estimate the sales volume. Even then, the estimate is tentative because people do not always carry out their stated intentions.

1
Marketing Strategy Development Suppose concept 1 for the electric car tests out best. The next step calls for developing a preliminary marketing strategy for introducing this car into the market.

The marketing strategy statement consists of three parts. The first part describes the size, structure, and behavior of the target market, the planned product positioning, and the sales, market share, and profit goals sought in the first few years. Thus:

> The target market consists of households that need a second car for shopping trips and visits to friends. The car will be positioned as more economical to buy and operate, and more fun to drive, than cars currently available to this market. The company will aim to sell five hundred thousand cars in the first year, at a loss not exceeding $3 million. The second year will aim for sales of seven hundred thousand cars with a planned profit of $5 million.

The second part of the marketing strategy statement outlines the product's planned price, distribution strategy, and marketing budget for the first year:

> The electric car will be offered in three colors and will have optional air-conditioning and power-drive features. It will sell at a retail price of $6,000, with 15% off the list price to dealers. Dealers who sell over ten cars per month will get an additional discount of 5% on each car sold that month. An advertising budget of $6 million will be split 50:50 between national and local advertising. Advertising copy will emphasize the car's economy and fun. During the first year, $100,000 will be spent on marketing research to monitor who is buying the car and their satisfaction levels.

The third part of the marketing strategy statement describes the planned long-run sales and profit goals and the marketing mix strategy over time:

> The company intends to ultimately capture 6% of the total auto market and realize an after-tax return on investment of 15%. To achieve this, product quality will start high and be further improved over time through technical research. Price will be raised in the second and third years if competition permits. The total advertising budget will be boosted each year by about 10%. Marketing research will be reduced to $60,000 per year after the first year.

2
Business Analysis Once management has decided on the product concept and marketing strategy, it can evaluate the business attractiveness of the proposal. Management must review the sales, costs, and profit projections to determine whether they satisfy the company's objectives. If they do, the product can move to the product development step.

3
Product Development If the product concept passes the business analysis test, it moves to R&D and/or engineering to be developed into a physical product. Up to now it existed only as a word description, a drawing, or a very crude mock-up. This step will answer whether the product idea can be translated into a technically and commercially workable product.

A prototype of an electric car. This vehicle has a top speed of 60 miles per hour and an in-city driving range of 80 miles.

Courtesy Copper Development Association Inc.

The R&D department will develop one or more physical versions of the product concept. It hopes to find a prototype that satisfies the following criteria: (1) Consumers see it as having the key attributes described in the product concept statement; (2) the prototype performs safely under normal use and conditions; (3) the prototype can be produced for the budgeted manufacturing costs.

Developing a successful prototype can take days, weeks, months, or even years. The prototype must incorporate the required functional characteristics and also convey the intended psychological characteristics. The electric car, for example, should strike consumers as being well built and safe. Management must learn how consumers decide whether or not a car is well built. One consumer practice is to slam the car door to hear its "sound." If the car does not have "solid-sounding" doors, then consumers will think it is poorly built.

When the prototypes are ready, they must be tested. Functional tests are conducted under laboratory and field conditions to make sure that the product performs safely and effectively. The new car must start well; its tires must not fall off; it must be able to maneuver corners without overturning. Consumer tests involve asking consumers to test-drive the car and rate the car and its attributes. (For an actual example of product development and testing, see exhibit 9-3.)

Market Testing   If the car has passed the functional and consumer tests, the company will manufacture a small number to be used in further market testing. Market testing is the stage where the product and marketing program are introduced into more authentic consumer settings to learn how consumers and dealers react to handling, using, and repurchasing the product, and how large the market is.

Market testing methods vary with the type of product (see exhibit 9-4 for an example of market testing). Companies testing frequently purchased consumer

Exhibit **9-3**

Brunswick Goes Through the Process of Product Development and Testing

After World War II, Brunswick Corporation, the market leader in bowling and billiard equipment, searched for a new-product area. The company wished to use its experience in making large wooden objects. Brunswick finally selected the school furniture market.

To identify the needs in the market, Brunswick interviewed three hundred educators. Many educators expressed dissatisfaction with the heavy furniture of the typical classroom. Brunswick decided to develop a line of light, movable classroom furniture. This furniture would aid team teaching, small-group learning, and the use of classroom television.

The initial step in the new-product development process was to develop sketches of the new furniture. Educators and school officials were asked to react to these sketches. Some educators thought that the chairs looked flimsy, and others raised questions about the orthopedics of the chair. This led to a series of revised sketches. Then Brunswick produced a set of handmade prototypes that it tested in the company's offices.

A final prototype was then selected, and a limited number of chairs were produced for further testing. Educators and children were exposed to these chairs to see how the chairs would be used and would withstand various kinds of maltreatment. Children were placed in a room and photographed as they used the chairs with and without supervision. Also, model classrooms were constructed using the full Brunswick furniture line. These classrooms served as places to observe chair use as well as to display the furniture to educators.

When Brunswick determined that the furniture met the educators' needs and would survive abuse, it introduced its chair line at the annual National Education Association convention. It sold out the entire first year's production capacity before the convention ended.

This was not, however, the end of product development and testing. As reports of field usage came back to Brunswick, the chair was modified to cope with unforeseen problems. For example, in California it became a craze among high-school students to peel the desk arm away from the chair. The chair was redesigned to prevent this.

There were other inputs for chair modification. Many cost-cutting changes were initiated in the manufacturing process. The wooden chair gave way to fiberglass models, with the cost per chair dropping from $18 to $5.

Exhibit **9-4**

Test Marketing Saves a Product—Dream Whip

After conducting extensive product tests and consumer home-use tests, General Foods decided that it was ready to put its Dream Whip, a new whipped cream, into several test markets to see how many consumers would buy it under real market conditions. General Foods chose five sites for test marketing—Indianapolis, Huntington, Louisville, Columbus, and Cincinnati—because this number of cities would permit testing different marketing mixes and budgets. Furthermore, one or two cities might yield atypical results because of weather conditions, competitive maneuvers, and so on.

Dream Whip was introduced in October and the response was very positive. However, by the following June, inventory started building up. Mail from consumers started to come in about the product's failure to perform. General Foods' researchers examined the complaints and discovered that hot weather caused a high failure rate in whipping. Management decided to delay national introduction. Instead, management opened a few additional test markets in Boston, Detroit, and Pittsburgh during the cold weather months to collect more consumer response data and to trim inventories. Meanwhile, the research and development department searched for a solution, which it found a year later, and modified the formula. The new formula for Dream Whip was successful in the test markets during warm weather. The new product was finally ready for national introduction. The expense of test marketing was minor compared with the huge losses the company would have suffered had it gone straight into national marketing.

packaged goods will want to estimate when and how frequently consumers buy the goods. From these estimates, total sales can be forecast.[3] The company hopes to find a high estimate. Too often, however, it will find many consumers trying the product but not rebuying it, thus showing a lack of product satisfaction. Or it might find that consumers repurchase the item once, but rarely after that. Or it might find high adoption but low frequency of purchase (as in the case of many gourmet frozen foods) because the buyers have decided to use the product only on special occasions.

Commercialization Market testing gives management enough information to make a final decision about whether to launch the new product. If the company goes ahead with commercialization, it will face high costs. The company will have to build or rent a full-scale manufacturing facility. And it may have to spend, as in the case of a new consumer-packaged product, between $10 million and $50 million for advertising and sales promotion alone in the first year.

In launching a new product, the company must decide: when, where, to whom, and how.

WHEN. The first decision is whether it is the right time to introduce the new product. If the electric car will cannibalize the company's other cars, its introduction may be delayed.[4] Or if the electric car can be improved further, the company may prefer to launch it next year. Or if the economy is depressed, the company may prefer to wait.

WHERE. The company must decide whether to launch the new product in a single location, a region, several regions, the national market, or the international market. Few companies have the confidence, money, and capacity to launch new products into full national distribution. They will develop a planned market rollout over time. Small companies, in particular, will select an attractive city and put on a blitz campaign to enter the market. They will enter other cities one at a time. Large companies will introduce their product into a whole region and then move to the next region. Companies with national distribution networks, such as auto companies, often will launch their new models in the national market.

TO WHOM. Within the rollout markets, the company must direct its promotion to the best targets. Presumably the company has already profiled the prime segments on the basis of earlier market testing. Prime segments for a new consumer product would ideally have four characteristics:[5] (1) They would be early adopters; (2) they would be heavy users; (3) they would be opinion leaders and talk favorably about the product; (4) they could be reached at low cost.

HOW. The company must develop an action plan for introducing the new product into the rollout markets. It must prepare the marketing budget for marketing mix elements and various activities. Thus the electric car's launch may be preceded by a publicity campaign after it arrives in the showrooms, and then by offers of gifts to draw more people into the showrooms. The company must prepare a separate marketing plan for each new market.

Product Life-Cycle Strategies

After launching the new product, management prays that the product will enjoy a long and happy life. Although they do not expect the product to sell forever, management wants to earn a decent profit to cover all the effort and risk that went into it. Management hopes that sales will be high and last long. Management is aware that each product will have a life cycle, although the exact shape and length are not easily known in advance.

The typical product life cycle is a curve, as shown in figure 9-2. It is marked by four distinct stages:

1. *Introduction* is a period of slow sales growth as the product is being introduced in the market. Profits are nonexistent in this stage because of the heavy expenses of product introduction.

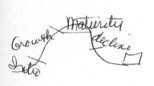

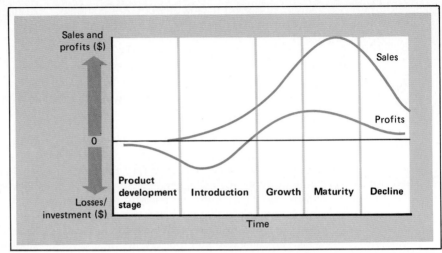

FIGURE 9-2

Sales and Profits over
the Product's Life
Cycle from
Development to
Decline

*When product (Bold) begins
to decline - you must
start a new product
such as Bolder) or
Bounty or New Bounty*

*Everytime you
reintroduce a
new kind you
keep sales going
up rather than
declining*

2. *Growth* is a period of rapid market acceptance and increasing profits.
3. *Maturity* is a period of slowdown in sales growth because the product has achieved acceptance by most of the potential buyers. Profits stabilize or decline because of increased expenses to defend the product against competition.
4. *Decline* is the period when sales show a strong downward drift and profits erode.

While the product life-cycle curve is typical, not all curves follow this pattern. A typical variation is a "cycle-recycle" pattern (figure 9-3a).[6] The second "hump" in sales is caused by a promotional push in the decline stage. Another common pattern is "scalloped" (figure 9-3b), consisting of a succession of life cycles based on the discovery of new-product characteristics, new uses, or new users. Nylon's sales, for example, show a scalloped pattern because of the many new uses—parachutes, hosiery, shirts, carpeting—discovered over time.

The product life cycle can describe a product class (gasoline-powered automobiles), a product form (convertibles), or a brand (Mustang). The concept is applied differently in each case. Product classes have the longest life cycles. The sales of many product classes stay in the mature stage for a long time. Product forms, on the other hand, tend to have the typical product life-cycle curve. Product forms, such as the dial telephone and cream deodorants, pass through a regular history of introduction, rapid growth, maturity, and decline. An individual brand's sales history depends on the brand's success and on changing competitive attacks and counterattacks. The brand life cycles of several well-known car brands are shown in figure 9-4.

The product life-cycle concept can also be applied to what are known as styles, fashions, and fads. Their special life-cycle features are described in exhibit 9-5.

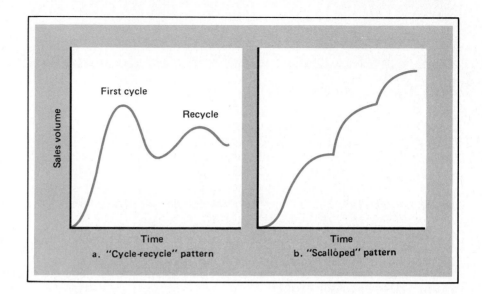

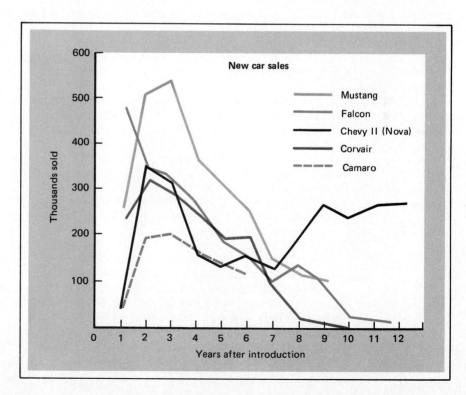

Exhibit 9-5

Style, Fashion, and Fad Cycles

In markets where style and fashion are influential, sales cycles take place, and marketers need to understand and predict them.

A *style* is a basic and distinctive mode of expression appearing in a field of human activity. For example, styles appear in homes (colonial, ranch, Cape Cod), clothing (formal, casual, funky), and art (realistic, surrealistic, abstract). Once a style is invented, it may last for generations, coming in and out of vogue. A style exhibits a cycle showing several periods of renewed interest.

A *fashion* is a currently accepted or popular style in a given field. For example, jeans are a fashion in today's clothing, and new-wave is a fashion in today's dance. Fashions pass through four stages. In the distinctiveness stage, some consumers take an interest in something new to set themselves apart from other consumers. The product may be custom-made or produced in small quantities by some manufacturers. In the copying stage, other consumers take an interest out of a desire to copy the fashion leaders, and additional manufacturers begin to produce larger quantities of the product. In the mass fashion stage, the fashion has become extremely popular and manufacturers have geared up for mass production. Finally, in the decline stage, consumers start moving toward other fashions that are beginning to catch their eye. Thus fashions tend to grow slowly, remain popular for awhile, and decline slowly. The length of a particular fashion cycle is hard to predict.

Fads are fashions that come quickly into the public eye, are adopted with great zeal, peak early, and decline very fast. Their acceptance cycle is short, and they tend to attract only a limited following. They often have a

Different marketing strategies are appropriate for different stages of the product life cycle.

Introduction Stage The introduction stage starts when the new product is first distributed and made available for purchase. Introduction takes time, and sales growth is apt to be slow. Such well-known products as instant coffee, frozen orange juice, and powdered coffee creamers waited for many years before they entered a stage of rapid growth. The slow growth may be due to: (1) delays in the expansion of production capacity; (2) technical problems ("working out the bugs"); (3) delays in making the product available to customers, especially in obtaining adequate distribution through retail outlets; (4) customer reluctance to change established

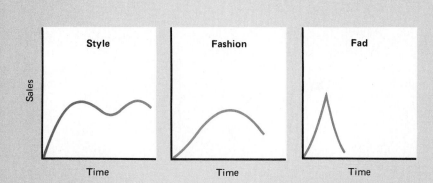

novel or quirky aspect, as when people start buying "pet rocks" or run naked and "streak." Fads appeal to people who are searching for excitement or who want to distinguish themselves from others or have something to talk about to others. Fads do not survive because they normally do not satisfy a strong need or satisfy it well. It is difficult to predict whether something will only be a fad and, if so, how long it will last—a few days, weeks, or months. The amount of media attention it receives, along with other factors, will influence its duration.

Sources: Compiled by the author from various sources, including Chester R. Wasson, "How Predictable Are Fashion and Other Product Life Cycles?" *Journal of Marketing*, July 1968, pp. 36–43; William H. Reynolds, "Cars and Clothing: Understanding Fashion Trends," *Journal of Marketing*, July 1968, pp. 44–49; and Dwight E. Robinson, "Style Changes: Cyclical, Inexorable and Foreseeable," *Harvard Business Review*, November-December 1975, pp. 121–31.

behavior patterns.[7] In the case of expensive new products, sales growth is retarded by additional factors, such as the small number of buyers who can adopt and afford the new product.

In this stage, profits are negative or low because of the low sales and heavy distribution and promotion expenses. Promotion expenses are at their highest "because of the need for a high level of promotional effort to (1) inform potential consumers of the new and unknown product, (2) induce trial of the product, and (3) secure distribution in retail outlets."[8]

There are only a few producers, and they produce basic versions of the product, since the market is not ready for product variations. The firms focus their selling on those buyers who are the readiest to buy, usually the higher-income groups. Prices tend to be on the high side.[9]

In the growth stage, an increasing number of consumers inspect and buy the product.
Laimute E. Druskis

Growth Stage

If the new product satisfies the market, sales will start climbing substantially. The early adopters will continue to buy it, and conventional consumers will start following their lead, especially if they hear favorable word of mouth. New competitors will enter the market, attracted by the opportunity. They will introduce new-product features, and this will expand the market. The increased number of competitors leads to an increase in the number of distribution outlets, and factory sales jump just to fill the pipelines.

Prices remain where they are or fall only slightly as demand increases. Companies maintain their promotion expenditures at the same or at a slightly higher level to meet competition and continue making the public aware of the product.

Profits increase during this stage as promotion costs are spread over a large sales volume, and manufacturing costs fall. The firm uses several strategies to sustain rapid market growth as long as possible:

1. The firm improves product quality and adds new-product features and models.
2. It enters new market segments.
3. It enters new distribution channels.
4. It shifts some advertising from making the public aware to making the public buy.
5. It lowers prices at the right time to attract more customers.

The firm that pursues these market expanding strategies will improve its competitive position.

Maturity Stage

At some point a product's rate of sales growth will slow down, and the product will enter a stage of maturity. This stage normally lasts longer than the previous stages, and it poses strong challenges to marketing management. Most products are in the maturity stage of the life cycle, and therefore most of marketing management deals with the mature product.

The slowdown in the rate of sales growth leaves many producers with many products to sell. This leads to intensified competition. Competitors engage more frequently in markdowns and off-list pricing. They increase their advertising and trade and consumer deals. They increase their R&D budgets to find better versions of the product. These steps mean lower profits. Some of the weaker competitors start dropping out. The industry eventually consists of well-entrenched competitors.

The product manager should not simply defend the product. A good offense is the best defense. He or she should consider strategies of market, product, and marketing mix modification.

MARKET MODIFICATION. Here the manager tries to increase the consumption of the existing product. The manager looks for new users and market segments. The manager also looks for ways to stimulate increased usage among present customers. The manager may want to reposition the brand to appeal to a larger or faster-growing segment.

PRODUCT MODIFICATION. The product manager can also modify product characteristics—such as product quality, features, or style—to attract new users and increased usage.

During the maturity stage, companies modify the features and style of their products.

Courtesy Sony Corporation of America

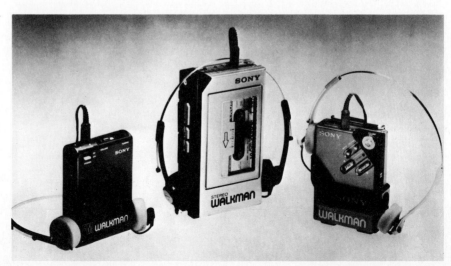

A strategy of *quality improvement* aims at increasing the functional performance of the product—its durability, reliability, speed, taste. This strategy is effective to the extent that (1) the quality can be improved, (2) buyers believe the claim of improved quality, and (3) a sufficient number of buyers want higher quality.

A strategy of *feature improvement* aims at adding new features that expand the product's versatility, safety, or convenience. Feature improvement has been a successful strategy of Japanese makers of watches, calculators, copying machines, and so on. For example, Sony keeps adding new playing features to its Walkman line of miniature stereo players.

A strategy of *style improvement* aims at increasing the attractiveness of the product. Thus car manufacturers restyle their cars periodically to attract buyers who want a new look.

MARKETING MIX MODIFICATION. The product manager should also try to stimulate sales by modifying one or more marketing mix elements. Prices can be cut in order to attract new buyers and competitors' customers. A more effective advertising campaign can be sought. Aggressive sales promotion—trade deals, cents-off coupons, gifts, and contests—can be used. The company can move into higher-volume market channels, particularly mass merchandisers, if these channels are growing. The company can offer new or improved services to buyers.

Decline Stage

The sales of most product forms and brands eventually dip. The sales decline may be slow, as in the case of oatmeal cereal; or rapid, as in the case of the Edsel automobile. Sales may plunge to zero, or they may stay at a low level and continue for many years at that level.

Sales decline for a number of reasons, including technological advances, consumer shifts in tastes, and increased domestic and foreign competition. As sales and profits decline, some firms withdraw from the market. Those remaining may reduce the number of their product offerings. They may drop smaller market segments and marginal trade channels. They may cut the promotion budget and reduce their prices further.

Carrying a declining product can be very costly to the firm. The product may consume too much of management's time; it often requires frequent price and inventory adjustment; it has high production costs; it requires both advertising and sales-force attention that might better be diverted to making newer products more profitable; its declining success can cause customers to wonder about the company as a whole. The biggest cost may well lie in the future. By not being eliminated at the proper time, declining products delay the aggressive search for replacement products. They also create a lopsided product mix, long on "yesterday's breadwinners" and short on "tomorrow's breadwinners," and they depress current profitability and weaken the company's foothold on the future.

For these reasons, a company needs to pay more attention to its aging products. The first task is to identify those products in the declining stage by

Table 9-1				
Product Life Cycle: Characteristics and Responses				
	INTRODUCTION	GROWTH	MATURITY	DECLINE
Characteristics:				
Sales	Low	Fast growth	Slow growth	Declining
Profits	Negligible	Peak levels	Declining	Low or zero
Customers	Innovative	Mass market	Mass market	Laggards
Competitors	Few	Growing	Many rivals	Declining number
Responses:				
Strategic Focus	Expand market	Market penetration	Defend share	Productivity
Marketing Expenditures	High	High (declining %)	Failing	Low
Marketing Emphasis	Product awareness	Brand preference	Brand loyalty	Selective
Distribution	Patchy	Intensive	Intensive	Selective
Price	High	Lower	Lowest	Rising
Product	Basic	Improved	Differentiated	Rationalized

Source: Peter Doyle, "The Realities of the Product Life Cycle," *Quarterly Review of Marketing,* Summer 1976, p. 5.

periodically reviewing the sales, market shares, costs, and profit trends on each of its products.[10] For each declining product, management has to decide whether to maintain, harvest, or terminate it. Management may decide to maintain its brand in the hope that competitors will leave the industry. For example, Procter & Gamble remained in the declining liquid soap business as others withdrew, and it made good profits. Or management may decide to harvest the product, which means reducing various costs (plant and equipment, maintenance, R&D, advertising, sales force, and so on) and hoping that sales hold up fairly well for a while. If successful, harvesting will increase the company's profits in the short run. Or management may decide to drop the product from the line. It can sell it to another firm or simply stop producing it.

The key characteristics of each stage of the product life cycle are summarized in table 9-1. The table also lists the marketing responses made by companies in each stage.[11]

Summary

Organizations are increasingly recognizing the necessity and advantages of developing new products and services. Their current products face shorter life spans and must be replaced by newer products.

New products, however, can fail. The risks of innovation are as great as the rewards. The key to successful innovation lies in developing a good organization for handling new-product ideas and developing sound research and decision procedures at each stage of the new-product development process.

The new-product development process consists of eight stages: idea generation, screening, concept development and testing, marketing strategy development, business analysis, product development, market testing, and commercialization. The purpose of each stage is to decide whether the idea should be further developed or dropped. The company wants to minimize the chances of poor ideas moving forward and good ideas being rejected.

Each commercialized product has a life cycle marked by a changing set of problems and opportunities. The sales history of the typical product follows a curve made up of four stages. The introduction stage is marked by slow growth and minimal profits as the product is being pushed into distribution. If successful, the product enters a growth stage, marked by rapid sales growth and increasing profits. During this stage the company attempts to improve the product, enter new market segments and distribution channels, and reduce its prices slightly. There follows a maturity stage, in which sales growth slows down and profits stabilize. The company seeks innovative strategies to renew sales growth, including market, product, and marketing mix modification. Finally, the product enters a decline stage, in which sales and profits deteriorate. The company's task during this stage is to identify the declining products and decide in each case whether to maintain, harvest, or drop it. In the last case, the product can be sold to another firm or ended.

Questions for Discussion

1. Polaroid, an acknowledged leader in photographic technology, introduced an "instant movie" system, Polavision, with substantial promotional expenditures to retailers and consumers. It lost $60 million in the first two years after introduction, never gaining wide acceptance. Why, do you think, did Polavision fail, given Polaroid's previous record of new-product successes?
2. IBM's entry into the home computer market may help its competitors rather than hurt them. Comment.
3. The guiding principle in the idea generation stage is to limit the number of new-product ideas that are proposed. Comment.
4. At what stage in the new-product development process is the consumer first contacted? Explain briefly.
5. Discuss the type of market testing you would suggest for the following new products: (a) Clairol hair-care product, (b) American Motors line of trucks, and (c) Samsonite plastic suitcases.
6. Discuss the role and importance of promotional expenses in each stage of the product life cycle.
7. Discuss one of the strategies discussed in the maturity stage that the following companies utilized: (a) Arm & Hammer baking soda, (b) State Farm insurance, and (c) Ford Mustang.
8. There is nothing the manager can do once a product reaches the decline stage. Comment.

Key Terms in Chapter 9

Business analysis   A review of sales, costs, and profit projections to determine whether a product concept and marketing strategy meet the company's objectives.

Commercialization   The launching of a new product.

Concept development   The elaboration of a product idea into meaningful consumer terms.

Concept testing   Trying out a product concept on a target group of consumers, asking them to respond to the product, and using their responses to determine whether the product has strong consumer appeal.

Decline stage   The eventual drop in a product's sales that follows the stages of introduction, growth, and maturity.

Growth stage   The increase in sales of a new product as early adopters continue to buy it and conventional consumers start to follow.

Idea generation   The systematic search for new product ideas.

Introduction stage   Making a new product available for purchase.

Marketing strategy development   The creation of a preliminary marketing strategy once a new-product concept has been developed.

Market testing   The stage of new-product development in which the product and marketing program are introduced into authentic consumer settings to learn how consumers and dealers react to handling, using, and repurchasing the product, and how large the market is.

Maturity stage   The eventual slowdown in a product's rate of sales growth.

New-product development   The development of an original product, an improved product, or a modified product consumers will see as "new."

Product development   The development of a physical version of the product concept in hopes that consumers will see the prototype as having the key attributes described in the product concept, that it performs safely, and that it can be produced for the budgeted costs.

Product life cycle   The course of a product's sales and profits that involves four stages: introduction, growth, maturity, and decline.

Screening   In the new-product development process, the elimination of poor ideas.

Cases for Chapter 9

Case 7   Hanes Corporation: From L'eggs to Children's Books? (p. 501)

Can Hanes use the same new-product development and life-cycle strategies for children's books as for panty hose? This case considers that question.

Case 8   Kraft, Inc.: A La Carte Retort Pouch Foods (p. 501)

What strategies can Kraft use to gain acceptance for retort packages? This chapter provides some answers.

Chapter 10

Pricing Products: Pricing Objectives and Policies

Objectives

After reading this chapter, you should be able to:

1. List and define the four types of market competition.
2. Explain how companies determine the demand for their products.
3. Discuss how companies select a pricing method.
4. Name three factors that influence a product's final price.

In the mid-1970s, the British Parliament passed an act requiring its top museums to charge admission for the first time in history. This created a storm of protest. The proponents of the admission price supplied the following arguments: (1) The government could no longer afford all of the annual cost of $44 million to maintain the museums; (2) visitors from abroad were getting something free by not being charged; (3) visitors would better appreciate the institutions if they were charged an admission fee; (4) museum directors would have the incentive to put on better shows and be more responsive; (5) the money could be used to finance extensions and better collections; and (6) museums on the Continent and in the United States charged admission fees. Those who opposed the admission price countered with the following arguments: (1) The charge would discourage attendance by slum children, students, and the old; (2) the cost of collecting the money—more attendants, gates at the entrance, more paperwork—would reduce much of the benefit; and (3) museums should not be forced to go into the entertainment business to please the public but should concentrate on presenting serious exhibits. Despite these counterarguments, the act was passed, and the British museums began to consider the best form of charging admission. They examined three major pricing approaches: (1) Museums could charge daily admission except for one day of the week. A free day could allow the poor or young to visit the museum. The admission charge could be varied for different visitors, being lower (or waived) for children and students, people over 65, handicapped people, and veterans. (2) Museums could encourage donations from visitors rather than charge a fixed price. At the Metropolitan Museum in New York, people are encouraged to contribute $4.00, or anything they can. The voluntary nature of the donation allows the poor and young to enter without cost if they choose. (3) The museums could charge a small admission fee and also sponsor a membership plan that provides members with special benefits, such as a monthly magazine, an annual report, invitations to exhibit openings, a discount at the gift shop, and a waiver of admission charges. The museum would establish different levels of membership and membership privileges, with dues going from $15 (regular membership) to $100 (special membership) to $500 (life membership).

The various museums considered these and other alternatives, and soon realized that the key issue was what objectives they were seeking to accomplish through the pricing mechanism.[1]

All profit organizations and many nonprofit organizations face the task of setting a price on their products or services. Price goes by many names:

> Price is all around us. You pay *rent* for your apartment, *tuition* for your education, and a *fee* to your physician or dentist. The airline, railway, taxi, and bus companies charge you a *fare;* the local utilities call their price a *rate;* and the local bank charges you *interest* for the money you borrow. The price for driving your car on Florida's Sunshine Parkway is a *toll,* and the company that insures your car charges you a *premium.* The guest lecturer charges an *honorarium* to tell you about a government official who took a *bribe* to help a shady character steal *dues* collected by a trade association. Clubs or societies to which you belong may make a special *assessment* to pay unusual expenses. Your regular lawyer may ask for a *retainer* to cover her services. The "price" of an executive is a *salary,* the price of a salesperson may be a *commission,* and the price of a worker is a *wage.* Finally, although economists would disagree, many of us feel that *income taxes* are the price we pay for the privilege of making money.[2]

How are prices set? Historically, prices were set by buyers and sellers negotiating with each other. Sellers would ask for a higher price than they expected to receive, and buyers would offer less than they expected to pay. Through bargaining, they would arrive at an acceptable price.

Setting one price for all buyers is a relatively modern idea. It became common only with the development of large-scale retailing at the end of the nineteenth century. F. W. Woolworth, Tiffany and Co., John Wanamaker, J. L. Hudson, and others advertised a "strictly one-price policy" because they carried so many items and supervised so many employees.

Historically, price has been the major determinant of buyer choice. This is still true in poorer nations, among poorer groups, and with commodity-type products. However, nonprice factors—such as promotion, distribution, and customer service—have become relatively more important in buyer choice in recent decades.

Companies handle pricing in a variety of ways. In small companies, prices are often set by top management. In large companies, pricing is typically handled by divisional and product line managers. Even here, top management sets the general pricing objectives and policies and often approves the prices proposed by lower levels of management. In industries where pricing is a key factor (aerospace companies, railroads, oil companies), companies will often establish a pricing department to set prices or assist others in setting appropriate prices. Others who influence pricing include sales managers, production managers, finance managers, and accountants.

In this and the next chapter, we will look at the problem of pricing products. This chapter will examine how the company can set the basic price of a product. We will show a six-step procedure consisting of selecting pricing objectives, determining demand, estimating costs, analyzing competitors' prices, selecting a pricing method, and selecting the final price. In the next chapter, we will look at specific pricing strategies that lead to adjusting the basic price to important situational factors. The price-adjusting strategies include geographic pricing, discount pricing, promotional pricing, discriminatory pricing, new-product pricing, and product-mix pricing. We will also look at the problems of initiating price cuts and responding to competitors' price changes.

Pricing in Different Types of Markets

Before examining price-setting procedures, we need to recognize that the seller's pricing policies depend on the type of market. Economists name four types of markets, with each presenting a different pricing challenge. These markets are described below.

Pure Competition A **pure competitive market** consists of many buyers and sellers trading in a like commodity such as wheat, copper, or financial securities. No single buyer or seller has much influence on the going market price. A seller cannot charge more than the market price because buyers can obtain as much as they need at this price. Nor would sellers charge less than the market price because they can sell all they want at the market price. Sellers in these markets do not spend much time on marketing strategy, since the role of marketing research, product development, pricing, advertising, sales promotion, and so on, is minimal as long as the market stays purely competitive.

Monopolistic Competition A **monopolistically competitive market** consists of many buyers and sellers who transact over a range of prices rather than a single market price. The reason for the price range is that sellers are able to vary their products for the buyers. Either the physical product can be varied in quality, features, or style, or the

In monopolistic competition, as in the small electronic product field, many sellers compete over a wide range of products.
Teri Leigh Stratford

accompanying services can be varied. Buyers can see different offers and are willing to pay different amounts. Sellers try to develop different offers for different customer segments and freely use branding, advertising, and personal selling, in addition to price, to distinguish their offer. Because there are many competitors, each firm is less affected by competitors' marketing strategies than in oligopolistic markets.

Oligopolistic Competition

An **oligopolistic market** consists of a few sellers who are highly sensitive to each other's pricing and marketing strategies. The product can be like (steel, aluminum) or unlike (cars, computers). The reason for the few sellers is that it is difficult for new sellers to enter the market. Each seller is alert to competitors' strategies and moves. If a steel company slashes its prices by 10%, buyers will quickly switch to this supplier. The other steelmakers will have to respond by lowering

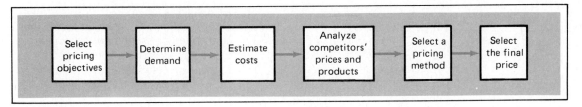

FIGURE 10-1

Procedure for Setting the Basic Price

their prices or increasing their services. An oligopolist is never sure that it will gain anything permanent through a price cut. On the other hand, if the oligopolist raises prices, competitors might not follow this lead. The oligopolist would have to retract the price increases or risk losing customers to competitors.

Pure Monopoly

A **pure monopoly** consists of only one seller. The seller may be a government monopoly (U.S. Postal System), a private regulated monopoly (Con Edison), or a private nonregulated monopoly (Du Pont when it introduced nylon). Pricing is handled differently in each case. A government monopoly can pursue a variety of pricing objectives. It might set a price below cost because the product is important to buyers and they cannot afford to pay full cost. Or the price might be set to cover costs or to produce good revenue. Or it might be set quite high to discourage consumption. In a regulated monopoly, the government permits the company to set rates that will yield a "fair return," one that will enable the company to maintain and expand its plant as needed. Nonregulated monopolies, on the other hand, are free to set any price the market will bear. However, they do not always charge the full price for a number of reasons: fear of government regulation, desire not to attract competition, desire to penetrate the market faster with a low price.

Thus pricing opportunities and challenges vary with the type of market. Except in pure competitive markets, companies need a systematic procedure for setting a basic price on their product. Figure 10-1 shows a price-setting procedure consisting of six steps. These steps are examined in the remainder of this chapter.

Select Pricing Objectives

The company first has to decide what objectives it has for the particular product. If the company has selected its target market and market positioning carefully, then its marketing mix strategy, including price, will be fairly straightforward. Pricing strategy is largely determined by the prior decision on market positioning.

At the same time, the company may have other objectives. The clearer a firm is about its objectives, the easier it is to set prices. Examples of other common objectives are survival, current profit maximization, market-share leadership, and product quality leadership.

Survival Companies set <u>survival</u> as their major objective if the market has too many producers, intense competition, or changing consumer wants. To keep their plants going and their products selling, companies must set a low price, hoping that consumers will react to it. Profits are less important than survival. Troubled companies such as Chrysler and International Harvester have resorted to large price-rebate programs in order to survive. As long as their prices cover costs, they can stay in business for a while.

Current Profit Maximization Many companies want to <u>set a price</u> that will <u>maximize</u> current <u>profits</u>. They estimate the demand and costs associated with alternative prices and choose the price that will produce the maximum current profit, cash flow, or rate of return on investment. In all cases, the company is emphasizing current financial performance rather than long-run performance.

Market-Share Leadership Other companies want to be the leaders in market share. They believe that the company owning the largest market share will enjoy the lowest costs and highest long-run profit. They go after market-share leadership by setting prices as low as possible. A variation of this objective is to pursue a specific market-share gain:

A company that establishes itself as a product quality leader normally charges a high price to cover higher production and development costs.
Courtesy Seagram Distillers Co.

How dare The Glenlivet be so expensive?

How dare we place such a premium on our 12-year-old Scotch? The same reason vintage wines and fine cognacs are so expensive. Superior taste. Just one sip and you'll know that The Glenlivet has a taste that's decidedly superior.

The Glenlivet is Scotland's first and finest single malt Scotch. Nothing but 100% Highland malt whisky, distilled from natural spring water and fine malt barley, aged in oaken casks, just as it always has been.

Only our time-honored methods can truly achieve The Glenlivet's unequaled taste. A taste that sets it apart. Its smoothness, body and bouquet are qualities found only in this unique Scotch.

Of course, you may elect to purchase a good Scotch that's less expensive. But for a truly superior taste, you have to pay the greater price.

The Glenlivet
12-year-old unblended Scotch. About $20 the bottle.

FIGURE 10-2

Two Possible
Demand Curves

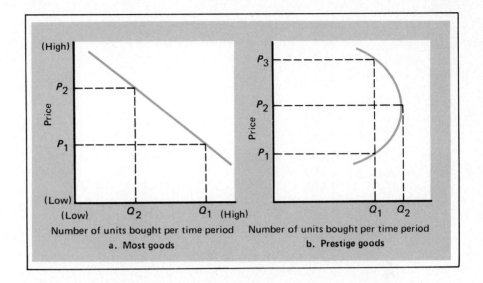

Number of units bought per time period
a. Most goods

Number of units bought per time period
b. Prestige goods

Say the company wants to increase its market share from 10% to 15% in one year. It will search for the price and marketing mix that will achieve this.

Product Quality Leadership   A company might have the objective of having the highest-quality product on the market. This normally calls for charging a high price to cover the high product quality and high cost of R&D. Michelin, the tire manufacturer, is a prime example of a firm pursuing product quality leadership. It keeps introducing new tire features and longer-lasting tires, and it charges high prices for its tires.

Determine Demand

Each price that the company charges will lead to a different level of demand for the product. The relation between the price charged and the resulting demand level is shown in the familiar demand curve shown in figure 10-2a. The demand curve shows the number of units that the market will buy in a given time period at alternative prices that might be charged during the period. In the normal case, demand and price are inversely related, that is, the higher the price, the lower the demand. Similarly, the lower the price, the higher the demand. Thus the company would sell less if it raised its price from P_1 to P_2. Presumably, consumers with a limited budget who face alternative products will buy less of something if its price is too high.

Most demand curves slope downward in either a straight or a curved line, as in figure 10-2a. In the case of prestige goods, however, the demand curve is sometimes positively sloped, as in figure 10-2b. A perfume company found that by raising its price from P_1 to P_2, it sold more perfume rather than less! Consumers felt the higher price meant a better or more desirable perfume. However, if too high a price is charged (P_3), the level of demand will be lower than at P_2.

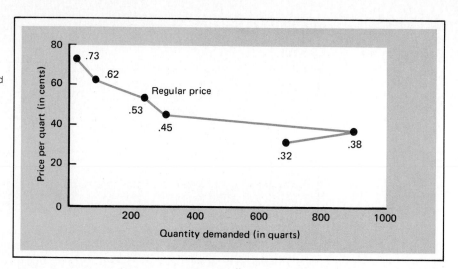

FIGURE 10-3

Demand Curve for Quaker State Motor Oil

Source: Sidney Bennett and J. B. Wilkinson, "Price-Quantity Relationships and Price Elasticity under In-Store Experimentation," *Journal of Business Research,* January 1974, pp. 30–34.

As price drops the greater the demand

Methods of Estimating Demand Curves

Most companies make some attempt to measure their demand curves. The type of market makes a difference. In a pure monopoly, the demand curve shows that the total demand for the product is based on the price the company charges. If there is one or more competing companies, however, the demand curve will vary, depending on whether the competitors' prices remain the same or change. Here, we will assume that the competitors' prices remain the same. (We will discuss what happens when competitors' prices change later in this chapter.)

To measure a demand requires estimating demand at different prices. Figure 10-3 shows the estimated demand curve for Quaker State Motor Oil.

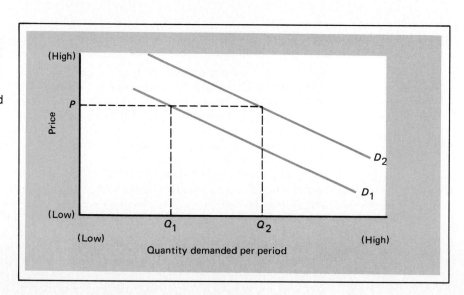

FIGURE 10-4

Effects of Promotion and Other Nonprice Factors on Demand Are Shown through Shifts of the Demand Curve

Demand rises as the price is lowered from 73¢ to 38¢. At 32¢, however, demand falls, possibly because people think that the oil is too cheap and may damage their car.

In measuring the price/demand relationship, the market researcher must remember that other factors besides price can affect demand. If Quaker State raised its advertising budget when it lowered its price, we would not know how much of the increased demand was due to the lower price and how much to the increased advertising. The same problem arises if a holiday weekend occurs when the lower price is established, because more travel and purchase of motor oil take place on holidays.

Economists show the impact of nonprice factors on demand through shifts of the demand curve, rather than movements along the demand curve. Suppose the initial demand curve is D_1, as in figure 10-4. The seller is charging P and selling Q_1 units. Suppose, too, the economy suddenly improves, or the seller doubles the advertising budget. The higher demand generated is reflected through an upward shift of the demand curve from D_1 to D_2. Without changing the price P, the seller's demand is now Q_2.

Price Elasticity of Demand

Marketers need to know how responsive demand will be to a change in price. Consider the two demand curves in figure 10-5. In figure 10-5a, a price increase from P_1 to P_2 leads to a relatively small decline in demand from Q_1 to Q_2. In figure 10-5b, the same price increase leads to a substantial drop in demand from Q_1' to Q_2'. If demand hardly changes with a small change in price, we say the demand is inelastic. If demand changes considerably, we say the demand is elastic.

What determines the price elasticity of demand? Demand is likely to be less elastic under the following conditions: (1) There are few or no substitutes or

FIGURE 10-5

Inelastic and
Elastic Demand

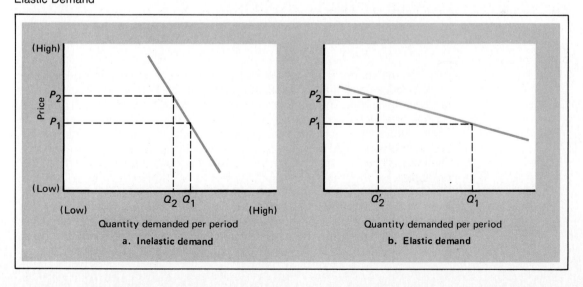

a. Inelastic demand

b. Elastic demand

competitors; (2) buyers do not readily notice the higher price; (3) buyers are slow to change their buying habits and search for lower prices; (4) buyers think the higher prices are justified by quality improvements, normal inflation, and so on.

If demand is elastic rather than inelastic, sellers will consider lowering their price. A lower price will produce more total revenue. This makes sense as long as the costs of producing and selling more do not increase disproportionately.

Estimate Costs

Demand tends to set the top price that the company can charge for its product. And company costs set the low price. The company wants to charge a price that covers all of its costs of producing, distributing, and selling the product, including a fair return for its effort and risk.

Types of Costs A company's costs take two forms, fixed and variable. *Fixed costs* (also known as overhead) are costs that do not vary. Thus a company must pay bills each month for rent, heat, interest, executive salaries, and so on. Fixed costs exist, regardless of the production level.

Variable costs vary directly with the level of production. Each hand calculator produced by Texas Instruments (TI) involves a cost of plastic, wires, packaging, and so on. These costs tend to be constant per unit produced. They are called variable because their total varies with the number of units produced.

Total costs are the sum of the fixed and variable costs for any given level of production. Management wants to charge a price that will at least cover the total production costs at a given level of production.

Analyze Competitors' Prices and Products

Although market demand might set a top price and costs set a low price, competitors' prices and their possible reactions help the firm establish an average range for its prices. The company needs to learn the price and quality of competitors' products. This can be done in several ways. The firm can send out comparison shoppers to price and compare competitors' products. The firm can get competitors' price lists and buy competitors' equipment and take it apart. The firm can ask buyers how they perceive the price and quality of competitors' products.

Once the company is aware of competitors' prices and products, it can use them as a starting point for its own pricing. If the firm's product is similar to a major competitors' product, then the firm will have to price close to the competitor or lose sales. If the firm's product is inferior, the firm will not be able to charge as much as the competitor. If the firm's product is superior, the firm can charge more than the competitor. Basically, the firm will use price to position its offer in relation to competitors.

Select a Pricing Method

Given the demand schedule, estimated costs, and competitors' prices, the company is now ready to select a price. The price will be somewhere between one that is too low to produce a profit and one that is too high to create any demand. Figure 10-6 summarizes the three major considerations in price setting. Product costs set a bottom possible price. Unique product features in the company's offer establish the top possible price. Competitors' prices and the prices of substitutes provide an intermediate point that the company has to consider in setting its price.

Companies settle the pricing issue by selecting a pricing method that includes one or more of these three considerations. The pricing method will lead, it is hoped, to a specific price. We will examine the following price-setting methods: cost-plus pricing, break-even analysis and target profit pricing, perceived-value pricing, going-rate pricing, and sealed-bid pricing.

Cost-Plus Pricing The most simple pricing method is to add a standard markup to the cost of the product. Thus an appliance retailer might pay a manufacturer $20 for a toaster and mark it up to sell at $30, which is a 50% markup on cost. The retailer's gross margin is $10. If the store's operating costs amount to $8 per toaster sold, the retailer's profit margin will be $2. (The arithmetic of markups is discussed in Appendix A: Marketing Arithmetic.)

The manufacturer who made the toaster also probably used cost-plus pricing. If the manufacturer's standard cost of producing the toaster was $16, it might have added a 25% markup, setting the price to the retailer at $20. Construction companies submit job bids by estimating the total project cost and adding a standard markup for profit. Lawyers and other professionals typically price by adding a standard markup to their costs. Some sellers tell their customers they will charge them their cost plus a specified markup; for example, aerospace companies price this way to the government.

FIGURE 10-6

Major Considerations in Setting a Price

Too low price		Possible price		Too high price
No possible profit at this price	Product costs	Competitors' prices and prices of substitutes	Unique product features	No possible demand at this price

Markups vary considerably among different goods. Some common markups (on price, not cost) in department stores are 20% for tobacco goods, 28% for cameras, 34% for books, 41% for dresses, 46% for costume jewelry, and 50% for millinery.[3] In the retail grocery industry, coffee, canned milk, and sugar tend to have low markups, while frozen foods, jellies, and some canned products have high markups. Quite a range of markups is found. Within the frozen-foods category, for example, markups on retail price range from a low of 13% to a high of 53%.[4] The varying markups reflect differences in unit costs, sales, turnover, and manufacturers' versus private brands.[5]

Does the use of standard markups to set prices seem logical? Generally, no. Any pricing method that ignores current demand and competition is not likely to lead to the best price. The retail graveyard is full of merchants who insisted on using standard markups in the face of competitors who had gone into discount pricing.

Still, markup pricing remains popular for a number of reasons. First, sellers know more about costs than demand. By tying the price to cost, sellers simplify their own pricing task; they do not have to make frequent adjustments as demand changes. Second, where all firms in the industry use this pricing method, their prices tend to be similar. Price competition is therefore minimized. Third, many people feel that cost-plus pricing is fairer to both buyers and sellers. Sellers do not take advantage of buyers when buyers' demand becomes great; yet the sellers earn a fair return on their investment.

Break-even Analysis and Target Profit Pricing

try to calculate sales needed to break even

Another cost-oriented pricing approach is that of target profit pricing. The firm tries to determine the price that will produce the profit it is seeking. Target pricing is used by General Motors, which prices its cars to achieve a 15% to 20% profit on its investment. This pricing method is also used by public utilities, which are constrained to make a fair return on their investment.

Target pricing uses the concept of a break-even chart. A break-even chart shows the total cost and total revenue expected at different sales volume levels. Figure 10-7 shows a hypothetical break-even chart. Fixed costs are $6 million regardless of sales volume. Total costs (fixed costs plus variable costs) rise with volume. The total revenue curve starts at zero and rises with each unit sold. The slope of the total revenue curve reflects the price. Here the price is $15 (for example, the company's revenue is $12 million on 800,000 units, which comes out to $15 per unit).

At $15, the company must sell at least 600,000 units to break even, that is, for total revenue to cover total cost. If the company seeks a target profit of $2 million, it must sell at least 800,000 units at a price of $15 each. If the company is willing to charge a higher price, say $20, then it will not need to sell as many units to achieve its target profit. However, the market may not buy even this lower volume at the higher price—much depends on the price elasticity of demand. This is not shown in the break-even chart. This pricing method requires the company to consider different prices, their impact on the volume necessary to pass the break-even point and realize target profits, and the likelihood that this will happen with each possible price.

FIGURE 10-7

Break-even Chart for
Determining Target
Price

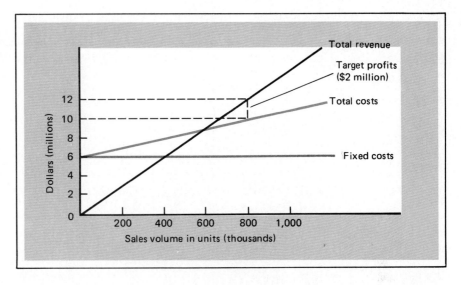

Perceived-Value Pricing An increasing number of companies are basing their prices on their products' perceived value. They see the buyers' perception of value, not the seller's cost, as the key to pricing. They use the nonprice factors in the marketing mix to build up perceived value in the buyers' minds. Prices are set to match the perceived value.

Consider the various prices that different restaurants charge for identical items. A consumer who wants a cup of coffee and a slice of apple pie may pay $1.25 at a drugstore counter, $1.50 at a family restaurant, $1.75 at a hotel coffee shop, $3.00 for hotel room service, and $4.00 at an elegant restaurant. Each successive restaurant can charge more because of the value added by the place's atmosphere.

The company using perceived-value pricing must establish the value of competing products in buyers' minds. In the previous example, consumers could be asked how much they would pay for the same coffee and pie in the different surroundings. Sometimes consumers could be asked how much they would pay for each benefit added to the offer. Exhibit 10-1 shows how Caterpillar uses the value of different benefits to price its construction equipment.

If the seller charges more than the buyer-recognized value, the company's sales will be lower than what they could be. Many companies overprice their products, and their products sell poorly. Other companies underprice their products. These products sell extremely well, but they produce less revenue than they would if their price was raised to the perceived-value level.[6]

Going-Rate Pricing In going-rate pricing, the firm bases its price largely on competitors' prices, with less attention paid to its own costs or to demand. The firm might charge the same, more, or less than its major competitor(s). In oligopolistic industries that

Consumers often judge the quality of products by the price charged.
Irene Springer

sell a commodity such as steel, paper, or fertilizer, firms normally charge the same price. The smaller firms "follow the leader." They change their prices when the market leader's prices change, rather than when their own demand or costs change. Some firms may charge a slight premium or give a slight discount, but they preserve the amount of difference. Thus minor gasoline retailers usually charge a few cents less than the major oil companies, without letting the difference increase or decrease.

Going-rate pricing is quite popular. Where demand elasticity is difficult to measure, firms feel that the going price represents the collective wisdom of the industry concerning the price that will yield a fair return. They also feel that conforming to the going price will preserve industrial harmony.

Sealed-Bid Pricing

Competitive-oriented pricing is also used when firms bid for jobs. The firm bases its own price on expectations of how competitors will price rather than on a relation to its own costs or to demand. The firm wants to win the contract, and this requires pricing lower than the other firms. Yet the firm cannot set its price below cost, or it will hurt itself financially.

Exhibit **10-1**

How Caterpillar Uses Perceived-Value Pricing

Caterpillar uses perceived value to set prices on its construction equipment. It might price a tractor at $24,000, although a similar competitor's tractor might be priced at $20,000. And Caterpillar will get more sales than the competitor! When prospective customers ask a Caterpillar dealer why they should pay $4,000 more for the Caterpillar tractor, dealers answer:

$20,000 is the tractor's price if it is only equivalent to the competitor's tractor

3,000 is the price premium for superior durability

2,000 is the price premium for superior reliability

2,000 is the price premium for superior service

1,000 is the price for the longer warranty on parts

$28,000 is the price to cover the value package

4,000 discount

$24,000 final price

Stunned customers learn that although they are being asked to pay a $4,000 premium for the Caterpillar tractor, they are in fact getting a $4,000 discount! They end up choosing the Caterpillar tractor because they are convinced that the lifetime operating costs of the Caterpillar tractor will be smaller.

Select the Final Price

The purpose of the previous pricing methods is to narrow the price range from which to select the final price. Before selecting the final price, however, the company must look at some additional considerations.

Psychological Pricing Sellers should consider the psychology of prices and not simply their economics. Many consumers use price as an indicator of quality. When Fleischmann raised the price of its gin from $4.50 to $5.50 a fifth, its liquor store sales went up, not down. Prestige pricing is especially effective with ego-sensitive products, such as perfumes and expensive cars. A $100 bottle of perfume may contain $10 worth of scent, but people are willing to pay $100 because this suggests something special.

Exhibit **10-2**

Price Decisions and Public Policy

Sellers must understand the law in pricing their products. They must avoid the following practices.

- *Price fixing:* Sellers must set prices without talking to competitors. Otherwise price collusion is suspected. Price fixing is illegal; the government does not accept any excuses for price fixing. The only exception is where price agreements are carried out under the supervision of a government agency, as in many local milk industry agreements, in the regulated transportation industries, and in fruit and vegetable cooperatives.
- *Resale price maintenance:* A manufacturer cannot require dealers to charge a specified retail price for its product. The seller can propose, however, a manufacturer's suggested retail price to dealers. The manufacturer cannot refuse to sell to a dealer who takes independent pricing action, nor punish the dealer by shipping late or denying advertising allowances. However, the manufacturer can refuse to sell to a dealer on other grounds presumably not related to the dealer's pricing.
- *Price discrimination:* The Robinson-Patman Act seeks to ensure that sellers offer the same price terms to a given level of trade. For example, every re- tailer is entitled to the same price terms whether the retailer is Sears or the local bicycle shop. However, price discrimination is allowed if the seller can prove its costs are different when selling to different retailers; for example, the seller has to prove that it costs less to sell a large volume of bicycles to Sears than to sell a few bicycles to a local dealer. Or the seller can discrimi- nate in its pricing if the seller manufactures different qualities of the same product for different retailers. The seller has to prove that these differences

Many sellers believe that prices should end in an odd number. Instead of pricing a stereo amplifier at $300, it should be priced at $299. Many customers will see this as a price in the $200 range rather than the $300 range. Newspaper ads are dominated with prices ending in odd numbers.[7]

Company Pricing Policies The possible price should be checked for consistency with company pricing policies. Many companies define the price image they want, their policy on price discounts, and their philosophy of meeting competitors' prices.

exist and that the price differences are proportional. Price differentials may also be used to "meet competition" in "good faith," providing the firm is trying to meet competitors at its own level of competition and that the price discrimination is temporary, localized, and defensive rather than offensive.

- *Minimum pricing:* A seller is not allowed to sell below cost with the intention to destroy competition. Wholesalers and retailers in over half the states face laws requiring a minimum percentage markup over their cost of merchandise plus transportation. These laws are called Unfair Trade Practices and attempt to protect small merchants from larger merchants who might sell items below cost to attract customers.

- *Price increases:* Companies are free to increase their prices to any level except in times of price controls. The major exception to the freedom of pricing is regulated public utilities. Since utilities have monopolistic power, their rates are regulated in the public interest. The government has used its influence from time to time to discourage major industry price hikes during periods of shortages or inflation.

- *Deceptive pricing:* Deceptive pricing is more common in the sale of consumer goods than business goods, because consumers typically possess less information and buying acumen. In 1958, the Automobile Information Disclosure Act required auto manufacturers to affix on auto windshields a statement of the manufacturer's suggested retail price, the prices of optional equipment, and the dealer's transportation charges. In the same year, the FTC issued its Guides against Deceptive Pricing, warning sellers not to advertise a price reduction unless it is a saving from the usual retail price, not to advertise "factory" or "wholesale" prices unless this is true, not to advertise comparable value prices on imperfect goods, and so forth.

Impact of Price on Other Parties

Management must also consider other parties' reactions to the contemplated price. How will the distributors and dealers feel about it? Will the company sales force be willing to sell at this price or will they complain that it is too high? How will competitors react to this price? Will suppliers raise their prices when they see the company's price? Will the government intervene and prevent this price from being charged? In the last case, marketers need to know the laws affecting price and make sure that their pricing policies are defensible. The major laws affecting prices are summarized in exhibit 10-2.

Summary

In spite of the increased role of nonprice factors in the modern marketing process, price remains an important element and is especially challenging in markets characterized by monopolistic competition or oligopoly.

In setting the price on a product, the company follows a six-step procedure. First, the company carefully establishes its marketing objective(s), such as survival, current profit maximization, market-share leadership, or product quality leadership. Second, the company determines the demand curve that shows the probable quantity purchased per period at alternative price levels. The more inelastic the demand, the higher the company can set its price. Third, the company estimates how its costs vary at different production levels. Fourth, the company examines competitors' prices as a basis for positioning its own price. Fifth, the company selects one of the following pricing methods: cost-plus pricing, break-even analysis and target profit pricing, perceived-value pricing, going-rate pricing, and sealed-bid pricing. Sixth, the company selects its final price, expressing it in the most effective psychological way, and checking to make sure that it conforms to company pricing policies and that it will prevail with the distributors and dealers, company sales force, competitors, suppliers, and government.

Questions for Discussion

1. What are the most influential factors affecting the setting of price in each of the four market types discussed in this chapter?
2. If product A's price elasticity of demand is -5 and product B's elasticity is -2, which would lose less from a price increase?
3. If you had a chance to open a car wash where annual fixed costs were $100,000, variable costs were $0.50 per car washed, and you determined that a competitive price would be $1.50 per car, would you invest in this business?
4. In setting prices, it is essential to establish only target market objectives. Comment.
5. Relate the main factors in developing pricing policies and constraints to Adidas's decision to price a new line of shoes.
6. What are the major types of cost-oriented pricing strategies? Give a company example for each type.
7. If a company is to respond accurately to price changes, it must thoroughly understand its competitors. Comment.
8. Public policy makers regulate what major pricing practices?

Key Terms in Chapter 10

Break-even pricing Pricing based on the cost of producing, marketing, and distributing a product and the profit the company is seeking.

Cost-plus pricing The addition of a standard markup to the cost of a product.

Elastic demand The tendency for demand for a

product to change because of a small price change.

Going-rate pricing Pricing based largely on competitors' prices rather than the company's own costs.

Inelastic demand The tendency for demand for a product to remain the same despite small changes in price.

Monopolistically competitive market Buyers and sellers who transact over a range of prices rather than a single market price.

Oligopolistic market A situation in which a few sellers, who are highly sensitive to each other's pricing and marketing strategies, sell to many buyers.

Perceived-value pricing Pricing based on the buyers' perception of value rather than the seller's cost.

Price The amount of money charged for a particular product.

Pure competitive market Buyers and sellers trading in a like commodity; a situation in which no single buyer or seller has much influence on the going market price.

Pure monopoly The presence of just one seller in a particular product market.

Sealed-bid pricing Pricing based on a firm's expectations of how competitors will price rather than on a relation to its own costs or to demand; used when companies bid for jobs.

Cases for Chapter 10

Case 9   Texas Instruments, Inc.: Learning-Aid Products That Talk (p. 503)

Texas Instruments must establish pricing objectives and determine demand for its product before it can tell if its pricing strategy will work. The chapter tells how they would go about it.

Case 10   Loctite Corporation (p. 505)

Loctite must choose pricing strategies for its new adhesives and sealants. This case looks at the factors Loctite must consider.

Chapter 11

Pricing Products: Pricing Strategies

Objectives

After reading this chapter, you should be able to:

1. Describe how a company sets a price for a new product.
2. List and define five types of discounts.
3. Discuss how pricing interacts with the other *P*'s in the marketing mix.
4. Explain why companies decide to change their prices.

Heublein, Inc., produces Smirnoff, the leading brand of vodka, which has 23% of the American market. In the 1960s, Smirnoff was attacked by another brand, Wolfschmidt, priced at one dollar less a bottle and claiming to be of the same quality. Heublein saw a real danger of customers switching to Wolfschmidt. Heublein considered the following possible counterstrategies:

1. Lower Smirnoff's price by one dollar to hold on to its market share.
2. Maintain Smirnoff's price but increase advertising and promotion expenditures.
3. Maintain Smirnoff's price and let its market share fall.

All three strategies would lead to lower profits. It seemed that Heublein faced a no-win situation.

At this point a fourth strategy occurred to Heublein's marketers, and it was brilliant. Heublein raised the price of Smirnoff by one dollar! It introduced a new brand, Relska, to compete with Wolfschmidt. And it introduced another brand, Popov, at a lower price than Wolfschmidt. This product-line strategy positioned Smirnoff as the elite brand and Wolfschmidt as an ordinary brand. Heublein's clever maneuvers produced a substantial increase in its overall profits.

The irony is that Heublein's three brands are pretty much the same in their taste and cost of manufacture. Heublein has learned how to sell substantially the same product at different prices by building effective concepts for each.

In this chapter we will look at pricing strategies. Companies do not set a single price. They create a pricing structure that covers different products and items in the product line and reflects variations in geographic costs, demand, purchase timing, and other factors. The company also faces a changing competitive environment and considers initiating price changes at times and responding to them at other times. This chapter will examine major pricing strategies available to management.

Pricing Strategies

Companies set their basic price and then modify it to meet varying factors in the environment. We will look at the following pricing strategies: new-product pricing, product-mix pricing, geographic pricing, discount pricing and allowances, promotional pricing, and discriminatory pricing.

New-Product Pricing A company's pricing strategy is based in part on the product life cycle. The introductory stage is especially challenging. We can distinguish between pricing a genuine product innovation that is protected by a patent and pricing a product that imitates existing products.

PRICING AN INNOVATIVE PRODUCT. Companies launching a patent-protected innovative product can choose between **market skimming pricing** and **market penetration pricing**.

Market skimming pricing. Many companies that invent new patent-protected products set high prices initially to "skim" the market. Du Pont often uses market skimming. On its new discoveries—cellophane, nylon, and so on—it estimates the highest price it can charge. Du Pont sets a price that makes it just worthwhile for some segments of the market to adopt the new material. After the initial sales slow down, it lowers the price to draw in the next price-sensitive layer of customers. In this way, Du Pont skims a maximum amount of revenue from various segments of the market. Polaroid also practices market skimming: It first introduces an expensive version of a new camera and gradually introduces simpler, lower-priced models to draw in new segments.

Market skimming makes sense under the following conditions: (1) a sufficient number of buyers have a high current demand; (2) the costs of producing a small volume are not so much higher that they cancel the advantage of market skimming; (3) the high initial price will not attract more competitors; (4) the high price supports the image of a superior product.

Market penetration pricing. Other companies set a relatively low price on their innovative product, hoping to attract a large number of buyers and win a large

		Price		
		High	Medium	Low
Product quality	High	1. Premium strategy	2. Penetration strategy	3. Superb-value strategy
	Medium	4. Overcharging strategy	5. Average strategy	6. Good-value strategy
	Low	7. Rip-off strategy	8. Cheap-flashy strategy	9. Cheap-value strategy

FIGURE 11-1

Nine Marketing Mix Strategies on Price/Quality

market share. Texas Instruments (TI) often uses market penetration pricing. TI will build a large plant, set its price as low as possible, win a large market share, experience falling costs, and cut its price further as costs fall.

The following conditions favor setting a low price:[1] (1) The market is highly price-sensitive, and a low price leads to more market growth; (2) production and distribution costs fall with more production; and (3) a low price discourages actual and potential competition.

PRICING AN IMITATIVE NEW PRODUCT. A company that plans to develop an imitative new product faces a product-positioning problem. It must decide where to position the product on quality and price. Figure 11-1 shows nine possible price/quality strategies. If the existing market leader falls into box 1 by producing the premium product and charging the highest price, the newcomer might prefer to use one of the other strategies. The newcomer could design a high-quality product and charge a medium price (box 2), design an average-quality product and charge an average price (box 5), and so on. The newcomer must consider the size and growth rate of the market in each cell and the particular competitors.

Product-Mix Pricing The strategy of setting a price on a product is different when the product is part of a product mix. In this case, the firm looks for a set of prices that maximize the profits on the total product mix. Pricing is difficult because the various products are related in terms of demand and cost and are subject to different degrees of competition. We will look at four situations.

PRODUCT-LINE PRICING. Companies normally develop product lines rather than single products. For example, Panasonic offers five different color video sound cameras, ranging from a simple one weighing 4.6 pounds to a complex one weighing 6.3 pounds that includes automatic focusing, fade control, and two speed zoom lenses. Each successive camera in the line offers additional features. Management must decide on the price steps to establish between the various cameras. The price steps should take into account cost differences between the cameras, customer evaluations of the different features, and com-

The different cameras in Panasonic's product line have prices to match costs, features, and consumers' perceptions of quality.

Photos courtesy of Panasonic

petitors' prices. If the price difference between two successive cameras is small, buyers will buy the more advanced cameras. If the price difference is large, customers will buy the less advanced cameras.

In many lines of trade, sellers use well-established price points for the products in their line. Thus men's clothing stores might carry men's suits at three price levels: $150, $220, and $310. The customers will associate low-, average-, and high-quality suits with the three price "points." Even if the three prices are moderately raised, men will normally buy suits at their preferred price point. The seller's task is to establish perceived quality differences that support the price differences.

OPTIONAL PRODUCT PRICING. Many companies offer to sell optional or accessory products along with their main product. The automobile buyer can order electric window controls, defoggers, and light dimmers. However, pricing these options is a sticky problem. Automobile companies have to decide which items to build into the price and which ones to offer as options. General Motors' normal pricing strategy is to advertise a stripped-down model for $6,000 to pull people into the showrooms and devote most of the showroom space to displaying loaded cars at $8,000 or $9,000. The economy model is stripped of so many comforts and conveniences that most buyers reject it. When GM launched its new front-wheel drive J-cars in the spring of 1981, it took a cue from the Japanese auto makers and included in the sticker price a number of useful items previously sold only as options. Now the advertised price represented a well-equipped car. Unfortunately, however, the price was over $8,000, and many car shoppers balked.

CAPTIVE PRODUCT PRICING. Companies in certain industries produce products—called captive products—that must be used with the main product. Examples of captive products are razor blades and camera film. Manufacturers of the main products (razors and cameras) often price the main products low and set high markups on the captive products. Thus Kodak prices its cameras low because it makes money on selling film. Those camera makers who do not sell film have to price their cameras higher in order to make the same overall profit.

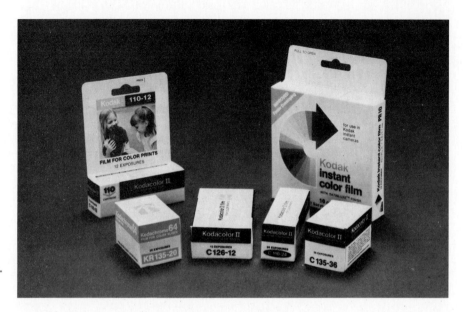

Kodak uses a captive product strategy for its film.
Courtesy Eastman Kodak Company

BY-PRODUCT PRICING.   In producing processed meats, petroleum products, and other chemicals, there are often by-products. If the by-products have no value and disposing of them is costly, this will affect the pricing of the main product. The manufacturer will seek a market for these by-products and will often accept any price that is higher than the cost of storing and delivering them. This will let the seller reduce the main product's price to make it more competitive.

Geographic Pricing

higher prices in diff local because of transportation

Geographic pricing involves the company's decision on pricing its products to customers located in different parts of the country. It costs more for a company to ship goods to a distant customer than to a near one. Should the company charge higher prices to distant customers to cover the higher shipping costs and thereby risk losing their business? Or should the company charge the same to all customers regardless of location? We will look at five major geographic pricing strategies in connection with the following hypothetical situation:

The Peerless Paper Company is located in Atlanta, Georgia, and sells paper products to customers all over the United States. The cost of freight is high and affects the companies from which customers buy their paper. Peerless wants to establish a geographic pricing policy. Management is trying to determine how to price a $100 order to three specific customers: customer A (Atlanta); customer B (Bloomington, Indiana); and customer C (Compton, California).

FOB ORIGIN PRICING.   Peerless can ask each customer to pay the shipping cost from the Atlanta factory to the customer's specific destination. All three customers would pay the same factory price of $100, with customer A paying, say, $10 for shipping, customer B paying $15, and customer C paying $25.

Called **FOB origin pricing**, it means that the goods are placed *free on board* a carrier, at which point the title and responsibility pass to the customer, who pays the freight from the factory to the destination.

Advocates of FOB origin pricing feel that this is the fairest way to assess freight charges, because each customer picks up its own cost. The disadvantage, however, is that Peerless will be a high-cost firm to distant customers. If Peerless's main competitor is in California, this competitor would outsell Peerless in California. In fact, the competitor would outsell Peerless in most of the West while Peerless would dominate the East. A vertical line could be drawn on a map connecting the cities where the two companies' price plus freight would be equal. Peerless would have the price advantage east of this line, and its competitor would have the price advantage west of this line.

UNIFORM DELIVERED PRICING. **Uniform delivered pricing** is the exact opposite of FOB pricing. Here the company charges the same price plus freight to all customers regardless of their location. The freight charge is set at the average freight cost. Suppose this is $15. Uniform delivered pricing therefore results in a high charge to the Atlanta customer (who pays $15 freight instead of $10) and a lower charge to the California customer (who pays $15 instead of $25). The Atlanta customer would prefer to buy paper from another local paper company that uses FOB origin pricing. On the other hand, Peerless has a better chance to win the California customer. Other advantages are that uniform delivered pricing is relatively easy to administer and allows the firm to have a nationally advertised price.

ZONE PRICING. **Zone pricing** falls between FOB origin pricing and uniform delivered pricing. The company establishes two or more zones. All customers within a zone pay the same total price, but this price is higher in the more distant zones. Peerless might set up an East zone and charge $10 freight to all customers in this zone; a Midwest zone and charge $15; and a West zone and charge $25. In this way, the customers within a given price zone receive no price advantage. Customers in Atlanta and Boston pay the same total price to Peerless. A complaint, however, is that the Atlanta customer is subsidizing the Boston customer's freight cost. In addition, a customer on the west side of the line dividing the East and Midwest pays more than one on the east side of the line, although they may be within a few miles of each other.

BASING-POINT PRICING. **Basing-point pricing** allows the seller to name some city as a basing point and charge all customers the freight cost from that city to the customer location regardless of the city from which the goods are actually shipped. For example, Peerless might establish Chicago as the basing point and charge all customers $100 plus the cost for freight from Chicago to the customer location. This means that an Atlanta customer pays the freight cost from Chicago to Atlanta even though the goods may be shipped from Atlanta. In its favor, using a basing-point location other than the factory raises the total price to customers near the factory and lowers the total price to customers far from the factory.

If all the sellers used the same basing-point city, delivered prices would be the same for all customers, and price competition would be eliminated. Such industries as sugar, cement, steel, and automobiles used basing-point pricing for years, but this method is less popular today. Some companies establish multiple basing points to create more flexibility. They quote freight charges from the basing-point city nearest to the customer.

FREIGHT ABSORPTION PRICING. The seller who is anxious to do business with a particular customer or geographic area might use **freight absorption pricing**. This involves absorbing all or part of the actual freight charges in order to get business. The seller might reason that if it can get more business, its average costs will fall and more than compensate for the extra freight costs. Freight absorption pricing is used to penetrate new markets and also to hold on to increasingly competitive markets.

Discount Pricing and Allowances Most companies will modify their basic price to reward customers for certain acts, such as early payment of bills, volume purchases, and buying off season. These price adjustments—called discounts and allowances—are described below.

CASH DISCOUNTS. A **cash discount** is a price reduction to buyers who pay their bills promptly. A typical example is "2/10, net 30." This means that payment is due within thirty days, but the buyer can deduct 2% from the cost by paying the bill within ten days. The discount must be given to all buyers meeting these terms. Such discounts are customary in many industries and help to improve the sellers' liquidity and reduce credit collection costs and bad debts.

QUANTITY DISCOUNTS. A **quantity discount** is a price reduction to buyers who buy large volumes. A typical example is "$10 per unit for less than 100 units; $9 per unit for 100 or more units." Quantity discounts must be offered to all

While ski manufacturers and resorts charge top prices in winter, they often offer discounts in other seasons.
Killington Photo/Bob Perry

customers and must not exceed the cost savings to the seller associated with selling large quantities. These savings include reduced expenses of selling, inventory, and transportation. Discounts provide an incentive to the customer to buy more from a given seller rather than buying from multiple sources.

FUNCTIONAL DISCOUNTS.   A functional discount (also called a trade discount) is offered by manufacturers to trade channel members who perform certain functions, such as selling, storing, and record keeping. Manufacturers may offer different functional discounts to different trade channels because of the varying services they perform, but manufacturers must offer the same functional discounts within each trade channel.

SEASONAL DISCOUNTS.   A **seasonal discount** is a price reduction to buyers who buy merchandise or services out of season. Seasonal discounts allow the seller to maintain steadier production during the year. Ski manufacturers will offer seasonal discounts to retailers in the spring and summer to encourage early ordering. Hotels, motels, and airlines will offer seasonal discounts in their slower selling periods.

ALLOWANCES.   **Allowances** are other types of reductions from the list price. For example, trade-in allowances are price reductions granted for turning in an old item when buying a new one. Trade-in allowances are most common in the auto industry and are also found in some other durable-goods categories. Promotional allowances are payments or price reductions to reward dealers for participating in advertising and sales-support programs.

Promotional Pricing

Under certain circumstances, companies will temporarily price their products below the list price, and sometimes even below cost. **Promotional pricing** takes several forms:

1. Supermarkets and department stores will price a few products as *loss leaders* to attract customers to the store in the hope that they will buy other things at normal markups.
2. Sellers will also use *special-event pricing* in certain seasons to draw in more customers. Thus white sales are run every January to attract shopping-weary customers into stores.
3. Manufacturers will sometimes offer *cash rebates* to consumers who buy the product from dealers within a specified time period. The manufacturer sends the rebate directly to the customer. Rebates are a flexible tool for trimming inventories during difficult selling periods without cutting list prices. They have recently been popular with Chrysler and other auto makers, and also with other big-ticket items such as Fedders, Polaroid, and Minolta.
4. Sellers often offer *discounts* from normal prices. One example of promotional discounting is seen in exhibit 11-1.

A white sale—a form of promotional pricing.
Anita Duncan

Exhibit **11-1**

Moving Mink Coats Through Promotional Discounting

Irwin and Carol Ware lease and operate the fur salon in the posh I. Magnin department store on North Michigan Avenue in Chicago. To move the sluggish inventory of fur coats, they decided to run a one-day sale. Fur coats were marked down from 50% to 70%. They loaded the racks with furs, with one rack bearing the sign "Everything on this rack below $2,000." To announce the sale, hype-type television advertising was used, as well as newspaper ads publicizing this as the sale of one's lifetime. Customers learned that they could take twenty-four months to pay.

Did this hard-sell, bargain-basement advertising work? No question about it. Carol Ware had over two hundred customers that day, with 50% leaving the store with newly purchased fur coats. The average salon sale: $4,500.

Source: Adapted from "Sale of Mink Coats Strays a Fur Piece from the Expected," *Wall Street Journal*, March 20, 1980, p. 1.

Discriminatory Pricing
Companies will often modify their basic price to allow for differences in customers, products, locations, and so on. In **discriminatory pricing**, the company sells a product or service at two or more prices that are not based on different costs. Discriminatory pricing takes several forms:

1. *Customer basis:* Different customers pay different amounts for the same product or service. Museums will charge students and senior citizens a lower admission fee.
2. *Product-form basis:* Different versions of the product are priced differently but not in proportion to their differences in costs. SCM Corporation prices its most expensive Proctor-Silex fabric iron at $54.95, which is five dollars more than its next most expensive iron. The top model has a light that signals when the iron is ready to use. Yet the extra feature costs less than one dollar to make.
3. *Place basis:* Different locations are priced differently even though the cost of offering each location is the same. A theater varies its seat prices because of audience preferences for certain locations.
4. *Time basis:* Prices are varied seasonally, by the day, and even by the hour. Public utilities vary their prices to commercial users by time of day and weekend versus weekday.

If price discrimination is to work, certain conditions must exist.[2] First, the market must be segmentable, and the segments must show different intensities

Airlines may use discriminatory pricing, charging different fares for different passengers under different circumstances.
Courtesy Delta Air Lines

of demand. Second, members of the segment paying the lower price should not be able to turn around and resell the product to the segment paying the higher price. Third, competitors should not be able to undersell the firm in the segment being charged the higher price. Fourth, the cost of segmenting and watching the market should not exceed the extra revenue from price discrimination. Fifth, the practice should not lead to customer resentment and ill will. Sixth, the particular form of price discrimination should not be considered illegal under the law.

With the current deregulation taking place in certain industries, such as air transportation and trucking, companies in these industries have increased their use of discriminatory pricing. Consider the price discrimination introduced by airlines:

> At one point, the passengers on a plane bound from Cleveland to Miami were paying as many as eleven different fares for the same flight due to the heated-up competition between Eastern, United, and three other airlines flying this route. Many of the fares were aimed at segments of the market. The eleven possible fares were (1) $218 for first class, (2) $168 for standard economy class, (3) $136 for night coach, (4) $134 for weekend excursion, (5) $130 for Job Corps volunteers, (6) $128 for midweek excursion, (7) $118 for group-excursion tours, (8) $112 for military personnel, (9) $112 for youth fares, (10) $103 for weekend fares, and (11) $95 for charter.

Initiating Price Changes

After developing their price structure and strategies, companies will face occasions when they will want to cut or raise prices.

Initiating Price Cuts Several circumstances may lead a firm to consider cutting its price. One circumstance is excess capacity. Here the firm needs additional business and cannot get it through increased sales efforts, product improvements, or other measures. In the late 1970s, various companies abandoned "follow-the-leader pricing" and turned to "flexible pricing" to boost their sales.[3]

Another circumstance is falling market share in the face of vigorous price competition. Several American industries—automobiles, consumer electronics, cameras, watches, and steel—have been losing their market share to Japanese competitors, whose high-quality products carry lower prices than American products. Zenith, General Motors, and other American companies have resorted to more aggressive pricing action. General Motors, for example, cut its subcompact car prices by 10% on the West Coast, where Japanese competition is strongest.

Companies will also initiate price cuts in a drive to dominate the market through lower costs. Either the company starts with lower costs than its competitors, or it initiates price cuts in the hope of gaining a market share that will lead to falling production costs through larger volume.

Initiating Price Increases Many companies have had to raise prices in recent years. They do this knowing that the price increases will be resented by customers, distributors, and the company's own sales force. Yet a successful price increase can increase profits considerably. For example, if the company's profit margin is 3% of sales, a 1% price increase will increase profits by 33% if sales volume is unaffected.

or maintain a profit margin

A major circumstance leading to price increases is the persistent worldwide cost inflation.[4] Rising costs unmatched by productivity gains squeeze profit margins and lead companies to regular rounds of price increases. Companies often raise their prices by more than the cost increase in anticipation of further inflation or government price controls. Companies hesitate to make long-run price commitments to customers—they fear that cost inflation will erode their profit margins. Companies are able to increase their prices in a number of ways to fight inflation.[5]

Another factor leading to price increases is overdemand. When a company cannot supply all of its customers' needs, it can raise its prices, ration the product to customers, or both. Prices can be raised almost invisibly by dropping discounts and adding higher-priced units to the line. Or prices can be pushed up openly.

Customers' Reactions to Price Changes Whether the price is raised or lowered, the action will surely affect customers, competitors, distributors, and suppliers and may interest government as well. Here we will consider buyers' reactions.

Customers do not always put a straightforward interpretation on price changes.[6] A price cut can be interpreted in the following ways:[7] (1) The item is about to be replaced by a later model; (2) the item has some fault and is not selling well; (3) the firm is in financial trouble and may not stay in business to

When inventory ↗ recession is nearby

Exhibit 11-2

The Price War in the Home Computer Market

There's a war on. A price war, that is, and the battleground is the home computer market. As recently as the fall of 1982, the lowest-priced home computers sold for around $200 to $300. Six months later the manufacturers of those computers, companies like Texas Instruments (TI), Commodore International Ltd., and Atari, in fierce competition with one another, were forced to drop prices even lower, to around $99. Timex now sells the lowest-priced home computer for $45.

A result of the price cutting, not surprisingly, has been a dramatic increase in home computer sales: The number of home computers shipped in 1983 was twice that of 1982. The two leaders in sales that have emerged from this price war are Commodore, with 33% of sales, and Texas Instruments, with 22%.

For manufacturers there are some serious drawbacks to the recent price cuts, despite the increases in sales. One is that price reductions mean much smaller profit margins. Another is that very rapid changes in price can cause some models to become obsolete even before they are available to consumers. For example, a company can design a low-priced model as an alternative to one of its more sophisticated models. If the manufacturer is suddenly forced to drop the price of the more expensive model, producing the new low-priced model becomes pointless. Something like this has happened to Texas Instruments. The company was busy designing its 99/2 models to be available at $99.95 when price reductions by other companies forced TI to drop the price of its more sophisticated 99/4A to $99. Texas Instruments will now probably have to drop the 99/2 altogether.

Until recently another type of home electronics machine—the video games player—was thought to be designed for another market. Today, however, the low price of the home computer is leading the two markets to combine. Because the home computer can be used as a video games player, as well as performing a variety of other tasks, consumers consider the home computer a more economical choice than the video games player. Now manufacturers of video games players, including Mattel and Coleco, are dropping games machines and introducing their own home computers into an already crowded market.

So far, though, some of the computer industry's most influential companies, such as IBM, Apple, and several Japanese companies, have not entered the home computer market. The personal computers made by these companies cost more than $1,500. IBM and Apple are both planning to introduce computers for under $1,000, however. Industry analysts predict that when these giants enter the home computer competition, smaller companies will be forced to drop out.

Source: "A Price War Blasts Open the Home Market," *Business Week*, June 13, 1983, pp. 104–10.

supply future parts; (4) the price will come down even further, and it pays to wait; or (5) the quality has been reduced.

A price increase, which would normally deter sales, may carry some positive meanings to the buyers: (1) The item is very "hot" and may be unobtainable unless it is bought soon; (2) the item is an unusually good value; or (3) the seller is greedy and is charging what the traffic will bear.

Competitors' Reactions to Price Changes A firm that is contemplating a price change has to worry about competitors' as well as customers' reactions. Competitors are very likely to react where the number of firms is small, the product is similar to others, and the buyers are highly informed.

How can the firm anticipate the likely reactions of its competitors? Assume that the firm faces one large competitor. The competitor may react in a set way to price changes. In that case, the competitor's reaction can be anticipated. Or the competitor may treat each price change as a fresh challenge and react according to self-interest at the time. In that case, the company will have to determine the competitor's self-interest at the time, such as boosting sales or stimulating demand.

When there are several competitors, the company must guess each competitor's likely reaction. All the competitors may behave alike, or they may behave differently because of critical differences in size, market shares, or policies. If some competitors will match the price change, there is good reason to expect that the rest will also match it.

Responding to Price Changes

Here we reverse the question and ask how a firm should respond to a price change initiated by a competitor. The firm needs to consider the following issues: (1) Why did the competitor change the price? Is it to steal the market, to use excess capacity, to meet changing costs, or to lead an industry-wide price change? (2) Does the competitor plan to make the price change temporary or permanent? (3) What will happen to the company's market share and profits if it doesn't respond? Are other companies going to respond? (4) What are the competitor's and other firms' responses likely to be to each possible reaction?

Besides these issues, the company must make a broader analysis. The company has to consider the product's stage in the life cycle, its importance in the company's product mix, the intentions and resources of the competitor, the price and value sensitivity of the market, the behavior of costs with volume, and the company's other opportunities.

An extended analysis of company alternatives is not always feasible at the time of a price change. The competitor may have spent considerable time in preparing for this decision, but the company may have to react decisively within hours or days. About the only way to cut down price-reaction decision time is to anticipate the competitor's possible price changes and prepare responses ahead of time.

Summary

Companies apply a variety of pricing strategies to the basic price. One is geographic pricing, where the company decides how to price to distant customers, choosing from such alternatives as FOB pricing, uniform delivered pricing, zone pricing, basing-point pricing, and freight absorption pricing. A second is discount pricing and allowances, where the company establishes cash discounts, quantity discounts, functional discounts, seasonal discounts, and allowances. A third is promotional pricing, where the company decides on loss-leader pricing, special-event pricing, and cash rebates. A fourth is discriminatory pricing, where the company establishes different prices for different customers, product forms, places, and times. A fifth is new-product pricing, where the company decides between introducing a patent-protected product innovation with skimming versus market penetration pricing. It decides on one of nine price/quality strategies for introducing an imitative product. A sixth is product-mix pricing, where the company decides on the price points for several products in a product line, and on the pricing of optional products, captive products, and by-products.

When a firm considers initiating a price change, it must carefully consider customers' and competitors' reactions. Customers' reactions are influenced by the meaning customers see in the price change. Competitors' reactions flow from either a set reaction policy or a fresh appraisal of each situation. The firm initiating the price change must also anticipate the probable reactions of suppliers, distributors, and government.

The firm that faces a price change initiated by a competitor must try to understand the competitor's intent and the likely duration of the change. If swiftness of reaction is desirable, the firm should preplan its reactions to different possible price actions by competitors.

Questions for Discussion

1. Armco, a major steel company, has developed a new process for galvanizing steel sheets so that they can be painted (previously not possible) and used in auto-body parts to prevent rust. What factors should Armco consider in setting a price for this product?
2. GE has invented a revolutionary new household light bulb that will last five times longer than the typical 1,000-hour life of ordinary light bulbs and use only one-third as much electricity. It is thinking of pricing the light bulb at $10 (this will save $20 over the light bulb's rated life in lower electric bills). What problems might GE have with this pricing policy? What suggestions would you make?
3. In 1981 and 1982, auto makers resorted to aggressive rebate programs in an attempt to sell more cars. What dangers exist with this pricing strategy?
4. Discuss whether the following companies practice market penetration or market skimming in pricing their products: (a) McDonald's, (b) Curtis Mathes television sets, and (c) Bic Corporation. Why?
5. Discuss the psychological pricing tactics that you think the following marketers use: (a) Hart Schaffner and Marx, (b) Safeway, (c) K mart, and (d) Kinney Shoes.

6. Discuss the two major discount pricing tactics that Head Skis might use in dealing with the retail outlets that carry its products.
7. In recent years the majority of price changes made by marketers have been price increases. Why?

Key Terms in Chapter 11

Allowance   A payment or price reduction granted for participation in certain programs, such as trade-ins of durable goods.

Basing-point pricing   A geographic pricing strategy in which the seller names a city as a basing point and charges all customers the freight cost from that city regardless of the city from which the goods are actually shipped.

Cash discount   A price reduction to buyers who pay their bills promptly.

Discriminatory pricing   The selling of a product at two or more prices that are not based on different costs.

FOB origin pricing   A geographic pricing strategy in which goods are placed free on board a carrier, and the customer pays the freight charges from the factory to the destination.

Freight absorption pricing   The practice of absorbing all or part of the freight charges in order to get business.

Functional discount   The manufacturer's discount offered to trade channel members who perform certain functions, such as selling, storing, and record keeping.

Market penetration pricing   The practice of setting a relatively low price on an innovative product in order to attract a large number of buyers and win a large market share.

Market skimming pricing   The practice of setting the price of a newly invented product as high as possible so that it is just worthwhile for some segments to adopt the product and the company receives the maximum amount of revenue.

Promotional pricing   The temporary pricing of products below the list price, sometimes below cost.

Quantity discount   A price reduction to buyers who buy large volumes.

Seasonal discount   A price reduction to buyers who buy merchandise or services out of season.

Uniform delivered pricing   A geographic pricing strategy in which a company charges the same price plus freight to all customers regardless of their location.

Zone pricing   A geographic pricing strategy in which all customers within a zone pay the same total price; this price is higher in the more distant zones.

Cases for Chapter 11

Case 9   Texas Instruments, Inc.: Learning-Aid Products That Talk (p. 503)
Which pricing strategy should Texas Instruments use for its learning-aid products? This case looks at why it may choose a certain strategy.

Case 10   Loctite Corporation (p. 505)
When Loctite chooses prices for its new adhesives and sealants, it must consider many factors. This case examines the factors.

Chapter 12

Placing Products: Distribution Channels and Physical Distribution

Objectives

After reading this chapter, you should be able to:

1. List the levels and functions of a distribution channel.
2. Identify the major channel alternatives open to a company.
3. Discuss how a company develops physical distribution objectives.
4. Compare the five major transportation modes.

At the end of the last century, many wealthy families built green-houses on their estates so that they could enjoy the sight and smell of freshly cut flowers in their homes. Bouquets of flowers brightened formal parties in the ballroom and afternoon tea in the parlor.

Large-scale commercial flower growing began in the early 1900s, when the general public took up the practice of buying fresh flowers for special occasions. To serve this expanding market, commercial growers began raising flowers in greenhouses located just outside large cities. Wholesalers entered the business to transport flowers from the growers to city flower shops. These businesses could operate only locally and on a small scale because of the product's perishability. Flowers have to be cut, transported, and sold to retailers very quickly in order to be available to the consumer while still fresh.

Air transportation caused major changes in the flower industry, however. The ability to move flowers rapidly over long distances allowed growers to produce large quantities of flowers in warm climates, such as California and Florida, and sell them to wholesalers for distribution to any part of the country.

Today jet transportation has further meaning for the flower industry: Foreign growers can compete in the American market. Colombian growers, for instance, are responsible for a major portion of the carnations and pompons sold in U.S. shops. The cost of flying a jetload of flowers from Colombia to the East Coast is about the same as the cost of flying a jetload from California. While Colombians must pay a U.S. duty to sell their flowers here, their labor costs are considerably lower than those of our own growers. An additional advantage for the Colombians is a warmer climate than in either California or Florida, where greenhouse heating costs are often staggering. Other countries competing in the American flower market include Holland and Israel. The result of foreign competition is that some American growers have been

4P
Prod
Pric
Prom
Place (where
        you
        distrib it)
right place
many places

forced out of the business. Others have had to switch to growing types of flowers that they know are not being imported.

The growers are not the only members of the flower industry that are having business problems. Retailers and wholesalers are troubled by the fact that Americans just don't buy enough flowers. In 1982, the average U.S. consumer spent approximately $20 for flowers. Wholesalers claim retailers are at fault for the poor sales. Most shops keep flowers in refrigerators behind a counter, an arrangement that discourages browsing, according to wholesalers. Street vendors, in contrast, sell their product right out in the open, making flowers directly accessible to passersby, a practice wholesalers would like to encourage retailers to adopt.

Wholesalers say that the flower industry is not likely to expand until retailers promote flowers for everyday use. At the moment, Americans tend to buy flowers only for formal occasions, like weddings and funerals. One retailer who agrees with wholesalers on this issue is Al Felly of Madison, Wisconsin. Felly points out that if each of the 80,000 homes in his town bought a $3 bouquet each week, annual revenues for local flower shops would total about $12 million. Actual revenues for 1980 were only about $200,000.

To increase sales, the American flower industry might follow a European example. Several years ago, the European flower industry developed the consumer habit of buying flowers for everyday use. The remedy involved three steps. The first was to improve distribution so that flowers would get into the stores more quickly. Second, retailers reduced markups, attracting more customers and enabling them to buy in larger volumes. Finally, European retailers offered a greater variety of flowers. The U.S. flower industry could benefit from changing its marketing and distribution procedures in similar ways because, as one wholesaler asks sadly, "What other industry do you know that has a product that everybody loves and nobody buys?"[1]

Distribution channel decisions are among the most critical decisions facing management. The company's chosen channels directly affect every other marketing decision. The company's pricing depends upon whether it uses large and high-quality dealers or medium-size, medium-quality dealers. The firm's sales-force decisions depend on how much selling and training the dealers will need. In addition, the company's channel decisions involve relatively long-term commitments to other firms. When a truck manufacturer signs up independent dealers, it cannot easily replace them with company-owned branches if conditions change. Therefore, management must choose channels with an eye on tomorrow's likely selling environment as well as today's.

In this chapter we will examine three major issues: (1) What is the nature of distribution channels? (2) What problems do companies face in designing and managing their channels? (3) What role do physical distribution decisions play in attracting and satisfying customers? In chapter 13 we will examine distribution channel issues from the perspective of retailers and wholesalers.

The Nature of Distribution Channels

Most producers work with middlemen to bring their product to market. They try to forge a distribution channel.

> A **distribution channel** is the set of firms and individuals that take title, or assist in transferring title, to the particular product or service as it moves from the producer to the consumer.

Why Are Middlemen Used? Why is the producer willing to give some of the selling job to middlemen? This means giving up some control over how and to whom the products are sold. Producers feel, however, that they gain certain advantages in using middlemen. These advantages are described below.

Many producers lack the financial resources to carry out direct marketing. For example, General Motors sells its automobiles through over eighteen thousand independent dealers. Even General Motors would be hard pressed to raise the cash to buy out its dealers.

Direct marketing would require many producers to become middlemen for the products of other producers in order to achieve mass-distribution economies. For example, the Wm. Wrigley Jr. Company would not find it practical to establish small retail gum shops throughout the country or to sell gum door to door or by mail order. It would have to sell gum along with many other small products and would end up in the drugstore or foodstore business. Wrigley finds it easier to work through the extensive network of privately owned distributors.

Even if producers can afford to establish their own channels, they can often earn a greater return by increasing their investment in their main business. If a company earns a 20% rate of return on manufacturing and foresees only a 10% return on retailing, it will not want to undertake its own retailing.

The use of middlemen largely boils down to their superior efficiency in making goods widely available and accessible to target markets. Middlemen, through their contacts, experience, specialization, and scale of operation, offer the firm more than it can usually achieve on its own.

Figure 12-1 shows one major source of the economies gained by the use of middlemen. Part a shows three producers each using direct marketing to reach three customers. This system requires nine different contacts. Part b shows the three producers working through one distributor, who contacts the three custom-

FIGURE 12-1

How a Distributor
Reduces the Number
of Direct Contacts

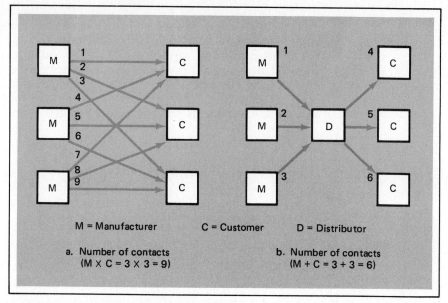

FIGURE 12-1

How a Distributor
Reduces the Number
of Direct Contacts

M = Manufacturer   C = Customer   D = Distributor

a. Number of contacts
   (M X C = 3 X 3 = 9)

b. Number of contacts
   (M + C = 3 + 3 = 6)

ers. This system requires only six contacts. In this way, middlemen reduce the amount of work that must be done.

Distribution Channel Functions

A distribution channel moves goods from producers to consumers. It overcomes the major time, place, and possession gaps that separate goods and services from those who would use them. Members of the distribution channel perform a number of key functions:[2]

1. Research—gathering information necessary for planning and aiding exchange.
2. Promotion—developing and spreading persuasive communications about the product.
3. Contact—finding and communicating with prospective buyers.
4. Matching—shaping and fitting the product to the buyer's requirements. This includes such activities as manufacturing, grading, assembling, and packaging.
5. Negotiation—attempting to agree on price and other terms so that transfer of ownership or possession can happen.
6. Physical distribution—transporting and storing the goods.
7. Financing—acquiring and using funds to cover the costs of the channel work.
8. Risk taking—taking on the risks in connection with carrying out the channel work.

The first five functions help complete transactions; the last three help fulfill the completed transactions.

The question is not *whether* these functions need to be performed—they must be—but rather *who* is to perform them. All the functions have three things in common: They use up scarce resources, they can often be performed better through specialization, and they can be performed by different channel members. To the extent that the manufacturer performs them, its costs go up and its prices have to be higher. When some functions are shifted to middlemen, the producer's costs and prices are lower, but the middlemen must add a charge to cover their work. The issue of who should perform various channel functions is one of relative efficiency and effectiveness. If the functions can be performed more efficiently, the channel will change.

Number of Channel Levels

Distribution channels can be described by the number of channel levels. Each middleman that performs some work in bringing the product and its title closer to the final buyer is a *channel level.* Since the producer and the final consumer both perform some work, they are part of every channel. We will use the number of intermediary levels to name the length of a channel. Figure 12-2 illustrates several marketing channels of different lengths.

A *zero-level channel* (also called a *direct marketing channel*) consists of a manufacturer selling directly to consumers. The three major ways of direct selling are door to door, mail order, and manufacturer-owned stores. Avon's sales representatives sell cosmetics to homemakers on a door-to-door basis; Franklin Mint sells collectible objects through mail order; and Singer sells its sewing machines through its own stores.

A *one-level channel* contains one middleman. In consumer markets, this middleman is typically a retailer; in industrial markets, it is often a sales agent or a broker.

FIGURE 12-2

Examples of Different Channel Levels

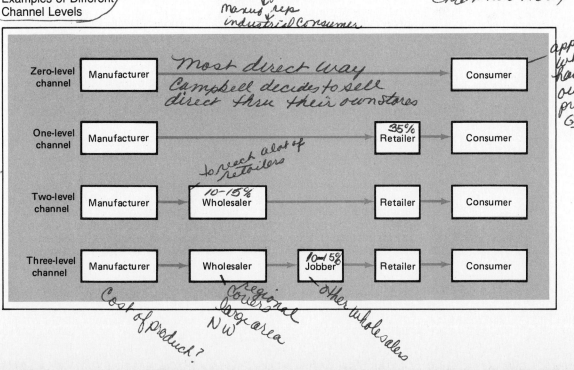

A *two-level channel* contains two middlemen. In consumer markets, they are typically a wholesaler and a retailer; in industrial markets, they may be an industrial distributor and dealers.

A *three-level channel* contains three middlemen. For example, in the meat-packing industry, jobbers usually come between wholesalers and retailers. Jobbers buy from wholesalers and sell to the smaller retailers, who generally are not serviced by the large wholesalers.

Distribution channels with more levels are also found, but with less frequency. From producers' points of view, the higher the number of channel levels, the less control they have.

Channels in the Service Sector

The concept of distribution channels is not limited to the distribution of physical goods. Producers of services and ideas also face the problem of making their output available and accessible to target populations. They develop "educational dissemination systems" and "health delivery systems." They must figure out agencies and locations for reaching a widespread population:

> Hospitals must be located in geographic space to serve the people with complete medical care, and we must build schools close to the children who have to learn. Fire stations must be located to give rapid access to potential conflagrations, and voting booths must be placed so that people can cast their ballots without expending unreasonable amounts of time, effort, or money to reach the polling stations. Many of our states face the problem of locating branch campuses to serve a burgeoning and increasingly well-educated population. In the cities we must create and locate playgrounds for the children. Many overpopulated countries must assign birth control clinics to reach the people with contraceptive and family planning information.[3]

Service businesses must develop their own distribution systems to fit their products. One example is Delta Airlines, as is shown in exhibit 12-1. Distribution channels also are used in "person" marketing. Before 1940, professional comedians could reach audiences through seven channels: vaudeville houses, special events, nightclubs, radio, movies, carnivals, and theaters. In the 1950s, television emerged as a strong channel, and vaudeville disappeared. Politicians also must find cost-effective channels—mass media, rallies, coffee hours—for distributing their messages to voters.

Channels normally describe a forward movement of products. We can also talk about *backward* channels. According to Zikmund and Stanton:

> The recycling of solid wastes is a major ecological goal. Although recycling is technologically feasible, reversing the flow of materials in the channel of distribution—marketing trash through a "backward" channel—presents a challenge. Existing backward channels are primitive, and financial incentives are inadequate. The consumer must be motivated to undergo a role change and become a producer—the initiating force in the reverse distribution process.[4]

The authors identify several middlemen that can play a role in "backward" chan-

Exhibit **12-1**

Delta Airline's "Hub-and-Spoke" Concept of Flight Scheduling

For many years, Delta has been the world's most profitable airline. Contributing to Delta's consistent lead are a number of factors, including its ability to make long-range business plans and stick to them and its excellent relations with employees. Perhaps the most important key to the airline's success, though, is its innovative distribution system for its product: airline flights.

Delta's system is known as the "hub-and-spoke" concept of flight scheduling. The "hub," or center of the system, is the airline's headquarters in Atlanta, Georgia; its routes to certain other U.S. cities form the "spokes." Delta schedules its short flights from those cities so that they all interconnect in Atlanta. Flights arrive in this central location and depart from it in groups. Ten times per day, thirty or more Delta flights all land at Atlanta's airport within minutes of one another. Then, in what the airline's employees refer to as the "big push," another group of thirty or so flights take off in all directions.

The system coordinates Delta's service so that the airline can match passengers who have to change planes in Atlanta with planes about to depart for a variety of destinations. For passengers, the hub-and-spoke system means convenient flight connections and short waiting times. For the airline, the system means that passengers are more likely to choose Delta than any other airline for connecting flights. A study of sales over a six-month period showed that almost 90% of Delta's passengers who fly into Atlanta on their way to other cities transfer to other Delta flights.

There are potential problems with this system, however. Because the flights are scheduled to coordinate with one another, bad weather in Atlanta can cause massive delays throughout the entire route system. Another snag occurs when flights are delayed before they reach Atlanta: Holding departing flights for the late incoming ones also spreads delays.

Overall, though, Delta's system works. Centralizing service has kept the airline's sales high. Most other airlines have now adopted similar hub-and-spoke systems with good results. But Delta remains the master of this distribution system.

Source: Based on "Delta: The World's Most Profitable Airline," *Business Week,* August 31, 1981, pp. 68–72.

nels, including (1) manufacturers' redemption centers, (2) "Clean-up Days" community groups, (3) traditional middlemen, such as soft-drink middlemen, (4) trash-collection specialists, (5) recycling centers, (6) modernized "rag and junk dealers," (7) trash-recycling brokers, and (8) central-processing warehousing.

Growth of Vertical Marketing Systems

One of the most significant recent channel developments has been the vertical marketing systems that have emerged to challenge conventional distribution channels. Figure 12-3 contrasts the two types of channel arrangements. A typical conventional distribution channel consists of an independent producer, wholesaler(s), and retailer(s). Each is a separate business seeking to maximize its own profits, even if that is at the expense of maximizing the profits for the system as a whole. No channel member has complete or substantial control over the other members.

A vertical marketing system (VMS), by contrast, consists of the producer, wholesaler(s), and retailer(s) acting as a unified system. Either one channel member owns the others, or franchises them, or has so much power that they all cooperate. The vertical marketing system can be dominated by the producer, wholesaler, or retailer.[5] VMSs came into being to control channel behavior and eliminate the conflict that results from independent channel members pursuing their own objectives. They are economical through their size, bargaining power, and elimination of duplicated services. VMSs have become the dominant mode of distribution in consumer marketing, serving as much as 64% of the total market.

We will now examine three major types of VMSs, which are shown in figure 12-4.

CORPORATE VMS. A **corporate VMS** combines successive stages of production and distribution under single ownership. As examples:

> Sherwin-Williams currently owns and operates over 2,000 retail outlets . . . Sears reportedly obtains 50 percent of its throughput from manufacturing facilities in which it has an equity interest . . . Holiday Inns is evolving into a self-supply network that includes a carpet mill, a furniture manufacturing plant, and numerous captive redistribution facilities. In short, these and other organizations are massive, vertically integrated systems. To describe them as "retailers," "manufacturers," or "motel operators" oversimplifies their operating complexities and ignores the realities of the marketplace.[6]

CONTRACTUAL VMS. A **contractual VMS** consists of independent firms linked by contracts and coordinating their programs to obtain more economies and/or

FIGURE 12-3

Comparison of Conventional Distribution Channel with Vertical Marketing System

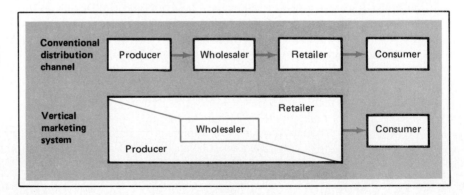

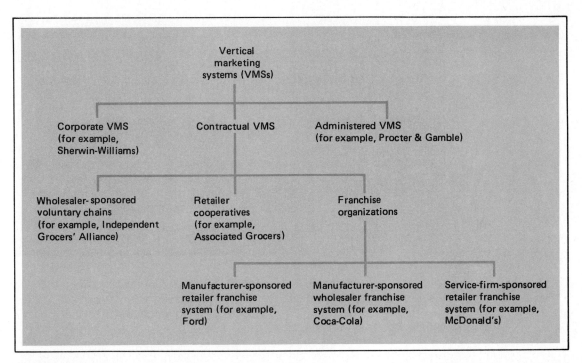

FIGURE 12-4

Types of Vertical
Marketing Systems

sales impact than they could achieve alone. Contractual VMSs have expanded
the most in recent years and are one of the most significant developments in the
economy. There are three types of contractual VMSs.

Wholesaler-sponsored voluntary chains. Wholesalers organize voluntary
chains of independent retailers to help them compete with large chain organizations. The wholesaler develops a program in which independent retailers stan-
dardize their selling practices and achieve buying economies that help the group
compete effectively with chain organizations. An example is the Independent
Grocers' Alliance.

and sponsor a chain

Retailer cooperatives. Retailers may take the initiative and organize a new
business entity to carry on wholesaling and possibly production. Members concentrate their purchases through the retailer co-op and plan their advertising
jointly. Profits are passed back to members in proportion to their purchases.
Nonmember retailers may also buy through the co-op but do not share in the
profits. An example is the Associated Grocers.

Franchise organizations. A channel member called a franchiser might link
several successive stages in the production-distribution process. Franchising
has been the fastest-growing and most interesting retailing development in recent years. Although the basic idea is an old one, some forms of franchising are
quite new. Three forms of franchises can be distinguished.

A franchise is part of a vertical marketing system, linked by contract to the producer.
Marc Anderson

The first is the *manufacturer-sponsored retailer franchise system,* found in the automobile industry. Ford, for example, licenses dealers to sell its cars, the dealers being independent business people who agree to meet various conditions of sales and service.

The second is the *manufacturer-sponsored wholesaler franchise system,* which is found in the soft-drink industry. Coca-Cola, for example, licenses bottlers (wholesalers) in various markets, who buy its syrup concentrate and then carbonate, bottle, and sell it to retailers in local markets.

The third is the *service-firm-sponsored retailer franchise system.* Here a service firm organizes a whole system for bringing its service efficiently to consumers. Examples are found in the auto rental business (Hertz, Avis), fast-food service business (McDonald's, Burger King), and motel business (Howard Johnson, Ramada Inn). This type of franchising system is discussed further in chapter 13.

ADMINISTERED VMS. An **administered VMS** coordinates successive stages of production ond distribution not through common ownership but through the size and power of one of the parties. Manufacturers of a top brand are able to gain strong cooperation and support from resellers. Thus General Electric, Procter & Gamble, Kraft, and Campbell Soup are able to command unusual cooperation from their resellers in connection with displays, shelf space, promotions, and price policies.

Growth of Horizontal Marketing Systems
Another development in distribution channels is the readiness of two or more companies to follow an emerging marketing opportunity together. Each company lacks the capital, know-how, production, or marketing resources to venture alone, or it is afraid of the risk, or it sees a substantial gain in joining with another company. The companies may work with each other on a temporary or permanent basis, or create a separate company. For example, Dr Pepper lacked

bottlers for its soft drink and decided to license Coca-Cola bottlers to bottle Dr. Pepper.

Growth of Multichannel Marketing Systems
Companies are increasingly using multichannel marketing systems to reach the same or different markets. For example, the John Smythe Company, a Chicago-based furniture retailer, sells a full line of furniture through its company-owned furniture stores as well as through its Homemakers Division, which operates furniture warehouse showrooms. Furniture shoppers can find many of the same items in both channels, usually finding lower prices at the latter. As another example, J. C. Penney operates department stores, mass-merchandising stores (called The Treasury), and specialty stores.

Many companies operate multichannel marketing systems that serve different customers.[7] For example, General Electric sells large home appliances both through independent dealers (department stores, discount houses, catalog retailers) and also directly to large housing tract builders. The independent dealers would like General Electric to get out of the business of selling to tract builders. General Electric defends itself by pointing out that builders and retailers need very different marketing approaches.

Channel Cooperation, Conflict, and Competition
Different degrees of cooperation, conflict, and competition can be found within and between distribution channels.

Channel cooperation is usual among members of the same channel. Manufacturers, wholesalers, and retailers complement each other's needs, and their cooperation normally produces greater profits than each participant could have obtained individually. By cooperating, they can more effectively sense, serve, and satisfy the target market.

Channel conflict, however, often arises within the channel. Sometimes, the conflict is among firms at the same channel level. Some Ford car dealers in Chicago complain about other Ford dealers in the city being too aggressive in their pricing and advertising and stealing sales from them. Some Pizza Inn franchisees complain about other Pizza Inn franchisees cheating on the ingredients, maintaining poor service, and hurting the overall Pizza Inn image. In these cases, the channel captain must establish clear and enforceable policies and take quick action to control this type of conflict.

Conflict can also occur between different levels of the same channel. For example, General Motors came into conflict with its dealers some years ago in trying to enforce policies on service, pricing, and advertising. And Coca-Cola came into conflict with its bottlers who agreed to bottle Dr Pepper.

Channel competition occurs between firms and systems trying to serve the same target markets. For example, department stores, discount stores, and catalog houses all compete for consumers' appliance dollars. This competition should result in consumers' enjoying a wider range of product choices, prices, and services. Competition also occurs between different whole systems serving a given market. For example, food consumers are served by conventional distribution channels, corporate chains, wholesale-sponsored voluntary chains, retailer-cooperatives, and food franchise systems.

Channel Design Decisions

We will now examine several channel decision problems facing manufacturers. In designing distribution channels, manufacturers have to struggle between what is ideal and what is available. A new firm is usually local or regional, selling in a limited market. Since it has limited capital, it usually uses existing middlemen. The number of middlemen in any local market is apt to be limited: a few manufacturers' sales agents, a few wholesalers, several established retailers, a few trucking companies, and a few warehouses. Deciding on the best channels might not be a problem. The problem might be to convince one or a few available middlemen to handle the product.

If the new firm is successful, it might branch out to new markets. Again, the manufacturer will tend to work through the existing middlemen, although this might mean using different types of distribution channels in different areas. In the smaller markets, the firm might sell directly to retailers; in the larger markets, it might sell through wholesalers. In rural areas, it might work with general-goods merchants; in urban areas, with limited-line merchants. In one part of the country, it might grant exclusive franchises because the merchants normally work this way; in another, it might sell through all outlets willing to handle the merchandise. Thus the manufacturer's channel system evolves in response to local opportunities and conditions.

Identifying the Major Channel Alternatives

Suppose a manufacturing company has defined its target market and desired positioning. It should next identify its major channel alternatives in terms of the types of middlemen and the number of middlemen.

TYPES OF MIDDLEMEN. The firm should identify the types of middlemen available to carry on its channel work. Consider the following example:

> A manufacturer of test equipment developed an audio device for detecting poor mechanical connections in any machine with moving parts. The company executives felt that this product would have a market in all industries where electric, combustion, or steam engines were used or manufactured. This meant such industries as aviation, automobile, railroad, food canning, construction, and oil. The company's sales force was small, and the problem was how to reach these diverse industries effectively. The following channel alternatives came out of management discussion: (1) Expand the company's direct sales force. Assign sales representatives to territories and give them responsibility for contacting all prospects in the area. Or develop separate company sales forces for the different industries. (2) Hire manufacturers' agencies in different regions or industries to sell the new test equipment. (3) Find distributors in the different regions and/or industries who will buy and carry the new line.[8] Give them exclusive distribution, adequate profit margins, product training, and promotional support.

Companies should also search for more innovative marketing channels. This happened when the Conn Organ Company decided to merchandise organs through department and discount stores, thus drawing more attention than organs had ever enjoyed in small music stores. A daring new channel was used

Tobacco products, magazines, and candy are usually sold through intensive distribution.

Marc Anderson

when the Book-of-the-Month Club decided to sell books through the mails. Other sellers followed soon after with Record-of-the-Month clubs, Fruit-of-the-Month clubs, and dozens of others.

Sometimes a company has to develop a channel other than the one it prefers because of the difficulty or cost of using the preferred channel. The decision sometimes turns out extremely well. For example, the U.S. Time Company originally tried to sell its inexpensive Timex watches through regular jewelry stores. But most jewelry stores refused to carry them. The company looked for other channels and managed to get its watches into mass-merchandising outlets. This turned out to be a wise decision because of the rapid growth of mass merchandising.

NUMBER OF MIDDLEMEN.   Companies have to decide on the number of middlemen to use at each level. Three strategies are available.

Intensive distribution.   Producers of convenience goods and common raw materials typically seek **intensive distribution**—that is, stocking their product in as many outlets as possible. These goods must have place utility. Cigarettes, for example, sell in over a million outlets to create maximum brand exposure and convenience.

Exclusive distribution.   Some producers deliberately limit the number of middlemen handling their products. The extreme form of this is **exclusive distribution**, where a limited number of dealers are granted the exclusive right to distribute the company's products in their respective territories. It often goes with *exclusive dealing,* where the manufacturer requires these dealers not to carry competing lines. Exclusive distribution is found to some extent in the distribution of new automobiles, some major appliances, and some women's apparel brands. Through granting exclusive distribution, the manufacturer hopes for more aggressive and knowledgeable selling and more control over middlemen's policies on prices, promotion, credit, and various services. Exclusive distribution tends to enhance the product's image and allow higher markups.

Selective distribution.   Between intensive and exclusive distribution is **selective distribution**—the use of more than one but less than all of the middlemen who are willing to carry a particular product. The company does not have to spread its efforts over many outlets, including many marginal ones. It can develop a good working relationship with the selected middlemen and expect a better-than-average selling effort. Selective distribution enables the producers to gain adequate market coverage with more control and less cost than intensive distribution.

Channel Management Decisions

As a result of reviewing its channel alternatives, the company will decide on the most effective channel design. Now its task is to manage the chosen channel. Channel management calls for selecting and motivating individual middlemen and evaluating their performance over time.

money

Selecting Channel Members Producers vary in their ability to recruit qualified middlemen. Some producers have no trouble. For example, Ford was able to attract twelve hundred new dealers for its ill-fated Edsel. In some cases, the promise of exclusive or selective distribution will draw a sufficient number of applicants.

At the other extreme are producers who have to work hard to line up qualified middlemen. When Polaroid started, it could not get photographic equipment stores to carry its new cameras and was forced to go to mass-merchandising outlets. And small food producers normally find it hard to get grocery stores to carry their products.

Motivating Channel Members Middlemen must be continuously motivated to do their best job. Most producers see the problem as finding ways to gain middlemen's cooperation.[9] They will use the carrot-and-stick approach. They will use such positive motivators as higher profit margins, special deals, premiums, cooperative advertising allowances, display allowances, and sales contests. At times they will use negative motivators, such as threatening to reduce the margins, slow down deliveries, or terminate the relationship. The weakness of this approach is that the producer has not really studied the needs, problems, strengths, and weaknesses of the distributors.

More sophisticated companies try to forge a long-term partnership with their distributors. The manufacturer develops a clear sense of what it wants from its distributors and what its distributors can expect. The manufacturer seeks an agreement from its distributors on various policies and may base compensation on their adhering to these policies.

Distribution programming is the most advanced arrangement. McCammon defines this as building a planned, professionally managed, vertical marketing system that incorporates the needs of both the manufacturer and the distributors.[10] The manufacturer establishes a department within the marketing department called *distributor relations planning,* and its job is to identify the distributors' needs and build up merchandising programs to help each distributor operate as fully as possible. This department and the distributors jointly plan the merchandising goals, inventory levels, space and visual merchandising plans, sales training requirements, and advertising and promotion plans. The aim is to make the distributors see that they make their money by being part of a sophisticated vertical marketing system.

Evaluating Channel Members The producer must periodically evaluate middlemen's performance against such standards as reaching sales quotas, average inventory levels, customer delivery time, treatment of damaged and lost goods, cooperation in company promotional and training programs, and middleman services owed to the customer.

The producer typically sets sales quotas for the middlemen. After each period, the producer might circulate a list showing the sales performance of each middleman. This list should motivate middlemen at the bottom to do better and middlemen at the top to maintain their performance. Middlemen's sales performance can be compared with their performance in the preceding periods. The average percentage improvement for the group can be used as a norm.

Exhibit **12-2**

Distribution Decisions and Public Policy

For the most part, manufacturers are free under the law to develop whatever channel arrangements suit them. In fact, the law affecting channels seeks to make sure that manufacturers are not excluded from using channels as the result of the tactics of others. But this places them under obligation to proceed cautiously in their own possible use of exclusionary tactics. Most of the law is concerned with mutual rights and duties of the manufacturer and channel members once they have formed a relationship.

- *Exclusive dealing:* Many manufacturers and wholesalers like to develop exclusive channels for their products. Both parties benefit from exclusive dealing—the seller gets more dependable outlets without having to invest capital in them, and the distributors get a steady source of supply and seller support. However, the result is that other manufacturers are excluded from selling to these dealers. This has brought exclusive-dealing contracts under the control of antitrust laws. They are legal as long as they do not substantially lessen competition, or tend to create a monopoly, and both partners enter into the agreement voluntarily.
- *Exclusive territorial distributorships:* Exclusive dealing often includes exclusive territorial agreements. The seller may agree not to sell to other distributors in the area, and/or the buyer may agree to confine sales to its own territory. The first practice is fairly normal under franchise systems as a way to increase dealer enthusiasm and investment in the area. A seller is under no legal compulsion to sell through more outlets than it wishes. The second practice, where the manufacturer tries to restrain each dealer to sell only in its own territory, has become a major legal issue.
- *Tying agreements:* Manufacturers of a strongly demanded brand occasionally sell it to dealers on condition that the dealers take some or all of the rest of the line. This practice is called *full-line forcing.* Such tying agreements are not illegal in themselves, but they do violate antitrust laws if they tend to lessen competition substantially. Buyers are being prevented from freely choosing among competing suppliers of other brands.
- *Dealers' rights:* Sellers are free to select their dealers, but their right to terminate dealerships is somewhat qualified. In general, sellers can drop dealers "for cause." But they cannot drop dealers, for example, if the dealers refuse to cooperate in a questionable legal arrangement, such as some kinds of exclusive-dealing or tying agreements.

Manufacturers need to be sensitive to their dealers. Manufacturers who treat their dealers carelessly risk losing their support and finding themselves in legal trouble. Exhibit 12-2 describes various rights and duties of manufacturers and their channel members.

Physical Distribution Decisions

We are now ready to look at the physical distribution, that is, how companies store, handle, and move goods so that they will be available to customers at the right time and place. Customers are highly influenced by the seller's physical distribution system. Here we will consider the nature, objective, and organizational aspects of physical distribution.

The Nature of Physical Distribution

The main elements of the physical distribution mix are shown in figure 12-5. We define physical distribution as follows:

Physical distribution is made up of the tasks involved in planning, implementing, and controlling the physical flow of materials and final goods from points of origin to points of use to meet the needs of customers at a profit.

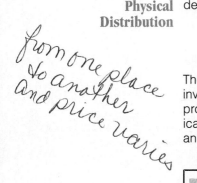

from one place to another and price varies

The major physical distribution cost is transportation, followed by warehousing, inventory carrying, receiving and shipping, packaging, administration, and order processing. Management has become concerned about the total cost of physical distribution, which amounts to 13.6% of sales for manufacturing companies and 25.6% for reseller companies.[11]

FIGURE 12-5

Elements of Physical Distribution, as a Percent of Total Physical Distribution Costs

Source: Based on B. J. LaLonde and P. H. Zinszer, *Customer Service: Meaning and Measurement* (Chicago: National Council of Physical Distribution Management, 1976).

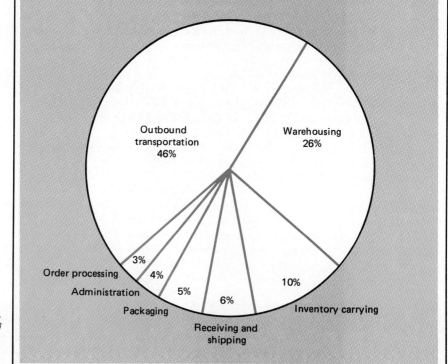

Physical distribution is not only a cost but also a potent tool in demand creation. Companies can attract additional customers by offering better service or lower prices through physical distribution improvements. Companies lose customers when they fail to supply goods on time. In the summer of 1976, Kodak launched its national advertising campaign for its new instant camera before it had delivered enough cameras to the stores. Customers found that it was not available and bought a Polaroid instead.

The Physical Distribution Objective

Many companies state their physical distribution objective as getting the right goods to the right places at the right time for the least cost. Unfortunately, no physical distribution system can maximize customer service and minimize distribution cost at the same time. Maximum customer service implies large inventories, premium transportation, and multiple warehouses, all of which raise distribution costs. Minimum distribution costs imply cheap transportation, low inventory, and few warehouses.

Physical distribution costs interact, often in an inverse way:

- The traffic manager favors rail shipment over air shipment whenever possible. This reduces the company's freight bill. However, because the railroads are slower, this ties up working capital longer, delays customer payment, and may cause customers to buy from competitors offering faster service.
- The shipping department uses cheap containers to minimize shipping costs. This leads to a high rate of damaged goods in transit and customer ill will.
- The inventory manager favors low inventories to reduce inventory cost. However, this increases stockouts, back orders, paperwork, special production runs, and high-cost fast-freight shipments.

Given that physical distribution activities involve strong trade-offs, decisions must be made on a total system basis.

The starting point for designing the physical distribution system is to study what customers want and what competitors are offering. Customers are interested in several things: (1) on-time delivery, (2) supplier willingness to meet customer emergency needs, (3) careful handling of merchandise, (4) supplier willingness to take back defective goods and resupply them quickly, and (5) supplier willingness to carry inventory for the customer.

The company has to research the relative importance of these services to customers. For example, service repair time is very important to buyers of photocopying equipment. Xerox therefore developed a service delivery standard that can "put a disabled machine anywhere in the continental United States back into operation within three hours after receiving the service request." Xerox runs a service division consisting of twelve thousand service and parts personnel.

The company must look at competitors' service standards in setting its own. It will normally want to offer at least the same level of service as competitors. But the objective is to maximize profits, not sales. The company has to look at the costs of providing higher levels of service. Some companies offer less service but charge a lower price. Other companies offer more service than competitors and charge a premium price to cover their higher costs.

The company ultimately has to establish physical distribution objectives to guide its planning. For example, Coca-Cola wants "to put Coke within an arm's length of desire." Companies go further and define standards for each service factor. One appliance manufacturer has established the following service standards: (1) to deliver at least 95% of the dealer's orders within seven days of order receipt, (2) to fill the dealer's order with 99% accuracy, (3) to answer dealer inquiries on order status within three hours, and (4) to ensure that damage to merchandise in transit does not exceed 1%.

Given a set of physical distribution objectives, the company is ready to design a physical distribution system that will minimize the cost of achieving these objectives. The major decision issues are:

1. How should orders be handled? (*order processing*)
2. Where should stock be located? (*warehousing*)
3. How much stock should be kept on hand? (*inventory*)
4. How should goods be shipped? (*transportation*)

We will now examine these four elements and their implications for marketing.

Order Processing Physical distribution begins with a customer order. The order department prepares invoices and sends them to various departments. Items out of stock are back-ordered. Shipped items are accompanied by shipping and billing documents, with copies going to various departments.

The company and customers benefit when these steps are carried out quickly and accurately. Ideally, sales representatives send in their orders every evening, in some cases phoning them in. The order department processes these quickly. The warehouse sends the goods out as soon as possible. Bills go out as soon as possible. The computer is used to speed up the order-shipping-billing cycle. For example, General Electric operates a computer-oriented system, which, upon receipt of a customer's order, checks the customer's credit standing and whether and where the items are in stock. The computer issues an order to ship, bills the customer, updates the inventory records, sends a production order for new stock, and relays the message back to the sales representative that the customer's order is on its way, all in less than fifteen seconds.[12]

Warehousing Every company has to store its goods while they wait to be sold. Storage is necessary because production and consumption cycles rarely match. Many agricultural commodities are produced seasonally, but demand is continuous. Storage overcomes these differences.

The company must decide on a desirable number of stocking locations. More stocking locations mean that goods can be delivered to customers more quickly. However, costs go up. Decisions on the number of stocking locations must be made by balancing the level of customer service and distribution costs.

Some company stock is kept at or near the plant, and the rest is located in warehouses around the country. The company might own private warehouses and rent space in public warehouses. Companies have more control if they own warehouses, but they tie up their capital and face some inflexibility if desired locations change. Public warehouses, on the other hand, charge for the rented space and provide additional services (at a cost) for inspecting goods, packaging them, shipping them, and invoicing them. In using public warehouses, companies have a wide choice of locations and warehouse types.

Companies use storage warehouses and distribution warehouses. *Storage warehouses* store goods for moderate to long periods of time. *Distribution warehouses* receive goods from various plants and suppliers and move them out as soon as possible. For example, Wal-Mart Stores, Inc., a regional discount chain, operates four distribution centers. One center covers 400,000 square feet on a ninety-three-acre site. The shipping department loads fifty to sixty trucks daily, delivering merchandise on a twice-weekly basis to its retail outlets. This is less expensive than supplying each retail outlet from each plant directly.

The older multistoried warehouses with slow elevators and inefficient materials-handling procedures are getting competition from newer single-storied *automated warehouses* with advanced materials-handling systems under the control of a central computer. In these automated warehouses, costing $10 million to $20 million each, only a few employees are necessary. The computer reads store orders, directs lift trucks and electric hoists to gather goods and move them to loading docks, and issues invoices. These warehouses have reduced worker injuries, labor costs, pilferage, and breakage and have improved inventory control.

Inventory   Inventory levels represent another physical distribution decision affecting customer satisfaction. Marketers would like their companies to carry enough stock to fill all customer orders immediately. However, it is not cost-effective for a company to carry this much inventory. Inventory costs increase at an increasing rate as the level of customer service rises. Management would need to know whether sales and profits would increase enough to justify higher inventories. Management can then decide when to order new stock and how much stock to order.

Transportation   Marketers need to take an interest in their company's transportation decisions. The choice of transportation carriers will affect the pricing of the products, on-time delivery performance, and the condition of the goods when they arrive, all of which will affect customer satisfaction.

In shipping goods to warehouses, dealers, and customers, the company can choose among five transportation modes: rail, water, truck, pipeline, and air. Each transportation mode's characteristics are summarized in table 12-1 and discussed in the following paragraphs.

RAIL.   Railroads are the nation's largest transportation carrier, accounting for 30% of the nation's total cargo ton-miles. Railroads are one of the most cost-effective modes for shipping carload quantities of bulk products—coal, sand, minerals, farm and forest products—over long land distances. Railroads have recently begun to increase customer-oriented services. They have designed new equipment to handle special categories of merchandise more efficiently, provided flatcars for carrying truck trailers by rail (piggyback), and provided

Placing Products: Distribution Channels and Physical Distribution

Table 12-1			
Characteristics of Major Transportation Modes			
TRANSPORTATION MODE	1980 CARGO TON-MILES (billions)	PERCENTAGE OF TOTAL	TYPICAL SHIPPED PRODUCTS
Rail	858.1	30.0%	Farm products, minerals, sand, chemicals, autos
Water	827.2	28.7%	Oil, grain, sand, gravel, metallic ores, coal
Truck	602.0	21.0%	Clothing, books, computers, paper goods
Pipeline	585.2	20.2%	Petroleum, coal, chemicals
Air	4.6	00.1%	Technical instruments, perishable food

Source: U.S. Department of Transportation, *National Transportation Statistics,* DOT-TSC-RSPA-81-8, September 1981.

Trucks taking on cargo to be delivered to many small retailers.
Courtesy Shell Oil Company, Inc.

in-transit services, such as diversion of shipped goods to other destinations en route and processing of goods en route.

WATER. A substantial amount of goods moves by ships and barges on coastal and inland waterways. The cost of water transportation is very low for shipping bulky, low-value, nonperishable products, such as sand, coal, grain, oil, and metallic ores. On the other hand, water transportation is the slowest transportation mode and is often affected by the weather.

TRUCK. Motor trucks have steadily increased their share of transportation and now account for 21% of total cargo ton-miles. They account for the largest portion of transportation within cities. Trucks are highly flexible in their routing and time schedules. They can move merchandise door to door, saving shippers the need to transfer goods from truck to rail and back again. Trucks are an efficient mode of transportation for short hauls of high-value merchandise. Their rates are competitive with railway rates in many cases, and trucks can usually offer faster services.

PIPELINE. Pipelines are a specialized means of shipping petroleum, coal, and chemicals from sources to markets. Pipeline shipment of petroleum products is less expensive than rail shipment, although more expensive than waterway shipment. Most pipelines are used by their owners to ship their own products.

AIR. Air carriers transport less than 1% of the nation's goods but are becoming more important as a transportation mode. Although airfreight rates are considerably higher than rail or truck freight rates, airfreight is ideal where speed is essential and/or distant markets have to be reached. Among the most frequently airfreighted products are perishables (such as fresh fish, cut flowers) and high-value, low-bulk items (such as technical instruments, jewelry). Companies find that airfreight reduces their required inventory levels, number of warehouses, and costs of packaging.

Choosing Transportation Modes

In choosing a transportation mode for a particular product, shippers consider as many as six criteria. Table 12-2 ranks the various transportation modes according to these criteria. Thus if a shipper seeks speed, air and truck are the prime choices. If the goal is low cost, then water and pipeline are the prime choices. Trucks appear to offer the most advantages, thus explaining their growing share.

Shippers are increasingly combining two or more transportation modes, thanks to containerization. Containerization consists of putting the goods in boxes or trailers that are easy to transfer between two transportation modes. Piggyback describes the use of rail and trucks; fishyback, water and trucks; trainship, water and rail; and airtruck, air and trucks. Each coordinated mode of transportation offers specific advantages to the shipper. For example, piggyback is cheaper than trucking alone and yet provides flexibility and convenience.

Transportation decisions must consider the complex trade-offs between various transportation modes and their implications for other distribution elements, such as warehousing and inventory. As the relative costs of different transportation modes change over time, companies need to reanalyze their options in the search for optimal physical distribution arrangements.

Organizational Responsibility for Physical Distribution

We can now see that decisions on warehousing, inventory, and transportation require the highest degree of coordination. A growing number of companies have set up a permanent committee composed of managers responsible for different physical distribution activities. This committee meets periodically to develop policies for improving overall distribution efficiency. Some companies have appointed a vice-president of physical distribution, who reports to the

Table 12-2

Transportation Modes Ranked According to Major Shipper Criteria

	SPEED (door-to-door delivery time)	FREQUENCY (scheduled shipments per day)	DEPENDABILITY (meeting schedules on time)	CAPABILITY (ability to handle various products)	AVAILABILITY (no. of geographic points served)	COST (per ton-mile)
Rail	3	4	3	2	2	3
Water	4	5	4	1	4	1
Truck	2	2	2	3	1	4
Pipeline	5	1	1	5	5	2
Air	1	3	5	4	3	5

Note: 1 = Most Favorable Rank.

Source: Adapted from James L. Heskett, Robert J. Ivie, and Nicholas A. Glaskowsky, *Business Logistics* (New York: Ronald Press, 1964), pp. 71ff. Copyright by John Wiley & Sons, Inc. Reprinted by permission.

marketing vice-president or manufacturing vice-president in most cases, or to the president. The location of the physical distribution department within the company is a secondary concern. The important thing is that the company coordinate its physical distribution and marketing activities in order to create high market satisfaction at a reasonable cost.

Summary

Distribution channel decisions are among the most complex and challenging decisions facing a firm. Each channel system creates a different level of sales and costs. Once a particular marketing channel has been chosen, the firm must usually stick with it for a substantial period. The chosen channel will significantly affect and be affected by the other elements in the marketing mix.

Each firm needs to identify alternative ways to reach its market. They vary from direct selling to using one, two, three, or more intermediary channel levels. Distribution channels are characterized by continuous and sometimes dramatic change. Three of the most significant trends are the growth of vertical, horizontal, and multichannel marketing systems. These trends have important implications for channel cooperation, conflict, and competition.

Channel design calls for identifying the major channel alternatives in terms of the types of middlemen and the number of middlemen. Channel management calls for selecting qualified middlemen and motivating them. Individual channel members must be periodically evaluated, comparing their sales performance with their past performance and with other channel members' sales performance.

Just as the marketing concept is receiving increased recognition, more business firms are paying attention to the physical distribution concept. Physical distribution is an area of potentially high cost savings and improved customer satisfaction. When order processors, warehouse planners, inventory managers, and transportation managers make decisions, they affect each other's costs and the capacity to handle demand. The physical distribution concept calls for treating all these decisions within a unified framework. The task becomes that of designing physical distribution arrangements that minimize the total cost of providing a desired level of customer services.

Questions for Discussion

1. "In a battle between giants like Procter & Gamble and Safeway [supermarket chain] five years ago, P&G would have prevailed. Now Safeway can call the tune." What has caused the change in power?
2. Why are middlemen used? Explain by using a concrete example.
3. Discuss how many channel levels are commonly used by the following companies: (a) Sears, (b) Fuller Brush, and (c) A&P.
4. Channels of distribution do not differ for services and physical products. Comment.
5. Distinguish between the three major types of vertical marketing systems. Give an example of each.

6. There is no way to eliminate channel conflict. Comment.
7. Discuss which of the following products would be intensively, exclusively, and selectively distributed, and why: (a) Rolex watches, (b) Volkswagen automobiles, (c) Gillette blades, and (d) Estée Lauder perfume.
8. How do physical distribution decisions differ from channel decisions? What is the main objective of physical distribution?
9. In what ways has the computer aided physical distribution?
10. Discuss which mode of transportation would probably be used to distribute the following products: (a) beer, (b) expensive jewelry, (c) natural gas, and (d) farm machinery.

Key Terms in Chapter 12

Administered VMS A vertical marketing system that coordinates successive stages of production and distribution not through common ownership but through the size and power of one of the parties.

Contractual VMS Independent firms linked by contracts and coordinating their programs to obtain more economies and/or sales impact than they could achieve alone.

Conventional marketing channel An independent producer, wholesaler(s), and retailer(s), each a separate business seeking to maximize its own profits, even if that is at the expense of maximizing the profits for others or for the system as a whole.

Corporate VMS The combination of successive stages of production and distribution under single ownership.

Distribution channel The set of firms and individuals that take title, or assist in transferring title, to the particular product or service as it moves from the producer to the consumer.

Exclusive distribution Granting a limited number of dealers the exclusive right to distribute a product in their own territories.

Intensive distribution The stocking of a product in as many outlets as possible.

Physical distribution The tasks involved in planning, implementing, and controlling the physical flow of materials and final goods from points of origin to points of use to meet the needs of customers at a profit.

Selective distribution The use of more than one but less than all of the middlemen who are willing to carry a particular product.

Vertical marketing system (VMS) The producer, wholesaler(s), and retailer(s) acting as a unified system; either one channel member owns the others, or franchises them, or has so much power that they all cooperate.

Cases for Chapter 12

Case 11   Gould, Inc.: Focus 800 BAT-TERY (p. 506)

Due to a changing market, Gould is changing its distribution objectives and distribution channels. This case presents the factors that management must consider in making these changes.

Case 12   Fotomat Corporation (p. 508)

What are Fotomat's physical distribution alternatives? How have competition and the growth of new products affected Fotomat's distribution channel objectives? This case looks at these questions.

Chapter 13

Placing Products: Retailing and Wholesaling

Objectives

After reading this chapter, you should be able to:

1. Discuss the roles of retailers and wholesalers in physical distribution.
2. List five types of retailers and give examples of each.
3. List four types of wholesalers and give examples of each.
4. Describe the marketing decisions facing retailers and wholesalers.

Customers at Spag's, a discount store in Massachusetts, are not surprised by any kind of merchandise they might see in the store. At the lowest possible retail price, customers might find computers, Nestlés Cocoa Mix, rat poison, golf balls, Oriental rugs, motor oil, and brass beds on a particular day. On the other hand, they might not find any of these things but an entirely different array of goods.

At Spag's, the principle behind its successful operation is to buy merchandise in bulk at a cost below wholesale prices and then sell it to customers at a very low markup. The key to Spag's profits is high-volume sales. On some days, 10,000 customers pass in and out of this bargain hunter's heaven.

The store occupies three huge adjoining buildings. Following no apparent system, merchandise is everywhere—stacked on the floor to dangling from the ceiling. There are no shopping carts because the store's owner, Anthony "Spag" Borgatti, Jr. ("Spag" is short for "Spaghetti," his nickname), believes they would occupy too much valuable space. Borgatti prefers to see every possible inch used for his low-priced merchandise. And he likes to see that merchandise move as quickly as possible out of the store, making room for more. "Turnover," says Borgatti, "is everything." Borgatti must have turned over quite a bit in the decades he's been operating because many say the store has made him a millionaire.

Spag's is one store operating in a growing retail trend—off-price retailing. This selling strategy consists of buying merchandise at reduced prices and passing the savings along to consumers. Off-price retailing has doubled its volume of sales during a recent five-year period. One retailing analyst predicts sales from this form of retailing will increase by an annual 15% during the next several years. Off-price retailers generally try to keep their overhead expenses down by occupying low-rent stores, employing a minimum number of salespeople, and accepting only cash for purchases.

One large group of off-price retailers specializes in clothing. These merchants often attract customers by offering designer merchandise at lower prices than those of department stores. "The essence of the business," says one expert, "is getting price breaks because you're picking up off-season merchandise, overstocks, and irregulars." An off-price retailer might be able to buy a line of designer dresses at a low price just several weeks after they've appeared in department stores.

The earliest off-price retail store was Loehmann's, a women's clothing store that opened in Brooklyn in 1920. Stores like Saks Fifth Avenue, Best's, and Lord & Taylor, selling the same clothing at higher prices, were outraged at being undersold. Because of pressure from these influential retailers, manufacturers convinced Loehmann's to remove the clothing's labels before putting it on the racks. In its chain of stores, Loehmann's is still snipping out labels.

Another successful off-price chain is Syms, operating along the entire East Coast. Syms does not remove labels. On the contrary, according to Syms's TV and radio advertisements, "If a garment doesn't have a recognizable label, it's not advisable to buy it." Aldo Papone, Vice Chairman of Dayton Hudson, an expanding midwestern chain, expresses this philosophy another way. "These people don't want cheap steak," Papone points out, "they want steak cheap."

A chain of stores centered in California, Pic-N-Save, offers a variety of miscellaneous off-price products. Founder and Chairman William Zimmerman looks for products that have been test-marketed and have failed, products that have outlived their stylishness, and overstocked items. One of Zimmerman's strategies for finding merchandise to fill his 78 stores is to attend merchandiser's trade shows. Instead of looking for new products at the shows, Zimmerman questions manufacturers about products that have recently bombed—items that he might be able to buy at a low price. Recent Pic-N-Save bargains have included half-price green Cēpacol mouthwash (a failed marketing experiment—usually the product is yellow); Cool-Ray sunglasses bought when the parent company decided to drop sunglasses; and Yoda T-shirts acquired when E.T. had become the craze.[1]

This chapter will focus on the institutions that make up the retailing and wholesaling sectors of the economy. In the first section on retailing, we ask the following questions: (1) What is the nature and importance of retailing? (2) What are the major types of retailers? (3) What marketing decisions do retailers make? In the second section, we ask the same questions about wholesalers.

Retailing

What is retailing? We all know that Sears is a retailer, but what about the Avon lady knocking at the door, the contractor phoning a family about home repair services, the doctor seeing patients, a hotel advertising a low-price weekend? Yes, they are all retailers. We define retailing as follows:

> **Retailing** includes all the activities involved in selling goods or services directly to final consumers for their personal, nonbusiness use.

Any institution that does this is doing retailing. It does not matter how the goods or services are sold (by personal selling, mail, telephone, or vending machine) or where they are sold (in a store, on the street, or in the consumer's home).

Retailing is one of the major industries in the United States. Retail stores constitute approximately 25% of all U.S. businesses and are the third-largest source of employment in the nation, with almost 16 million employees. The industry is composed of over 1.5 million single-unit establishments and over 340,000 multiunit organizations, and it generated a total of approximately $1,038,000,000 in sales in 1981.[2]

Who are the nation's largest retailers? The ten largest ones and their sales in billions in 1981 were Sears Roebuck ($27.3), Safeway Stores ($16.5), K mart ($16.6), J. C. Penney ($11.8), Kroger ($11.2), F. W. Woolworth ($7.2), American Stores ($7.1), Lucky Stores ($7.2), Federated Department Stores ($7.0), and A&P ($6.8).[3] The largest retailers are primarily general merchandise department store chains and supermarket chains.

Whether selling to a class or a mass market, retailers have learned over the years that they are operating in a rapidly changing environment. Yesterday's retailing formulas may not work today, and most probably will not work tomorrow. Where are W. T. Grant (one of the nation's oldest and largest chain of variety stores) and Food Fair (the country's eighth-largest supermarket chain)? Both are in bankruptcy. Whatever happened to the great A&P? "Formerly considered a colossal near-monopoly, nemesis of small competitors, and trustbuster target, A&P has come to look like a mangy, toothless old lion."[4] What about the great Montgomery Ward (the nation's fourth-largest general merchandise chain)? It is searching for a strategy to regain its glory. Even Sears is in trouble:

> During the 1970s Sears painfully discovered the risks of a changing environment. Its strategies for each decade since its founding in 1886 were right on target, and it took over the number-one spot from the older Montgomery Ward's in the 1940s. Sears bet on economic growth in the postwar period, and Ward's bet on economic stagnation. Sears won the bet. Sears opened hundreds of new stores in the suburbs, renovated its old stores, and added new and nontraditional lines, such as insurance, savings banks, and paintings. It prospered through the early 1970s when it decided to change its strategy from expansion to upgrading. It decided to pursue affluent consumers by adding higher-quality lines and even designer merchandise. But its timing was bad. The boom turned into a bust, and Sears customers were in no mood to pay higher prices. They shifted their shopping to K Marts and

other discount merchandisers. Nor did the new strategy attract the more affluent buyers. In 1974 Sears experienced its first profit slump in thirteen years, a 24.8 percent decline. After its retailing profits peaked in 1976 at $441.2 million, they fell to $363.9 million for 1977 and $330.7 million for 1978.[5]

What is Sears doing in the 1980s to regain its position? It is carrying out the following strategies: Recognizing that its strongest market is "middle-class America," it is no longer pursuing more affluent consumers. Rather, it is strengthening its relationship with its present credit customers and is aiming its merchandise and services at this market. In 1981, for example, Sears bought a real estate firm and an investment firm in order to be able to offer these services to their customers. In another move, Sears is now selling the Levi Strauss brand of jeans and clothing in its stores.

Modern retailers have to watch for signs of change and be ready to shift their strategy—not too early and not too late. But even a decision to shift is not easy to carry out. The large retailer is often tied to its own policies, which its managers have accepted as the "conventional wisdom." And it is tied to its public image, which consumers retain long after the store's reality has changed.

Retailing also includes the small "mom-and-pop" store. Small retailers are important for several reasons: (1) They often create new retailing forms that the large stores later copy; (2) they offer greater convenience to consumers because they are everywhere; (3) they often are more adaptable and give more personal service; and (4) they offer people a chance to be their own boss.

Types of Retailers

The millions of retailing units in this country come in all sizes and shapes. Furthermore, new retailing forms keep emerging and combining the features of older forms. For example, a modern K mart store combines the features of the supermarket and the discount store. Since customers vary in the forms they prefer, businesses with different levels of customer service can exist and be successful at the same time. Figure 13-1 shows four levels of service and the retailing institutions typically using them.

Self-service retailing grew rapidly in this country in the 1930s as a result of depressed economic conditions. Today self-service retailing is used by customers in all walks of life, especially for obtaining convenience goods and some shopping goods. Self-service is the basis of all discount operations. Many customers are willing to carry out their own "locate-compare-select" process to save money.

In *self-selection retailing* a salesclerk is available for assistance if desired. Customers complete their transactions by finding a salesclerk and paying for the item. Self-selection institutions have somewhat higher operating expenses than self-service operations because of the additional staff requirements.

In *limited-service retailing,* such as that found in large department store chains like Sears, the quality of sales assistance is somewhat higher because these stores carry more shopping goods and customers need more information. The stores also offer services such as credit and merchandise return not normally found in less service-oriented stores. Thus, their operating costs are higher.

DECREASING SERVICES ⟵⟶ INCREASING SERVICES			
Self-service	**Self-selection**	**Limited-service**	**Full-service**
Attributes Very few services Price appeal Staple goods Convenience goods	Restricted services Price appeal Staple goods Convenience goods	Small variety of services Shopping goods	Wide variety of services Fashion merchandise Specialty merchandise
Examples Warehouse retailing Grocery stores Discount stores Mail-order retailing Automatic vending	Discount retailing Variety stores Mail-order retailing	Door-to-door sales Department stores Telephone sales Variety stores	Specialty stores Department stores

FIGURE 13-1

Classification of Retailers Based on the Amount of Customer Service

Source: Adapted from Larry D. Redinbaugh, *Retailing Management: A Planning Approach* (New York: McGraw-Hill, 1976), p. 12.

In *full-service retailing,* such as in classy department stores, salesclerks are ready to assist personally in every phase of the locate-compare-select process. Customers who like to be "waited on" prefer this type of store. The high staffing cost, the higher proportion of specialty goods and slower-moving items (fashions, jewelry, cameras), the more liberal merchandise return policies, various credit plans, free delivery, home servicing of durables, and customer facilities such as lounges and restaurants, all result in high costs. It is not surprising that full-service retailing has been declining for several decades.

In describing types of retailing, we will use several bases for classification: product line sold, relative price emphasis, nature of business premises, ownership of store, and type of store cluster. The types are shown in table 13-1 and described below.

Table 13-1

Different Ways to Classify Retail Outlets

PRODUCT LINE SOLD	RELATIVE PRICE EMPHASIS	NATURE OF BUSINESS PREMISES	OWNERSHIP OF STORE	TYPE OF STORE CLUSTER
Specialty store	Discount store	Mail-and- telephone- order retailing	Corporate chain	Central business district
Department store	Warehouse		Voluntary chain and retailer cooperative	Regional shopping center
Supermarket	Catalog showroom			
Convenience store		Automatic vending	Consumer cooperative	Community shopping center
Combination store, superstore, and hypermarché		Buying service	Franchise organization	Neighborhood shopping center
Service business		Door-to-door retailing	Merchandising conglomerate	

PRODUCT LINE SOLD.   The first basis for classifying retailing institutions is according to the product line sold. There are grocery stores, liquor stores, furniture stores, and so on. More broadly, we can look at the length and depth of the product assortment and distinguish some major store types. Among the most important ones are the **specialty store**, **department store**, **supermarket**, **convenience store**, and **superstore**.

Specialty store.   A specialty store carries a narrow product line with a deep assortment within that line. Examples of specialty retailers are clothing stores, sporting goods stores, furniture stores, florists, and bookstores. Specialty stores can be subclassified by the narrowness in their product line. A clothing store would be a *single-line store;* a men's clothing store would be a *limited-line store;* and a men's custom shirt store would be a *superspecialty store.* Some analysts think that superspecialty stores will grow the fastest in the future to take advantage of increasing opportunities for market segmentation, market targeting, and product specialization. Some of the successful current examples are Athlete's Foot (sport shoes only), Tall Men (tall men's clothing), The Gap (primarily jeans), and Calculators, Inc. (primarily calculators).

The recent growth of specialty stores is tied to the boom of shopping centers, which typically have one or two department stores and many specialty stores. Often 60% to 70% of the total shopping space is occupied by specialty stores. Although most specialty stores are independently owned, chain specialty stores are showing the strongest growth. The most successful specialty chain stores zero in on the needs of specific target markets.

The Limited specializes in high-fashion clothes for the woman who is eighteen- to thirty-five-years old and is willing to pay a little more to get just the right look. The merchandise is presented in coordinated outfits, the employees are fashionably dressed and of the same age as the target market, and the store has a contemporary atmosphere. Having defined its target

Specialty stores, such as The Limited, can focus on the needs and tastes of a specific market segment.
Courtesy The Limited Stores, Inc.

Exhibit 13-1

The Fading Stereo Boom

During the 1970s, stereo stores did a booming business. Stores like Tech Hi-Fi, Pacific Stereo, and Playback grew into profitable chains selling only stereo equipment. Most buyers were young people, particularly college students. Today, however, many stereo stores have closed or are suffering severe financial losses.

The reasons for the drop in stereo sales have to do with changes in both the economy and electronics technology. Young people today generally have less money to spend than did a similar group a decade ago. But perhaps a more direct cause of the stereo boom's collapse is the fact that there are so many more electronics products available for those who can afford them. Among college students, money is as likely to go toward video equipment or a personal computer as it is to buy a stereo.

Stereo stores that have survived are those that have expanded their product lines and changed their marketing strategies. Team Central, Inc., centered in Minneapolis, now sells home computers, video equipment, and telephones in addition to stereos. Instead of aiming its advertising at college students, this company is going after an older crowd—homeowners. Crazy Eddie, Inc., of New York has also expanded its stock with additional electronics products.

Unfortunately, video equipment and computers bring a new set of problems for retailers. Because video prices have dropped sharply in the past few years, the large number of retailers dealing in these products are forced into price competition. While retailers can charge 30% to 35% over cost on stereo equipment, the markup on video products is only about 10% to 15%. Meanwhile, a new group of stores specializing in computers is tough competition for retailers offering a variety of electronics products. Computer stores can offer a wider selection because they handle just one product, and they can offer lower prices. Sales of telephones give dealers some consolation, as they have higher retail margins than other products.

Today, selling stereos is not enough. Retailers are forced to choose between turning their stores into "electronics supermarkets" or going out of business.

Source: Bob Davis, "Hi-Fi Boom Fades, Forcing Stores to Go Beyond Stereo or Close Down," *Wall Street Journal*, March 8, 1983, p. 37.

market carefully, The Limited can study the fashion interests of eighteen- to thirty-five-year-old women, pretest new fashion ideas, build a unique image, aim its advertising carefully, and locate in shopping centers.

Specialty stores can, however, run into trouble if they specialize in products that lose popularity. For an example, see exhibit 13-1.

Department store.   A department store carries several product lines, typically clothing, home furnishings, and household goods. Each line is operated as a separate department managed by specialist buyers or merchandisers. Examples of well-known department stores are Bloomingdale's (New York), Marshall Field (Chicago), and Filene's (Boston).

Some writers believe that the department store grew out of the general store (because it carries several product lines); others believe that it grew out of the dry goods store (because many department store founders first ran dry goods stores). The Bon Marché, established in Paris in 1852, is considered to be the first department store.[6] It introduced four innovative principles: (1) low markups and rapid turnover, (2) marking and displaying the prices of merchandise, (3) encouraging customers to look around without any pressure or obligation to purchase, and (4) a liberal complaints policy.

The earliest department stores in America included Jordan Marsh, Macy's, Wanamaker's, and Stewart's. These stores were housed in huge impressive buildings in fashionable central locations. They sold the concept of "shopping for enjoyment." This was a far cry from the specialty stores of the period, which had little on display and which discouraged customers from looking around.

Starting in the post–World War II period, department stores' share of total retailing and profitability declined. Many observers believe that these stores are in the declining stage of the retail life cycle. They point to (1) the increased competition among department stores, which has raised their costs; (2) the increased competition coming from other types of retailers, particularly discount stores, specialty chain stores, and warehouse retailers; and (3) the heavy traffic, poor parking, and deterioration in central cities, which have made downtown shopping less appealing.

The result has been the closing of some department stores and the merging of others. Department stores are waging a "comeback" war, however. Many have opened branches in suburban shopping centers, where the population is increasing and there are higher incomes and better parking. Others have added "bargain basements" to meet the discount threat. Still others are remodeling their stores, including "going boutique." Some are experimenting with mail-order and telephone shopping. Others, like Dayton-Hudson, have diversified into other store types, such as discount and specialty stores. Some department stores are cutting back on the number of employees, product lines, and customer services such as delivery and credit, but this strategy may hurt their major appeal, namely, better service.

Supermarket.   A supermarket is a relatively large, low-cost, low-margin, high-volume, self-service operation "designed to serve the consumer's total needs for food, laundry, and household maintenance products."[7] A supermarket store can be independently owned, although most supermarket stores are operated by supermarket chains. The largest ones (in billions of 1981 dollars) are Safeway ($16.5), Kroger ($11.2), Lucky ($7.2), American Stores ($7.1), A&P ($6.8), Winn-Dixie ($6.2), and Jewel ($5.1).

The supermarket can be traced to two sources: John Hartford's introduction of the cash-and-carry Great Atlantic & Pacific Tea Company (A&P) food stores in 1912; and Clarence Saunders's Piggly-Wiggly stores, which introduced in 1916 the principles of self-service, customer turnstiles, and checkout counters. However, supermarkets did not achieve great popularity until the 1930s. Michael "King" Kullen is credited with starting the first successful supermarket in 1930, a self-service, cash-and-carry grocery operation with 6,000 square feet of selling space as opposed to 800 square feet in conventional stores at the time. Kullen drew enough business to operate profitably with a gross margin of 9% to 10% of sales, which was half that of food stores at that time. Within the next two years, 300 supermarkets were opened, and by 1939 there were approximately 5,000, accounting for 20% of total grocery sales. Today there are over 37,000 supermarkets in operation, accounting for 76% of total grocery sales.

Several factors accounted for the supermarket takeoff in the 1930s. The Great Depression forced consumers to be price conscious and allowed operators to get merchandise at low prices from distressed sources and occupy large buildings at low rentals. The mass ownership of automobiles made distance less important and increased weekly shopping, thus reducing the need for small neighborhood stores. The advances in refrigeration technology allowed supermarkets and consumers to store perishables longer. New packaging technology allowed food products to be marketed in storable consumer-size packages (cans and boxes) rather than the distributor-size containers (barrels and crates). This stimulated the selling of a brand through advertising, which reduced the number of salesclerks needed in the store. Finally, the integration of grocery, meat, and produce departments made one-stop shopping possible and attracted customers from considerable distances, thus giving supermarkets the needed volume for success.

Supermarkets have moved in several directions to further build their sales volume. They have opened larger stores, with today's selling space occupying approximately 18,000 square feet as opposed to 11,700 square feet in the mid-1950s. Most of the chains now operate fewer but larger stores. Supermarkets carry a large number and variety of items. A typical supermarket handled three thousand items in 1946 and now handles around eight thousand. The most significant increase has been in the number of nonfood items carried—nonprescription drugs, beauty aids, housewares, magazines, books, toys—which now account for 8% of total supermarket sales. This "scrambled merchandising" is continuing, and many supermarkets are moving into prescriptions, appliances, records, sporting goods, hardware, garden supplies, and even cameras, hoping to find high-margin lines to improve profitability. Supermarkets are also upgrading their facilities, with more expensive locations, larger parking lots, carefully planned architecture and decor, longer store hours and Sunday openings, and a wide variety of customer services, such as check cashing, rest rooms, and background music. Supermarkets have also increased promotional competition in the form of heavy advertising, trading stamps, and games of chance. And supermarkets have moved heavily into private brands to reduce their dependence on national brands and increase their profit margins. Supermarket chains are also expanding their outlets in the Sun Belt states, where economic growth is stronger.[8]

Convenience store. Convenience food stores are relatively small stores, located near residential areas, open long hours seven days a week, and carrying a limited line of high-turnover convenience products. Examples are 7-Elevens and White Hen Pantries. Their long hours and their use by consumers mainly for "fill-in" purchases make them relatively high-priced operations. Yet they satisfy an important consumer need, and people seem willing to pay for the convenience. The number of convenience stores increased from approximately 2,000 in 1957 to 37,800 in 1981, with sales of $14.1 billion in 1981.[9]

Convenience food retailing has recently spread to the food-gasoline store. Customers drive up to a service station that carries about one hundred convenience items—bread, milk, cigarettes, coffee, and soft drinks—and can charge their purchases to their oil company credit cards.

Combination store, superstore, and hypermarché. At the other end of the spectrum are three types of stores that are larger than the conventional supermarket. *Combination stores* represent a diversification of the supermarket store into the growing drug and prescription field. Combination supermarkets and drugstores average 55,000 square feet of selling space. Three basic designs are used. The Kroger chain locates its supermarkets and its Super X discount drugstores side by side. Each store can be run as a distinct operation. The Jewel Company prefers a single store with drugs on one side and food on the other, offering easier access and convenience to the consumer and probably generating more sales "synergy" than the side-by-side design. Borman's in Detroit displays the drugs between the food to create more cross-shopping and greater sales "synergy."

Superstores are larger than conventional supermarkets (30,000 instead of 18,000 square feet of selling space) and aim at meeting the consumer's total needs for routinely purchased food and nonfood items. They usually offer such services as laundry, dry cleaning, shoe repair, check cashing and bill paying, and bargain lunch counters.[10] Superstores often charge 5% to 6% higher prices over conventional supermarkets due to the wider assortment. Many leading chains are moving toward the superstore concept. For example, Kroger plans to build 114 superstores averaging 30,000 square feet of selling space.

Hypermarchés are even larger than superstores, ranging between 80,000 and 220,000 square feet. The hypermarché (a term not used in the U.S. but common in Europe) combines supermarket, discount, and warehouse retailing principles. Its product assortment goes beyond routinely purchased goods and includes furniture, heavy and light appliances, clothing items, and many other things. The hypermarché has price discounts in contrast to the normal pricing by superstores. Like a warehouse, it has many products that come prepacked in wire "baskets" direct from manufacturers and stacks them on five-tier metal racks to a height of twelve to fifteen feet. The restocking is done by forklift trucks, which move through the wide aisles during selling hours. The basic approach is bulk display and minimum handling by store personnel, with discounts offered to customers who are willing to carry heavy appliances and furniture out of the store. The original hypermarché was opened by Carrefour in a Paris suburb in 1963, and it was an immediate success. The real boom occurred in the late 1960s and early 1970s, particularly in France and Germany where a few hundred now operate. American chains are proceeding cautiously, preferring to open superstores instead, although a few operations such as J. C. Penney's The

Treasury and the Jewel's Grand Bazaar have adopted some of the hypermarché's operating principles.

Service business. We want to briefly mention those business enterprises whose "product line" is service rather than goods. Service retailers include hotels and motels, banks, airlines, colleges, hospitals, movie theaters, tennis clubs and bowling alleys, restaurants, repair services, and various personal service businesses, such as barber and beauty shops, dry cleaners, and funeral homes. Service retailers in the United States are growing at a faster rate than product retailers. Banks are looking for new ways to distribute their services efficiently, including the use of automatic tellers and eventually telephones for paying bills by telephone. Health maintenance organizations (HMOs) are revolutionizing the way consumers get and pay for their health services. The amusement industry has created Disneyworld and its imitators. Groups such as Transcendental Meditation, est, and Silva Mind Control have applied franchise and chain organization principles to mass-distribute personal growth services. And H & R Block has built a franchised network of accountants and tax specialists ready to help consumers pay as little as possible to Uncle Sam.

RELATIVE PRICE EMPHASIS. Retail stores can also be classified according to their price image. Most stores offer medium prices and normal levels of customer service. Some stores offer higher-quality goods and services, along with higher prices. Gucci's justifies its high prices by saying, "You will remember the goods long after the prices are forgotten." **Discount stores**, on the other hand, sell goods for less than their normal prices because they run lower-cost, lower-service operations. Discount stores will be examined here, along with two offshoots, **warehouse stores** and **catalog showrooms**.

Discount store. A discount store sells standard merchandise at lower prices by accepting lower profit margins and selling a higher volume. The mere use of discount pricing and specials from time to time does not make a discount store. Nor does the selling of cheap and inferior goods at low prices. A true discount store exhibits five elements: (1) The store regularly sells its merchandise at lower prices than those prevailing in high-margin, low-turnover outlets; (2) the store emphasizes national brands, so that low price does not suggest inferior quality; (3) the store operates on a self-service, minimum-facilities basis; (4) the location tends to be in a low-rent area, drawing customers from relatively long distances; and (5) the fixtures are simple and functional.[11] In 1981, there were an estimated 8,282 discount department stores, with almost $73 billion in sales.[12]

Discount retailing has a long history, having been practiced before World War II by Alexander's and Mays, well-known New York discount department stores. But the real explosion of discount retailing took place in the late 1940s when it moved from soft goods (clothing, toiletries) to hard goods (refrigerators, appliances, washing machines, dishwashers, air conditioners, furnishings, sporting goods). Early postwar discounters such as Masters, Korvette, and Two Guys were successful for a number of reasons. After the war, many hard goods became highly standardized, reducing the need for in-store salesmanship. Furthermore, a vast new group of price-conscious but affluent consumers emerged.

The early discount stores operated from almost warehouse facilities in low-rent but heavily traveled districts, slashing services, advertising widely, and carrying a reasonable width and depth of branded products. They operated with expenses of 12% to 18% of sales compared with 30% to 40% for the department and specialty stores. By 1960, discount stores accounted for one-third of all sales of household appliances, and the average turnover of stock was fourteen per year compared with four for a conventional department store.

In recent years, intense competition among discount stores, and between discount and department stores, has led many discount retailers to enhance their image. They have improved their decor, added new lines such as wearing apparel, added more services such as check cashing and easy returns, and opened new branches in suburban shopping centers, all leading to higher costs and higher prices. Furthermore, department stores often cut their prices to compete with the discounters, with the distinction between the two growing progressively blurred. Several major discount chains folded in the 1970s as a result of rising costs and the loss of their price edge.

Discount retailing has moved beyond general merchandise into special merchandise stores, such as discount sporting goods stores, discount stereo equipment stores, and discount bookstores. Discount food retailing has been one of the most interesting developments. In 1956, the Shop-Rite supermarket food chain dropped its trading stamps and launched a bold discount strategy. Economies were created by operating fewer hours, reducing nonessential services, and having "everyday low prices." Its greater efficiency permitted prices that were approximately 4% below those of conventional supermarkets, and the chain met with great success.

Warehouse store. A warehouse store is a no-frill, discount, reduced-service operation that seeks to move a high volume of products at low prices. In its broad form, it includes hypermarchés and box food discount stores. One of its most interesting forms is the furniture showroom warehouse. Conventional furniture stores have run warehouse sales for years to clear out old stock, but it took two brothers, Ralph and Leon Levitz, to build it into a new merchandising concept in 1953. By 1977, they had built sixty-one furniture warehouse showrooms. Shoppers enter a football-field-sized warehouse located in a suburban low-rent area. They pass through the warehouse section, where they see a large amount of inventory piled in neat tiers: approximately fifty-two thousand items worth about $2 million. They enter the showroom section containing approximately two hundred rooms of attractively displayed furniture. Customers make their selections and place orders with salespeople. By the time the customer pays, leaves, and drives to the loading entrance, the merchandise is ready. Heavy goods can be delivered in a few days (compared with the many weeks of waiting with conventional furniture stores) or loaded on the customer's vehicle.

The whole operation is targeted to buyers of medium-priced brand-name furniture who are seeking discount prices and immediate availability. The shoppers enjoy a wide brand selection and low prices, but on the other hand they often complain about the limited customer service. Levitz stores have attracted a number of competitors. The profit picture is mixed because these stores have high inventory costs, spend a lot on promotion to attract enough customers, and often face too many competitors in the same markets.[13]

Catalog showroom. A catalog showroom applies catalog and discounting principles to a wide selection of high-markup, fast-moving, brand-name goods. These include jewelry, power tools, luggage, cameras, and photographic equipment. These stores emerged in the late 1960s and have become one of retailing's hottest new forms, even posing a threat to the traditional discounter. Catalog showroom sales in 1982 totaled $9.27 billion, a jump from the $750 million ten years earlier. The industry is dominated by publicly owned companies such as Best Products Co., Service Merchandise, and Modern Merchandising. Currently, approximately four hundred companies operate about two thousand catalog showrooms in the United States.[14]

The catalog showrooms issue four-color catalogs, often five hundred pages long, and supplement them with smaller seasonal editions. They are available in the showroom and are also mailed to past buyers. Each item's list price and discount price are shown. The customer can order an item over the phone and pay delivery charges or drive to the showroom, examine it firsthand, and buy it out of stock.

Catalog showrooms make their money by carrying national brands in non-fashion goods categories, leasing stores in low-rent areas, doing with one-third fewer salespeople, minimizing opportunities for shoplifting by their case display, and operating largely on a cash basis.

NATURE OF BUSINESS PREMISES. Although the overwhelming majority of goods and services are sold through stores, nonstore retailing has been growing much faster than store retailing. In 1977, nonstore retailing amounted to $75 billion, or 12% of all consumer purchases. Some observers foresee as much as a third of all general merchandise retailing being done through nonstore channels by the end of the century.[15] Others predict remote retailing, where consumers will order their goods by using home computers and receive or pick them up, without stepping into stores.[16] In this section we will examine four forms of nonstore retailing: **mail-and-telephone-order retailing**, **vending machines**, **buying services**, and **door-to-door selling and in-house parties**.

Mail-and-telephone-order retailing. Mail-and-telephone-order retailing covers any selling that involves using the mail or telephone to get orders and/or using them to aid in the delivery of goods. Mail order originated when customers mailed their orders to manufacturers or merchants. After the Civil War, merchants attempted to stimulate customer orders by sending out catalogs, primarily to people living in rural areas. Montgomery Ward was established in 1872 in Chicago and was followed fourteen years later by Sears, Roebuck. By 1918, these two concerns were conducting giant catalog mail-order businesses, and there were some twenty-five hundred other mail-order houses. In the 1930s and 1940s, many retailers halted their mail-order operations as chain stores opened branches in smaller towns and brought more merchandise to their inhabitants and as the number of automobiles and good roads increased. But today, far from declining, the mail-and-telephone-order business is booming.

There are eleven thousand mail-and-telephone-order businesses in the United States, with sales of over $8 billion. The mail-and-telephone-order business takes several forms.

1. *Mail-order catalog:* Sellers usually mail catalogs to select lists of customers and make the catalogs available on their premises, either at no charge or at a nominal charge. This approach is used by general merchandise mail-order houses carrying a full line of merchandise. Sears is the industry giant, with over $3 billion in catalog operations, and it sends out 300 million catalogs annually.[17] J. C. Penney is number two, selling over a billion dollars' worth of merchandise. These giant merchandisers also operate catalog counters in their stores and catalog offices in small communities where customers can examine the catalogs and place orders. Orders are shipped from central warehouses to these catalog desks, and upon arrival, the customers are phoned to pick up their orders. Recently, specialty department stores, such as Neiman-Marcus and Saks Fifth Avenue, have begun sending out catalogs to cultivate an upper-middle-class market for high-priced, often exotic, merchandise, such as "his and her" bathrobes, designer jewelry, and gourmet foods (see exhibit 13-2).

2. *Direct response:* A direct marketer will sometimes run an ad in a newspaper, a magazine, or on radio or television describing some product, and the customer can write or phone for it. The direct marketer selects the media that will produce the greatest number of orders for a given advertising expenditure. This strategy works well with such products as phonograph records and tapes, books, and small appliances.

3. *Direct mail:* Direct marketers often send mailing pieces—letters, fliers, and foldouts—to prospects whose names are on special mailing lists of high-potential buyers of the product category. The mailing lists are purchased from mailing list brokerage houses. Direct mail has proved very successful in promoting books, magazine subscriptions, and insurance and is increasingly being used to sell novelty items, clothing apparel, and even gourmet foods. The major charities use direct mail to raise $21.4 billion, or over 80% of their total contributions.[18]

4. *Telephone selling:* Direct marketers are increasingly using the telephone to sell everything from home repair services to newspaper subscriptions to zoo memberships. Some telephone marketers have developed computerized phoning systems where households are dialed automatically and computerized messages presented.

Several factors have stimulated the increase in mail-and-telephone-order selling. The movement of women into the work force has cut down on their available shopping time. Other factors have made shopping less pleasant: the rising costs of driving; traffic congestion and parking headaches; shoppers moving to the suburbs and avoiding crime-plagued urban shopping areas; and the shortage of sales help and having to queue at checkout counters. In addition, many chain stores have dropped slower-moving specialty items, thus creating an opportunity for direct marketers to promote these items. Finally, the development of "toll-free" phone numbers and the willingness of direct marketers to accept telephone orders at night or on Sundays have boosted this form of retailing.

Automatic vending. Automatic vending through coin-operated machines has been a major post–World War II growth area, with total sales soaring to $13.8

Exhibit **13-2**

Buying through Catalogs—Armchair Shopping

One form of retailing lets consumers buy almost anything without ever set-ting foot inside a store. An increasing number of retailers are selling every imaginable product through mail-order catalogs.

You can order your very own sheepskin-lined logger's boots from L. L. Bean, a sexy nightie from Victoria's Secret, fruit-of-the-month from Harry and David, or boneless loin roast of milk-fed veal from the Pfaelzer Collection. If none of these items strikes your fancy, there are plenty more. How about a one-third-scale Corvette, an unobtrusive toilet bowl cleaner, a personalized pet collar, or a chess robot? These, too, are yours for the ordering.

According to a recent study, sales through catalogs are increasing by about 15% per year, as compared to only 3% growth in store sales. In 1982, over five billion catalogs were mailed to U.S. consumers—that's an average of forty catalogs stuffed into the mailbox of the average American house-hold.

Buying and selling through catalogs offers advantages for both con-sumer and retailer. Women continue to do most of the shopping in this country, even though a major portion of American women are now em-ployed. Buying through catalogs, or armchair shopping, offers a time- and trouble-saving alternative to shopping in stores, particularly for those on a tight schedule. For retailers this method cuts the costs of labor and over-head and virtually eliminates shoplifting.

A catalog business is only as good as its mailing list, though. Many re-tailers find they get the best results by targeting their mailings to high-income neighborhoods. For up to $250,000, the U.S. Bureau of the Census provides lists of zip codes and the average income level for each area. Us-ing such a list, retailers can choose where to mail their catalogs based on neighborhoods' income level.

Several merchants even offer a catalog version of window shopping, an activity that consists of browsing through pages of the ultimate luxury items available for the most exorbitant prices. J S & A Group Products That Think invites you to order a seat on the first commercial space shuttle flight; Sakowitz of Texas has offered a full-sized wooden roller coaster for $2,430,000; Neiman-Marcus has offered his and hers airplanes; and one store offered a bathtub full of diamonds. From the most economical, utilitarian necessities to the most extravagant trinkets, gadgets, and baubles, if you want it, you can order it from a catalog.

Source: Based on "Catalog Cornucopia," *Time,* November 8, 1982, pp. 73–78.

billion by 1980 (1.5% of the total retail trade). Automatic vending is not new, and one study cites a 215 B.C. book describing an Egyptian coin-actuated device for selling sacrificial water.[19] In the 1880s, the Tutti-Frutti Company began installing chewing-gum machines at train stations. But today's machines have come a long way and have benefited from space-age and computer technology. The new machines can accept coins or bills and make the proper change. Automatic vending has been applied to a considerable number of products, including impulse convenience goods (cigarettes, soft drinks, candy, newspapers, and hot and cold beverages) and other products (cosmetics, paperbacks, record albums, film, T-shirts, insurance policies, shoeshines, and even fishing bait).

Vending machines are found in factories, offices, large retail stores, gasoline stations, and even railway dining cars. They are usually owned by companies that lease space in favorable locations and service the machines. According to the National Automatic Merchandising Association, over seven thousand machine operators in the United States operate more than 6 million machines.

Vending machines offer customers the advantages of twenty-four-hour selling, self-service, and less damaged merchandise. At the same time, automatic vending is a relatively expensive distribution channel, and prices of vended merchandise are often 15% to 20% higher. Vendor costs are high because of frequent restocking at widely scattered locations, frequent machine breakdowns, and the high pilferage rate in certain locations. For the customer, the biggest irritations are machine breakdowns, out-of-stock items, and the fact that merchandise cannot be returned.

Buying service.   A buying service helps a specific clientele—usually the employees of large organizations, such as schools, hospitals, unions, and government agencies—buy from a selective list of retailers at a discount. A customer looking for a video recording machine would get a form from the buying service, take it to an approved retailer, and buy the appliance at a discount. The retailer would then pay a small fee to the buying service. United Buying Service, for example, offers its 900,000 members the opportunity to buy merchandise at "cost plus 8%."

Door-to-door selling.   This form of selling—which started centuries ago with traveling peddlers—has grown into a $6 billion industry, with over six hundred companies selling either door to door, office to office, or at home sales parties. One of the pioneers, the Fuller Brush Company, still employs about 10,000 sales representatives to sell its brushes, combs, brooms, and other products. Other pioneers include vacuum cleaner companies, like Electrolux, and Bible-selling companies, like the Southwestern Company of Nashville. Encyclopedia companies have used door-to-door selling for years; World Book became the leader by hiring and training schoolteachers to sell its encyclopedias part time. Avon entered the industry with its concept of the homemakers' friend and beauty consultant—the Avon lady (see p. 185). Its army of 1,340,000 representatives worldwide produced over $3 billion in sales in 1982, making it the world's largest cosmetics firm and the number-one door-to-door marketer. Avon is several times larger than the next two leading door-to-door marketers, Electrolux and Tupperware. Tupperware helped popularize home sales parties, in which several friends and neighbors are invited to a party in someone's home where Tupperware is demonstrated and sold. Tupperware handles about 140 different products and works through 50,000 independent dealers.[20]

Door-to-door selling meets the needs of people for the convenience and personal attention that are part of in-home buying. The prices of the items are not low, since door-to-door selling is expensive (the sales representatives get a 20% to 50% commission), and there are the costs of hiring, managing, and motivating the sales force. The future of door-to-door retailing is somewhat uncertain. With a majority of American households today consisting of single-person or two-person families (with both members working full time), the likelihood of finding anyone home during the day is falling. And with the new telecommunication technologies expected to grow in the 1980s, the door-to-door sales representative may well be replaced by a home computer.

OWNERSHIP OF STORE. Retailing institutions can be classified according to their form of ownership. About 80% of all retail stores are independents, and they account for two-thirds of all retail sales. Several other forms—the corporate chain, voluntary chain and retailer cooperative, consumer cooperative, franchise organization, and merchandising conglomerate—represent alternative ownership forms.

Corporate chain. The chain store is one of the most important retail developments in the twentieth century. **Chain stores** are two or more outlets that are commonly owned and controlled, sell similar lines of merchandise, have central buying and merchandising, and may use a similar architectural motif.[21]

Common ownership and control is the unique feature of the corporate chain. It sells similar lines of merchandise. Headquarters plays a key role in deciding on the chain's product assortment, placing bulk orders for the goods to get quantity discounts, distributing the goods to the individual store units, and establishing pricing, promotion, and other standard merchandising policies for the units. Finally, the chains often develop a similar architectural motif to increase each unit's visibility and identifiability in the public eye.

The success of corporate chains is based on their ability to achieve a price advantage over independents by moving toward high volume and low margins. Chains achieve their efficiency in several ways. First, their size allows them to buy large quantities to take maximum advantage of quantity discounts and lower transportation costs. Second, chains have been able to develop superior organizations by hiring good managers and developing special procedures in the areas of sales forecasting, inventory control, pricing, and promotion. Third, the chains are able to integrate wholesaling and retailing functions, while independent retailers have to deal with many wholesalers. Fourth, the chains get promotional economies by buying advertising that benefits all their stores and whose cost is spread over a large volume. And fifth, the chains permit their units some freedom to meet variations in consumer preferences and competition in local markets.

In addition to the corporate chain, there is the voluntary chain, which is a wholesaler-sponsored group of independent retailers, and the retailer cooperative, which is a set of independent retailers who have organized themselves.

Consumer cooperative. A consumer cooperative (or co-op) is any retail firm that is owned by its customers. Consumer co-ops are started by the residents of a community when they feel that local retailers are not serving them well, either charging too high prices or providing poor-quality products. The residents contribute money to open their own store, and they vote on its policies and elect a group to manage it. The store may set its prices low or, alternatively, set normal prices with the members receiving a dividend based on the individual level of purchases. Many successful cooperatives are based on an ideology, and several are found in college communities. Although there are a few thousand consumer cooperatives in the United States, they have never become an important force in distribution. The opposite is true in some European countries, especially in the Scandinavian countries and Switzerland.

> A striking example is Migros in Switzerland, a consumer cooperative that accounts for 11% of the entire Swiss retail volume! Migros was founded in 1925 by Gottlieb Duttweiler as a corporate chain in the grocery business that is dedicated to challenging entrenched high-markup competitors in the grocery field. He was so successful that in 1946 he turned Migros into a consumer cooperative by selling one share of stock to each of his eighty-five thousand registered customers. Today Migros is a huge federation of 440 branch stores, 74 specialty stores, and numerous other enterprises essentially owned by its customers.

Franchise organization. A franchise organization is an association formed by a contract between a franchiser (who may be a manufacturer, wholesaler, or service organization) and franchisees (who are independent business people who buy the right to own and operate one or more units in the franchise system). The contract covers the financial arrangements and the responsibilities of both the franchiser and franchisee. The main distinction between franchise organizations and other contractual systems (voluntary chains and retailer cooperatives) is that franchise organizations are normally based on some unique product or service, or on a method of doing business, or on a trade name, goodwill, or patent that the franchiser has developed.

In 1982, there were approximately 466,000 franchise outlets, with sales of $437 billion. Their heaviest concentration in terms of number of units is in gasoline service stations (32.4%), automobile and truck dealers (6.4%), and fast-food restaurants (7.3%). Among the fast-food restaurants, the market-share leaders as of 1979 were McDonald's (18.1%), Burger King (5.7%), Kentucky Fried Chicken (5.5%), Wendy's (4.1%), and International Dairy Queen (3.8%). McDonald's and other fast-food franchisers are currently facing difficult challenges in rising labor and food costs, forcing them to raise their prices to customers. New competitors continue to emerge, offering new foods such as tacos and gyros. Some of the franchisers are opening smaller units in small towns, where there is less competition. Others are moving into large factories, office buildings, colleges, and even hospitals. Still others are experimenting with new products that they hope will appeal to the public and be profitable to the firm.

Merchandising conglomerate. Merchandising conglomerates are free-form corporations that combine several diversified retailing lines and forms under central ownership, along with some integration of their distribution and management functions.[22] Major examples include Federated Department Stores, Allied Stores, Dayton Hudson, and J. C. Penney. Among the most profitable of the diversified retailers are the Melville Corporation, which operates the Thom McAn, Miles, and Vanguard shoe chains; Chess King, a string of 326 young men's fashion stores; Foxmoor, a women's junior apparel store; Clothes Ben, a chain of discount women's apparel stores; CVS, a chain of health and beauty-aid stores; and Marshall, Inc., a regional chain that carries all kinds of name-brand clothing.[23]

TYPE OF STORE CLUSTER. The last principle for retail classification is whether consumers face a single store or several clustered stores. Most stores today cluster in shopping districts, both because of zoning ordinances and to offer more convenience through one-stop shopping. Just as supermarkets and department stores save consumers time and energy in finding what they need, so do clustered stores. The four main types are the central business district, the regional shopping center, the community shopping center, and the neighborhood shopping center.

Central business district. Central business districts were the main form of retail cluster until the 1950s. Every large city and town had a central business district containing department stores, specialty stores, banks, and major movie houses. Smaller business districts could be found in neighborhood and outlying areas. Then, in the 1950s, people began to migrate to the suburbs. Suburbanites reduced their shopping in the central business district, wishing to avoid the heavy traffic, expensive parking, and the deteriorating central city. These central business districts deteriorated further and forced centrally located merchants to open branches in the growing suburban shopping centers. These merchants also made an effort to revitalize the downtown area by building shopping malls and underground parking and by renovating their stores. Some central business districts have made a comeback, but others are in a state of slow and possibly irreversible decline.

Regional shopping center. A **shopping center** is "a group of commercial establishments planned, developed, owned, and managed as a unit related in location, size, and type of shop to the trade area that it services, and providing on-site parking in definite relationship to the types and sizes of stores it contains."[24] Of these, the regional shopping center is the most dramatic and competitive with the central business district and neighborhood shopping areas.

A regional shopping center is like a mini-downtown and contains from forty to over one hundred stores. To be profitable, it must serve a population of from one hundred thousand to one million customers who live within thirty minutes' driving time. In its early form, the regional shopping center often contained two strong department stores at the two ends of a mall and a set of specialty stores in between. This arrangement encouraged comparison shopping because the specialty stores typically carried goods that competed with the lines carried by the department stores. Thus a customer wishing to buy jeans could comparison-shop at Sears, Lord & Taylor, Just Jeans, The Gap, and The County Seat. Regional shopping centers have added new types of retailers over the years, such as dentists, health clubs, and even branch libraries. Larger regional malls now have several department stores and are laid out to encourage freely moving traffic so that all the stores can get exposure. Many of the newer malls in the North are enclosed under one roof so that shoppers can shop under any weather conditions.

Community shopping center. A community shopping center contains fifteen to fifty retail stores serving between twenty thousand and one hundred thousand residents, with 90% living within one and one-half miles of the center. There is normally one primary store, usually a branch of a department store or a variety store. The shopping center is likely to include a supermarket, convenience goods stores, and professional offices—and sometimes a bank. The primary store will usually be located at the corner of the L in the case of L-shaped shopping centers, or in the center in the case of line-shaped shopping centers. The stores nearest to the primary store normally sell shopping goods, and the more distant stores normally sell convenience goods.

Neighborhood shopping center. The largest number of shopping centers are those serving neighborhoods. Neighborhood shopping centers contain five to fifteen stores and serve a population of less than twenty thousand residents. Customers walk to these centers or drive no more than five minutes. These are convenience shopping centers with the supermarket as the principal tenant and several service establishments, such as a dry cleaner, self-service laundry, shoe repair store, and beauty shop. In contrast to the larger shopping centers, this is usually an unplanned strip of stores.

Shopping centers now account for approximately one-third of all retail sales, but they may be reaching their saturation point. Sales per square foot are dropping and vacancy rates are climbing; some bankruptcies have occurred. Shopping center developers are planning to build smaller shopping centers in medium-sized and smaller cities and in the fastest-growing areas, such as the Southwest.[25] Meanwhile, some people predict a different future for shopping centers in the next few years: "Although you will still be able to find shopping centers in 1985, you may not be able to recognize them. They will be smaller, fewer in number, and their occupants will be dramatically different. Doctors, lawyers, dentists, clinics, contractors, churches, counselling centers, local government offices—and even the public library—will have found a place among the few surviving retail tenants."[26]

Retailer Marketing Decisions We will now look at the major marketing decisions facing retailers in the following areas: target market, product assortment and services, price, promotion, and place.

TARGET MARKET DECISION. A retailer's most important decision concerns the target market. Until the target market has been defined and profiled, the retailer cannot make consistent decisions on product assortment, store decor, advertising messages and media, price levels, and so on. Some stores are able to define their target markets quite well. A fashionable women's apparel store in

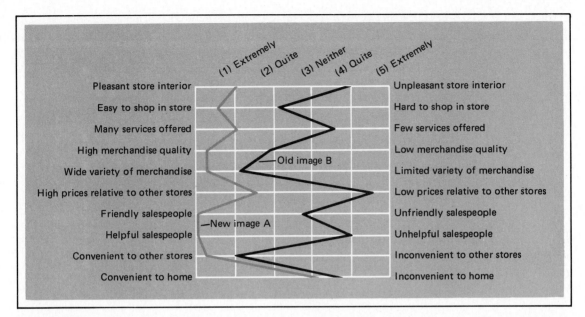

	(1) Extremely	(2) Quite	(3) Neither	(4) Quite	(5) Extremely	
Pleasant store interior						Unpleasant store interior
Easy to shop in store						Hard to shop in store
Many services offered						Few services offered
High merchandise quality						Low merchandise quality
Wide variety of merchandise		Old image B				Limited variety of merchandise
High prices relative to other stores						Low prices relative to other stores
Friendly salespeople	New image A					Unfriendly salespeople
Helpful salespeople						Unhelpful salespeople
Convenient to other stores						Inconvenient to other stores
Convenient to home						Inconvenient to home

FIGURE 13-2

A Comparison between the Old and New Image of a Store Seeking to Appeal to a Target Market

Source: Adapted from David W. Cravens, Gerald E. Hills, and Robert B. Woodruff, *Marketing Decision Making: Concepts and Strategy* (Homewood, Ill.: Richard D. Irwin, 1976), p. 234. © 1976 Richard D. Irwin, Inc.

Palm Springs knows that its primary market is upper-income women, primarily between thirty and fifty-five years of age, living within thirty minutes' driving time from the store. However, too many retailers have not clarified their target markets or are trying to satisfy some incompatible target markets, satisfying none of them well. Even Sears, which services so many different people, must develop a better definition of which groups it will make its major target customers so that it can achieve more precision in its product assortment, prices, locations, and promotions with these groups.

A retailer should carry out periodic marketing research to check that it is satisfying its target customers. Consider a store that seeks to attract wealthy consumers, but whose image as a store is the one shown by the black line in figure 13-2. The store's image does not appeal to its target market, and it has to serve either the mass market or redesign itself into a "classier store." Suppose it decides on the latter. Sometime later the store interviews customers again. The store image is now shown by the orange line in figure 13-2. The store has succeeded in bringing its image closer to its target market.

PRODUCT ASSORTMENT AND SERVICES DECISION. Retailers have to decide on three major "product" variables: product assortment, services mix, and store atmosphere.

The retailer's product assortment must match the shopping expectations of the target market. In fact, it becomes a key element in the competitive battle among similar retailers. The retailer has to decide on product assortment width (narrow or wide) and depth (shallow or deep). Thus, in the restaurant business, a restaurant can offer a narrow and shallow assortment (small lunch counter), a narrow and deep assortment (delicatessen), a wide and shallow assortment (cafeteria), or a wide and deep assortment (large restaurant). Another product

Table 13-2		
Typical Retail Services		
PREPURCHASE SERVICES	POSTPURCHASE SERVICES	ANCILLARY SERVICES
1. Accepting telephone orders	1. Delivery	1. Check cashing
2. Accepting mail orders (or purchases)	2. Regular wrapping (or bagging)	2. General information
3. Advertising	3. Gift wrapping	3. Free parking
4. Window display	4. Adjustments	4. Restaurants
5. Interior display	5. Returns	5. Repairs
6. Fitting rooms	6. Alterations	6. Interior decorating
7. Shopping hours	7. Tailoring	7. Credit
8. Fashion shows	8. Installations	8. Rest rooms
9. Trade-ins	9. Engraving	9. Baby attendant services
	10. COD delivery	

Source: Carl M. Larson, Robert E. Weigand, and John S. Wright, *Basic Retailing,* 2nd ed. (Englewood Cliffs, N.J.: Prentice-Hall, 1982), p. 384. © 1982 by Prentice-Hall. Reprinted by permission.

assortment dimension is the quality of the goods. The customer is interested not only in the range of choice but also in the quality of the product.

Retailers also must decide on the services mix to offer customers. The old "mom-and-pop" grocery stores offered home delivery, credit, and conversation, services that today's supermarkets have completely eliminated. Table 13-2 lists some of the major services that full-service retailers can offer. The services mix is one of the key tools of nonprice competition for differentiating one store from another.

The store's atmosphere is a third element in its product arsenal. Every store has a physical layout that makes it hard or easy to move around. Every store has a "feel"—one store is dirty, another is charming, a third is palatial, a fourth is somber. The store must embody a planned atmosphere that suits the target market and influences them toward making a purchase. A funeral parlor should be quiet, somber, and peaceful, and a discothèque should be bright, loud, and vibrating. The atmosphere is designed by creative people who know how to combine visual, aural, olfactory, and tactile stimuli to achieve the desired effect.[27]

PRICE DECISION. The retailers' prices are a key competitive factor and reflect the quality of goods carried and services offered. Retailers' ability to buy intelligently is a key ingredient in successful retailing. Beyond this, they must price carefully in a number of other ways. Low markups can be set on some items so that they can work as traffic builders or loss leaders, in the hope that customers will buy additional items with a higher markup once they are in the store. In addition, retail management has to be adept in its use of markdowns on slower-moving merchandise. Shoe retailers, for example, expect to sell 50% of their shoes at a 60% markup, 25% at a 40% markup, and the remaining 25% at cost. Their initial pricing anticipates these expected markdowns.

Exhibit **13-3**

The Great Retailers

Managers in six different retail industries were asked to cite the person who had done the most for his or her industry in the last fifty years. Here are this half-century's great retailers:

- Man of the Half-Century in the General Merchandise/Department Store field—the late James Cash Penney: " . . . among his contributions are the first profit-sharing programs. He was a pioneer respondent to consumerism before it was recognized by that name; not only a believer in but an ardent practitioner of the Golden Rule."
- Man of the Half-Century in the Food Service field—Ray A. Kroc, chairman of the McDonald's Corp.: " . . . for bringing to the restaurant industry the most advanced concepts of franchising and for the application of the advanced marketing and operational techniques to the food service industry."
- Man of the Half-Century in the Supermarket field—Sidney R. Rabb, chairman of the Stop & Shop Co.: " . . . reorganized the Super Market Institute into the kind of organization it is today. An industry leader in innovative merchandising and operations' techniques; renowned for introducing modern personnel relations concepts in the food field."
- Man of the Half-Century in the Discount Department Store field—Harry B. Cunningham, honorary chairman of the S. S. Kresge Co.: " . . . was the driving force behind the founding of K Mart, which not only revolutionized his own company but set a model for industry leadership."
- Man of the Half-Century in the Chain Drug field—the late Charles R. Walgreen, Sr.: " . . . the pioneer who envisioned a chain drug industry when there was none, then built his chain into that industry's leading retailer."
- Man of the Half-Century in the Home Improvement Center field—John A. Walker, executive vice president of Lowe's Companies, Inc.: " . . . he introduced sophisticated marketing concepts to the lumberyard field, thereby creating a new retail apparatus, the modern home improvement center."

Source: "The Man of the Half-Century Awards," *Chain Store Age*, September 1975, pp. 76–77. © 1975 by Lebhar-Friedman Inc. Reprinted by permission.

PROMOTION DECISION. Retailers use the normal promotional tools— advertising, personal selling, sales promotion, and publicity—to reach consumers. Retailers advertise in newspapers, magazines, radio, and television. The advertising is occasionally supplemented by hand-delivered circulars and direct-mail pieces. Personal selling requires careful training of salespeople in how to greet customers, meet their needs, and handle their doubts and complaints. Sales promotion may take the form of in-store demonstrations, trading stamps, grand prizes, and visiting celebrities. Publicity is always available to retailers who have something interesting to say. Consider the range of promotional styles available to three art galleries that opened in Chicago:

> The Seaburg-Isthmus Gallery edged quietly into the local art world last month with a model of promotional-making-with-words, when a simple and informative letter announced its opening. . . . Our second example is Origin, which received a lurid public-relations blast that embarrassed the young artist (Matt) and is enough to scare off the very people he would like to see in his studio-gallery. Somehow the hard sell and art mix poorly. . . . Our third example is a prime instance of non-sell. With no name but the address, 1017 Armitage, the workshop of Julian Frederick Harr has a tidy gallery up front and behind is a cluttered, chip-and-shaving sculptor's studio. . . . In the long run, Harr, quietly building his people-traps, is better off than Matt, who will have to live down his own well-intentioned publicity. But the Seaburg-Isthmus soft sell is by far the most effective.[28]

PLACE DECISION. The retailer's choice of location is a key competitive factor in its ability to attract customers. For example, customers primarily choose a bank that is nearest to them. Department store chains, oil companies, and fast-food franchisers are particularly careful in selecting locations and using advanced methods of site selection and evaluation.

Wholesaling

Nature and Importance of Wholesaling

What is wholesaling? We can recognize commercial distribution firms as wholesalers, but a small retail bakery selling pastry to a local hotel is also engaging in wholesaling at that point.

> **Wholesaling** includes all the activities involved in selling goods or services to those who are buying for purposes of resale or business use.

In this chapter, we will use the terms *wholesalers* and *wholesaling* to describe firms that are engaged primarily in wholesaling activity.

Wholesalers differ from retailers in a number of ways. First, wholesalers pay less attention to promotion, atmosphere, and location because they are dealing with business customers rather than final consumers. Second, wholesale transactions are usually larger than retail transactions, and wholesalers usually cover a larger trade area than retailers. Third, the government deals with wholesalers and retailers differently in regard to legal regulations and taxes.

Why are wholesalers used at all? Manufacturers could bypass them and sell directly to retailers or final consumers. The answer lies in the efficiencies that wholesalers bring about. First, small manufacturers with limited financial resources cannot afford to develop direct-selling organizations. Second, even manufacturers with sufficient capital may prefer to use their funds to expand production rather than carry out wholesaling activities. Third, wholesalers are likely to be more efficient at wholesaling because of their scale of operation, their wider number of retail contacts, and their specialized skills. Fourth, retailers who carry many lines often prefer to buy assortments from a wholesaler rather than buy directly from each manufacturer.

Thus retailers and manufacturers have reasons for using wholesalers. Wholesalers are used when they are more efficient in performing one or more of the following functions:

1. *Selling and promoting:* Wholesalers provide a sales force that helps manufacturers reach many small customers at a relatively low cost. The wholesaler has more contacts and is often more trusted by the buyer than is the distant manufacturer.
2. *Buying and assortment building:* Wholesalers are able to select items and build assortments needed by their customers, thus saving the customer considerable work.
3. *Bulk breaking:* Wholesalers achieve savings for their customers by buying in carload lots and breaking bulk.
4. *Warehousing:* Wholesalers hold inventories, thereby reducing the inventory costs and risks to suppliers and customers.
5. *Transportation:* Wholesalers provide quicker delivery to buyers because they are closer than the manufacturers.
6. *Financing:* Wholesalers finance their customers by granting credit, and they finance their suppliers by ordering early and paying their bills on time.
7. *Risk bearing:* Wholesalers absorb some risk by taking title and bearing the cost of theft, damage, spoilage, and obsolescence.
8. *Market information:* Wholesalers supply information to their suppliers and customers about competitors' activities, new products, price development, and so on.
9. *Management services and counseling:* Wholesalers often help retailers improve their operations by training their salesclerks, helping with stores' layouts and displays, and setting up accounting and inventory control systems.

A number of major economic developments have contributed to wholesaling's growth over the years. They include: (1) the growth of mass production in large factories located away from the principal users of the output; (2) the growth of production in advance of orders rather than in response to specific orders; (3) an increase in the number of levels of intermediate producers and users; and (4) the increasing need for adapting products to the needs of intermediate and final users in terms of quantities, packages, and forms.[29]

Types of Wholesalers In 1977 there were 383,000 wholesaling establishments in the United States doing a total annual volume of $1,258 billion. The wholesalers fall into four groups (see table 13-3). **Merchant wholesalers** take title to the goods. In 1977 they accounted for $676 billion, or over half the total wholesale sales volume of $1,258 billion.[30] **Brokers** and **agents** do not take title to the goods. They accounted for $130 billion, or about 10% of the total wholesale sales volume. **Manufacturers' sales branches and offices** are manufacturers' wholesaling operations. They

Table 13-3

Classification of Wholesalers

MERCHANT WHOLESALERS	BROKERS AND AGENTS	MANUFACTURERS' SALES BRANCHES AND OFFICES	MISCELLANEOUS WHOLESALERS

Full-service wholesalers
  Wholesale merchants
  Industrial distributors
Limited-service wholesalers
  Cash-and-carry wholesalers
  Truck wholesalers
  Drop shippers
  Rack jobbers
  Producers' cooperatives
  Mail-order wholesalers
	Brokers
	Agents
		Sales branches and
		  offices
		Purchasing offices
			Agricultural assemblers
			Petroleum bulk plants
			  and terminals
			Auction companies

accounted for $452 billion, or about 36% of the total wholesale sales volume. Miscellaneous wholesalers accounted for the remaining volume.

MERCHANT WHOLESALERS. Merchant wholesalers are independently owned businesses that take title to the merchandise they handle. In different trades they may be called jobbers, distributors, or mill supply houses. They are the largest single group of wholesalers, accounting for roughly 50% of all wholesaling (in sales volume and in number of establishments). Merchant wholesalers fall into two broad types: full-service wholesalers and limited-service wholesalers.

Full-service wholesalers. Full-service wholesalers provide such services as carrying stock, using a sales force, offering credit, making deliveries, and providing management assistance. They are either wholesale merchants or industrial distributors.

Wholesale merchants sell primarily to retailers and provide a full range of services. They vary mainly in the width of their product line. *General merchandise wholesalers* carry several merchandise lines to meet the needs of both general merchandise retailers and single-line retailers. *General-line wholesalers* carry one or two lines of merchandise in a greater depth of assortment. Major examples are hardware wholesalers, drug wholesalers, and clothing wholesalers. *Specialty wholesalers* specialize in carrying only part of a line in great depth. Examples are health food wholesalers, seafood wholesalers, and automotive parts wholesalers. They offer customers the advantage of deeper choice and greater product knowledge.

Industrial distributors sell to manufacturers rather than to retailers. They provide several services, such as carrying stock, offering credit, and providing delivery. They may carry a broad range of merchandise (often called a mill supply house), a general line, or a specialty line. Industrial distributors may concentrate on such lines as MRO items (*maintenance, repair,* and *operating* supplies, OEM items (*original equipment supplies,* such as ball bearings, and *m*otors), or equipment (such as hand and power tools and fork trucks). There are about 12,000 industrial distributors in the United States, and their sales were approximately $23.5 billion in 1974.

Limited-service wholesalers. Limited-service wholesalers offer fewer services to their suppliers and customers. There are several types of limited-service wholesalers.

Cash-and-carry wholesalers have a limited line of fast-moving goods, sell to small retailers for cash, and normally do not deliver. A small fish store retailer, for example, normally drives at dawn to a cash-and-carry fish wholesaler and buys several crates of fish, pays on the spot, and drives the merchandise back to the store and unloads it.

Truck wholesalers (also called truck jobbers) primarily sell and deliver. They carry a limited line of semiperishable merchandise (such as milk, bread, snack foods), which they sell for cash as they make their rounds of supermarkets, small groceries, hospitals, restaurants, factory cafeterias, and hotels.

Drop shippers operate in bulk industries such as coal, lumber, and heavy equipment. They do not carry inventory or handle the product. Once an order is received, they find a manufacturer, who ships the merchandise directly to the customer on the agreed terms and time of delivery. The drop shipper assumes title and risk from the time the order is accepted to the time it is delivered to the customer. Because drop shippers do not carry inventory, their costs are lower and they can pass on some savings to customers.

Rack jobbers serve grocery and drug retailers, mostly in the area of nonfood items. These retailers do not want to order and maintain displays of hundreds of nonfood items. The rack jobbers send delivery trucks to stores, and the delivery person sets up toys, paperbacks, hardware items, health and beauty aids, and so on. They price the goods, keep them fresh, set up point-of-purchase displays, and keep inventory records. Rack jobbers sell on consignment, which means that they retain title to the goods and bill the retailers only for the goods sold to consumers. Thus they provide such services as delivery, shelving, inventory carrying, and financing. They do little promotion because they carry many branded items that are highly advertised.

Producers' cooperatives are owned by farmer-members and assemble farm produce to sell in local markets. Their profits are distributed to members at the end of the year. They often attempt to improve product quality and promote a co-op brand name, such as Sun Maid raisins, Sunkist oranges, or Diamond walnuts.

Mail-order wholesalers send catalogs to retail, industrial, and institutional customers featuring jewelry, cosmetics, specialty foods, and other small items. Their main customers are businesses in small outlying areas. The orders are filled and sent by mail, truck, or other efficient means of transportation.

Rack jobbers set up and maintain the displays of a large number of grocery and drug store products.
Courtesy Frito-Lay's

BROKERS AND AGENTS. Agents and brokers differ from merchant wholesalers in two ways: They do not take title to goods, and they perform only a few functions. Their main function is to aid in buying and selling. For their services, they will earn a commission of anywhere from 2% to 6% of the selling price. Like merchant wholesalers, they generally specialize by product line or customer types. They account for 10% of the total wholesale volume.

Brokers.   The chief function of a broker is to bring buyers and sellers together and to assist in negotiation. Brokers are paid by the party who hired them. They do not carry inventory, get involved in financing, or assume risk. The most familiar examples are food brokers, real-estate brokers, insurance brokers, and security brokers.

Agents.   Agents represent either buyers or sellers on a more permanent basis. There are several types.

Manufacturers' agents (also called manufacturers' representatives) are more numerous than the other types of agent wholesalers. They represent two or more manufacturers of complementary lines. They enter into a formal written agreement with each manufacturer covering pricing policy, territories, order-handling procedures, delivery service and warranties, and commission rates. They know each manufacturer's product line and use their wide contacts to sell the manufacturer's products. Manufacturers' agents are used in such lines as apparel, furniture, and electrical goods. Most manufacturers' agents are small businesses, with only a few employees who are skilled sales representatives. They are hired by small manufacturers who cannot afford to maintain their own field sales force and by large manufacturers who want to use agents to open new territories or to represent them in territories that cannot support a full-time sales representative.

Selling agents are given contractual authority to sell a manufacturer's entire output. The manufacturer either is not interested in the selling function or feels unqualified. The selling agent serves as a sales department and has significant influence over prices, terms, and conditions of sale. The selling agent normally has no territorial limits. Selling agents are found in such product areas as textiles, industrial machinery and equipment, coal and coke, chemicals, and metals.

Purchasing agents generally have a long-term relationship with buyers and make purchases for them, often receiving, inspecting, warehousing, and shipping the merchandise to the buyers. One type consists of resident buyers in major apparel markets, who look for suitable lines of apparel that can be carried by small retailers located in small cities. They are knowledgeable and provide helpful market information to clients as well as obtaining the best goods and prices available.

Commission merchants (or houses) are agents who take physical possession of products and negotiate sales. They are normally not employed on a long-term basis. They are used most often in agricultural marketing by farmers who do not want to sell their own output and do not belong to producers' cooperatives. A commission merchant would take a truckload of commodities to a central market, sell it for the best price, deduct a commission and expenses, and send the balance to the producer.

MANUFACTURERS' SALES BRANCHES AND OFFICES.   The third major type of wholesaling consists of wholesaling operations conducted by sellers or buyers themselves rather than through independent wholesalers. There are two types.

Sales branches and offices.   Manufacturers often set up their own sales branches and offices to improve inventory control, selling, and promotion. *Sales*

A country auction. The auctioneers are acting as wholesalers, linking producer and customer.
Ken Karp

branches carry inventory and are found in such industries as lumber and automotive equipment and parts. *Sales offices* do not carry inventory and are most noticeable in dry goods and notion industries. Sales branches and offices account for about 11% of all wholesale establishments and 36% of all wholesale volume.

Purchasing offices.   Many retailers set up purchasing offices in major market centers such as New York and Chicago. These purchasing offices perform a role similar to that of brokers or agents but are part of the buyer's organization.

MISCELLANEOUS WHOLESALERS.   A few specialized types of wholesalers are found in certain sectors of the economy. *Agricultural assemblers* gather farm products from farmers and build them into larger lots for shipment to food processors, bakers, and government buyers. *Petroleum bulk plants and terminals* sell and deliver petroleum products to filling stations, other retailers, and business firms. *Auction companies* are important in industries where buyers want to see and inspect goods prior to purchase, such as in the tobacco and livestock markets.

Wholesaler Marketing Decisions

Wholesalers must make a number of marketing decisions. The main ones concern the choice of target market, product assortment and services, pricing, promotion, and place.

TARGET MARKET DECISION.   Wholesalers, like retailers, need to define their target market and not try to serve everyone. They can choose a target group of customers according to size criteria (such as only large retailers), type of cus-

Warehousing and transportation are services that wholesalers often provide to customers.

United Fresh Fruit and Vegetable Association

tomer (such as convenience food stores only), need for service (such as customers who need credit), or other criteria. Within the target group, they can identify the more profitable customers and design stronger offers and build better relationships with them. They can propose automatic reordering systems, set up management training and advisory systems, and even sponsor a voluntary chain. They can discourage less profitable customers by requiring larger orders or adding surcharges to smaller ones.

PRODUCT ASSORTMENT AND SERVICES DECISION.   The wholesalers' "product" is their assortment. Wholesalers are under great pressure to carry a full line and maintain sufficient stock for immediate delivery. But this can hurt profits. Wholesalers today are reexamining how many lines to carry and are choosing to carry only the more profitable ones.

Wholesalers are also reexamining which services count most in building strong customer relationships and which ones should be dropped or charged for. The key is to find a distinct mix of services valued by their customers.

PRICING DECISION.   Wholesalers usually mark up the cost of goods by a conventional percentage, say 20%, to cover their expenses. Expenses may run 17% of the gross margin, leaving a profit margin of approximately 3%. In grocery wholesaling, the average profit margin is often less than 2%. Wholesalers are beginning to experiment with new approaches to pricing. They may cut their margin on some lines in order to win important new customers. They will ask suppliers for a special price break when they can turn it into an opportunity to increase the supplier's sales.

PROMOTION DECISION.   Most wholesalers are not promotion-minded. Their use of trade advertising, sales promotion, publicity, and personal selling is largely haphazard. Personal selling is particularly behind the times in that wholesalers still see selling as a single sales representative talking to a single customer instead of a team effort to sell, build, and service major accounts. Wholesalers also need to adopt some of the nonpersonal promotion techniques used by retailers. They need to develop an overall promotion strategy. They also need to make greater use of supplier promotion materials and programs.

PLACE DECISION.   Wholesalers typically locate in low-rent, low-tax areas and put little money into their physical setting and offices. Often their systems for handling materials and processing orders lag behind the available technologies. To meet rising costs, progressive wholesalers have been developing new procedures. One development is the automated warehouse, where the orders are key-punched on tabulating cards and then fed into a computer. The items are picked up by mechanical devices and conveyed on a belt to the shipping platform where they are assembled. This type of mechanization is progressing rapidly, as is the mechanization of many office activities. Many wholesalers are turning to computers and word processing machines to carry out accounting, billing, inventory control, and forecasting.

Summary

Retailing and wholesaling consist of many organizations doing the work of bringing goods and services from the point of production to the point of use.

Retailing includes all the activities involved in selling goods or services directly to final consumers for their personal, nonbusiness use. Retailing is one of the major industries in the United States. Retailers can be classified in several ways: by product line sold (specialty stores, department stores, supermarkets, convenience stores, combination stores, superstores, hypermarchés, and service businesses); relative price emphasis (discount stores, warehouse stores, and catalog showrooms); nature of the business premises (mail-and-telephone-order retailing, automatic vending, buying services, and door-to-door retailing); ownership of store (corporate chains, voluntary chains, retailer cooperatives, consumer cooperatives, franchise organizations, and merchandising conglomerates); and the type of store cluster (central business districts, regional shopping centers, community shopping centers, and neighborhood shopping centers). Retailers make decisions on their target market, product assortment and services, pricing, promotion, and place. Retailers need to find ways to improve their professional management and increase their productivity.

Wholesaling includes all the activities involved in selling goods or services to those who are buying for the purpose of resale or for business use. Wholesalers help manufacturers deliver their products efficiently to the many retailers and industrial users across the nation. Wholesalers perform many functions, including selling and promoting, buying and assortment building, bulk breaking, warehousing, transporting, financing, risk bearing, supplying market information, and providing management services and counseling. Wholesalers fall into four groups. Merchant wholesalers take possession of the goods. They can be subclassified as full-service wholesalers (wholesale merchants, industrial distributors) and limited-service wholesalers (cash-and-carry wholesalers, truck wholesalers, drop shippers, rack jobbers, producers' cooperatives, and mail-order wholesalers). Agents and brokers do not take possession of the goods but are paid a commission for aid in buying and selling. Manufacturers' sales branches and offices are wholesaling operations conducted by nonwholesalers to bypass the wholesalers. Miscellaneous wholesalers include agricultural assemblers, petroleum bulk plants and terminals, and auction companies. Wholesaling is holding its own in the economy. Progressive wholesalers are adapting their services to the needs of target customers and are seeking ways to reduce the costs of transacting business.

Questions for Discussion

1. In two of its San Diego outlets, Montgomery Ward opened "Law Store" booths that provide a one-shot consultation for a $10 fee. Customers are ushered to a telephone boothlike enclosure where operators connect them to a central office of lawyers who respond to queries over the telephone. Discuss the retailer marketing decisions for the "Law Store."
2. What is the major difference between retailers and wholesalers? Explain by using an example of each.
3. Analyze the major differences between a warehouse store and a catalog showroom. What factors contributed to their growth?
4. Door-to-door selling will decline in the 1980s. Comment.
5. If friends of yours were planning to open a card shop, which type of store cluster would you recommend that they select? Why?
6. Is there a difference between the approach taken in retailer marketing decisions and that taken in product marketing decisions? Explain.
7. The major distinction between merchant wholesalers and agents/brokers is that the former offer more services to the buyer. Comment.
8. Would a small manufacturer of lawn and garden tools seek a manufacturer's agent or a selling agent to handle the merchandise? Why?
9. Why, do you think, has the promotion area of marketing strategy been traditionally weak for wholesalers?

Key Terms in Chapter 13

Agent   A wholesaler who represents either buyer or seller on a relatively permanent basis, performs only a few functions, and does not take title to merchandise.

Automatic vending   Selling through coin-operated machines.

Broker   A wholesaler who does not take title to goods and whose function is to bring buyers and sellers together and assist in negotiations.

Buying service   A retailer that helps a specific clientele—usually the employees of large organizations, such as schools, hospitals, unions, and government agencies—buy from a selective list of retailers.

Catalog showroom   A retail operation that applies catalog and discounting principles to a wide selection of high-markup, fast-moving, brand-name goods.

Chain stores Two or more outlets that are commonly owned and controlled, sell similar lines of merchandise, have central buying and merchandising, and may have a similar architectural motif.

Consumer cooperative Any retail firm that is owned by its customers.

Convenience store A relatively small store, located near a residential area, open long hours seven days a week, and carrying a limited line of high-turnover convenience products.

Department store A retail organization that carries several product lines, typically clothing, home furnishings, and household goods; each line is operated as a separate department managed by specialist buyers or merchandisers.

Discount store A retail institution that sells standard merchandise at lower prices by accepting lower profit margins and selling a higher volume.

Door-to-door retailing Selling in customers' homes, offices, or at home sales parties.

Franchise An organization that is formed by a contract between a manufacturer, wholesaler, or service organization (franchiser) and independent business people (franchisees) who buy the right to own and operate one or more units in the system.

Mail-and-telephone-order retailing Any selling that involves using the mail or telephone to get orders and/or using them to aid in the delivery of goods.

Manufacturers' sales branches and offices Wholesaling operations conducted by sellers or buyers themselves rather than through independent wholesalers.

Merchandising conglomerates Free-form corporations that combine several diversified retailing lines and forms under central ownership, along with some integration of their distribution and management functions.

Merchant wholesaler An independently owned business that takes title to the merchandise it handles.

Retailing All the activities involved in selling goods or services directly to final customers for their personal, nonbusiness use.

Shopping center "A group of commercial establishments planned, developed, owned, and managed as a unit related in location, size, and type of shop to the trade area that it services, and providing on-site parking in definite relationship to the types and sizes of stores it contains."

Specialty store A retail outlet that carries a narrow product line with a deep assortment within that line.

Supermarket A relatively large, low-cost, low-margin, high-volume, self-service operation "designed to serve the consumer's total needs for food, laundry, and household maintenance products."

Superstore A retail organization that is larger than conventional supermarkets and aims at meeting consumers' total needs for routinely purchased food and nonfood items.

Warehouse store A no-frill, discount, reduced-service operation that seeks to move a high volume of products at low prices.

Wholesaling All the activities involved in selling goods or services to those who are buying for the purposes of resale or business use.

Cases for Chapter 13

Case 11   Gould, Inc.: Focus 800 BAT-TERY (p. 506)
While deciding to expand its distribution channels, Gould considered the nature of retailing and its own relationship with retailers. This case looks at Gould's position.

Case 12   Fotomat Corporation (p. 508)
Fotomat must make many decisions about its retail outlets. This case presents the problems and factors Fotomat must consider.

Chapter 14

Promoting Products: Communication and Promotion Strategy

Objectives

After reading this chapter, you should be able to:

1. Name and define the four tools of the promotion mix.
2. List the six elements in the marketing communication process.
3. Explain how the promotion budget and mix are set.
4. Discuss four factors that affect the promotion mix.

Pizza Inn is a large food franchise system with over five hundred outlets. The system grosses over $50 million annually. Pizza Inn makes a special effort to train its five hundred independent franchisers to communicate a good image of the fast-food chain. If one outlet uses poor ingredients, prepares its food badly, gives slow service, or fails to keep the place clean, this hurts the other units in the system.

Pizza Inn's marketing communications manager is responsible for putting together an integrated communications program. In his or her mind, everything about Pizza Inn is a potential communication vehicle. He or she sees consumers receiving three kinds of impressions about Pizza Inn: those received before they ever visit it, those received when dining in a Pizza Inn for the first time, and those received after leaving it. These are called impressions of the first, second, and third kind.

Consumers receive their first impressions of Pizza Inn in three ways. They might be exposed to Pizza Inn advertisements in newspapers or on radio or television. Or they might observe a Pizza Inn store while walking or driving, in which case the store's exterior appearance communicates something. Or they might hear others talking about Pizza Inn, such as friends or employees.

Consumers receive their second impressions when they dine at a Pizza Inn for the first time. Customers enter and observe the store's interior appearance and ambiance, finding it either attractive or dull. Customers also observe the personnel's appearance and attitude, whether they are friendly and efficient or not. Even the menu's appearance and selection create an impression. Customers order and receive food that they either enjoy or find disappointing. They consider the food and dining experience in relation to the price to judge whether they received good value for the money.

Customers now leave, feeling either satisfied, indifferent, or disappointed. Yet they will not be through receiving impressions about Pizza Inn. They will still see or hear ads about Pizza Inn, see Pizza Inn as they drive by, and possibly hear others talk about it.

Clearly the marketing communications manager has much more to manage than an advertising budget. He or she must make sure that the whole enterprise and its employees communicate quality, service, and value to the target consumers.[1]

Modern marketing calls for more than developing a good product, pricing it attractively, and making it accessible to target customers. Companies must also communicate with their customers. What is communicated, however, should not be left to chance.

To communicate effectively, companies hire advertising agencies to develop effective ads; sales promotion specialists to design sales incentive programs; and public relations firms to develop the corporate image. They train their salespeople to be friendly and knowledgeable. For most companies the question is not whether to communicate, but how much to spend and in what ways.

A modern company manages a complex marketing communications system (see figure 14-1). The company communicates with its middlemen, consumers, and various publics. Its middlemen communicate with their consumers and various publics. Consumers engage in word-of-mouth communication with each other and with other publics. Meanwhile each group provides communication feedback to every other group.

The marketing communications mix (also called the promotion mix) consists of four major tools:

- **Advertising**—any paid form of nonpersonal presentation and promotion of ideas, goods, or services by an identified sponsor.

- **Sales promotion**—short-term incentives to encourage purchase or sale of a product or service.

- **Publicity**—nonpersonal stimulation of demand for a product, service, or business unit by planting commercially significant news about it in a published medium or obtaining favorable presentation of it on radio, television, or stage that is not paid for by the sponsor.

- **Personal selling**—oral presentation in a conversation with one or more prospective purchasers for the purpose of making sales.[2]

Within each category are specific communication tools, such as sales presentations, point-of-purchase displays, specialty advertising, trade shows, fairs, demonstrations, catalogs, literature, press kits, posters, contests, premiums, coupons, and trading stamps. At the same time, communication is more than these tools. The product's styling, its price, the package's shape and color, the salesclerk's manner and dress, all communicate something to buyers. The whole marketing mix, not just the promotion mix, must be coordinated for the maximum communication impact.

This chapter examines two major questions: What are the major steps in

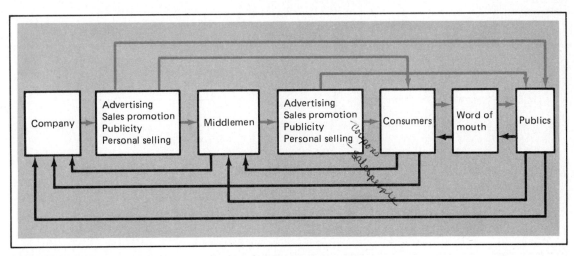

FIGURE 14-1

All of the
Communication and
Feedback Involved in
a Marketing
Communications
System

Get message across and consider target group —

developing effective marketing communication? How should the promotion mix be determined? Chapter 15 will focus on the mass-communication tools of advertising, sales promotion, and publicity. Chapter 16 will focus on the sales force as a communication and promotional tool.

Steps in Developing Effective Communication

Secret to Advertising short, sweet simple

Marketers need to understand how communication works. Communication involves the nine elements shown in the model in figure 14-2. Two elements are the major parties in a communication—sender and receiver. Another two are the major communication tools—message and media. Four are major communication functions—encoding, decoding, response, and feedback. The last element is the noise in the system. These elements are defined as follows:

- *Sender:* The party sending the message to another party.
- *Encoding:* The process of putting thought into symbolic form.
- *Message:* The set of symbols that the sender transmits.
- *Media:* The communication channels through which the message moves from sender to receiver.
- *Decoding:* The process by which the receiver assigns meaning to the symbols transmitted by the sender.
- *Receiver:* The party receiving the message sent by another party.
- *Response:* The set of reactions that the receiver has after being exposed to the message.
- *Feedback:* The part of the receiver's response that the receiver communicates back to the sender.
- *Noise:* The occurrence of unplanned static or distortion during the communication process that results in the receiver's receiving a different message than the sender sent.

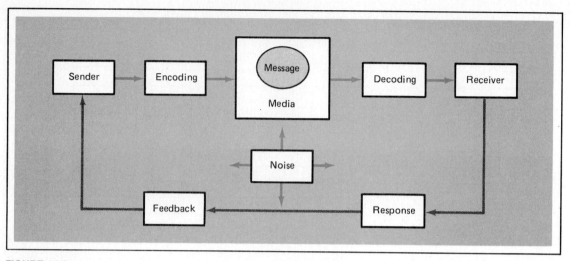

FIGURE 14-2

A Model Showing the Elements in the Communication Process

The model points out the key factors in effective communication. Senders must know what audiences they want to reach and what responses they want. They must be skillful in encoding messages that take into account how the target audience tends to decode messages. They must transmit the message through efficient media that reach the target audience. They must develop feedback channels so that they can know the audience's response to the message.

We will look at the elements in the communication model mainly in terms of the planning flow (from target audience back to the communicator). The marketing communicator must: (1) Identify the target audience, (2) determine the response sought, (3) choose a message, (4) choose the media, (5) select source attributes, and (6) collect feedback.

Identifying the Target Audience

A marketing communicator must start with a clear target audience in mind. The audience may be potential buyers of the company's products, current users, deciders, or influencers. The audience may be individuals, groups, particular publics, or the general public. The target audience will critically influence the communicator's decisions on *what* is to be said, *how* it is to be said, *when* it is to be said, *where* it is to be said, and *who* is to say it.

Determining the Response Sought

Once the target audience has been identified, the marketing communicator must determine what response is sought. The ultimate response, of course, is the purchase by the consumer. But purchasing is the result of a long process of consumer decision making. The marketing communicator needs to know where the target audience now stands and to which state it needs to be moved.

The target audience may be in any of the six buyer readiness states— *awareness, knowledge, liking, preference, conviction,* or *purchase*. These states are described in the following paragraphs.

AWARENESS.   The first thing to establish is how aware the target audience is of the product or organization. The audience may be unaware of it, know only its name, or know one or a few things about it. If most of the target audience is unaware, the communicator's task is to build awareness, perhaps just name recognition. This can be accomplished with simple messages repeating the name. Even then, building awareness takes time.

> Suppose a small Iowa college called Pottsville seeks applicants from Nebraska but has no name recognition in Nebraska. And suppose there are thirty thousand high-school seniors in Nebraska who may be potentially interested in Pottsville College. The college might set the objective of making 70% of these students aware of Pottsville's name within one year.

KNOWLEDGE.   The target audience might be aware of the company or its product but not know much more. Pottsville may want its target audience to know that it is a private four-year college in eastern Iowa with excellent programs in ornithology and thanatology. Pottsville College needs to learn how many people in the target audience have little, some, or much knowledge about Pottsville. The college may decide to build up product knowledge as its immediate communication objective.

LIKING.   If the target audience knows the product, how do they feel about it? We can develop a scale including: dislike very much, dislike somewhat, indifferent, like somewhat, like very much. If the audience looks unfavorably on Pottsville College, the communicator has to find out why and then develop a communications campaign to build up favorable feelings. If the unfavorable view is rooted in real inadequacies of the college, then a communications campaign will not do the job. The task would require improving the college and then communicating its quality. Good public relations calls for "good deeds followed by good words."

PREFERENCE.   The target audience might like the product but not prefer it to others. In this case, the communicator will try to build consumer preference. The communicator will praise the product's quality, value, performance, and other attributes. The communicator can check on the campaign's success by re-measuring the audience's preferences after the campaign.

CONVICTION.   A target audience might prefer a particular product but not develop a conviction about buying it. Thus some high-school seniors may prefer Pottsville but may not be sure they want to go to college. The communicator's job is to build conviction that going to college is the right thing to do.

PURCHASE.   Some members of the target audience might have conviction but not quite get around to making the purchase. They may be waiting for additional information, plan to act later, and so on. The communicator must lead these consumers to take the final step. Among purchase-producing devices are offering the product at a low price, offering a premium, offering an opportunity to try it on a limited basis, or indicating that it will soon be unavailable.

These six states reduce into three stages known as the cognitive (awareness, knowledge), affective (liking, preference, conviction), and behavioral (purchase). Buyers normally pass through these stages on their way to the purchase stage. The communicator's task is to identify the stage that most consumers are in and develop a communication campaign that will move them to the next stage.

Choosing a Message Having defined the desired audience response, the communicator moves to developing an effective message. Ideally, the message should get attention, hold interest, arouse desire, and obtain action (known as the AIDA model). In practice, few messages take the consumer all the way from awareness through purchase, but the AIDA framework suggests the desirable qualities.

Formulating the message will require solving three problems: what to say (message content), how to say it logically (message structure), and how to say it symbolically (message format).

jog your mind

run to your library

American Library Association

A communicator prepares an effective message by combining words and artwork in a way that captures the attention and interest of the reader. Here, the American Library Association is promoting use of the library.

Reprinted by permission of the American Library Association.

MESSAGE CONTENT.   The communicator has to figure out an appeal or theme that will produce the desired response. There are three types of appeals.

Rational appeals relate to the audience's self-interest. They show that the product will produce the claimed benefits. Examples would be messages demonstrating a product's quality, economy, value, or performance.

Emotional appeals attempt to stir up some negative or positive emotion that will motivate purchase. Communicators have worked with fear, guilt, and shame appeals in getting people to do things they should (for example, brushing their teeth, having an annual health checkup) or stop doing things they shouldn't (for example, smoking, drinking too much, drug abuse, overeating). Fear appeals are effective up to a point, but if the audience anticipates too much fear in the message, the audience will avoid it.[3] Communicators also use positive emotional appeals, such as love, humor, pride, and joy. Evidence has not established that a humorous message, for example, is necessarily more effective than a straight version of the same message.[4]

Moral appeals are directed to the audience's sense of what is right and proper. They are often used to urge people to support social causes, such as a cleaner environment, better race relations, equal rights for women, and aid to the disadvantaged. An example is the March of Dimes appeal: "God made you whole. Give to help those He didn't." Moral appeals are less often used in connection with everyday products.

MESSAGE STRUCTURE.   A message's effectiveness also depends on its structure. The communicator has to decide on three issues. The first is whether to draw a definite conclusion or leave it to the audience. Drawing a conclusion is usually more effective.[5] The second is whether to present a one-sided or two-sided argument. Usually a one-sided argument is more effective in sales presentations.[6] The third is whether to present the strongest arguments first or last. Presenting them first establishes strong attention but may lead to an anticlimactic ending.

MESSAGE FORMAT.   The communicator must develop a strong format for the message. If it is a print ad, the communicator has to decide on the headline copy, illustration, and color. To attract attention, advertisers use such devices as novelty and contrast, arresting pictures and headlines, distinctive formats, message size and position, and color, shape, and movement.[7] If the message is to be carried over the radio, the communicator has to carefully choose words, voice qualities (speech rate, rhythm, pitch, articulation), and vocalizations (pauses, sighs, yawns). The "sound" of an announcer promoting a used automobile has to be different from one promoting a quality bed mattress. If the message is to be carried on television or in person, then all of these elements plus body language (nonverbal clues) have to be planned. Presenters have to pay attention to their facial expressions, gestures, dress, posture, and hairstyle. If the message is carried by the product or its packaging, the communicator has to pay attention to texture, scent, color, size, and shape.

> Color plays a major communication role in food preferences. When homemakers sampled four cups of coffee that had been placed next to brown, blue, red, and yellow containers (all the coffee was identical, but this was unknown to the homemakers), 75% felt that the coffee next to the brown container was too strong; nearly 85% judged the coffee next to the red container to be the richest; nearly everyone felt that the coffee next to the blue container was mild and the coffee next to the yellow container was weak.

Choosing the Media The communicator must now select efficient channels of communication. Communication channels are of two broad types, *personal* and *nonpersonal*.

PERSONAL COMMUNICATION CHANNELS. Personal communication channels involve two or more persons communicating directly with each other. They might communicate face to face, person to audience, over the telephone, through the medium of television, or even through the mails on a personal correspondence basis. Personal communication channels are effective due to the opportunities the persons have for personal addressing and feedback.

A further distinction can be drawn between advocate, expert, and social channels of communication. *Advocate channels* consist of company salespeople contacting buyers in the target market. *Expert channels* consist of independent persons with expertise making statements to target buyers. *Social channels* consist of neighbors, friends, family members, and associates talking to target buyers. This last channel, known as *word-of-mouth influence,* is the most persuasive in many product areas.

Personal influence carries great weight in product categories that are expensive or risky. Buyers of automobiles and major appliances go beyond massmedia sources to seek the opinions of knowledgeable people. Personal influence is also influential for products with high social visibility.

Companies can take several steps to stimulate personal influence channels to work on their behalf. They can (1) identify influential individuals and companies and devote extra effort to them; (2) create opinion leaders by supplying certain people with the product on attractive terms; (3) work through local influential people, such as disc jockeys, class presidents, and presidents of women's organizations; (4) use influential people in testimonial advertising; and (5) develop advertising that has high "conversation value."[8]

NONPERSONAL COMMUNICATION CHANNELS. Nonpersonal communication channels are media that carry messages without personal contact or feedback. They include mass and selective media, atmospheres, and events. *Mass and selective media* consist of print media (newspapers, magazines, direct mail), electronic media (radio, television), and display media (billboards, signs, posters). Mass media are aimed at large, often undifferentiated, audiences; selective media are aimed at specialized audiences. (See exhibit 14-1 for an example of a selective medium.) *Atmospheres* are designed environments that create or reinforce the buyer's leanings toward purchase or consumption of the product. Thus lawyers' offices and banks are designed to communicate confidence and other things that might be valued by the clients.[9] *Events* are designed occurrences to communicate particular messages to target audiences. Public relations departments arrange news conferences or grand openings to achieve specific communication effects on an audience.

Although personal communication is often more effective than mass communication, mass media may be the major way to stimulate personal communication. Mass communications affect personal attitudes and behavior through a two-step flow-of-communication process. "Ideas often flow from radio and print to opinion leaders and from these to the less active sections of the population."[10]

This two-step communication flow has several implications. First, the influence of mass media on public opinion is not as direct, powerful, and automatic as supposed. Rather, *opinion leaders,* persons who belong to primary groups and whose opinions are sought in one or more product areas, form and carry the message to others.

Second, the hypothesis challenges the notion that people's buying styles are primarily influenced by a "trickle-down" effect from higher-status classes. Since people primarily interact within their own social class, they pick up their fashion and other ideas from people like themselves who are opinion leaders.

A third implication is that mass communicators would be more efficient by directing their message specifically to opinion leaders, letting the latter carry the message to others. Thus pharmaceutical firms first try to promote their new drugs with the most influential physicians.

Selecting Source Attributes The message's impact on the audience is influenced by how the audience perceives the sender. Messages delivered by highly credible sources are more persuasive. Pharmaceutical companies want doctors to testify about their products' benefits because doctors have high credibility. Antidrug crusaders will use ex-drug addicts to warn high-school students against drugs. Marketers will hire well-known personalities, such as newscasters or athletes, to deliver their messages.

But what factors make a source credible? The three factors most often identified are expertise, trustworthiness, and likability.[11] *Expertise* is the degree to which the communicator appears to possess the necessary authority to back the claim. Doctors, scientists, and professors rank high on expertise in their respective fields. *Trustworthiness* is related to how objective and honest the source is perceived to be. Friends are trusted more than strangers or salespeople. *Likability* describes the source's attractiveness to the audience. Such

Exhibit **14-1**

Marketing Strategy Makes a "Turkey" a Hit

Time magazine called it a "turkey," but Paramount expects its new movie to be a hit. The movie is *Staying Alive,* a continuation of the story begun in *Saturday Night Fever,* one that earned $150 million for Paramount in this country. The new movie stars John Travolta as a young man from Brooklyn trying to win success as a Broadway dancer. But plot is not one of this movie's strong points. *Staying Alive* is a movie in which the soundtrack is more important than the story, and dancing means more than drama. Paramount is not concerned about the fact that critics have panned *Staying Alive.* Planners at the film company are using some specific marketing techniques that they feel will bring in big profits, if not artistic acclaim.

One of Paramount's strategies has been to tailor the movie to appeal to a particular target audience: young people who like music and dancing. An important tool for reaching this audience in the marketing of *Staying Alive* has been MTV, the cable television station that shows videotapes to accompany rock songs. For MTV, Paramount has not only bought advertising time but has also provided the station with video clips from the movie. These 2- to 3-minute segments of music and dance fit closely with the MTV format and, Paramount hopes, will make MTV viewers want to see the full-length movie.

Paramount began the advertisements for *Staying Alive* quite early. Usually ads begin seven to ten days before a movie opens, but advertising for *Staying Alive* began three weeks before the movie opened. To add to audiences' early awareness of the movie, radio stations began playing songs by the BeeGees from the movie soundtrack almost three months before the opening date.

Paramount has used similar strategies for its recent movie *Flashdance.* This movie also has very little plot but a lot of music and dancing. The soundtrack album became popular on radio and MTV before the movie's release. "By the time *Flashdance* opened," says Frank Manusco of Paramount, "the music was known nationally." *Flashdance,* like *Staying Alive,* received exceptionally bad reviews, but the movie has grossed $60 million for Paramount. So Manusco has a point when he says, "Movies like these aren't made or broken on reviews."

If *Staying Alive* becomes the hit movie Paramount expects, the movie company plans to make more music-and-dance-oriented films in the future.

Source: Laura Landro, "Paramount Pictures' 'Staying Alive' Seen as Box Office Killer," *Wall Street Journal,* July 15, 1983.

qualities as candor, humor, and naturalness make a source more likable. The most highly credible source, then, would be a person who scored high on all three dimensions.

Collecting Feedback After spreading the message, the communicator must research its effect on the target audience. This involves asking the target audience whether they recognize or recall the message, how many times they saw it, what points they recall, how they felt about the message, and their previous and current attitudes toward the product and company. The communicator would like to collect behavioral measures of audience response, such as how many people bought the product, liked it, and talked to others about it.

Figure 14-3 provides an example of feedback measurement. Looking at brand A, we find that 80% of the total market are aware of brand A, 60% have tried it, and only 20% of those who have tried it are satisfied. This indicates that the communication program is effective in creating awareness but the product fails to meet consumer expectations. On the other hand, only 40% of the total market are aware of brand B, only 30% have tried it, but 80% of those who have tried it are satisfied. In this case, the communication program needs to be strengthened to take advantage of the brand's satisfaction-generating power.

FIGURE 14-3

Current Consumer States for Two Brands

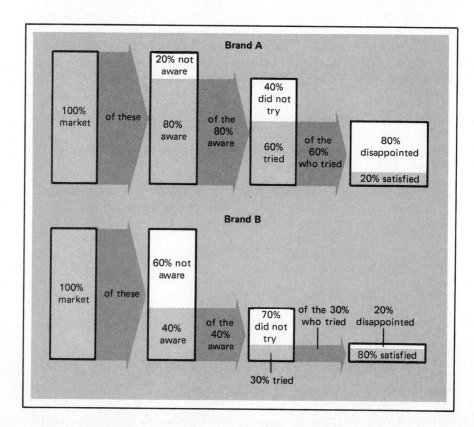

Setting the Total Promotion Budget and Mix

We have looked at the steps involved in planning and directing communications to a specific target audience. But how does the company decide on (1) the total promotion budget and (2) its division among the major promotional tools? We will examine these questions in that order.

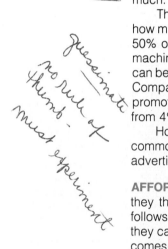

Establishing the Total Promotion Budget   One of the most difficult marketing decisions facing companies is how much to spend on promotion. John Wanamaker, the department store magnate, said: "I know that half of my advertising is wasted, but I don't know which half. I spend $2 million for advertising, and I don't know if that is half enough or twice too much."

Thus, it is not surprising that industries and companies vary considerably in how much they spend on promotion. Promotion spending may amount to 30% to 50% of sales in the cosmetics industry and only 10% to 20% in the industrial machinery industry. Within a given industry, low- and high-spending companies can be found. Philip Morris is a high spender. When it acquired the Miller Brewing Company, and later the Seven-Up Company, it substantially increased total promotion spending. The additional spending at Miller's raised its market share from 4% to 22% within a few years (see pp. 29–30).

How do companies decide on their promotion budget? We will describe four common methods used to set the total budget for any component, such as advertising.

AFFORDABLE METHOD.   Many companies set the promotion budget at what they think the company can afford. One executive explained this method as follows: "Why it's simple. First, I go upstairs to the controller and ask how much they can afford to give us this year. He says a million and a half. Later, the boss comes to me and asks how much we should spend and I say, 'Oh, about a million and a half.' "[12]

This method of setting budgets completely ignores the impact of promotion on sales volume. It leads to an uncertain annual promotion budget, which makes long-range market planning difficult.

PERCENTAGE-OF-SALES METHOD.   Many companies set their promotion budget at a specific percentage of sales (either current or anticipated) or of the sales price. A railroad company executive said: "We set our appropriation for each year on December 1 of the preceding year. On that date we add our passenger revenue for the next month, and then take 2% of the total for our advertising appropriation for the new year."[13] Automobile companies typically budget a fixed percentage for promotion based on the planned car price. Oil companies set the budget at some fraction of a cent for each gallon of gasoline sold under their own label.

A number of advantages are claimed for this method. First, the percentage-of-sales method means that promotion expenditures are likely to vary with what the company can "afford." This satisfies the financial managers, who feel that expenses should bear a close relation to the movement of corporate sales over the business cycle. Second, this method encourages management to think in terms of the relationship between promotion costs, selling price, and profit per unit. Third, this method encourages competitive stability to the extent that competing firms spend approximately the same percentage of their sales on promotion.

In spite of these advantages, the percentage-of-sales method has little to justify it. It uses circular reasoning in viewing sales as the cause of promotion rather than as the result. It leads to a budget set by the availability of funds rather than by the opportunities. It discourages experimenting with other types of promotion or aggressive spending. The promotion budget's dependence on year-to-year sales changes interferes with long-range planning. The method does not provide a logical basis for choosing the specific percentage, except what has been done in the past or what competitors are doing. Finally, it does not encourage building up the promotion budget by determining what each product and territory deserves.

COMPETITIVE-PARITY METHOD. Some companies set their promotion budget to match competitors' outlays. This thinking is illustrated by the executive who asked a trade source: "Do you have any figures which other companies in the builders' specialties field have used which would indicate what proportion of gross sales should be given over to advertising?"[14]

Two arguments support this method. One is that the competitors' expenditures represent the collective wisdom of the industry. The other is that maintaining a competitive parity helps prevent promotion wars.

Neither argument is valid. There are no grounds for believing that the competition has a better idea of what a company should be spending on promotion. Company reputations, resources, opportunities, and objectives differ so much that their promotion budgets are hardly a guide. Furthermore, there is no evidence that budgets based on competitive parity discourage promotion wars from breaking out.

OBJECTIVE-AND-TASK METHOD. The objective-and-task method calls upon marketers to develop their promotion budget by (1) defining their specific objectives, (2) determining the tasks that must be performed to achieve these objectives, and (3) estimating the costs of performing these tasks. The sum of these costs is the proposed promotion budget.

Ule showed how the objective-and-task method could be used to establish an advertising budget for a new filter tip cigarette, Sputnik (a fictitious name).[15] The steps are as follows:

1. *Establish the market-share goal.* The advertiser wants 8% of the market. Since there are 50 million cigarette smokers, the company wants to switch 4 million smokers to Sputnik.
2. *Determine the percent of the market that should be reached by Sputnik advertising.* The advertiser hopes to reach 80% (40 million smokers) with its advertising.
3. *Determine the percent of aware smokers that should be persuaded to try the brand.* The advertiser would be pleased if 25% of aware smokers, or 10 million smokers, tried Sputnik. This is because the advertiser estimates that 40% of all triers, or 4 million persons, would become loyal users. This is the market goal.

4. *Determine the number of advertising impressions per 1% trial rate.* The advertiser estimates that 40 advertising impressions (exposures) for every 1% of the population would bring about a 25% trial rate.

5. *Determine the number of gross rating points that would have to be purchased.* A gross rating point is one exposure to 1% of the target population. Since the company wants to achieve 40 exposures to 80% of the population, it will want to buy 3,200 (40 × 80) gross rating points.

6. *Determine the necessary advertising budget on the basis of the average cost of buying a gross rating point.* To expose 1% of the target population to one impression costs an average of $3,277. Therefore 3,200 gross rating points would cost $10,486,400 ($3,277 × 3,200) in the introductory year.

This method has the advantage of requiring management to spell out its assumptions about the relationship between dollars spent, exposure levels, trial rates, and regular usage.

The overall answer to how much weight promotion should receive in the total marketing mix (as opposed to product improvement, lower prices, more services, and so on) depends on where the company's products are in their life cycle, whether they are commodities or highly differentiable, whether they are routinely needed or have to be "sold," and other considerations. In theory, the total promotion budget should be established where the marginal profit from the last promotion dollar just equals the marginal profit from the last dollar in the best nonpromotional use. Implementing this principle, however, is not easy.

Establishing the Promotion Mix

Companies within the same industry differ considerably in how they divide their promotion budget. Avon concentrates its promotion funds on personal selling (its advertising is only 1.5% of sales), while Revlon spends heavily on advertising (about 7% of sales). In selling vacuum cleaners, Electrolux spends heavily on a door-to-door sales force, while Hoover relies more on advertising. Thus it is possible to achieve a given sales level with various mixes of advertising, personal selling, sales promotion, and publicity.

Companies are always searching for ways to gain efficiency by substituting one promotional tool for another as its economics become more favorable. Many companies have replaced some sales force activity with telephone sales and direct mail. Other companies have increased their sales promotion expenditures in relation to advertising to gain quicker sales. Since promotional tools can be substituted for each other, marketing functions need to be coordinated in a single marketing department.

Designing the promotion mix is even more complicated when one tool can be used to promote another. Thus when McDonald's decides to run Million Dollar Sweepstakes in its fast-food outlets (a form of sales promotion), it has to take out newspaper ads to inform the public. When General Mills develops a consumer advertising/sales promotion campaign to back a new cake mix, it has to set aside money to promote this campaign to the trade to win their support.

Many factors influence the marketer's choice of promotional tools. We will look at these factors in the following paragraphs.

Persuades you long time —

NATURE OF EACH PROMOTIONAL TOOL. Each promotional tool—advertising, personal selling, sales promotion, and publicity—has its own unique characteristics and costs. Marketers have to understand these characteristics in selecting them.

Advertising. Because of the many forms and uses of advertising, it is difficult to make general statements about its special qualities as a part of the promotion mix. Yet the following qualities can be noted:[16]

1. *It is public.* Advertising is a highly public mode of communication. Its public nature suggests that the product is legitimate and standard. Because many persons receive the same message, buyers know that their motives for purchasing the product will be publicly understood.
2. *It is pervasive.* Advertising is a pervasive medium that permits the seller to repeat a message many times. It also allows the buyer to receive and compare the messages of various competitors. Large-scale advertising by a seller says something positive about the seller's size, popularity, and success.
3. *It is expressive.* Advertising provides opportunities for dramatizing the company and its products through the artful use of print, sound, and color. Sometimes its very success, however, may dilute or distract from the message.
4. *It is impersonal.* Advertising cannot be as personal as a company sales representative. The audience does not feel that it has to pay attention or respond. Advertising is only able to carry on a monologue, not a dialogue, with the audience.

On the one hand, advertising can be used to build up a long-term image for a product (such as Coca-Cola ads), and, on the other, to trigger quick sales (as when Sears advertises a weekend sale). Advertising is an efficient way to reach many geographically dispersed buyers at a low cost per exposure. Certain forms of advertising, such as TV advertising, can require a large budget; other forms, such as newspaper advertising, can be done on a small budget.

Personal selling. Personal selling is the most effective tool at certain stages of the buying process, particularly in developing a buyer's preference, conviction, and purchase. The reason is that personal selling, when compared with advertising, has three distinctive qualities:[17]

1. *It is personal.* Personal selling involves an alive, immediate, and interactive relationship between two or more persons. Each person is able to observe the other's needs and characteristics at close hand and make immediate adjustments.
2. *It creates a relationship.* Personal selling permits all kinds of relationships to spring up, ranging from a matter-of-fact selling relationship to a deep personal friendship. The effective sales representative will normally keep the customer's interest at heart if he or she wants a long-run relationship.
3. *It leads to a response.* Personal selling makes the buyer feel under some obligation for having listened to the sales talk. The buyer has a greater need to attend and respond, even if the response is a polite "thank you."

Personal selling draws a response from a consumer and may make a consumer more ready to try a new product, such as a computer.

Courtesy Apple Computers, Inc.

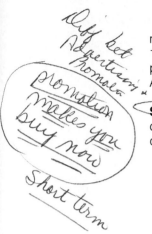

These distinctive qualities come at a cost. Personal selling is the company's most expensive tool, costing companies an average of $128 a sales call in 1980.[18] In 1977, American firms spent over $100 billion on personal selling compared with $38 billion on advertising. This money supported over 5.4 million Americans who are engaged in sales work.

Sales promotion.   Although sales promotion involves an assortment of tools—coupons, contests, premiums, and so on—these tools have three distinctive characteristics:

1. *They attract and communicate.* They gain attention and usually provide information that may lead the consumer to the product.
2. *They create an incentive to buy.* They offer some concession, inducement, or contribution that gives value to the consumer.
3. *They offer an invitation.* They include a distinct invitation to make the transaction now.

Companies use sales promotion tools to create a stronger and quicker response. Sales promotion can be used to dramatize product offers and to boost sagging sales. Sales promotion effects are usually short run, however, and are not effective in building long-run brand preference.

Publicity.   Publicity's appeal is based on its three distinctive qualities:

1. *It is believable.* News stories and features seem more authentic and credible to readers than ads.
2. *It catches buyers.* Publicity can reach many prospects who may avoid salespeople and advertisements. The message gets to the buyers as news rather than as a sales-directed communication.
3. *It is dramatic.* Publicity, like advertising, has a potential for dramatizing a company or product.

Marketers tend to underuse product publicity or use it as an afterthought. Yet a well-thought-out publicity campaign coordinated with the other promotion mix elements can be extremely effective. *PR*

FACTORS IN SETTING THE PROMOTION MIX.   Companies consider several factors in developing their promotion mix. These factors are examined below.

Type of product or market.   The effectiveness of promotional tools varies between consumer and industrial markets. The differences are shown in figure 14-4. Consumer-goods companies normally devote most of their funds to advertising, followed by sales promotion, personal selling, and, finally, publicity. Industrial-goods companies devote most of their funds to personal selling, followed by sales promotion, advertising, and publicity. In general, personal selling is more heavily used with expensive and risky goods and in markets with fewer and larger sellers (hence, industrial markets).

Although advertising is less important than sales calls in industrial markets, it still plays a significant role. Advertising can build product awareness and comprehension, develop sales leads, make a product legitimate, and reassure buyers. Advertising's role in industrial marketing is dramatically shown in a

FIGURE 14-4

Relative Importance of Promotional Tools in Consumer versus Industrial Markets

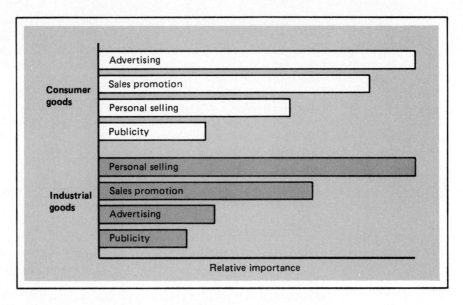

FIGURE 14-5

Advertising Has a Role to Play in Industrial Selling

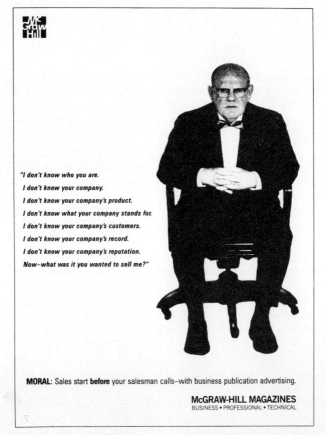

McGraw-Hill ad (see figure 14-5). Advertising could have prevented most of the statements the buyer makes in that ad. Morrill showed, in his study of industrial commodity marketing, that advertising combined with personal selling increased sales 23% over what they were with no advertising. The total promotion cost as a percent of sales was reduced by 20%.[19]

Similarly, personal selling can make a strong contribution in consumer-goods marketing. It is not simply the case that "salesmen put products on shelves and advertising takes them off." Well-trained consumer-goods sales representatives can sign up more dealers to carry the brand, influence them to devote more shelf space to the brand, and encourage them to cooperate in special promotions.

Push versus pull strategy. The promotion mix is heavily influenced by whether the company chooses a push or a pull strategy to create sales. The two strategies are contrasted in figure 14-6. A *push strategy* calls for using the sales force and trade promotion to push the product through the channels. The producer aggressively promotes the product to wholesalers, wholesalers aggressively promote the product to retailers, and retailers aggressively promote the product to consumers. A *pull strategy* calls for spending a lot of money on advertising and consumer promotion to build up consumer demand. If effective, consumers will ask their retailers for the product, the retailers will ask their wholesalers for the product, and the wholesalers will ask the producers for the product. Companies differ in their use of push or pull. For example, Lever Brothers relies more heavily on push, and Procter & Gamble on pull.

Buyer readiness stage. Promotional tools vary in their cost-effectiveness at different stages of buyer readiness.[20] Advertising, along with publicity, plays the major role in the awareness stage. Customer knowledge is primarily influenced by education, with advertising and personal selling playing secondary roles. Customer conviction is primarily influenced by personal selling, followed closely by advertising. Finally, closing the sale is mainly a function of personal selling. Clearly, personal selling, given its expensiveness, should be focused on the later stages of the customer buying process.

FIGURE 14-6

Push versus Pull Strategy

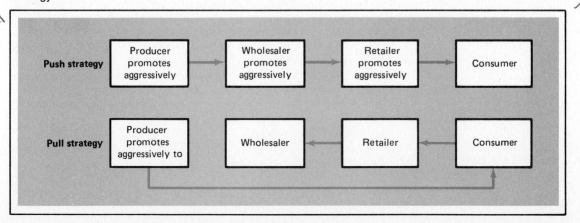

Product life-cycle stage. The promotional tools vary in their effectiveness at different stages of the product life cycle. In the introduction stage, advertising and publicity are most effective in producing high awareness, and sales promotion is useful in getting consumers to try the product. Personal selling is relatively expensive, although it must be used to get retailers to carry the product.

In the growth stage, advertising and publicity continue to be important, while sales promotion can be reduced because fewer incentives are needed.

In the mature stage, sales promotion becomes more important in relation to advertising. Buyers know the brands and need only to be reminded through advertising.

In the decline stage, advertising is used only to remind, publicity is eliminated, and sales representatives give the product only minimal attention. Sales promotion, however, might continue to be strong.

Summary

Promotion is one of the four major elements of the company's marketing mix. The main promotional tools—advertising, sales promotion, publicity, and personal selling—have separate and overlapping capabilities, and their effective coordination requires careful definition of communication objectives.

In preparing specific marketing communications, the communicator has to understand the nine elements of any communication process: sender, receiver, encoding, decoding, message, media, response, feedback, and noise. The communicator's first task is to identify the target audience and its characteristics. Next, the communicator has to define the sought response, whether it be awareness, knowledge, liking, preference, conviction, or purchase. Then a message should be constructed containing an effective content, structure, and format. Then the media must be selected, both for personal communication and non-personal communication. The message must be delivered by someone credible, namely, someone who is an expert, trustworthy, and likable. Finally, the communicator must monitor how much of the market becomes aware and tries the product and is satisfied in the process.

The company has to decide how much to spend for total promotion. The most popular approaches are to spend what the company can afford, use a percentage of sales, base promotion on competitors' expenditures, or base it on an analysis and costing of the communication objectives and tasks.

The company has to split the promotion budget among the major promotional tools. Companies are guided by the characteristics of each promotional tool, the type of product or market, whether the company prefers a push or a pull strategy, the buyer's readiness stage, and the product life-cycle stage.

Questions for Discussion

1. Apply the four major tools in the marketing communication mix to professional sports teams.
2. What two communication parties are used in marketing communication? Discuss how they relate to McDonald's.

3. How would the six buyer readiness states relate to your last purchase of beer or a soft drink?
4. Discuss the type of message content used by the following marketers: (a) Consolidated Edison, (b) Datsun, (c) American Lung Association, and (d) General Electric.
5. What major types of communication channels can an organization use? When should each be used?
6. State whether the following individuals are credible sources for market communication: (a) Reggie Jackson, (b) Neil Armstrong, and (c) Dorothy Hamill. Why?
7. How might a company set its promotion budget? Discuss the advantages of each approach.
8. The type of product being marketed has no relationship to the promotion mix employed by the marketer. Comment.

Key Terms in Chapter 14

Advertising Any paid form of nonpersonal presentation and promotion of ideas, goods, or services by an identified sponsor.

Decoding In communication, the process by which the receiver assigns meaning to the symbols transmitted by the sender.

Encoding In communication, the process of putting thought into symbolic form.

Feedback The part of the receiver's response that is communicated back to the sender.

Media The communication channels through which the message moves from sender to receiver.

Message The set of symbols that the sender transmits.

Noise The occurrence of unplanned static or distortion during the communication process that results in the receiver's receiving a different message than the sender sent.

Personal selling Oral presentation in a conversation with one or more prospective purchasers for the purpose of making sales.

Publicity Nonpersonal stimulation of demand for a product, service, or business unit by planting commercially significant news about it in a published medium or obtaining favorable presentation of it on radio, TV, or stage that is not paid for by the sponsor.

Receiver The party receiving the message sent by another party.

Response The set of reactions that the receiver communicates back to the sender.

Sales promotion Short-term incentives to encourage the purchase or sale of a product or service.

Sender In communication, the party sending the message to another party.

Cases for Chapter 14

Case 13   The Pillsbury Co.: Totino's Pizza (p. 510)

Totino's highly successful frozen pizza is facing increased competition, as described in this case. The company is developing a new promotion strategy, including a new promotion budget and promotion mix.

Case 14   Purex Industries, Inc. (p. 511)

Purex must look at the role of promotion in its marketing strategy. This case presents the factors that influence its decisions.

Chapter 15

Promoting Products: Advertising, Sales Promotion, and Publicity

Objectives

After reading this chapter, you should be able to:

1. Define the roles of advertising, sales promotion, and publicity in the promotion mix.
2. Describe how advertising messages are developed and sent to consumers.
3. Discuss how sales promotion and publicity campaigns are developed and implemented.
4. Explain how companies measure the effectiveness of their promotion campaigns.

Men at Work's first album, *Business as Usual,* sold over four million copies. A single from the album—"Who Can It Be Now?"—occupied the number-one position on the record sales charts for 15 weeks. Because of the album, the band won the 1982 Grammy Award for the Best New Artist. To the record industry, the album's success was "the most lucrative accident in record company history," according to one Columbia Records executive. The success of the album was considered accidental because Columbia Records had released it without providing a focus for the presentation of the band through its advertising, promotion, and publicity.

Columbia's problem recently was how to create that focus for the second Men at Work album, *Cargo.* The company's executives felt that to sustain Men at Work's success they needed to present a distinct, recognizable "face" for the band, the unique look that had been missing from the first album. At a meeting before *Cargo*'s release, Al Teller, senior vice-president and general manager of Columbia Records in New York, said, "Our main task is to give these guys some kind of image."

For that image to seem authentic and be effective, the record company had to find qualities in the band members themselves that could be built into a kind of trademark. By studying photographs and videotapes of the band, the people at Columbia Records found that one of Men at Work's most appealing qualities was their carefree, almost childlike playfulness. This was the image Columbia chose for the band to project, that of a funny, playful group. The band's performance of the song "Down Under" for the nationally televised Grammy Awards was the first chance to test this new image. The people at Columbia were pleased with this appearance and proceeded to put the rest of their *Cargo* plans into action.

Publicity for the album involved every conceivable medium. Marilyn Laverty, publicity director at Columbia, organized the band's appearances on the cover of *Rolling Stone* magazine, on the television show "Entertainment Tonight," and in four videotaped performances of songs from *Cargo* for cable television's MTV. Laverty's choices for Men at Work's publicity were national media that would show the band in the playful image Columbia had created. The *Rolling Stone* article began with a description of Men at Work playing cricket at home in Melbourne and featured a photograph of the band clowning with champagne glasses, a stethoscope, and a couple of funny hats. One MTV video featured lead singer Colin Hay frolicking in a Sherlock Holmes costume.

Barbara Cooke, director of product marketing, arranged for numerous point-of-purchase displays, attention-catching devices to spark consumer interest in record stores. Three days before *Cargo*'s release, Columbia mailed 30,000 posters, 85,000 display album covers, and cassette display cards to record stores all over the United States. One wall display was a large poster of the band reading comic books. *Cargo* album covers made up the display's background and border.

Paul Rappaport, head of Columbia's album-oriented radio department, arranged for disc jockeys across the country to receive an array of promotional materials: a 12-inch single and record sleeve, bio, and picture of the group. The disc jockeys also received a 90-minute taped interview with the band that stations could play for free on the condition that they aired the interview the weekend before *Cargo*'s release. After this bombardment of promotion, "it's just a matter of prayer," says Rappaport.

For Men at Work and Columbia Records, *Cargo* is another hit. In its first two weeks, the album sold 1.25 million copies. The band attributes its success to its music, a sound that before the arrival of Men at Work did not exist in the American music industry. Columbia Records executives believe that without a sharply focused image and strong advertising, publicity, and promotional support, far fewer Americans would have wanted to hear that unique sound.[1]

No matter how talented and creative it is, a band needs a distinct image and a carefully planned promotion campaign in order to be successful. Columbia Records developed a campaign for the band Men at Work, using the mass-promotion tools of advertising, sales promotion, and publicity. These tools are examined in this chapter.

Advertising

In 1981, advertising ran up a bill of $61.3 billion. We define advertising as follows:

> **Advertising** consists of nonpersonal forms of communication conducted through paid media under clear sponsorship.

The spenders included not only commercial firms but also museums, fund-raisers, and various social action organizations seeking to advertise their causes to various target publics. In fact, the twenty-fourth-largest advertising spender is a nonprofit organization—the U.S. government.

Within the commercial sector, the top one hundred national advertisers account for as much as one-fourth of all national advertising.[2] Table 15-1 lists the top ten advertisers in 1981. Procter & Gamble is the leading spender, accounting for almost $672 million, or 5.6% of its total sales of $11.4 billion. The other major spenders are found in the auto, food, retailing, communications, and tobacco industries. Advertising as a percentage of sales is low in the automobile industry and high in the food and drug industries. The highest-percentage spenders overall are in drugs, toiletries, and cosmetics, followed by gum, candy, and soaps. The Noxell Corporation spent a record 22.2% of its sales on advertising.

Advertising dollars go into various media: magazine and newspapers, radio and television, outdoor displays (posters, signs, skywriting), direct mail, novelties (matchboxes, blotters, calendars), cards (trains, buses), catalogs, directories, and circulars. And advertising has many uses: long-term buildup of an organization's image (*institutional advertising*), long-term buildup of a particular brand (*brand advertising*), information spreading about a sale, service, or event

Table 15-1				
The Top Ten National Advertisers in 1981				
RANK	COMPANY	TOTAL ADVERTISING IN MILLIONS	TOTAL SALES IN MILLIONS	ADVERTISING AS % OF SALES
1	Procter & Gamble	$671.7	$11,944	5.6%
2	Sears, Roebuck & Co.	544.1	27,360	2.0
3	General Foods Corp.	456.8	8,351	5.5
4	Philip Morris, Inc.	432.9	10,885	4.0
5	General Motors Corp.	401.0	62,698	0.6
6	K mart Corp.	349.6	16,527	2.1
7	Nabisco Brands Inc.	340.9	5,819	5.9
8	R. J. Reynolds Industries	321.2	11,691	2.7
9	AT&T	297.0	58,214	0.5
10	Mobil Corp.	293.1	68,587	4.3

Source: Reprinted with permission from the September 9, 1982, issue of *Advertising Age*. Copyright © 1982 by Crain Communications, Inc.

(*classified advertising*), announcement of a special sale (*sale advertising*), and advocacy of a particular cause (*advocacy advertising*).

Advertising's roots can be traced back to early history (see exhibit 15-1). Although advertising is primarily used by private enterprise, it is used in all the countries of the world, including socialist countries. Advertising is a cost-effective way to spread messages, whether it be to build brand preference for Coca-Cola all over the world or to motivate consumers to drink milk or practice birth control.

Organizations handle their advertising in different ways. In small companies, advertising is handled by someone in the sales department, who will occasionally work with an advertising agency. Large companies set up advertising departments, whose managers report to the vice-presidents of marketing. The advertising department's job is to develop the total budget, approve agency ads and campaigns, and handle direct-mail advertising, dealer displays, and other forms of advertising not ordinarily performed by the agency. Most companies use an outside advertising agency because it offers several advantages (see exhibit 15-2).

Marketing management must make five important decisions in developing an advertising program. These decisions are listed in figure 15-1 and are examined in the following sections.

FIGURE 15-1

Major Decisions in
Advertising

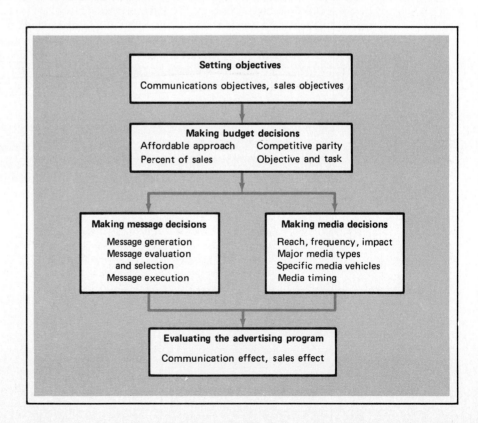

Exhibit 15-1

Historical Milestones in Advertising

Advertising practice goes back to the very beginning of recorded history. Archaeologists in the countries rimming the Mediterranean Sea have dug up signs announcing various events and offers. The Romans painted walls to announce gladiatorial contests, and the Phoenicians painted murals on prominent rocks along parade routes extolling their wares, a precursor of modern outdoor advertising. A Pompeii wall painting praised a politician and asked for the people's votes.

Another early form of advertising was the town crier. During the Golden Age in Greece, town criers circulated through Athens announcing the sale of slaves, cattle, and other goods. An early Athenian "singing commercial" went as follows: "For eyes that are shining, for cheeks like the dawn/For beauty that lasts after girlhood is gone/For prices in reason, the woman who knows/Will buy her cosmetics of Aesclyptos."

Another early form of advertising was the mark placed by artisans on their individual goods, such as pottery. As an artisan's reputation spread through word of mouth, buyers began to look for his distinctive mark, just as trademarks and brand names are used today. For example, Osnabrück linen was carefully controlled for quality and commanded a price 20% higher than unbranded Westphalian linens. As production became more centralized and markets became more distant, the mark took on more significance.

The turning point in the history of advertising came in the year 1450 when Gutenberg invented the printing press. Advertisers no longer had to produce extra copies of a sign by hand. The first printed advertisement in the English language appeared in 1478.

In 1622, advertising received a substantial boost with the launching of the first English newspaper, *The Weekly Newes*. Later Addison and Steele published the *Tatler* and became devotees of advertising. Addison included this advice to copy writers: "The great art in writing advertising is the finding out the proper method to catch the reader, without which a good thing may pass unobserved, or be lost among commissions of bankrupts." The September 14, 1710, issue of the *Tatler* contains ads for razor strops, patent medicines, and other consumer products.

Advertising had its greatest growth in the United States. Ben Franklin has been called the father of American advertising because his *Gazette,* first published·in 1729, attained the largest circulation and advertising volume of any·paper in colonial America. Several factors contributed to America's becoming the cradle of advertising. First, American industry led in the mechanization of production, which created surpluses and the need to convince consumers to buy more. Second, the development of a fine network of waterways, highways, and roads made the transportation of goods and advertising media to the countryside feasible. Third, the establishment in 1813 of compulsory public education increased literacy and the growth of newspapers and magazines. The invention of radio and, later, television created two more amazing media for the dissemination of advertising.

Exhibit 15-2

How Does an Advertising Agency Work?

Madison Avenue, USA, is a name familiar to most Americans and describes an avenue in New York City where some major advertising agencies are headquartered with their approximately thirty thousand employees. But most of the nation's six thousand agencies are found outside New York, and there are few cities that do not have at least one agency, even if it is a one-person shop. The seven largest U.S. agencies in terms of world billings in 1978 were J. Walter Thompson, McCann Erickson, Young & Rubicam, Ogilvy and Mather, BBDO, Ted Bates, and Leo Burnett. The world's largest advertising agency is located in Japan, and its name is Dentsu.

Even companies with a strong advertising department will use advertising agencies. Agencies employ creative and technical specialists who often can perform advertising tasks better and more efficiently than the company's staff. Agencies also bring an outside perspective to bear on the company's problems, as well as a broad range of experience from working with different clients and situations. Agencies are paid from media discounts and therefore cost the firm very little. In addition, since the firm can cancel its agency contract at any time, an agency has a strong incentive to perform effectively.

Advertising agencies are typically organized around four departments: *creative,* which handles the development and production of ads; *media,* which selects media and places ads; *research,* which determines audience characteristics and wants; and *business,* which handles the agency's business activities. Each account is supervised by an account executive, and personnel in each department are assigned to work on one or more accounts.

Agencies often attract new business through their reputation or size. Generally, however, a client invites a few agencies to make a competitive

---

Setting
Objectives

The first step in developing an advertising program is to set the advertising objectives. These objectives must flow from prior decisions on the target market, marketing positioning, and marketing mix. The marketing positioning and mix strategy defines the job that advertising must do in the total marketing program.

Many specific communication and sales objectives can be set for advertising.[3] They can be classified as to whether their aim is to inform, persuade, or remind. Table 15-2 lists some of these objectives.

Informative advertising figures heavily in the introduction stage of a product category, where the objective is to build *primary demand.* Thus, the yogurt industry initially had to inform consumers of yogurt's nutritional benefits and many uses.

Persuasive advertising becomes important in the growth stage, where a company's objective is to build *selective demand.* For example, the Stouffer's Lean Cuisine ad in figure 15-2 attempts to persuade an audience of weight-conscious consumers that this new product is terrific looking and tasting even though it is low-calorie food. Some persuasive advertising has moved into the

presentation for its business and then selects one of them.

Ad agencies receive compensation in the form of commissions and some fees. Typically, the agency receives 15% of the media cost as a rebate. Suppose the agency buys $60,000 of magazine space for a client. The magazine bills the advertising agency for $51,000 ($60,000 less 15%), and the agency bills the client for $60,000, keeping the $9,000 commission. If the client bought space directly from the magazine, it would have paid $60,000 because these commissions are only paid to accredited advertising agencies.

Both advertisers and agencies are becoming more and more dissatisfied with the commission system. Larger advertisers complain that they pay more for the same services received by smaller ones simply because they place more advertising. Advertisers also believe that the commission system drives agencies away from low-cost media and short advertising campaigns. Agencies are unhappy because they perform extra services for an account without receiving additional compensation. The trend today is toward compensation on either a straight fee basis or a combination commission and fee.

Other trends are also buffeting the advertising agency business. Full-service agencies are facing increasing competition from limited-service agencies specializing in media buying, or advertising copy writing, or advertising production. Business managers in agencies are getting more power and demanding more profit-mindedness from the creative staff. Some advertisers have opened in-house agencies, thus abandoning a long-standing relationship with their agency. Finally, the Federal Trade Commission wants agencies to share responsibility with the client for deceptive advertising. These trends will effect some changes in the industry, but agencies that do a good job will endure.

Table 15-2

Possible Advertising Objectives

TYPE OF ADVERTISING	OBJECTIVES OF THE ADVERTISING
Informative Advertising *Pioneering*	Telling the market about a new product or suggesting new uses for a product • Informing the market of a price change • Explaining how the product works • Describing available services • Correcting false impressions or reducing consumers' fears • Building a company image
Persuasive Advertising *Competitive*	Building brand preference • Encouraging switching to your brand • Changing customer's perception of product attributes • Persuading customer to purchase now • Persuading customer to receive a sales call
Reminder Advertising *Retentive*	Reminding consumers that the product may be needed in the near future • Reminding them where to buy it • Keeping it in their minds during off seasons • Maintaining its top-of-mind awareness

FIGURE 15-2

Advertising Creating a Position for a New Product

Stouffer's identified a market segment of weight-conscious consumers who love good-tasting food. The result was the Lean Cuisine line of frozen foods.

© 1983 Stouffer Foods Corporation

Hyatt uses persuasive advertising very effectively in its campaign showing its welcoming atmosphere for business clients.

© 1983 Hyatt Hotels Corp.

category of *comparison advertising,* which seeks to establish the superiority of one brand through specific comparison with one or more other brands in the product class.[4] Comparison advertising has been used in such product categories as deodorants, toothpastes, tires, and automobiles.

Reminder advertising is highly important in the mature stage to keep the consumer thinking about the product. The purpose of expensive Coca-Cola ads in magazines is to remind people about Coca-Cola, not to inform or persuade them. A related form of advertising is *reinforcement advertising,* which seeks to assure current purchasers that they have made the right choice. Automobile ads will often show satisfied customers enjoying some special feature of the car they bought.

Making Budget Decisions After determining advertising objectives, the company can proceed to establish its advertising budget for each product. The role of advertising is to increase demand for a product. The company wants to spend the amount required to achieve the sales goal. Four commonly used methods for setting the advertising budget were described in chapter 14. Companies such as Du Pont and Anheuser-Busch run advertising experiments as part of their advertising budgeting. Thus, Anheuser-Busch will spend higher-than-normal amounts in some territories and lower-than-normal amounts in others and will check the results against a control group of territories to measure what it gains or loses with higher or lower expenditures. Its findings enabled Anheuser-Busch to substantially cut its advertising expenditures with no loss in market share.[5]

Making Message Decisions Given the advertising objectives and budget, management has to develop a creative strategy. Advertisers go through three steps: message generation, message evaluation and selection, and message execution.

MESSAGE GENERATION. Creative people use different methods to generate advertising ideas to carry out advertising objectives. Many creative people get ideas by talking to consumers, dealers, experts, and competitors. The Schlitz campaign "When you are out of Schlitz you are out of beer" came about because the advertising agency executive overheard a customer say this to a bartender when the latter said he was out of Schlitz.

Some creative people try to figure out which of four types of reward—rational, sensory, social, or ego satisfaction—buyers expect from a product and through what experience they expect to receive the rewards. By combining the rewards with the types of experience, they can create many types of advertising messages.[6]

MESSAGE EVALUATION AND SELECTION. The advertiser needs to evaluate the possible messages. Twedt suggested that messages be rated on desirability, exclusiveness, and believability.[7] The message must first say something desirable or interesting about the product. The message must also say something exclusive or distinctive that does not apply to every brand in the product category. Finally, the message must be believable or provable.

For example, the March of Dimes searched for an advertising theme to raise money for its fight against birth defects.[8] Twenty possible messages came out of a brainstorming session. A group of young parents were asked to rate each message for interest, distinctiveness, and believability, assigning up to 100 points for each. For example, "Five hundred thousand unborn babies die each year from birth defects" scored 70, 60, and 80 on interest, distinctiveness, and believability, while "Your next baby could be born with a birth defect" scored 58, 50, and 70. The first message outperformed the second and was preferred for advertising purposes.

MESSAGE EXECUTION. The message's impact depends not only on what is said but also on how it is said. Message execution can be decisive for those products that are highly similar, such as detergents, cigarettes, coffee, and beer. The advertiser has to put the message across in a way that wins the target audience's attention and interest.

The advertiser usually prepares a copy strategy statement describing the objective, content, support, and tone of the desired ad. Here is a copy strategy statement for a Pillsbury product called "1869 Brand Biscuits":

> The *objective* of the advertising is to convince biscuit users that now they can buy a canned biscuit that's as good as homemade—Pillsbury's 1869 Brand Biscuits. The *content* consists of emphasizing the following product characteristics: (1) They look like homemade biscuits, (2) they have the same texture as homemade biscuits, and (3) they taste like homemade biscuits. *Support* for the "good as homemade" promise will be twofold: (1) 1869 Brand Biscuits are made from a special kind of flour (soft wheat flour) used to make homemade biscuits but never before used in making canned biscuits, and (2) the use of traditional American biscuit recipes. The *tone* of the advertising will be a news announcement, tempered by a warm, reflective mood emanating from a look back at traditional American baking quality.

Creative people must now find a style, tone, words, and format for executing the message.

Any message can be presented in different execution styles, such as:

1. *Slice-of-life*. This shows one or more persons using the product in a normal setting. A family seated at the dinner table might express satisfaction with a new biscuit brand.
2. *Life-style*. This emphasizes how a product fits in with a life-style. An ad for Scotch shows a handsome middle-aged man holding a glass of Scotch in one hand and steering his yacht with the other.
3. *Fantasy*. This creates a fantasy around the product or its use. Revlon's ad for Jontue features a barefoot woman wearing a chiffon dress and coming out of an old French barn, crossing a meadow, and confronting a handsome young man on a white steed, who carries her away.
4. *Mood or image*. This builds an evocative mood or image around the product, such as beauty, love, or serenity. No claim is made about the product except through suggestion. Many cigarette ads, such as those for Salem and Newport cigarettes, create moods.
5. *Musical*. This shows one or more persons or cartoon characters singing a

[handwritten marginalia: "better to use animated Person"]

song involving the product. Many cola ads have used this type of format.

6. *Personality* symbol. This creates a character that personifies the product. The character might be animated (<u>Green Giant,</u> Cap'n Crunch, Mr. Clean) or real (Marlboro man, Morris the Cat).

7. *Technical expertise.* This shows the company's expertise and experience in making the product. Thus, Hills Brothers shows one of its buyers carefully selecting the coffee beans, and Italian Swiss Colony emphasizes its many years of experience in winemaking.

8. *Scientific evidence.* This presents survey or scientific evidence that the brand is preferred to or outperforms one or more other brands. For years, Crest toothpaste has featured scientific evidence to convince toothpaste buyers of Crest's superior anticavity-fighting properties.

9. *Testimonial evidence.* This features a highly credible or likable source endorsing the product. It could be a celebrity like O. J. Simpson (Hertz Rent-a-Car) or ordinary people saying how much they like the product.

[handwritten marginalia: "problem/solution/result"]

The communicator must also choose an appropriate tone for the ad. Procter & Gamble is consistently positive in its tone: Its ads say something superlatively positive about the product. Humor is avoided so as not to take attention away from the message. On the other hand, Volkswagen's ads for its famous "Beetle" typically took on a humorous tone ("the Ugly Bug").

Memorable and attention-getting words must be found. The themes listed below on the left would have had much less impact without the creative phrasing on the right:[9]

Theme	Creative Copy
• 7-Up is not a cola.	• "The Un-Cola."
• Let us drive you in our bus instead of driving your car.	• "Take the bus, and leave the driving to us."
• Shop by turning the pages of the telephone directory.	• "Let your fingers do the walking."
• If you drink a beer, Schaefer is a good beer to drink.	• "The beer to have when you're having more than one."
• We don't rent as many cars, so we have to do more for our customers.	• "We try harder."

Format elements, such as ad size, color, and illustration, will make a difference in an ad's impact as well as cost. <u>A minor rearrangement of the elements within the ad can improve its attention-gaining power by several points.</u> Larger-size ads gain more attention, though not necessarily by as much as their difference in cost. Four-color illustrations instead of black and white increase ad effectiveness and ad costs.

Making Media Decisions The advertiser's next task is to chose advertising media to carry the advertising message. The steps are (1) deciding on reach, frequency, and impact; (2) choosing among major media types; (3) selecting specific media vehicles; and (4) deciding on media timing.

DECIDING ON REACH, FREQUENCY, AND IMPACT.   In order to select media, the advertiser must determine the desired reach, frequency, and impact needed to achieve the advertising objectives:

1. *Reach.* The advertiser must decide on how many persons in the target audience should be exposed to the ad campaign during the specified period of time. For example, the advertiser might seek to reach 70% of the target audience during the first year.
2. *Frequency.* The advertiser must also decide on how many times the average person in the target audience should be exposed to the message during the specified time period. For example, the advertiser might seek an average exposure frequency of three.
3. *Impact.* The advertiser must also decide on the impact that the exposure should have. Messages on television typically have more impact than messages on radio because television combines sight and sound, not just sound. Within a media form such as magazines, the same message in one magazine (say, *Good Housekeeping*) may deliver more credibility than in another (say, *Police Gazette*). For example, the advertiser may seek an impact of 1.5 where 1.0 is the impact of an ad in an average medium.

Now suppose the advertiser's product might appeal to a market of 1 million consumers. The goal is to reach 700,000 consumers (1,000,000 × 70%). Since the average consumer will receive three exposures, 2,100,000 exposures (700,000 × 3) must be bought. Since high-impact exposures of 1.5 are desired, a rated number of exposures of 3,150,000 (2,100,000 × 1.5) must be bought. If a thousand exposures with this impact cost $10, the advertising budget will have to be $31,500 (3,150 × $10). In general, the more reach, frequency, and impact the advertiser seeks, the higher the advertising budget will have to be.

CHOOSING AMONG MAJOR MEDIA TYPES.   The media planner has to know how well the major media types deliver reach, frequency, and impact. The major advertising media are profiled in table 15-3. The major media types, in order of their advertising volume, are newspapers, television, direct mail, radio, magazines, and outdoor. Each medium has certain advantages and limitations. Media planners make their choice among these media categories by considering several characteristics, the most important ones being:

1. *Target audience media habits.* For example, radio and television are the most effective media for reaching teenagers.
2. *Product.* Women's dresses are best shown in color magazines, and Polaroid cameras are best demonstrated on television. Media types have different potentials for demonstration, visualization, explanation, believability, and color.
3. *Message.* A message announcing a major sale tomorrow will require radio or newspapers. A message containing a great deal of technical data might require specialized magazines or mailings.
4. *Cost.* Television is very expensive, while newspaper advertising is inexpensive.

Table 15-3

Profiles of Major Media Types

MEDIUM	VOLUME IN BILLIONS (1980)	PERCENTAGE (1980)	EXAMPLE OF COST (1981)	ADVANTAGES	LIMITATIONS
Newspapers	$15.6	28.5%	$11,128 one page in weekday *Chicago Tribune*	Flexibility; timeliness; good local market coverage; broad acceptance; high believability	Short life; poor reproduction quality; small "pass-along" audience
Television	11.3	20.7	$2,000 for thirty seconds of prime time in Chicago	Combines sight, sound, and motion; appealing to the senses; high attention; high reach	High absolute cost; high clutter; fleeting exposure; less audience selectivity
Direct mail	7.7	14.0	$1,190 for the names and addresses of 34,000 veterinarians	Audience selectivity; flexibility; no ad competition within the same medium; personalization	Relatively high cost; "junk mail" image
Radio	3.7	6.7	$400 for one minute of prime time in Chicago	Mass use; high geographic and demographic selectivity; low cost	Audio presentation only; lower attention than television; nonstandardized rate structures; fleeting exposure
Magazines	3.2	5.9	$57,780 one-page, four-color ad in *Newsweek*	High geographic and demographic selectivity; credibility and prestige; high-quality reproduction; long life; good pass-along readership	Long ad purchase lead time; some waste circulation; no guarantee of position
Outdoor	0.6	1.1	$8,000 prime billboard cost per month in Chicago	Flexibility; high repeat exposure; low cost; low competition	No audience selectivity; creative limitations
Miscellaneous	12.6	23.1			
Total	$54.7	100.0%			

Note: Miscellaneous media include media expenditures of the first six types that were not classified.

Source: The figures in columns 2 and 3 are from *Advertising Age,* February 16, 1981. Copyright © 1981 by Crain Communications, Inc. Reprinted with permission.

Promoting Products: Advertising, Sales Promotion, and Publicity

Given the media characteristics, the media planner must decide how to allocate the budget to the major media types. For example, in launching its new biscuit, Pillsbury might decide to allocate $3 million to daytime network television, $2 million to women's magazines, and $1 million to daily newspapers in twenty major markets.

SELECTING SPECIFIC MEDIA VEHICLES. The media planner now chooses the specific media vehicles that will be most cost-effective. For example, if the advertisement is going to appear in magazines, the media planner looks up the circulation and costs for different ad sizes, color options, and ad positions and frequency. He or she then evaluates the magazines on characteristics such as credibility, prestige, geographic editioning, occupational editioning, reproduction quality, editorial climate, lead time, and psychological impact. The media planner decides which specific magazines deliver the best reach, frequency, and impact for the money.

The only newsweekly where you can buy a 4,600,000 circulation rate base.

The only newsweekly where you are guaranteed to get what you pay for.

On October 3, TIME's rate base jumps still further ahead of other newsweeklies, to 4,600,000.

At the same time, we introduce the Issue-By-Issue Tally system, a pricing innovation designed to assure you of getting the full value of your advertising dollars.

IBIT guarantees advertisers that the total circulation they pay for—in the issues in which they run and in their contract year—will average out to be *equal to or more than the rate base* for that period. If not, an appropriate adjustment will be made.

Now, more than ever, you can count on getting the most from TIME.

TIME

Specific media vehicles let potential advertisers know about their editorial climate and readership.

The cost-per-thousand criterion.   Media planners calculate the cost per thousand persons reached by a particular vehicle. If a full-page, four-color advertisement in *Newsweek* costs $58,000 and *Newsweek*'s estimated readership is 6 million persons, the cost of reaching each one thousand persons is approximately $10. The same advertisement in *Business Week* may cost $26,000 but reach only 2 million persons, at a cost per thousand of $13. The media planner would rank the various magazines according to cost per thousand and favor those magazines with the lower cost per thousand.

Several adjustments have to be applied to this initial measure. First, the measure should be adjusted for audience quality. For a baby lotion advertisement, a magazine read by one million young mothers would have an exposure value of one million, but if read by one million old men would have a zero exposure value. Second, the exposure value should be adjusted for the audience attention to ads. Readers of *Vogue,* for example, pay more attention to ads than readers of *Newsweek.* Third, the exposure value should be adjusted for the editorial quality (prestige and believability) that one magazine might have over another.

DECIDING ON MEDIA TIMING.   The advertiser has to decide how to schedule the advertising over the year considering the season and expected economic developments. Suppose sales of a particular product peak in December and wane in March. The seller can advertise heavily from December through March. Or the seller can advertise in May and June to try to raise sales at that time of year. Or the seller can advertise at the same degree throughout the year.

The advertiser also has to choose the pattern of the ads. Ad continuity is achieved by scheduling exposures evenly within a given period. *Pulsing* refers to scheduling exposures unevenly over the same time period. Thus, fifty-two exposures could be scheduled continuously at one per week throughout the year, or pulsed in several concentrated bursts. Those who favor pulsing feel that (1) the audience will learn the message more thoroughly and (2) money can be saved. Anheuser-Busch's research indicated that Budweiser could suspend advertising in a particular market and experience no adverse sales effect for at least a year and a half.[10] Then the company could introduce a six-month burst of advertising and restore the previous growth rate. This analysis led Budweiser to adopt a pulsing advertising strategy.

The decisions on media vehicles and timing can be displayed in a chart. The media schedule in figure 15-3 shows that "As the World Turns" will be used each weekday except for the summer months; "Hollywood Squares" will be used three times a week throughout the year; *Family Circle* will be used at the beginning of each month except for the summer months; and the *Reader's Digest* will be used every month.

Evaluating the Advertising Program

Advertising needs to be evaluated continuously. Researchers use several techniques to measure the communication and sales effects of advertising.

MEASURING THE COMMUNICATION EFFECT.   Measuring the communication effect tells whether an ad is communicating effectively. This technique, called

Promoting Products: Advertising, Sales Promotion, and Publicity

Medium	Jan.	Feb.	Mar.	Apr.	May	June	July	Aug.	Sept.	Oct.	Nov.	Dec.
Daytime TV "As the World Turns" (5 30-second commercials per week)												
"Hollywood Squares" (3 30-second commercials per week)												
Magazines *Family Circle* (9 pages)												
Reader's Digest (12 pages)												

FIGURE 15-3

A Sample Media Schedule

Source: S. Watson Dunn and Arnold M. Barban, *Advertising: Its Role in Modern Marketing*, 5th ed. Copyright © 1982 by CBS College Publishing. Reprinted by permission of Holt, Rinehart and Winston, CBS College Publishing.

copy testing, can be used before an ad is run and after it is printed or broadcast.

Before an ad is used, the advertiser can ask consumers whether they like the ad or whether its message stands out. After the ad is used, advertisers can measure whether consumers can recall the ad or recognize that they have seen it before.

MEASURING THE SALES EFFECT. What sales are generated by an ad that increases brand awareness by 20% and brand preference by 10%? This can be answered by measuring the sales effect. This is difficult, because other factors, such as features of the product itself, affect sales.

One way of measuring the sales effect of advertising is to compare past sales with past advertising expenditures. For example, Montgomery and Silk measured the impact of three promotional tools—direct mail, samples and literature, and journal advertising—on a pharmaceutical firm's sales.[11] Their statistical results indicated that the firm overdid direct mail and underspent on journal advertising.

Another way is to design the advertising program itself as an experiment. Du Pont was one of the first companies to design advertising experiments. Du Pont's paint department divided fifty-six sales territories into high, average, and low market-share territories.[12] In one-third of the group, Du Pont spent the normal amount for advertising; in another third, two and one-half times the normal amount; and in the remaining third, four times the normal amount. At the end of the experiment, Du Pont estimated how many extra sales had been created by

Exhibit **15-3**

Advertising Decisions and Public Policy

Companies must avoid deception or discrimination in their use of advertising. Here are the major issues:

- *False advertising*. Advertisers must not make false claims, such as asserting that a product cures something that it does not cure. Advertisers must avoid false demonstrations, such as using Plexiglas instead of sandpaper in a commercial to demonstrate that a razor blade can shave sandpaper.
- *Deceptive advertising*. Advertisers must not create ads that have the capacity to deceive, even though no one may be deceived. A floor wax cannot be advertised as giving six months' protection unless this is under typical conditions, and a diet bread cannot be advertised as having fewer calories if the only reason is that the slices are thinner. The problem is to distinguish between deception and puffery, the latter being acceptable.
- *Bait-and-switch advertising*. A seller should not attract buyers on false pretenses. For example, a seller advertises a $79 sewing machine and then refuses to sell the product, disparages its features, demonstrates a defective one, or imposes unreasonable delivery dates.
- *Promotional allowances and services*. The company must make promotional allowances and services available to all customers on proportionately equal terms.

Run ad that is different then what you get inside or they try to sell you something else.

higher levels of advertising expenditure. Du Pont found that higher advertising expenditure increased sales at a diminishing rate, and that the sales increase was weaker in Du Pont's high-market-share territories.

Advertising involves major sums of money that can easily be misspent by companies that fail to define their advertising objectives; make careful budget, message, and media decisions; and evaluate advertising's results. Advertising also draws considerable public attention and scrutiny, due to its power to influence life-styles and opinions. Advertising has been subjected to increased regulation designed to ensure that it performs responsibly. (See exhibit 15-3.)

Sales Promotion

Advertising is supplemented by other marketing mix tools. These are sales promotion and publicity.

Sales promotion consists of a wide variety of promotional tools designed to stimulate earlier and/or stronger market response.

These tools include *consumer promotion* (such as samples, coupons, money-refund offers, price packs, premiums, contests, trading stamps, demonstrations), *trade promotion* (such as buying allowances, free goods, merchandise allowances, cooperative advertising, push money, dealer sales contests), and *sales-force promotion* (such as bonuses, contests, sales rallies).

Sales promotion tools are used by most organizations, including manufacturers, distributors, retailers, trade associations, and nonprofit institutions. As examples of the latter, churches sponsor bingo games, theater parties, testimonial dinners, and raffles.

Sales promotion has grown rapidly in recent years. Between 1969 and 1976, sales promotion expenditures increased 9.4% per year compared with advertising's increase of 5.4%. Sales promotion expenditures exceeded $30 billion in 1976.[13]

Several factors have contributed to the rapid growth of sales promotion, particularly in consumer markets.[14] These include: (1) Promotion is now more accepted by top management as an effective sales tool; (2) more product managers are qualified to use sales promotion tools; (3) product managers are under greater pressure to increase their sales; (4) an increasing number of competitors have become more promotion-minded; (5) middlemen have demanded more deals from manufacturers; and (6) advertising efficiency has declined due to rising costs, media clutter, and legal restraints.

Sales promotion tools can be divided into those that are "consumer franchise building" and those that are not.[15] Those that are give a selling message along with the deal, as in the case of free samples, coupons when they include a selling message, and premiums when they are related to the product. Sales promotion tools that are not consumer franchise building include price packs, consumer premiums not related to a product, contests and sweepstakes, consumer refund offers, and trade allowances. Using consumer franchise-building promotions helps reinforce consumers' brand awareness and understanding.

Sales promotion seems most effective when used together with advertising. "In one study, point-of-purchase displays related to current TV commercials were found to produce 15% more sales than similar displays not related to such advertising. In another, a heavy sampling approach along with TV advertising proved more successful than either TV alone or TV with coupons in introducing a product.[16]

In using sales promotion, a company must establish the objectives; select the tools; develop the program; pretest, implement, and control it; and evaluate the results.

Establishing the Sales Promotion Objectives

Sales promotion objectives are based on the marketing objectives for the product. The specific objectives set for sales promotion will vary with the type of target market. For consumers, objectives include encouraging more usage and purchase of larger-size items, getting nonusers to try the product, and attracting users of competitors' brands. For retailers, objectives include encouraging the retailer to carry new items, higher levels of inventory and related items, offsetting competitive promotions, building the retailer's brand loyalty, and gaining entry into new retail outlets. For the sales force, objectives include encouraging support of a new product or model, encouraging more sales calls, and stimulating sales in off-season.

Selecting the Sales Promotion Tools Many tools are available to accomplish the sales promotion objectives. The marketing planner should take into account the type of market, sales promotion objectives, competitive conditions, and cost-effectiveness of each tool. The main tools are described below.

great but — who can afford it

SAMPLES, COUPONS, PRICE PACKS, PREMIUMS, AND TRADING STAMPS. These tools make up the bulk of consumer promotions. Samples are offers of a free amount or trial of a product to consumers.[17] The sample might be delivered door to door, sent in the mail, picked up in a store, found attached to another product, or featured in an advertising offer. Sampling is the most effective and most expensive way to introduce a new product. S. C. Johnson & Sons spent $12 million on sampling its new shampoo Agree.

Coupons are certificates entitling the bearer to a stated saving on the purchase of a specific product. Over 81 billion coupons were distributed in 1979, about 1,200 per household. Only 4% were redeemed. Coupons can be mailed, enclosed in other products, or inserted in ads. They can be effective in stimulating sales of a mature brand and getting consumers to try a new brand.

Price packs (also called cents-off deals) are offers to consumers of savings off the regular price of a product. They appear on the product's label or package. They may take the form of a *reduced-price pack,* which is a single package sold at a reduced price (such as two for the price of one); or a *banded pack,* which consists of two related products banded together (such as a toothbrush and toothpaste). Price packs are very effective—even more than coupons—in stimulating short-term sales.

Premiums are merchandise offered at a relatively low cost or free as an incentive to purchase a particular product. A with-pack premium accompanies the product inside (in-pack) or outside (on-pack) the package. The package itself, if a reusable container, may serve as a premium. A free-in-the-mail premium is an item mailed to consumers who send in a proof of purchase, such as a boxtop. A self-liquidating premium is an item sold below its normal retail price to consumers who request it. Manufacturers now offer consumers all kinds of premiums bearing the company's name: Budweiser fans can order T-shirts, hot-air balloons, and hundreds of other items with Bud's name on them.[18]

Trading stamps are a special type of premium received by customers making purchases that they can redeem for merchandise through stamp redemption centers. The first merchants who adopt trading stamps usually attract new business. Other merchants adopt them defensively, but eventually they become a burden to everyone, with some merchants deciding to drop them and offer lower prices instead.[19]

POINT-OF-PURCHASE DISPLAYS AND DEMONSTRATIONS. Point-of-purchase (POP) displays and demonstrations take place at the point of purchase or sale. A five-foot-high cardboard display of Cap'n Crunch next to Cap'n Crunch cereal boxes is an example. Unfortunately, many retailers do not like to handle the hundreds of displays, signs, and posters they receive from manufacturers each year. Manufacturers are responding by creating better POP materials, tying them in with television or print messages, and offering to set them up. The L'eggs panty hose display is one of the most creative in the history of POP materials and a major factor in the success of this brand.[20]

TRADE PROMOTION. Manufacturers use a number of techniques to secure the cooperation of wholesalers and retailers. Manufacturers may offer a buying allowance, which is an offer of money off on each case purchased during a stated period of time. The offer encourages dealers to buy a quantity or carry a new item that they might not ordinarily buy.

Manufacturers may offer a merchandise allowance to compensate dealers for featuring the manufacturer's products. An advertising allowance compensates dealers for advertising the manufacturer's product. A display allowance compensates them for carrying special displays of the product.

Manufacturers may offer free goods, which are extra cases of merchandise to middlemen who buy a certain quantity. They may offer push money, which is cash or gifts to dealers or their sales force to push the manufacturer's goods. Manufacturers may offer free specialty advertising items that carry the company's name, such as pens, pencils, calendars, paperweights, matchbooks, memo pads, ashtrays, and yardsticks.[21]

BUSINESS CONVENTIONS AND TRADE SHOWS. Industry associations organize annual conventions and typically sponsor a trade show at the same time. Firms selling to the particular industry display and demonstrate their products at the trade show. Over fifty-six hundred trade shows take place every year, drawing approximately eighty million people. The participating vendors expect several benefits, including generating new sales leads, maintaining customer contacts, introducing new products, meeting new customers, and selling more to present customers.[22]

Good place to show products

The National Association of Men's Sportswear Buyers convention provides an opportunity for clothing manufacturers to display their products.
Courtesy National Association of Men's Sportswear Buyers

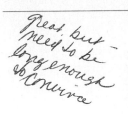

Great but — need to be long enough to convince

CONTESTS, SWEEPSTAKES, AND GAMES. Contests, sweepstakes, and games give consumers, dealers, or sales representatives the chance to win something—such as cash, vacation trips, or goods—as a result of luck or extra effort. A contest calls for consumers to submit an entry—a jingle, estimate, suggestion—to be examined by a panel of judges, who will select the best entries. A sweepstake calls for consumers to put their names in a drawing. A game gives something to consumers every time they buy—bingo numbers, missing letters—which may or may not help them win a prize. A sales contest is a contest involving dealers or the sales force to induce them to redouble their sales efforts over a stated period, with prizes going to the top performers.

Developing the Sales Promotion Program

The marketing planner must make some additional decisions about the full promotion program. In particular, the marketer must decide on how much incentive to offer, who can participate, how to advertise the sales promotion, how long it should last, when it should start, and how much to budget.

SIZE OF INCENTIVE. The marketer has to determine how much of an incentive to offer. A certain minimum incentive is necessary if the promotion is to succeed. A higher incentive will produce more sales response, but at a diminishing rate. Some of the large consumer packaged-goods firms have a sales promotion manager who studies the effectiveness of past promotions and recommends appropriate incentives to brand managers.

CONDITIONS FOR PARTICIPATION. Incentives might be offered to everyone or to select groups. A premium might be offered to only those who turn in boxtops. Sweepstakes might not be offered in certain states, or to families of company personnel, or to persons under a certain age.

DISTRIBUTION VEHICLE FOR PROMOTION. The marketer must decide how to promote and distribute the promotion program. A fifteen-cents-off coupon could be distributed in the package, store, mail, or advertising media. Each distribution method involves a different level of reach and cost.

DURATION OF PROMOTION. If the sales promotion period is too short, many consumers will not be able to take advantage of it, since they may not be re-purchasing at the time. If the promotion runs too long, the deal will lose some of its "act now" force.

TIMING OF PROMOTION. Brand managers need to develop calendar dates for promotions. The dates will be used by production, sales, and distribution. Some unplanned promotions will also be needed and require cooperation on short notice.

TOTAL SALES PROMOTION BUDGET. The sales promotion budget can be developed in two ways. The marketer can choose the promotions and estimate their total cost. The more common way is to take a percentage of the total budget for sales promotion.

Pretesting the Sales Promotion Program Sales promotion tools should be pretested when possible to determine if they are appropriate and offer the right incentive. Yet fewer than 42% of premium offers are ever pretested.[23]

Implementing the Sales Promotion Program Companies should establish plans for carrying out each promotion covering lead time and sell-off time. Lead time is the time necessary to prepare the program prior to launching it. Sell-off time begins with the launch and ends when the deal closes.

Evaluating the Sales Promotion Results Evaluation of sales promotion programs is crucial, but it is rarely given much attention.[24] When manufacturers do evaluate, they can use one of four methods. The most common method is to compare sales before, during, and after a promotion. Suppose a company has a 6% market share in the prepromotion period, which jumps to 10% during the promotion, falls to 5% immediately after the promotion, and rises to 7% after some time. The promotion evidently attracted new triers as well as more purchasing by existing customers. After the promotion, sales fell as consumers used up their inventories. The long-run rise to 7% indicates that the company gained some new users. If the brand's share returned to the prepromotion level, then the promotion only altered the time pattern of demand rather than the total demand.

Consumer panel data would reveal the kinds of people who responded to the promotion and what they did after the promotion. If more information is needed, consumer surveys can be conducted to learn how many recall the promotion, what they thought of it, how many took advantage of it, and how it affected their subsequent brand choice behavior. Sales promotions can also be evaluated through experiments that vary such attributes as incentive value, duration, and distribution media.

Clearly, sales promotion plays an important role in the total promotion mix. Its use requires defining the sales promotion objectives, selecting the appropriate tools, developing the sales promotion program, pretesting it, implementing it, and evaluating the results.

Publicity

In addition to sales promotion, another major promotional tool is publicity.

> **Publicity** involves "securing editorial space, as divorced from paid space, in all media read, viewed, or heard by a company's customers or prospects, for the specific purpose of assisting in the meeting of sales goals."[25]

Publicity's results can sometimes be spectacular. Consider the movie *Return of the Jedi:*

> In addition to being the third of the *Star Wars* movies, *Return of the Jedi* is a marketing phenomenon. Since the movie opened, sales of *Return of the Jedi*

posters, toys, T-shirts, and costumes have been booming. The storybook of the movie has topped best-seller lists around the country. Burger King is heavily advertising a sales promotion featuring glasses with pictures of *Jedi* characters. Pepperidge Farm is selling *Jedi* cookies: vanilla for the heroes, peanut butter for the creatures, and chocolate for the villains. *Time* ran a cover story on the movie. Newspapers and television news programs have told about dedicated fans standing in line for days to get tickets and have interviewed people planning to see the movie again and again and again.

Publicity is used to promote brands, products, persons, places, ideas, activities, organizations, and even nations. Trade associations have used publicity to rebuild interest in commodities such as eggs, milk, and potatoes. Organizations have used publicity to attract attention or to counter a poor image. Nations have used publicity to attract more tourists, foreign investment, and international support.

Publicity is part of a larger concept, that of public relations. Company public relations has several objectives, including obtaining favorable publicity for the company, building up a good "corporate citizen" image for the company, and handling adverse rumors and stories that break out. Public relations departments use several tools to carry out these objectives.[26]

1. *Press relations.* The aim of press relations is to place newsworthy information into the news media to attract attention to a person, product, or service.
2. *Product publicity.* Product publicity involves various efforts to publicize specific products.
3. *Corporate communications.* This activity covers internal and external communications to promote understanding of the institution.
4. *Lobbying.* Lobbying involves dealing with legislators and government officials to promote or defeat legislation and regulation.
5. *Counseling.* Counseling involves advising management about public issues and company positions and image.

Those skilled in publicity are usually found not in the company's marketing department but in its public relations department. The public relations department is typically located at corporate headquarters, and its staff is so busy dealing with various publics—stockholders, employees, legislators, city officials—that publicity to support product marketing objectives may be neglected. One solution is to add a publicity specialist to the marketing department.

Publicity is often described as a marketing stepchild because of its limited and infrequent use. Yet publicity can create a memorable impact on public awareness at a fraction of the cost of advertising. The company does not pay for the space or time in the media. It pays for a staff to develop and circulate the stories. If the company develops an interesting story, it could be picked up by all the media and be worth millions of dollars in equivalent advertising. Furthermore, it would have more credibility than advertising.

In considering when and how to use product publicity, management should establish the publicity objectives, choose the publicity messages and vehicles, implement the publicity plan, and evaluate the publicity results.

Establishing the Publicity Objectives

The first task is to set specific objectives for the publicity. The Wine Growers of California hired the public relations firm of Daniel J. Edelman, Inc., in 1966 to develop a publicity program to support two major marketing objectives: (1) Convince Americans that wine drinking is a pleasurable part of good living, and (2) improve the image and market share of California wines among all wines. The following publicity objectives were established: (1) Develop magazine stories about wine and get them placed in top magazines (*Time, House Beautiful*) and in newspapers (food columns, feature sections); (2) develop stories about wine's many health values and direct them to the medical profession; and (3) develop specific publicity for the young adult market, college market, government agencies, and various ethnic communities. These objectives were turned into specific goals so that the final results could be evaluated.

Choosing the Publicity Messages and Vehicles

The publicist next identifies interesting stories to tell about the product. Suppose a relatively unknown college wants more public recognition. The publicist will search for possible stories. Do any faculty members have unusual backgrounds, or are any working on unusual projects? Are any new and unusual courses being taught? Are any interesting events taking place on campus? Usually this search will uncover hundreds of stories that can be fed to the press. The stories chosen should reflect the image the college wants.

If the number of stories is insufficient, the publicist should propose newsworthy events that the college could sponsor. Here the publicist gets into creating news rather than finding news. The ideas include hosting major academic conventions, inviting celebrity speakers, and developing news conferences. Each event is an opportunity to develop many stories directed at different audiences.

Event creation is a particularly important skill in publicizing fund-raising drives for nonprofit organizations. Fund-raisers have developed a large repertoire of special events, including anniversary celebrations, art exhibits, auctions, benefit evenings, bingo games, book sales, cake sales, contests, dances, dinners, fairs, fashion shows, parties in unusual places, phonothons, rummage sales, tours, and walkathons. No sooner does one type of event get created, such as a walkathon, than competitors spawn new versions such as readathons, bikeathons, and jogathons.

Implementing the Publicity Plan

Implementing publicity requires care. Take the matter of placing stories in the media. A great story is easy to place. But most stories are less than great and may not get past busy editors. One of the chief assets of publicists is their personal relationship with media editors. Publicists are often ex-journalists who know many media editors and know what they want. Publicists look at media editors as a market to satisfy so that these editors will continue to use their stories.

Evaluating the Publicity Results

Publicity's contribution is difficult to measure because it is used with other promotional tools. If it is used before the other tools come into action, its contribution is easier to evaluate.

The easiest measure of publicity effectiveness is the number of exposures

Exhibit **15-4**

Two Examples of Successful Publicity Campaigns

A publicist is able to find or create stories around even mundane products. Some years ago, the Potato Board decided to finance a publicity campaign to encourage more potato consumption. A national attitude and usage study indicated that many consumers perceived potatoes as too fattening, not nutritious enough, and not a good source of vitamins and minerals. These attitudes were disseminated by various opinion leaders, such as food editors, diet advocates, and doctors. Actually, potatoes have far fewer calories than most people imagine, and they contain several important vitamins and minerals. The Potato Board decided to develop separate publicity programs for consumers, doctors, and dieticians, nutritionists, home economists, and food editors. The consumer program consisted of disseminating many stories about the potato for network television and women's magazines, developing and distributing *The Potato Lover's Diet Cookbook,* and placing articles and recipes in food editors' columns. The food editors' program consisted of food editor seminars conducted by nutrition experts.

Publicity can also be highly effective in brand promotion. One of the top brands of cat food is Star-Kist Foods' 9-Lives. Its brand image revolves around Morris the Cat. The advertising agency of Leo Burnett, which created Morris for its ads, wanted to make him more of a living, breathing, real-life feline to whom cat owners and cat lovers could relate. It hired a public relations firm, which then proposed and carried out the following ideas: (1) Launch a Morris "Look-Alike" contest in nine major markets, with Morris booked for personal appearances and extensive stories appearing about the search for a look-alike; (2) write a book called *Morris, An Intimate Biography,* describing the adventures of this famous feline; (3) establish a coveted award called "The Morris," a bronze statuette given to the owners of award-winning cats selected at local cat shows; (4) sponsor an "Adopt-a-Cat Month," with Morris as the official "spokescat" urging people to adopt stray cats as Morris once was; and (5) distribute a booklet called "The Morris Method" on cat care. These publicity steps strengthened the brand's market share in the cat food market.

created in the media. Publicists supply the client with a "clippings book" showing all the media that carried news about the product and a summary statement such as the following:

Media coverage included 3,500 column inches of news and photographs in 350 publications with a combined circulation of 79.4 million; 2,500 minutes of air time on 290 radio stations and an estimated audience of 65 million; and 660 minutes of air time on 160 television stations with an estimated audience of 91 million. If this time and space had been purchased at advertising rates, it would have amounted to $1,047,000.[27]

Measuring exposure this way is not very satisfying. There is no indication of how many people actually read or heard the message and what they thought afterward. There is no information on the net audience reached, since publications overlap in readership.

A better measure is the change in product awareness/comprehension/attitude resulting from the publicity campaign (after allowing for the impact of other promotional tools). This requires surveying the before-and-after levels of these variables. The Potato Board learned, for example, that the number of people who agreed with the statement "Potatoes are rich in vitamins and minerals" went from 36% before the campaign to 67% after the campaign, a significant improvement in product comprehension. (See exhibit 15-4.)

The sales and profit impact is the most satisfactory measure if obtainable. For example, 9-Lives sales increased 43% at the end of the "Morris the Cat" publicity campaign. However, advertising and sales promotion had been stepped up, and their contribution has to be excluded.

Summary

Three major tools of promotion are advertising, sales promotion, and publicity. They are mass-marketing tools as opposed to personal selling, which targets specific buyers.

Advertising—the use of paid media by a seller to communicate persuasive information about its products, services, or organization—is a potent promotional tool. American marketers spend over $61 billion annually on advertising, and it takes many forms (national, regional, local; consumer, industrial, retail; product, brand, institutional, and so on). Advertising decision making is a five-step process consisting of setting objectives; making budget, message, and media decisions; and then evaluating the advertising program. Advertisers should establish clear goals as to whether the advertising is supposed to inform, persuade, or remind buyers. The advertising budget can be established on the basis of what is affordable, as a percentage of sales, on the basis of competitors' expenditures, or on the basis of objectives and tasks. The message decision calls for generating messages, evaluating and choosing among them, and executing them effectively. The media decision calls for defining the reach, frequency, and impact goals; choosing among major media types; selecting specific media vehicles; and scheduling the media. Finally, campaign evaluation calls for evaluating the communication and sales effects of advertising before, during, and after the advertising campaign.

Sales promotion covers a wide variety of short-term incentive tools—coupons, premiums, contests, buying allowances—designed to stimulate consumer markets, the trade, and the organization's own sales force. Sales promotion expenditures have been growing at a faster rate than advertising in recent years. Sales promotion calls for establishing the sales promotion objectives; selecting the tools; developing, pretesting, and implementing the sales promotion program; and evaluating the results.

Publicity—which is the securing of free editorial space or time—is the least utilized of the major promotional tools, although it has great potential for building awareness and preference in the marketplace. Publicity involves establishing the publicity objectives; choosing the publicity messages and vehicles; implementing the publicity plan; and evaluating the results.

Questions for Discussion

1. Technological advances have added several new media to the list of promotional tools. For each of the following media, list its advantages and disadvantages, and state when it could best be used:

   —Machines that automatically dial telephone numbers in sequence and then play recorded messages by well-known celebrities selling everything from cosmetics to political candidates.

   —Two-way cable TV that permits viewers to use a console to order goods directly after seeing them in an advertisement.

   —Sears catalogs and videocassettes that permit product demonstration and voice-over descriptions.

   —Electronic newspapers that can display the classifieds or real estate listings from anywhere in the country on a viewer's home computer screen.

2. Many firms have had to contend with negative rumors about their products in recent years—K mart coats from Taiwan with poisonous snakes nesting in them, McDonald's using worms in its hamburger meat, Pop Rocks candy making your stomach explode, bubble gum containing spider eggs. How can a company best deal with these rumors when using public relations and advertising?

3. The major objective of advertising is to inform. Comment.

4. Explain the major aspects of the message decision and relate them to a specific product.

5. Sales promotion tools are only effective when used for consumer promotion. Comment.

6. Which sales promotion tools are the most widely used for supermarket products? Why?

7. How might Del Monte evaluate whether its national sales promotion campaign was successful?

8. Discuss how you would develop a publicity campaign for the American Cancer Society.

Key Terms in Chapter 15

Advertising   Nonpersonal forms of communication conducted through paid media under clear sponsorship.

Publicity   "Securing editorial space, as divorced from paid space, in all media read, viewed, or heard by a company's customers or prospects, for the specific purpose of assisting in the meeting of sales goals."

Sales promotion   A wide variety of promotional tools designed to stimulate earlier and/or stronger market response.

Cases for Chapter 15

Case 13   The Pillsbury Co.: Totino's Pizza (p. 510)
Totino's must develop the best possible promotion mix, taking into consideration many of the points made in this chapter.

Case 14   Purex Industries, Inc. (p. 511)
Purex's key marketing strategies are directly related to the promotion mix. This case looks at factors that may lead Purex to change the mix.

Chapter 16

Promoting Products: Personal Selling and Sales Management

Objectives

After reading this chapter, you should be able to:

1. Discuss the role of a company's sales representative.
2. Describe the three sales-force structures and the advantages and disadvantages of each.
3. List and define the steps in the selling process.
4. Explain how companies evaluate the effectiveness of their sales representatives.

Ray Henderson spends a lot of his time waiting to see doctors, even when he's in the best of health. Henderson is a sales representative for the Merck Sharp & Dohme division of Merck & Co., Inc., a producer of prescription drugs. His territory is northeastern Tennessee. Every working day, he travels from town to town, using his 22 years of experience to get past receptionists and into doctors' private offices, talking with busy doctors in whatever time they can spare about his company's new drugs, and leaving samples for the doctors to "try" by prescribing them to patients. In the pharmaceuticals industry, sales representatives like Henderson are still known as detail men, even though many of them today are women. The name refers to the fact that these sales representatives provide doctors with details about new drugs.

Henderson's firm, as well as Henderson himself, makes sure that he is well informed about the company's products. In their first year, Merck's sales representatives spend 12 weeks in biology and pharmacology courses. Then the new sales representatives receive additional instruction by joining young doctors, still completing their own training, on hospital rounds. To make sure these sales representatives stay informed throughout their careers, Merck tests them four times a year on the properties of some currently available drugs. To add to the education his company provides, Henderson studies a lot on his own. Waiting in doctors' offices gives him some time to read the medical books he carries with him when he's on the road.

Recently, the use of a knowledgeable sales force to promote their products directly to doctors has become more important to drug companies than ever before. The industry has been enjoying an especially productive period: In the early 1980s, drug companies introduced more new products than in any other period since the early 1960s. Busy doctors find that staying informed about the large numbers of new drugs is more and more difficult. Drug companies worry that unless they make sure that doctors know about their new drugs, the doctors won't prescribe them. So that physicians don't miss any of its products, Merck has recently increased its sales force by 55%—to 1,400.

Besides his office visits, Ray Henderson has other duties. One of them is to set up meetings between well-known specialists in particular areas of medicine and the local physicians in his territory. These meetings provide physicians with valuable opportunities for exchanging ideas and information.

Many people feel that doctors should not depend on sales representatives for their information about drugs. In their eagerness to increase sales, critics feel, sales representatives might give biased, overly positive information about their company's drugs. To offset this criticism, the companies downplay the importance of their company's sales force, and in general, the sales representatives have a reputation for honesty. People like Ray Henderson have worked hard to earn and maintain that reputation. "You gotta be true," says Henderson. "All you have to do is fool a doctor once and he'll never trust you again." While doctors don't usually depend on sales representatives as their only source of information on new drugs, they often appreciate any additional facts that the sales representatives can provide. Sometimes that information can be about other companies' products. As one doctor says about the value of visits from these sales representatives, "It's a real fine way to find out the side effects of their competition's drugs. They'll always tell you that."

Sales representatives also enable doctors to communicate with drug companies. When a Merck drug produces an unexpected side effect, northeastern Tennessee doctors can let the company know about it through Henderson. Because of this function, a Merck vice-president calls the sales representatives "a link between the researcher and the physician."[1]

Robert Louis Stevenson observed that "everyone lives by selling something." A sales force can be found in nonprofit as well as profit organizations. College recruiters are the college's sales-force arm for attracting students. Churches use membership committees to attract new members. The U.S. Agricultural Extension Service sends agricultural specialists to sell farmers on using new farming methods. Hospitals and museums use fund-raisers to contact and raise money from donors.

The people who do the selling are called by various names: sales representatives, account executives, sales consultants, sales engineers, field representatives, agents, service representatives, and marketing representatives. Selling is one of the oldest professions in the world (see exhibit 16-1).

There are many stereotypes of sales representatives. "Salesmen" may bring to mind the image of Arthur Miller's pitiable Willy Loman in *Death of a Salesman* or Meredith Willson's cigar-smoking, back-slapping, joke-telling Harold Hill in *The Music Man*. Sales representatives are typically pictured as loving sociability—although many sales representatives actually dislike it. They are criticized for forcing goods on people—although buyers often search out sales representatives.

Actually the term **sales representative** covers a broad range of positions in our economy, where the differences are often greater than the similarities. Mc-Murry devised the following classification of sales positions:[2]

1. Positions where the sales representative's job is predominantly to deliver the product, for example, milk, bread, fuel, oil.
2. Positions where the sales representative is predominantly an inside order taker, such as the haberdashery sales representative standing behind the counter.
3. Positions where the sales representative is also predominantly an order taker but works in the field, as the packing house, soap, or spice sales representative does.
4. Positions where the sales representative is not expected or permitted to take an order but is called on only to build goodwill or to educate the actual or potential user . . . the distiller's "missionary person" or the medical "detail man" representing an ethical pharmaceutical house.
5. Positions where the major emphasis is placed on technical knowledge, for example, the engineering sales representative who is primarily a consultant to "client" companies.
6. Positions that demand the creative sale of tangible products, like vacuum cleaners, refrigerators, siding, and encyclopedias.
7. Positions requiring the creative sale of intangibles, such as insurance, advertising services, or education.

FIGURE 16-1

Major Decisions in
Sales-Force
Management

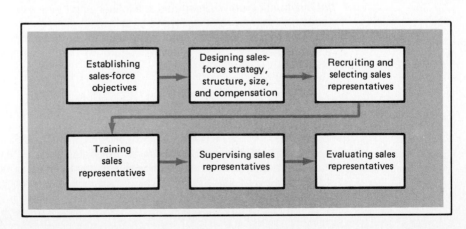

Exhibit 16-1

Milestones in the History of Selling and Salesmanship

Selling goes back to the dawn of history. Paul Hermann described a Bronze Age traveling salesman's sample case: ". . . a solid wooden box, 26 inches in length, containing in specially hollowed compartments various types of axes, sword blades, buttons, etc." Early sellers and traders were not held in high esteem. The Roman word for salesman meant "cheater," and Mercury, the god of cunning and barter, was regarded as the patron deity of merchants and traders.

The buying and selling of commodities flourished over the centuries and centered in market towns. Traveling peddlers carried goods to the homes of prospective customers who were unable to get to the market towns.

The first salesmen in the United States were Yankee peddlers (pack peddlers), who carried clothing, spices, household wares, and notions in backpacks from East Coast manufacturing centers to settlers in the western frontier regions. The pack peddlers also traded with the Indians, exchanging knives, beads, and ornaments for furs. Many traders came to be viewed as shrewd, unprincipled tricksters who would not think twice about putting sand in the sugar, dust in the pepper, and chicory in the coffee. They often sold colored sugar water as "medicine" guaranteed to cure all possible ills.

In the early 1800s, some of the peddlers began to use horse-drawn wagons and to stock heavier goods, such as furniture, clocks, dishes, weapons, and ammunition. Some of these wagon peddlers settled in frontier villages and opened the first general stores and trading posts.

The larger retailers traveled once or twice a year to the nearest major city to replenish their stock. Eventually, wholesalers and manufacturers

This list of positions ranges from the least to the most creative types of selling. The earlier jobs call for maintaining accounts and taking orders, while the latter require hunting down prospects and influencing them to buy. Our discussion will focus on the more creative types of selling.

The major decisions that companies face in building and managing an effective sales force are shown in figure 16-1 and examined in the following sections.

Establishing Sales-Force Objectives

Companies set different objectives for their sales force. IBM's sales representatives are responsible for "selling, installing, and upgrading" customer computer equipment; AT&T sales representatives are responsible for "developing, selling, and protecting" accounts. Sales representatives generally are responsible for one or more of the following: finding and cultivating new customers; commu-

hired greeters, or drummers, who would seek out and invite retailers to visit the displays of their employers. The drummers would meet incoming trains and ships to beat their competitors. In time, the drummers traveled to their customers' places of business. Prior to 1860, there were fewer than one thousand traveling salesmen, many of whom were credit investigators who also took orders for goods. By 1870 there were seven thousand, by 1880 twenty-eight thousand, and by 1900 ninety-three thousand traveling salesmen.

Modern selling and sales management techniques were refined by John Henry Patterson (1844–1922), widely regarded as the father of modern salesmanship. Patterson ran the National Cash Register Company (NCR). He asked his best salesmen to demonstrate their sales approaches to the other salesmen. The best sales approach was printed in a "Sales Primer" and distributed to all NCR salesmen to be followed to the letter. This was the beginning of the canned sales approach. In addition, Patterson assigned his salesmen exclusive territories and sales quotas to stretch their effort. He held frequent sales meetings that served as both sales training sessions and social gatherings. He sent his salesmen regular communcations on how to sell. One of the young men trained by Patterson was Thomas J. Watson, who later founded IBM. Patterson showed other companies the way to turn a sales force into an effective tool for building sales and profits.

Sources: Written by the author based on various sources, including Paul Hermann, *Conquest by Man* (New York: Harper & Row, 1954), p. 38; Frederic Russell, Frank Beach, and Richard Buskirk, *Textbook of Salesmanship* (New York: McGraw-Hill, 1969), pp. 8–10; Bertrand Canfield, *Salesmanship: Practices and Principles* (New York: McGraw-Hill, 1950), p. 6; and Thomas and Marva Belden, *The Lengthening Shadow* (Boston: Little, Brown, 1962), p. 44.

nicating information about the company's products and services; selling, including approaching, presenting, answering objections, and closing sales; providing services; carrying out market research and intelligence work and filling out call reports; and allocating—sales representatives are able to evaluate customer quality and allocate scarce products during product shortages.

Individual companies become more specific about their sales-force objectives and activities. For example, one company advises its sales representatives to spend 80% of their time with current customers and 20% with prospects, and 85% of their time on established products and 15% on new products.[3] If norms are not established, sales representatives tend to spend most of their time selling established products to current accounts and neglect new products and new prospects.

As a company increases its market orientation, its sales force needs to become more market-oriented. Sales representatives should know how to produce customer satisfaction and company profit. They should know how to analyze sales data, measure market potential, gather market intelligence, and develop marketing strategies and plans. Sales representatives need analytical marketing skills. This becomes especially critical at the higher levels of sales management. Marketers believe that a market-oriented rather than a sales-oriented sales force will be more effective in the long run.

Designing the Sales Force

Once the company has established its sales-force objectives, it is ready to face questions of sales-force strategy, structure, size, and compensation.

Sales-Force Strategy The company will be competing with others to get orders from customers. It must base its strategy in an understanding of the customer buying process. It can use one or more of five sales approaches:

1. *Sales representative to buyer.* A sales representative talks to a prospect or customer in person or over the phone.
2. *Sales representative to buyer group.* A sales representative makes a sales presentation to a buying group.
3. *Sales team to buyer group.* A sales team (such as a company officer, a sales representative, and a sales engineer) makes a sales presentation to a buying group.
4. *Conference selling.* The sales representative brings resource people from the company to meet with one or more buyers to discuss problems and mutual opportunities.
5. *Seminar selling.* A company team conducts an educational seminar for a technical group in a customer company about state-of-the-art developments.

Thus the sales representative often acts as the "account manager" who arranges contacts between various people in the buying and selling organizations. Selling increasingly calls for teamwork, requiring the support of other personnel. These include top management, which is increasingly involved in the sales process, especially when national accounts[4] or major sales[5] are at stake; technical people, who supply technical information to the customer before, during, or after the purchase of the product; customer service representatives, who provide installation, maintenance, and other services to the customer; and an office staff consisting of sales analysts, order expediters, and secretaries.

particular territories

Sales-Force Structure Sales-force strategy also deals with structuring the sales force to have maximum effectiveness in the marketplace. This structure is obvious if the company sells one product line to one industry with customers in many locations. In that case the company would use a **territorial-structured sales force**. If the company sells many products to many types of customers, it might need a **product-structured** or **customer-structured sales force**. These structures are discussed below.

TERRITORIAL-STRUCTURED SALES FORCE.   This is the simplest sales-force structure. Each sales representative is assigned an exclusive territory in which to represent the company's full line. This structure has a number of advantages. First, the sales representative's responsibilities are clearly defined. As the only sales representative working the territory, he or she bears the credit or blame for area sales. Second, territorial responsibility increases the sales representative's incentive to cultivate local business and personal ties. These ties contribute to the sales representative's selling effectiveness and personal life. Third, travel expenses are relatively small, since each sales representative travels within a small geographic area.

A territorial sales organization is supported by a hierarchy of sales management positions. Several territories will be supervised by a district sales manager, several districts will be supervised by a regional sales manager, and several regions will be supervised by a national sales manager or sales vice-president.

PRODUCT-STRUCTURED SALES FORCE.   Sales representatives must know their products, especially when the products are technically complex, highly unrelated, or very numerous. This, together with the development of product divisions and product management, has led many companies to structure their sales force along product lines.

This structure, however, may lead to a duplication of efforts. For example, the American Hospital Supply Corporation has several product divisions, each with its own sales force. It is possible that several sales representatives from the American Hospital Supply Corporation could call on the same hospital on the same day. This means that company sales personnel travel over the same routes, and each waits to see the customer's purchasing agents. These extra costs must be weighed against the benefits of more knowledgeable product representation.

CUSTOMER-STRUCTURED SALES FORCE.   Companies often set up their sales force along customer lines. There may be a separate sales force for various industries, for major versus regular accounts, and for current versus new-business development. The most obvious advantage of customer specialization is that each sales force can become knowledgeable about specific customer needs. At one time, General Electric's sales representatives specialized in products (fan motors, switches, and so forth). It later changed to specialization in markets, such as the air-conditioning market and auto market, because that is how customers saw the problem of fan motors, switches, and so forth.

The major disadvantage of a customer-structured sales force arises when the various types of customers are scattered throughout the country. This means extensive travel by each sales force.

Sales-Force Size   Once the company has set its sales-force strategy and structure, it is ready to consider its sales-force size. Sales representatives are one of the company's most productive and expensive assets. Increasing their number will increase both sales and costs.

Most companies use the workload approach to establish the sales-force size.[6] The company might think as follows:

Suppose we have one thousand A accounts and two thousand B accounts in the nation. A accounts require thirty-six calls a year and B accounts twelve calls a year. This means we need a sales force that can make sixty thousand sales calls a year. Suppose the average sales representative can make one thousand calls a year. We need sixty full-time sales representatives.

Sales-Force Compensation

To attract the desired number of sales representatives, the company has to develop an attractive compensation plan. The level of compensation must bear some relation to the "going market price" for the type of sales job and abilities required. For example, the average earnings of the experienced salesperson in 1981 amounted to $30,444.[7]

This compensation is made up of several elements—a fixed amount, a variable amount, expenses, and fringe benefits. The fixed amount, which might be salary or a drawing account, is intended to give the sales representative some stable income. The variable amount, which might be commissions, bonuses, or profit sharing, is intended to stimulate and reward greater effort. Expense allowances help the sales representatives undertake selling efforts that are considered necessary or desirable. And fringe benefits, such as paid vacations, sickness or accident benefits, pensions, and life insurance, are intended to provide security and job satisfaction.

Compensation for this top Mary Kay Cosmetics sales representative includes public recognition at a company seminar and a fur coat.
Courtesy Mary Kay Cosmetics

Recruiting and Selecting Sales Representatives

Having established the strategy, structure, size, and compensation for the sales force, the company now has to make a number of other decisions. Specifically, the company has to set up systems for sales-force recruiting and selecting, training, supervising, and evaluating.

Importance of Careful Selection At the heart of a successful sales-force operation is the selection of effective sales representatives. The performance levels of an average and a top sales representative are quite different. A survey of over five hundred companies revealed that 27% of the sales force brought in over 52% of the sales.[8] Beyond the differences in sales productivity are the great wastes in hiring the wrong people. Of the sixteen thousand sales representatives who were hired by the surveyed companies, only 68% still worked for the company at the end of the year, and only 50% of these were expected to remain throughout the following year.

What Makes a Good Sales Representative? Selecting sales representatives would not be a problem if one knew what traits to look for. If effective sales representatives are outgoing, aggressive, and energetic, these characteristics could be checked in applicants. But many successful sales representatives are introverted, mild-mannered, and far from energetic. Successful sales representatives include men and women who are tall and short, articulate and inarticulate, well groomed and slovenly.

Nevertheless the search continues for the magic combination of traits that spells surefire sales ability. Many lists have been drawn up. McMurry wrote: "It is my conviction that the possessor of an *effective* sales personality is a *habitual 'wooer,' an individual who has a compulsive need to win and hold the affection of others.*"[9] McMurry listed five additional traits of the super sales representative: "A high level of energy, abounding self-confidence, a chronic hunger for money, a well-established habit of industry, and a state of mind that regards each objection, resistance, or obstacle as a challenge."[10]

Mayer and Greenberg offered one of the shortest lists.[11] They concluded that the effective sales representative has at least two basic qualities: (1) empathy, the ability to feel as the customer does; and (2) ego drive, a strong personal need to make the sale. These two traits led in predicting good subsequent performance of applicants for sales positions in three different industries.

Recruitment Procedures After management has developed its selection criteria, it must recruit. The personnel department seeks applicants by various means, which include getting names from current sales representatives, using employment agencies, placing job ads, and contacting college students. Recruiting, if successful, will attract many applicants, and the company will need to select the best ones. The selection procedures can vary from a single informal interview to prolonged testing and interviewing, not only of the applicant but also of the applicant's family.

Many companies give formal tests to sales applicants. Although test scores are only one information element in a set that includes personal characteristics, references, past employment history, and interviewer reactions, they are weighted quite heavily by such companies as IBM, Prudential, Procter & Gamble, and Gillette. Gillette claims that tests have reduced turnover by 42% and have predicted the subsequent progress of new sales representatives in the sales organization.

Training Sales Representatives

Many companies used to send their new sales representatives into the field almost immediately after hiring them. They would be supplied with samples, order books, and instructions to sell west of the Mississippi. Training programs were luxuries. A training program meant making large outlays for instructors, materials, and space; paying a person who was not yet selling; and losing opportunities because he or she was not in the field.

Today's new sales representatives may spend a few weeks to several months in training. The average training period is twenty-eight weeks in industrial-products companies, twelve in service companies, and four in consumer-products companies.[12] At IBM, new sales representatives are not on their own for two years! And IBM expects its sales representatives to spend 15% of their time each year in additional training.

The training programs have several goals:

Most companies today have formal training programs for sales representatives and sales managers.

Paul Sequeira/Photo Researchers

1. *Sales representatives need to know and identify with the company*. Most companies devote the first part of the training program to describing the company's history and objectives, the organization and lines of authority, the chief officers, the company's financial structure and facilities, and the chief products and sales volume.

2. *Sales representatives need to know the company's products.* Sales trainees are shown how the products are produced and how they function in various uses.

3. *Sales representatives need to know customers' and competitors' characteristics.* Sales representatives learn about the different types of customers and their needs, buying motives, and buying habits. They learn about the company's and competitors' strategies and policies.

4. *Sales representatives need to know how to make effective sales presentations.* Sales representatives receive training in the principles of salesmanship. In addition, the company outlines the major sales arguments for each product, and some provide a sales script.

5. *Sales representatives need to understand field procedures and responsibilities.* Sales representatives learn how to divide time between active and potential accounts; how to use the expense account, prepare reports, and route effectively.

Principles of Salesmanship Many sales representatives do not know how to sell (see exhibit 16-2). One of the major objectives of sales training programs is to train sales representatives in the art of selling. Companies spend hundreds of millions of dollars for seminars, books, cassettes, and other materials. Almost a million copies of books on selling are purchased every year, with such tantalizing titles as *How to Outsell the Born Salesman, How to Sell Anything to Anybody, The Power of Enthusiastic Selling, How Power Selling Brought Me Success in 6 Hours, Where Do You Go from No. 1,* and *1000 Ways a Salesman Can Increase His Sales.* One of the most enduring books is Dale Carnegie's *How to Win Friends and Influence People.*

All of the sales training approaches try to convert a sales representative from being a passive order taker to being an active order getter. *Order takers* operate on the following assumptions: (1) Customers know their needs; (2) they would resent any attempt at influence; and (3) they prefer sales representatives who are courteous and self-effacing. An example of order taking is a Fuller Brush sales representative who knocks on dozens of doors each day, simply asking if the consumer needs any brushes.

In training salespeople to be order getters, there are two basic approaches, a sales-oriented approach and a customer-oriented approach. The first one trains the salesperson in high-pressure selling techniques, such as those used in selling encyclopedias and automobiles. The techniques include overstating the product's merits, criticizing competitive products, using a slick canned presentation, selling yourself, and offering some concession to get the order on the spot. This form of selling assumes that (1) the customers are not likely to buy except under pressure; (2) they are influenced by a slick presentation and ingratiating manner; and (3) they will not be sorry after signing the order, or if they are, it doesn't matter.

The other approach trains sales personnel in customer problem solving. The salesperson learns how to identify customer needs and propose effective solutions. This approach assumes that (1) customers have hidden needs that constitute company opportunities; (2) they appreciate good suggestions; and (3) they will be loyal to sales representatives who have their long-term interests at heart.

Exhibit **16-2**

How Well Trained Are Sales Reps?

A vice-president of a major food company spent one week watching fifty sales presentations to a busy buyer for a major supermarket chain. Here are some of his reactions:

- I watched a soap company representative come in to the buyer. He had three separate new promotional deals to talk about with six different dates. He had nothing in writing. . . . After the salesman left, the buyer looked at me and said, "It will take me 15 minutes to get this straightened out."
- I watched another salesman walk in to the buyer and say, "Well, I was in the area, and I want you to know that we have a great new promotion coming up next week." The buyer said, "That's fine. What is it?" He said, "I don't know. . . . I'm coming in next week to tell you about it." The buyer asked him what he was doing there today. He said, "Well, I was in the area."
- Another salesman came and said, "Well, it's time for us to write that order now . . . getting ready for the summer business." The buyer said, "Well, fine, George, how much did I buy last year in total?" The salesman looked a little dumbfounded and said, "Well, I'll be damned if I know. . . ."
- The majority of salesmen were ill-prepared, unable to answer basic questions, uncertain as to what they wanted to accomplish during the call. They did not think of the call as a studied, professional presentation. They didn't have a real idea of the busy retailer's needs and wants.

Source: From an address given by Donald R. Keough at the Twenty-seventh Annual Conference of the Super-Market Institute in Chicago, April 26–29, 1964.

Under the marketing concept, the problem solver is a more compatible image for the sales representative than the hard seller or order taker.

Most sales training programs view the **selling process** as consisting of several steps that the sales representative must master. These steps are shown in figure 16-2 and are discussed below.[13]

PROSPECTING AND QUALIFYING. The first step in the selling process is to identify prospects. Although the company supplies leads, sales representatives need skill in developing their own leads. Leads can be developed in the following ways: (1) asking current customers for the names of prospects; (2) cultivating other referral sources, such as suppliers, dealers, noncompeting sales representatives, bankers, and trade association executives; (3) joining organizations to which prospects belong; (4) engaging in speaking and writing activities that will draw attention; (5) examining data sources (newspapers, directories) in search of names; (6) using the telephone and mail to track down leads; and (7) dropping in unannounced on various offices.

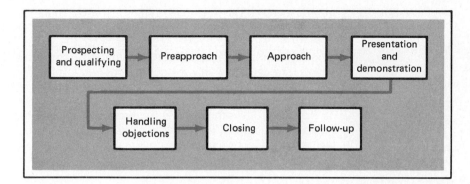

FIGURE 16-2
Major Steps in
Effective Selling

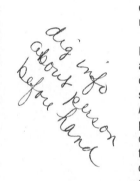

Sales representatives need to know how to screen out poor leads. Prospects can be qualified by examining their financial ability, volume of business, special requirements, location, and likelihood of continuous business.

PREAPPROACH. The sales representative should learn as much as possible about the prospect company (what it needs, who is involved in the purchase decision) and its buyers (their personal characteristics and buying styles). The sales representative can consult standard sources (*Moody's, Standard and Poor's, Dun and Bradstreet*), acquaintances, and others to learn about the company. The sales representative should set call objectives, which might be to qualify the prospect, or gather information, or make an immediate sale. Another task is to decide on the best approach, which might be a personal visit, a phone call, or a letter. The best timing should be thought out because many prospects are busy at certain times. Finally, the sales representative should give thought to an overall sales strategy for the account.

APPROACH. The sales representative should know how to meet and greet the buyer to get the relationship off to a good start. This involves the sales representative's appearance, the opening lines, and the follow-up remarks. The sales representative should wear clothes similar to what the buyer wears; show courtesy and attention to the buyer; and avoid distracting mannerisms, such as pacing the floor or staring at the customer. The opening lines should be positive, such as "Mr. Smith, I am Bill Jones from the ABC Company. My company and I appreciate your willingness to see me. I will do my best to make this visit profitable and worthwhile for you and your company." This might be followed by some key questions or the showing of a display or sample to attract the buyer's attention and curiosity.

PRESENTATION AND DEMONSTRATION. The sales representative now tells the product "story" to the buyer, showing how the product will make or save money. The sales representative describes the product features but concentrates on selling the customer benefits. The sales representative will follow the AIDA formula of getting *attention,* holding *interest,* arousing *desire,* and obtaining *action.*

Companies use three styles of sales presentation. The oldest is the *canned*

A Johnson & Johnson sales representative can describe how his company's products will solve problems for this dentist's patients.

Courtesy Johnson & Johnson

approach, which is a memorized sales talk covering the main points. An encyclopedia sales representative might describe the encyclopedia as "a once-in-a-lifetime buying opportunity" and focus on some beautiful four-color pages of sports pictures, hoping to trigger desire for the encyclopedia. Canned presentations are used primarily in door-to-door and telephone selling.

The *formulated approach* first identifies the buyer's needs and buying style and then uses a formulated approach to this type of buyer. The sales representative initially draws the buyer into a discussion in a way that indicates the buyer's needs and attitudes. Then the sales representative moves into a formulated presentation that shows how the product will satisfy that buyer's needs.

The *need-satisfaction approach* starts with a search for the customer's real needs by encouraging the customer to do most of the talking. This approach calls for good listening and problem-solving skills. It is well described by an IBM sales representative: "I get inside the business of my key accounts. I uncover their key problems. I prescribe solutions for them, using my company's systems and even, at times, components from other suppliers. I prove beforehand that my systems will save money or make money for my accounts. Then I work with the account to install the system and make it prove out."[14]

Sales presentations can be improved with demonstration aids, such as booklets, flip charts, slides, movies, and actual product samples. To the extent that the buyer can see or handle the product, he or she will better remember its features and benefits.

HANDLING OBJECTIONS. Customers almost always pose objections during the presentation or when asked to place an order. Their resistance can be psychological or logical. To handle objections, the sales representative maintains a positive approach, asks the buyer to clarify the objection, questions the buyer in such a way that the buyer has to answer his or her own objection, denies the validity of the objection, or turns the objection into a reason for buying.

CLOSING. The sales representative now attempts to close the sale. Some sales representatives do not get to this stage or do not handle it well. They lack confidence, or feel guilty about asking for the order, or do not recognize the right psychological moment to close the sale. Sales representatives need to know how to recognize closing signals from the buyer, including physical actions, statements or comments, and questions. Sales representatives can use one of several closing techniques. They can ask for the order, go over the points of the agreement, offer to help the office personnel write up the order, ask whether the buyer wants A or B, get the buyer to make minor choices such as the color or size, or indicate what the buyer will lose if the order is not placed now. The sales representative may offer the buyer specific inducements, such as a special price, an extra quantity at no charge, or a gift.

FOLLOW-UP. This last step is necessary if the sales representative wants to ensure customer satisfaction and repeat business. Immediately after closing the sale, the sales representative should complete any necessary details on delivery time, purchase terms, and other matters. The sales representative should schedule a follow-up call when the initial order is received to make sure there is proper installation, instruction, and servicing. This visit would detect any problems and assure the buyer of the sales representative's interest.

Supervising Sales Representatives

New sales representatives are given more than a territory, a compensation package, and training—they are given supervision. Through supervision, employers hope to direct and motivate the sales force to do a better job.

Directing Sales Representatives Companies vary in how closely they supervise their sales representatives. Sales representatives who are paid mostly on commission and who are expected to hunt down their own prospects are generally left on their own. Those who are salaried and must cover definite accounts are likely to be closely supervised.

DEVELOPING CUSTOMER TARGETS AND CALL NORMS. Most companies classify customers into A, B, and C accounts, reflecting the account's sales volume, profit potential, and growth potential. They establish the desired number of calls per period on each account class. Thus, A accounts may receive nine calls a year; B, six calls; and C, three calls.

DEVELOPING PROSPECT TARGETS AND CALL NORMS. Companies often specify how much time their sales force should spend prospecting for new accounts. Spector Freight, for example, wants its sales representatives to spend 25% of their time prospecting and to stop calling on a prospect after three unsuccessful calls.

Companies set up prospecting standards for a number of reasons. If left alone, many sales representatives will spend most of their time with current customers. Current customers are better-known quantities. Sales representatives can depend on them for some business, whereas a prospect may never deliver any business. Unless sales representatives are rewarded for opening new accounts, they may avoid new-account development.

USING SALES TIME EFFICIENTLY. Sales representatives need to know how to use their time efficiently. One tool is the annual call schedule that shows which customers and prospects to call on in which months, and which activities to carry out. The activities include participating in trade shows, attending sales meetings, and carrying out marketing research projects.

The other tool is time-and-duty analysis. The sales representative spends time traveling, eating and taking breaks, waiting, selling, and doing administrative chores. The actual selling time may be as little as 15% of total working time! If it could be raised from 15% to 20%, this would be a 33% improvement. Companies are constantly seeking more time-effective methods. This takes the form of training sales representatives in the use of "phone power," simplifying the record-keeping forms, using the computer to develop call and routing plans, and supplying marketing research reports on customers.

Motivating Sales Representatives   Some sales representatives will do their best without any special coaching from management. To them, selling is the most fascinating job in the world. They are ambitious and self-starters. But most sales representatives require encouragement and special incentives to work at their best level. Management can influence the sales force's morale and performance through its organizational climate, sales quotas, and positive incentives.

ORGANIZATIONAL CLIMATE.   Organizational climate describes the feeling that sales representatives get regarding their opportunities, value, and rewards for a good performance. Some companies treat sales representatives as if they were of minor importance. Other companies treat their sales representatives as the prime movers and allow unlimited opportunity for income and promotion. The company's attitude toward its sales representatives acts as a self-fulfilling prophecy. If they are held in low esteem, there is much turnover and poor performance; if they are held in high esteem, there is little turnover and high performance.

The personal treatment from the sales representative's immediate supervisor is an important aspect of organizational climate. An effective sales manager keeps in touch with the sales force through correspondence and phone calls, personal visits in the field, and evaluation sessions in the home office. At different times the sales manager acts as the sales representative's boss, companion, coach, and confessor.

SALES QUOTAS.   Many companies set sales quotas for their sales representatives, specifying what they should sell during the year by product. Their compensation is often related to how well they fill their quotas.

Sales quotas are developed in the process of developing the annual marketing plan. The company first decides on a sales forecast that is reasonably achievable. This becomes the basis for planning production, work-force size, and financial requirements. Then management establishes sales quotas for its regions and territories that typically add up to more than the sales forecast. Sales quotas are set higher than the sales forecast in order to stretch the sales managers and sales representatives to their best effort. If they fail to make their quotas, the company may still make its sales forecast.

POSITIVE INCENTIVES.   Companies use several incentives to stimulate sales-force effort. Periodic sales meetings provide a social occasion, a break from routine, a chance to meet and talk with "company brass," and a chance to air feelings and to identify with a larger group. Companies also sponsor sales contests to spur the sales force to a special selling effort above what would normally be expected. Other motivators include honors, awards, and profit-sharing plans.

Evaluating Sales Representatives

We have been describing how management communicates what the sales representatives should be doing and motivates them to do it. But there is more to sales management. Managers must get regular information from sales representatives to evaluate their performance.

Exhibit **16-3**

Personal Selling and Public Policy

Sales representatives must follow the rules of "fair competition" in trying to obtain orders. Certain activities are illegal or heavily regulated. Sales representatives are to refrain from offering bribes to buyers, purchasing agents, or other influence sources. It is illegal to get technical or trade secrets of competitors through espionage or bribery. They must not disparage competitors or their products by suggesting things that are not true. They must not sell used items as new or mislead the customer about the buying advantages. They must inform customers of their rights, such as the 72-hour "cooling-off" period in which customers can return merchandise and receive their money back. They must not discriminate against buyers on the basis of their race, sex, or creed.

Source: Adapted from Ovid Riso, ed., *The Dartnell Sales Manager's Handbook,* 11th ed. (Chicago: Dartnell Corporation, 1968), pp. 320–22.

Sources of Information Management obtains information about its sales representatives in several ways. The most important source is sales reports. These include plans for future activities and reports on the number and productivity of sales calls. Additional information comes through personal observation, customers' letters and complaints, customer surveys, and conversations with other sales representatives.

Formal Evaluation of Performance The sales reports, along with other reports and observations, supply the raw materials for evaluating members of the sales force. Formal evaluation leads to at least three benefits. First, management has to develop and communicate clear standards for judging sales performance. Second, management is motivated to gather well-rounded information about each sales representative. And third, sales representatives know they will have to sit down one morning with the sales manager and explain their performance or failure to achieve certain goals.

COMPARING SALES REPRESENTATIVES' PERFORMANCE. One type of evaluation is to compare and rank the sales performance of the various sales representatives. Such comparisons, however, can be misleading. Relative sales performances are significant only if there are no variations in territory market potential, workload, degree of competition, company promotional effort, and so forth. Furthermore, sales are not the indicator of achievement. Management should be more interested in how much each sales representative contributes to net profits. And this requires examining each sales representative's sales mix and sales expenses.

COMPARING CURRENT SALES WITH PAST SALES. A second type of evaluation is to compare a sales representative's current performance with his or her past performance. This should provide a direct indication of progress. The comparison can show how profits and sales have increased (or decreased) over the years for that particular sales representative. It can also show the sales representative's record on making sales calls and developing new customers.

QUALITATIVE EVALUATION OF SALES REPRESENTATIVES. The evaluation usually includes the sales representative's knowledge of the company, products, customers, competitors, territory, and responsibilities. Personality characteristics can be rated, such as general manner, appearance, speech, and temperament. The sales manager can also review any problems in motivation or compliance. The sales manager should check to make sure that the sales representative knows the law (see exhibit 16-3). Each company must decide what would be most useful to know. It should communicate these criteria to sales representatives so that they understand how their performance is judged and can make an effort to improve it.

Summary

Most companies use sales representatives, and many companies assign them the key role in the marketing mix. The high cost of this resource calls for an effective process of sales management consisting of six steps: establishing sales-force objectives; designing sales-force strategy, structure, size, and compensation; recruiting and selecting; training; supervising; and evaluating.

As an element of the marketing mix, the sales force is very effective in achieving certain marketing objectives and carrying on certain activities, such as prospecting, communicating, selling, servicing, information gathering, and allocating. Under the marketing concept, the sales force needs skills in marketing analysis and planning in addition to the traditional selling skills.

Once the sales-force objectives have been decided, sales-force strategy answers the questions of what type of selling would be most effective (solo selling, team selling, and so on), what type of sales-force structure would work best (territorial, product, or customer-structured), how large the sales force should be, and how the sales force should be compensated in terms of pay level and elements such as salary, commissions, bonuses, expenses, and fringe benefits.

Sales representatives must be recruited and selected carefully to hold down the high costs of hiring the wrong people. Sales training programs familiarize new salespeople with the company's history, its products and policies, the characteristics of the customers and competitors, and the art of selling. The art of selling involves a seven-step sales process: prospecting and qualifying, preapproach, approach, presentation and demonstration, handling objections, closing, and follow-up. Sales representatives need supervision and continuous encouragement because they must make many decisions and are subject to many frustrations. Periodically, the company must evaluate their performance to help them do a better job.

Questions for Discussion

1. How does personal selling differ from advertising?
2. Relate the six tasks of selling to an automobile sales representative.
3. In what alternative ways can a sales force be structured? Relate each to a specific company that sells industrial products.
4. A combination of straight salary and commission is probably the best way to compensate a sales force. Comment.
5. What two personal qualities do you think are most important to a successful sales representative? Why?
6. You have just been hired by World Book Encyclopedia Company to be a sales representative for the summer. Discuss how you would progress through the steps in effective selling.
7. What major tasks must those who supervise sales representatives undertake?
8. How would your manager in question 6 go about evaluating your selling job for World Book at the end of the summer?

Key Terms in Chapter 16

Customer-structured sales force An organizational structure for a sales force based on customer needs and on customer, industry, or market specialization.

Product-structured sales force An organizational structure for a sales force based on product lines.

Sales representative An individual acting for a company who performs one or more of the following activities: prospecting, communicating, selling, servicing, information gathering, and allocating.

Selling process The steps a sales representative follows when selling, which include prospecting and qualifying, preapproach, approach, presentation and demonstration, handling objections, closing, and follow-up.

Territorial-structured sales force An organizational structure for a sales force based on a geographic area.

Case for Chapter 16

Case 14   Purex Industries, Inc. (p. 511)
Personal selling plays a key role in Purex's marketing strategy, as can be seen in this case.

Chapter 17

Strategy, Planning and Control

Objectives

After reading this chapter, you should be able to:

1. Describe how companies develop mission statements and objectives.
2. Name and define three company growth strategies.
3. List and describe the parts of a marketing plan.
4. Explain the three ways in which companies control their marketing plans.

United Bank (a fictitious name) is a major Chicago bank engaged in retail and commercial banking. The latter is handled by its commercial department, which is divided into separate industry groups such as transportation, communication, utilities, and small manufacturers.

The bank's transportation group deals with airlines, trucking firms, railroads, bus companies, and barge companies. For twenty years it was headed by a lending officer who was considered a successful manager. His group increased the bank's loans to the transportation industry by 5% to 15% annually. He did not operate from a plan but instead encouraged his staff to spend a lot of time with transportation executives and seize opportunities as they arose. When his staff's performance occasionally slipped, he put pressure on them to go after business more aggressively.

After the officer retired, the bank appointed a younger man with an M.B.A. degree. He approached the job very differently. He asked the bank's marketing research department to estimate the total loans made by all area banks to transportation companies; the marketing strategies and market shares of the banks competing for this business; and the major financial needs of transportation companies in the future. One of the major findings was that this bank was realizing less than 50% of its sales potential in this market. The new lending officer then designed a planning and control system that called for setting goals, strategies, and action programs for different market segments within transportation. He assigned market segment managers who were responsible for developing market segment plans and controls. As a result of the marketing planning and control system, the new lending officer doubled the bank's outstanding loans to the transportation industry in two years.

FIGURE 17-1

The Relationship between Planning, Organization, and Control

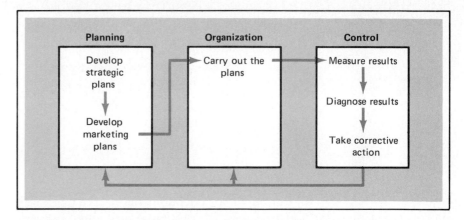

Clearly, many companies need to improve their formal planning and control systems. Making various, continuous decisions is not the same as planning. Planning is a higher-order company activity that often leads to improved sales and profit performance.

In this chapter we will examine how the components of the marketing mix are assembled into total plans and are carried out and controlled. The relationship between planning and control is shown in figure 17-1.

Planning consists of two parts—strategic planning and marketing planning.

Control consists of measuring and diagnosing the results of the strategic and marketing plans and taking corrective action.

The plans are carried out by the marketing organization. (Organizational structure is discussed in chapter 2.)

Strategic Planning

Many companies operate without formal plans. In new companies, managers are so busy that they have no time for planning. In mature companies, many managers argue that they have done well without formal planning and therefore it cannot be too important. They resist taking the time to prepare a written plan. They argue that the marketplace changes too fast for a plan to be useful—it would end up collecting dust. For these and other reasons, many companies have not introduced formal planning systems.

Yet, formal planning can yield a number of benefits. Melville Branch lists these benefits as follows: (1) Planning encourages systematic thinking ahead by management; (2) it leads to a better coordination of company efforts; (3) it leads to the development of performance standards for control; (4) it causes the company to sharpen its objectives and policies; (5) it makes the company better prepared for sudden developments; (6) it brings about a more vivid sense in the participating executives of their interacting responsibilities.[1]

Since strategic planning sets the stage for the rest of the planning in the firm, we turn to it first. We define strategic planning as follows:

> **Strategic planning** is the managerial process of developing and maintaining a strategic fit between the organization's goals and capabilities and its changing marketing opportunities. It relies on developing a clear company mission, supporting objectives and goals, a sound business portfolio, and a growth strategy.

The steps in strategic planning are illustrated in figure 17-2 and discussed below.

Company Mission

An organization exists to accomplish something in the larger environment. Its specific purpose or mission is usually clear at the beginning. Over time, its mission may become unclear as the organization grows and adds new products and markets. Or the mission may remain clear but some managers may no longer be interested in it. Or the mission may remain clear but may no longer be appropriate to the new conditions in the environment.

When management senses that the organization is drifting, it must renew its search for purpose. It is time to ask:[2] "What is our business? Who is the customer? What is value to the customer? What will our business be? What should our business be? These simple-sounding questions are among the most difficult the company will ever have to answer. Successful companies continuously raise these questions and answer them thoughtfully and thoroughly.

Many organizations develop formal mission statements to answer these questions. A well-worked-out mission statement provides corporate personnel with a shared sense of opportunity, direction, significance, and achievement. The mission statement should define the business domain(s) in which the organization will operate. Business domains can be defined in terms of products, technologies, customer groups, customer needs, or some combination. Companies have traditionally defined their business domain in product terms, such as "We manufacture slide rules," or in technological terms, such as "We are a chemical-processing firm." Some years ago, Theodore Levitt proposed that market-oriented definitions of a business are superior to product or technological definitions of a business.[3] He argued that a business must be viewed as a

FIGURE 17-2

Steps in Strategic Planning

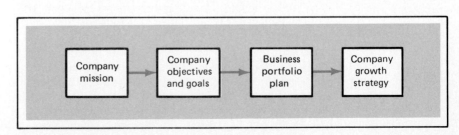

FIGURE 17-3

Successive
Expansion of a Prune
Company

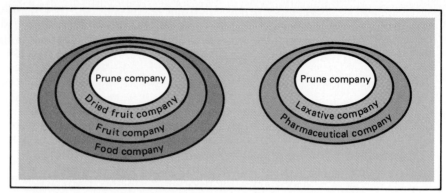

customer-satisfying process, not a goods-producing process. Products and technologies eventually become obsolete, whereas basic market needs may endure forever. Thus, a slide rule manufacturer will go out of business as soon as electronic calculators appear unless the manufacturer defines its business as meeting calculation needs, not making slide rules. A market-oriented mission statement defines the business in terms of serving particular customer groups and/or needs.

In developing a market-oriented statement of mission, management should avoid making its mission too narrow or too broad. A lead pencil manufacturer that says it is in the business of making communication equipment is stating its mission too broadly. A useful approach is to move from the current product to higher levels of business opportunities and then decide on the most workable opportunities available to the company. Figure 17-3 shows a prune company's options. A prune company can see itself as a dried fruit company, a fruit company, or, ultimately, a food company. Alternatively, it can see itself as a laxative company or, ultimately, a pharmaceutical company. Each broadening step suggests new opportunities but may also lead the company into unrealistic business ventures beyond its capabilities.

Company Objectives and Goals

The company's mission needs to be turned into a detailed set of supporting objectives for each level of management. Each manager should have objectives and be responsible for their accomplishment. This system is known as *management by objectives.*

As an illustration, the International Minerals and Chemical Corporation is in several businesses, including the fertilizer business. The fertilizer division does not say that its mission is to produce fertilizer. Instead, it says that its mission is "to fight world hunger." This mission leads to a definite hierarchy of objectives (see figure 17-4).[4] The mission to fight world hunger leads to the company objective of increasing agricultural productivity. Agricultural productivity can be increased by researching new fertilizers that promise higher yields. But research is expensive and requires improved profits to plow back into research programs. So a major objective becomes profit improvement.

Profits can be improved by increasing the sales of current products, reducing current costs, or both. Sales can be increased by increasing the company's market share in the domestic market and entering new foreign markets. These become the company's current marketing objectives.

Marketing strategies must be developed to support these marketing objectives. To increase its domestic market share, the company will increase its product's availability and promotion. To enter new foreign markets, the company will cut prices and call on large farms. These are the broad marketing strategies.

Each marketing strategy would have to be spelled out in greater detail. For example, increasing the product's promotion will call for more salespeople and advertising, both of which will have detailed strategies. In this way the firm's mission is translated into a specific set of objectives for the current period.

The objectives should be turned into specific measurable goals where possible. The objective to "increase market share" is not as good as "increase market share to 15% by the end of the second year." Managers use the term *goals* to describe objectives that have been made specific with respect to size and time. Turning objectives into goals makes it easier to plan and control.

Business Portfolio Plan The major tool in strategic planning is business portfolio analysis. This involves management evaluating its portfolio, or the businesses making up the company. A "business" can be a company division, a product line, or a single product or brand.

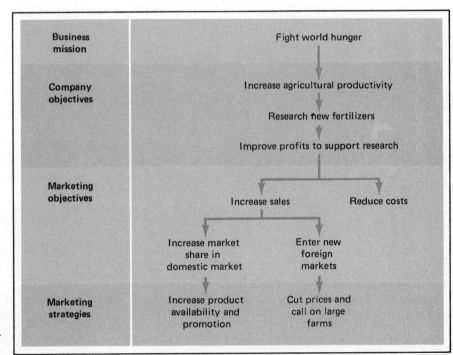

FIGURE 17-4

Hierarchy of Objectives for the International Minerals and Chemical Corporation, Fertilizer Division

The analysis itself calls for determining which are the company's more profitable or weaker businesses and deciding what to do with each of them. The company will want to put strong resources into its more profitable businesses and phase down or withdraw from its weaker businesses. It can keep its portfolio of businesses up to date by strengthening or adding growing businesses and withdrawing from declining businesses.

For example, General Electric has an approach to business portfolio analysis that includes looking at several factors in two areas. To evaluate the attractiveness of a specific industry, it looks at market size, market growth rate, profit margin, intensity of competition, cyclicality and seasonality, and falling unit costs based on large-scale production or accumulated experience on the part of management. General Electric looks at business strength in terms of relative market share, price competitiveness, product quality, the company's knowledge of its market, sales effectiveness, and geographic advantages. The best businesses are those that have strengths in these areas; the worst are those that have weaknesses. On the basis of its analysis, General Electric will allocate its resources among its businesses.

Company Growth Strategy

Beyond evaluating current businesses, strategic planning must determine future businesses and business directions that the company should consider. We will illustrate company growth planning with the following illustration:

> Modern Publishing Company issues a leading health magazine that has a monthly circulation of three hundred thousand copies. The company's marketing environment is changing rapidly in terms of consumer interests, new competitors, and rising publishing costs. It is attempting to draw up a systematic plan for company growth during the next decade.

A company can develop a growth strategy by moving through three levels of analysis. The first level identifies opportunities available to the company within its current scope of operations (**intensive growth** opportunities). The second level identifies opportunities to integrate with other parts of the marketing system in the industry (**integrative growth** opportunities). The third level identifies opportunities lying outside the industry (**diversification growth** opportunities). Table 17-1 lists specific opportunities within each broad class.

Table 17-1

Major Classes of Growth Opportunities

INTENSIVE GROWTH	INTEGRATIVE GROWTH	DIVERSIFICATION GROWTH
Market Penetration	Backward Integration	Concentric Diversification
Market Development	Forward Integration	Horizontal Diversification
Product Development	Horizontal Integration	Conglomerate Diversification

INTENSIVE GROWTH. Intensive growth makes sense if the company has not fully exploited the opportunities in its current products and markets. Ansoff has proposed a useful device called a *product/market expansion grid* for identifying intensive growth opportunities.[5] This grid, shown earlier in chapter 2, p. 33, points out three major types of intensive growth opportunities.

1. **Market penetration** consists of the company's seeking increased sales for its current products in its current markets through more aggressive marketing. Modern Publishing can:
   a. Encourage current subscribers to increase their purchase quantity by giving gift subscriptions to friends.
   b. Try to attract competitors' customers by offering lower subscription rates or promoting its magazine as being superior to other health magazines.
   c. Try to convert new prospects who do not now read health magazines but have the same profile as current readers.
2. **Market development** consists of the company's seeking increased sales by taking its current products into new markets. Modern Publishing can:
   a. Distribute its magazine in new geographic markets—regional, national, or international—where it has not been available.
   b. Make the magazine attractive to new consumer segments by developing appropriate features.
   c. Try to sell its magazine to new institutional segments, such as hospitals, physicians' offices, and health clubs.
3. **Product development** consists of the company's seeking increased sales by developing new or improved products for its current markets. Modern Publishing can:
   a. Develop new and different magazines that will appeal to the readers of its health magazine.
   b. Create different regional versions of its health magazine.
   c. Develop a cassette version of its monthly magazine for markets that prefer listening to reading.

INTEGRATIVE GROWTH. Integrative growth makes sense if the industry is strong and/or the company can gain by moving backward, forward, or horizontally in the industry. **Backward integration** consists of the company's seeking ownership or increased control of its supply systems. Modern Publishing might buy a paper supply company or a printing company to increase its control over supplies. **Forward integration** consists of a company's seeking ownership or increased control of its distribution system. Modern Publishing might see an advantage in buying some magazine wholesaler businesses or subscription agencies. **Horizontal integration** consists of the company's seeking ownership or increased control of some of its competitors. Modern Publishing might buy out other health magazines.

DIVERSIFICATION GROWTH. Diversification growth makes sense if the industry does not present much opportunity for further company growth, or if the opportunities outside the industry are superior. Diversification does not mean

Diversification is one form of company growth strategy.
Johnson & Johnson/Photo by Mark DeAngeli

that the company should take just any opportunity. The company would identify fields that make use of its expertise or help it overcome particular weaknesses. There are three types of diversification:

1. **Concentric diversification**, or adding new products that have technological and/or marketing similarities with the existing product lines. These products will normally appeal to new classes of customers. Modern Publishing, for example, might start a paperback division to take advantage of its network of magazine distributors.
2. **Horizontal diversification**, or adding new products that could appeal to its current customers although they are not related to its current product line. For example, Modern Publishing might open up health clubs in the hope that readers of its health magazine would become club members.
3. **Conglomerate diversification**, or adding new products that have no relationship to the company's current technology, products, or markets. These products will normally appeal to new classes of customers. Modern Publishing might want to enter new business areas, such as personal computers, real-estate office franchising, or fast-food service.

Marketing Planning

The company's strategic plan establishes the kinds of businesses that the company will be in and its objectives for each business. More detailed planning has to take place for each business. If the business consists of several product lines, products, brands, and markets, plans must be written for each of these. Thus we hear of business plans, product plans, brand plans, and market plans.

We will use the term *marketing plan* to describe all of these. We want to examine the major parts of marketing plans and the steps in developing the marketing budget.

The Parts of a Marketing Plan

How does a marketing plan look? Our discussion will focus on product or brand plans. A product or brand plan should contain the following sections: executive summary, current marketing situation, threats and opportunities, objectives and issues, marketing strategies, action programs, budgets, and controls (see figure 17-5).

EXECUTIVE SUMMARY. The plan should open with a short summary of the main goals and recommendations to be presented. Here is an example:

> The 1983 Marketing Plan seeks to generate a significant increase in company sales and profits over the preceding year. The sales target is set at $80 million, which represents a planned 20% sales gain. This increase is deemed attainable because of the improved economic, competitive, and distribution picture. The operating margin is forecasted at $8 million, which represents a 25% increase over last year. To achieve these goals, the sales promotion budget will be $1.6 million, which represents 2% of projected sales. The advertising budget will be $2.4 million, which represents 3% of projected sales. . . . [The continuation of the summary gives more details.]

The executive summary helps higher management to quickly grasp the major thrust of the plan. A table of contents should follow the executive summary.

CURRENT MARKETING SITUATION. The first major section of the plan describes the nature of the target market and the company's position in it. The marketing planner describes the market in terms of its size, major segments, customer needs, and special environmental factors; reviews the major products; identifies the competition; and defines the distribution channel.

THREATS AND OPPORTUNITIES. This section requires the manager to look ahead and visualize the major threats and opportunities facing the product. The

FIGURE 17-5

Components of a Marketing Plan

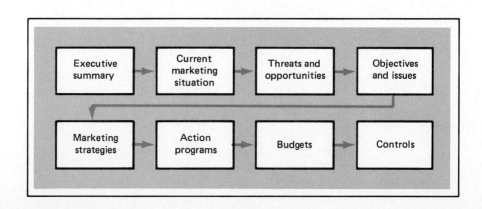

purpose is to make the manager anticipate important developments that can have a significant effect on the firm. Managers should list as many threats and opportunities as they can imagine. Suppose the manager at a cigarette company comes up with the following list:

1. The U.S. Surgeon General is asking Congress to pass a law requiring that every cigarette brand include a skull and crossbones on the front of the package and the warning: "Scientific evidence shows that daily smoking shortens a person's life by an average of seven years."
2. An increasing number of public places are prohibiting smoking or are setting up separate sections for smokers and nonsmokers.
3. A new insect is attacking tobacco-growing areas, leading to the possibility of smaller crops in the future and larger price increases if some means cannot be found to control it.
4. The company's research lab is on the verge of finding a way to turn lettuce into harmless tobacco. If successful, the new tobacco will be enjoyable and harmless.
5. Cigarette smoking is rapidly increasing in foreign markets, especially in developing nations.
6. Several groups are pressing for the legalization of marijuana so that it can be grown openly and sold through retail outlets.

Each item has implications for the cigarette business. The first three can be classified as threats, which can be defined as follows:

A **threat** is a challenge posed by an unfavorable trend or specific event that would lead, in the absence of purposeful marketing action, to product stagnation or demise.

The last three items in the list can be classified as company marketing opportunities, which can be defined as follows:

A **company marketing opportunity** is an attractive arena for company marketing action in which a particular company would enjoy a competitive advantage.

The manager should assess each threat and opportunity according to its potential for happening and the implications for the company.

OBJECTIVES AND ISSUES. Having studied the product's threats and opportunities, the manager is now in a position to set objectives and consider issues that will affect them. The objectives should be stated as goals that the company would like to reach during the plan's term. For example, the manager might want to achieve a 15% market share, a 20% pretax profit on sales, and a 25% pretax profit on investment. Suppose that the current market share is only 10%. This poses a key issue, namely, how can the market share be increased? The manager will want to consider the major issues involved in trying to increase market share.

MARKETING STRATEGIES. In this section, the manager outlines the broad marketing strategy or "game plan" for reaching the objectives. We define marketing strategy as follows:

> **Marketing strategy** is the marketing logic by which the business unit hopes to achieve its marketing objectives. Marketing strategy consists of specific strategies bearing on target markets, marketing mix, and marketing expenditure level.

Target markets. Marketing strategy should spell out the market segments on which the company will focus. These segments differ in their preferences, responses to marketing effort, and profitability. The company would be smart to concentrate its effort and energy on those market segments it can best serve from a competitive point of view. It should develop a marketing strategy for each targeted segment.

Marketing mix. The manager should outline specific strategies in regard to such marketing mix elements as new products, field sales, advertising, sales promotion, prices, and distribution. Reasons should be provided for each strategy that responds to the threats, opportunities, and key issues spelled out in earlier sections of the plan.

Marketing expenditure level. The manager should also spell out the marketing budget that will be needed to carry out the various marketing strategies. The manager knows that higher budgets will probably produce more sales but is looking for the marketing budget that will produce the best overall profit picture.

ACTION PROGRAMS. The marketing strategies should be turned into specific action programs that answer the following questions: (1) *What* will be done? (2) *When* will it be done? (3) *Who* is responsible for doing it? and (4) *How much* will it cost? For example, the manager may want to intensify sales promotion as a key strategy for winning market share. A sales promotion action plan should be drawn up and should outline special offers and their dates, trade shows participation, new point-of-purchase displays, and so on. The action plans are subject to change during the year as new problems and opportunities arise.

BUDGETS. The action plans allow the manager to make a supporting budget that is essentially a projected profit and loss statement. On the revenue side, it shows the forecasted number of items that would be sold and the average net price. On the expense side, it shows the cost of production, physical distribution, and marketing. The difference is the projected profit. Higher management will review the budget and approve or modify it. Once approved, the budget is the basis for buying materials, production scheduling, manpower planning, and marketing operations.

CONTROLS. The last section of the plan outlines the controls that will be applied to monitor the plan's progress. Typically, goals and budgets are spelled out for each month or quarter. This means that higher management can review the results each period and spot businesses that are not reaching their goals. The managers of these businesses have to offer an explanation and indicate what corrective actions they will take.

Developing the Marketing Budget   We will now examine the task of developing a marketing budget to reach a given level of sales and profits. We will first illustrate a common marketing budget-setting approach and then describe certain improvements.

TARGET PROFIT PLANNING.   Suppose John Smith, the ketchup product manager at Heinz, has to prepare his annual marketing plan. He will probably follow the procedure shown in table 17-2 called *target profit planning*. The steps in this procedure are as follows:

- Step 1: Smith starts by estimating the total market for ketchup for the coming year. The estimate is formed by applying the recent growth rate of the market (6%) to this year's market size (23,600,000 cases). This projects a market size of 25,000,000 cases for next year.
- Step 2: Smith forecasts Heinz's share of the ketchup market for the next year. In this case, he assumes that the past market share of 28% will continue.
- Step 3: Smith forecasts Heinz's sales for next year. The market share (28%) times the total market (25,000,000 cases) produces a forecast of 7,000,000 cases.
- Step 4: Smith sets a price to the distributor of $4.45 per case.
- Step 5: Smith can now calculate expected sales revenue for next year of $31,150,000. This figure is produced by multiplying the forecasted sales (7,000,000 cases) by the price per case ($4.45).
- Step 6: Smith estimates the variable costs at $2.75 per case. This figure is based on the costs of the following items: Tomatoes and spices ($.50) + bottles and caps ($1.00) + labor ($1.10) + physical distribution ($0.15).
- Step 7: By subtracting the variable costs ($2.75 per case) from the sales price ($4.45 per case) and multiplying that figure by the forecasted sales (7,000,000 cases), Smith can estimate the contribution margin to cover fixed costs, profits, and marketing. The figure is $11,900,000.
- Step 8: Smith estimates the fixed costs by multiplying the fixed charge per case of $1.00 by the 7,000,000 cases for a total of $7,000,000.
- Step 9: In step 7, Smith had estimated $11,900,000 as the contribution margin to cover fixed costs, profits, and marketing. By subtracting the fixed costs of $7,000,000 from that figure, Smith comes up with an estimate of $4,900,000 as the contribution margin to cover profits and marketing.
- Step 10: The estimated target profit goal for ketchup is $1,900,000.
- Step 11: Subtracting the target profit goal ($1,900,000) from the contribution margin to cover profits and marketing ($4,900,000) leaves $3,000,000 available for marketing.
- Step 12: Smith splits the $3,000,000 marketing budget into its mix elements, such as advertising, sales promotion, and marketing research. The split is normally in the same proportion as the preceding year's split, with two-thirds of the money for advertising, almost one-third on sales promotion, and the remainder on marketing research.

Table 17-2	
Target Profit Plan	
STEPS IN THE TARGET PROFIT PLAN	RESULT
1. Forecast of total market	25,000,000 cases
2. Forecast of market share	28%
3. Forecast of sales volume	7,000,000 cases
4. Price to distributor	$4.45 per case
5. Estimate of sales revenue	$31,150,000
6. Estimate of variable costs	$2.75 per case
7. Estimate of contribution margin to cover fixed costs, profits, and marketing	$11,900,000
8. Estimate of fixed costs	$7,000,000
9. Estimate of contribution margin to cover profits and marketing	$4,900,000
10. Estimate of target profit goal	$1,900,000
11. Amount available for marketing	$3,000,000
12. Split of the marketing budget:	
Advertising	$2,000,000
Sales Promotion	$ 900,000
Marketing Research	$ 100,000

PROFIT OPTIMIZATION PLANNING. Target profit planning produces satisfactory profits, but not necessarily top profits. We now want to consider how to find the optimal profit plan. Profit optimization requires that the manager identify the relationship between sales volume and the various elements of the marketing mix. We will use the term *sales response function* to describe the relationship between sales volume and one or more elements of the marketing mix.

> A **sales response function** forecasts the likely sales volume during a specified time period associated with different possible expenditure levels of one or more marketing mix elements.

Figure 17-6 shows a possible sales response function. This function indicates that the more the company spends in a given period on marketing, the higher its sales are likely to be. The particular function is S-shaped, although other shapes are possible. The S-shaped function shows that low levels of marketing expenditure ($100,000) are not likely to produce much sales. Too few buyers will be reached, or reached effectively, by the company's message. Higher levels of marketing expenditure ($200,000) will produce much higher levels of sales. Very high expenditures ($300,000), however, might not add much more sales and would represent "marketing overkill."

Sales diminish at very high levels of expenditure for a number of reasons. First, there is an upper limit to the total potential demand for any particular product. The easier sales prospects buy almost immediately, leaving the more difficult sales prospects. As the upper limit is approached, it becomes increasingly expensive to attract the remaining buyers. Second, as a company

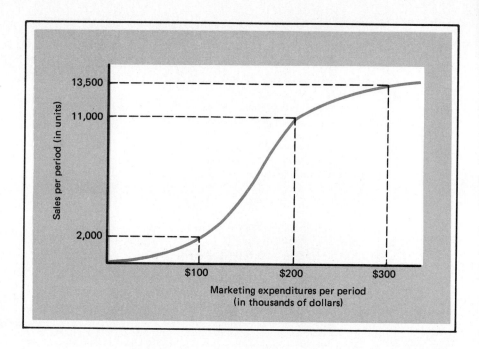

FIGURE 17-6

A Possible Sales
Response Function

steps up its marketing effort, its competitors are likely to do the same, with the result that each company experiences increasing sales resistance. And third, if sales were to increase at an increasing rate throughout, natural monopolies would result. A single firm would take over each industry. Yet this is not what happens.

How can marketing managers estimate the sales response functions that apply to their business? Three methods are available. The first is the *statistical method,* where the manager gathers data on past sales and levels of marketing mix variables and estimates the sales response functions through statistical techniques.[6] The second is the *experimental method,* which calls for varying the marketing expenditure and budget split in similar geographic or other units and noting the resulting sales volume.[7] The third is the *judgmental method,* where experts are asked to make intelligent guesses about the needed levels.[8]

Once the sales response functions have been estimated, how are they used in profit organizations? In figure 17-7, we introduce some more curves to find the point of optimal marketing expenditure. The key function that we start with is the sales response function. It resembles the S-shaped sales response function in figure 17-6 except for two differences. First, sales response is expressed in terms of sales dollars instead of sales units so that we can find the profit-maximizing marketing expenditure. Second, the sales response function is shown as starting above zero sales since some sales might take place even without any marketing expenditures.

To find the optimal marketing expenditure, the marketing manager subtracts all nonmarketing costs from the sales response function to come up with the gross profit function. Next, the marketing expenditure function is represented as

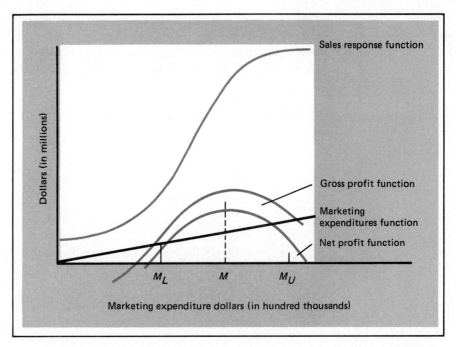

FIGURE 17-7

Relationship between Sales Volume, Marketing Expenditures, and Profits

a straight line starting at the origin and rising at the rate of one dollar of marketing expenditure on the horizontal axis for every $10 on the vertical axis. The marketing expenditure function is then subtracted from the gross profit function to come up with the net profit function. The net profit function shows positive net profits with marketing expenditures between M_L and M_U. This becomes the rational range of marketing expenditure. The net profit function reaches a maximum of M. Therefore the marketing expenditure that would maximize net profit is M.

The graphic solution can also be carried out numerically or algebraically; indeed, it has to be if sales volume is a function of more than one marketing mix variable.[9]

Marketing Control

Because many surprises will occur during the carrying out of marketing plans, the marketing department has to maintain constant control. Marketing control systems are essential in making sure that the company operates efficiently and effectively. Marketing control, however, is far from being a single process. Three types of marketing control can be distinguished (see table 17-3).

Annual plan control consists of marketing personnel's checking ongoing performance against the annual plan and taking corrective action when necessary. *Profitability control* consists of determining the actual profitability of different products, territories, market segments, and trade channels. *Strategic control*

Table 17-3			
Types of Marketing Control			
TYPE OF CONTROL	PRIME RESPONSIBILITY	PURPOSE OF CONTROL	APPROACHES
Annual plan control	Top management Middle management	To examine whether the planned results are being achieved	Sales analysis Market-share analysis Marketing expense-to-sales analysis Customer attitude tracking
Profitability control	Marketing controller	To examine where the company is making and losing money	Profitability by: Product Territory Market segment Trade channel Order size
Strategic control	Top management Marketing auditor	To examine whether the company is pursuing its best marketing opportunities and doing this efficiently	Marketing audit

consists of periodically examining whether the company's basic strategies are well matched to its opportunities. We now turn to these three types of marketing control.

Annual Plan Control The purpose of annual plan control is to ensure that the company achieves the sales, profits, and other goals established in its annual plan. Four steps are involved (see figure 17-8). First, management must state the monthly or quarterly goals in the annual plan. Second, management must measure its performance in the marketplace. Third, management must determine the causes of any seri-

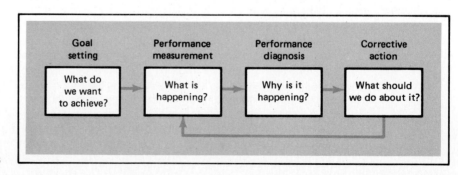

FIGURE 17-8
The Control Process

ous performance failures. Fourth, management must take corrective action to close the gaps between its goals and its performance. This may require changing the action programs, or even changing the goals.

What specific control tools are used by management to check on plan performance? The four main tools are sales analysis, market-share analysis, marketing expense-to-sales analysis, and customer attitude tracking. If one of these tools shows that the plan performance is inadequate, then corrective action is taken.

SALES ANALYSIS.   **Sales analysis** consists of measuring and evaluating actual sales in relation to sales goals. The company can start by looking at sales figures. Suppose the annual plan called for selling 4,000 widgets in the first quarter at $1 a widget, or $4,000. At quarter's end, only 3,000 widgets were sold at $0.80 a widget, or $2,400. Sales were $1,600, or 40% below expected sales. The company should look closely into why its expected sales volume was not achieved.[10]

The company can also look at whether specific products, territories, and so forth, produced their expected share of sales. Suppose the company sells in three territories and expected sales were 1,500 units, 500 units, and 2,000 units, respectively, adding up to 4,000 widgets. The actual sales volume was 1,400 units, 525 units, and 1,075 units, respectively. Thus, territory one fell short by 7%; territory two had a 5% surplus; and territory three fell short by 46%. Territory three is causing most of the trouble. The sales vice-president can check into territory three to see what is causing the poor performance.

MARKET-SHARE ANALYSIS.   Company sales do not reveal how well the company is doing relative to competitors. Suppose a company's sales increase. This could be due to improved economic conditions in which all companies gained. Or it could be due to improved company performance in relation to its competitors. Management needs to track the company's market share. If the company's market share goes up, it is gaining on competitors; if its market share goes down, it is losing to competitors.

MARKETING EXPENSE-TO-SALES ANALYSIS.   Annual plan control requires making sure that the company is not overspending to achieve its sales goals. Watching the ratio of marketing expense to sales will help keep marketing expenses in line.

CUSTOMER ATTITUDE TRACKING.   Alert companies use various systems to track the attitudes of customers, dealers, and other marketing system participants. By monitoring changing customer attitudes before they affect sales, management can take earlier action. The main customer attitude tracking systems are complaint and suggestion systems, customer panels, and customer surveys.[11]

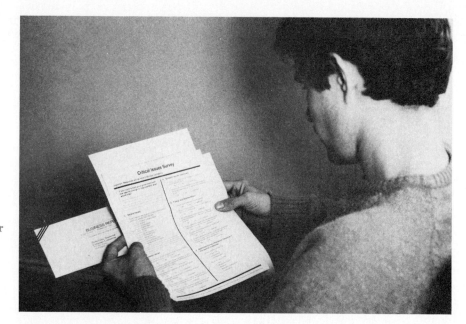

Surveys help companies monitor the attitudes of customers and other environmental forces.
Teri Leigh Stratford

CORRECTIVE ACTION. When actual performance varies too much from the annual plan goals, companies take corrective actions. Consider the following case:

> A larger fertilizer company's sales were lagging behind its goals. The industry was marked by excess capacity and rampant price cutting. In trying to save the situation, the company adopted a series of increasingly drastic actions: (1) The company ordered cutbacks in production. (2) The company began to cut its prices selectively. (3) The company put more pressure on its sales force to meet their quotas. The sales representatives started "beating down" doors, pressuring customers to buy more or buy before the end of the year. (4) The company cut the budgets for personnel hiring and training, advertising, public relations, charities, and research and development. (5) The company began to lay off, retire, or fire personnel. (6) The company undertook some fancy bookkeeping to produce a better picture. (7) The company began to cut its investment in plant and equipment. (8) The company decided to sell some of its product lines to other companies. (9) The company started to consider selling out or merging with another company.

Many companies find they can take less drastic actions to correct the variations from the annual plan.

Profitability Control Besides annual plan control, companies also need to measure the profitability of their various products, territories, market segments, trade channels, and order sizes. This information will help management determine whether any products or marketing activities should be expanded, reduced, or eliminated.[12] Consider the following example:

The marketing vice-president of a lawn mower company wants to determine the profitability of selling its lawn mower through three types of retail channels: hardware stores, garden supply shops, and department stores.

The first step involves identifying all the expenses involved in selling, advertising, packing, delivering, and billing for the product. The second step is to see how much of which expenses are involved in selling through each type of channel. Once the expenses are determined, the third step is to prepare a profit and loss statement for each channel. The company may find that it is actually losing money by selling through garden supply shops, that it just breaks even in hardware stores, and that it is making almost all of its money through department store sales.

DETERMINING THE BEST CORRECTIVE ACTION. It would be naive to conclude that garden supply shops and possibly hardware stores should be dropped in order to concentrate on department stores. The following questions would need to be answered first:

- To what extent do buyers buy on the basis of the type of retail outlet versus the brand? Would they seek out the brand in those channels that are not eliminated?
- What are the trends with respect to the importance of these three channels?
- Have company marketing strategies directed at the three channels been optimal?

On the basis of the answers, marketing management can evaluate a number of alternatives and then take action.

Strategic Control From time to time, companies must undertake a critical review of their overall marketing effectiveness. Marketing is an area where objectives, policies, strategies, and programs rapidly become obsolete. Each company should periodically reassess its overall approach to the marketplace, using the tool known as the marketing audit.[13] We define marketing audit as follows:

> A **marketing audit** is a comprehensive, systematic, independent, and periodic examination of a company's—or business unit's—marketing environment, objectives, strategies, and activities with a view to determining problem areas and opportunities and recommending a plan of action to improve the company's marketing performance.

The marketing auditor should be given free rein to interview managers, customers, dealers, sales representatives, and others who might throw light on the organization's marketing performance. Figure 17-9 is a guide to the kinds of questions that the marketing auditor will ask. Not all of these questions are important in every situation. The auditor will develop a set of findings and recommendations based on this information. The findings may come as a surprise, and sometimes a shock, to management. Management decides which recommendations make sense and how and when to implement them.

FIGURE 17-9
Parts of a Marketing Audit

PART I—MARKETING ENVIRONMENT AUDIT

The Macroenvironment

A. Demographic
   1. What major demographic developments and trends pose opportunities or threats to this company?
   2. What actions has the company taken in response to these developments and trends?

B. Economic
   1. What major developments in income, prices, savings, and credit will impact the company?
   2. What actions has the company been taking in response to these developments and trends?

C. Natural
   1. What is the outlook for the cost and availability of natural resources and energy needed by the company?
   2. What concerns have been expressed about the company's role in pollution and conservation, and what steps has the company taken?

D. Technological
   1. What major changes are occurring in product technology;? In process technology? What is the company's position in these technologies?
   2. What major generic substitutes might replace this product?

E. Political
   1. What laws now being proposed could affect marketing strategy and tactics?
   2. What federal, state, and local actions should be watched? What is happening in the areas of pollution control, equal employment opportunity, product safety, advertising, price control, and so forth, that affects marketing strategy?

F. Cultural
   1. What is the public's attitude toward business and toward the products produced by the company?
   2. What changes in consumer and business life-styles and values have a bearing on the company?

The Task Environment

A. Markets
   1. What is happening to market size, growth, geographic distribution, and profits?
   2. What are the major market segments?

B. Customers
   1. How do customers and prospects rate the company and its competitors on reputation, product quality, service, sales force, and price?
   2. How do different customer segments make their buying decisions?

C. Competitors
   1. Who are the major competitors? What are their objectives and strategies, their strengths and weaknesses, their sizes and market shares?
   2. What trends will affect future competition and substitutes for this product?

D. Distribution and Dealers
   1. What are the main trade channels for bringing products to customers?
   2. What are the efficiency levels and growth potentials of the different trade channels?

E. Suppliers
   1. What is the outlook for the availability of key resources used in production?
   2. What trends are occurring among suppliers in their pattern of selling?

F. Facilitators and Marketing Firms
   1. What is the cost and availability outlook for transportation services?
   2. What is the cost and availability outlook for warehousing facilities?
   3. What is the cost and availability outlook for financial resources?
   4. How effectively is the advertising agency performing?

G. Publics
   1. What publics represent particular opportunities or problems for the company?
   2. What steps has the company taken to deal effectively with each public?

PART II—MARKETING STRATEGY AUDIT

A. Business Mission
   1. Is the business mission clearly stated in market-oriented terms? Is it feasible?

B. Marketing Objectives and Goals
   1. Are the corporate and marketing objectives stated in the form of clear goals to guide marketing planning and performance measurement?
   2. Are the marketing objectives appropriate, given the company's competitive position, resources, and opportunities?

C. Strategy
   1. What is the core marketing strategy for achieving the objectives? Is it sound?
   2. Are enough resources (or too many resources) budgeted to accomplish the marketing objectives?
   3. Are the marketing resources allocated optimally to market segments, territories, and products?
   4. Are the marketing resources allocated optimally to the major elements of the marketing mix—such as product quality, service, sales force, advertising, promotion, and distribution?

PART III—MARKETING ORGANIZATION AUDIT

A. Formal Structure
   1. Does the marketing officer have adequate authority and responsibility over company activities that affect the customer's satisfaction?
   2. Are the marketing activities optimally structured along functional, product, end user, and territorial lines?

B. Functional Efficiency
   1. Are there good communication and working relations between marketing and sales?
   2. Is the product management system working effectively? Are product managers able to plan profits or only sales volume?
   3. Are there any groups in marketing that need more training, motivation, supervision, or evaluation?

C. Interface Efficiency
   1. Are there any problems between marketing and manufacturing, R&D, purchasing, or financial management that need attention?

PART IV—MARKETING SYSTEMS AUDIT

A. Marketing Information System
   1. Is the marketing intelligence system producing accurate, sufficient, and timely information about marketplace developments?
   2. Is marketing research being adequately used by company decision makers?

B. Marketing Planning System
   1. Is the marketing planning system well conceived and effective?
   2. Is sales forecasting and market potential measurement soundly carried out?
   3. Are sales quotas set on a proper basis?

C. Marketing Control System
   1. Are the control procedures adequate to ensure that the annual plan objectives are being achieved?
   2. Does management periodically analyze the profitability of products, markets, territories, and channels of distribution?
   3. Are marketing costs being examined periodically?

(Continued)

D. New-Product Development System
1. Is the company well organized to gather, generate, and screen new-product ideas?
2. Does the company do adequate concept research and business analysis before investing in new ideas?
3. Does the company carry out adequate product and market testing before launching new products?

PART V—MARKETING PRODUCTIVITY AUDIT

A. Profitability Analysis
1. What is the profitability of the company's different products, markets, territories, and channels of distribution?
2. Should the company enter, expand, contract, or withdraw from any business segments, and what should be the short- and long-run profit consequences?

B. Cost-Effectiveness Analysis
1. Do any marketing activities seem to have excessive costs? Can cost-reducing steps be taken?

PART VI—MARKETING FUNCTION AUDITS

A. Products
1. What are the product line objectives? Are these objectives sound? Is the current product line meeting the objectives?
2. Are there products that should be phased out?
3. Are there new products that are worth adding?
4. Would any products benefit from quality, feature, or style modifications?

B. Price
1. What are the pricing objectives, policies, strategies, and procedures? To what extent are prices set on cost, demand, and competitive criteria?
2. Do the customers see the company's prices as being in line with the value of its offer?
3. Does the company use price promotions effectively?

C. Distribution
1. What are the distribution objectives and strategies?
2. Is there adequate market coverage and service?
3. Should the company consider changing its degree of reliance on distributors, sales representatives, and direct selling?

D. Advertising, Sales Promotion, and Publicity
1. What are the organization's advertising objectives? Are they sound?
2. Is the right amount being spent on advertising? How is the budget determined?
3. Are the ad themes and copy effective? What do customers and the public think about the advertising?
4. Are the advertising media well chosen?
5. Is sales promotion used effectively?
6. Is there a well-conceived publicity program?

E. Sales Force
1. What are the organization's sales-force objectives?
2. Is the sales force large enough to accomplish the company's objectives?
3. Is the sales force organized along the proper principles of specialization (territory, market, product)?
4. Does the sales force show high morale, ability, and effort?
5. Are the procedures adequate for setting quotas and evaluating performances?
6. How is the company's sales force rated in relation to competitors' sales forces?

Summary

Not all companies use formal planning or use it well. Yet formal planning can yield several benefits, including more systematic thinking, better coordination of company efforts, sharper objectives and improved performance measurement, and so on—all of which should lead to improved sales and profits.

Strategic planning sets the scene for the rest of company planning. The strategic planning process consists of defining the company's mission, objectives and goals, business portfolio, and growth strategy.

Developing a sound mission statement is a challenging undertaking. The mission statement should be market-oriented, feasible, motivating, and specific if it is to direct the firm to its best opportunities.

From there, strategic planning calls for evaluating each of the company's businesses in terms of whether it should be built up, maintained, harvested, or terminated.

To achieve company growth, strategic planning calls for identifying market opportunities where the company would enjoy a differential advantage over competitors. The company can identify relevant opportunities by considering intensive growth opportunities within its present product/market scope (market penetration, market development, and product development), integrative growth opportunities within its industry (backward, forward, and horizontal integration), and diversification growth opportunities outside its industry (concentric, horizontal, and conglomerate diversification).

Once the strategic plans have been set, each business has to prepare marketing plans for its products, brands, and markets. The main components of a marketing plan are: executive summary, current marketing situation, threats and opportunities, objectives and issues, marketing strategies, action programs, budgets, and controls. The marketing budget section of the plan can be developed either by setting a target profit goal or by using sales response functions to identify the profit-optimizing marketing plan.

Marketing organizations carry out three types of marketing control: annual plan control, profitability control, and strategic control.

Annual plan control consists of monitoring the current marketing efforts and results to make sure that the annual sales and profit goals will be achieved. The main tools are sales analysis, market-share analysis, marketing expense-to-sales analysis, and customer attitude tracking.

Profitability control calls for identifying the expenses and determining the actual profitability of the firm's products, territories, market segments, trade channels, and order sizes.

Strategic control is the task of making sure that the company's marketing objectives, strategies, and programs are optimally adapted to the current and forecasted marketing environment. It uses the marketing audit, which is a comprehensive, systematic, independent, and periodic examination of the organization's marketing environment, objectives, strategies, and activities. The purpose of the marketing audit is to determine marketing opportunities and problem areas and recommend short-run and long-run actions to improve the organization's overall marketing performance.

Questions for Discussion

1. Scott Paper Company has faced increased competition from P&G, Georgia Pacific, Fort Howard Paper, and unbranded generics in the past decade, losing its market share and being forced into developing the first strategic plan in the company's 101-year history. Discuss what you believe such a strategic plan might include.
2. Develop a mission statement for Capitol Records. Also, discuss each of the essential characteristics of this statement for Capitol.
3. How do the major classes of growth opportunities differ? Into which class or classes would you place the following companies—McDonald's, IBM, and Tenneco?
4. Briefly discuss the aspects of the current marketing situation analysis that a marketing planner for Gallo wine would have to consider.
5. What major decisions constitute the marketing strategy phase of the marketing plan? Why is it so essential that they be well coordinated?
6. Some friends of yours are planning to open a discotheque. They realize that marketing "control" is essential for success. How would you advise them on the options they have for exercising marketing control in their new venture?
7. What are the relative advantages and disadvantages of customer attitude tracking when compared with the other annual plan control approaches?
8. The heart of the strategic control process is the marketing audit. Briefly discuss the characteristics and purpose of this concept.

Key Terms in Chapter 17

Backward integration A company's seeking ownership or increased control of its supply systems.

Company marketing opportunity An attractive arena for company marketing action in which a particular company would enjoy a competitive advantage.

Concentric diversification A company's addition of new products that have technological and/or marketing similarities with its existing product lines.

Conglomerate diversification A company's addition of new products that have no relationship to its current technology, products, or markets.

Control Measuring and diagnosing the results of the strategic and marketing plans and taking corrective action.

Diversification growth opportunities A company's opportunities that lie outside the industry.

Forward integration A company's seeking ownership or increased control of its distribution systems.

Horizontal diversification A company's addition

of new products that could appeal to its current customers although they are not related to its current product line.

Horizontal integration A company's seeking ownership or increased control of some of its competitors.

Integrative growth opportunities A company's opportunities to integrate with other parts of the marketing system in the industry.

Intensive growth opportunities Opportunities available to a company within its current scope of operations.

Market development A company's seeking increased sales by taking its current products into new markets.

Marketing audit A comprehensive, systematic, independent, and periodic examination of a company's marketing environment, objectives, strategies, and activities with a view to determining problem areas and opportunities and recommending a plan of action to improve the company's marketing performance.

Marketing strategy The marketing logic by which

a business hopes to achieve its marketing objectives; consists of specific strategies bearing on target markets, marketing mix, and marketing expenditure level.

Market penetration A company's seeking increased sales for its current markets through more aggressive marketing.

Planning A formal design to improve a company's sales and profit performance that includes two components—strategic planning and marketing planning.

Product development A company's seeking increased sales by developing new or improved products for its current markets.

Sales analysis Measurement and evaluation of actual sales in relation to sales goals.

Sales response function A forecast of the likely sales volume during a specified time period associated with different possible expenditure levels of one or more marketing mix elements.

Strategic planning The managerial process of developing and maintaining a strategic fit between the organization's goals and capabilities and its changing marketing opportunities.

Threat A challenge posed by an unfavorable trend or specific event that would lead, in the absence of purposeful marketing action, to product stagnation or demise.

Cases for Chapter 17

Case 16   Minnetonka, Inc.: Softsoap (p. 516)
Minnetonka must review and revise its marketing objectives and strategy for Softsoap. This case looks at the factors that will affect a new marketing plan.

Case 17   Maytag Co.: Laundry Equipment (p. 518)
Should Maytag change its marketing strategy? What growth plans should the company make? This case suggests some answers.

Chapter 18

International Marketing

After reading this chapter, you should be able to:

1. Discuss how the economic, political-legal, and cultural environments affect international marketing.
2. Describe three strategies for entering foreign markets.
3. Explain how the marketing mix is adapted for foreign markets.
4. List and describe three forms of international marketing organization.

Campbell Soup Company is clearly America's soup market leader, with over 80% of the wet-soup sales in this country. But when it has ventured abroad, its performance has often been much less impressive.

One of Campbell's early calamitous experiences occurred in Great Britain. It introduced its famous small red-and-white-label cans of condensed soup in that country in the 1960s and used U.S. advertising themes. Campbell eventually lost $30 million on this venture. The reason: The consumers saw the small-size cans next to the large-size cans of the uncondensed British soups and thought Campbell soup was expensive. What they failed to appreciate was that Campbell's soup was condensed and, with the addition of a cup of water, was really less expensive than the other soups.

In 1978, Campbell entered the Brazilian market in a joint venture with a Brazilian company. Campbell invested $6 million. This time Campbell's offerings consisted mainly of vegetable-and-beef combinations packed in extra-large cans bearing the familiar red-and-white label. Initial sales were satisfactory, but then they went flat. After three years and $2 million worth of advertising campaigns, Campbell decided to close down its consumer soup business in Brazil.

What went wrong this time? In subsequent interviews with Brazilian homemakers, Campbell learned that these women felt that they were failing to fulfill their roles as homemakers by not serving their family a soup that they had made themselves. They preferred to buy the dehydrated products of Knorr and Maggi to start a soup and add their own ingredients and flair. Households bought Campbell soup only to have around as an emergency soup in case they needed something quickly. Apparently Campbell had not done much in-depth marketing research before coming to Brazil.

Campbell's inability to read a foreign market correctly for its product has been repeated by many American firms. A few months following Campbell's failure in Brazil, Gerber announced that it was closing down its baby-food operation in Brazil after an eight-year struggle to make it pay off. Apparently Brazilian homemakers did not consider prepared baby food a good substitute for fresh food made by themselves or their live-in maids. They might buy some prepackaged baby food only when they visit their family or go on vacation.[1]

Because of the large size of the U.S. market and some bad marketing experiences abroad, many American companies have avoided aggressive international marketing. Most American firms prefer domestic to foreign marketing. Domestic marketing is simpler and safer. Managers do not have to learn another language, deal with a different currency, face political and legal uncertainties, or adapt the product to different customer needs and expectations.

Two factors draw American companies into international marketing. First, they might be *pushed* by a weakening of marketing opportunities or changing business conditions at home. GNP growth might slow down; government might become antibusiness; the tax burden might become too heavy; the government might push business into expanding abroad in order to earn more foreign currency and reduce the U.S. trade deficit.[2] Second, American companies might be *pulled* into foreign trade by growing opportunities for their product in other countries. Without abandoning the domestic market, they might find foreign markets attractive even allowing for the extra costs and problems they face in operating abroad.

American exports accounted for 11.5% of the U.S. gross national product in 1982.[3] This makes the United States the world's largest exporting nation in absolute dollars. Other countries are more involved in world trade. The United Kingdom, Belgium, the Netherlands, and New Zealand have to sell more than half their output abroad in order to have high employment and pay for imported goods. International marketing is second nature to the companies in these countries.

Some companies here and abroad have gone into world marketing on such a large scale that they can be called **multinational companies**. Among American companies receiving more than 40% of their revenue from abroad in 1982 were Exxon (75%), Texaco (69%), Citicorp (67%), Mobil (61%), Caterpillar Tractor (57%), Dow Chemical (52%), IBM (45%), Coca-Cola (43%), and Xerox (42%). American companies face formidable multinational competitors, such as Royal Dutch/Shell, British Petroleum, Unilever, Philips, Volkswagenwerk, Nippon Steel, Siemens, Toyota Motor, and Nestlé.

While some American companies have aggressively expanded abroad, many foreign companies have entered the American market. Their names and

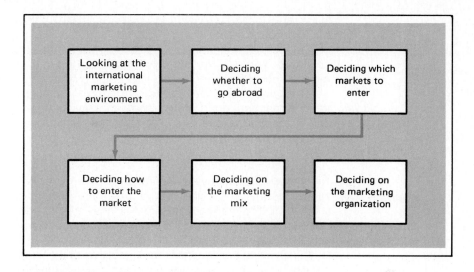

FIGURE 18-1

Major Decisions in
International
Marketing

brands have become household words, such as Sony, Honda, Datsun, Nestlé, Perrier, Norelco, Mercedes Benz, and Volkswagen, with many Americans showing a preference for these brands over domestic brands. There are many other products that appear to be produced by American firms but are really produced by foreign multinationals. This group includes Bantam Books, Baskin-Robbins Ice Cream, Capitol Records, Kiwi Shoe Polish, Lipton Tea, and Saks Fifth Avenue. America is also attracting huge foreign investment in tourist and real-estate ventures, notably Japanese land purchases in Hawaii, Kuwait's resort development off the South Carolina coast, and Arab purchases of Manhattan office buildings—and one offer by a Saudi Arabian sheik to buy the Alamo for his son.

One might ask whether international marketing involves any new principles. Obviously the principles of setting marketing objectives, choosing target markets, developing marketing positions and mixes, and carrying out marketing control still apply. The principles are not new, but the differences between nations can be so great that the international marketer needs to understand foreign environments and institutions and be prepared to revise the most basic assumptions about how people respond to marketing stimuli.

In the rest of this chapter, we will examine the six basic decisions that a company faces in considering international marketing. (See figure 18-1.)

Looking at the International Marketing Environment

A company has to learn many things before deciding whether to sell abroad. The company has to acquire a thorough understanding of the international marketing environment. The international marketing environment has changed greatly since 1945, creating both new opportunities and new problems. The most significant changes are (1) the internationalization of the world economy reflected in the rapid growth of world trade and investment; (2) the gradual erosion of the U.S.'s dominant position and its attendant problems of an unfavorable balance of trade and the changing value of the dollar in world markets; (3) the rising economic power of Japan in world markets; (4) the establishment of an international financial system offering improved currency convertibility; (5) the shift in world income since 1973 to the oil-producing companies; (6) the increasing trade barriers put up to protect domestic markets against foreign competition; and (7) the gradual opening up of major new markets, namely, China, the USSR, and the Arab countries.[4]

The International Trade System

The American company looking abroad must understand the restrictions as well as the opportunities in the international trade system. In attempting to sell to another country, the American firm will face various trade restrictions. The most common is the **tariff**, which is a tax levied by the foreign government against certain imported products. The tariff may be designed to raise revenue (revenue tariff) or to protect domestic firms (protective tariff). The exporter may also face a **quota**, which sets limits on the amount of goods that the importing country will accept in certain product categories. The purpose of the quota is to conserve on foreign currency and protect local industry and employment. An **embargo** is the ultimate form of quota in that some kinds of imports are totally banned. Trade is also discouraged by **exchange control**, which regulates the amount of available foreign currency and its exchange rate against other currencies. The American company may also find a set of **nontariff barriers**, such as discrimination against American company bids, and product standards that discriminate against American products. For example, the Dutch government bars tractors that run faster than ten miles an hour, which means that most American-made tractors are barred.

At the same time, certain countries have formed **economic communities** the most important of which is the European Economic Community (EEC, also known as the Common Market). The EEC's members are the major Western European nations, and they are striving to reduce tariffs and prices and expand employment and investment within the community. Since EEC's formation, other economic communities have been formed, notably the Latin American Free Trade Association (LAFTA), the Central American Common Market (CACM), and the Council for Mutual Economic Assistance (CMEA) formed for the Eastern European countries.

Each nation has unique features that must be grasped. A nation's readiness for different products and services and its attractiveness as a market to foreign firms depend on its economic, political-legal, and cultural environment.

Economic Environment

In considering foreign markets, the international marketer must study each country's economy. Two economic characteristics reflect the country's attractiveness as an export market.

The first is the country's industrial structure. The country's industrial structure shapes its product and service requirements, income levels, employment levels, and so on. There are four types of industrial structure.

SUBSISTENCE ECONOMIES.   In a subsistence economy, the vast majority of people engage in simple agriculture. They consume most of their output and barter the rest for simple goods and services. They offer few opportunities for exporters. Examples include Bangladesh and Ethiopia.

RAW-MATERIALS EXPORTING ECONOMIES.   These economies are rich in one or more natural resources but poor in other respects. Much of their revenue comes from exporting these resources. Examples are Chile (tin and copper), Zaire (rubber), and Saudi Arabia (oil). These countries are good markets for extractive equipment, tools and supplies, materials-handling equipment, and trucks. Depending on the number of foreign residents and wealthy native rulers and landholders, they are also a market for Western-style commodities and luxury goods.

INDUSTRIALIZING ECONOMIES.   In an industrializing economy, manufacturing is beginning to account for between 10% and 20% of the country's gross national product. Examples include Egypt, the Philippines, India, and Brazil. As manufacturing increases, the country relies more on imports of textile raw materials, steel, and heavy machinery, and less on imports of finished textiles, paper products, and automobiles. The industrialization creates a new rich class and a small but growing middle class, both demanding new types of goods, some of which can be satisfied only by imports.

INDUSTRIAL ECONOMIES.   Industrial economies are major exporters of manufactured goods. They trade manufactured goods among themselves and also export them to other types of economies in exchange for raw materials and semifinished goods. The large and varied manufacturing activities of these industrial nations and their sizable middle class make them rich markets for all sorts of goods. The United States and Western Europe have industrial economies.

The second economic characteristic is the country's income distribution. Income distribution is related to a country's industrial structure but is also affected by the political system. The international marketer distinguishes countries with five different income distribution patterns: (1) very low family incomes, (2) mostly low family incomes, (3) very low and very high family incomes, (4) low, medium, and high family incomes, and (5) mostly medium family incomes. Consider the market for Lamborghinis, an automobile costing more than $50,000. The market would be very small in countries with type 1 or type 2 income patterns. The largest single market for Lamborghinis turns out to be Portugal (income pattern 3), the poorest country in Europe but one with enough wealthy status-conscious families who can afford them.

Political-Legal Environment   Nations differ greatly in their political-legal environment. At least four factors should be considered in deciding whether to do business in a particular country.

ATTITUDES TOWARD INTERNATIONAL BUYING.   Some nations are very receptive, indeed encouraging, to foreign firms, and others are very hostile. As an example of the former, Mexico for a number of years has been attracting foreign investment by offering investment incentives and site-location services. On the other hand, India has required exporters to deal with import quotas, blocked currencies, stipulations that a high percentage of the management teams be nationals, and so on. IBM and Coca-Cola made the decision to leave India because of all the "hassles."

POLITICAL STABILITY. The country's future stability is another issue. Governments change hands, sometimes quite violently. Even without a change, a regime may decide to respond to new popular feelings. The foreign company's property may be expropriated; or its currency holdings may be blocked; or import quotas or new duties may be imposed. Where political instability is high, international marketers may still find it profitable to do business in that country, but the situation will affect how they handle financial and business matters.[5]

MONETARY RESTRICTIONS. A third factor concerns any restriction on or problems with monetary exchange. Sometimes a government will block its currency, or forbid it from being converted into foreign currency. Normally sellers want their profits to be in a currency they can use. In the best case, they can be paid in their own currency. Short of this, sellers might accept a blocked currency if they can buy other goods in that country that they need or that they can sell elsewhere for a useful currency. In the worst case with a blocked currency, sellers may have to take their money out of the host country in the form of unmarketable goods that they can sell elsewhere only for a loss. Besides currency restrictions, a fluctuating foreign exchange rate also creates high risks for sellers overseas.

GOVERNMENT BUREAUCRACY. A fourth factor is the extent to which the host government runs an efficient system for assisting foreign companies: efficient customs handling, adequate market information, and other factors favorable to doing business. A common shock to Americans is the extent to which impediments to trade disappear if a suitable payment (bribe) is made to some official(s).

Cultural Environment

Each country has its own folkways, norms, and taboos. The way foreign consumers think about and use certain products must be checked out by the seller before planning the marketing program. Here is a sampling of some of the surprises in the consumer market:

- The average Frenchman uses almost twice as many cosmetics and beauty aids as does his wife.
- The Germans and the French eat more packaged, branded spaghetti than the Italians.
- Italian children like to eat a bar of chocolate between two slices of bread as a snack.
- Women in Tanzania will not give their children eggs for fear of making them bald or impotent.

Not being aware of the cultural environment reduces a company's chances of success. Some of America's most successful marketers have fumbled when they went abroad. Kentucky Fried Chicken opened eleven outlets in Hong Kong, but they all failed within two years. Apparently Hong Kong citizens found it too messy to eat chicken with their hands. McDonald's located its first European outlet in a suburb of Amsterdam, but sales were disappointing. McDonald's missed the fact that most Europeans live in the central city and are less mobile.

Business norms and behavior also vary from country to country. U.S. business executives need to be briefed on these before negotiating in another country. Here are some examples of different foreign business behavior:

- South Americans are accustomed to talking business in close physical proximity with other persons—in fact, almost nose to nose. The American business executive retreats, but the South American pursues. And both end up being offended.
- In face-to-face communications, Japanese business executives rarely say no to an American business executive. Americans are frustrated and don't know where they stand. Americans come to the point quickly. Japanese business executives find this offensive.
- In France, wholesalers don't care to promote a product. They ask their retailers what they want and deliver it. If an American company builds its strategy around French wholesalers' cooperation, it is likely to fail.

Each country (and even regional groups within each country) has cultural traditions, preferences, and taboos that the marketer must study.[6]

Deciding Whether to Go Abroad

Companies get involved in international marketing in one of two ways. Someone—a domestic exporter, a foreign importer, a foreign government—asks the company to sell abroad. Or the company starts to think on its own about going abroad. It might face overcapacity at home or see better marketing opportunities in other countries.

Before going abroad, the company should try to define its international marketing objectives and policies. First, it should decide what proportion of foreign to total sales it will seek. Most companies start small when they venture abroad. Some plan to stay small, seeing foreign operations as a small part of their business. Other companies will have grander plans, seeing foreign business as ultimately equal to or even more important than their domestic business.

Second, the company must choose between marketing in a few countries and marketing in many countries. The Bulova Watch Company made the latter choice and expanded into over one hundred countries. It spread itself too thin, made profits in only two countries, and lost around $40 million.[7]

Third, the company must decide on the types of countries to consider. The countries that are attractive will depend on the product, geographic factors, income and population, political climate, and other factors. The seller may favor certain country groups or parts of the world.

Deciding Which Markets to Enter

After developing a list of possible foreign markets, the company will have to screen and rank them. Consider the following example:

> CMC's market research in the computer field revealed that England, France, West Germany, and Italy offer us significant markets. England, France, and Germany are about equal-size markets, while Italy represents about two-thirds the potential of any one of those countries. . . . Taking everything into consideration, we decided to set up first in England because its market for our products is as large as any and its language and laws are similar to ours. England is different enough to get your feet wet, yet similar enough to the familiar U.S. business environment so that you do not get in over your head.[8]

The market choice seems relatively simple and straightforward. Yet one can question whether the reason for selecting England—the compatibility of its language and culture—should have been given this prominence. The candidate countries should be ranked on several criteria, such as (1) market size, (2) market growth, (3) cost of doing business, (4) competitive advantage, and (5) risk level. The goal is to figure out which market will allow for the greatest long-term return on investment by the company.[9]

Deciding How to Enter the Market

Once a company has decided to sell to a particular country, it must determine the best mode of entry. Its choices are **exporting**, **joint venturing**, and **direct investment abroad**[10] Each succeeding strategy involves more commitment, risk, and possible profits. The three market entry strategies are shown in figure 18-2, along with the various options under each.

Export The simplest way to get involved in a foreign market is through export. *Occasional exporting* is a passive level of involvement where the company exports surpluses from time to time and sells goods to resident buyers representing foreign companies. *Active exporting* takes place when the company makes a commitment to expand exports to a particular market. In either case the company produces all of its goods in the home country. It may or may not modify them for the export market. Of the three choices, exporting involves the least change in the company's product lines, organization, investments, or mission.

A company can export its product in two ways. It can hire independent international marketing middlemen (indirect export) or handle its own exporting (direct export). Indirect export is more common in companies just beginning their exporting. First, it involves less investment. The firm does not have to develop an overseas sales force or a set of contacts. Second, it involves less risk. International marketing middlemen—domestic-based export merchants or agents,

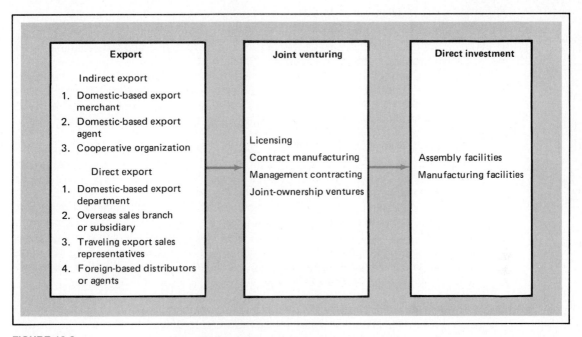

Export	Joint venturing	Direct investment
Indirect export		
1. Domestic-based export merchant		
2. Domestic-based export agent		
3. Cooperative organization	Licensing	
	Contract manufacturing	Assembly facilities
Direct export	Management contracting	Manufacturing facilities
1. Domestic-based export department	Joint-ownership ventures	
2. Overseas sales branch or subsidiary		
3. Traveling export sales representatives		
4. Foreign-based distributors or agents		

FIGURE 18-2

Market Entry
Strategies

or cooperative organizations—bring know-how and services to the relationship, and the seller will normally make fewer mistakes.

Joint Venturing A second broad method of entering a foreign market is to join with businesses in a host country to set up production and marketing facilities. Joint venturing differs from exporting in that a partnership is formed that leads to some production facilities abroad, and it differs from direct investment in that an association is formed with someone in that country. There are four types of joint venture.

LICENSING. **Licensing** is a simple way for a manufacturer to become involved in international marketing. The licensor enters an agreement with a licensee in the foreign market, offering the right to use a manufacturing process, trademark, patent, trade secret, or other item of value for a fee or royalty. The licensor gains entry into the market at little risk; the licensee gains production expertise, or a well-known product or name, without having to start from scratch. Gerber introduced its baby foods in the Japanese market through a licensing arrangement. Coca-Cola carried out its international marketing by licensing bottlers around the world—or, more technically, franchising bottlers, because it supplies the syrup needed to produce the product.

Licensing has potential disadvantages in that the firm has less control over the licensee than if it had set up its own production facilities. Furthermore, if the licensee is very successful, the firm has given up these profits, and if and when the contract ends, it may find it has created a competitor.

CONTRACT MANUFACTURING.   Another option is to contract with local manufacturers to produce the product. Sears used this method in opening up department stores in Mexico and Spain. Sears found qualified local manufacturers to produce many of the products it sells.

Contract manufacturing has the drawback of less control over the manufacturing process and the loss of potential profits from manufacturing. On the other hand, it offers the company a chance to start faster, with less risk, and with the opportunity to form a partnership or buy out the local manufacturer later.

MANAGEMENT CONTRACTING.   Here the domestic firm supplies the management know-how to a foreign company that supplies the capital. The domestic firm is exporting management services rather than products. Hilton uses this arrangement in managing hotels around the world.

Management contracting is a low-risk method of getting into a foreign market, and it yields income from the beginning. On the other hand, the arrangement is not sensible if the company has limited management talent that can be put to better uses or if there are greater profits to be made by undertaking the whole venture. Management contracting prevents the company from setting up its own operations for a period of time.

JOINT-OWNERSHIP VENTURES.   Joint-ownership ventures consist of foreign investors joining with local investors to create a local business in which they share joint ownership and control. The foreign investor may buy an interest in a local company, a local company may buy an interest in an existing operation of a foreign company, or the two parties may form a new business venture.

A jointly owned venture may be necessary or desirable for economic or political reasons. The firm may lack the financial, physical, or managerial resources to undertake the venture alone. Or the foreign government may require joint ownership as a condition for entry.

Joint ownership has certain drawbacks. The partners may disagree over investment, marketing, or other policies. Where many American firms like to reinvest earnings for growth, local firms often like to take out these earnings. Where American firms give a large role to marketing, local investors may rely only on selling. Furthermore, joint ownership can hamper a multinational company from carrying out specific manufacturing and marketing policies on a worldwide basis.

Direct Investment   The ultimate involvement in a foreign market is investment in foreign-based assembly or manufacturing facilities. As a company gains experience in export, and if the foreign market appears large enough, foreign production facilities offer distinct advantages. First, the firm may save money in the form of cheaper labor or raw materials, foreign government investment incentives, freight savings, and so on. Second, the firm will gain a better image in the host country because it creates jobs. Third, the firm develops a deeper relationship with government, customers, local suppliers, and distributors, enabling it to adapt its products better to the local marketing environment. Fourth, the firm retains full control over the investment and can therefore develop manufacturing and marketing policies that serve its long-term international objectives.

Deciding on the Marketing Mix

Companies that operate in one or more foreign markets must decide how much, if at all, to adapt their marketing mix to local conditions. At one extreme are companies that use a *standardized marketing mix* worldwide. Standardization of the product, advertising, distribution channels, and other elements of the marketing mix promises the lowest costs because no major changes have been introduced. This thinking is behind the idea that Coca-Cola should taste the same around the world and Ford should produce a "world car" that suits the needs of most consumers in most countries. At the other extreme is the idea of a *customized marketing mix,* where the producer adjusts the marketing mix elements to each target market, bearing more costs but hoping for a larger market share and return. Nestlé, for example, varies its product line and its advertising in different countries. Between these two extremes, many possibilities exist. Thus Levi Strauss can sell the same jeans worldwide but can vary the advertising theme in each country.

We will now examine possible adaptations of a company's product, promotion, price, and distribution as it goes abroad.

Product Keegan distinguished five adaptation strategies of product and promotion to a foreign market (see figure 18-3).[11] Here we will examine the three product strategies and later look at the two promotion strategies.

Straight extension means introducing the product in the foreign market without any change. Top management instructs its marketing people: "Take the product as is and find customers for it." The first step, however, should be to determine whether the foreign consumers use that product. Deodorant usage among men ranges from 80% in the United States to 55% in Sweden, 28% in Italy, and 8% in the Philippines. Many Spaniards do not use such common products as butter and cheese.

Straight extension has been successful in some cases but a disaster in others. General Foods introduced its standard powdered Jell-O in the British market only to find that British consumers prefer the solid-wafer or cake form. Straight extension is tempting because it involves no additional R&D expense,

FIGURE 18-3

Five International
Product and
Promotion Strategies

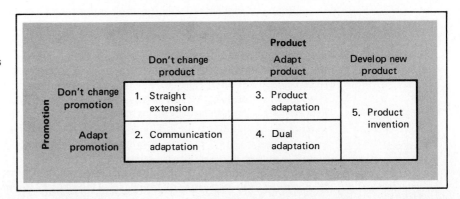

		Product		
		Don't change product	Adapt product	Develop new product
Promotion	Don't change promotion	1. Straight extension	3. Product adaptation	5. Product invention
	Adapt promotion	2. Communication adaptation	4. Dual adaptation	

manufacturing retooling, or promotion modification. But it can be costly in the long run.

Product adaptation involves altering the product to meet local conditions or preferences. Heinz varies its baby-food products: In Australia it sells a baby food made from strained lamb brains, and in the Netherlands, a baby food made from strained brown beans. General Foods blends different coffees for the British (who drink their coffee with milk), the French (who drink their coffee black), and Latin Americans (who want a chicory taste).

Product invention consists of creating something new. This can take two forms. *Backward invention* is the reintroducing of earlier product forms that happen to be well adapted to the needs of that country. The National Cash Register Company reintroduced its crank-operated cash register that could sell at half the cost of a modern cash register and sold substantial numbers in the Orient, Latin America, and Spain. This illustrates the existence of international product life cycles, where countries stand at different stages of readiness to accept a particular product.[12] *Forward invention* is creating a brand new product to meet a need in another country. There is an enormous need in less-developed countries for low-cost, high-protein foods. Companies such as Quaker Oats, Swift, and Monsanto are researching the nutritional needs of these countries, formulating new foods, and developing advertising campaigns to gain product trial and acceptance. Product invention seems to be a costly strategy, but the payoffs might make it worthwhile.

Promotion   Companies can either adopt the same promotion strategy they are using in the home market or change it for each local market.

Consider the message. Many multinational companies use a standardized advertising theme around the world. Exxon used "Put a tiger in your tank" and gained international recognition. The advertising is varied in minor ways, such as changing the colors to avoid taboos in other countries. Purple is associated with death in most of Latin America; white is a mourning color in Japan; and green is associated with jungle sickness in Malaysia. Even names have to be modified. In Germany, *mist* means "manure" and *scotch* (Scotch tape) means "schmuck"; in Spain, Chevrolet's *Nova* translates as *no va,* which means "it doesn't go"! In Sweden, Helene Curtis changed the name of Every Night Shampoo to Every Day because Swedes wash their hair in the morning.

Other companies encourage their international divisions to develop their own ads. The Schwinn Bicycle Company might use a pleasure theme in the United States and a safety theme in Scandinavia.

Media also require international adaptation because media availability varies from country to country. Commercial TV time is available for one hour each evening in Germany, and advertisers must buy time months in advance. In Sweden, commercial TV time is nonexistent. Commercial radio is nonexistent in France and Scandinavia. Magazines are a major medium in Italy and a minor one in Austria. Newspapers are national in the United Kingdom and local in Spain.

Price   Manufacturers often price their products lower in foreign markets. Incomes may be low, and a low price is necessary to sell the goods. The manufacturer may set

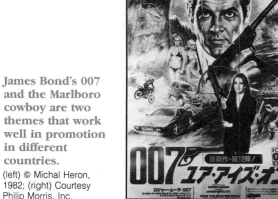

James Bond's 007 and the Marlboro cowboy are two themes that work well in promotion in different countries.

(left) © Michal Heron, 1982; (right) Courtesy Philip Morris, Inc.

low prices to build a market share. Or the manufacturer may want to dump goods that have no market at home. If the manufacturer charges less in the foreign market than in the home market, this is called *dumping*. The Zenith Company accused Japanese television manufacturers of dumping their TV sets on the U.S. market. If the U.S. Customs Bureau finds dumping, it can levy a dumping tariff.

Distribution Channels The international company must take a whole-channel view of the problem of distributing products to the final consumers.[13] Figure 18-4 shows the three major links between the seller and the ultimate buyer. The first link, the seller's headquarters organization, supervises the channels and is part of the channel itself. The second link, channels between nations, gets the products to the borders of the foreign nations. The third link, channels within nations, gets the products from their foreign entry point to the ultimate consumers. Too many American manufacturers think their job is done once the product leaves their hands. They should pay more attention to how it is handled within the foreign country.

Within-country channels of distribution vary considerably from country to country. There are striking differences in the number and type of middlemen

FIGURE 18-4

Whole-Channel Concept for International Marketing

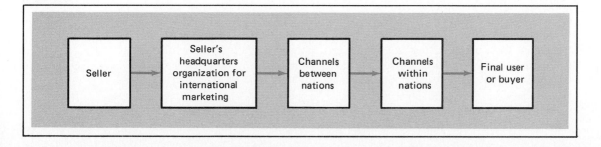

Exhibit **18-1**

The Americans Are Coming—With Popcorn

The American government wants the British to eat more popcorn. So does the Popcorn Institute of Chicago, whose members produce 85% of the world's popcorn. Americans spend more than $1 billion per year on popcorn, while the British spend only $4.7 million. Turning the British into popcorn eaters would mean an increase in profits for American farmers and exporters. To convince skeptical Britons of popcorn's virtues, the agricultural trade office of the American Embassy has teamed up with the Popcorn Institute in a three-year popcorn-promoting campaign. The drive has focused on popcorn's low cost, its nutritional value, and new ways to serve it. Some of the suggested new ways include chunky peanut butter popcorn, popcorn soaked in brandy, and pizza-flavored popcorn in a sauce for steak. A more conventional idea—but one not familiar to the British—is to serve it with salt and butter.

Until now, Britons have been accustomed to eating only caramel-coated popcorn at amusement arcades and at the movies. The Popcorn Institute is looking for other areas of British life where popcorn might fit in. One potential new group of popcorn eaters is the pub crowd. Since the pub is a center of British social life, the Popcorn Institute is trying to convince owners to offer popcorn as a give-away snack to go along with beer and other drinks. Although pub owners are reluctant to spend the minimum of $475 for a commercial corn popper, Wilson Lynn Abbott, director of the agricultural trade office, argues that the cost is an investment with a sure payoff. He tells pub owners, "Studies have shown that you can increase beer intake per customer by 30 to 40 percent by offering popcorn." Abbott also points out that the popcorn itself costs less than potato chips and peanuts, snacks that owners typically choose as give-aways.

Americans eat most of their popcorn at home, presumably while watching television. With this in mind, the Popcorn Institute is going after Britain's large television audience as its second, and possibly its biggest, potential market. Here again, the campaign stresses popcorn's low cost in comparison with other snacks.

Because diet is such a common concern today, the promotional campaign also emphasizes popcorn's nutritional assets: eaten alone, without any added flavorings, it's not fattening; it provides fiber; and it even contains protein, vitamins, and minerals. Some British schools have used it as a substitute for sugared snacks. Ann Attfield, in charge of the kitchen at St. Angela's Roman Catholic Girls School in Stevenage, has even covered popcorn with melted cheese and herbs and served it to students as a vegetable dish.

Encouraged by an early market survey, one American company, West Bend, will soon begin selling an electric corn popper for home use. While it's unlikely that popcorn will replace the vegetable on many British dinner plates, the campaign is making the British increasingly fond of this American snack.

Source: Based on "Selling the U.S. Popcorn Habit in Britain," *New York Times*, January 26, 1983, p. C-9.

serving each foreign market. To get soap into Japan, Procter & Gamble has to work through what is probably the most complicated distribution system in the world. It must sell to a general wholesaler, who sells to a basic product specialty wholesaler, who sells to a specialty wholesaler, who sells to a regional wholesaler, who sells to a local wholesaler, who finally sells to retailers. All of these distribution levels may combine to result in a doubling or tripling of the consumer's price over the importer's price.[14] If P&G takes the same soap to tropical Africa, the company sells to an import wholesaler, who sells to a mammy, who sells to a petty mammy, who sells the soap door to door.[15]

Another difference lies in the size and character of retail units abroad. Whereas large-scale retail chains dominate the U.S. scene, most foreign retailing is in the hands of many small independent retailers. In India, millions of retailers operate tiny shops or sell in open markets. Their markups are high, but the real price is brought down through bargaining. Supermarkets could conceivably bring down prices, but they are difficult to start because of many economic and cultural barriers.[16]

Deciding on the Marketing Organization

Companies manage their international marketing activities in at least three different ways. Most companies first organize an export department, then create an international division, and ultimately become a multinational organization.

Export Department A firm normally gets into international marketing by simply shipping out the goods. If its international sales expand, the company organizes an export department consisting of a sales manager and a few assistants. As sales increase further, the export department is expanded to include various marketing services so that it can go after business more aggressively. If the firm moves into joint ventures or direct investment, the export department will no longer be adequate.

International Division Many companies get involved in several international markets and ventures. A company may export to one country, license in another, have a joint-ownership venture in a third, and own a subsidiary in a fourth. Sooner or later it will create an international division or subsidiary to handle all its international activity. The international division is headed by an international division president, who sets goals and budgets and is responsible for the company's growth in the international market.

Multinational Organization Some firms pass beyond the international division stage and become multinational organizations. They stop thinking of themselves as national marketers who venture abroad and start thinking of themselves as global marketers. The top corporate management and staff are involved in the planning of worldwide manufacturing facilities, marketing policies, financial flow, and logistical systems. The global operating units report directly to the chief executive or executive committee, not to the head of an international division. Executives are trained in worldwide operations, not just domestic or international. Management is recruited from many countries; components and supplies are purchased where they can be obtained at the lowest cost; and investments are made where the anticipated returns are greatest.

Major companies must go more multinational in the 1980s if they are going to grow. As foreign companies successfully invade the domestic market, U.S. companies will have to move more aggressively into foreign markets. They will have to evolve from ethnocentric companies treating their foreign operations as secondary, to geocentric companies where they view the entire world as a single market.[17]

Summary

Companies undertake international marketing for a variety of reasons. Some are pushed by poor opportunities in the domestic market, and some are pulled by attractive opportunities abroad. Given the risk of international marketing, companies need a systematic way to make their international marketing decisions.

The first step is to understand the international marketing environment, particularly the international trade system. In considering a particular foreign market, its economic, political-legal, and cultural characteristics must be assessed. Second, the company must consider what proportion of foreign to total sales it will seek, whether it will do business in a few or many countries, and what types of countries it wants to market in. The third step is to decide which particular markets to enter, and this calls for evaluating the probable rate of return on investment against the level of risk. Fourth, the company has to decide how to enter each attractive market, whether through exporting, joint venturing, or direct investment. Many companies start as exporters, move to joint venturing, and finally undertake direct investment. Companies must decide on the extent to which their products, promotion, price, and distribution should be adapted to each foreign market. Finally, the company must develop an effective organization for pursuing international marketing. Most firms start with an export department and graduate to an international division. A few pass to a multinational organization, which means that worldwide marketing is planned and managed by the top officers of the company.

Questions for Discussion

1. In looking at the international marketing environment, the economic environment of the country is the most important consideration for the firm. Comment.
2. Discuss the relevant aspects of the political-legal environment that might affect K mart's decision to open retail outlets in Italy.
3. What steps are involved in deciding which markets to enter? Relate these steps to a consumer product example.

4. Briefly discuss the three major strategies that a firm might use to enter a foreign market.
5. How does licensing differ from the other joint-venture possibilities?
6. What product strategy possibilities might Hershey's consider in marketing its chocolate bars in South American countries?
7. The price of products sold in foreign markets is usually lower than in the domestic market. Why?
8. Discuss the type of international marketing organization you would suggest for the following companies: (a) Huffy Bicycles is planning to sell three models in the Far East; (b) a small manufacturer of toys is going to market its products in Europe; and (c) Dodge is contemplating selling its full line of cars and trucks in Kuwait.

Key Terms in Chapter 18

Direct investment abroad   Involvement in a foreign market through foreign-based assembly or manufacturing facilities.

Economic community   A group of nations organized for the purpose of working toward common goals in the regulation of international trade; an example is the European Economic Community (EEC).

Embargo   A ban on the import of a certain product.

Exchange control   Regulation of the amount of available foreign currency and its exchange rate against other currencies.

Exporting   A company's selling of products to another country either by hiring independent marketing middlemen (indirect export) or by marketing the products itself (direct export).

Joint venturing   A method of entering a foreign market by joining businesses in a host country to set up production and marketing facilities.

Licensing   A method of entering international marketing by establishing an agreement in a foreign market that offers the right to use a manufacturing process, trademark, or other valuable item for a fee or royalty.

Multinational company   A firm that has a major part of its operations outside its home country.

Nontariff barriers   Restrictions on international trade involving such obstructions as discrimination against bids from a particular country or product standards that discriminate against a country's products.

Quota   A limit on the amount of goods that an importing country will accept in certain product categories; designed to conserve on foreign currency and to protect local industry and employment.

Tariff   A tax on certain imported or exported products; designed to raise revenue or to protect domestic firms.

Case for Chapter 18

Case 15   STP Corporation (p. 514)
This case looks at the marketing strategy of the STP Corporation. Should it change its strategy in its international markets?

Chapter **19**

Services Marketing and Nonprofit Marketing

After reading this chapter, you should be able to:

1. Define service and describe four characteristics that affect service marketing.
2. Explain why and how organizations market themselves.
3. Discuss why persons and places are marketed.
4. Relate the four *P*'s of marketing to a social marketing campaign.

The Evanston Hospital, serving the North Shore area of Chicago, appointed Dr. John McLaren as its first vice-president of marketing. Hospitals have had vice-presidents of development and public relations, but this appointment raised a number of eyebrows both inside and outside the hospital.

Before 1970, hospitals had the problem of too many patients. The situation turned around drastically in the 1970s, and hospitals experienced declining admissions and patient-days. Given the high fixed costs and rising labor costs, their declining patient census could spell the difference between being in the black and being in the red.

Hospitals began to scramble for ways to get a larger share of the available patients. Since most patients go to their physician's hospital, the key market target was physicians. Every hospital began to ponder how it could attract more of the "high-yield" physicians to its staff. The key was in knowing what physicians want—things like the latest equipment, good colleagues and nursing staffs, and a good hospital image.

The more hospitals looked at the problem, the more complex the marketing challenges appeared. Hospitals had to research the community's health needs, images of competing hospitals, how patients felt about hospital services, and so on. Individual hospitals began to realize that they could no longer offer every kind of medical service; this led to expensive duplication of equipment and services and underutilized capacity. Hospitals began to pick and choose medical specialties—heart, pediatrics, burn treatment, psychiatry.

Meanwhile some hospitals went overboard in making a pitch for patients. Sunrise Hospital in Las Vegas ran a large ad showing a ship with the caption "Introducing the Sunrise Cruise—Win a Once-in-a-Lifetime Cruise Simply by Entering Sunrise Hospital on Any Friday or Saturday: Recuperative Mediterranean Cruise for Two." St. Luke's Hospital in Phoenix introduced nightly bingo games for all patients (except cardiac cases), producing immense patient interest and an annual profit of $60,000. A Philadelphia hospital served candlelight dinners with steak and champagne to parents of newborn children.

Then what is Dr. John McLaren's job at the Evanston Hospital? His job is to promote particular hospital services (services marketing), the hospital itself (organization), some key physicians (person marketing), Evanston as an attractive community (place marketing), and ideas on better health (idea marketing).

Marketing as a discipline developed initially in connection with selling physical products, such as toothpaste, cars, steel, and equipment. The physical product focus may cause people to overlook the many other types of products that are marketed, namely, services, organizations, persons, places, and ideas.

Services Marketing

One of the major developments in America has been the phenomenal growth of service industries. Service businesses now provide 73% of the payroll jobs of the nonfarm work force. In contrast, Germany has 41% of its work force in the service sector and Italy has 35%. As a result of rising affluence, more leisure, and the growing complexity of products that require servicing, the United States has become the world's first service economy.

Service industries are quite varied. The government sector, with its courts, employment services, hospitals, loan agencies, military services, police and fire departments, post office, regulatory agencies, and schools, is in the service business. The private nonprofit sector, with its museums, charities, churches, colleges, foundations, and hospitals, is in the service business. A good part of the business sector, with its airlines, banks, computer service bureaus, hotels, insurance companies, law firms, management consulting firms, medical practices, motion picture companies, plumbing repair companies, and real-estate firms, is in the service business.

Not only are there traditional service industries but new types keep popping up all the time:

> For a fee, there are now companies that will balance your budget, baby-sit your philodendron, wake you up in the morning, drive you to work, or find you a new home, job, car, wife, clairvoyant, cat feeder, or gypsy violinist. Or perhaps you want to rent a garden tractor? A few cattle? Some original paintings? . . . If it is business services you need, other companies will plan your conventions and sales meetings, design your products, handle your data processing, or supply temporary secretaries or even executives.[1]

Nature and Characteristics of a Service

A wide range of activities and businesses are classified as services. We define service as follows:

> A **service** is any activity or benefit that one party can offer to another that is essentially intangible and does not result in the ownership of anything. Its production may or may not be tied to a physical product.

Renting a hotel room, depositing money in a bank, traveling on an airplane, visiting a psychiatrist, having a haircut, having a car repaired, watching a professional sport, seeing a movie, having clothes cleaned in a dry-cleaning establishment, getting advice from a lawyer—all involve buying a service.

Services have four characteristics that must be considered when designing marketing programs.

INTANGIBILITY. Services are intangible. They cannot be seen, tasted, felt, heard, or smelled before they are bought. The woman getting a "face lift" cannot see the result before the purchase, and the patient in the psychiatrist's office cannot know the outcome in advance. The buyer has to have faith in the service provider.

Service providers can do certain things to improve the client's confidence. First, they can increase the product's tangibility. A plastic surgeon can make a drawing showing how the patient's face will look after the surgery. Second, service providers can emphasize the service's benefits rather than just describing its features. Thus, a college admissions officer can talk to prospective students about the great jobs its alumni have found instead of only describing life on the campus. Third, service providers can develop brand names for their service to increase confidence, such as Magikist cleaning, United Airlines' Red Carpet service, and Transcendental Meditation. Fourth, service providers can use a celebrity to create confidence in the service, as Hertz has done with O. J. Simpson.

INSEPARABILITY. A service is inseparable from its source, whether it be a person or a machine. But a physical product exists whether or not its source is present. Consider going to a Rolling Stones concert. The entertainment value is inseparable from the performer. It is not the same service if an announcer tells the audience that Mick Jagger is indisposed and Donny and Marie Osmond will substitute. This means that the number of people who can buy this service—watching Mick Jagger perform live—is limited to the amount of time that Mick Jagger gives to concerts.

Several strategies exist for getting around this limitation. The service provider can learn to work with larger groups. Psychotherapists have moved from one-on-one therapy to small-group therapy to groups of over three hundred people in a hotel ballroom getting "therapized." The service provider can learn to work faster—the psychotherapist can spend 30 minutes with each patient instead of 50 minutes and can see more patients. The service organization can train more service providers and build up client confidence, as H & R Block has done with its national network of trained tax consultants.

VARIABILITY.   Services are highly variable, as they depend on who provides them and when and where they are provided. A Vidal Sassoon haircut will be of higher quality than one performed by a newly trained hair stylist. And Sassoon's haircuts may vary with his energy and mental set at the time of each appointment. Service buyers are frequently aware of this high variability and talk to others before selecting a service provider.

Service firms can take two steps toward quality control. The first is investing in good personnel selection and training. Airlines, banks, and hotels spend substantial sums to train their employees in providing good service. One should find the same friendly and helpful personnel in every Marriott Hotel. The second step is monitoring customer satisfaction through suggestion and complaint systems, customer surveys, and comparison shopping so that poor service can be detected and corrected.[2]

PERISHABILITY.   Services cannot be stored. The reason many doctors charge patients for missed appointments is that the service value only existed at that point when the patient did not show up. The perishability of services is not a problem when demand is steady, because it is easy to staff the services in advance. When demand fluctuates, service firms have difficult problems. For example, public transportation companies have to own much more equipment because of rush-hour traffic demand than they would if demand were even throughout the day.

Sasser has described several strategies for producing a better match between demand and supply in a service business.[3]

On the demand side:

1. Differential pricing will shift some demand from peak to off-peak periods. Examples include low early-evening movie prices and weekend discount prices for car rentals.
2. Nonpeak demand can be cultivated. McDonald's opened its Egg McMuffin breakfast service, and hotels developed their mini-vacation weekend.
3. Complementary services can be developed during peak time to provide

When demand for a service fluctuates, the service firm must be able to meet peak demand. Thus, a public transportation company must own enough buses and trains to handle rush-hour traffic.

WMATA Photo by Phil Portlock

alternatives to waiting customers, such as cocktail lounges to sit in while waiting for a table and automatic tellers in banks.

4. Reservation systems are a way to manage the demand level. Airlines, hotels, and physicians employ them extensively.

On the supply side:

1. Part-time employees can be hired to serve peak demand. Colleges add part-time teachers when enrollment goes up, and restaurants call in part-time waitresses when needed.
2. Peak-time efficiency routines can be introduced. Employees perform only essential tasks during peak periods. Paramedics assist physicians during busy periods.
3. Increased consumer participation in tasks can be encouraged, as when consumers fill out their own medical records or bag their own groceries.
4. Shared services can be developed, as when several hospitals share medical equipment purchases.
5. Facilities making potential expansion possible can be developed, as when an amusement park buys surrounding land for later development.

Classification of Services

The types of services available vary considerably. Services can be classified in a number of ways. First, is the service people-based or equipment-based? A psychiatrist needs virtually no equipment, but a pilot needs an airplane. Within people-based services, there are those involving professionals (accounting, management consulting), skilled labor (plumbing, car repair), and unskilled labor (janitorial service, lawn care). In equipment-based services, there are those involving automated equipment (automated car washes, vending machines), equipment operated by relatively unskilled labor (taxis, motion picture theaters), and equipment operated by skilled labor (airplanes, computers).[4] Even within a specific service industry, different service providers vary in the amount of equipment they use—contrast James Taylor with his single guitar and the Rolling Stones with their tons of audio equipment. Sometimes the equipment adds value to the service (stereo amplification), and sometimes it exists to reduce the amount of labor needed (automated car washes).

Second, is the client's presence necessary to the service? A client must be present during brain surgery, but not during a car repair. If the client must be present, the service provider has to be considerate of his or her needs. Thus, beauty shop operators will decorate their shops, play background music, and engage in light conversation with the client.

Third, what about the client's purchase motive? Does the service meet a personal need (personal services) or a business need (business services)? Physicians will price physical examinations for private patients differently from those for company employees on a retainer. Service providers typically develop different marketing programs for personal and business markets.

Fourth, what about the service provider's motives (profit or nonprofit) and form (private or public)? These two characteristics, when crossed, produce four quite different types of service organizations. Clearly the marketing programs of a private investor hospital will differ from those of a private charity hospital or a Veterans Administration hospital.

The Extent and Importance of Marketing in the Service Sector

Service firms typically lag behind manufacturing firms in their use of marketing. Many of them are small (shoe repair stores, barbershops) and think of marketing as expensive or irrelevant. There are also service businesses (law and accounting firms) that believe that it is unprofessional to use marketing. Other service businesses (colleges, hospitals) had so much demand in the past that they had no need for marketing until recently.

Today, as competition intensifies, as costs rise, as productivity stagnates, and as service quality deteriorates, more service firms are taking an interest in marketing. Airlines were one of the first service industries to study their consumers and competition and take positive steps to make travelers' trips easier and more pleasant. Banks are another industry that moved toward more active use of marketing in a relatively short period of time. At first, banks thought of marketing as consisting mainly of promotion and friendliness, but they have now set up marketing organization, information, planning, and control systems.[5] Stockbrokers, insurance companies, and hotels have used marketing unevenly, with some leaders taking major marketing steps (Merrill Lynch, Hyatt Regency) and most firms lagging behind.

As competition intensifies, more service businesses are using marketing. Leading the way are producers who are moving into service industries. For example, Sears moved into services marketing years ago—insurance, banking, income tax consulting, car rentals. Xerox Corporation operates a major sales-training business (Xerox Learning), and Gerber Products runs nursery schools and sells insurance.

Organization Marketing

Often organizations will carry out marketing activities to "sell" the organization itself.

Organization marketing consists of the activities undertaken to create, maintain, or alter attitudes and/or behavior of target audiences toward particular organizations.

Organization marketing has traditionally been handled by the public relations department. This is evident from the following definition of public relations:

Public relations is the management function that evaluates public attitudes, identifies the policies and procedures of an individual or an organization with the public interest, and plans and executes a program of action to earn public understanding and acceptance.[6]

Public relations is essentially marketing management shifted from a product or service to an organization.[7] The same skills are needed: knowledge of audience needs, desires, and psychology; communication skills; and ability to design and carry out programs that influence behavior. The similarities between marketing and public relations have led some companies to combine both func-

The 1982 New York City Marathon, co-sponsored by Manufacturers Hanover

The marketplace only accepts achievement.

Manufacturers Hanover succeeds.

Consistency, quality, loyalty. Three qualities that clearly show themselves in Alberto Salazar's victory in the 1982 New York Marathon.

Consistency of winning, not once, or twice, but three consecutive times. Winning in spite of increasingly strong competition each year.

Quality of performance to call on extra effort, break away from the pack and be one of the best.

Loyalty of spirit to commit to endless training and mental preparation.

These same core values, witnessed by millions of our neighbors as they experienced this extraordinary event,

have enabled Manufacturers Hanover to emerge as a $64 billion diversified financial services organization, with a network of over 700 offices worldwide.

To compete demands acceptance of the challenges in the marketplace. And rising to accept those challenges. Consider the source.

MANUFACTURERS HANOVER
The financial source. Worldwide.

Member FDIC

As part of public relations programs, companies support the arts, community groups, and sporting events.

tions under a single control. General Electric appointed a vice-president of marketing and public affairs who "will be responsible for all corporate activities in advertising, public affairs, and public relations. He [or she] will also handle corporate marketing, including research and personnel development."

Organization marketing calls for assessing the organization's current image and developing a marketing plan to improve its image.

Image Assessment

The first step in image assessment is to research the organization's current image among key publics. *The way an individual or a group sees an object is called its image.* Different individuals can have different images of the same object. The organization might be pleased with its public image or might find that it has serious image problems.

Image Planning and Control

The next step calls for the organization to identify the image that it would like to have. It must not aim for the "impossible." Assume that a management consulting firm decides that it would like to be seen as more innovative, more friendly, more knowledgeable, and larger.

The firm now develops a marketing plan to shift its actual image toward the desired one. Suppose that it wants to put the most emphasis on increasing its reputation as a knowledgeable firm. The key step, of course, is to hire better consultants. If the firm has highly knowledgeable consultants but they are not visible, then it needs to give them more exposure. Its knowledgeable consultants should be encouraged to join business and trade associations, give speeches, write articles, and develop public seminars on "hot" new topics.[8]

The firm must resurvey its publics periodically to see whether its activities are improving its image. Image modification cannot be accomplished overnight because of limited funds and the "stickiness" of public images. If the firm is making no progress, either its substance or its communications are deficient.

Person Marketing

Persons, as well as services and organizations, are marketed. We define person marketing as follows:

> **Person marketing** consists of activities undertaken to create, maintain, or alter attitudes and/or behavior toward particular persons.

Two common forms of person marketing are celebrity marketing and political candidate marketing. A third form, personal marketing, is described in appendix B, "Careers in Marketing."

Celebrity Marketing

Although celebrity marketing has a long history going back to the ancient Greeks and Romans, in recent times it has been associated with the buildup of Hollywood stars and entertainers. Hollywood actors and actresses would hire press agents to promote their stardom. The press agent would place news about the star in the mass media and also schedule appearances in highly visible locations. One of the great promoters was the late Brian Epstein, who managed the Beatles' rise to stardom and received a larger share of the money than any Beatle. Today, celebrities are promoted by entire organizations. After he became the World Series most valuable player, Bucky Dent asked the William Morris Agency to manage his public life.[9] The agency lined him up to visit children's hospitals, Little Leagues, and conventions; to co-host "A.M. New York" and appear on the Merv Griffin show; to have posters made and marketed; to make a commercial for a car manufacturer; and to get spreads in *Playboy* and other magazines.

Celebrity marketers cannot work miracles; much depends on the star. If the star is a born promoter, there is no limit. Elton John, who has made more money than the Beatles or Elvis Presley, wears one of over two hundred pairs of glasses, pounds the piano with his feet, bats tennis balls into the crowd, and hires actors to wander around the stage dressed as Frankenstein or Queen Elizabeth. Whether these are his ideas or his manager's, he carries them off well.

Celebrity marketers recognize that celebrity life cycles are quite varied and often short (see figure 19-1). The head of marketing for Polygram, a major record firm, likens a performer's career to a crate of strawberries that must be packaged, brought to the market, and sold before they spoil and become worthless. A national publicity director for Mercury Records describes a typical meeting: "We get together every six weeks. We'll go down our sales figures. If we decide a group is getting 'no action'—meaning no airplay or sales—we'll drop them. If promotion doesn't get results, you don't just throw away more money."[10] Some "has-been" celebrities, such as singer Eddie Fisher, try to relaunch their careers, but they find it difficult to get back to the top.[11]

Political Candidate Marketing

Political candidate marketing has become a major industry and area of special-ization.[12] Every few years the public is treated to numerous campaigns for local, state, and national offices. Political campaigns consist of the candidate's going into the voter market and using marketing research and commercial advertising to maximize voter "purchase."

Interest in the marketing aspects of elections has been stimulated by the spectacular growth in political advertising, scientific opinion polling, computer analysis of voting patterns, and professional campaign management firms.

> The personal handshake, the local fund-raising dinner, the neighborhood tea, the rally, the precinct captain and the car pool to the polls are still very much with us . . . the new campaign has provided a carefully coordinated strate-gic framework within which the traditional activities are carried out in keeping with a Master Plan. It centers on a shift from the candidate-controlled, loosely knit, often haphazard "play-it-by-ear" approach to that of a precise, central-ized "team" strategy for winning or keeping office. Its hallmarks include the formal strategic blueprint, the coordinated use of specialized propaganda skills, and a more subtle approach to opinion measurement and manipu-lation. And, though there is a world of difference between selling a candidate and merchandising soap or razor blades, some of the attributes of commer-cial advertising have been grafted onto the political process.[13]

FIGURE 19-1

Celebrity Career Life Cycles

Source: Charles Seton, "The Marketing of a Free Lance Fashion Photographer" (unpublished student paper, January 20, 1978).

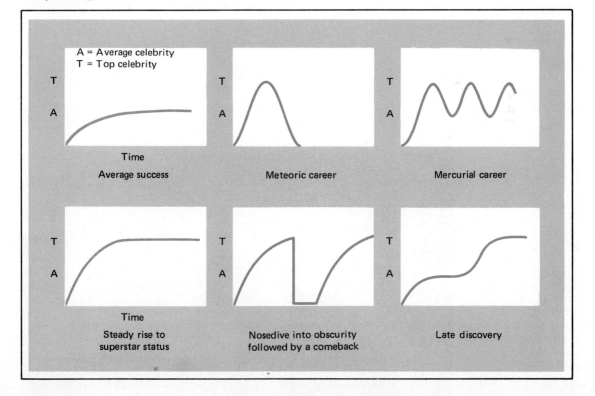

Place Marketing

People searching for new homes or vacation spots are familiar with place marketing.

Place marketing involves activities undertaken to create, maintain, or alter attitudes and/or behavior toward particular places.

Four types of place marketing can be distinguished.

Domicile Marketing Domicile marketing involves developing and/or promoting the sale or rental of single-family dwellings, apartments, and other types of housing units. It has traditionally relied on classified want ads and real-estate agents. Advanced marketing has emerged in connection with condominium selling and the development of total communities.[14] Large builders research housing needs and develop housing products aimed at the price ranges and preferences of specific market segments. Some high-rise apartments have been built for the jet set and others for the geriatric set—filled with the features, symbols, and services appropriate to each. Entire housing communities have been designed for specific target markets.

Business Site Marketing Business site marketing involves developing, selling, or renting business sites or properties, such as factories, stores, offices, and warehouses. Large developers will research companies' land needs and respond with real-estate solutions, such as industrial parks, shopping centers, and new office buildings. Most states operate industrial development offices that try to sell companies on the advantages of locating new plants in their states. They spend large sums on advertising and offer to fly prospects to the site at no cost. Troubled cities, such as New York,

Developers of new communities, such as this one in Florida, could market the climate, the pleasures of having palm trees on the lawn and ocean in the backyard, and the attractiveness of the homes.
Courtesy General Development Corporation

Detroit, and Atlanta, have appointed task forces to raise their city's image and draw new business to their area. Foreign nations, such as Ireland, Greece, and Turkey, have marketed their homeland as good locations for business investment.

Land Investment Marketing Land investment marketing involves developing and selling land for investment. The buyers—corporations, doctors, small investors, speculators—hope to sell the land when it rises sufficiently in value. Land investment marketing has been instrumental in developing large parts of Florida and the Far West. Land developers have elaborate marketing programs to interest possible investors in their land. The programs include mass-media advertising and publicity, direct mail, personal sales calls, free dinner meetings, and even free flights to the sites.

Vacation Marketing Vacation marketing involves attracting vacationers to spas, resorts, cities, states, and even entire nations. The effort is carried on by travel agents, airlines, motor clubs, oil companies, hotels, motels, and government agencies. The power of place marketing was demonstrated in the career of the late Steve Hannagan: "He built monuments to his skill and the power of press-agentry in making the Memorial Day auto races at Indianapolis a national event and in making Miami Beach and Sun Valley into nationally known resorts."[15]

Today almost every city and state publicizes its tourist attractions. Miami Beach is considering making gambling legal in order to attract more tourists, and the Virgin Islands want to "repopularize" the islands after some bad tourist incidents. Some places, however, are trying to demarket themselves. Palm Beach, Florida, is letting its beach erode to discourage tourists; Oregon has publicized its bad weather; Yosemite National Park may ban snowmobiling, conventions, and private car usage; and Finland wants to discourage tourists from vacationing in certain areas where they feel the damage of mass tourism exceeds the revenues.

Idea Marketing

Ideas can also be marketed. In one sense, all marketing is the marketing of an idea, whether it be the idea of brushing one's teeth, the idea that Crest is the most effective decay preventer, or anything else. In this section we will confine our discussion to the marketing of social ideas, such as public health campaigns to reduce smoking, alcoholism, drug abuse, and overeating; environmental campaigns to promote wilderness protection, clean air, and conservation; and other campaigns, such as family planning, women's rights, and racial equality. This area has been called social marketing:[16]

> **Social marketing** is the design, implementation, and control of programs seeking to increase the acceptability of a social idea, cause, or practice in a target group(s). It uses market segmentation, consumer research, concept development, communications, facilitation, incentives, and exchange theory to maximize target group response.

Social marketers can pursue different objectives: (1) produce understanding (knowing the nutritional value of different foods); (2) trigger a one-time action (participating in a mass-immunization campaign); (3) attempt to change behavior (auto seat-belt campaign); (4) change a basic belief (convincing antiabortionists to believe in a woman's right to abortion).

The Advertising Council of America has carried out dozens of social advertising campaigns, including "Smokey the Bear," "Keep America Beautiful," "Join the Peace Corps," "Buy Bonds," and "Go to College." But social marketing is much broader. Many public advertising campaigns fail because they use only advertising and fail to develop and use all the marketing mix tools.

The social marketer, in designing a social change strategy, goes through a normal marketing planning process. The first step is to define the objective. Suppose the objective is "to reduce the percentage of teenagers who smoke from 60% to 40% within five years." The next step is to analyze the beliefs, attitudes, values, and behavior of teenagers. The major forces that support teenage smoking are also analyzed. This is followed by concepts that might dissuade teenagers from smoking (see exhibit 19-1). The next step calls for evaluating alternative communication and distribution approaches to the target market. This is followed by the development of a marketing plan and a marketing organization to carry it out. Finally, provision is made to monitor ongoing results and take corrective action.

Exhibit **19-1**

Can Social Marketing Reduce Cigarette Smoking?

The weight of scientific evidence demonstrates a link between cigarette smoking and lung cancer, heart disease, and emphysema. Most cigarette smokers are aware of the bad effects of cigarette smoking. The problem is to give them the means or the will to reduce their cigarette consumption. The four *P*'s suggest several possible approaches:

1. Product
   a. Require manufacturers to add a tart or bitter ingredient to the tobacco.
   b. Cut down further on the tar and nicotine in cigarettes.
   c. Find a new type of tobacco for cigarettes that tastes as good but is safe.
   d. Promote other products that will help people relieve their tensions, such as chewing gum.

2. Promotion
   a. Increase fear of early death among smokers.
   b. Create guilt or shame among cigarette users.
   c. Strengthen other goals of smokers that surpass their satisfaction from smoking.
   d. Urge smokers to cut down the number of cigarettes they smoke or to smoke only the first half of the cigarette.

3. Place
   a. Make cigarettes harder to obtain or unavailable.
   b. Make it easier for cigarette smokers to attend antismoking clinics.
   c. Make it harder to find public places that allow cigarette smoking.

4. Price
   a. Raise the price of cigarettes substantially.
   b. Raise the cost of life and health insurance to smokers.
   c. Offer a monetary or nonmonetary reward to smokers for each period they forgo smoking.

Social marketing is still too new to evaluate its effectiveness in comparison with other social change strategies. Social change is hard to produce with any strategy, let alone one that relies on voluntary response. Social marketing has been mainly applied to family planning,[17] environmental protection,[18] energy conservation, improved nutrition, auto driver safety, and public transportation, with some encouraging successes. More applications will have to take place before we can determine social marketing's contributions to social change.

Summary

Marketing has been broadened in recent years to cover "marketable" entities other than products, namely, services, organizations, persons, places, and ideas.

The United States is the world's first service economy in that most Americans work in service industries. Services are activities or benefits that one party can offer to another that are essentially intangible and do not result in the ownership of anything. Services are intangible, inseparable, variable, and perishable. Services can be classified according to whether they are people- or equipment-based, whether the client's presence is necessary, whether the client is a consumer or business, and whether the service provider is a profit or nonprofit firm in the private or public sector. Service industries lag behind manufacturing firms in adopting and using marketing concepts. Yet rising costs and increasing competition are forcing service industries to search for ways to increase their productivity. Marketing makes a contribution by calling for more systematic planning of service concepts and their pricing, distribution, and promotion.

Organizations can also be marketed. Organization marketing is undertaken to create, maintain, or alter attitudes and/or behavior of target audiences toward particular organizations. It calls for assessing the organization's current image and developing a marketing plan for bringing about an improved image.

Person marketing consists of activities undertaken to create, maintain, or alter attitudes and/or behavior toward particular persons. Two common forms are celebrity marketing and political candidate marketing.

Place marketing involves activities undertaken to create, maintain, or alter attitudes and/or behavior toward particular places. The four most common types are domicile marketing, business site marketing, land investment marketing, and vacation marketing.

Idea marketing involves efforts to market ideas. In the case of social ideas it is called social marketing and consists of the design, implementation, and control of programs seeking to increase the acceptability of a social idea, cause, or practice in a target group. Social marketing goes further than public advertising in coordinating advertising with the other elements of the marketing mix. The social marketer proceeds by defining the social change objective, analyzing consumer attitudes and competitive forces, developing and testing alternative concepts, developing appropriate channels for the idea's communication and distribution, and finally, monitoring the results. Social marketing has been applied to family planning, environmental protection, antismoking campaigns, and other public issues.

Questions for Discussion

1. In 1981, the U.S. government was ranked twenty-fourth among the leading advertisers in the United States based on total expenditures, while the Canadian government was the leading advertiser in that country, spending twice as much as General Foods, the second-ranked advertiser. In your opinion, why was there

such a difference between the relative rankings of these two governments in advertising expenditures?

2. Many banks have been hiring marketing executives with consumer packaged-goods marketing experience. In your opinion, why has this trend occurred, and what problems, if any, might result from this hiring practice?

3. Relate the four distinctive characteristics of services to the purchase of a movie ticket.

4. Producers of services have historically been more marketing-oriented than producers of products. Comment.

5. Explain how distribution channels are important to the following service marketers: (a) Coopers and Lybrand ("Big 8" accounting firm), (b) Paramount Pictures, (c) Joe's Repair Shop, and (d) the local repertory theater.

6. What is the primary purpose of the individual charged with organization marketing? Explain.

7. The only places that can be effectively marketed are those that people enjoy visiting. Comment.

8. What distinguishes social marketing from social advertising? Explain.

Key Terms in Chapter 19

Organization marketing The activities undertaken to create, maintain, or alter attitudes and/or behavior of target audiences toward particular organizations.

Person marketing Activities undertaken to create, maintain, or alter attitudes and/or behavior toward particular persons.

Place marketing Activities undertaken to create, maintain, or alter attitudes and/or behavior toward particular places.

Public relations The management function that evaluates public attitudes, identifies the policies and procedures of an individual or an organization with the public interest, and plans and ex-

ecutes a program of action to earn public understanding and acceptance.

Service Any activity or benefit that one party can offer to another that is essentially intangible and does not result in the ownership of anything.

Social marketing The design, implementation, and control of programs seeking to increase the acceptability of a social idea, cause, or practice in a target group(s); uses market segmentation, consumer research, concept development, communications, facilitation, incentives, and exchange theory to maximize target group response.

Cases for Chapter 19

Case 18   Consumers Union of the United States, Inc. (p. 520)
The Consumers Union, a nonprofit organization, has to market itself to the public. This case looks at some of the factors involved.

Case 19   H & R Block: Legal Services (p. 521)
Not only does H & R Block have to market its new legal clinics, but it also has to market the idea of legal services. This case considers some of the problems.

Chapter 20

Marketing and Society

Objectives

After reading this chapter, you should be able to:

1. List and respond to ten social criticisms of marketing.
2. Explain how consumerism and environmentalism affect marketing strategies.
3. Describe five principles followed by socially responsible marketers.
4. Discuss the role of ethics in marketing.

Northern California experienced a severe drought starting in 1977. The lack of water threatened to destroy much fruit and vegetables that California supplied to the nation, cause power shortages, increase fire hazards, destroy green lawns, and limit opportunities for fishing and boating. Long-run solutions, such as weather modification, water desalinization, and better irrigation, would not be ready to help in the current crisis. Each community had to adopt strong measures to encourage major user segments—homes, industry, agriculture, and government—to cut down on their water consumption. For example, the community of Palo Alto initially sought a 10% reduction in water consumption in its area. To accomplish this, the community undertook a large number of actions, including:

1. Water consumption quotas were established for households and other types of users. For example, households were required to reduce their consumption by a certain percentage of their consumption in the previous year.
2. The price of water was raised but not expected to deter much usage by itself.
3. Citizens were sent water flow restrictors to use on their faucets.
4. Extraordinary media coverage was given to the water crisis on radio and television and in newspapers. Brochures were mailed to all homeowners.
5. Citizens were asked to reexamine each water use and to bring it down. This meant fewer showers, fewer toilet flushes, less washing of clothes and dishes, less watering of lawns, less car washing, and so on.

The many campaigns were so effective in producing citizen awareness, interest, desire, and action that water consumption dropped by 17% in Palo Alto. Palo Alto residents, it appeared, competed in conspicuous nonconsumption, trying to outdo each other with stories of how they found ways to cut down on water. Some claimed, with civic pride, not to have taken a bath for a month. Other sectors, including business firms and government agencies, also managed to effect substantial reductions in their water consumption.[1]

Responsible marketers will interpret buyer wants and respond with appropriate products, priced to yield good value to the buyers and profit to the producer. The *marketing concept* is a philosophy of service and mutual gain. Its practice leads the economy by an invisible hand to satisfy the many and changing needs of millions of consumers.

Not all marketing practice follows this theory. Some individuals and companies use questionable marketing practices. And some private marketing transactions, seemingly innocent in themselves, have deep implications for the larger society. Consider the sale of cigarettes. Ordinarily, companies should be free to sell cigarettes, and smokers should be free to buy them. However, the public is interested in this transaction. First, the smoker may be shortening his or her own life. Second, this places a burden on the smoker's family and on society at large. Third, other people in the presence of the smoker may have to inhale the smoke and may experience discomfort and harm. This is not to say that cigarettes should be banned. Rather, it shows that private transactions may involve questions of public policy.

This chapter looks at the social consequences of private marketing practices. It addresses the following questions: (1) What are the most frequent social criticisms of marketing? (2) What steps have private citizens taken to curb marketing ills? (3) What steps have legislators and government agencies taken to curb marketing ills? (4) What steps have enlightened companies taken to carry out socially responsible marketing?

Social Criticisms of Marketing

Some social critics claim that marketing hurts individual consumers, society as a whole, and other businesses.

Marketing's Impact on Individual Consumers Critics have accused the American marketing system of harming consumers through (1) high prices, (2) deceptive practices, (3) high-pressure selling, (4) shoddy or unsafe products, (5) planned obsolescence, and (6) poor service to disadvantaged consumers.

HIGH PRICES.   Many critics charge that the American marketing system causes prices to be higher than they would be under more "sensible" arrangements. They point to three factors.

High costs of distribution.   A long-standing charge is that greedy middlemen mark up prices beyond the value of their services. One of the most thorough studies of distribution costs appeared in *Does Distribution Cost Too Much?* The study was done after observing that selling and distribution costs rose from 20% of product costs in 1850 to 50% of product costs in 1920. The authors concluded that distribution cost too much and pointed their finger at ". . . duplication of sales efforts, multiplicity of sales outlets, excessive services, multitudes of brands, and unnecessary advertising . . . misinformed buying on the part of consumers . . . and, among distributors themselves, lack of a proper knowledge of costs, too great zeal for volume, poor management and planning, and unwise price policies."[2]

How do retailers answer these charges? They argue as follows: First, middlemen perform work that would otherwise have to be performed by the manufacturers or the consumers. Second, the rising markup reflects improved services that consumers want: more convenience, larger stores and assortment, longer store hours, return privileges, and so on. Third, the costs of operating stores keep rising and force retailers to raise their prices. Fourth, retail competition is so intense that profit margins are actually quite low. For example, supermarket chains are barely left with 1% profit on their sales after taxes.

High advertising and promotion costs.   Modern marketing is also accused of pushing up prices because of heavy advertising and sales promotion. For example, a dozen tablets of a well-known brand of aspirin sell for the same price as one hundred tablets of lesser-known brands. Critics feel that if "commodity" products were sold in bulk, their prices would be considerably lower. Differentiated products—cosmetics, detergents, toiletries—include costs of packaging and promotion that can amount to 40% or more of the manufacturer's price to the retailer. Much of the packaging and promotion adds psychological rather than functional value to the product. Retailers themselves undertake additional promotion—advertising, trading stamps, games of chance, and so on—thereby adding several more cents to retail prices.

Business people have answers to these charges. First, consumers are not interested only in the functional aspects of products. They also buy concepts, such as products that make them feel affluent, beautiful, or special. The manufacturer develops concepts for the market that consumers are willing to pay for. If they want, consumers can usually buy functional versions of the product at a lower price. Second, branding exists to give confidence to buyers. A brand name signifies a certain quality, and consumers are willing to pay for well-known brands even if they cost a little more. Third, heavy advertising is a necessary, cost-effective way to inform the millions of potential buyers of the existence and merits of a brand. If consumers want to know what is available on the market, they must expect manufacturers to spend large sums of money on advertising. Fourth, heavy advertising and promotion are necessary for the firm when competitors are doing it. The individual enterprise would lose "share of mind" if it did not match competitive expenditures. At the same time, companies are very cost conscious about promotion and try to spend their money wisely. And fifth, heavy sales promotion is necessary from time to time because goods are produced ahead of demand in a mass-production economy. Special incentives have to be offered to buyers in order to sell inventories.

Excessive Markups. Critics charge that certain industries are particularly guilty of marking up goods excessively. They point to the drug industry, where a pill costing five cents to manufacture may cost the consumer forty cents; they point to the pricing tactics of funeral homes that prey on the emotions of bereaved relatives;[3] they point to the high charges of television and auto repair people.

Business people respond to these criticisms with the following observations: First, there are some unscrupulous business owners who take advantage of consumers. They should be reported to the Better Business Bureau and other consumer protection groups. Second, most businesses deal fairly with consumers because they want their repeat business. Third, consumers often do not understand the reason for high markups. Pharmaceutical markups have to cover the cost of purchasing, promoting, and distributing existing medicines and the high research and development costs spent in the search for new and improved medicines.

DECEPTIVE PRACTICES. Business people are often accused of deceptive practices that lead consumers into believing they will get more value than they actually do. Certain industries draw a higher than average number of complaints. Among the worst offenders are insurance companies (claiming that policies are "guaranteed renewable" or underwritten by the government), publishing companies (approaching subscribers under false pretenses), mail-order land-sales organizations (misrepresenting land tracts or improvement costs), home improvement contractors (using bait-and-switch tactics), automotive repair shops (advertising ultra-low repair prices and then "discovering" a necessary major repair), home freezer plans (falsely representing the savings), correspondence schools (overstating employment opportunities after course completion), vending machine companies (falsely guaranteeing top locations), studios offering dance instruction (signing up elderly people for lessons beyond their life expectancy), and companies selling medical devices (exaggerating therapeutic claims).

Deceptive practices have given rise to legislative and administrative remedies. In 1938, the Wheeler-Lea Act gave the Federal Trade Commission (FTC) power to regulate "unfair or deceptive acts or practices." The FTC has published several guidelines listing deceptive practices. The toughest problem is distinguishing between puffery and deception in advertising. Shell Oil advertised that Super Shell with platformate consistently gave more mileage than the same gasoline without platformate. Now this is true, but what Shell did not say is that almost all automotive gasoline includes platformate. Its defense was that it had never claimed that platformate was an exclusive Shell feature. The FTC, however, felt that the ad's intent was to deceive, although the message was literally honest.

Defenders of advertising freedom offer three arguments: First, most business people avoid deceptive practices because such practices would harm their businesses in the long run. Consumers would fail to get what they expected and would switch to more reliable entrepreneurs. Second, most consumers recognize advertising exaggeration and exercise a healthy skepticism when they buy. And third, some advertising puffery is inevitable and even desirable.

HIGH-PRESSURE SELLING.   Sales representatives in certain industries are accused of applying high-pressure selling techniques that get people to buy goods they had no thought of buying. It is often said that encyclopedias, insurance, real estate, and jewelry are sold, not bought. The sales representatives are trained in delivering smooth canned talks to entice purchase. They sell hard because sales contests promise big prizes to those sales representatives who sell the most.

Business people recognize that buyers can often be talked into buying things they did not start out wanting or needing. Recent legislation requires door-to-door salespeople to announce their purpose at the door—to sell the product. Buyers are allowed a "three-day cooling-off period" in which they can cancel their contract after rethinking it. In addition, consumers can complain to the Better Business Bureau when they feel that undue selling pressure was applied.

SHODDY OR UNSAFE PRODUCTS.   Another criticism is that products lack the quality they should have. One type of complaint is that products are not made well. "If [the consumer] somehow escapes rattles, pings, loose buttons, or missing knobs there probably will be dents, mismatched sizes, static fluttering, leaking, or creaking."[4] Automobiles receive a higher than average number of complaints. Consumers Union, an independent testing agency that publishes *Consumer Reports,* tested thirty-two cars and found something wrong with all of them. "Cars were delivered with rain leaks, fender dents, nonaligned windows, broken distributor caps, ignition locks that wouldn't lock."[5] Complaints have also been lodged about home and auto repair services, various appliances, and clothing.

A second type of complaint concerns whether certain products deliver any benefit. Consumers got a shock on hearing that dry breakfast cereal may have little nutritional value. Robert B. Choate, a nutritional specialist, told a Senate subcommittee: "In short, [the cereals] fatten but do little to prevent malnutrition. . . . The average cereal . . . fails as a complete meal even with milk added."[6] Choate added that consumers could often get more nutrition by eating the cereal package than the contents.

A third type of complaint has to do with products' safety characteristics. For years, Consumers Union has reported various hazards in tested products—electrical dangers in appliances, carbon monoxide poisoning from room heaters, finger risks in lawn mowers, and faulty steering in automobiles. Product quality has been a problem in certain industries for a number of reasons, including occasional manufacturer indifference, increased product complexity, poorly trained labor, and insufficient quality control.

On the other hand, several forces also lead manufacturers to have an interest in producing good quality. First, large manufacturers are very concerned with

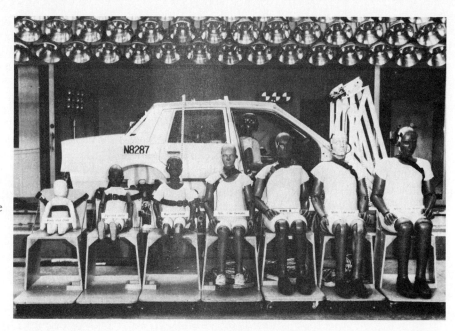

In response to consumers' complaints about unsafe products, some companies developed extensive product testing programs. This is a family of dummies used by General Motors to evaluate human reactions to collisions.

Courtesy General Motors

their reputations. A customer who is disappointed with one of their products may avoid buying their other products (see exhibit 20-1). Second, large retailers are developing their own name for quality, both in their selection of national brands and in their private brands. Third, consumer groups keep an eye out for poorly made or unsafe products.

PLANNED OBSOLESCENCE. Critics have charged that producers in certain industries cause their products to become obsolete before they actually need replacement. There are three types of obsolescence.

Planned style obsolescence is a strategy used by producers to change users' concepts of acceptable appearance. Manufacturers of women's apparel, men's apparel, automobiles, furniture, and even homes have been accused of this. The annual style change of Detroit automobiles is another example.

Planned functional obsolescence means a deliberate policy by manufacturers to "withhold fully developed attractive features whose present absence and subsequent introduction may be used to encourage an earlier replacement of the product. . . ."[7] An example would be the withholding by automobile manufacturers of a whole set of improvements with respect to safety, pollution reduction, and gasoline economy.

Planned material obsolescence means that manufacturers choose materials and components that are subject to higher breakage, wear, rot, or corrosion. For example, many drapery manufacturers are using a higher percentage of rayon in their drapes. They argue that rayon reduces the price of the drapes and has better holding power. Critics assert that rayon will cause the drapes to fall apart in two cleanings instead of four.

Exhibit **20-1**

A Contrast in Company Responses to Unsafe Products

This is the story of two companies, one that moved too slowly after its tire failures allegedly killed twenty-nine people and injured fifty, and another that moved very swiftly when its toy killed two children.

Concern over the performance of the Firestone 500 radial tire arose in 1976 when a Ralph Nader group started receiving consumer complaints. The National Highway Traffic Safety Administration (NHTSA) investigated after receiving more than five hundred complaints. Over fourteen thousand consumer complaints were compiled. Then Firestone sought an injunction against release of the NHTSA report. The Firestone Company waited until it was forced by the government to recall the thirteen million Firestone radial tires.

Parker Brothers, the toy company that is a subsidiary of General Mills, voluntarily recalled a spectacularly successful toy called Riviton, a kit consisting of plastic parts, rubber rivets, and a riveting tool. When Parker Brothers heard of the first death, it was assumed to be a freak accident never to be repeated. When the second death was caused by the same part of the toy, "the decision was very simple. Were we supposed to sit back and wait for death No. 3?" said Randolph Barton, president of Parker Brothers. In support of Parker Brothers' swift behavior, Susan King, chairman of the Consumer Product Safety Commission, stated that the company was "a model of social responsibility."

Business people answer these charges as follows: First, consumers like style changes. They get tired of the old products. People want a new look in fashion or a new-styled automobile. No one has to buy the new look. If enough people did not like it, it would fail. Second, companies withhold new functional features when they are not adequately tested, when they add more cost to the product than consumers are willing to pay, and for other good reasons. They do this at the risk of having a competitor introduce the new feature and steal the market. Third, companies often substitute new materials in order to lower their costs and prices. They do not design their products to break down earlier because they would lose their customers to other brands. Fourth, much of so-called planned obsolescence is the working out of dynamic competitive and technological forces in a free society, leading to ever-improving goods and services.

POOR SERVICE TO THE DISADVANTAGED CONSUMER. The American marketing system has been accused of poorly serving disadvantaged consumers. According to David Caplovitz in his *The Poor Pay More,* the urban poor often have to shop in smaller stores that carry inferior goods and charge higher prices.[8] The former chairman of the FTC, Paul Rand Dixon, summarized a Washington, D.C., study:

> The poor pay more—nearly twice as much—for appliances and furniture sold in Washington's low-income area stores. . . . Goods purchased for $100 at wholesale sold for $225 in the low-income stores compared with $159 in the general market stores. . . . Installment credit is a major marketing factor in selling to the poor . . . some low-income market retailers imposed effective annual finance charges as high as 33 percent. . . . [9]

Yet ironically, the merchants' profits were not exorbitant:

> The findings of the economic study suggest that the marketing system for distribution of durable goods to low-income areas is costly. Low-income market retailers have markedly higher costs, partly because of bad debt expenses, but to a greater extent because of higher selling, wage, and commission costs. These expenses reflect in part greater use of home demonstration selling, and expenses associated with the collection and processing of installment contracts. Thus, although their markups are often two or three times higher than general market retailers, on the average low-income market retailers do not make particularly high profits.[10]

Clearly, better marketing systems must be built in low-income areas, and low-income people need consumer protection. The FTC has taken action against merchants who advertise false values, sell old merchandise as new, or charge too much for credit. It is trying to make it harder for merchants to win court judgments and garnishments against low-income people who were wheedled into buying something. Another hope is to encourage large-scale retailers to open outlets in low-income areas.[11]

Marketing's Impact on Society as a Whole

The American marketing system has been accused of contributing to several "bads" in American society—excessive materialism, false wants, insufficient social goods, cultural pollution, and excessive political power.

EXCESSIVE MATERIALISM. Critics have charged that the American business system encourages excessive interest in material possessions. People are judged by what they own rather than by what they are. People are not considered successful unless they own a suburban home, two cars, and the latest clothes and appliances.

Some of this may be changing. Some Americans are losing their drive for possessions. They are relaxing more, playing more, and learning to get along with less. "Small is beautiful" and "less is more" describe this ideology. More emphasis is being placed on cultivating close relationships and simple pleasures than on being "hooked on things."

FALSE WANTS. The interest in things is not seen as a natural state of mind but rather as one created by Madison Avenue. Business hires Madison Avenue to stimulate people's desires for goods. Madison Avenue uses the mass media to create materialistic models of the good life. Conspicuous consumption on the part of some creates envy in others. People work harder to earn the necessary money. Their purchases increase the output and productive capacity of Industrial America. In turn, Industrial America makes greater use of Madison Avenue to stimulate desire for the industrial output. Thus people are seen as the manipulated link between production and consumption. Wants come to depend on output.

This summary probably exaggerates the power of business to create or stimulate wants. Under normal social conditions, people see and choose among conflicting life-styles. In addition, people have normal defenses against the mass media—selective attention, perception, distortion, and retention. The mass media are most effective when they appeal to existing needs rather than attempt to create new ones. Furthermore, people seek information with respect to larger purchases and do not rely on single sources of information. Even small purchases, which may be influenced by advertising messages, lead to repeat purchases only if the product's performance meets the expectations. Finally, the high failure rate of new products contradicts the claim that companies are able to control demand.

On a deeper level, our wants and values are influenced not only by marketers but also by family, peer groups, religion, ethnic background, and education. If Americans are highly materialistic, it is because their value system arose out of basic socialization processes that go much deeper than business and mass media could produce alone.

INSUFFICIENT SOCIAL GOODS.   Business has been accused of overstimulating demand for private goods (such as automobiles) at the expense of public goods (the roads the automobiles are driven on). As private goods increase, they require a proportionate number of public services that are usually not forthcoming. According to economist John Kenneth Galbraith:

> An increase in the consumption of automobiles requires a facilitating supply of streets, highways, traffic control, and parking space. The protective services of the police and the highway patrols must also be available, as must those of the hospitals. Although the need for balance here is extraordinarily clear, our use of privately produced vehicles has, on occasion, got far out of line with the supply of the related public services. The result has been hideous road congestion, an annual massacre of impressive proportions, and chronic colitis in the cities.[12]

Thus Galbraith sees private consumption leading to a "social imbalance" and "social costs" that neither the producers nor the consumers appear willing to pay for. A way must be found to restore a social balance between private goods and public goods. Manufacturing firms could be required to bear the full social costs of their operations. In this way, they would build these costs into the price. Where buyers did not find the private goods worth the price, those firms would disappear and resources would move to those uses that could support the sum of the private and social costs.

CULTURAL POLLUTION.   Critics charge the marketing system with creating *cultural pollution*. People's senses are constantly being assaulted by advertising.

Serious programs are interrupted by commercials; printed matter is lost between pages of ads; magnificent landscapes are marred by billboards. These interruptions intrude sex, power, or status continuously into people's consciousness.

Business people answer the charges of commercial noise with these arguments: First, they hope that their ads primarily reach the target audience. Because of mass-communication channels, some ads are bound to reach people who have no interest in the product and are therefore bored or irritated. People who buy magazines addressed to their interests—such as *Vogue* or *Fortune*—rarely complain about the ads because they advertise products of interest. Second, the ads make commercial radio and television free media and keep down the costs of magazines and newspapers. Most people think commercials are a small price to pay.

EXCESSIVE POLITICAL POWER. Another criticism is that business wields too much political power. There are "oil," "cigarette," and "auto" senators who support particular industries' interests against the public interest. Business is accused of holding too much power over the mass media, limiting their freedom to report independently and objectively. One critic said: "How can *Life, Post,* and *Reader's Digest* afford to tell the truth about the scandalously low nutritional value of most packaged foods . . . when these magazines are being subsidized by such advertisers as General Foods, Kellogg's, Nabisco, and General Mills? . . . The answer is *they cannot and do not.*"[13]

American industries do promote and protect their interests. They have a right to representation in Congress and the mass media, although their influence could become too extensive. Fortunately, many powerful business interests thought to be untouchable have been tamed in the public interest. Standard Oil was dismantled in 1911, and the meat-packing industry was disciplined after the exposures of Upton Sinclair. Ralph Nader inspired legislation requiring the auto industry to build more safety into its vehicles, and the Surgeon General's Report required cigarette companies to include a health warning on their packages. The media are becoming more courageous in featuring editorial material designed to interest different market segments. Excessive business power tends to produce countervailing forces to check and offset these powerful interests.

Marketing's Impact on Other Businesses

Critics also charge that many companies ride roughshod over other companies. Three problems are involved: anticompetitive mergers, artificial barriers to entry, and predatory competition.

ANTICOMPETITIVE ACQUISITION. A recurrent accusation is that many firms expand by acquiring other firms rather than by internally developing new and needed products. Within a certain time period, the nine leading ethical drug companies developed eight new businesses internally and acquired sixteen other businesses.[14] As another example, Procter & Gamble (P&G) acquired Clorox, the major producer of household liquid bleach.[15] The Supreme Court ruled that P&G's acquisition would deprive the industry of potential competition not only from P&G, had it entered the market on its own, but also from smaller firms that might now be discouraged from entering this market.

Acquisition is a complicated subject. Acquisitions can be beneficial to the society under the following circumstances: (1) when the acquiring company can produce goods more economically, leading to lower costs and lower prices; (2) when a well-managed company takes over a poorly managed company and improves its efficiency; and (3) when an industry that was noncompetitive becomes competitive after the acquisition. Acquisitions can also be harmful, particularly when a vigorous young competitor is absorbed and fewer firms dominate the industry.

BARRIERS TO ENTRY.   Critics have charged that marketing practices add substantial barriers to entry into an industry by new companies. These barriers take the form of patents, substantial promotion requirements, tie-ups of suppliers or dealers, and so on.

People concerned with antitrust regulation recognize that some barriers are associated with the economic advantage of large-scale enterprise. Other barriers could be challenged by existing and new laws. For example, some critics have proposed a progressive tax on advertising expenditures to reduce the role of selling costs as a major barrier to entry.

PREDATORY COMPETITION.   Some firms have been known to use competitive tactics with the intention of hurting or destroying other firms. They may set their prices below costs, threaten to cut off business with suppliers, or disparage the competitor's products.

Various laws have been designed to prevent predatory competition. It is difficult, though, to establish that the intent or action was really predatory. In a classic case, A&P, a large retailer, was able to charge lower prices than small mom-and-pop grocery stores. The question is whether this was predatory competition or the healthy competition of a more efficient retailing institution against the less efficient.[16]

Citizen Actions to Regulate Marketing

Because some people have viewed business as the cause of many economic and social ills, grass-roots movements have arisen from time to time to discipline business. The two major antibusiness movements have been *consumerism* and *environmentalism*.

Consumerism   American business firms have been the target of an organized consumer movement on three occasions. The first consumer movement took place in the early 1900s and was fueled by rising prices, Upton Sinclair's exposés of conditions in the meat industry, and the ethical-drug scandals. The second consumer movement, in the mid-1930s, was sparked by an upturn in consumer prices in the midst of the Depression and another drug scandal. The third movement began in the 1960s. Consumers had become better educated; products had become increasingly complex and hazardous; discontent with American institutions was widespread; influential writings by John Kenneth Galbraith, Vance Packard, and Rachel Carson accused big business of wasteful and manipulative practices; a

1962 presidential speech by John F. Kennedy declared that consumers have the right to safely, to be informed, to choose, and to be heard; there were congressional investigations of certain industries; and, finally, Ralph Nader appeared on the scene to force many of the issues.[17]

Since then, many consumer groups have been organized and several consumer laws have been passed. The consumer movement has spread internationally and has become very strong in Scandinavia and the Low Countries. But what is the consumer movement?

Consumerism is an organized movement of citizens and government to enhance the rights and power of buyers in relation to sellers.

The traditional sellers' rights include:

1. The right to introduce any product in any size and style, provided it is not hazardous to personal health or safety; or, if it is, to introduce it with the proper warning and controls.
2. The right to price the product at any level, provided there is no discrimination among similar classes of buyers.
3. The right to spend any amount of money to promote the product, provided it is not defined as unfair competition.
4. The right to use any product message, provided it is not misleading or dishonest in content or execution.
5. The right to introduce any buying incentive schemes they wish.

The traditional buyers' rights include:

1. The right not to buy a product that is offered for sale.
2. The right to expect the product to be safe.
3. The right to expect the product to perform as claimed.

Comparing these rights, many believe that the balance of power lies on the sellers' side. True, the buyer can refuse to buy. But critics feel that the buyer has insufficient information, education, and protection to make wise decisions when facing highly sophisticated sellers. Consumer advocates call for the following additional consumer rights:

4. The right to be adequately informed about the more important aspects of the product.
5. The right to be protected against questionable products and marketing practices.
6. The right to influence products and marketing practices in directions that will enhance the "quality of life."

Consumers have not only rights but responsibilities to protect themselves instead of leaving this to someone else. Consumers who feel they got a bad deal have several remedies available, including writing to the company president or to the media; contacting federal, state, or local agencies; and filing claims in small-claims courts.

Environmentalism Where consumerists focus on whether the marketing system is efficiently serving consumer wants, environmentalists focus on marketing's impact on the environment and the costs of serving these needs and wants. In 1962, Rachel Carson's *Silent Spring* presented a documented case of pesticidal pollution of the environment.[18] It was no longer a matter of wasted resources but of human survival. In 1970, the Ehrlichs coined the term "eco-catastrophe" to symbolize the harmful impact of certain American business practices on the environment.[19] And in 1972, the Meadowses published *The Limits to Growth,* which warned people that the quality of life would inevitably decline in the face of unchecked population growth, spreading pollution, and continued exploitation of natural resources.[20] These concerns underpin environmentalism.

Environmentalists want companies to operate on ecological principles.

United Press International Photo

> **Environmentalism** is an organized movement of concerned citizens and government to protect and enhance people's living environment.

Environmentalists are concerned with strip mining, forest depletion, factory smoke, billboards, and litter, with the loss of recreational opportunity, and with the increase in health problems due to bad air and water and chemically sprayed food.

Environmentalists are not against marketing and consumption; they simply want them to operate on ecological principles. They do not think the marketing system's goal should be to maximize consumption, consumer choice, or consumer satisfaction. The marketing system's goal should be to maximize life quality. And life quality means not only the quantity and quality of consumer goods and services but also the quality of the environment.

Environmentalism has hit certain industries hard. Steel companies and public utilities have had to invest billions of dollars in pollution-control equipment and costlier fuels. The auto industry has had to introduce expensive emission controls in cars. The soap industry has had to develop low-phosphate detergents. The packaging industry has had to develop ways to reduce litter and increase biodegradability in its products. The gasoline industry has had to formulate new low-lead and no-lead gasolines. These industries resent environmental regulations, especially when imposed too rapidly to allow the companies to make the proper adjustments. These companies have absorbed large costs and have passed them on to buyers.

Public Actions to Regulate Marketing

Citizen agitation against specific marketing practices will usually stimulate public debate and lead to legislative proposals. The bills will be debated, and many will be defeated, others will be modified and sometimes made "toothless," and a few will emerge in really workable form.

We listed many of the laws bearing on marketing in chapter 4. The task is to translate these laws into the language that marketing executives understand as they make decisions in the areas of competitive relations, products, price, promotion, and channels of distribution. Figure 20-1 summarizes the major issues facing marketing management when making decisions. The specific dos and don'ts have already been reviewed in the appropriate chapters.

Business Actions toward Socially Responsible Marketing

At the present time, most companies have come around to accepting the new consumer rights in principle. They might oppose specific pieces of legislation as not being the best way to solve particular consumer problems. But they recognize consumers' rights to information and protection. In this section we will examine responsible and creative business responses to the changing marketing environment. We first outline a concept of enlightened marketing and then consider marketing ethics. Enlightened marketing holds that the company's marketing should support the best long-run performance of the marketing system. Enlightened marketing embodies five principles.

CONSUMER-ORIENTED MARKETING. The company should view and organize its marketing activities from consumers' point of view. It should strive to effec-

FIGURE 20-1

Major Marketing Decision Areas that May Be Called into Question under the Law

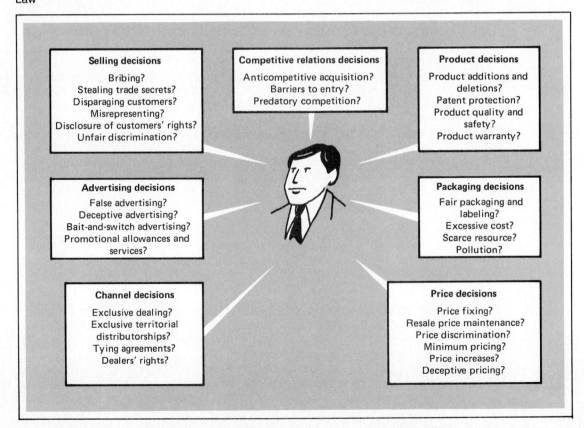

Selling decisions	Competitive relations decisions	Product decisions
Bribing? Stealing trade secrets? Disparaging customers? Misrepresenting? Disclosure of customers' rights? Unfair discrimination?	Anticompetitive acquisition? Barriers to entry? Predatory competition?	Product additions and deletions? Patent protection? Product quality and safety? Product warranty?

Advertising decisions		Packaging decisions
False advertising? Deceptive advertising? Bait-and-switch advertising? Promotional allowances and services?		Fair packaging and labeling? Excessive cost? Scarce resource? Pollution?

Channel decisions		Price decisions
Exclusive dealing? Exclusive territorial distributorships? Tying agreements? Dealers' rights?		Price fixing? Resale price maintenance? Price discrimination? Minimum pricing? Price increases? Deceptive pricing?

tively and efficiently sense, serve, and satisfy a defined set of needs of a defined group of customers. Consider the following example:

> Barat College, a women's college in Lake Forest, Illinois, published a college catalog that candidly spelled out Barat College's strong and weak points. Among the weak points it shared with applicants were the following: "An exceptionally talented student musician or mathematician . . . might be advised to look further for a college with top faculty and facilities in that field. . . . The full range of advanced specialized courses offered in a university will be absent. . . . The library collection is average for a small college, but low in comparison with other high-quality institutions."

The effect of "telling it like it is" is to build confidence so that applicants really know what they will find at Barat College and to emphasize that Barat College will strive to improve its consumer value as rapidly as time and funds permit.

INNOVATIVE MARKETING. The company should continuously seek real product and marketing improvements. The company that overlooks new and better ways to do things will eventually be challenged by a company that has found a better way. One of the best examples of an innovative marketer is Procter & Gamble (P&G):

> P&G's approach to markets is to search for benefits that customers might be missing. In the case of Crest toothpaste, P&G spent years seeking a toothpaste that would be effective in reducing tooth decay, since most toothpastes either made no such claim or implied some effectiveness at fighting tooth decay without really being effective. Some time later P&G decided to enter the shampoo market and develop a benefit that many customers wanted but no brand provided, that of dandruff control. After years of research, it launched Head and Shoulders, which became an instant market leader. P&G then looked for a way to enter the paper products business. It noticed a need on the part of new parents for a "disposable" diaper that would be low enough in price to replace the chores of handling and washing cloth diapers. After years of research, P&G developed an effective paper diaper at a cost that most families could afford. The product was named Pampers, and it immediately won market leadership.

VALUE MARKETING. The company should put most of its resources into value marketing that builds the value of its products. A number of things marketers do—one-shot sales promotions, minor packaging changes, advertising puffery—may raise sales in the short run but add less value in improving the product's quality, features, or convenience.

SENSE-OF-MISSION MARKETING. The company should define its mission in broad social terms rather than narrow product terms. When a company defines a social mission, company personnel feel better about their work and have a clearer sense of direction. Consider the mission statement of the International Minerals and Chemical Corporation:

> We're not merely in the business of selling our brand of fertilizer. We have a sense of purpose, a sense of where we are going. The first function of cor-

porate planning is to decide what kind of business the company is in. Our business is *agricultural productivity*. We are interested in anything that affects plant growth, now and in the future.[21]

SOCIETAL MARKETING. An enlightened company will make marketing decisions by considering consumers' wants, the company's requirements, consumers' long-run interests, and the society's long-run interests. The company is aware that neglecting the last two considerations is a disservice to consumers and society.

A societally oriented marketer wants to design not only pleasing but salutary products. The distinction is shown in figure 20-2. Current products can be classified according to their degree of immediate consumer satisfaction and long-run consumer benefit. *Desirable products* combine high immediate satisfaction and high long-run benefits, such as tasty, nutritious breakfast foods. *Pleasing products* give high immediate satisfaction but may hurt consumers in the long run, such as cigarettes. *Salutary products* have low appeal but are also highly beneficial to consumers in the long run, such as low-phosphate detergents. Finally, *deficient products* have neither immediate appeal nor salutary qualities, such as bad-tasting patent medicine. The challenge posed by pleasing products is that they sell extremely well but may ultimately hurt the consumer. The product opportunity, therefore, is to add salutary qualities without diminishing the product's pleasing qualities. For example, Sears developed a phosphate-free laundry detergent that was very effective. The challenge posed by salutary products is to add some pleasing qualities so that they will become more desirable in consumers' minds.

Marketing Ethics Even the conscientious marketers will face many moral dilemmas. The best thing to do will often be unclear. Since not all executives have fine moral sensitivity, companies need to develop corporate marketing policies. Policies are "broad, fixed guidelines that everyone in the organization must adhere to, and that are not subject to exception."[22] They cover distributor relations, advertising standards, customer service, pricing, product development, and general ethical standards.

Figure 20-3 lists fourteen ethically difficult situations that marketers could

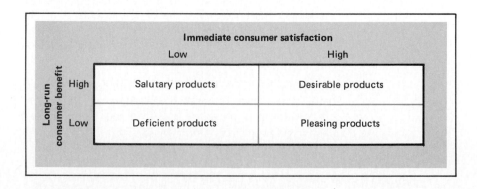

| | | Immediate consumer satisfaction | |
		Low	High
Long-run consumer benefit	High	Salutary products	Desirable products
	Low	Deficient products	Pleasing products

FIGURE 20-2

Classification of New-Product Opportunities

1. You work for a cigarette company and up to now have not been convinced that cigarettes cause cancer. A recent report has come across your desk that clearly establishes the connection between cigarette smoking and cancer. What would you do?
2. Your R&D department has modernized one of your products. It is not really "new and improved," but you know that putting this statement on the package and in the advertising will increase sales. What would you do?
3. You have been asked to add a stripped-down model to the low end of your line that could be advertised to attract customers. The product won't be very good, but the sales representatives could be depended upon to persuade buyers to buy the higher-priced units. You are asked to give the green light for developing this stripped-down version. What would you do?
4. You are interviewing a former product manager who just left a competitor's company. You are thinking of hiring her. She would be more than happy to tell you all the competitor's plans for the coming year. What would you do?
5. One of your dealers in an important territory has had family troubles recently and his sales have slipped. He was one of the company's top producers in the past. It is not clear how long it will take before his family troubles straighten out. In the meantime, many sales are being lost. There is a legal way to terminate the dealer's franchise and replace him. What would you do?
6. You have a chance to win a big account that will mean a lot to you and your company. The purchasing agent hinted that he would be influenced by a "gift." Your assistant recommends sending a color television set to his home. What would you do?
7. You have heard that a competitor has a new product feature that will make a big difference in sales. She will have a hospitality suite at the annual trade show and unveil this feature at a party thrown for her dealers. You can easily send a snooper to this meeting to learn what the new feature is. What would you do?
8. You are eager to win a big contract, and during sales negotiations you learn that the buyer is looking for a better job. You have no intention of hiring him, but if you hinted that you might, he would probably give you the order. What would you do?
9. You have to choose between three ad campaigns outlined by your agency for your new product. The first (A) is a soft-sell, honest information campaign. The second (B) uses sex-loaded emotional appeals and exaggerates the product's benefits. The third (C) involves a noisy, irritating commercial that is sure to gain audience attention. Preliminary tests show that the commercials are effective in the following order: C, B, and A. What would you do?
10. You are a marketing vice-president working for a beer company, and you have learned that a particularly lucrative state is planning to raise the minimum legal drinking age from 18 to 21. You have been asked to join other breweries in lobbying against this bill and make contributions. What would you do?
11. You want to interview a sample of customers about their reactions to a competitive product. It has been suggested that you invent an innocuous name like Marketing Research Institute and interview people. What would you do?
12. You produce an antidandruff shampoo that is effective with one application. Your assistant says that the product would turn over faster if the instructions on the label recommended two applications. What would you do?
13. You are interviewing a capable woman applicant for a job as sales representative. She is better qualified than the men just interviewed. At the same time, you suspect that some of your current salesrepresentatives (all men) will react negatively to her hiring, and you also know that some important customers may be ruffled. What would you do?
14. You are a sales manager in an encyclopedia company. A common way for encyclopedia representatives to get into homes is to pretend they are taking a survey. After they finish the survey, they switch to their sales pitch. This technique seems to be very effective and is used by most of your competitors. What would you do?

FIGURE 20-3

Some Morally Difficult
Situations in
Marketing

face during their careers. If marketers favor the immediate sales-producing actions in all fourteen cases, their marketing behavior might well be described as immoral or amoral. If they refuse to go along with *any* of the actions, they might be ineffective as marketing managers and unhappy because of the constant moral tension. Obviously managers need a set of principles that will help them determine the moral gravity of each situation and how far they can go in good conscience.

Each marketer must work out a philosophy of proper behavior. Every moral system is based on some conception of the good life and the relation of one's welfare to that of others. Once the marketer works out a clear philosophy, he or she can deal with the many knotty questions posed by marketing and other human activities.

Marketing executives of the 1980s will face many challenges. They will have abundant marketing opportunities because of technological advances in solar energy, home computers and robots, cable television, modern medicine, and new forms of transportation, recreation, and communication. At the same time, forces in the socioeconomic environment will increase the constraints under which marketing can be carried out. Those companies that are able to create new values and practice societally responsible marketing will have a world to conquer.

Summary

A marketing system should function to sense, serve, and satisfy consumer needs and enhance the quality of consumers' lives. In endeavoring to meet consumer needs, business people may take certain actions that are not to everyone's liking or benefit. Marketing executives should be aware of the main criticisms.

Marketing's impact on consumer welfare has been criticized for high prices, deceptive practices, high-pressure selling, shoddy or unsafe products, planned obsolescence, and poor service to disadvantaged consumers. Marketing's impact on society has been criticized for excessive materialism, false wants, insufficient social goods, cultural pollution, and excessive political power. Marketing's impact on business competition has been criticized for anticompetitive acquisition, high barriers to entry, and predatory competition.

These felt abuses of the marketing system have given rise to citizen action movements, specifically consumerism and environmentalism. Consumerism is an organized social movement seeking to strengthen the rights and power of consumers in relation to sellers. Resourceful marketers will recognize it as an opportunity to serve consumers better by providing more consumer information, education, and protection. Environmentalism is an organized social movement seeking to minimize the harm done by marketing practices to the environment and quality of life. It calls for intervening when the satisfaction of consumers' wants would create too much environmental cost.

Citizen action has led to the passage of many laws to protect consumers in the area of product safety, truth in lending, ingredient labeling, open dating, and truth in advertising.

Although many businesses initially opposed these social movements and laws, most of them now recognize a need for positive consumer information, education, and protection. Some companies have pursued a policy of enlightened marketing based on the principles of consumer orientation, innovation, value creation, social mission, and societal orientation. These companies have formulated company policies and guidelines to help their executives deal with moral dilemmas.

Questions for Discussion

1. Which two criticisms of marketing's impact on individual consumer welfare are the most legitimate? Briefly defend your position.
2. Those critics of marketing's impact on society are really condemning our American business system rather than just the area of marketing. Comment.
3. The Federal Trade Commission is proposing to restrict mergers between large (over $2 billion in sales) corporations. Which criticisms of marketing's impact on other businesses would this help to alleviate? Why?
4. How does consumerism differ from environmentalism? Which poses the greater threat to marketing? Explain.
5. Discuss the five principles of enlightened marketing.
6. Ethical issues facing marketing will decrease in the 1980s. Comment.
7. If you were the marketing manager at Dow Chemical Company, how would you deal with the principle of curbing potential harm with regard to water pollution?
8. How might the scarcity of natural resources, including energy, affect the principles of economic efficiency and innovation in the future?

Key Terms in Chapter 20

Consumerism An organized movement of citizens and government to enhance the rights and power of buyers in relation to sellers.

Environmentalism An organized movement of concerned citizens and government to protect and enhance people's living environment.

Case for Chapter 20

Case 20 Ronco, Inc. (p. 522)
Evaluating the case of Ronco requires an understanding of all of the material presented in this book.

Appendix A

Marketing Arithmetic

One aspect of marketing that is not discussed within the text is marketing arithmetic. The calculation of sales, costs, and certain ratios is important for many marketing decisions. The purpose of this appendix is to describe three major areas of marketing arithmetic: the operating statement, analytic ratios, and markups and markdowns.

Operating Statement

The operating statement and the balance sheet are the two main financial statements used by companies. The balance sheet shows the assets, liabilities, and net worth of a company at a given point in time. The operating statement (also called profit and loss statement or income statement) is the more important of the two for marketing information. It shows company sales, cost of goods sold, and expenses during the given time period. By examining the operating statement from one time period to the next, the firm can spot favorable or unfavorable trends and take the appropriate action.

Figure A-1 shows the 1983 operating statement for Dale Parsons, a small men's wear specialty store in the Midwest. This statement is for a retailer; the operating statement for a manufacturer would be somewhat different. Specifically, the section on purchases within the "cost of goods sold" area would be replaced by "cost of goods manufactured."

The operating statement's outline follows a logical sequence of steps to arrive at this firm's $5,000 net profit figure:

Net sales	$60,000
Cost of goods sold	− 35,000
Gross margin	$25,000
Expenses	− 20,000
Net profit	$ 5,000

Let us examine the major elements of the operating statement separately.

The first element of the operating statement details the amount that Parsons received for the goods he sold during the year. The sales figures consist of three

Gross Sales		$65,000
Less: Sales returns and allowances		5,000
Net Sales		**$60,000**
Cost of Goods Sold:		
Beginning inventory, January 1, at cost	$12,000	
Gross purchases	$33,000	
Less: Purchase discounts	3,000	
Net purchases	$30,000	
Plus: Freight-in	2,000	
Net cost of delivered purchases	32,000	
Costs of goods available for sale	$44,000	
Less: Ending inventory, December 31, at cost	9,000	
Cost of goods sold		35,000
Gross Margin		**$25,000**
Expenses:		
Selling expenses		
Sales, salaries, and commissions	$ 8,000	
Advertising	1,000	
Delivery	1,000	
Total selling expenses	$10,000	
Administrative expenses		
Office salaries	$ 4,000	
Office supplies	1,000	
Miscellaneous (outside consultant)	1,000	
Total administrative expenses	$ 6,000	
General expenses		
Rent	$ 2,000	
Heat, light, and telephone	1,000	
Miscellaneous (insurance, depreciation)	1,000	
Total general expenses	$ 4,000	
Total expenses		$20,000
Net Profit		**$ 5,000**

FIGURE A-1

Operating Statement for Dale Parsons for the Year Ending December 31, 1983

items: gross sales, returns and allowances, and net sales. Gross sales is the total amount charged to customers during the year for merchandise purchased in Parsons's store. As expected, some customers returned merchandise because of damage or a change of mind. If the customer receives a full refund or full credit on a purchase, we refer to this exchange as a "return." The customer may decide to keep the item if Parsons will reduce the price to reflect damage done to the merchandise. This is called an "allowance." By reducing the gross sales figure by the returns and allowances, we arrive at net sales—what Parsons earned in revenue after a year of selling merchandise:

Gross sales	$65,000
Returns and allowances	−5,000
Net sales	$60,000

The cost of goods sold for Dale Parsons in 1983 merits discussion. Of course, the stock of inventory in the store at the beginning of the year must be included. During the year, $33,000 worth of suits, slacks, shirts, ties, jeans, and so forth, was purchased. One company provided a discount of $3,000 to the store, and thus net purchases were $30,000. Since the store is located in a small town and requires a special delivery route, Parsons had to pay an additional $2,000 to get the merchandise delivered to him, giving him a net cost of $32,000. When the beginning inventory was added to this figure, the cost of goods available for sale amounted to $44,000. The $9,000 ending inventory of clothes in the store on December 31 was then subtracted to come up with the $35,000 "cost of goods sold" figure. Here again we follow a logical series of steps to arrive at the cost of goods sold:

Amount Parsons started with (beginning inventory)	$12,000
Net amount Parsons purchased	+30,000
Any added costs to obtain these purchases	+ 2,000
Total cost of goods Parsons had available for sale during year	$44,000
Amount Parsons had left over (ending inventory)	− 9,000
Cost of merchandise that was actually sold	$35,000

The difference between what Parsons paid for the merchandise ($35,000) and what he received ($60,000) is called the gross margin ($25,000).

In order to show what Parsons "cleared" at the end of the year, the gross margin must be reduced by the "expenses" incurred in generating that volume of business. The selling expenses for Dale Parsons included two part-time employees; local newspaper, radio, and television advertising; and the cost of delivering merchandise to customers after alterations. Selling expenses amounted to $10,000 for the year. Administrative expenses included the salary for a part-time bookkeeper, office supplies (stationery, business cards, etc.), and a miscellaneous expense of an administrative audit conducted by an outside consultant. Administrative expenses were $6,000 in 1983. Finally, the general expenses of rent, utilities, insurance, and depreciation came to $4,000. Total expenses were therefore $20,000 for the year. By subtracting expenses ($20,000) from gross margin ($25,000), we arrive at the net profit of $5,000 for Parsons during 1983.

Analytic Ratios

The operating statement supplies the data needed for deriving several key ratios. Typically these ratios are referred to as operating ratios—the ratio of selected items on the operating statement to net sales—and allow marketers to compare their performance in one year with that in previous years (or industry standards and competitors in the same year) in order to determine the overall success of the firm. The most commonly computed operating ratios are the gross margin percentage, the net profit percentage, the operating expense percentage, and the returns and allowances percentage.

RATIO	FORMULA	COMPUTATION FROM FIGURE A-1
Gross margin percentage	$= \dfrac{\text{Gross margin}}{\text{Net sales}}$	$= \dfrac{\$25{,}000}{\$60{,}000} = 42\%$
Net profit percentage	$= \dfrac{\text{Net profit}}{\text{Net sales}}$	$= \dfrac{\$5{,}000}{\$60{,}000} = 8\%$
Operating expense percentage	$= \dfrac{\text{Total expenses}}{\text{Net sales}}$	$= \dfrac{\$20{,}000}{\$60{,}000} = 33\%$
Returns and allowances percentage	$= \dfrac{\text{Returns and allowances}}{\text{Net sales}}$	$= \dfrac{\$5{,}000}{\$60{,}000} = 8\%$

Another ratio that is useful for analytical purposes is the stockturn rate. The stockturn rate is the number of times that an inventory turns over or is sold during a specified time period (usually one year). It may be computed on a cost, selling, or unit price basis. Thus the formula can be:

$$\text{Stockturn rate} = \frac{\text{Cost of goods sold}}{\text{Average inventory at cost}}$$

or the formula can be:

$$\text{Stockturn rate} = \frac{\text{Selling price of goods sold}}{\text{Average selling price of inventory}}$$

or it can be:

$$\text{Stockturn rate} = \frac{\text{Sales in units}}{\text{Average inventory in units}}$$

We will use the first formula:

$$\frac{\$35{,}000}{\dfrac{\$12{,}000 + \$9{,}000}{2}} = \frac{\$35{,}000}{\$10{,}500} = 3.3$$

That is, Parsons's inventory turned over 3.3 times in 1983. Normally, the higher the stockturn rate, the higher the management efficiency and company profitability.

Return on investment (ROI) is a frequently used measure of managerial effectiveness that uses data from the firm's operating statement and balance sheet. A commonly used formula for computing ROI is as follows:

$$\text{ROI} = \frac{\text{Net profit}}{\text{Sales}} \times \frac{\text{Sales}}{\text{Investment}}$$

Two questions may arise when looking at this formula: Why use a two-step process when ROI could be computed simply as net profit over investment? What exactly is "investment"?

Insight for answering the first question can be gained by observing how each component of the formula can affect the ROI. Suppose Dale Parsons computed his ROI as follows:

$$\text{ROI} = \frac{\text{Net profit } \$5,000}{\text{Sales } \$60,000} \times \frac{\text{Sales } \$60,000}{\text{Investment } \$30,000}$$

$$8.3\% \qquad \times \qquad 2 \qquad = 16.6\%$$

If Parsons had believed that increasing his share of the clothing market had certain marketing advantages, he might have generated the same ROI if his sales had doubled and profit and investment remained the same (accepting a lower profit ratio but generating a higher turnover and market share):

$$\text{ROI} = \frac{\text{Net profit } \$5,000}{\text{Sales } \$120,000} \times \frac{\text{Sales } \$120,000}{\text{Investment } \$30,000}$$

$$4.16\% \qquad \times \qquad 4 \qquad = 16.6\%$$

Parsons might have increased his ROI by generating a higher net profit figure through more efficient marketing planning, implementation, and control:

$$\text{ROI} = \frac{\text{Net profit } \$10,000}{\text{Sales } \$60,000} \times \frac{\text{Sales } \$60,000}{\text{Investment } \$30,000}$$

$$16.6\% \qquad \times \qquad 2 \qquad = 33.2\%$$

Another way to increase ROI is to find some way to generate the same levels of sales and profits while decreasing investment (perhaps by cutting the size of Parsons's average inventory):

$$\text{ROI} = \frac{\text{Net profit } \$5,000}{\text{Sales } \$60,000} \times \frac{\text{Sales } \$60,000}{\text{Investment } \$15,000}$$

$$8.3\% \qquad \times \qquad 4 \qquad = 33.2\%$$

What is "investment" in the ROI formula? Investment is often thought of as the total assets of the firm. However, many analysts have now turned to other measures of return to assess managerial performance. Some of these measures are return on net assets (RONA), return on stockholders' equity (ROE), or return on assets managed (ROAM). Since investment is measured at a particular point in time, it is usual for ROI to be computed as the average investment between two time periods (for example, January 1 and December 31 of the same year). ROI can also be measured as an "internal rate of return" by using discounted cash flow analysis (see any financial textbook dealing with this technique). The objective in using any of these measures is to determine how effectively the company has been utilizing its resources. As inflation, competitive pressures, and cost of capital show greater upward movement, these measures become increasingly important barometers of marketing and corporate management performance.

Markups and Markdowns

For retailers and wholesalers, an understanding of the concepts of markup and markdown is essential. The marketer must make a profit to stay in business, and thus the markup percentage is an important strategic consideration. Both markups and markdowns are expressed in percentage terms.

There are two different ways to compute markups—on cost or on selling price:

$$\text{Markup percentage on cost} = \frac{\text{Dollar markup}}{\text{Cost}}$$

$$\text{Markup percentage on selling price} = \frac{\text{Dollar markup}}{\text{Selling price}}$$

Dale Parsons must decide which formula to use; otherwise much confusion may result. If Parsons bought shirts for $8 and wanted to mark them up $4, his markup percentage on cost would be $4/$8 = 50%. If he based his markup on selling price, the percentage would be $4/$12 = 33.3%. In figuring markup percentage, most retailers use the selling price rather than the cost.

Suppose Parsons knew his cost ($10) and desired margin (25%) for a man's tie and wanted to compute the selling price, using the markup as a percentage of the selling price formula. The formula is:

Selling price = Cost + (Margin × Selling price)
Selling price = $10 + 25% of Selling price
75% of Selling price = $10
Selling price = $13.33

As a product moves through the channel of distribution, each channel member adds his markup to the product before selling it to the next member. This "markup chain" is illustrated for a suit purchased by a Parsons customer for $200:

		$ AMOUNT	% OF SELLING PRICE	
	Cost	$108	90%	
Manufacturer	Markup	12	10	markup
	Selling price	$120	100%	
	Cost	$120	80%	
Wholesaler	Markup	30	20	markup
	Selling price	$150	100%	
	Cost	$150	75%	
Retailer	Markup	50	25	markup
	Selling price	$200	100%	

The retailer whose markup is 25% does not necessarily enjoy more profit than a manufacturer whose markup is 10%. Profit also depends on how many items with that profit margin can be sold (stockturn rate) and on operating efficiency (expenses, etc.).

Sometimes a retailer would like to be able to convert markups based on selling price to cost, and vice versa. The formulas are:

$$\text{Markup percentage on selling price} = \frac{\text{Markup percentage on cost}}{100\% + \text{Markup percentage on cost}}$$

$$\text{Markup percentage on cost} = \frac{\text{Markup percentage on selling price}}{100\% - \text{Markup percentage on selling price}}$$

Suppose Parsons found out that his competitor was using a markup percentage of 30% based on cost and he wanted to know what this would be on a percentage of selling price. The calculation would be:

$$\frac{30\%}{100\% + 30\%} = \frac{30\%}{130\%} = 23\%$$

Since Parsons was using a 25% markup on the selling price for suits, he felt that his markup was compatible with that of his competitor.

Near the end of the summer Parsons found that he had an inventory of summer slacks in stock. Thus he knew that a markdown, a reduction from the original selling price, was necessary. He had purchased twenty pairs originally at $10 each and had sold ten pairs at $20 each. He marked down the other pairs to $15 and sold five pairs. His markdown ratio (percentage) is computed as follows:

$$\text{Markdown percentage} = \frac{\text{Dollar markdown}}{\text{Total net sales in dollars}}$$

The dollar markdown is $25 (5 pairs × $5 each) and total net sales are $275, which is (10 pairs × $20) + (5 pairs × $15). The ratio, then, is $25/$275 = 9%.

Markdown ratios are typically computed for each department, rather than for individual items, so that a measure of relative marketing efficiency for that department can be calculated and compared over time. Parsons will use markdown ratios to gauge the relative efficiency of the buyers and salespeople in the store's various departments.

Appendix B

Careers in Marketing

Now that you have completed your first course in marketing, you have some knowledge of what this field entails. You may have decided that marketing has what you are seeking in a career—constant challenge, stimulating problems, working with people, and almost unlimited advancement opportunities. Marketing is a very broad field with a wide variety of tasks involving the analysis, planning, implementation, and control of marketing programs. Marketing positions are available in all types and sizes of institutions. This appendix will acquaint you with entry-level and higher-level marketing opportunities and suggest steps you might follow in selecting a career path and marketing yourself.

Description of Marketing Jobs

Between one-fourth and one-third of the civilian labor force are employed in marketing-related positions. Consequently, there are an enormous number of marketing careers. Positions in marketing are thought to be excellent training for the highest levels in the organization because of the knowledge of products and consumers gained in these jobs. A 1976 profile of the *Fortune* 500 chief executives showed more CEOs with backgrounds in marketing and distribution than any other career emphasis.

Remuneration in the marketing area of the firm will vary. Starting salaries for marketing usually rank slightly below those for engineering and chemistry but are equal to or higher than those for economics/finance, accounting, general business, and the liberal arts. In 1981, sales trainees with bachelor's degrees received a starting salary of $17,000, and with master's degrees, $25,000. If you are successful in the entry-level marketing position, you will quickly be promoted to higher levels of responsibility and salary. Table B-1 shows average salaries plus bonuses for marketing executives in 1980.

Marketing has become an attractive career for some individuals who have not traditionally considered this field. One trend is the growing number of women entering marketing. Women have historically been employed in the retail sector of marketing. They are now moving into all types of sales and marketing positions. According to *Business Week,* women accounted for 2% of sales recruits in

Table B-1	
Annual Salaries for Marketing Positions	
POSITION	SALARY RANGE
Marketing Research Analyst	$16,000–$29,000
Marketing Research Manager	$23,000–$43,000
Assistant Brand Manager	$21,000–$34,000
Brand Manager	$25,000–$42,000
Group Brand Manager	$27,000–$55,000
Director of Marketing	$34,000–$60,000+
International Marketing Manager	$31,000–$50,000+
Sales Promotion Manager	$24,000–$42,000
Copywriter	$18,000–$41,000+
Creative Director	$24,000–$43,000+
Media Buyer	$16,000–$31,000+
Account Executive	$21,000–$41,000
Director of Public Relations	$26,000–$46,000+

Note: The best paid marketing executive (Nicholas DiBari of Comdisco) earned $637,879 in 1980.

Source: Adapted from "Annual Salaries for Marketing Positions," *Advertising Age*, January 4, 1982, p. S–2.

the insurance industry in 1971 and 12% in 1978. Women are very successful in sales careers in pharmaceutical companies, publishing companies, banks, and an increasing number of industrial selling jobs. Their ranks are also growing in product and brand manager positions.

Another trend is the growing acceptance of marketing by nonprofit organizations. Colleges, arts organizations, libraries, and hospitals are increasingly applying marketing to their problems. They are beginning to hire marketing directors and marketing vice-presidents to manage their varied marketing activities.

Here are brief descriptions of important marketing jobs.

Advertising Advertising is an important business activity that requires skill in planning, fact gathering, and creativity. Although compensation for advertising personnel is comparable with that in other business fields, opportunities for rapid advancement in advertising are usually greater than in other fields because of less emphasis on age or length of employment. Typical jobs in advertising agencies are described below.[1]

Copywriters produce the concepts that become written words and visual images of advertisements. They dig for facts, read voraciously, borrow ideas. They talk to customers, suppliers, and *anybody* who can possibly give them a clue about how to attract the target audience's attention and interest.

[1]Descriptions of advertising positions are based on Jack Engle, *Advertising: The Process and Practice* (New York: McGraw-Hill, 1980), pp. 429–34.

Artists are the other part of the creative team. Their major function is to translate copywriters' ideas into dramatic visuals called "layouts." Ad agency artists develop print layouts, package designs, television layouts (called "story-boards"), corporate logotypes, trademarks, and symbols. They specify style and size of typography, paste the type in place, and arrange all details of the ad so that it can be reproduced by engravers and printers. A particularly perceptive art director or copy chief becomes the agency's creative director and oversees all the agency's advertising. The creative director is high in the ad agency's structure.

Account executives are the liaison between client and agency. Their major responsibility is to know marketing and its components. They explain client plans and objectives to their creative teams and supervise the development of the total advertising plan for their accounts. Their main task is to keep the client happy with the agency! Because "account work" is essentially a job of personal relationships, account executives are usually personable, diplomatic, and bright.

Media buyers have the task of selecting the best media for clients. Media representatives flock to the buyer's office whenever they hear that a buy is under consideration. They come armed with statistics to prove that *their* numbers are better, *their* costs per thousand are less, and *their* medium delivers more ripe audiences than competitive media. Media buyers have to evaluate these claims. Media buyers also bargain with the broadcast media for the best rates and make deals with the print media for good ad positions.

Large ad agencies maintain an active marketing research department to provide market information for the development of new ad campaigns and to assess current campaigns. Those interested in marketing research should consider possible employment in ad agencies.

Brand and Product Management

Brand and product managers plan, direct, and control business and marketing efforts for their products. They are concerned with research and development, packaging, manufacturing, sales and distribution, advertising, promotion, market research, and business analysis and forecasting. In consumer goods companies, the newcomer (who usually needs an M.B.A.) joins a brand team and learns the ropes by doing numerical analyses and watching the senior brand people. This person, if competent, eventually heads the team and is later assigned a larger brand to manage. Several industrial-goods companies also have product managers. Product management is considered one of the best training grounds for future corporate officers.

Customer Affairs

Some large consumer-goods companies have established the position of customer affairs representative to act as a liaison between the customer and the firm. The representatives handle complaints, suggestions, and problems concerning the company's products, determine what action is required, and coordinate the activities required to solve the problem. The position requires a person who is empathetic, diplomatic, and capable of working with a wide range of people inside and outside the firm.

Industrial Marketing People interested in industrial marketing careers can go into sales, service, product design, marketing research, and so on. They usually need a technical background. Most people start in sales and spend time in training and making calls with senior salespeople. If they stay in sales, they may advance to district, regional, and higher sales positions. Or they may go into product management and work closely with customers, suppliers, manufacturing, and sales engineering.

International Marketing As U.S. firms increase their international business, they seek qualified people who have some foreign language fluency and are willing to travel to and/or relocate in foreign cities. For such assignments, most companies select experienced personnel who have proven themselves in domestic operations. An M.B.A. is often an asset but not always a requirement.

Marketing Management Science and Systems Analyst Individuals who have been trained in management science, quantitative methods, and systems analysis can become consultants to managers facing difficult marketing problems, such as demand measurement and forecasting, market structure analysis, and new-product evaluation. Career opportunities exist primarily within larger marketing-oriented firms, management consulting firms, and public institutions concerned with health, education, or transportation. An M.B.A. or an M.S. is usually required.

Marketing Research Marketing researchers work with their managers in defining problems and identifying the information needed to resolve the problems. They will design the research project, including the questionnaires and samples, and will handle data tabulation, analysis, report preparation, and presentation of findings with recommendations to management. An understanding of statistics, psychology, and sociology is desirable at a master's degree level. Career opportunities exist with manufacturers, retailers, some wholesalers, trade and industry associations, marketing research firms, advertising agencies, and governmental and private nonprofit agencies.

New-Product Planning Persons interested in new-product planning can find opportunities in a large variety of organizations. They usually need a good background in marketing, marketing research, and sales forecasting; they need organizational skills to motivate and coordinate others; and they may need a technical background. Usually the person works first in some other marketing positions before joining the new-product department.

Physical Distribution Physical distribution is a large and dynamic field, with many career opportunities. Major transportation carriers, manufacturers, wholesalers, and retailers all employ physical distribution specialists. Courses in quantitative methods, finance, accounting, and marketing will provide students with the necessary skills.

Public Relations Most organizations have a public relations person or staff to anticipate public problems, handle complaints, deal with the media, build the corporate image, and so on. Persons interested in public relations should be able to speak and write clearly and persuasively and should preferably have a background in journalism, communications, or the liberal arts. The challenges in this job are highly varied and very people-oriented.

Purchasing Purchasing agents are playing a growing role in firms' profitability during periods of rising material costs and shortages. In retail organizations, being a "buyer" has frequently been a route to the top. Purchasing agents in industrial concerns play a key role in holding down manufacturing costs. A technical background is useful in some purchasing positions, along with a knowledge of credit, finance, and physical distribution.

Retailing Management Retailing companies provide people with an early opportunity to take on marketing responsibilities. The market growth of large-scale retailing has brought increased emphasis on "professional training" as part of the preparation for a career in retailing. Although, historically, starting salaries and job assignments in retailing have been at lower levels than in manufacturing or advertising, the gap is narrowing. The major routes to top management in retailing are merchandise management and store management. The progression in merchandise management is from buyer trainee to assistant buyer to buyer to merchandise division manager. In store management, the progression is from management trainee to assistant department (sales) manager to department manager to store (branch) manager. Whereas buyers are primarily concerned with assortment selection and promotion, department managers are concerned with sales-force management and display. Large-scale retailing offers the new recruit an opportunity to move in a few years into the management of a branch or part of a store doing as much as $5 million in sales.

Sales and Sales Management Sales and sales management opportunities exist in a wide range of profit and nonprofit organizations and in product and service organizations, including financial, insurance, consulting, and government. People have to carefully match their backgrounds, interests, technical skills, and academic training with available sales opportunities. Training programs vary greatly in form and length, ranging from a few weeks to two years. Career paths lead from salesperson to district, regional, and higher levels of sales management and, in many cases, to the top management of the firm.

Other Marketing Careers We have excluded descriptions of many other marketing-related jobs, such as sales promotion, wholesaling, packaging, pricing, and credit management. But information on these positions can be gathered through library sources.

Choosing and Getting a Job

In this section we want to describe how to go about choosing and getting a job. This calls for the application of marketing skills, particularly marketing analysis and planning. The following are eight suggested steps for choosing a career and finding that first job.

Make Self-Assessment Self-assessment is the most important part of a job search. Unless you have some very specific notion of what you want—a mild climate, a city with an opera company, a firm that is no bigger than the school from which you got your B.A., or a job in France—you are likely to end up with something that is suboptimal. Self-assessment is largely a process of clarifying and articulating ideas you may already hold in fuzzy or ambiguous form. To assist in self-assessment, you might look at the following books, which raise many questions you should consider:

1. *What Color Is Your Parachute?* by Richard Bolles
2. *Three Boxes in Life and How to Get Out of Them* by Richard Bolles
3. *Guerilla Tactics in the Job Market* by Tom Jackson

Also avail yourself of the counseling service at your school. Tests such as the Strong-Campbell Interest Inventory will help profile your interests.

Examine Job Descriptions Now examine various job descriptions to see what positions best match your interests, desires, and abilities. Descriptions can be found in the *Occupation Outlook Handbook* and the *Dictionary of Occupational Titles* published by the U.S. Department of Labor. These volumes describe what workers in various occupations do, the specific training and education needed, and the availability of jobs in each field as well as possibilities for advancement and earnings.

Develop Job-Search Objectives Your initial career "shopping" list should be broad and flexible. Do not make the mistake of being narrow in your concept of ways to achieve your objectives. For example, if marketing research is your goal, consider the public as well as the private sector and regional as well as national firms. Only after exploring many options should you begin to focus on specific sectors of industries and initial job assignments that may be right for you. You need to set down a list of basic goals. Your list might say: a job in a small company, in a large city, in the Sun Belt, doing marketing research, with an electronic data processing firm.

Examine Job Market and Assess Opportunities You must now examine the market for those positions to get an idea of how many openings you can expect to be available. For an up-to-date listing of marketing-related job openings, refer to the latest edition of the *College Placement Annual* available at school placement offices. This publication is revised annually to show current job openings for hundreds of companies seeking college graduates for entry-level positions. Companies seeking experienced or advanced-degree personnel are also listed. Use the services of your placement office to the fullest extent at this stage to discover openings and to set up interviews with firms looking to fill marketing positions that are of interest to you. Take the time to thoroughly analyze the industries and companies in which you are interested. Some suggested information sources are business magazines, annual reports, business reference books, faculty members, and fellow students. Try to analyze the future growth and profit pattern of the company and industry, chances for advancement, salary levels, entry positions, amount of travel that is necessary, and so on.

Develop Search Strategies
You might use one or more strategies to contact the firm. Strategy possibilities include (1) on-campus interviews, (2) phoning or writing, and (3) asking marketing professors and/or school alumni for possible contacts.

Develop Résumé and Cover Letter
Your résumé should capture your abilities, education, background, training, work experience, and personal qualifications—but it should also be brief, usually one page. The goal of the résumé is to gain a positive response from potential employers.

The cover letter is, in some ways, more difficult to write than the résumé. The cover letter must be persuasive, professional, and interesting. Ideally, it should set you above and apart from the other candidates for the position. Each letter should look and sound original, that is, individually typed and tailored to the specific organization being contacted. It should describe the position you are applying for, arouse interest, describe your qualifications, and indicate how you can be contacted. The cover letter should be addressed to an individual rather than a title. The letter should also be followed up with a telephone call.

Obtain Interviews
Here is some advice to follow before, during, and after your interviews.
Preparation for the interview:

1. Interviewers have extremely diverse styles—for example, the "chitchat" let's-get-to-know-each-other-style; the quasi-interrogation style of question after question; and the tough-probing why, why, why style, to name a few. Be ready for anything.
2. Practice being interviewed with a friend, and ask for a critique.
3. Ask at least five good questions that are not readily answered in the company's literature.
4. Anticipate possible interview questions and frame suitable answers.
5. Avoid "back-to-back" interviews, as they can be exhausting.
6. Dress for the interview in conservative styles rather than high-fashion styles.
7. Plan to arrive about ten minutes early to collect your thoughts before being called. Check your name on the interview schedule, noting the name of the interviewer and the room number.
8. Review the major points you intend to cover.

During the interview:

1. Give a firm handshake when greeting the interviewer. Introduce yourself using the same form the interviewer has used. Make a good initial impression.
2. Retain your poise. Relax. Smile occasionally. Maintain enthusiasm throughout the interview.
3. Good eye contact, good posture, and distinct speech are musts. Don't clasp your hands or fiddle with jewelry, hair, etc. Sit comfortably in your chair. Do not smoke, even if asked.
4. Have extra copies of your résumé with you.
5. Have your story down pat. Present your selling points. Answer questions directly. Avoid one-word answers, but don't be wordy.
6. Most times, let the interviewer take the initiative, but don't be passive. Find an appropriate opportunity to direct the conversation to those things you want the interviewer to hear.
7. The latter part of the interview is the best time to make your most important point or to ask a pertinent question, in order to end the session on a high note.
8. Don't be afraid "to close": You might say, "I'm very interested in the position, and I have enjoyed this interview."

After the interview:

1. Upon leaving, record the key points. Be sure to record who is to follow up on the interview and when a decision can be expected.
2. Objectively analyze the interview with regard to the questions asked, the answers given, your overall interview presentation, and the interviewer's response (interest, boredom, etc.) to specific points.
3. Send a thank-you letter mentioning any additional things and your availability to supply further information.
4. If you do not hear within the time specified, write or call the interviewer to determine your status.

Follow-up If you are successful, you will be invited to visit the organization. The in-company interview will run from a few hours to a whole day. Your interest, maturity, enthusiasm, assertiveness, logic, and company and functional knowledge will all be scrutinized. You should be asking questions that are important to you. Find out about the environment, job role, responsibilities, opportunities, current industrial issues, and the "firm's personality." If all goes well, you may be working for the organization at some future time. You can avoid embarrassment later if you remember the names of the people you meet.

Cases

1 Sony Corporation: Walkman

Sony introduced the Walkman at the end of 1979. In 1980 it shipped 550,000 of these gadgets worldwide, and in 1981 the figure was more than three times that number. At least twenty companies entered the market with similar products. The Walkman and its competitors provide high-quality playback through lightweight earphones attached to a lightweight cassette player worn on the belt or around the neck. Sony management must now determine whether the Walkman-type product will continue to be popular and how it should compete in this market.

The Walkman was created by a young engineer who made it for fun. In time it was shown to Mr. Akio Morita, Sony's chairman, who adopted it for his personal use and enthusiastically served as the product development project leader, reducing to six months the time between planning the product and its marketing instead of the usual one to two years. Product development and marketing ideas were obtained from high-school and university students as they used and discussed the Walkman in a room especially equipped for observation.

In Japan the Walkman virtually sold itself following special presentations for newspaper and magazine reporters. Many articles appeared in magazines, but few in newspapers. Special events were planned for young people, who were encouraged to try the Walkman while enjoying all kinds of activities in public places, such as skateboarding, cycling, jogging, and skipping rope.

In the United States the product has been used by people as they work, bicycle, drive, roller-skate, sun themselves, ski, converse, and block out the sounds of the world. The Walkman in use in public places was a form of promotion in itself and helped to create an ever-spiraling demand that spread worldwide, as the Hula-Hoop had done twenty years earlier.

The retail list prices of the Walkman Models I and II are about $100 and $180, respectively, in the United States. They are sold in a variety of retail outlets. Competitive products with a range of features are sold in essentially the same retail outlets at list prices ranging from $75 to $250. Price cutting is common.

In planning its marketing efforts for the Walkman in the United States, Sony is interested in knowing whether the product is simply a novelty, as some observers contend, in which case the demand could dry up rather quickly. On the other hand, if it is felt that the product serves one or more useful basic functions, even in the short run, the market could be quite large and could include segments other than the youth market. If other market segments are to be cultivated, Sony will have to decide whether it should concentrate on one or two models for all parts of the market or offer models designed especially for different markets, as well as the features each model should possess.

Questions

1. What groups of potential buyers exist for the Walkman?
2. What can Sony do to increase the sale of the product to each of these groups?

2 Minnetonka, Inc.: ShowerMate™

Minnetonka, Inc., experienced rapid growth in the sale of its Softsoap, a liquid detergent in a pump dispenser package. In three years its sales grew from virtually nothing to a 75% share of the $80-million-a-year home liquid-soap market.

Research indicated that liquid soap was being used in the home primarily as a hand soap at wash basins or sinks, whereas most bar soaps, almost 75% of the $1 billion bar-soap sales, were being used in showers or bathtubs. Seeking to gain an early competitive edge in this virtually untapped market segment for liquid soap, Minnetonka launched ShowerMate, its liquid-soap product in a squeeze tube with a hook on one end, which could be hung on a shower head or on a towel bar during use. The company introduced ShowerMate in a few markets and soon thereafter announced that it would be rolling out nationally with advertising support at a level of $10 to $15 million a year. Initial markets were Houston; Orlando and Jacksonville, Florida; Denver; Portland, Oregon; Seattle; and Minneapolis-St. Paul.

A number of competitive shower/tub liquid products were already available. Among them were Shower of Capri from S. C. Johnson & Co. and Shower Up from Jo Go Industries. Both Armour/Dial and Procter & Gamble had products in test markets.

ShowerMate, in a twelve-ounce squeeze bottle with built-in hook, sells for about $2.00 retail, whereas Shower Up and Shower of Capri, in eight-ounce and eleven-ounce squeeze bottles, respectively, sell for about $1.50 and $1.70. All are backed with extensive advertising and are sold through grocery, drug, general, and mass-merchandise outlets.

As a liquid detergent soap, however, ShowerMate is subject to such misconceptions as the following:

1. Synthetic detergents are easily compounded and it is difficult to do anything special to differentiate them. (*Chemical Week,* May 14, 1981, p. 34)
2. Despite claims by liquid-soap advertisers, liquid soaps are less economical than bar soaps. (*Consumer Reports* questioned these claims. See the March 1981 issue, p. 161.)
3. Liquid soap is more difficult to use in the shower. However, bar-soap usage patterns must be broken and a new set of squeeze-bottle usage habits established. But it is almost impossible to squeeze out the right amount and keep the soap from being washed away before it can be used.
4. Detergents are harder on the skin than soap. Some women believe that detergents may produce irritation of the more sensitive parts of the

body. ShowerMate carries the following warning label: "Avoid getting ShowerMate™ into eyes—if it does, rinse eyes with water." (This may not represent a serious problem, but the warning does create a cautious attitude.)

Skeptics in the industry claim that liquid soap is a small specialty market that is approaching its upper limit on a per capita basis, that liquid soap is not suited for shower or bath, and that its importance will diminish after initial purchases prove disappointing. The skeptics also claim that beyond a small segment, liquid soap may be a novelty item suitable for the gift market or for display in the home when there are guests.

Questions

1. What is your judgment regarding the future of liquid soap in the shower/tub segment?
2. What recommendations would you offer Minnetonka so that it could make the best of this opportunity?

3 Great Waters of France, Inc.: Perrier

The sales of Perrier sparkling mineral water from France skyrocketed in the United States from $1 million to almost $80 million per year, then declined somewhat. Perrier now accounts for 80% of the currently declining U.S. mineral-water imports and 29% of the $225 million per year retail bottled-water market, which is growing at the rate of 9% annually. A trade source reports that the American public has been trading down in price, even to the extent of drinking club soda and seltzer in place of mineral water.

Perrier's early phenomenal success added a segment to the soft-drink market that surprised everyone, including its management, and attracted numerous large and small competitors as well as state and federal regulators. The Perrier management is now faced with the problem of deciding how to market the product in the new, highly competitive environment in which Perrier is no longer the subject of word-of-mouth advertising and publicity and consumers have fewer dollars to spend. The advertising agency has recommended the creation and launching of a plan designed to regain Perrier's "newsworthiness."

Perrier is a naturally carbonated spring water with smaller bubbles and a distinct flavor when compared with competing products, most of which are charged with machine-made carbon dioxides. The distinctively shaped green-tinted bottle, the equally distinctive label, the premium price, and the advertising all combine to have a snob appeal and build an elitist image.

Perrier's sales success has been based upon a carefully planned and executed strategy, which positions the product as a healthful alternative to soft drinks or alcoholic beverages, bought by affluent adults and those who try to be like them, and sold for 69¢ to 79¢, significantly above the price of the average soft drink. Prior to the mass-marketing thrust, it was available primarily in gourmet shops at around $1 a bottle.

An integral part of the Perrier plan involved shifting distribution emphasis from gourmet shops to the soft-drink sections of supermarkets. Ironically, price competition here runs rampant, shelf display space demands are severe, and costly promotions and trade allowances are essential.

In this environment, Perrier's elitist image is being given its most severe test. Some marketers believe that all the elitist image-building efforts may not be able to offset the soft-drink section ambiance and competitive behavior. They feel that it is only a matter of time until this highly visible item will be sold as a "price special" to draw customers.

Perrier's shift from gourmet shops to supermarkets was accompanied by advertising, promotional, and publicity efforts. Advertising stressed Perrier's origins and later shifted to show affluent youthful adults drinking the product in different situations. Trend setters drinking the product were shown on society pages. Perrier T-shirts and beach towels appeared. A nationwide fitness program included sponsorship of Perrier Paracourse Fitness Circuits and co-sponsorship of athletic events. Every participant in major marathons throughout the United States was given a Perrier T-shirt and a bottle of cold Perrier. The publicity and word-of-mouth advertising resulting from these efforts did much to build sales.

Some contend that Perrier is a fad in this country and that its long life in France as a leading beverage will not be repeated in the United States. Bruce Nevins, president of Great Waters of France, Inc., who developed his marketing abilities at Levi Strauss & Co., admits that Perrier's great growth was aided by Americans' rising concern with diet and health. He adds that Perrier is no more a fad than health is. Perrier is being challenged at the upper end of the market in a few major cities by Khisu Mineral Water, which is said to have cured Korean King Sejong of all his ailments in the year 1445. King Sejong called it "miracle water," but it is being sold in New York as "mineral water" for about $2 for a fourteen-ounce bottle, in contrast to 95¢ for a bottle of Perrier water. At the 21 Club in New York, Khisu is $4.50 and Perrier is $3.10 a bottle. Khisu advertising asks, "Can you afford a miracle?"

To regain Perrier's "newsworthiness," Perrier's advertising agency has recommended developing and launching a radio campaign that would get people talking about it again. The proposed campaign would center on such well-known historical characters as Julius Caesar, Dracula, Socrates, and Ponce de León. In the Dracula commercial, the narrator would describe how the vampire kneels beside a beautiful sleeping woman, caresses her, and lovingly plunges "his teeth into the milky whiteness of her throat." Then Dracula would speak the key line that the advertising agency wants to make famous: "It's good, but it is not Perrier." According to one of the agency's executives, the key line would be spoken by all the historical characters in some fifteen different commercials, which could resemble a radio soap opera with people looking forward to the next episode.

Questions

1. Should the advertising agency's idea be accepted?
2. How should Perrier be promoted at this stage in its life?

4 Levi Strauss & Co.

Levi Strauss & Co. has decided to distribute through J. C. Penney Co. and Sears, Roebuck & Co., thereby reducing its reliance on jean specialty chains, jean boutiques, and upscale department stores. This decision was evidently caused by a sustained slump in the apparel and retailing industries, a substantial drop in the company's earnings, and the apparent maturing of the market for jeans. The management must now determine how to make the change, keeping in mind the best interests of its old retailer-customers, its new ones (Sears and Penney), and the company itself.

Many retailers, manufacturers, and security analysts believe that the jeans business has finally matured. Reasons cited are the aging U.S. population and the declining interest in designer jeans and the western look. It was pointed out that people were buying dressier, more fashionable clothes, that the preppy look was gaining acceptance, and that chinos were considered a comfortable alternative to denim. Levi Strauss officials said they did not believe that jeans' popularity was declining. Instead, they felt that the increased interest in the dress-up look meant that people were expanding their wardrobes and thereby creating an opportunity for the company, the largest apparel company in the United States.

Levi's plan to sell through mass merchandisers will have an impact on several interest groups. Some of Levi's longtime retailers were shocked by the possible change and the added competition it would bring. Independent and chain specialty stores whose businesses were built around Levi's had mixed reactions. Upscale department stores were especially upset by the plan.

Some observers believe that the company will shift more of its advertising attention to other "moderate-to-better" lines of jeans. The head of a large jeans specialty chain believes that the plan will help Levi Strauss and its retailers in geographic areas where they are now weak. Others fear price competition. Sears and Penney, especially the latter, have been promoting their own brands of jeans against Levi's. It is not clear whether they want to stock Levi jeans as traffic builders, image builders, or direct contributors to profits. What they do will be critical to Levi Strauss and its current retailers. In any event, it will take many months to stock their stores and evaluate what actually happens. In the meantime, Levi's management is planning to increase the advertising budget to help retailers. It is also formulating criteria and guidelines for determining what types of goods it should sell through Sears and Penney.

It was reported that Levi's executives acknowledged their debt to their retailer-customers but made it clear that sentiment would not sway them. The proposal to expand distribution had been discussed a number of times over the years, but the management evidently felt that the present might be the right time to make the move. The company had experienced a poor year; competition in the jeans market was severe; consumer demand had weakened, especially for designer jeans and the western look; and broadened distribution would expose Levi jeans to more potential consumers as well as increase sales to new retailers as they stocked their shelves.

Earlier, Levi's Canadian subsidiary had announced the "555," a limited-edition jeans—limited to between 30,000 and 50,000 pairs. The "555" carried a retail price of $33.95—a few dollars more than the best-selling nonregistered Levi jeans. Distribution was exclusively through a Canadian specialty jean chain, Thrifty's Just Pants. The "555" was a straight-leg jean with a button fly front and other details similar to the original 1849 gold rush blue jeans. Levi's two-horse trademark appeared on a leather patch on the rear pocket. A small copper plate carried a five-digit serial number, which was registered in the company's archives when the buyer returned the postage-paid card provided at the time of purchase. Buyers received a certificate documenting their ownership and a token that was good for a 10% discount on the purchase of another Levi Strauss item. The subsidiary's director of marketing believes the "limited edition" idea is as successful with apparel as it has been with books, works of art, and other collectibles. A museum director was quoted as saying that the "555" could in time become a museum piece.

Questions

1. What responses to Levi's new distribution plan are likely to occur on the consumer and retail levels? What action should the company take to gain the greatest benefits?
2. What further use, if any, should the company make of the "limited-edition jeans" idea?

5 Maytag Co.: Microwave Ovens

In early 1981, the Maytag Co. of Newton, Iowa, a manufacturer of laundry equipment and dishwashers, acquired the Cleveland, Tennessee-based, Hardwicke Stove Co., makers and marketers of gas and electric ranges and microwave ovens for the residential market. Although it was announced that the two companies would continue to operate separately, Maytag's chairman of the board and chief executive officer (CEO) stated in the company's annual report: "We have the talent and resources to do much more together than we could have done separately." The meaning of this statement was not clarified, but several appliance manufacturers, appliance retailers, and security analysts were reported to have felt that there were good reasons why Maytag should introduce a Maytag countertop microwave oven using Hardwicke's experience and facilities.

Maytag, with annual sales of $350 to $450 million, is seen by many consumers as a manufacturer of high-performance products. This is supported by favorable ratings in *Consumer Reports* for Maytag's laundry equipment and dishwashers. Hardwicke's products, on the other hand, have been in the medium- and low-priced bracket. Hardwicke's annual sales have been between $40 and $50 million. The 100-year-old company has been managed conservatively and, like Maytag, has been proud that it had no debt.

Microwave ovens for the home first caught on in the 1950s, but their growth was slow until the early 1970s. At that time the problems involved in microwave cooking included uneven cooking, meats that could not be browned, foil-wrapped foods that could not be put in the oven, few cookbooks available, and real or imagined personal radiation danger associated with microwaves.

As soon as these problems were overcome, sales took off. By the late 1970s the countertop microwave ovens were no longer considered a luxury. With more and more working women, the ovens' appeal became stronger, and they are now being used in almost 20% of U.S. households. Retailers sold about 3.5 million units in 1981, representing an annual increase of almost five hundred thousand units for the past several years. Microwave ovens, which range in price from $200 to $500, have been one of the fastest-selling items in the appliance business. Industry analysts foresee a market penetration of these cooking units comparable with that of color television sets.

Five of the forty or so producers of microwave ovens have well over 50% of the consumer market. Litton and Amana are the leaders, but Sears, General Electric, and Sharp are not far behind. Sunbeam, a recent entry, has a well-respected name with consumers. Japanese firms selling microwave ovens for the home include Sharp, Panasonic, Sanyo, Hitachi, and Toshiba. It is estimated that Japanese imports account for roughly 20% of the units sold. Manufacturers and retailers believe that a shakeout of microwave producers is on the horizon. Retail prices are frequently discounted, and advertising expenditures are fairly heavy.

Questions

1. Should Maytag market a countertop microwave oven using the Maytag name?
2. What are your recommendations and reasons?

6 American Cyanamid Co.

The American Cyanamid Company is a diversified, multinational company involved in the research, development, manufacturing, and marketing of more than twenty-five hundred products. The company has operating divisions in agricultural, pharmaceutical, specialty chemical, and consumer products. Cyanamid sees itself primarily as a research and development company with a strong ability to develop a basic chemical product and turn it into a family of diversified products.

One of Cyanamid's many products is its Cyalume® light stick. First marketed in 1971, this chemical light was the result of ten years of research at American Cyanamid. The Cyalume light stick is a clear, wand-shaped plastic tube, six inches in length, containing two liquid chemical components. One liquid is held in an inner glass vial apart from the other, which is contained only by the plastic tube. The chemicals react and produce excited molecules that give off a visible yellow-green light.

Since the device utilizes a chemical process, it produces no heat and does not require any form of ignition to operate. As a result, the device can be activated and used under water, as well as in other situations where battery or electrical power is not available, or where a spark from conventional lighting devices might be dangerous. For example, the light stick is safe for illuminating the scenes of mining or industrial accidents, where explosive concentrations of gases or fumes may be present.

Each light stick is a self-contained unit capable of producing light for eight hours. However, only the first three hours of this light output are considered to be useful working light. The product is dependable, with a shelf life of at least two years when stored under normal conditions. In addition, the product is safe— both of the chemical liquids contained within the tube are nontoxic and require no special measures in case of contact with the skin or eyes. The light stick is also flameless, cool, waterproof, windproof, lightweight, compact, and noncorrosive.

The light stick, however, does have some limitations. The intensity of the light produced by the light stick is low and shines in all directions. The light cannot be confined to a narrow beam, such as that produced by a flashlight. Light cannot be shut off once activated, and it is affected by temperature. Maximum light is emitted at temperatures ranging from 70° to 80° F. At temperatures below 32° F., there is a very substantial reduction in light emission. The light stick is also sensitive to humidity. It is wrapped in an airtight outer foil wrapper. If the wrapper is punctured and the light stick is not used within a few days, the light emission will be reduced. If it is left in the damaged wrapper for a longer period of time, it may be totally deactivated.

The technology used in the Cyalume light stick is unique and is protected by several U.S. patents held by the American Cyanamid Company. The patents are effective for a number of years, and a new generation of patents is a strong possibility. The product has been approved or accepted by the U.S. Bureau of Mines, the Federal Aviation Administration, the U.S. Navy, and the General Services Administration for special use as a marker or for lighting work areas.

After several years of production and distribution of the light stick by the Organic Chemicals Division to industrial and military users, sales increased significantly. The OCD has in the past avoided selling to novelty users, fearing that such displays would detract from the more serious uses for a product, especially those of an emergency nature.

Corporate management believed there was a large untapped potential in both the consumer and the industrial/military markets. Both divisions were requested to prepare independent reports recommending major markets for the product and general approaches by which they could be reached at a profit. The memorandum included the following statements:

> I want your suggestions as to what markets look promising and strategies we should adopt if we go into these markets. I do not expect you to provide any quantitative data in your report—especially with respect to the strategies you suggest we use in entering these markets. Thus, your reports will be essentially qualitative in nature. You are to present your reports at our next executive meeting with the understanding that once we, as a group, are agreed on what general strategies we have to adopt if we are to have any reasonable chance of being successful, that you and your staffs will be assigned the responsibility of detailing the precise strategies to be employed and the expenditures required. Following this we will meet and decide whether such an investment is feasible and desirable.

These reports were to be rough in the sense that specific data were not required. Essentially, they were to be reports that would take the planners through the planning process in a quick and rough way to get the "feel" of the problem and give corporate management ideas as a basis for further thought. Special attention was to be given to how the product would be used, why it would be selected over other modes, who would buy it, where it would be bought, and how important price would be.*

Questions

1. What four or five major questions would you ask to help you prepare a report on either the consumer or industrial market?
2. Diagram a market planning process you might use in drawing up a rough plan for the chemical light.
3. What opportunities for the chemical light exist in the consumer market? Industry? Government? Other not-for-profit organizations?

*Condensed from a case prepared by Mr. Willard Moran, V. P. Consumer Products, American Cyanamid Company. Cyalume® is a registered trademark of American Cyanamid Company.

7 Hanes Corporation: From L'eggs to Children's Books?

The outstanding success of L'eggs panty hose encouraged Hanes to launch other products using L'eggs marketing ideas with the hope of duplicating their success. The marketing director for new products is working on a plan for marketing high-quality children's paperback books under the name Starbooks. He called a meeting of his staff to get their ideas and provide a training opportunity.

These books would be aimed at preschool readers, early readers, and readers up to twelve years of age and would retail between $0.60 and $1.69. The licensing rights to two hundred titles from several publishers would be available. Children's books are sold through book and department stores, direct mail, book clubs, and other retail outlets, with supermarkets and drugstores each accounting for 6% of the total children's book sales. Milwaukee, Rochester, Kansas City, and Salt Lake City would be considered possible test markets if the company decided to go ahead.

The marketing director's reasons for focusing on children's books include the following:

- The large market that exists—$600 million a year.
- The many competitors with small market shares (Western Publishing Company's Golden Books are probably the best known).
- An absence of aggressive marketing efforts.
- A trend toward one-store shopping that favors supermarkets and large chain drugstores.
- The existing market for children's books in supermarkets and drugstores.
- The higher percentage gross margin on children's books than on most items in supermarkets.
- A L'eggs marketing plan that seems to fit children's books, at least in part.
- The L'eggs direct distribution network that is already in place.

A few days before the meeting, it was learned that a new marketing plan for Golden Books was soon to be launched by Racine-based Western Publishing Company, recently acquired by Mattel, Inc., the well-known toy and game marketer. Western Publishing had not been innovative or aggressive in the past, and the Hanes marketing director did not believe the new plan would change the competitive situation very much.

Questions

1. What recommendations concerning the Starbooks proposal would you make to the marketing director?
2. What product mix decisions must Hanes make concerning the Starbooks proposal?

8 Kraft, Inc.: A La Carte Retort Pouch Foods

Kraft's A La Carte retort pouch foods are made with an innovative packaging technology that some analysts believe could create the new major food category of the future. It appears to be the most important breakthrough in food processing and marketing since Clarence Birdseye perfected the frozen-food process over fifty years ago. The flexible vacuum-sealed retort pouch makes it possible to combine frozen-food quality with shelf-stable convenience, without putting the product into a can or keeping it in a freezer. Its fresh taste is said to surpass that of canned products and to be equal to frozen. Retort pouch foods are ready to eat after boiling the pouch for five minutes. Energy usage is reduced by at least half during preparation, processing, and storage. It is also less in retail outlets and homes.

The retort pouch was developed by the U.S. military about twenty years ago and has received considerable attention as an alternative processing technique to canning and freezing. The Food and Drug Administration did not allow commercial use of the pouch in this country until 1977. American Pouch Food Co., a minority-owned-and-operated company, was awarded a large contract to supply the military's ready-to-eat program, which is intended to replace the C- and K-type field rations. Apollo astronauts took retort pouch foods, processed by Swift & Co., on their trip to the moon because they were easy to store and fast to prepare.

Consumer retort pouch entrée lines are being marketed in the United States by Kraft, Inc., and the ITT-Continental Baking Co. under the names "A La Carte" and "Continental Kitchens Flavor Seal," respectively. Retail prices range from $1.39 to $2.49, depending upon the brand and item. Gourmet entrées include such dishes as beef burgundy, beef Stroganoff, sweet and sour pork, creamed chicken, beef stew, Salisbury steak, and macaroni and beef.

Retort pouch foods face the unusual marketing challenge of being a shelf product with primary competition from frozen foods. Complicating the matter further, there are two polarized market targets for the single-service gourmet entrées—the young (both singles and marrieds) and the older "empty-nesters"—rather than the classic mass market of traditional households with children.

Retort pouch food, despite its advantages, has met consumer resistance in the United States. High prices and skepticism have combined to keep product trial low. In contrast, consumer acceptance has been good for several years in Europe and Japan. One industry observer said that in the United States the gourmet items were positioned directly against the frozen prepared products, but since people were not dissatisfied with frozen products, they had little incentive to switch.

Kraft and ITT-Continental, which pioneered retort pouches in U.S. supermarkets, face the difficult job of helping consumers understand an unfamiliar form of packaging. Most shoppers just don't understand the retort process. Moreover, Kraft has chosen to emphasize the product's convenience of storage and shorter heating time rather than explain the process technology.

Research from test-market efforts showed low trial and very high repeat purchase rates. Projection of test-market sales results indicates a national market of $40 to $50 million annually for the two major competitors out of a total of $1.4 billion for the retail prepared-food categories in which their entrées are positioned. A supplier of retort pouches to the food processors indicates the very large potential for retort pouch foods by pointing out that in the United States some 34 billion cans of food are produced and sold each year, as well as 17 billion pounds of frozen food.

Retailers have a great interest in reducing ever-increasing energy costs, which now amount to more than rent for some stores. With an increasingly significant share of all supermarket expenses consisting of buying and operating frozen-food cases and storage facilities, some supermarket chains have started cutting back on space allowed frozen foods in new stores, even though frozen foods have a higher gross margin than meat and produce and have lower labor costs.

In reviewing the situation, it seemed clear that there existed both a short-run and a long-run market opportunity for retort pouch foods. The competitors seemed satisfied to develop the market slowly. Pouch-filling equipment was still slow and expensive, making for high costs and limited product availability. Kraft's A La Carte and ITT-Continental's Continental Kitchens Flavor Seal sales were said to be above expectations, admittedly conservative, in the limited number of market areas in which they were being sold.

The only new significant development seemed to be ITT-Continental's introduction of its "Deli On Your Shelf," a lower-priced line of pouch foods aimed at families in the Atlanta and Florida markets.*

Questions

1. What changes, if any, should Kraft make in its market development plan for consumer retort pouch foods?
2. How have the forces in Kraft's marketing environment affected the success of retort pouches?

9 Texas Instruments, Inc.: Learning-Aid Products That "Talk"

Texas Instruments' drive into consumer markets has expanded beyond pocket calculators. A few years ago it introduced several new hand-held learning-aid products (LAPs) at relatively low prices. The Little Professor, Dataman, and First Watch have numerical memories and displays. The first two teach math, and the third teaches how to tell time. The Spelling B and Speak & Spell teach how to spell and they have both numerical and alphabetical memories and displays. Speak & Spell is further distinguished by its voice capability. Recent additions are Speak & Read and Speak & Math.

Although the LAPs differ significantly in both form and function from other TI consumer products (calculators and watches) and are in the introductory stage of the product life cycle, the marketing strategy is virtually identical to that used for the company's more mature products. Their educational value suggests that they could be sold to schools as a supplementary learning aid. Only a limited effort has been made to develop either the educational or the entertainment markets. As with any new-product introduction, TI is faced with assessing market potential and familiarizing potential customers with a previously unheard-of product. These problems are particularly acute in this case because the products were developed as an outgrowth of technological innovation rather than in response to consumer needs.

The company is at the point where it must decide what strategies and action programs it should use to ensure successful participation in the market for small electronic learning-aid products. A major aspect is the pricing strategy.

The learning aids began in 1972 when TI, along with such firms as Bowmar, National Semiconductor, and Commodore, packaged inexpensive calculators

*Reprinted with permission from the February 23, 1981, issue of *Advertising Age*. Copyright 1981 by Crain Communications, Inc.

with game books. By 1975, National Semiconductor had introduced the Quiz Kid, an owl-shaped, hand-held machine in which users inputted simple math problems and what they believed to be the correct answers. The device then indicated with a green or a red light whether the answers were right or wrong.

TI's Little Professor, introduced in 1976, was further refined one year later with the introduction of Dataman. This machine had specific math problems preprogrammed in its memory. The Dataman extended the Little Professor's capability by adding game-playing capabilities and a fluorescent "stadium scoreboard" display for correct answers.

In 1978, Spelling B and Speak & Spell were introduced. These products are noteworthy for their alphabetic capabilities. Speak & Spell uses TI's new voice synthesizer technology. It contains 230 of the most commonly misspelled words in order of difficulty. It asks you to spell a word that it clearly pronounces. When you finish spelling the word, you press a button, and if you are right it says, "That is correct, now spell *treasure*." If you misspelled the word, it says, "Wrong, try again," and you have another chance. If you miss again, the unit says, "The correct spelling is T-R-E-A-S-U-R-E." The unit also automatically displays the number of right and wrong answers at the end of a block of ten words. Speak & Spell can be used as a pronunciation guide and as the basis for a number of games, and it will accept additional small memory cartridges that raise the spelling difficulty. The new technology involved holds enormous potential, since voice-command control will eventually be an important aspect of life.

The speech synthesis chip, which has brought such wide attention to Speak & Spell, is a far more advanced (and compact) version of the circuit and chip systems in commercial and industrial "talking machines," such as those used by banks and for disconnected and new-number messages by telephone companies. The memory capability of Speak & Spell is more than twice that of any previous portable voice memory system. The speech synthesis capability of Speak & Spell was hailed as a major innovation and, as a result, has received a great deal of attention.

The high levels of consumer interest and user involvement, along with the company's leading technological position, have indicated a strong basis for a well-planned line of voice-synthesized learning aids to be aggressively marketed throughout the year. This would be in contrast to past efforts involving year-end promotions for two or three items.

Several future uses have been proposed for voice synthesis chips, including foreign language education and electronic games (such as chess and backgammon). An example of the potential is the electronic dictionary, already being offered by at least two firms. It can translate as many as fifteen hundred English words and phrases into a foreign language, such as French, German, Spanish, Russian, and Japanese. Languages can be changed by switching cartridges or cassettes, available at $25 to $50 each. Both the Lexicon and the Craig are pocket-size and sell for about $200.

The direct sales force for TI's Consumer Products Group sells LAPs as well as calculators, and until a few years ago digital watches, to major retail chains. Smaller stores either place their orders directly with TI or purchase through distributors. In a recent year, advertising amounted to about $1 million and was confined to the four weeks following Thanksgiving. The sole advertising medium used was television (prime and fringe time), with very heavy exposure. The company used some trade magazine advertising, but the program was not extensive. Cooperative advertising was also offered to retailers.

TI reached its dominant position in pocket calculator and digital watches sales by using a low-margin, high-volume strategy. Relatively low prices were established on a few models in the hope that large production volumes, coupled with accumulated experience in manufacturing and marketing (the experience curve), would result in a series of unit cost decreases. This would in turn permit still lower prices and thereby result in a dominant market share and presumably profit for Texas Instruments.

On numerous occasions Speak & Spell has been in short supply. Moreover there are no close substitutes. The retail price for Speak & Spell has varied considerably by year and by type of retail outlet. The range has been from less than $45 to over $60. This has raised the question of whether the company's experience-curve pricing strategy, basic to the nonconsumer business, was appropriate for the consumer-oriented learning-aid products.

Questions

1. For the learning-aid products line, should the company use the low-price strategy it used for digital watches and pocket calculators?
2. What are your recommendations for developing and aggressively marketing a line of learning aids featuring the TI voice/sound synthesizer?

10 Loctite Corporation

Loctite is a highly profitable and rapidly growing manufacturer and marketer of adhesives and sealants and related specialty chemicals, with annual sales of almost $200 million. The company's growth has been with the "wonder glues" (specifically the anaerobic type), which cure quickly in the absence of air, and the "crazy glues" (cyanoacrylates), which cure instantly upon exposure to moisture that is present in trace amounts on surfaces to be bonded. In the industrial market, this product sells for over $60 per pound, which contains roughly thirty thousand drops and is generally applied a few drops at a time. Consumer packages are much smaller, containing about one-tenth of an ounce and selling for up to $2 per tube, or about $20 or more per ounce.

The company's phenomenal success in the industrial market has attracted competitors, including some large and aggressive ones, such as Esmark and the 3M Company. Competitive anaerobic and cyanoacrylate products are being marketed in most countries where the company conducts business. The company has patent protection on its anaerobics in the United States and, to a lesser extent, in a number of foreign countries. Nearly all competitive anaerobic sealants and adhesives are sold at prices lower than Loctite's. Although the company has selectively reduced prices to meet competition from time to time, it believes that attention to technical service and customer needs has generally enabled it to maintain its market position without significant price reductions.

The company plans to intensify its "application engineering" approach, which helped it overtake Eastman Kodak in the more competitive "crazy glue," or cyanoacrylates, market. This approach casts well-trained technical service personnel as customer problem solvers using Loctite's products, often especially formulated for the customer's application. The company has three principal user markets for its products: the industrial market, the consumer market, and the automotive aftermarket. In the Industrial Products Group, approximately 60% of sales are made through independent distributors, some of which sell adhesives and sealants made by others, and the remainder of sales are made directly to end users. The company maintains close and continued contact with its distributors and major end users to provide technical assistance and support for the use of its products. In the United States and Canada, sales are made through approximately 120 technically trained district managers, sales engineers, and approximately 2,800 independent industrial distributors.

The Industrial Products Division faces the problem of pricing three new products. The details are as follows:

- *Bond-a-matic:* This is an instant glue applicator for assembly lines and is targeted at small and medium-sized manufacturers that put a lot of parts together. The product avoids "adhesive clog," a common and costly problem. The company is so confident of the product's performance that it will mail a demonstration kit for a thirty-day free trial. The product should be priced low enough so that it can be bought by production managers without the approval needed for a capital expenditure.
- *Quick Repair Kit:* This includes an assortment of materials to make quick minor repairs requiring fast-curing adhesives and/or sealants to keep equipment running and minimize wasting materials in small shops and factories. The kit includes a pair of Vice-Grip pliers as a premium.
- *Quick-Metal:* This is a puttylike adhesive for temporary repair of worn metal bearings and other machine parts. Equipment is ready to run in one hour compared with twelve hours for "metalizers," the most commonly used alternative method. Loctite claims that the product can save the user over $4,000 in time and labor. It is packaged in 50cc tubes.

All of these products are to be sold through the Industrial Products Division's distributors. In determining the suggested price to be charged by the distributors for each product, assume the following hypothetical data:

	BOND-A-MATIC	QUICK REPAIR KIT	QUICK-METAL
Loctite:			
Cost to make	$27.00	$ 6.25	$1.50
All other costs	23.00	5.75	3.50
Total cost per unit	$50.00	$12.00	$5.00
Distributor:			
Usual gross margin on this type of product is 33⅓% of selling price.			

Questions
1. What factors should be considered in determining the price that Loctite should suggest its distributors charge their customers?
2. What price would you recommend that Loctite suggest to its distributors?

11 Gould, Inc.: Focus 800 BAT-TERY

Gould, Inc., a diversified manufacturer of electrical equipment, is launching a major test of an innovative plan for direct consumer sales to help it gain a larger share of the sagging $2.5 million replacement auto battery market. Gould invented the maintenance-free battery and produces about one out of seven car batteries made in the United States, but almost all of its batteries are sold under private labels, mostly through oil companies and mass merchandisers. The new direct marketing plan will bring the company into competition with some of its own biggest private-label customers, such as J. C. Penney, K mart, and Mobil's Montgomery Ward. The plan is now being tested in the seven-county Chicago area.

The 800 BAT-TERY plan calls for the establishment of a roadside service for standard motorists by maintaining a fleet of leased "Rover" vans in the Chicago area and equipping them with a stock of fresh batteries. A motorist unable to start his or her car can dial the 800 BAT-TERY number toll free between 6 A.M. and 10 P.M. seven days a week. If the dispatcher, after a diagnostic dialogue with the caller, believes it is a battery problem, a van is dispatched and will usually arrive within an hour. If roadside tests show a battery is needed, one is sold and installed by the van driver at a price ranging from $49.50 to $69.50. If the battery is not faulty and the car can be started, the charge is $15.00 payable to the van driver by cash, check, or credit card (credit risk is verified by the dispatcher when the call is first received). If the car cannot be started, there is no charge. The plan is believed to be quite attractive to consumers because it offers greater convenience at no higher cost compared with batteries purchased at traditional outlets.

Most replacement batteries are purchased at national retail chains (such as Sears, K mart, and Penney's) or through gas stations. Gould supplies both types of retailers as well as some vehicle manufacturers, but its batteries are always sold under their brand name rather than the Gould name. Consequently, a dissatisfied retailer can easily switch to another supplier without affecting consumer demand. Since there is overcapacity in the industry, all manufacturers are anxious to supply retailers. This puts the battery manufacturers in a difficult bargaining position, which has resulted in battery sales being more profitable for the retailers than the manufacturers.

Gould could have decided to develop a chain of retail outlets, as has been done by the big tire manufacturers, such as Goodyear, Firestone, and General. However, it was unlikely that batteries would draw as well as tires because they are usually purchased on an emergency basis and less frequently. To attract motorists, other merchandise or services would have to be offered. Even then, the stores would have little to distinguish them from competing stores. Moreover, if the capital investment in each store was $200.000 and the interest rate 15% per year, the interest charge alone would be $30,000 per year per store. Considering the number of stores necessary to service adequately the seven-county Chicago area (not to mention the entire country!), the retail store option requires a substantial capital investment.

An examination of the experience of Federal Express revealed that a leased van fleet could be operated for much less money and with more time and space flexibility than retail stores. In fact, the cost of leasing twenty-four vans in the Chicago area was estimated to be $7,000 a month (*Business Week,* June 15, 1981, p. 82). There are other costs associated with entering the retail battery market, such as advertising to establish consumer awareness, but these costs would be approximately the same for the van or store plan.

Before establishing this system, Gould undertook consumer research to determine the demand. There are approximately 47 million replacement battery sales per year, with the possibility of even more as new-car price increases encourage drivers to keep and maintain their existing cars. Replacement sales can be categorized as *anticipatory* or *distress*. Anticipatory sales are those in which serviceable batteries are replaced because the owner feels that the battery may fail under tough starting conditions. Anticipatory sales are about 20% of total replacement sales but are highly seasonal. They represent 50% of replacement sales in September. Distress sales make up 80% of replacement sales and are also highly seasonal. Automobiles require extra starting power in cold weather, and batteries deliver less power as the temperatures drop. Peak demand is experienced on extremely cold mornings.

Gould tested the new approach in Wilkes-Barre, Pa., and raised its market share by five percentage points. That area was used because it could be serviced by one of the company's nearby battery plants. If the Chicago area test is successful, Gould will eventually extend it to forty-two markets.*

Questions

1. What opportunities and threats does the plan face?
2. How should management deal with these opportunities and threats?

12 Fotomat Corporation

Fotomat Corporation markets photographic film and processing services through a chain of thirty-eight hundred drive-through kiosks located in high-traffic areas and five hundred retail stores. Photofinishing services accounted for 90% of its $237 million in revenues in 1980. Fotomat has about 10% of the photofinishing market, making it a distant second to Kodak with over 50%. Fotomat owns and operates twelve processing plants. The company has expanded its operations in the past four years by adding some kiosks and most of the five hundred retail stores, all under the Fotomat name.

The retail stores were developed from a small nucleus of Detroit area camera stores acquired in 1977 as a means of entering the general camera market and attracting the more serious photographer. The stores provide much more display and inventory space, but at the same time the question arises, How should the stores differ from the kiosks with respect to role, products, services, location, appearance, store hours, advertising, and type of personnel? The details can be clarified only after this basic question has been answered.

When Fotomat was founded in 1968, Kodak had well over 90% of the market. How could Fotomat hope to compete with a very large firm that manufactures cameras, film, processing chemicals, and supplies and provides processing, printing, and enlarging services? Richard D. Irwin, Fotomat's president, answered this question as follows:

> By building a better mousetrap. The key to this business is that it is a service oriented industry and you have to offer people convenience. So we locate our kiosks where people can trade with us easily, and on a drive-thru basis. We put our kiosks near high traffic areas like shopping centers and offer quality service. We do not necessarily try to be lowest priced. (*Commercial and Financial Chronicle*, June 6, 1975)

*Case 11 was prepared by Professor Richard Yalch, School of Business Administration, University of Washington, Seattle 98195. Although all of the case information was taken from published news stories, the writer benefited from a class presentation at Northwestern University by Richard Melrose of Gould, Inc.

Kiosks are staffed by part-time "Fotomates," usually homemakers or high-school students who are paid the minimum wage. The company favors this system because the labor costs are low and part-time help is difficult to unionize. But Fotomat has fallen victim to rising minimum-wage requirements that have increased labor costs and cut into profit margins. Prime kiosk locations are becoming scarce, as is part-time labor in urban areas. Competitive price cutting is common, and sales per kiosk have been falling in recent years. All of this translates into lower profit margins for Fotomat.

In the early years, the company found its strength in convenience, reliability, speedy service, and a guarantee. Fotomat offers to replace any film that does not turn out properly—even if due to customer negligence. The company focused on the "Instamatic" photographer, who was not as concerned with picture quality as with speed and convenience in getting back prints or slides.

Fotomat has encountered major problems with its kiosks in recent years. Higher costs, increasing competition, and changing markets have lowered its sales per outlet and reduced its profit margins. As a result, Fotomat has explored different products to supplement sales at the kiosks. These attempts include panty hose, key making, shoe repair, and instant printing. Each attempt has proved to be less than promising, prompting one astute observer to quip, "The only common thread throughout the product line is desperation."

In 1978, Fotomat began selling blank videocassette tapes and a service that transfers 8-mm home movies to videotape cassettes. The transfer business, although profitable, has grown slowly. On the other hand, blank tape sales are growing rapidly and are quite profitable.

Fotomat was not the only company that learned that giant Kodak could be forced to concede some of its share in the processing market. Competition arrived in many forms. There have been increasing numbers of local and regional processors, as well as new kiosk chains following Fotomat's lead. Supermarkets, drugstores, and discount chains have made major investments in photofinishing services. "Minilabs" make it possible for one-day, on-the-spot film-processing services to be offered by many stores.

The rash of new competitors has made it difficult for Fotomat to sell its services near a store that quite possibly could process film faster and cheaper and could provide the customer with one-stop shopping. And the greater convenience of direct-mail processing firms not only has attracted some photofinishing consumers but also has increased these firms' market share.

Competition in the market is not the only change confronting Fotomat. Forty-five percent of all cameras sold in a recent year were instants (the Polaroid type). This kind of camera requires no film-processing service. Conventional camera sales grew at about 10%, most of which were 35-mm units. Thirty-five-millimeter photofinishing grew rapidly. The number of 35-mm camera owners increased quite dramatically. This presented Fotomat with an image problem because of its concentration on Instamatic cameras and film. These 35-mm consumers are more quality-conscious and less concerned with convenience. They buy more prints and enlargements and are also in the market for accessories and supplies.

Fotomat's president belatedly recognized that the company had missed the significant shift from the Instamatic cameras and film, which he said "made up around 90% of the business" in the early 1970s, to 35-mm film, which represents over 50% of the exposures today. Forecasts indicate that it will rise to about 80% to 90% by 1990. To correct the damage done by its myopia, Fotomat introduced, in late 1978, the Series 35, a merchandising effort to capture the 35-mm market by stressing higher-quality processing and larger prints. The program brought an increase in 35-mm photofinishing work and helped to improve Fotomat's image among serious photographers. To accommodate these customers, Fotomat has been replacing some of its kiosks with a larger and different kind of retail store. What products and services should be offered here has again become a problem. Also, whether to use the stores to support kiosk operations, and vice versa, needs to be explored.

Two new threats developed in late 1981. First, Technicolor announced a five-year plan to build a one-thousand-unit chain of one-hour photofinishing stores. Technicolor's prestigious name and professional experience in the movie industry could make it a strong competitor if a significant demand exists for one-hour service. This move by Technicolor was said to be an effort to offset declining revenues, which will drop even more as movie companies increasingly do their own film processing. Second, Kodak has introduced a new mass-market small camera, using twenty small film frames mounted on a disc. What impact this will have on other processors is not clear.

Fotomat's efforts to make a profit on the rental of prerecorded movies have been unsuccessful. Innovative ideas are needed by management to improve results. The present plan makes it possible for a customer to order a videotaped movie by calling a toll-free number and within twenty-four hours have it available at a nearby Fotomat kiosk or store. Rental fees are competitive. A deposit to cover the purchase price is required.

The videocassette recorder/player business is growing rapidly and represents a huge potential market for both programs and equipment. How and where Fotomat should try to take advantage of this great market opportunity has yet to be determined. A number of options are available:

1. In addition to movies, rent videotaped material, such as golf and tennis lessons and video music.
2. Sell prerecorded movies and other materials, in both videotape and videodisc form.
3. Sell video equipment, starting with video cameras, which are increasing in popularity as prices decline, performance improves, and they become lighter and less bulky.
4. Also consider selling videotape recorder/players and possibly videodisc players.

Questions

1. What should Fotomat offer in its kiosks? In its camera stores?
2. What other recommendations do you think Fotomat's management should consider?

13 The Pillsbury Co.: Totino's Pizza

Totino's Inc., a Minneapolis-based frozen-pizza company, was acquired by the Pillsbury Co. in 1975, when the annual sales growth rate was 20%. Within two years, Totino's revolutionary crisp crust technology had been developed, and the company was ready to put into action an aggressive marketing plan designed to make it the leader in consumer frozen pizza. The key aspects of the plan were product improvement, aggressive promotional efforts, and the three basic segments of the market: high, medium, and low price.

The plan was successful, and within three years Totino's was the leading brand of frozen pizza in the United States despite the new competitive entries sponsored by General Mills (Saluto), H. J. Heinz (La Pizzeria), Nestlé (Stouffer's), Quaker Oats (Celeste), and more vigorous competition from over one hundred smaller regional firms.

Jeno's Inc. of Duluth, Minnesota, the former leader in the frozen-pizza market and more recently second, sought to regain leadership by attempting to nullify Totino's advantage in the crisp crust and distinctive package. Jeno's followed Totino's by two years in introducing its "crisp and tasty crust." The package for its "regular" size (about 12 ounces) could easily be confused with Totino's package for the same size.

Totino's management must now reconsider its marketing objectives and activities in view of the new competitive situation, especially the advertising and promotion aspects.

Advertising expenditures for the industry are about 2% of sales, among the lowest for food products and at a rate usually associated with commodity-type products. On the other hand, a considerable amount is spent at the retail level in the form of display, advertising, and other types of allowances as sales incentives. Consumers are also offered incentives—promotional price specials and coupons have been the principal ones. Hardly a week goes by without some special promotion for items in the frozen-pizza case.

Retailers favor profit-producing brands. With limited freezer cabinet space, they favor the seller who spends the most on advertising and promotion, especially trade allowances that directly improve profitability. On the other hand, Totino's and other manufacturers recognize that such allowances and most types of sales promotion efforts are only short-term sales stimulators and build little consumer loyalty. Totino's management wants to spend its advertising and promotional dollars effectively to build customer loyalty—such as a strong consumer franchise. Yet competitors spend for immediate sales stimulation. This is especially true of marginal manufacturers.

Totino's management is concerned about what it believes to be the excessive use of short-term sales stimulators in the industry. It would like to cut back on both consumer and retailer incentives. This would enable it to shift money to advertising that is dedicated to consumer franchise building.

Questions

1. What recommendations would you give Totino's management concerning the marketing of the product, particularly advertising and sales promotion?
2. What moves by competitors must Totino's expect and plan for?

14 Purex Industries, Inc.

Purex is a manufacturer and marketer of industrial and consumer products, primarily price-promoted items in both the branded and nonbranded categories. The company is the fourth-largest maker of household cleaning products and the largest producer and distributor of private-label household cleaning products. Purex claims a 25% share of the home liquid-bleach market, second only to

Clorox; and it claims a substantial share of the clothes-dryer, fabric-softener market, second only to Procter & Gamble.

The following internal and external developments have recently brought about a new competitive situation that may call for changes in Purex's consumer products' marketing efforts, especially those relating to the household cleaning products.

1. Private label and generic products now represent a significant and growing share of industry sales, particularly in the paper goods and household cleaning categories. Consumers are showing greater acceptance as a result of economic conditions and other influences, but acceptance varies by product, retail outlet, and area.

2. Retailers, eager to attract price-conscious consumers and improve their profits, are moving toward nonbranded products and "no-frills" retailing in conventional supermarkets. New types of "no-frills" retail food stores, such as Aldi, A & P's Plus, and Jewel's T Box, as well as warehouse stores that place great emphasis on value, are becoming more numerous. Some outlets have reduced the number of categories of goods stocked, while others carry only the two or three leading brands in each category.

3. Nationally advertised brand manufacturers, suffering from the inroads made by generics and private labels, are bringing out more price-oriented brands. Scott Paper Company, the leading producer of toilet paper, has products at both ends of the price spectrum. Procter & Gamble has launched an economy-priced unadvertised line of paper products under the name Summit. P&G has also introduced an economy-priced Ivory shampoo, but in its test markets did not stress price as a selling point. It is not clear how much advertising support is planned.

4. Purex itself has taken several steps toward adjusting to changing conditions. It has:
   a. Purchased the Decatur, Illinois-based A. E. Staley Company's assets and business in household products and retail food products, which gave Purex additional laundry products, fabric softeners, corn starch and syrup products, and four manufacturing facilities in the United States.
   b. Purchased the New York-based Witco Chemical Company's two strategically located low-cost spray-drying detergent manufacturing plants, thus increasing Purex's capacity to five such units.
   c. Sold some of its losing or marginal industrial and agricultural businesses and shifted, on a royalty basis, the manufacture and sale of its drugstore products to Jeffrey Martin Inc., an international marketing firm that scored a great success with its Porcelana skin spot fade cream. The brands shifted include Ayds appetite suppressant products, Doan's pills, and Cuticura medicated skin-care products. These actions have increased Purex's available cash, allowing reallocation of assets.
   d. Realigned its operations to give separate worldwide organizations to consumer and industrial products and services.

Historically, Purex's first product was household liquid bleach, and its principal competition was, and is, Clorox. Each company sought to differentiate in the minds of consumers its brand of this commodity-type product through advertising, packaging, and product labels. The product itself was and is chemically the same. Over the years Purex acquired a number of well-known brand products, sometimes after they had passed their peak. Among them were Old

Dutch scouring cleanser, Bo-Peep ammonia, LaFrance bluing, Cameo copper cleanser, Fels Naptha laundry bar soap, Sweetheart soap products, Dobie cleaning pads, Brillo soap pads, Ellio's pizza, Pope brand tomatoes, and other Italian products. The company also developed products to give it a full line of household cleaning items.

Purex's management has attributed much of the company's success with its branded products to (1) its "key account" selling plan aimed at retailers and (2) its "price/value" concept aimed at consumers and retailers.

The "key account" concept involves working effectively with a limited number of large retail chains, which account for a disproportionately large share of Purex's consumer product sales. By working closely with these key accounts, learning their needs, coordinating activities, and fulfilling these needs, the company's key account representatives have been highly successful with retailers. This successful Purex approach—that is, cultivating mutually beneficial relationships with selected large retailers—has become more widely accepted by competitors, thereby decreasing one of Purex's earlier advantages.

The Purex price/value marketing concept elements are: competitive quality at lower prices, relatively light advertising support, and heavy retailer incentives. Purex has claimed that the retailers' gross profit margin on Purex products is significantly higher than on competitors'. The company's "Symbol of Value" logo, consisting of a circle around an outstretched hand holding a bar of Purex soap above the words "Symbol of Value," appears in almost all advertisements and on product packages. Such value is somewhat difficult to demonstrate. Procter & Gamble, on the other hand, has claimed that its products provide superior product performance that can be perceived by consumers. This can be demonstrated.

Purex sold price-promoted products under the price/value concept through the 1960s, but in the 1970s it pushed the concept more aggressively by adjusting the price downward even more sharply. Purex-brand bleaches and detergents were priced at 30% below top-selling brands. Trade observers now believe that competition will become even more severe for Purex if generics become more accepted and economy-priced branded products are increased by major premium-brand manufacturers. The success of the price/value concept depends upon whether consumers believe they are getting a good value at a low price.

Household liquid bleach, a commodity-type product, is a case in point. The active ingredient in all liquid bleaches sold for household use in the United States is sodium hypochlorite—5.25%. The remaining 94.75% is water. Yet the following prices for various branded and nonbranded bleaches have been observed in a large chain supermarket:

	NATIONAL	REGIONAL	PRIVATE LABEL	GENERIC
1 qt.	$ .52			
2 qts.	.88		$ .59	
4 qts.	1.05	$ .79	.79	$ .61
6 qts.	1.57			

Price differences of this type exist in most outlets where liquid bleach is sold even though all the bottles contain essentially the same bleach solution. Whether these price differences continue will depend on whether sellers are able to make meaningful differentiations in the minds of consumers. At one time, Purex tried to differentiate its product by increasing the active ingredient to 5.75%, thus allowing it to claim a stronger, more effective product. Later the 5.25% formulation was restored and has continued. Clorox has developed a convenient nondrip bottle.

It is estimated that nonbranded products, including the private label and generics, now account for almost 35% of Purex's household cleaning product sales. Some observers consider this a potential problem because this price-sensitive business comes in large orders with no consumer loyalty. Purex and other nonbranded product suppliers recognize the strong bargaining power of large retail chain buyers, especially when a supplier becomes overly dependent on one or a few buyers.

For many years Purex has enjoyed the advantage of its price/value marketing concept. In view of the new competitive situation, the question is whether the concept and marketing plans based on it will be sufficient for Purex to maintain its reasonably good growth and earnings record.

Questions

1. What recommendations would you make to the Purex management?
2. What other pricing strategies could Purex use for its household cleaning products?

15 STP Corporation

The STP Corporation is a marketer of oil and gasoline additives and other branded and packaged auto consumer products in the United States and more than 130 other countries. After a period of rapid expansion involving major policy and ownership changes, there is need for a critical audit of the corporation's activities, particularly its product lines and markets served.

STP markets a variety of branded consumer products that are bought by the owners of the more than 100 million autos in use today in the United States alone. It focuses on satisfying the needs of the rapidly developing population of do-it-yourself consumers. STP is in an ideal position to take advantage of the economic factors that have forced consumers to keep their cars longer and to maintain them personally.

STP Oil Treatment, the company's original product, remains the cornerstone of the product line. Over 40 million cans were sold last year, and this product continues to be the overwhelming favorite oil additive for motorists around the world.

In the United States, STP markets many products ranging from oil and gas additives and a carburetor cleaner to a comprehensive line of oil, gas, and air filters, PCV valves, and breather elements. It was the first company in the auto aftermarket to introduce nationally a multigrade motor oil developed to extend oil drain intervals to fifteen thousand miles or one year (whichever comes first) under normal driving conditions for cars in good mechanical condition.

STP Double Oil Filters continue to help the sale of other products in the marketplace and are a stable profit contributor.

STP Gas Treatment was a significant factor in STP's growth, and the new easy-to-pour plastic packaging, coupled with the improved formula, should result in continued gains. Trade response has been favorable to the new space-age-shaped packaging.

Prior to its acquisition by Esmark, STP had been involved in ongoing discussions with the Federal Trade Commission with regard to certain of the company's advertising claims for STP Oil Treatment. Even earlier, *Consumer Reports* had published an unfavorable rating of the same product and the claims made. Some of the early advertising messages were delivered by Andy Granatelli, former chairman of STP. The FTC matter was settled in February 1978, and advertising for that product, which had been stopped temporarily, resumed.

STP extended its product line beyond the limitations of an automobile engine by introducing domestically and internationally "Son of a Gun!"—a multipurpose restorer and beautifier of leather, wood, vinyl, and rubber. It is a product that has uses for the home as well as for the automobile, and one that includes women as significant potential buyers. Son of a Gun!—like so many of STP's other successful products—has shown itself to be highly responsive to effective advertising and sales promotion activities.

STP has achieved exposure and visibility for its products and its distinctive red, white, and blue STP logo. Primary to this marketing posture is radio, television, and print advertising supplemented by point-of-sale promotions. Merchandising techniques include retailer utilization of a variety of effective display units, mobiles, and informative brochures. Beyond this is the visibility and excitement of STP's auto-racing activities, which range from participation in drag racing and Indy car races to sponsorship of six-time world stock-car champion Richard Petty.

Products bearing the STP label are sold in more than 130 countries. More than thirty STP-branded international items are currently in the product line, including such diverse items as an all-purpose silicon spray lubricant, insect sprays, brake fluid, car wax, radiator cleaner and flush, multipurpose spray penetrant, and radiator treatment.

This dedication to an expanded product line has been accelerated. The international division plans to introduce more than a dozen new car-care products into the marketplace, along with a program to make the package designs more adaptable to different languages and cultures.

Some of the other products considered for possible addition to the product line are oils for boats, motorcycles, diesel engines, and machinery and an aerosol insecticide.*

Questions

1. How do you account for the success of the STP Corporation?
2. What should be the company's market product line criteria? Evaluate each of the new products mentioned in the last paragraph, indicating whether they should be added to the line.
3. What differences, if any, exist between marketing STP products in the United States and marketing them in foreign countries? What changes should STP make in its marketing activities for the United States? For foreign markets?

*This case is based on the 1978 Esmark, Inc., annual report and form 10-K filed with the SEC by the company.

16 Minnetonka, Inc.: Softsoap™

In 1978, Minnetonka, Inc., a Chaska, Minnesota, firm dealing primarily in bath products, introduced Softsoap, an inexpensive, pump-dispensed, liquid hand soap. One industry analyst asserted that Softsoap was the "first major innovation in the hand soap market since Procter and Gamble introduced Ivory, 'the soap that floats,' a century ago." Softsoap's meteoric success, with almost an 8% market share in its first year, has attracted the interest of such marketing giants as Procter & Gamble, Colgate-Palmolive, Lever Brothers, and Armour-Dial. Initially slow to react, these slumbering goliaths with a substantial stake in the bar-soap industry are awakening to the threat posed by Softsoap. Minnetonka must decide how to respond.

Starting out with a $3,000 investment in 1964, Robert Taylor, a Stanford M.B.A., began manufacturing scented soaps in attractive packages in his basement. In subsequent years he expanded his line into bubble baths, fruit shampoos, and fancy bar soaps, moved out of his basement, and formed Minnetonka. By 1968, Taylor's initial investment had grown into a $650,000 business. Flushed with his early success, he diversified Minnetonka outside of the bath-related products with lines ranging from candles and cosmetics to real estate. Taylor optimistically hoped to boost sales over the $100 million mark.

Problems quickly arose in managing such a diverse portfolio. With the added difficulties brought on by the 1974 economic recession, Taylor was faced with a $1.6 million loss. He responded by retrenching, divesting of most of his bath-unrelated lines, and concentrating once again on innovative, attractively packaged soap products primarily for the gift market. Back on familiar ground, Taylor managed to turn Minnetonka around while successfully expanding his existing lines—Village Bath, Dirty Kids—and acquiring Claire Burke, Inc. Minnetonka, in 1976, was a growing firm dealing mostly in specialty bath products for the gift market. Utilizing a highly creative approach to manufacturing and packaging, Minnetonka developed such products as fruit shampoos, "War Paint" bubble baths, the "Incredible Soap Machine" liquid-soap dispenser, and fancy bar soaps. Its products were primarily distributed through specialty stores for the gift market.

In 1978, working from information garnered in focus group sessions on the Incredible Soap Machine, a Village Bath entry in the liquid/fancy soap category, Taylor set out to offer a liquid-soap product positioned against the bar soaps. The focus groups had indicated a favorable reaction to the convenience and neatness of the Incredible Soap Machine, but the price, $4.94, was considered too high for regular use.

In response, Minnetonka came out with Softsoap at $1.59 for 10.5 ounces and retailed it through grocery/food outlets and drugstores primarily using food brokers. Softsoap is attractively packaged in a plastic, pump-dispensing bottle with a clear plastic overcap. The package comes in four colors: yellow, brown, blue, and green, and all colors feature a decorative wicker motif.

The sales rollout in April 1980 was supported by a heavy national television advertising schedule, plus magazine and Sunday supplement coupon offers. Softsoap was so successful that within days many stores were completely sold out of their initial order.

Beyond having an appealing and effective product that answers a need for some consumers, the key to Softsoap's success has been extremely strong distribution in grocery, drug, and mass-merchandising outlets. By the end of

1980, Softsoap brand was being sold in nearly all the supermarkets in the U. S.

The product is shipped from geographically dispersed manufacturing sites by independent trucking firms to independent and chain warehouses. Purchases are usually allotted by the truckload. Units are shipped in cases containing a dozen bottles, all of the same color.

The successful advertising campaign that began in 1980 was expanded in 1981, bringing the "Soap without the soapy mess" message to consumers through television, magazines, newspapers, and outdoor advertising. Softsoap was the number-one advertiser in its product category during 1981.

In 1981, the company's new-product introduction increased the shelf impact of the Softsoap line in retail stores. The current Softsoap line includes the 10.5- and 16.5-ounce sizes in four colors; a 22-ounce refill bottle; Work Soap™, a heavy-duty liquid hand soap that removes soil and grease while conditioning the skin and leaving the hands smooth; ShowerMate™; and Soap on Tap™, a higher-priced brand of liquid soap that is being sold by the Softsoap sales force through the same outlets as the Softsoap brand.

The primary use of Softsoap is as a hand soap, usually in the place of bar soap at bathroom and kitchen sinks. It is against this primary use category that product positioning and promotions are based. The product is broadly targeted for homemakers. The target segment is currently defined by the distribution channels and, in an encompassing sense, includes all consumers who use those retail outlets where the product appears.

Softsoap is distributed to retailers with a suggested retail price of $1.59 for 10.5 ounces. Actual shelf prices range between $1.29 and $1.77, not including deals or coupon offers, which may at times reduce the price to as little as $0.99. The retailer receives a 30% markup compared with an industry average markup on bar soaps of around 15%. Private-label brands and generics sell for as little as $1.00.

By early 1982, there were more than forty competitors eager to capture a portion of the estimated $80 million (1981) liquid-soap market. The ultimate threat lies in the hands of the four major soapers—Armour-Dial, Procter & Gamble, Colgate-Palmolive, and Lever Brothers. Each was reportedly in the research and development stage on products for the liquid-soap class. In late 1981, the long-anticipated test marketing of both Procter & Gamble's Rejoice and Armour-Dial's Liqua 4 took place. Rejoice is positioned for use "instead of a bar" and claims to "condition your skin as it cleans, leaving it soft and smooth." Liqua 4 comes in a 5-ounce soap-shaped container and is being touted as a "liquid formula" that replaces bar soap with "complete skin care." In addition to the advertised brands, dealer-sponsored private-label brands and generic liquid soap in quite similar pump-dispenser bottles have appeared at much lower prices.

As a market leader, Softsoap is now positioned in the middle or mainstream of the market; that is, it is a moderate-quality soap at a moderate price appealing to the market generally. Competitors have already started to fragment the liquid-soap market with products designed for (1) those who want a higher-priced cleansing, a skin-care product (Yardley's and Jovan), (2) the baby-care market (Yardley's), and (3) the shower/bath market (the company's ShowerMate is described on page 494).

The company could try to discourage further competition by entering liquid-soap products in these and other major segments ahead of major competition. In addition to, or in place of, segmenting the market, Minnetonka could launch a line of personal-care products based on the pump-dispensing bottle idea— hand lotions, shampoo, and toothpaste, for example.

The most fundamental decision is whether or not Minnetonka should continue in the mass market competing against major soap companies or sell specialty products in smaller markets. It could sell its mass-market products, Softsoap and ShowerMate, to another company as a going business and return to its original business, personal specialty products for the gift market. If it decides to compete against the major soap companies, then a plan for doing so must be formulated. Should the company compete head-on, or is some other strategy more promising? A logical approach would be built on the strengths of the company relative to market opportunities and competitive strengths.*

Questions

1. What changes should Minnetonka make in its marketing objectives and strategy, if any?
2. Develop a marketing plan for Softsoap, taking into consideration your answer to question 1.

17 Maytag Co.: Laundry Equipment

The Maytag Co., a limited-line appliance manufacturer, has been one of the most profitable firms in the appliance business in recent years, with annual sales of between $350 million and $450 million. Its basic strategy has been to make the best product and charge for it accordingly. Its sales have been primarily to the upper end of the replacement market. Neither the newly formed household market nor the builder's market has been targeted. Maytag's laundry equipment has the reputation of being trouble-free, and the company has featured "Ol' Lonely," the Maytag repairman, in its advertising. Changing conditions make it desirable that the company consider whether its long-held strategy should be changed.

Maytag's laundry equipment is still regarded as the top of the line, but despite much effort and favorable ratings in *Consumer Reports*, many consumers and members of the industry still consider its dishwasher to be second to Hobart's Kitchen-Aid, long the leader in the high-quality, high-price niche. Maytag is, however, narrowing the gap. It has launched an extensive comparative advertising campaign aimed at Kitchen-Aid. The headline of one ad asks, "Which of these two great dishwashers is best—Kitchen-Aid or Maytag?" The message gives a detailed point-by-point comparison and has been delivered in fifty-eight major markets using spot TV and newspapers.

The premium-quality niche for laundry and kitchen appliances targeted by both Maytag and Kitchen-Aid may be eroding. Although there is no solid evidence of this, there is an increasingly prevalent feeling in the trade and among consumers that the quality difference between high-priced and medium-priced major laundry and kitchen appliances is becoming smaller and the price difference relatively larger.

In 1981, Maytag acquired the Cleveland, Tennessee-based, Hardwicke Stove Co., makers and marketers of gas and electric ranges and microwave ovens sold through conventional outlets in medium- and low-price brackets.

Some of the major developments in the industry are as follows:

*Case 16 was prepared in part by Karen Balch, Mike Hutter, John Monson, Jeff Steinhilber, and Meeks Vaughan.

1. The structure of the industry is changing, through mergers and acquisitions, with a few large full-line companies producing most of the industry output. Design and Manufacturing Co. of Connersville, Indiana, produces dishwashers that account for over half the dollars spent without selling a single unit under its own name. It supplies such buyers as Sears, Magic Chef, Roper, Western Auto, Gambles, and Tappan.
2. Competition, always keen in this industry, has become even more so.
   a. Low-cost producers, such as White Consolidated Industries, are constantly driving for lower costs.
   b. General Electric has undertaken a major project focused on its dishwashers and designed to improve product quality and reliability but at the same time reduce production costs through the increased use of industrial robots.
   c. Marketing efforts have been intensified, with greater emphasis being given to quick sales stimulants, such as factory rebates, special factory-authorized sales, and additional incentives for consumers and dealers. Advertising also has an important role.
3. Products are being designed with fewer electromechanical and more electronic components to control operations. Microprocessors and other advanced technology require greater technological resources not only for the design and manufacture of equipment but also for service and repairs.
4. Service is becoming a major problem. Special tools and well-trained service personnel are required for major repairs. Service calls are costly to make. The need for, and cost of, service calls are resented by consumers, especially when repairs are minor. Most companies would rather not be bothered with them. Few make a profit, although it is believed that in the appliance industry the Sears service operation is profitable because of its large volume of maintenance service contracts.
5. General Electric hopes to reduce the problem by starting a "Quick Fix System." This is offered through franchised dealers, where customers can purchase detailed repair manuals for GE appliances and commonly needed replacement parts at a special display. GE surveys show that 40% of the appliance repairs are currently being done by consumers who get little help from manufacturers. Moreover, 25% of consumer repairs are made by women.

Maytag's marketing strategy has worked well for its laundry equipment but not so well for its dishwasher, but this seems to be improving. However, the basic changes now occurring suggest that Maytag would be wise to evaluate its basic strategy and consider what new growth directions the company should take, especially in view of the mature market for laundry equipment. Some of the possibilities are as follows:

1. New-product types—for example, stoves, refrigerators, cooking equipment?
2. New markets—for example, builder, institutional, international?
3. New channels—for example, sell to Sears, Montgomery Ward, K mart?
4. Develop a cheaper line of products? If so, should they be sold under the Maytag name or some other brand name?

Questions
1. Should Maytag change its basic marketing strategy?
2. What are your recommendations and reasons?

18 Consumers Union of the United States, Inc.

According to the charter of the Consumers Union of the United States, Inc., it was established in 1936 as a nonprofit organization "to provide for consumer information and counsel on consumer goods and services . . . to give information and assistance on all matters relating to expenditures of family income . . . and to initiate and cooperate with individual and group efforts seeking to create and maintain decent living standards."

Today, Consumers Union is the most important and influential organization in the consumer movement. From its inception, CU has concerned itself with a wide range of issues beyond product testing. In recent years it has increasingly come to view the promotion of consumer education as one of its major roles. CU has undertaken to inform consumers about all phases of their relationship with the marketplace, including such topics as interest rates, guarantees and warranties, life insurance, product safety, and the selection of a doctor. It has helped to finance a variety of activities in the consumer movement area, including David Caplovitz's research on the problem of low-income consumers as well as the development of an international organization of product-testing associations (the International Organization of Consumers Unions), and it has occasionally provided expert testimony at regulatory and legislative hearings.

Most of CU's $20 million income in 1978 came from more than 2 million subscribers and newsstand buyers of *Consumer Reports,* a monthly publication of test results with product ratings and consumer information. The *Buying Guide* issue has in the past consisted of about 450 pages, with more than twenty-three hundred ratings by brand and model. Subscription rates in 1983 were $14.00 for one year, $24.00 for two years, $34.00 for three years. The newsstand price of a single copy was $1.50, and the *Buying Guide* issue was $3.50. Some income was derived from book sales and, on rare occasions, from a government grant. In an effort to protect its independence, CU has not accepted advertising, gifts, donations, subsidies, or private grants. CU defends its impartiality and independence by taking legal action against those who use the name "Consumers Union" or CU test results for commercial purposes. CU members act as watchdogs, and CU has lost few, if any, cases.

In a speech in 1970, Colston E. Warne, president of the Consumers Union of the United States, Inc., mentioned the following as imperfections in the consumer movement:

1. Narrow focus on products, particularly technically complex products
2. Lack of emphasis on nutritional testing

In another speech during the same year, Dr. Warne listed the following as the major complaints of the consumer public regarding Consumers Union's testing methods:

1. Infrequent testing of major items
2. Inaccessibility of products tested and availability of products yet to be tested
3. Postponement of test results to the point of obsolescence
4. Insufficient coverage of door-to-door and mail-order items
5. Excessive emphasis on minor advantages and disadvantages, and insufficient emphasis on performance and durability

In one of its reports, CU mentions the following priorities:

1. Focus on environmental issues
2. Expansion of the basic staff
3. Coordinated effort to see that legislative, regulatory, and legal actions correct the inequalities that CU has exposed
4. Creation and maintenance of a Washington office
5. Experimental research in areas more useful to disadvantaged consumers
6. Formation of a Consumer Interests Foundation, Inc., which will probe more deeply into broader areas of consumer concern

CU's management is reappraising the organization and its operations with an eye to the future. Management is specifically interested in getting recommendations indicating how CU can serve consumers most effectively with its limited resources.

Questions

1. From a marketing point of view, what changes, if any, should CU make in its product-testing service program for consumers, including *Consumer Reports* magazine? Briefly indicate your ideas and reasons for each of the following categories: (a) target market(s), (b) product/service line, (c) pricing/fund raising, (d) distribution/place, and (e) communication (advertising, publicity, promotion, personal selling).
2. What should be CU's role in the consumer movement? (a) What services should be offered beyond product testing? (b) How should each be financed?
3. Should Consumers Union take an active role in sponsoring causes, as advocated by Ralph Nader when he was a director of the organization?

19 H & R Block: Legal Services

H & R Block is a leader in the tax field, preparing over 10% of the individual returns in the United States. The company has agreed with Hyatt Legal Services to open jointly hundreds of legal clinics nationwide over the next few years. They will share quarters with Block's tax offices, starting in Pennsylvania and Ohio, where Hyatt now has nine clinics. The plan is to do for legal clinics what H & R Block did for income tax preparation, that is, make low-cost legal services as available as Block's tax preparation services.

Only one legal-clinic chain, Jacoby & Meyers, with over fifty clinics in California and New York, has grown beyond a few offices in the four years since the Supreme Court approved legal advertising. Marketing, administration, and inadequate capital are the major problems inhibiting expansion. Many lawyers are not good businessmen.

The new Hyatt Legal Clinics will be supported by the newly created Block Management Co. Fees will be charged for office space, secretarial and legal assistants, and access to word processing and computer equipment. It will also provide expert marketing and financial services to the joint venture.

Present fees are scaled to attract low- and average-income clients. An initial consultation costs $15, and the basic, more-or-less routine legal services, such as wills, real-estate transactions, and uncontested divorces, are available in most cases at lower prices than those charged by traditional law firms.

Some questions remain to be resolved. Will the clinics be able to attract the masses of people who have not used a lawyer and do not believe they have legal problems despite the opinions of lawyers that they do? While everyone files a tax return, not everyone needs low-cost legal help. Will those who become involved in a legal situation clearly requiring a lawyer be inclined to use a legal clinic? Will reduced fees be an attraction or a deterrent? Can adequate quality control measures be installed so that clients will get good service at low cost?

An aggressive educational marketing plan is needed to persuade potential clients to recognize when they need legal help and that good low-cost service is available at the Hyatt clinics.*

Questions

1. What are your recommendations concerning a marketing plan for the Hyatt Legal Clinics?
2. How do the features of the Hyatt Legal Clinics' products affect the marketing plan?

20 Ronco, Inc.

Ronco, Inc., a longtime leader in the carnival-pitchman era in TV advertising, sells such household gadgetry items as the Miracle Broom, Smokeless Ashtray, Egg Scrambler, and Mr. Microphone, but is changing the marketing strategy it has used for almost twenty years. The company's great success attracted imitators who have caused Ronco's advertising effectiveness to decline. In the past the company has been a gift-oriented promotional house, which resulted in 60% of its sales in the fourth quarter. It hopes to smooth out its sales and become more profitable. To do this it plans to make changes as follows:

- *Products:* Move away from inexpensive, "gimmicky" products to more lasting ones. Stress healthful, high-quality products—for example, a small air-cleaning machine and a back vibrator, both costing over $20.
- *Packaging:* Make it more sophisticated.
- *Distribution:* Increase the number of retail outlets to 60,000 from 23,000 and include more supermarkets, drugstores, and other types, especially more of the smaller outlets.
- *Pricing and terms of sale:* Carry only higher-priced items ranging from $10 to $25. Consider the use of consignment selling to increase in-store availability and better control of retail prices, as opposed to current guaranteed sale.
- *Advertising:* Increase the advertising budget from $7 million to $14 million, the extra $7 million to be spent throughout the year. It is expected that doubling advertising dollars will double sales.

One of management's ideas consists of providing retailers with a colored

*See "H & R Block: Expanding Beyond Taxes for Faster Growth," *Business Week,* December 9, 1980.

cardboard display rack supporting a large sign announcing: "RONCO ALL OCCASION GIFT CENTER: As Advertised on TV."

The assortment of ideas available for use in the display racks includes the following:

- Egg Scrambler $12.88
- Phono Record Vacuum   14.88
- Miracle Broom   14.88
- Smokeless Ashtray   16.88
- Mr. Microphone   17.88
- Mr. Microphone with AM/FM radio   19.45
- Back Relief Electric Vibrator   24.88
- Battery Tester   11.94
- Egg Beater   15.45
- Food Dehydrator   23.95

The founder and chairman of Ronco, Inc., is Ronald Popeil. In his early years he hawked vegetable slicers and similar gadgets in five-and-ten and department stores and learned much from his employer-father, Sam Popeil, one-time king of household gadgetry and founder of Popeil Bros.

Sam Popeil's success resulted from his great ability to fiddle with existing products and make them better; select ear-catching names, such as Dial-o-Matic, Kitchen Magic, Veg-o-Matic, and Pocket Fisherman; deftly demonstrate them in stores and later on TV; and induce distributors and retailers to handle them on a consignment basis. Unsold goods were returned for credit at the end of the season and refurbished for sale the next season.

In 1979, Sam Popeil lost his business because of mounting losses, excessive inventory, lack of fresh ideas, and need for more effective management. Popeil blames his downfall partly on his distributors, Ronco and K-Tel, which became so successful that they went public and added competing products so as not to be overly dependent on one manufacturing source.

The housewares industry has long been one area where small entrepreneurs have been able to introduce innovative single items that succeed or fail on their own merit. In competition with them are some well-known brand product lines and firms whose products are recognized as families of quality products, such as Ecko and Rubber Maid, so that one product in the line helps to cross-sell other items.

Some observers have questioned whether Ronco, Inc., can successfully shift to its proposed new strategy of selling a line of products from a display rack in view of its past lower-priced, single-product promotions characterized by a high-pressure, carnival-pitchman, gadget orientation. The higher-priced units seem to be out of line in supermarkets and drugstores, especially for gift items.*

Questions
1. What is your evaluation of the situation?
2. What are your recommendations to the Ronco management?

*See "Ronco Trades Shlock for Some Sophistication," *Advertising Age,* July 20, 1981; "Gadget King Popeil Sees Empire Crumble," *Chicago Tribune,* September 12, 1979; "Mom and Pop's Last Stand," *Forbes,* November 13, 1978.

References

Chapter 1

1. Peter F. Drucker, *Management: Tasks, Responsibilities, Practices* (New York: Harper & Row, 1973), pp. 64–65.
2. Here are some other definitions: "Marketing is the performance of business activities that direct the flow of goods and services from producer to consumer or user." "Marketing is getting the right goods and services to the right people at the right place at the right time at the right price with the right communication and promotion." "Marketing is the creation and delivery of a standard of living."
3. Kelvin J. Lancaster, "A New Approach to Consumer Theory," *Journal of Political Economy* 14 (1966): 132–57.
4. For further discussion, see Wroe Alderson, "Factors Governing the Development of Marketing Channels," in *Marketing Channels for Manufactured Products,* ed. Richard M. Clewett (Homewood, Ill.: Richard D. Irwin, 1957), pp. 211–14.
5. "Texas Instruments Shows U.S. Business How to Survive in the 1980s," *Business Week,* September 18, 1978, pp. 66ff; and "The Long-Term Damage from TI's Bombshell," *Business Week,* June 15, 1981, p. 36.
6. See "So We Made a Better Mousetrap," *President's Forum,* Fall 1962, pp. 26–27.
7. See Theodore Levitt's classic article, "Marketing Myopia," *Harvard Business Review,* July-August 1960, pp. 45–56.
8. See Irving J. Rein, *Rudy's Red Wagon: Communication Strategies in Contemporary Society* (Glenview, Ill.: Scott, Foresman, 1972).
9. See Joseph McGinness, *The Selling of the President* (New York: Trident Press, 1969).
10. See John B. McKitterick, "What Is the Marketing Management Concept?" in *The Frontiers of Marketing Thought and Action* (Chicago: American Marketing Association, 1957), pp. 71–82; Fred J. Borch, "The Marketing Philosophy as a Way of Business Life," in *The Marketing Concept: Its Meaning to Management,* Marketing Series, No. 99 (New York: American Management Association, 1957), pp. 3–5; and Robert J. Keith, "The Marketing Revolution," *Journal of Marketing,* January 1960, pp. 35–38.
11. Levitt, "Marketing Myopia."
12. Carlton P. McNamara, "The Present Status of the Marketing Concept," *Journal of Marketing,* January 1972, pp. 50–57.
13. Peter M. Banting and Randolph E. Ross, "The Marketing Masquerade," *Business Quarterly* (Canada), Spring 1974, pp. 19–27. Also see Philip Kotler, "From Sales Obsession to Marketing Effectiveness," *Harvard Business Review,* November-December 1977, pp. 67–75.
14. Laurence P. Feldman, "Societal Adaptation: A New Challenge for Marketing," *Journal of Marketing,* July 1971, pp. 54–60; and Martin L. Bell and C. William Emery, "The Faltering Marketing Concept," *Journal of Marketing,* October 1971, pp. 37–42.
15. The societal marketing concept goes by different names. See Leslie M. Dawson, "The Human Concept: New Philosophy for Business," *Business Horizons,* December 1969, pp. 29–38; James T. Rothe and Lissa Benson, "Intelligent Consumption: An Attractive Alternative to the Marketing Concept," *MSU Business Topics,* Winter 1974, pp. 29–34; and George Fisk, "Criteria for a Theory of Responsible Consumption," *Journal of Marketing,* April 1973, pp. 24–31.
16. Richard D. Farmer, "Would You Want Your Daughter to Marry a Marketing Man?" *Journal of Marketing,* January 1967, p. 1.

17. Sterling Hayden, *Wanderer* (New York: Knopf, 1963).
18. William J. Stanton, *Fundamentals of Marketing,* 5th ed. (New York: McGraw-Hill, 1978), p. 7.
19. Sir Winston Churchill.
20. Ralph Z. Sorenson II, "U.S. Marketers Can Learn from European Innovators," *Harvard Business Review,* September-October 1972, pp. 89–99.
21. Thomas V. Greer, *Marketing in the Soviet Union* (New York: Holt, Rinehart & Winston, 1973).
22. Donald L. Pike, "The Future of Higher Education: Will Private Institutions Disappear in the U.S.?" *Futurist,* December 1977, p. 374.

Chapter 2

1. Written by the author and based on "Turmoil among the Brewers: Miller's Fast Growth Upsets the Beer Industry. Can It Topple the U.S. Leader?" *Business Week,* November 8, 1976, pp. 58–67; and other sources.
2. H. Igor Ansoff, "Strategies for Diversification," *Harvard Business Review,* September-October 1957, pp. 113–24.
3. This example is described in detail in Glen L. Urban and John R. Hauser, *Design and Marketing of New Products* (Englewood Cliffs, N.J.: Prentice-Hall, 1980), pp. 187, 221, and elsewhere.
4. The "four *P*'s" classification was first suggested by E. Jerome McCarthy in *Basic Marketing: A Managerial Approach* (Homewood, Ill.: Richard D. Irwin, 1960).
5. For details, see "General Foods Corporation: Post Division," in *Organization Strategy: A Marketing Approach,* ed. E. Raymond Corey and Steven H. Star (Boston: Division of Research, Graduate School of Business Administration, Harvard University, 1971), pp. 201–30.
6. See David J. Luck, "Interfaces of a Product Manager," *Journal of Marketing,* October 1969, pp. 32–36.
7. See B. Charles Ames, "Dilemma of Product/Market Management," *Harvard Business Review,* March-April 1971, pp. 66–74.

Chapter 3

1. Based on "Key Role of Research in Agree's Success Is Told, *Marketing News,* January 12, 1979.
2. This definition is adapted from "Marketing Information Systems: An Introductory Overview," in *Readings in Marketing Information Systems,* ed. Samuel V. Smith, Richard H. Brien, and James E. Stafford (Boston: Houghton Mifflin, 1968), p. 7.
3. Dik Warren Twedt, ed., *1978 Survey of Marketing Research* (Chicago: American Marketing Association, 1978).
4. For example, see Paul E. Green and Donald S. Tull, *Research for Marketing Decisions,* 4th ed. (Englewood Cliffs, N.J.: Prentice-Hall, 1978).
5. Andris A. Zoltners and P. Sinha, "Integer Programming Models for Sales Resource Allocation," *Management Science,* March 1980, pp. 242–60.
6. T. E. Hlavac, Jr., and J. D. C. Little, "A Geographic Model of an Automobile Market," Working Paper No. 186-66 (Cambridge: Massachusetts Institute of Technology, Alfred P. Sloan School of Management, 1966).
7. See John D. C. Little and Leonard M. Lodish, "A Media Planning Calculus," *Operations Research,* January-February 1969, pp.1–35.
8. See Glen L. Urban and John R. Hauser, *Design and Marketing of New Products* (Englewood Cliffs, N.J.: Prentice-Hall, 1980).
9. For an excellent annotated reference to major secondary sources of business and marketing data, see Thomas C. Kinnear and James R. Taylor, *Marketing Research: An Applied Approach* (New York, McGraw-Hill, 1979), pp. 128–31, 138–71.
10. For more information on experiments, see Seymour Banks, *Experimentation in Marketing* (New York, McGraw-Hill, 1965).
11. For an overview of mechanical devices, see Roger D. Blackwell, James S. Hensel, Michael B. Phillips, and Brian Sternthal, *Laboratory Equipment for Marketing Research* (Dubuque, Iowa: Kendall/Hunt, 1970), pp. 7–8.
12. Bobby J. Calder, "Focus Groups and the Nature of Qualitative Marketing Research," *Journal of Marketing Research,* August 1977, pp. 353–64.
13. The Allegheny Airlines example is based on Harry T. Chandis, "The Birth of USAir," *Marketing Communications,* January 1980, pp. 30–32; and Grant F. Winthrop, " 'Agony Airlines' Becomes a High Flyer," *Fortune,* June 30, 1980, pp. 104–8.

Chapter 4

1. See John Gruen, "Dancevision," *Dance Magazine,* December 1982, p. 91; Tom Nicholson, "Cable TV's First Casualty," *Newsweek,* September 27, 1982, p. 65; "Sifting through the Fallout of CBS Cable," *Broadcasting,* Sep-

tember 27, 1982, pp. 28–30; Harry F. Waters, "Culture Shock on Cable," *Time,* October 6, 1981.

2. The statistical data in this chapter have been drawn from the *Statistical Abstract of the United States, 1982–83,* and other sources.

3. See Ellen Graham, "Advertisers Take Aim at a Neglected Market: The Working Woman," *Wall Street Journal,* July 5, 1977, p. 1.

4. A SMA consists of a county or group of contiguous counties with a total population of at least 100,000 and a central city with a minimum population of 50,000 (or two closely located cities with a combined population of 50,000).

5. Rachel Carson, *Silent Spring* (Boston: Houghton Mifflin, 1962).

6. *First Annual Report of the Council on Environmental Quality* (Washington, D.C.: Government Printing Office, 1970), p. 158.

7. See "The Coming Boom in Solar Energy," *Business Week,* October 9, 1978, pp. 88–104.

8. See Karl E. Henion II, *Ecological Marketing* (Columbus, Ohio: Grid, 1976).

9. Alvin Toffler, *Future Shock* (New York: Bantam, 1970), pp. 25–30.

10. For an excellent and comprehensive list of possible future products, see Dennis Gabor, *Innovations: Scientific, Technological, and Social* (London: Oxford University Press, 1970). Also see Charles Panat, *Breakthroughs* (Boston: Houghton Mifflin, 1980); and "Technologies for the '80s," *Business Week,* July 6, 1981, pp. 48ff.

11. Dennis D. Fisher, "ReaLemon Sales Tactics Hit," *Chicago Sun-Times,* July 4, 1974.

12. Leo Greenland, "Advertisers Must Stop Conning Customers," *Harvard Business Review,* July-August 1974, p. 18.

13. See Edward Meadows, "Bold Departures in Antitrust," *Fortune,* October 5, 1981, pp. 180–88.

14. See Bill Abrams, "'Middle Generation' Growing More Concerned with Selves," *Wall Street Journal,* January 21, 1982, p. 25.

Chapter 5

1. Prepared by the author from material in "The $100 Million Object Lesson," *Fortune,* January 1971; and "The End of Corfam," *Wall Street Journal,* March 17, 1971, p. 1.

2. *Statistical Abstract of the United States, 1980.*

3. See Kevin A. Wall, "New Market: Among Blacks, the Haves Are Now Overtaking the Have-Nots," *Advertising Age,* February 11, 1974, pp. 35–36; Mary Jane Schlinger and Joseph T. Plummer, "Advertising in Black and White," *Journal of Marketing Research,* May 1972, pp. 149–53; and Raymond A. Bauer and Scott M. Cunningham, "The Negro Market," *Journal of Advertising Research,* April 1970, pp. 3–12.

4. See Melvin Helitzer and Carl Heyel, *The Youth Market* (New York: Media Books, 1970), p. 58; George W. Schiele, "How to Reach the Young Consumer," *Harvard Business Review,* March-April 1974, pp. 77–86.

5. See "The Graying of America," *Newsweek,* February 28, 1977, pp. 50–65.

6. See Rena Bartos, "What Every Marketer Should Know about Women," *Harvard Business Review,* May-June 1978, pp. 73–85.

7. See A. H. Kizilbash and E. T. Garman, "Grocery Retailing in Spanish Neighborhoods," *Journal of Retailing,* Winter 1975–76, pp. 15–22ff.

8. See Leon G. Schiffman and Leslie Lazar Kanuk, *Consumer Behavior* (Englewood Cliffs, N.J.: Prentice-Hall, 1978), pp. 343–56.

9. See Harry L. Davis, "Decision Making within the Household," *Journal of Consumer Research,* March 1976, pp. 241–60; Harry L. Davis and Benny P. Rigaux, "Perception of Marital Roles in Decision Processes," *Journal of Consumer Research,* June 1974, pp. 51–60; and Harry L. Davis, "Dimensions of Marital Roles in Consumer Decision-Making," *Journal of Marketing Research,* May 1970, pp. 168–77.

10. See "Flaunting Wealth: It's Back in Style," *U.S. News & World Report,* September 21, 1981, pp. 61–64.

11. Gail Sheehy, *Passages: Predictable Crises in Adult Life* (New York: Dutton, 1974); and Roger Gould, *Transformations* (New York: Simon & Schuster, 1978).

12. Sidney J. Levy, "Symbolism and Life Style," in *Toward Scientific Marketing,* ed. Stephen A. Greyser (Chicago: American Marketing Association, 1964), pp. 140–50.

13. See Raymond L. Horton, "Some Relationships between Personality and Consumer Decision-Making," *Journal of Marketing Research,* May 1979, pp. 244–45.

14. For more reading, see Edward L. Grubb and Harrison L. Grathwohl, "Consumer Self-Concept, Symbolism, and Market Behavior: A Theoretical Approach," *Journal of Marketing,* October 1967, pp. 22–27; Ira J. Dolich, "Congruence Relationships between Self-Images and Product Brands, *Journal of Marketing Re-*

search, February 1969, pp. 40–47; and E. Laird Landon, Jr., "The Differential Role of Self-Concept and Ideal Self-Concept in Consumer Purchase Behavior," *Journal of Consumer Research,* September 1974, pp. 44–51.

15. Abraham H. Maslow, *Motivation and Personality* (New York: Harper & Row, 1954), pp. 80–106.

16. Bernard Berelson and Gary A. Steiner, *Human Behavior: An Inventory of Scientific Findings* (New York: Harcourt Brace Jovanovich, 1964), p. 88.

17. This relationship is known as Weber's law and is one of the main laws in psychophysics.

18. See David Krech, Richard S. Crutchfield, and Egerton L. Ballachey, *Individual in Society* (New York: McGraw-Hill, 1962), chap. 2.

19. Several models of the consumer buying process have been developed by marketing scholars. The most prominent models are those of John A. Howard and Jagdish N. Sheth, *The Theory of Buyer Behavior* (New York: John Wiley, 1969); Francesco M. Nicosia, *Consumer Decision Processes* (Englewood Cliffs, N.J.: Prentice-Hall, 1966); and James F. Engel, Roger D. Blackwell, and David T. Kollat, *Consumer Behavior,* 3d ed. (New York: Holt, Rinehart & Winston, 1978).

20. See Chem L. Narayana and Ron J. Markin, "Consumer Behavior and Product Performance: An Alternative Conceptualization," *Journal of Marketing,* October 1975, pp. 1–6. These various sets are an elaboration of the concept of an *evoked set,* which was originally proposed by Howard and Sheth, *Theory of Buyer Behavior,* p. 26. They defined *evoked set* as the set of brands "that become alternatives in the buyer's choice decision."

21. James H. Myers and Mark L. Alpert, "Semantic Confusion in Attitude Research: Salience vs. Importance vs. Determinance," in *Advances in Consumer Research* (Proceedings of the Seventh Annual Conference of the Association of Consumer Research, October 1976), pp. 106–10.

22. See Paul E. Green and Yoram Wind, *Multiattribute Decisions in Marketing: A Measurement Approach* (Hinsdale, Ill.: Dryden Press, 1973), chap. 2.

23. See Jagdish N. Sheth, "An Investigation of Relationships among Evaluative Beliefs, Affect, Behavioral Intention, and Behavior," in *Consumer Behavior: Theory and Application,* ed. John U. Farley, John A. Howard, and L. Winston Ring (Boston: Allyn & Bacon, 1974), pp. 89–114.

24. See Martin Fishbein, "Attitudes and Prediction of Behavior," in *Readings in Attitude Theory and Measurement,* ed. Martin Fishbein (New York: John Wiley, 1967), pp. 477–92.

25. See John E. Swan and Linda Jones Combs, "Product Performance and Consumer Satisfaction: A New Concept," *Journal of Marketing Research,* April 1976, pp. 25–33.

26. The following discussion leans heavily on Everett M. Rogers, *Diffusion of Innovations* (New York: Free Press, 1962).

27. Ibid.

28. See James Coleman, Elihu Katz, and Herbert Menzel, "The Diffusion of an Innovation among Physicians," *Sociometry,* December 1957, pp. 253–70.

29. See J. Bohlen and G. Beal, *How Farm People Accept New Ideas,* Special Report No. 15 (Ames: Iowa State College Agricultural Extension Service, November 1955).

30. Elihu Katz and Paul F. Lazarsfeld, *Personal Influence* (New York: Free Press, 1955), p. 234.

Chapter 6

1. Some of this information is drawn from "The College Caterers Are Dropping Out," *Business Week,* April 23, 1979, pp. 36–37.

2. Frederick E. Webster, Jr., and Yoram Wind, *Organizational Buying Behavior* (Englewood Cliffs, N.J.: Prentice-Hall, 1972), p. 2.

3. Patrick J. Robinson, Charles W. Faris, and Yoram Wind, *Industrial Buying and Creative Marketing* (Boston: Allyn & Bacon, 1967).

4. Webster and Wind, *Organizational Buying Behavior,* p. 6.

5. Ibid., pp. 78–80.

6. See Murray Harding, "Who Really Makes the Purchasing Decision?" *Industrial Marketing,* September 1966, p. 76. This point of view is further developed in Ernest Dichter, "Industrial Buying Is Based on Same 'Only Human' Emotional Factors That Motivate Consumer Market's Housewife," *Industrial Marketing,* February 1973, pp. 14–16.

7. Webster and Wind, *Organizational Buying Behavior,* pp. 33–37.

8. Robinson, Faris, and Wind, *Industrial Buying and Creative Marketing,* p. 14.

9. Albert W. Frey, *Marketing Handbook,* 2d ed. (New York: Ronald Press, 1965), p. 21.

10. See Leonard Groeneveld, "The Implications of Blanket Contracting for Industrial Purchasing and Marketing," *Journal of Purchasing,* November 1972, pp. 51–58; and H. Lee Math-

ews, David T. Wilson, and Klaus Backhaus, "Selling to the Computer Assisted Buyer," *Industrial Marketing Management* 6 (1977): 307–15.

11. Stanley E. Cohen, "Looking in the U.S. Government Market," *Industrial Marketing,* September 1964, pp. 129–38.

12. See "Out of the Maze," *Sales and Marketing Management,* April 9, 1979.

Chapter 7

1. Based on "Coke's Big Marketing Blitz," *Business Week,* May 30, 1983, pp. 58–64.

2. See "R. J. Reynolds Stops a Slide in Market Share," *Business Week,* January 26, 1976, p. 92.

3. "Can the Baby Toy Market Be Segmented 12 Ways?" *Business Week,* February 14, 1977, p. 62.

4. "Dog Food Concept Turns into a Scrap," *Business Week,* April 19, 1976, pp. 137–38.

5. Joseph T. Plummer, "Life Style Patterns: New Constraint for Mass Communications Research," *Journal of Broadcasting,* Winter 1971–72, pp. 79–89.

6. Quoted in Franklin B. Evans, "Psychological and Objective Factors in the Prediction of Brand Choice: Ford versus Chevrolet," *Journal of Business,* October 1959, pp. 340–69.

7. Ralph Westfall, "Psychological Factors in Predicting Product Choice," *Journal of Marketing,* April 1962, pp. 34–40.

8. Shirley Young, "The Dynamics of Measuring Unchange," in *Attitude Research in Transition,* ed. Russell I. Haley (Chicago: American Marketing Association, 1972), pp. 61–82.

9. Russell L. Ackoff and James R. Emshoff, "Advertising Research at Anheuser-Busch, Inc. (1968–74)," *Sloan Management Review,* Spring 1975, pp. 1–15.

10. See Daniel Yankelovich, "New Criteria for Market Segmentation," *Harvard Business Review,* March-April 1964, p. 85.

11. Frank M. Bass, Douglas J. Tigert, and Ronald T. Lonsdale, "Market Segmentation: Group versus Individual Behavior," *Journal of Marketing Research,* August 1968, p. 276.

12. This classification was adapted from George H. Brown, "Brand Loyalty—Fact or Fiction?" *Advertising Age,* June 1952-January 1953, a series of articles.

13. For more on consumer segmentation variables, see Ronald Frank, William Massy, and Yoram Wind, *Market Segmentation* (Englewood Cliffs, N.J.: Prentice-Hall, 1972).

14. See Wendell R. Smith, "Product Differentiation and Market Segmentation as Alternative Marketing Strategies," *Journal of Marketing,* July 1956, pp. 3–8; and Alan A. Roberts, "Applying the Strategy of Market Segmentation," *Business Horizons,* Fall 1961, pp. 65–72.

15. Natalie McKelvy, "Shoes Make Edison Brothers a Big Name," *Chicago Tribune,* February 23, 1979, Sec. 5, p. 9.

16. R. William Kotrba, "The Strategy Selection Chart," *Journal of Marketing,* July 1966, pp. 22–25.

17. These maps must be interpreted with care. Not all customers share the same perceptions. The map shows the average perceptions.

Chapter 8

1. See *Marketing Definitions: A Glossary of Marketing Terms,* compiled by the Committee on Definitions of the American Marketing Association (Chicago: American Marketing Association, 1960).

2. Systems selling is described in chapter 6.

3. See Harper W. Boyd, Jr., and Sidney J. Levy, "New Dimensions in Consumer Analysis," *Harvard Business Review,* November-December 1963, pp. 129–40.

4. Theodore Levitt, *The Marketing Mode* (New York: McGraw-Hill, 1969), p. 2.

5. The three definitions can be found in *Marketing Definitions*.

6. The first three definitions can be found in *Marketing Definitions*. For further reading on this classification of goods, see Richard H. Holton, "The Distinction between Convenience Goods, Shopping Goods, and Specialty Goods," *Journal of Marketing,* July 1958, pp. 53–56; and Gordon E. Miracle, "Product Characteristics and Marketing Strategy," *Journal of Marketing,* January 1965, pp. 18–24.

7. The first four definitions can be found in *Marketing Definitions*.

8. See Bill Paul, "It Isn't Chicken Feed to Put Your Brand on 78 Million Birds," *Wall Street Journal,* May 13, 1974, p. 1.

9. "Research Suggests Consumers Will Increasingly Seek Quality," *Wall Street Journal,* October 15, 1981, p. 1.

10. See Theodore R. Gamble, "Brand Extension," in *Plotting Marketing Strategy,* ed. Lee Adler (New York: Simon & Schuster, 1967), pp. 170–71. For several more recent examples, see "Name Game," *Time,* August 31, 1981, pp. 41–42.

11. See Robert W. Young, "Multibrand Entries," in

Adler, *Plotting Marketing Strategy,* pp. 143–64.

12. "General Foods—Post Division (B)," Case M-102, Harvard Business School, 1964.

13. "Product Tryouts: Sales Tests in Selected Cities Help Trim Risks of National Marketing," *Wall Street Journal,* August 10, 1962, p. 1.

14. Peter G. Banting, "Customer Service in Industrial Marketing: A Comparative Study," *European Journal of Marketing* 10, no. 3 (1976): 140.

15. See Ralph S. Alexander and Thomas L. Berg, *Dynamic Management in Marketing* (Homewood, Ill.: Richard D. Irwin, 1965), pp. 419–28.

16. See Benson P. Shapiro, *Industrial Product Policy: Managing the Existing Product Line* (Cambridge, Mass.: Marketing Science Institute, 1977), pp. 9–10.

17. This definition can be found in *Marketing Definitions.*

Chapter 9

1. Written by the author and based on some notes of Professor Harold W. Fox, as well as "P&G's Aren't Chips Off the Old Spud, but They Are Selling," *Wall Street Journal,* March 28, 1974; and "In Spite of Huge Losses, Procter & Gamble Tries Once More to Revive Pringle's Chips," *Wall Street Journal,* October 7, 1981.

2. David S. Hopkins and Earl L. Bailey, "New Product Pressures," *Conference Board Record,* June 1971, pp. 16–24.

3. See Edward M. Tauber, "Forecasting Sales Prior to Test Market," *Journal of Marketing,* January 1977, pp. 80–84. Also see Robert Blattberg and John Golanty, "Tracker: An Early Test Market Forecasting and Diagnostic Model for New Product Planning," *Journal of Marketing Research,* May 1978, pp. 192–202.

4. See Roger A. Kerin, Michael G. Harvey, and James T. Rothe, "Cannibalism and New Product Development," *Business Horizons,* October 1978, pp. 25–31.

5. Philip Kotler and Gerald Zaltman, "Targeting Prospects for a New Product," *Journal of Advertising Research*, February 1976, pp. 7–20.

6. William E. Cox, Jr., "Product Life Cycles as Marketing Models," *Journal of Business,* October 1967, pp. 375–84.

7. Robert D. Buzzell, "Competitive Behavior and the Product Life Cycle," in *New Ideas for Successful Marketing,* ed. John S. Wright and Jac L. Goldstucker (Chicago: American Marketing Association, 1966), p. 51.

8. Ibid., p. 51.

9. Ibid., p. 52.

10. Several systems are in use. See Philip Kotler, "Phasing Out Weak Products," *Harvard Business Review,* March-April 1965, pp. 107–18; and Paul W. Hamelman and Edward M. Mazze, "Improving Product Abandonment Decisions," *Journal of Marketing,* April 1972, pp. 20–26.

11. For further reading on the product life-cycle concept, see Theodore Levitt, "Exploit the Product Life Cycle," *Harvard Business Review,* November-December 1965, pp. 81–94; Nariman K. Dhalla and Sonia Yuspeh, "Forget the Product Life Cycle Concept!" *Harvard Business Review,* January-February 1976, pp. 102–12; and the special section of articles on the product life cycle in the Fall 1981 issue of the *Journal of Marketing.*

Chapter 10

1. Philip Kotler, *Marketing for Nonprofit Organizations* (Englewood Cliffs: N.J.: Prentice-Hall, 1982), pp. 303–4. © 1982 by Prentice-Hall. Reprinted by permission.

2. David J. Schwartz, *Marketing Today: A Basic Approach,* 3d ed. (New York: Harcourt Brace Jovanovich, 1981), p. 271.

3. *Departmental Merchandising and Operating Results of 1965* (New York: National Retail Merchants Association, 1965).

4. See Lee E. Preston, *Profits, Competition, and Rules of Thumb in Retail Food Pricing* (Berkeley: University of California Institute of Business and Economic Research, 1963), p. 31.

5. Ibid., pp. 29–40.

6. See Daniel A. Nimer, "Pricing the Profitable Sales Has a Lot to Do with Perception," *Sales Management,* May 19, 1975, pp. 13–14.

7. For further discussion, see Edward R. Hawkins, "Price Policies and Theory," *Journal of Marketing,* January 1954, pp. 233–40.

Chapter 11

1. See Joel Dean, *Managerial Economics* (Englewood Cliffs, N.J.: Prentice-Hall, 1951), pp. 420ff.

2. See George Stigler, *The Theory of Price,* rev. ed. (New York: Macmillan, 1952), pp. 215ff.

3. See "Flexible Pricing," *Business Week,* December 12, 1977, pp. 78–88.

4. See "Pricing Strategy in an Inflation Economy," *Business Week,* April 6, 1974, pp. 43–49.

5. Norman H. Fuss, Jr., "How to Raise Prices—

Judiciously—to Meet Today's Conditions," *Harvard Business Review,* May-June 1975, pp. 10ff.

6. For an excellent review, see Kent B. Monroe, "Buyers' Subjective Perceptions of Price," *Journal of Marketing Research,* February 1973, pp. 70–80.

7. See Alfred R. Oxenfeldt, *Pricing for Marketing Executives* (San Francisco: Wadsworth, 1961), p. 28.

Chapter 12

1. Based on Russell Leavitt, "Billions in Blossoms," *Fortune,* May 18, 1981, pp. 68–75.

2. For other lists, see Edmund D. McGarry, "Some Functions of Marketing Reconsidered," in *Theory in Marketing,* ed. Reavis Cox and Wroe Alderson (Homewood, Ill.: Richard D. Irwin, 1950), pp. 269–73; and Louis P. Bucklin, *A Theory of Distribution Channel Structure* (Berkeley: Institute of Business and Economic Research, University of California, 1966), pp. 10–11.

3. Ronald Abler, John S. Adams, and Peter Gould, *Spatial Organization: The Geographer's View of the World* (Englewood Cliffs, N.J.: Prentice-Hall, 1971), pp. 531–32.

4. William G. Zikmund and William J. Stanton, "Recycling Solid Wastes: A Channels-of-Distribution Problem," *Journal of Marketing,* July 1971, p. 34.

5. Bert C. McCammon, Jr., "Perspectives for Distribution Programming," in *Vertical Marketing Systems,* ed. Louis P. Bucklin (Glenview, Ill.: Scott Foresman, 1970), pp. 32–51.

6. Ibid., p. 45.

7. See Robert E. Weigand, "Fit Products and Channels to Your Markets," *Harvard Business Review,* January-February 1977, pp. 95–105.

8. For reading on industrial distributors, see Frederick E. Webster, Jr., "The Role of the Industrial Distributor," *Journal of Marketing,* July 1976, pp. 10–16.

9. See Bert Rosenbloom, *Marketing Channels: A Management View* (Hinsdale, Ill.: Dryden Press, 1978), pp. 192–203.

10. McCammon, "Perspectives for Distribution Programming," p. 43.

11. B. J. LaLonde and P. H. Zinszer, *Customer Service: Meaning and Measurement* (Chicago: National Council of Physical Distribution Management, 1976).

12. Jurgen F. Ringer and Charles D. Howell, "The Industrial Engineer and Marketing," in *Industrial Engineering Handbook* (2d ed.), ed. Har-

old Bright Maynard (New York: McGraw-Hill, 1963), pp. 10, 102–3.

Chapter 13

1. Liz Roman Gallese, "The Cheese at Spag's Is Next to the Rugs—Over by the Golf Balls," *Wall Street Journal,* January 28, 1983, p. 1; "The Discount Twist in Suburban Shopping Malls," *Business Week,* July 7, 1980, pp. 94–96; Walter McQuade, "The Man Who Makes Millions on Mistakes," *Fortune,* September 6, 1982, pp. 106–16; and John Merwin, "Lemons to Lemonade," *Forbes,* August 30, 1982, pp. 60–61.

2. *Statistical Abstract of U.S., 1982–83.*

3. Standard and Poor's Industry Surveys, *Retailing,* June 1983.

4. John Dennis McDonald, *The Game of Business* (New York: Doubleday, 1975), p. 102.

5. Phyllis Berman, "Too Big for Miracles," *Forbes,* June 15, 1977, p. 26. Reprinted by permission.

6. Ernest Samhaber, *Merchants Make History* (New York: Harper & Row, 1964), pp. 345–48.

7. The quoted part of the definition is from Walter J. Salmon, Robert D. Buzzell, Stanton G. Cort, and Michael R. Pearce, *The Super Store—Strategic Implications for the Seventies* (Cambridge, Mass.: Marketing Science Institute, 1972), p. 83.

8. See "Supermarkets Eye the Sunbelt," *Business Week,* September 27, 1976, p. 61.

9. Standard and Poor's Industry Surveys, *Retailing,* June 1983.

10. Salmon et al., *The Super Store,* p. 4.

11. Ronald R. Gist, *Retailing Concepts and Decisions* (New York: John Wiley, 1968), pp. 45–46. The list of elements is slightly modified from Gist's.

12. Standard and Poor's Industry Surveys, *Retailing,* June 1983.

13. See Jonathan N. Goodrich and Jo Ann Hoffman, "Warehouse Retailing: The Trend of the Future?" *Business Horizons,* April 1979, pp. 45–50.

14. "Catalog Showroom Hot Retailer," *Chicago Tribune,* December 6, 1978, Sec. 4, p. 12; and Standard and Poor's Industry Surveys, *Retailing,* June 1983.

15. Leo Bogart, "The Future in Retailing," *Harvard Business Review,* November-December 1973, p. 26.

16. Belden Menkus, "Remote Retailing a Reality by 1985?" *Chain Store Age Executive,* September 1975, p. 42.

17. "Millions by Mail," *Forbes,* March 15, 1976, p. 82.

18. For an excellent text on direct-mail techniques, see Bob Stone, *Successful Direct Marketing Methods,* 2d, rev. ed. (Chicago: Crain Books, 1979).

19. G. R. Schreiber, *A Concise History of Vending in the U.S.A.* (Chicago: Vend, 1961), p. 9.

20. See "How the 'New Sell' Is Raking in Billions," *U.S. News & World Report,* May 8, 1978, pp. 74–75.

21. See Ronald R. Gist, *Marketing and Society: Text and Cases,* 2d ed. (Hinsdale, Ill.: Dryden Press, 1974), p. 334.

22. See Rollie Tillman, "Rise of the Conglo-merchant," *Harvard Business Review,* November-December 1971, pp. 44–51.

23. See Phyllis Berman, "Melville Corp.: Discounting with a Difference," *Forbes,* April 16, 1979, pp. 93–94.

24. This definition is from the Urban Land Institute and can be found in Roger A. Dickinson, *Retail Management: A Channels Approach* (Belmont, Calif.: Wadsworth, 1974), p. 9.

25. David Elsner, "Shopping Center Boom Appears to Be Fading Due to Overbuilding," *Wall Street Journal,* September 7, 1976, p. 1.

26. Menkus, "Remote Retailing," p. 42.

27. For more discussion, see Philip Kotler, "Atmospherics as a Marketing Tool," *Journal of Retailing,* Winter 1973–74, pp. 48–64.

28. Harold Haydon, "Galleries: A Little Push Is Better Than Too Much or No Promotion at All," *Chicago Sun-Times,* October 30, 1970, p. 55.

29. David A. Revzan, *Wholesaling in Marketing Organization* (New York: John Wiley, 1961), pp. 10–11.

30. See *Statistical Abstract of U.S., 1982–83.*

Chapter 14

1. Written by the author, based on a Pizza Inn brochure.

2. The definitions, except for *sales promotion,* are from *Marketing Definitions: A Glossary of Marketing Terms* (Chicago: American Marketing Association, 1960). The AMA definition of *sales promotion* covers, in addition to incentives, such marketing media as displays, shows and exhibitions, and demonstrations that can better be classified as forms of advertising, personal selling, or publicity. Some marketing scholars have also suggested adding *packaging* as a fifth element of the promotion mix, although others classify it as a product element.

3. Michael L. Ray and William L. Wilkie, "Fear: The Potential of an Appeal Neglected by Marketing," *Journal of Marketing,* January 1970, pp. 55–56; and Brian Sternthal and C. Samuel Craig, "Fear Appeals: Revisited and Revised," *Journal of Consumer Research,* December 1974, pp. 22–34.

4. See Brian Sternthal and C. Samuel Craig, "Humor in Advertising," *Journal of Marketing,* October 1973, pp. 12–18.

5. Carl I. Hovland and Wallace Mandell, "An Experimental Comparison of Conclusion-Drawing by the Communication and by the Audience," *Journal of Abnormal and Social Psychology,* July 1952, pp. 581–88.

6. See C. I. Hovland, A. A. Lumsdaine, and F. D. Sheffield, *Experiments on Mass Communication,* vol. 3 (Princeton, N.J.: Princeton University Press, 1948), chap. 8.

7. For further discussion, see James F. Engel, Roger D. Blackwell, and David T. Kollat, *Consumer Behavior,* 3d ed. (Hinsdale, Ill.: Dryden Press, 1978), pp. 346–48.

8. See Thomas S. Robertson, *Innovative Behavior and Communication* (New York: Holt, Rinehart & Winston, 1971), chap. 9.

9. See Philip Kotler, "Atmospherics as a Marketing Tool," *Journal of Retailing,* Winter 1973–74, pp. 48–64.

10. P. F. Lazarsfeld, B. Berelson, and H. Gaudet, *The People's Choice,* 2d ed. (New York: Columbia University Press, 1948), p. 151.

11. Herbert C. Kelman and Carl I. Hovland, "Reinstatement of the Communication in Delayed Measurement of Opinion Change," *Journal of Abnormal and Social Psychology* 48 (1953): 327–35.

12. Quoted in Daniel Seligman, "How Much for Advertising?" *Fortune,* December 1956, p. 123.

13. Albert Wesley Frey, *How Many Dollars for Advertising?* (New York: Ronald Press, 1955), p. 65.

14. Ibid., p. 49.

15. G. Maxwell Ule, "A Media Plan for 'Sputnik' Cigarettes," *How to Plan Media Strategy* (American Association of Advertising Agencies, 1957 Regional Convention), pp. 41–52.

16. See Sidney J. Levy, *Promotional Behavior* (Glenview, Ill.: Scott, Foresman, 1971), chap. 4.

17. Ibid.

18. *Sales and Marketing Management,* February 23, 1981, p. 34.

19. *How Advertising Works in Today's Marketplace: The Morrill Study* (New York: McGraw-Hill, 1971), p. 4.

20. "What IBM Found about Ways to Influence Selling," *Business Week,* December 5, 1959, pp. 69–70. Also see Harold C. Cash and William J. Crissy, "Comparison of Advertising and Selling," in *The Psychology of Selling,* vol. 12 (Flushing, N.Y.: Personal Development Associates, 1965).

Chapter 15

1. Bob Spitz, "Caution: Men at Work on Men at Work," *Esquire,* July 1983, pp. 105–9; Kurt Loder, "Men at Work: Out to Lunch," *Rolling Stone,* June 23, 1983, pp. 16–19, 87, 88.
2. Statistical information in this chapter on advertising's size and composition draws on the special issue of *Advertising Age* on the one hundred leading national advertisers, February 16, 1981, and September 10, 1981; and on the *Statistical Abstract of the U.S., 1982–83.*
3. See Russell H. Colley, *Defining Advertising Goals for Measured Advertising Results* (New York: Association of National Advertisers, 1961).
4. See William L. Wilke and Paul W. Farris, "Comparison Advertising: Problem and Potential," *Journal of Marketing,* October 1975, pp. 7–15.
5. See Russell L. Ackoff and James R. Emshoff, "Advertising Research at Anheuser-Busch, Inc. (1963–68)," *Sloan Management Review,* Winter 1975, pp. 1–15.
6. John C. Maloney, "Marketing Decisions and Attitude Research," in *Effective Marketing Coordination,* ed. George L. Baker, Jr. (Chicago: American Marketing Association, 1961), pp. 595–618.
7. Dik Warren Twedt, "How to Plan New Products, Improve Old Ones, and Create Better Advertising," *Journal of Marketing,* January 1969, pp. 53–57.
8. See William A. Mindak and H. Malcolm Bybee, "Marketing's Application to Fund Raising," *Journal of Marketing,* July 1971, pp. 13–18.
9. L. Greenland, "Is This the Era of Positioning?" *Advertising Age,* May 29, 1972.
10. Philip H. Dougherty, "Bud 'Pulses' the Market," *New York Times,* February 18, 1975, p. 40.
11. David B. Montgomery and Alvin J. Silk, "Estimating Dynamic Effects of Market Communications Expenditures," *Management Science,* June 1972, pp. 485–501.
12. See Robert D. Buzzell, "E. I. Du Pont de Nemours & Co.: Measurement of Effects of Advertising," in his *Mathematical Models and Marketing Management* (Boston: Division of

Research, Graduate School of Business Administration, Harvard University, 1964), pp. 157–79.
13. Roger A. Strang, "Sales Promotion—Fast Growth, Faulty Management," *Harvard Business Review,* July-August 1976, pp. 115–24.
14. Ibid., pp. 116–19.
15. See Roger A. Strang, Robert M. Prentice, and Alden G. Clayton, *The Relationship between Advertising and Promotion in Brand Strategy* (Cambridge, Mass.: Marketing Science Institute, 1975), chap. 5.
16. Strang, "Sales Promotion," p. 124.
17. Most of the definitions in this section have been adapted from John F. Luick and William Lee Siegler, *Sales Promotion and Modern Merchandising* (New York: McGraw-Hill, 1968).
18. For further reading, see Carl-Magnus Seipel, "Premiums—Forgotten by Theory," *Journal of Marketing,* April 1971, pp. 26–34.
19. See Fred C. Allvine, "The Future for Trading Stamps and Games," *Journal of Marketing,* January 1969, pp. 45–52.
20. "Our L'eggs Fit Your Legs," *Business Week,* March 27, 1972.
21. See Walter A. Gaw, *Specialty Advertising* (Chicago: Specialty Advertising Association, 1970).
22. See Suzette Cavanaugh, "Setting Objectives and Evaluating the Effectiveness of Trade Show Exhibits," *Journal of Marketing,* October 1976, pp. 100–105.
23. Russell D. Bowman, "Merchandising and Promotion Grow Big in Marketing World," *Advertising Age,* December 1974, p. 21.
24. Strang, "Sales Promotion," p. 120.
25. George Black, *Planned Industrial Publicity* (Chicago: Putnam Publishing, 1952), p. 3.
26. Adapted from Scott M. Cutlip and Allen H. Center, *Effective Public Relations,* 3d ed. (Englewood Cliffs, N.J.: Prentice-Hall, 1964), pp. 10–14.
27. Arthur M. Merims, "Marketing's Stepchild: Product Publicity," *Harvard Business Review,* November-December 1972, pp. 111–12.

Chapter 16

1. Michael Waldholz, "How a 'Detail Man' Promotes New Drugs to Tennessee Doctors," *Wall Street Journal,* November 8, 1982. Used with permission.
2. Robert N. McMurry, "The Mystique of Super-Salesmanship," *Harvard Business Review,* March-April 1961, p. 114.
3. See William R. Dixon, "Redetermining the Size of the Sales Force: A Case Study," in *Changing*

Perspectives in Marketing Management, ed. Martin R. Warshaw (Ann Arbor: University of Michigan, 1962), p. 58.

4. Roger M. Pegram, Selling and Servicing the National Account (New York: Conference Board, 1972).

5. William H. Kaven, Managing the Major Sale (New York: American Management Association, 1971); and Benson P. Shapiro and Ronald S. Posner, "Making the Major Sale," Harvard Business Review, March-April 1976, pp. 68–78.

6. Walter J. Talley, "How to Design Sales Territories," Journal of Marketing, January 1961, pp. 7–13.

7. Marketing News, February 5, 1982, p. 1.

8. The survey was conducted by the Sales Executives Club of New York and was reported in Business Week, February 1, 1964, p. 52.

9. McMurry, "Mystique of Super-Salesmanship," p. 117.

10. Ibid., p. 118.

11. David Mayer and Herbert M. Greenberg, "What Makes a Good Salesman?" Harvard Business Review, July-August 1964, pp. 119–25.

12. "Double-Digit Hikes in 1974 Sales Training Costs," Sales and Marketing Management, January 6, 1975, p. 54.

13. Some of the discussion on the selling process is based on W. J. E. Crissy, William H. Cunningham, and Isabella C. M. Cunningham, Selling: The Personal Force in Marketing (New York: John Wiley, 1977), pp. 1.19–29.

14. Mark Hanan, "Join the Systems Sell and You Can't Be Beat," Sales and Marketing Management, August 21, 1972, p. 44. Also see Mark Hanan, James Cribbin, and Herman Heiser, Consultative Selling (New York: American Management Association, 1970).

Chapter 17

1. Melville C. Branch, The Corporate Planning Process (New York: American Management Association, 1962), pp. 48–49.

2. See Peter Drucker, Management: Tasks, Responsibilities, Practices (New York: Harper & Row, 1973), chap. 7.

3. Theodore Levitt, "Marketing Myopia," Harvard Business Review, July-August 1960, pp. 45–56.

4. For a useful discussion of objectives setting, see Charles H. Granger, "The Hierarchy of Objectives," Harvard Business Review, May-June 1964, pp. 63–74.

5. H. Igor Ansoff, "Strategies for Diversification,"

Harvard Business Review, September-October 1957, pp. 113–24.

6. For examples of empirical studies using fitted sales response functions, see Doyle L. Weiss, "Determinants of Market Share," Journal of Marketing Research, August 1968, pp. 290–95; Donald E. Sexton, Jr., "Estimating Marketing Policy Effects on Sales of a Frequently Purchased Product," Journal of Marketing Research, August 1970, pp. 338–47; and Jean-Jacques Lambin, "A Computer On-Line Marketing Mix Model," Journal of Marketing Research, May 1972, pp. 119–26.

7. See Russell Ackoff and James R. Emshoff, "Advertising Research at Anheuser-Busch," Sloan Management Review, Winter 1975, pp. 1–15.

8. See Philip Kotler, "A Guide to Gathering Expert Estimates," Business Horizons, October 1970, pp. 79–87.

9. See Philip Kotler, Marketing Decision Making (New York: Holt, Rinehart & Winston, 1971).

10. For further discussion, see James M. Hulbert and Norman E. Toy, "A Strategic Framework for Marketing Control," Journal of Marketing, April 1977, pp. 12–20.

11. For an application to a hotel chain, see Arthur J. Daltas, "Protecting Service Markets with Consumer Feedback," Cornell Hotel and Restaurant Administration Quarterly, May 1977, pp. 73–77.

12. For a basic text, see Donald R. Longman and Michael Schiff, Practical Distribution Cost Analysis (Homewood, Ill.: Richard D. Irwin, 1955).

13. For further discussion, see Philip Kotler, William Gregor, and William Rodgers, "The Marketing Audit Comes of Age," Sloan Management Review, Winter 1977, pp. 25–43. A preliminary marketing audit tool is described in Philip Kotler, "From Sales Obsession to Marketing Effectiveness," Harvard Business Review, November-December 1977, pp. 67–75.

Chapter 18

1. Written by the author and based on "Brazil: Campbell Soup Fails to Make It to the Table," Business Week, October 12, 1981; and "Brazil: Gerber Abandons a Baby-Food Market," Business Week, February 8, 1982.

2. See "The Reluctant Exporter," Business Week, April 10, 1978, pp. 54–66.

3. Bureau of Economic Analysis, U.S. Department of Commerce.

4. See Warren J. Keegan, "Multinational Product Planning: New Myths and Old Realities," in Multinational Product Management (Cam-

bridge, Mass.: Marketing Science Institute, 1976), pp. 1–8.

5. For a system of rating the political stability of different nations, see F. T. Haner, "Rating Investment Risks Abroad," *Business Horizons,* April 1979, pp. 18–23.

6. For more examples, see David A. Ricks, Marilyn Y. C. Fu, and Jeffery S. Arpan, *International Business Blunders* (Columbus, Ohio: Grid, 1974).

7. Igal Ayal and Jehiel Zif, "Market Expansion Strategies in Multinational Marketing," *Journal of Marketing,* Spring 1979, pp. 84–94.

8. James K. Sweeney, "A Small Company Enters the European Market," *Harvard Business Review,* September-October 1970, pp. 127–28.

9. See David S. R. Leighton, "Deciding When to Enter International Markets," in *Handbook of Modern Marketing,* ed. Victor P. Buell (New York: McGraw-Hill, 1970), pp. 23–28.

10. The discussion of entry strategies in this section is based on the discussion in Gordon E. Miracle and Gerald S. Albaum, *International Marketing Management* (Homewood, Ill.: Richard D. Irwin, 1970), chaps. 14–16.

11. Warren J. Keegan, "Multinational Product Planning: Strategic Alternatives," *Journal of Marketing,* January 1969, pp. 58–62.

12. Louis T. Wells, Jr., "A Product Life Cycle for International Trade?" *Journal of Marketing,* July 1968, pp. 1–6.

13. See Miracle and Albaum, *International Marketing Management,* pp. 317–19.

14. See William D. Hartley, "How Not to Do It: Cumbersome Japanese Distribution System Stumps U.S. Concerns," *Wall Street Journal,* March 2, 1972, pp. 1, 8.

15. For a description of the distribution systems in selected countries, see Wadi-Nambiaratchi, "Channels of Distribution in Developing Economies," *Business Quarterly,* Winter 1965, pp. 74–82.

16. For further discussion, see Arieh Goldman, "Outreach of Consumers and the Modernization of Urban Food Retailing in Developing Countries," *Journal of Marketing,* October 1974, pp. 8–16.

17. See Yoram Wind, Susan P. Douglas, and Howard V. Perlmutter, "Guidelines for Developing International Marketing Strategies," *Journal of Marketing,* April 1973, pp. 14–23.

Chapter 19

1. "Services Grow While the Quality Shrinks," *Business Week,* October 15, 1971, p. 50.

2. For a good discussion of quality control systems at the Marriott Hotel chain, see G. M. Hostage, "Quality Control in a Service Business," *Harvard Business Review,* July-August 1975, pp. 98–106.

3. See W. Earl Sasser, "Match Supply and Demand in Service Industries," *Harvard Business Review,* November-December 1976, pp. 133–40.

4. See Dan R. E. Thomas, "Strategy Is Different in Service Businesses," *Harvard Business Review,* July-August 1978, p. 161.

5. See Daniel T. Carroll, "Ten Commandments for Bank Marketing," *Bankers Magazine,* Autumn 1970, pp. 74–80; also see G. Lynn Shostack, "Banks Sell Services—Not Things," *Bankers Magazine,* Winter 1977, pp. 40–45.

6. *Public Relations News,* October 27, 1947.

7. For this argument, see Philip Kotler and William Mindak, "Marketing and Public Relations," *Journal of Marketing,* October 1978, pp. 13–20.

8. For additional ways to market the services of a professional services firm, see Philip Kotler and Richard A. Connor, Jr., "Marketing Professional Services," *Journal of Marketing,* January 1977, pp. 71–76.

9. Carol Oppenheim, "Bucky Dent: The Selling of a Sudden Superstar," *Chicago Tribune,* December 16, 1978, sec. 2, p. 1.

10. "In the Groove at Mercury Records," *Chicago Daily News,* October 16, 1976.

11. John E. Cooney, "Eddie Fisher Discovers That Regaining Fame Is a Daunting Goal," *Wall Street Journal,* February 20, 1978, p. 1.

12. Theodore White, *The Making of the President 1960* (New York: Atheneum, 1961); and Joe McGinness, *The Selling of the President 1968* (New York: Trident Press, 1969).

13. See E. Glick, *The New Methodology* (Washington, D.C.: American Institute for Political Communication, 1967), p. 1. Also see Philip Kotler and Neil Kotler, "Business Marketing for Political Candidates," *Campaigns and Elections,* Summer 1981, pp. 24–33.

14. For a description of the marketing of a "new town" in Texas called The Woodlands, see Betsy D. Gelb and Ben M. Enis, "Marketing a City of the Future," in *Marketing Is Everybody's Business* (Santa Monica, Calif.: Goodyear, 1977).

15. See Scott Cutlip and Allen H. Center, *Effective Public Relations,* 3d ed. (Englewood Cliffs, N.J.: Prentice-Hall, 1964), p. 10.

16. See Philip Kotler and Gerald Zaltman, "Social Marketing: An Approach to Planned Social

Change," *Journal of Marketing,* July 1971, pp. 3–12.

17. See Eduardo Roberto, *Strategic Decision-Making in a Social Program: The Case of Family-Planning Diffusion* (Lexington, Mass.: Lexington Books, 1975).

18. See Karl E. Henion II, *Ecological Marketing* (Columbus, Ohio: Grid, 1976).

Chapter 20

1. Adapted from Peter T. Hutchinson, Don E. Parkinson, and Charles B. Weinberg, "Water Conservation in Palo Alto," in Christopher H. Lovelock and Charles B. Weinberg, eds., *Cases in Public and Nonprofit Marketing* (Palo Alto, Calif.: Scientific Press, 1971), pp. 183–96.

2. Paul W. Stewart and J. Frederick Dewhurst with Louis Field, *Does Distribution Cost Too Much?* (New York: Twentieth Century Fund, 1939).

3. Jessica Mitford, *The American Way of Death* (New York: Simon & Schuster, 1963).

4. Rattles, Pings, Dents, Leaks, Creaks—And Costs," *Newsweek,* November 25, 1968, p. 92.

5. Ibid.

6. "The Breakfast of Fatties?" *Chicago Today,* July 24, 1970.

7. Gerald B. Tallman, "Planned Obsolescence as a Marketing and Economic Policy," in *Advancing Marketing Efficiency,* ed. L. H. Stockman (Chicago: American Marketing Association, 1958), pp. 27–39.

8. David Caplovitz, *The Poor Pay More* (New York: Free Press, 1963).

9. A speech delivered at Vanderbilt University Law School, reported in *Marketing News,* August 1, 1968, pp. 11, 15.

10. Ibid.

11. For further reading, see Alan R. Andreasen, *The Disadvantaged Consumer* (New York: Free Press, 1975).

12. John Kenneth Galbraith, *The Affluent Society* (Boston: Houghton Mifflin, 1958), p. 255.

13. From an advertisement for *Fact* magazine, which does not carry advertisements.

14. Mark Hanan, "Corporate Growth through Venture Management," *Harvard Business Review,* January-February 1969, p. 44.

15. FTC v. Procter & Gamble, 386 U.S. 568 (1967).

16. See Morris Adelman, "The A & P Case: A Study in Applied Economic Theory," *Quarterly Journal of Economics,* May 1949, p. 238.

17. For more details, see Philip Kotler, "What Consumerism Means for Marketers," *Harvard Business Review,* May-June 1972, pp. 48–57. Also see Paul N. Bloom and Stephen A. Greyser, "The Maturing of Consumerism," *Harvard Business Review,* November-December 1981, pp. 130–39.

18. Rachel Carson, *Silent Spring* (Boston: Houghton Mifflin, 1962).

19. Paul R. Ehrlich and Ann H. Ehrlich, *Population, Resources, Environment: Issues in Human Ecology* (San Francisco: W. H. Freeman, 1970).

20. Donnella H. Meadows, Dennis L. Meadows, Jorgen Randers, and William W. Behrens III, *The Limits to Growth* (New York: Universe Books, 1972).

21. Gordon O. Pehrson, quoted in "Flavored Algae from the Sea?" *Chicago Sun-Times,* February 3, 1965, p. 54.

22. Earl L. Bailey, *Formulating the Company's Marketing Policies: A Survey* (New York: Conference Board, Experiences in Marketing Management, No. 19, 1968), p. 3.

Glossary

Administered VMS A system that coordinates successive stages of production and distribution not through common ownership but through the size and power of one of the parties. (p. 282)

Advertising Any nonpersonal form of communication conducted through paid media under clear sponsorship. (pp. 332 and 353)

Agent A wholesaler who represents either buyer or seller on a relatively permanent basis and who does not take title to merchandise. (p. 321)

Allowance A payment or price reduction granted for participation in certain programs, such as trade-ins of durable goods. (p. 264)

Attitude A person's enduring favorable or unfavorable cognitive evaluations, emotional feelings, and action tendencies toward some object or idea. (p. 123)

Automatic vending Selling through coin-operated machines. (p. 310)

Backward integration A company's seeking ownership or increased control of its supply systems. (p. 405)

Basing-point pricing A geographic pricing strategy in which the seller names a city as a basing point and charges all customers the freight cost from that city regardless of the city from which the goods are actually shipped. (p. 262)

Belief A descriptive thought that a person holds about something. (p. 123)

Brand A name, term, sign, symbol, or design, or a combination of them, which is intended to identify the goods or services of one seller or group of sellers. (p. 192)

Brand extension strategy Any effort to use a successful brand name to launch product modifications or new products. (p. 197)

Brand mark That part of a brand which can be recognized but is not utterable, such as a symbol, design, or distinctive coloring or lettering. (p. 192)

Brand name That part of a brand which can be vocalized. (p. 192)

Break-even pricing Pricing based on the cost of producing, marketing, and distributing a product and the profit the company is seeking. (p. 248)

Broker A wholesaler who does not take title to goods and whose function is to bring buyers and sellers together and assist in negotiations. (p. 321)

Business analysis A review of sales, costs, and profit projections to determine whether a product concept and marketing strategy meet the company's objectives. (p. 221)

Buying service A retailer that helps a specific clientele—usually the employees of large organizations, such as schools, hospitals, unions, and government agencies—buy from a selective list of retailers. (p. 312)

Capital items Goods that enter the finished product partly; they include two groups—installations and accessory equipment. (p. 191)

Cash discount A price reduction to buyers who pay their bills promptly. (p. 263)

Catalog showroom A retail operation that applies catalog and discounting principles to a wide selection of high-markup, fast-moving, brand-name goods. (p. 309)

Chain stores Two or more outlets that are commonly owned and controlled, sell similar lines of merchandise, have central buying and merchandising, and may have a similar architectural motif. (p. 313)

Commercialization The launching of a new product. (p. 224)

Company marketing opportunity An attractive arena for company marketing action in which a particular company would enjoy a competitive advantage. (pp. 36 and 408)

Company's marketing environment The actors and forces that are outside the firm and that affect the marketing management's ability to develop and maintain successful transactions with its target customers. (p. 77)

Concentrated marketing Focusing marketing efforts on a large share of one or a few submarkets, rather than going after a small share of a large market. (p. 178)

Concentric diversification A company's addition of new products that have technological and/or marketing similarities with its existing product lines. (p. 406)

Concept development The elaboration of a product idea into meaningful consumer terms. (p. 219)

Concept testing Trying out a product concept on a target group of consumers, asking them to respond to the product, and using their responses to determine whether the product has strong consumer appeal. (p. 220)

Conglomerate diversification A company's addition of new products that have no relationship to its current technology, products, or markets. (p. 406)

Consumer cooperative Any retail firm that is owned by its customers. (p. 314)

Consumer market All the individuals and households who buy or acquire goods and services for personal consumption. (p. 106)

Consumerism An organized movement of citizens and government to enhance the rights and power of buyers in relation to sellers. (p. 470)

Contractual VMS Independent firms linked by contracts and coordinating their programs to obtain more economies and/or sales impact than they could achieve alone. (p. 280)

Control Measuring and diagnosing the results of the strategic and marketing plans and taking corrective action. (p. 400)

Convenience goods Goods that the customer usually purchases frequently, immediately, and with the minimum of effort in comparison buying. (p. 189)

Convenience store A relatively small store, located near a residential area, open long hours seven days a week, and carrying a limited line of high-turnover convenience products. (p. 305)

Conventional marketing channel An independent producer, wholesaler(s), and retailer(s), each a separate business seeking to maximize its own profits, even if that is at the expense of maximizing the profits for the system as a whole. (p. 280)

Copyright The exclusive legal right to reproduce, publish, and sell the matter and form of a literary, musical, or artistic work. (p. 192)

Corporate VMS The combination of successive stages of production and distribution under single ownership. (p. 280)

Cost-plus pricing The addition of a standard markup to the cost of a product. (p. 247)

Customer-structured sales force An organizational structure for a sales force based on customer, industry, or market specialization. (p. 385)

Decline stage The eventual drop in a product's sales that follows the stages of introduction, growth, and maturity. (p. 232)

Decoding In communication, the process by which the receiver assigns meaning to the symbols transmitted by the sender. (p. 333)

Demands Human wants that are backed by purchasing power. (p. 3)

Demography The study of human populations in respect to characteristics such as size and density. (p. 85)

Department store A retail organization that carries several product lines, typically clothing, home furnishings, and household goods; each line is operated as a separate department managed by specialist buyers or merchandisers. (p. 304)

Differentiated marketing Operating in several segments of the market and designing separate offers for each. (p. 177)

Direct investment abroad Involvement in a foreign market through foreign-based assembly or manufacturing facilities. (p. 434)

Discount store A retail institution that sells standard merchandise at lower prices by accepting lower profit margins and selling a higher volume. (p. 307)

Discriminatory pricing The selling of a product at two or more prices that are not based at different costs. (p. 265)

Distribution channel The set of firms and individuals that take title, or assist in transferring title, to the particular product or service as it moves from the producer to the consumer. (p. 275)

Diversification growth opportunities A company's opportunities that lie outside the industry. (p. 404)

Door-to-door retailing Selling in customers' homes, offices, or at home sales parties. (p. 312)

Durable goods Tangible goods that normally survive many uses. (p. 188)

Economic community A group of nations organized for the purpose of working toward common goals in the regulation of international trade; an example is the European Economic Community (EEC). (p.428)

Elastic demand The tendency for demand for a product to change because of a small price change. (p. 245)

Embargo A ban on the import of a certain product. (p. 428)

Encoding In communication, the process of putting thought into symbolic form. (p. 333)

Environmentalism An organized movement of concerned citizens and government to protect and enhance people's living environment. (p. 471)

Exchange The act of obtaining a desired object from someone by offering something in return. (p. 7)

Exchange control Regulation of the amount of available foreign currency and its exchange rate against other currencies. (p. 428)

Exclusive distribution Granting a limited number of dealers the exclusive right to distribute a product in their respective territories. (p. 285)

Exporting A company's selling of products to another country either by hiring independent marketing middlemen (indirect export) or by marketing the products themselves (direct export). (p. 432)

Feedback The part of the receiver's response that the receiver communicates back to the sender. (p. 333)

FOB origin pricing A geographic pricing strategy in which goods are placed free on board a carrier, and the customer pays the freight charges from the factory to the destination. (p. 262)

Forward integration A company's seeking ownership or increased control of its distribution systems. (p. 405)

Franchise An organization that is formed by a contract between a manufacturer, wholesaler, or service organization (franchiser) and independent business people (franchisees) who buy the right to own and operate one or more units in the system. (p. 314)

Freight absorption pricing The practice of absorbing all or part of the freight charges in order to get business. (p. 263)

Functional discount The manufacturer's discount offered to trade channel members who perform certain functions, such as selling, storing, and record keeping. (p. 264)

Functional organization A group of marketing specialists who are in charge of different marketing activities and who report to a marketing vice-president. (p. 44)

Geographic organization Organizing a company's national sales force along geographic lines. (p. 44)

Going-rate pricing Pricing based largely on competitors' prices rather than the company's own costs. (p. 249)

Government market Government units—federal, state, and local—that purchase or rent goods for carrying out the main functions of government. (p. 152)

Growth stage The increase in sales of a new product as early adopters continue to buy it and conventional consumers start to follow their lead. (p. 230)

Horizontal diversification A company's addition of new products that could appeal to its current customers although they are not related to its current product line. (p. 406)

Horizontal integration A company's seeking ownership or increased control of some of its competitors. (p. 405)

Human need A person's feeling of deprivation. (p. 2)

Human want The form that a human need takes as shaped by a person's culture and individuality. (p. 3)

Idea generation The systematic search for new product ideas. (p. 218)

Industrial market All the individuals and organizations who buy goods and services that enter into the production of other products or services that are sold, rented, or supplied to others. (p. 139)

Inelastic demand The tendency for demand for a product to remain the same despite small changes in price. (p. 245)

Integrative growth opportunities A company's opportunities to integrate with other parts of the marketing system in the industry. (p. 404)

Intensive distribution The stocking of a product in as many outlets as possible. (p. 285)

Intensive growth opportunities Opportunities available to a company within its current scope of operations. (p. 404)

Introduction stage Making a new product available for purchase. (p. 228)

Joint venturing A method of entering a foreign market by joining businesses in a host country to set up production and marketing facilities. (p. 433)

Learning Changes in an individual's behavior resulting from experience. (p. 122)

Licensing A method of entering international marketing by establishing an agreement in a foreign market that offers the right to use a manufacturing process, trademark, or other valuable item for a fee or royalty. (p. 433)

Life-style A person's pattern of living in the world as expressed in his or her activities, interests, and opinions. (p. 119)

Macroenvironment The larger societal forces that affect the microenvironment, such as the demographic, economic, natural, political, and cultural forces. (p. 77)

Mail-and-telephone-order retailing Any selling that involves using the mail or telephone to get orders and/or using them to aid in the delivery of goods. (p. 309)

Manufacturers' sales branches and offices Wholesaling operations conducted by sellers or buyers themselves rather than through independent wholesalers. (p. 324)

Market The set of actual and potential buyers of a product. (p. 9)

Market development A company's seeking increased sales by taking its current products into new markets. (p. 405)

Market management organization A form of marketing organization in which major markets are the responsibility of market managers, who work with the various functional specialists in the company to develop and achieve their plans for the market. (p. 46)

Market penetration A company's seeking increased sales for its current markets through more aggressive marketing. (p. 405)

Market penetration pricing The practice of setting a relatively low price on an innovative product in order to attract a large number of buyers and win a large market share. (p. 258)

Market positioning Arranging for a product to occupy a clear, distinctive, and desirable place in the market and in the minds of target customers. Also, the act of creating a competitive positioning for the product and a detailed marketing mix. (pp. 41 and 162)

Market segment Consumers who respond in a similar way to a given set of marketing stimuli. (p. 38)

Market segmentation The process of classifying customers into groups with different needs, characteristics, and/or behavior. Also, the act of dividing a market into distinct groups of buyers who might need separate products and/or marketing mixes. (pp. 38 and 162)

Market skimming pricing The practice of setting the price of a newly invented product as high as possible so that it is just worthwhile for some segments to adopt the product and the company receives the maximum amount of revenue. (p. 258)

Market targeting The act of evaluating and selecting one or more of the market segments to enter. (p. 162)

Market testing The stage of new-product development in which the product and marketing program are introduced into authentic consumer settings to learn how consumers and dealers react to handling, using, and repurchasing the product, and how large the market is. (p. 222)

Marketing Human activity directed at satisfying needs and wants through exchange processes. (p. 2)

Marketing audit A comprehensive, systematic, independent, and periodic examination of a company's marketing environment, objectives, strategies, and activities with a view to determining problem areas and opportunities and recommending a plan of action to improve the company's marketing performance. (p. 417)

Marketing concept The idea that the key to achieving organizational goals consists in determining the needs and wants of target markets and delivering the desired satisfactions more effectively and efficiently than competitors. (p. 15)

Marketing information system A continuing and interacting structure of people, equipment, and procedures to gather, sort, analyze, evaluate, and distribute pertinent, timely, and accurate information for use by marketing decision makers to improve their marketing planning, execution, and control. (p. 55)

Marketing intelligence system The set of sources and procedures by which executives obtain their everyday information about developments in the commercial environment. (p. 56)

Marketing intermediaries Firms that aid the company in promoting, selling, and distributing its goods to customers, including middlemen, physical distribution firms, marketing services agencies, and financial intermediaries. (p. 79)

Marketing management The analysis, planning, implementation, and control of programs designed to create, build, and maintain beneficial exchanges with target buyers for the purpose of achieving organizational objectives. (p. 11)

Marketing management process A procedure that consists of (1) analyzing market opportunities, (2) selecting target markets, (3) developing the marketing mix, and (4) managing the marketing effort. (p. 31)

Marketing manager An employee of a company who is involved in analysis, planning, implementation, and/or control activities. (p. 12)

Marketing mix The set of controllable marketing variables that the firm blends to produce the response it wants in the target market. (p. 41)

Marketing research The systematic design, collection, analysis, and reporting of data and findings relevant to a specific marketing situation facing the company. (p. 57)

Marketing strategy The marketing logic by which a business hopes to achieve its marketing objectives; consists of specific strategies bearing on target markets, marketing mix, and marketing expenditure level. (p. 409)

Marketing strategy development The creation of a preliminary marketing strategy once a new-product concept has been developed. (p. 221)

Mass marketing Mass production, mass distribution, and mass promotion of one product to all buyers. (p. 161)

Materials and parts Goods that enter the manufacturer's product completely; they fall into two classes—raw materials and manufactured materials and parts. (p. 190)

Matrix organization A marketing organization that uses both product and market managers. (p. 47)

Maturity stage The eventual slowdown in a product's rate of sales growth. (p. 231)

Media The communication channels through which the message moves from sender to receiver. (p. 333)

Merchandising conglomerates Free-form corporations that combine several diversified retailing lines and forms under central ownership, along with some integration of their distribution and management functions. (p. 314)

Merchant wholesaler An independently owned business that takes title to the merchandise it handles. (p. 322)

Message The set of symbols that the sender transmits. (p. 333)

Microenvironment The forces close to the company that affect its ability to serve its customers, namely, the company, marketing intermediaries, customers, competitors, and publics. (p. 77)

Monopolistically competitive market Buyers and sellers who transact over a range of prices rather than a single market price. (p. 239)

Motive A need that is sufficiently pressing to direct a person to seek a way to satisfy it. (p. 119)

Multinational company A firm that has a major part of its operations outside of its home country. (p. 426)

New-product development The development of an original product, an improved product, or a modified product that consumers will see as "new." (p. 215)

Noise The occurrence of unplanned static or distortion during the communication process that results in the receiver's receiving a different message than the sender sent. (p. 333)

Nondurable goods Tangible goods that normally are consumed in one or a few uses. (p. 188)

Nontariff barriers Restrictions on international trade involving such obstructions as discrimination against bids from a particular company or product standards that discriminate against a country's products. (p. 428)

Oligopolistic market A situation in which a few sellers, who are highly sensitive to each other's pricing and marketing strategies, sell to many buyers. (p. 240)

Organization marketing The activities undertaken to create, maintain, or alter attitudes and/or behavior of target audiences toward particular organizations. (p. 448)

Organizational buying "The decision-making process by which formal organizations establish the need for purchased products and services, and identify, evaluate, and choose among alternative brands and suppliers." (p. 139)

Packaging   The activities of designing and producing the container or wrapper for a product. (p. 198)

Perceived-value pricing   Pricing based on the buyers' perception of value rather than the seller's cost. (p. 249)

Perception   "The process by which an individual selects, organizes, and interprets information inputs to create a meaningful picture of the world." (p. 121)

Person marketing   Activities undertaken to create, maintain, or alter attitudes and/or behavior toward particular persons. (p. 450)

Personal selling   Oral presentation in a conversation with one or more prospective purchasers for the purpose of making sales. (p. 332)

Personality   A person's distinguishing psychological characteristics that lead to relatively consistent and enduring responses to his or her environment. (p. 118)

Physical distribution   The tasks involved in planning, implementing, and controlling the physical flow of materials and final goods from points of origin to points of use to meet the needs of customers at a profit. (p. 288)

Place marketing   Activities undertaken to create, maintain, or alter attitudes and/or behavior toward particular places. (p. 452)

Place utility   Positioning a product in a location that is accessible to customers. (p. 79)

Planning   A formal design to improve a company's sales and profit performance that includes two components—strategic planning and marketing planning. (p. 400)

Possession utility   Making products available to consumers when they want to use them. (p. 79)

Price   The amount of money charged for a particular product. (p. 238)

Primary data   Data that consist of originally collected information for the specific purpose at hand. (p. 61)

Product   Anything that can be offered to a market for attention, acquisition, use, or consumption that might satisfy a want or need; includes physical objects, services, persons, places, organizations, and ideas. (pp. 4 and 187)

Product concept   The idea that consumers will favor those products that offer the most quality, performance, and features, and therefore the organization should devote its energy to making continuous product improvements. (p. 14)

Product development   A company's seeking increased sales by developing new or improved products for its current markets. Also, the development of a physical version of the product concept in hopes that consumers will see the prototype as having the key attributes described in the product concept, that it performs safely, and that it can be produced for the budgeted manufacturing costs. (pp. 221 and 405)

Product-differentiated marketing   Producing two or more products that exhibit different features, styles, quality, sizes, and so on. (p. 161)

Product item   A distinct unit that is distinguishable by size, price, appearance, or some other attribute. (p. 187)

Product life cycle   The course of a product's sales and profits that involves four stages: introduction, growth, maturity, and decline. (p. 225)

Product line   A group of products that are closely related, either because they function in a similar manner, are sold to the same customer groups, are marketed through the same types of outlets, or fall within a given price range. (p. 205)

Product management organization   A form of marketing organization in which products are the responsibility of product managers, who work with the various functional specialists in the company to develop and achieve their plans for the product. (p. 45)

Product mix   The set of all product lines and items that a particular seller offers for sale to buyers. (p. 207)

Product-structured sales force   An organizational structure for a sales force based on product lines. (p. 385)

Production concept   The idea that consumers will favor those products that are available and highly affordable, and therefore management should concentrate on improving production and distribution efficiency. (p. 14)

Promotional pricing   The temporary pricing of products below the list price, sometimes below cost. (p. 264)

Public   Any group that has an actual or potential interest in or impact on an organization's ability to achieve its objectives. (p. 82)

Public relations   The management function that evaluates public attitudes, identifies the policies and procedures of an individual or an organization with the public interest, and plans and executes a program of action to earn public understanding and acceptance. (p. 448)

Publicity   Nonpersonal stimulation of demand for a product, service, or business unit by planting commercially significant news about it in a published medium or obtaining favorable presentation of it on radio, TV, or stage that is not paid for by the sponsor. (pp. 332 and 372)

Purchasing agents   Professionally trained buyers of industrial goods. (p. 141)

Pure competitive markets   Buyers and sellers trading in a like commodity; a situation in which no single buyer or seller has much influence on the going market price. (p. 239)

Pure monopoly   The presence of just one seller in a particular product market. (p. 241)

Quantity discount   A price reduction to buyers who buy large volumes. (p. 263)

Quota   A limit on the amount of goods that an importing country will accept in certain product categories; designed to conserve on foreign currency and to protect local industry and employment. (p. 428)

Receiver   The party receiving the message sent by another party. (p. 333)

Reference group   A group that has a direct (face-to-face) or indirect influence on a person's attitudes or behavior. (p.113)

Reseller market   All the individuals and organizations who acquire goods for the purpose of reselling or renting them to others at a profit. (p. 151)

Response   The set of reactions that the receiver communicates back to the sender. (p. 333)

Retailing   All the activities involved in selling goods or services directly to final customers for their personal, nonbusiness use. (p. 299)

Sales analysis   Measurement and evaluation of actual sales in relation to sales goals. (p. 415)

Sales promotion   Short-term incentives to encourage the purchase or sale of a product or service. Also, a wide variety of promotional tools designed to stimulate earlier and/or stronger market response. (pp. 332 and 367)

Sales representative   An individual acting for a company who performs one or more of the following activities: prospecting, communicating, selling, servicing, information gathering, and allocating. (p. 381)

Sales response function   A forecast of the likely sales volume during a specified time period associated with different possible expenditure levels of one or more marketing mix elements. (p. 411)

Sample   The segment of the population selected to represent the population as a whole. (p. 67)

Screening   In the new-product development process, the elimination of poor ideas. (p. 218)

Sealed-bid pricing   Pricing based on a firm's expectations of how competitors will price rather than on a relation to its own costs or to demand; used when companies bid for jobs. (p. 250)

Seasonal discount   A price reduction to buyers who buy merchandise or services out of season. (p. 264)

Secondary data   Data that consist of information already existing somewhere, having been collected for another purpose. (p. 61)

Selective distribution   The use of more than one but less than all of the middlemen who are willing to carry a particular product. (p. 285)

Selling concept   The idea that consumers will not buy enough of the organization's products unless the organization undertakes a substantial selling and promotion effort. (p. 15)

Selling process   The steps a sales representative follows when selling, which include prospecting and qualifying, preapproach, approach, presentation and demonstration, handling objections, closing, and follow-up. (p. 390)

Sender   In communication, the party sending the message to another party. (p. 333)

Service   Any activity or benefit that one party can offer to another that is essentially intangible and does not result in the ownership of anything. (p. 445)

Services   Activities, benefits, or satisfactions that are offered for sale. (p. 188)

Shopping center   "A group of commercial establishments planned, developed, owned, and managed as a unit related in location, size, and type of shop to the trade area that it services, and providing on-site parking in definite relationship to the types and sizes of stores it contains." (p. 315)

Shopping goods   Goods that the customer, in the process of selection and purchase, characteristically compares on such bases as suitability, quality, price, and style. (p. 189)

Social class   A relatively lasting group whose members share similar values, interests, and behavior; exists in a hierarchically ordered society. (p. 110)

Social marketing   The design, implementation, and control of programs seeking to increase the acceptability of a social idea, cause, or practice in a target group(s); uses market segmentation, consumer research, concept development, communications, facilitation, incentives, and exchange theory to maximize target group response. (p. 453)

Societal marketing concept The idea that the organization's task is to determine the needs, wants, and interests of target markets and to deliver the desired satisfactions more effectively and efficiently than competitors in a way that preserves or enhances the consumer's and society's well-being. (p. 18)

Specialty goods Goods with unique characteristics and/or brand identification for which a significant group of buyers is habitually willing to make a special purchase effort. (p. 189)

Specialty store A retail outlet that carries a narrow product line with a deep assortment within that line. (p. 302)

Strategic planning The managerial process of developing and maintaining a strategic fit between the organization's goals and capabilities and its changing marketing opportunities. (p. 401)

Supermarket A relatively large, low-cost, low-margin, high-volume, self-service operation "designed to serve the consumer's total needs for food, laundry, and household maintenance products." (p. 304)

Superstore A retail organization that is larger than conventional supermarkets and aims at meeting consumers' total needs for routinely purchased food and nonfood items. (p. 306)

Suppliers Business firms and individuals who provide resources needed by the company and its competitors to produce the particular goods and services. (p. 79)

Supplies and services Items that do not enter the finished product at all. (p. 191)

Target marketing Distinguishing between market segments, selecting one or more of these segments, and developing products and marketing mixes tailored to each. (p. 161)

Tariff A tax on certain imported or exported products; designed to raise revenue or to protect domestic firms. (p. 428)

Territorial-structured sales force An organizational structure for a sales force based on a geographic area. (p. 385)

Threat A challenge posed by an unfavorable trend or specific event that would lead, in the absence of purposeful marketing action, to product stagnation or demise. (p. 408)

Time utility The showing and delivering of a product at the time customers want to buy it. (p. 79)

Trademark A brand or part of a brand that is given legal protection; protects the seller's exclusive rights to use the brand name and/or brand mark. (p. 192)

Transaction A trade between two parties that involves at least two things of value, agreed-upon conditions, a time of agreement, and a place of agreement. (p. 7)

Transactional efficiency The degree to which a volume of exchanges can be accomplished smoothly and effectively with the fewest possible transactions. (p. 9)

Undifferentiated marketing Going after the whole market with one market offer, rather than focusing on one segment. (p. 176)

Uniform delivered pricing A geographic pricing strategy in which a company charges the same price plus freight to all customers regardless of their location. (p. 262)

Unsought goods Goods that the consumer does not know about or knows about but does not normally think of buying. (p. 190)

Vertical marketing system (VMS) The producer, wholesaler(s), and retailer(s) acting as a unified system; either one channel member owns the others, or franchises them, or has so much power that they all cooperate. (p. 280)

Warehouse store A no-frill, discount, reduced-service operation that seeks to move a high volume of products at low prices. (p. 308)

Wholesaling All the activities involved in selling goods or services to those who are buying for purposes of resale or business use. (p. 320)

Zone pricing A geographic pricing strategy in which all customers within a zone pay the same total price; this price is higher in the more distant zones. (p. 262)

Name Index

Subject Index